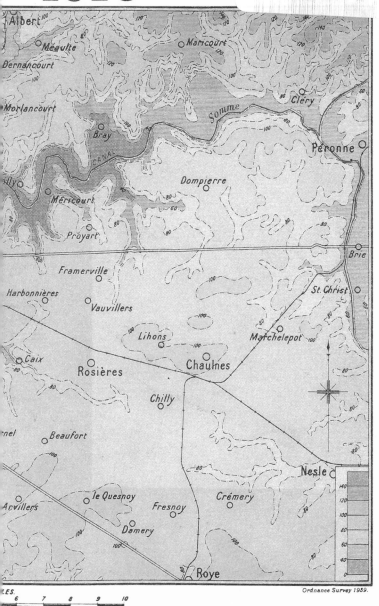

Albert ○ 100

○ Méaulte

Dernancourt

Morlancourt

○ Bray

lly ○

○ Méricourt

○ Proyart

Framerville

Harbonnières ○

○ Vauvillers

Lihons ○

○ Caix

Rosières ○

Chilly

nel

○ Beaufort

Arvillers ○

○ le Quesnoy

Fresnoy ○

○ Damery

Roye ○

○ Maricourt

○ Cléry

Somme

CANAL

Dompierre ○

Péronne ○

Brie

St. Christ ○

Marchelepot ○

Chaulnes ○

Nesle ○

Crémery ○

LES.
6   7   8   9   10

S.

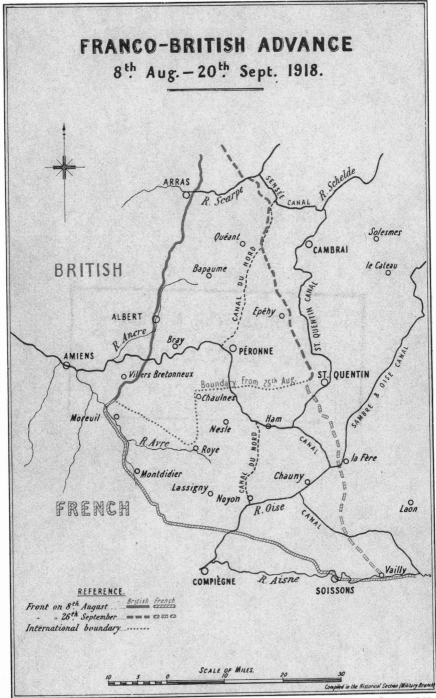

FRANCO-BRITISH ADVANCE
8th Aug. – 20th Sept. 1918.

REFERENCE.

Front on 8th August — British French
" " 26th September
International boundary

SCALE OF MILES.
10   5   0   10   20   30

Compiled in the Historical Section (Military Branch)

Ordnance Survey 1945.

HISTORY OF THE GREAT WAR

BASED ON OFFICIAL DOCUMENTS
BY DIRECTION OF THE HISTORICAL SECTION OF THE
COMMITTEE OF IMPERIAL DEFENCE

MILITARY OPERATIONS
FRANCE AND BELGIUM
1918

VOLUME IV

8th AUGUST — 26th SEPTEMBER

THE FRANCO-BRITISH OFFENSIVE

Edited by
BRIGADIER-GENERAL SIR JAMES E. EDMONDS, C.B., C.M.G.
HON. D. LITT. (*Oxon.*) R.E. (*Retired*) *p.s.c.* †

THE IMPERIAL WAR MUSEUM
Department of Printed Books

In Association With
THE BATTERY PRESS
Nashville

© Crown copyright 1947
Reprinted with the permission of the Controller of HMSO
Published jointly by
**The Imperial War Museum, London
Department of Printed Books
ISBN: 1-870423-05-4**
and
The Battery Press, Inc.
P.O. Box 198885
Nashville, Tennessee 37219
Twenty-seventh in The Battery Press Great War Series
1993
ISBN: 0-89839-191-1

Printed in the United States of America

INTRODUCTION

By

Dr. G. M. Bayliss

The Keeper, Department of Printed Books, Imperial War Museum

I am pleased to introduce this volume, one of a series of reprints of British official histories of military operations in the First World War. For some time I have hoped to make this invaluable source more widely available to students of the Great War; this has now been made possible by cooperation between the Imperial War Museum and Battery Press.

The original editions in the series were produced by the Historical Section of the Committee of Imperial Defence; the first appearing in 1922 and the last in 1949. Apart from Her Majesty's Stationery Office, two commercial publishers were also involved: Macmillan put their imprint on several volumes and Heinemann was responsible for the account of the Gallipoli Campaign. Due to the number of full-colour maps, costs of production were high and this has served to limit later attempts to reprint the series, which have foundered after the publication of text only volumes.

Battery Press, in conjunction with the Imperial War Museum's Department of Printed Books, have taken up the reprinting challenge. In order to make the project viable, we have also decided not to reprint the expensive map volumes. However, readers who wish to obtain copies of any maps in the series are welcome to contact the Imperial War Museum library for further assistance. Since no complete and accurate list of the series exists, the following represents an attempt to remedy this deficiency.

Constantinople

Edmonds, Brig. Gen. Sir James E.
> The Occupation of Constantinople 1918-1923. (Draft provisional history, prepared in 1944 but not printed. It is the intention of Battery Press to produce an expanded version in cooperation with the Imperial War Museum).

East Africa

Hordern, Lt. Col. Charles
> East Africa: Vol. I. August 1914-September 1916 [based on a draft by Major H. Fitz M. Stacke]. London: H.M.S.O., 1941.
> East Africa: Vol. II. [Never published; draft chapters exist in the Public Record Office, London].

Egypt and Palestine

MacMunn, Lieut. Gen. Sir George and Falls, Captain Cyril
> Egypt and Palestine: [Vol. I] From the outbreak of war with Germany to June 1917. London: H.M.S.O., 1928. Accompanying map case.

Falls, Captain Cyril
> Egypt and Palestine: [Vol. II] From June 1917 to the end of the War. Parts I and II. London: H.M.S.O., 1930. Accompanying map case.

France and Belgium
1914

Edmonds, Brig. Gen. Sir James E.
> France and Belgium 1914: [Vol. I] August-October. Mons, the retreat to the Seine, the Marne and the Aisne, August-October 1914. London: Macmillan, 1922 (2nd. ed. 1925; 3rd. ed. 1934). Accompanying map case. [Addenda and Corrigenda to '1914' Vol. I issued with the '1918' Vol. II]. Text volume only reprinted by Shearer Publications, Woking, Surrey, 1984.

Edmonds, Brig. Gen. Sir James E.
> France and Belgium 1914: [Vol. II] Antwerp, La Bassée, Armentiéres, Messines, and Ypres, October-November 1914. London: Macmillan, 1925. Accompanying map case. [Addenda and Corrigenda issued with '1915' Vol. I and '1915' Vol. II].

1915

Edmonds, Brig. Gen. Sir James E. and Wynne, Capt. G. C.
> France and Belgium 1915: [Vol. I] Winter 1914-15: Battle of Neuve Chapelle: Battle of Ypres. London: Macmillan, 1927 Accompanying

map case. [Addenda and Corrigenda issued with '1915' Vol. II and '1916' Vol. I, '1918' Vols. I and II].

Edmonds, Brig. Gen. Sir James E.
France and Belgium 1915: [Vol. II] Battle of Aubers Ridge, Festubert, and Loos. London: Macmillan, 1928. Accompanying map case.

1916

Edmonds, Brig. Gen. Sir James E.
France and Belgium 1916: [Vol. I] Sir Douglas Haig's command to the 1st July: Battle of the Somme. London: Macmillan, 1932. Accompanying appendices volume and map case. [Addenda and Corrigenda to '1916' Vol. I issued with the '1918' Vol. II]. Text volume only reprinted by Shearer Publications, Woking, Surrey, 1986.

Miles, Captain Wilfrid
France and Belgium 1916: [Vol. II]. 2nd July 1916 to the end of the Battles of the Somme: preface by Brig. Gen. Sir James E. Edmonds. London: Macmillan, 1938. Accompanying maps and appendices volume.

1917

Falls, Captain Cyril
France and Belgium 1917: [Vol. I]. The German retreat to the Hindenburg Line and the Battle of Arras: preface by Brig. Gen. Sir James E. Edmonds. London: Macmillan, 1940. Accompanying appendices volume.

Edmonds, Brig. Gen. Sir James E.
France and Belgium 1917: [Vol. II]7th June-10th November: Messines and Third Ypres (Passchendaele). London: H.M.S.O., 1948. [Volume begun by Cyril Falls and G. C. Wynne completed and edited by Edmonds].

Miles, Captain Wilfrid
France and Belgium, 1917: [Vol. III] The Battle of Cambrai; preface by Brig. Gen. Sir James E. Edmonds. London: H.M.S.O., 1948.

1918

Edmonds, Brig. Gen. Sir James E.
France and Belgium 1918: [Vol. I]. The German March offensive and its preliminaries. London: Macmillan, 1935. Accompanying appendices volume and map case. [Addenda and Corrigenda '1918' Vol. I issued with Vol. II].

Edmonds, Brig. Gen. Sir James E.
France and Belgium 1918: [Vol. II.] March-April: continuation of the

German offensives. London: Macmillan, 1937. Accompanying map case. [Special addendum to '1918' Vol. II. Further Addenda and Corrigenda issued with '1917' Vol. I and '1918' Vol. III].

Edmonds, Brig. Gen. Sir James E.
France and Belgium 1918: [Vol. III]. May-July: the German diversion offensives and the first Allied counter-offensive. London: Macmillan, 1939.

Edmonds, Brig. Gen. Sir James E.
France and Belgium 1918: [Vol. IV], 8th August-26th September: the Franco-British offensive. London: H.M.S.O., 1947

Edmonds, Brig. Gen. Sir James E.
France and Belgium 1918: [Vol. V]. 26th September-11th November: the advance to victory. London: H.M.S.O.., 1947

Gallipoli
Aspinall-Oglander, Brig. Gen. C. F.
Gallipoli: Vol. I: Inception of the campaign to May 1915. London: William Heinemann, 1929. Accompanying maps and appendices volume.

Aspinall-Oglander, Brig. Gen. C. F.
Gallipoli: Vol. II: May 1915 to the evacuation. London: William Heinemann, 1932. Accompanying maps and appendices volume.

Italy
Edmonds, Brig. Gen. Sir James E. and Davies, H. R.
Italy, 1915-1919. London: H.M.S.O., 1949.

Macedonia
Falls, Captain Cyril
Macedonia: [Vol. I] From the outbreak of war to Spring 1917. London: H.M.S.O., 1933. Accompanying map case.

Falls, Captain Cyril
Macedonia: [Vol. II] From the Spring of 1917 to the end of the war. London: H.M.S.O., 1935. Accompanying map case.

Mesopotamia
Moberly, Brig. Gen. F. J.
The Campaign in Mesopotamia 1914-1918. Vol. I: London: H.M.S.O., 1923. Vol. II: London: H.M.S.O., 1924. Vol. III: London: H.M.S.O., 1925. Vol. IV: London: H.M.S.O., 1927.

Persia

Moberly, Brig. Gen. F. J.

Operations in Persia, 1914-1919. Confidential edition. London: H.M.S.O., 1929. Public edition. London: H.M.S.O., [in association with the Imperial War Museum], 1987.

Rhineland

Edmonds, Brig. Gen. Sir James E.

The Occupation of the Rhineland, 1918-1929. Confidential edition. London: H.M.S.O., 1944. Public edition, with introduction by Dr. G. M. Bayliss, London: H.M.S.O., [in association with the Imperial War Museum], 1987.

Togoland and the Cameroons

Moberly, Brig. Gen. F. J.

Togoland and the Cameroons, 1914-1916. London: H.M.S.O., 1931.

OTHER RELATED VOLUMES

Order of Battle of Divisions

Becke, Major A. F.

Order of Battle of Divisions. Part 1: The Regular British Divisions. London: H.M.S.O., 1935. Part 2A: The Territorial Force Mounted Divisions and the 1st-Line Territorial Force Divisions (42-56). London: H.M.S.O., 1936. Part 2B: The 2nd-Line Territorial Force Divisions (57th-69th) with the Home Service Divisions. (71st-73rd) and 74th and 75th Divisions. London: H.M.S.O., 1937. Part 3A: New Army Divisions (9-26). London: H.M.S.O., 1938. Part 3B: New Army Divisions (30-41) and 63rd (R.N.) Division. London: H.M.S.O., 1945. Part 4: The Army Council, G. H. Q's, Army and Corps, 1914-1918. London: H.M.S.O., 1945.

Principal Events

Committee of Imperial Defence, Historical Section

Principal events 1914-1918. London: H.M.S.O., 1922.

Transportation on the Western Front

Henniker, Col. A. M.

Transportation on the Western Front 1914-1918; with introduction by Brig. Gen. Sir James E. Edmonds. London: H.M.S.O., 1937. Accompanying case of maps.

PREFACE

This volume covers the period of fifty days, from the 8th August, the "black day of the German Army", until the 26th September, 1918, when the British Armies were lined up opposite the main Hindenburg Position and its continuations northward to the sea, ready to play their part in the great combined Allied offensive which brought about the end of the war.

The volume therefore includes accounts of the preparations which ensured the complete surprise of the enemy on the 8th August by the Fourth Army, and of the failure to exploit that surprise to the full ; the entry of the Third and First Armies into the battle on the 21st August ; the wonderful feat of arms of the Australian Corps on the 30th August which resulted in the capture of Mont St. Quentin and Péronne ; the breaking of the Drocourt–Quéant Line (called by the Germans the Wotan Line) by the Canadian Corps on the 2nd September ; and the forcing of part of the Canal du Nord by the 42nd, New Zealand, 37th and 2nd Divisions on the 4th September, and of the south-north course of the Somme (canal and river) by the 32nd Division and 5th Australian Division on the 5th September.   It also describes the substantial advance made during August and early September by the Second and Fifth Armies between th La Bassée canal and Ypres.

The period was one of steady advance by the Allied forces, and in it, beside the main British thrust, the French Armie gained some ground between Soissons and the British right, and the American First Army, recently formed during the 12th–15th September, cleared the St. Mihiel Salient.   Under the constant pressure maintained on them, the German Armies gradually began to break up.

The operations are interesting from the tactical rather than the strategic point of view, the British successes being gained as a rule—counting by divisions—against superior numbers.   The German defence in depth, whose protagonist, General von Lossberg, was Chief of the General Staff of the Group of Armies opposite the main British attack, proved ineffectual, because the *Eingreif* (super counter-attack) divisions brought up, although they did attempt a few feeble counter-attacks, had generally to be employed as reinforcements to relieve beaten divisions in the line. Defence in depth, unless strong motorized forces are available, demands numbers almost equal to those of the assailant. Some reflections on the campaign will be found at the end of the text of the volume.

Greater results might have been obtained at even smaller cost had the French First Army, under General Debeney, on the immediate right of the B.E.F., pressed forward with the same energy as did first the Canadians and then the Australians next to it. If Sir Douglas Haig had had ample reserves at his disposal, the results might have been decisive. Unfortunately in early August he could provide only one division behind the Fourth Army and two behind the Third Army. In view of the number of German divisions on his front and the enemy reserves available, his frontage was already too extended, and it was actually increased at General Sir Henry Rawlinson's request for the 8th August ; for the commander of the Fourth Army had reasonable fears that his neighbour, General Debeney, would not co-operate whole-heartedly. Possibly anticipating that this might be the case, Maréchal Foch, with a view to ensuring thorough co-operation, had placed the French First Army under the British Commander-in-Chief, and later the Generalissimo strove " to get a move on " Generals Pétain and Debeney by messages which British commanders would regard as insulting.

The very young soldiers with whom the ranks of the British battalions had been filled up after the heavy fighting of March and April did remarkably well in the attack ; whether they would have fought equally well in defence was not put to the test.

Most readers will be surprised to learn of the heavy casualties which were suffered by the tanks and how small was their material effect. It was otherwise with their moral effect ; so it has pleased many Germans to attribute their defeat in the field to the tanks. This excuse will not bear examination. Incidentally, the Germans, one and all, claim on almost every occasion to have been assailed by superior numbers—for instance, when two German divisions were driven off Mont St. Quentin after a long fight by an Australian brigade numbering no more than 1,200 men, our opponents claim to have been ousted by vast superiority in guns, men and tanks. The *Alpine Corps*, although its nine *Jäger* battalions were turned out of Epéhy by a British reinforced brigade of five battalions, states in its history that it was attacked by two divisions.

An official history must take into account the movement of every division at least ; but it has not been feasible, in view of the very large forces employed, to enter into the details of every engagement. I have been forced, by consideration of space, to select certain operations such as those of the 8th August and the Outtersteene fight of the 18th August for lengthier treatment than others. Between the major events, during the German retirements the actions were monotonously alike—the engagement by British advanced guards of enemy rear guards consisting of machine guns and a few scattered field guns. The general reader is recommended to skip much of the narrative which records these daily movements and to gather what happened from the sketch maps.

A skeleton Order of Battle of corps and divisions only has been provided,[1] as details can be found in the " Order of Battle " volumes already published.

As in the case of previous volumes, I am greatly indebted to the combatants to whom the draft chapters were circulated for providing explanations, filling gaps and generally for furnishing corrections, additions and suggestions. Their names are too numerous to mention ; but I must specially thank Dr. C. E. W. Bean, M.A., Litt.D., the Australian Official Historian, for the loan of the typescript chapters of his volume dealing with the period,[2] and to Colonel A. Fortescue Duguid, D.S.O., the Canadian Official Historian, for his own comments and for obtaining those of Canadian officers on my draft chapters. Considerable use has been made of " The Story of the Fourth Army in the Battle of the Hundred Days August 8th to November 11th, 1918 ", published in 1919, by Major-General (now Field-Marshal) Sir Archibald Montgomery (now Montgomery-Massingberd), who was chief General Staff officer of the Fourth Army.

---

[1] Appendix I.
[2] See " A.O.A." in List of books.

For the French operations I have had the benefit of the French official account, Tome VII., Volume I, and the books of Colonel Grasset, Commandant Daille and Captain Gallini.

The allusions to the American forces and their employment have been checked by reference to General J. J. Pershing's " My Experiences in the World War ", and the two Order of Battle volumes prepared in the Historical Section of the U.S. Army War College.

The outbreak of war deprived me of the collaboration of the *Kriegsgeschichtliche Forschungsanstalt des Heeres*, the German Historical Section : so the statements as regards the German divisions engaged had to be compiled from the British Intelligence reports checked by the " Histories of " Two-Hundred and Fifty-one Divisions of the German Army " which participated in the War 1914–18, compiled from " records of the General Staff, American Expeditionary " Forces at General Headquarters 1919 ", and confirmed by the regimental histories of the units. When the name of a German division cropped up on the Intelligence maps, the process was to find from the " Histories " volume which were the units in the division, and then to verify from the unit histories that they were present at the particular place on the particular day. In some cases a unit history mentioned the presence of other divisions whose arrival was not known to the British Intelligence until a later date. The number of German divisions shown is certainly not more than were engaged and may be less ; only in one case did the Intelligence maps show a division which was not present, and then the division which did hold the particular frontage was omitted.

Full details of the 8th August from the German side were found in the Official Monograph, " Die Katastrophe des " 8 August 1918 ", and a good deal of general information about the period in the books of Crown Prince Rupprecht of Bavaria and General von Gallwitz, who commanded Groups of Armies ; of General Ludendorff ; of General von Kuhl, who was Crown Prince Rupprecht's Chief of the Staff and one of the military experts at the *Reichstag* Committee which enquired into the loss of the war ; of General von Lossberg, who was Chief of the Staff to General von Boehn's Group of Armies, opposite to the British ; and in the Bavarian one-volume official story of the war.

I have had the benefit of the invaluable criticism of the final draft by Mr. W. B. Wood, M.A. (Oxon.) and Major-General Sir Henry Thuillier.

The names of my assistants in the compilation appear opposite the title page.

All officers interested may not have seen the draft or proofs.   I beg, therefore, as I have done in previous volumes, that any corrections or additions, and criticisms thought necessary, may be sent to the Secretary of the Historical Section, Offices of the Cabinet.

At the same time, I offer my thanks to those who so kindly furnished corrections for the earlier volumes.

This volume was completed in TS in December, 1940, but owing to paper shortage its publication was postponed.

J. E. E.

NOTES

THE location of troops and places is written from right to left of the front of the Allied Forces unless otherwise stated. In translations from the German the order given is as in the original; otherwise enemy troops are enumerated like the British. Where roads which run through both the British and German lines are described by the names of towns or villages, the place in British hands is mentioned first, thus: "Albert–Bapaume road".

To save space and bring the nomenclature in line with "Division", "Infantry Brigade" has in the text been abbreviated to "Brigade", as distinguished from "Cavalry Brigade" and "Artillery Brigade"; "Regiment" similarly means "Infantry Regiment".

The convention observed in the British Expeditionary Force is followed as regards the distinguishing numbers of Armies, Corps, Divisions, etc., of the British and Allied Armies, e.g., they are written in full for Armies, in Roman figures for corps, and in Arabic for smaller formations and units, except Artillery Brigades, which are Roman; thus: Fourth Army, IV. Corps, 4th Cavalry Division, 4th Division, 4th Cavalry Brigade, 4th Brigade, IV. Brigade R.F.A.; but for artillery brigades with numbers higher than one hundred Arabic figures are used.

German formations and units, to distinguish them clearly from the Allies, are printed in italic characters, thus *First Army*, *I. Corps*, *1st Division*.

The usual abbreviations of regimental names have been used: for example, "2/R. West Kent" or "West Kent" for 2nd Battalion The Queen's Own Royal West Kent Regiment; K.O.Y.L.I. for the King's Own Yorkshire Light Infantry; K.R.R.C. for the King's Royal Rifle Corps. To avoid constant repetition, the "Royal" in regimental titles is sometimes omitted. To economize space the 63rd (Royal Naval) Division, the 14th (Light) Division, etc., are usually described by their numbers only. [1]

First-line and Second-line Territorial Force units are distinguished by a figure in front of the battalion or other number, thus: 1/8th London, 2/8th London, 1/3rd London or 2/3rd London Field Company, R.E., or when the First-line and Second-line had been amalgamated, simply 3/London; but in the case of First-line units the figure in front of the battalion number is sometimes omitted.

---

[1] The Yorkshire Regiment is usually called in the text by its ancient name "The Green Howards".

Abbreviations employed occasionally are :—
B.E.F. for British Expeditionary Force ;
D.A.N. for Détachment d' armée du Nord ;
G.A.C. for Groupe d'armées du Centre ;
G.A.E. for Groupe d'armées de l' Est ;
G.A.N. for Groupe d'armées du Nord ;
G.A.R. for Groupe d'armées de Réserve ;
G.H.Q. for British General Headquarters ;
G.Q.G. for French Grand Quartier-Général (usually spoken as " Grand Q.G.") ;

O.H.L. for German *Oberste Heeresleitung* (German Supreme Command). *N.B.*—" G.H.Q." in German means Grosses Haupt-Quartier, that is the Kaiser's Headquarters, political, military and naval, as distinguished from O.H.L.
R.I.R. (on maps) for Reserve Infantry Regiment.

The spellings of " lacrymatory " and " strongpoint " are arbitrary, and were selected as being shorter than the usual ones.

Officers are described by the rank which they held at the period under consideration. To save space the initials instead of the Christian names of knights are generally used.

The German pre-war practice of writing the plain name without " von ", when it is applicable and no rank or title is prefixed, has been adopted, *e.g.*, " Falkenhayn " and not " von Falkenhayn ".

Both belligerents had adopted Summer Time, the Allies on the night of the 9th–10th March and the Germans on that of the 14th–15th April, so throughout the volume German time is one hour ahead of British time.

Owing to printing restrictions, map references instead of being in the margin as in previous volumes, are given in footnotes.

MAPS AND SKETCHES

The operations are illustrated as far as possible by sketches bound in the text : the four maps judged indispensable, if reduced to double-page size would have made the details too small to be read with ease, are placed in a pocket.

The frontispiece shows the ground gained by the Allies between Soissons and Arras during the period dealt with. Besides this, the St. Mihiel Salient was captured by the Americans, for which see End–paper B, and progress was made north of the La Bassée canal, which is shown on Sketches 21 and 25.

The layered End-paper A shows the configuration of the ground over which the Battle of Amiens was fought. Large layered maps on the 1 : 100,000 scale of the whole area over which the hostilities described in this volume took place will be found as Map 1 of " 1918 " Volume I, which goes as far north as Lens, and Map 13 of " 1918 " Volume II, which gives the remainder of the British front from Lens to Ypres ; it was therefore thought unnecessary to provide one here.

End-paper B shows the German back positions on the Western Front.

The names of a number of small localities mentioned, probably only once, are omitted on the maps and sketches to avoid over-crowding ; their position is described in brackets with reference to some place which is marked. Thus, Prusle (2 miles east of Brie). In a few cases this device has been used in regard to villages marked on the sketches but not easy to find.

Armies are shown by " First," " Second " ; corps, by " XV," " XXXI," " CDN " (Canadian), " AUS " (Australian), and " CAV " (Cavalry) ; divisions, by Arabic figures, 42, 53 ; and brigades by small ordinal figures, 3rd, 17th.

The maps and sketches were drawn for reproduction by Mr. H. Burge.

ERRATA TO MAPS AND SKETCHES

Map 1. *for* Villers Bretonneu (*left centre*)
    read Villers Bretonneux.
    for Crepe Wd. (*right centre*)
    read Crépey Wd.

Map 3. *for* Sergueux (*left bottom corner*)
    read Serqueux.

Map 4. *for* Boir Becqierelle (*centre*)
    read Boiry Becquerelle.

Sketch   5. *for* Cerisy Gally (*right centre*)
             read Cerisy, *as in text.*

Sketch 14. *for* the *red* V. *under Bucquoy*
             read IV.

Sketch 17. *above* 54th (Brigade) (*left top corner*)
             add figure "18" (*for 18th Division*).

Sketch 25. *for* Richebourg Avoné (*top*)
             read Richebourg Avoué.

Sketch 28. *delete* "46" (*in red, left centre*).
             for Cornouivillers Wood (*lower centre*)
             read Cornouillers Wood.
             In the III. Corps area, for X Copse (*North of Y Copse*)
             read Z Copse.

---

[1] All dates are in 1918.

Chapter VII

Chapter VIII

Chapter IX

Chapter X

Chapter XI

Chapter XII

Chapter XIII

Chapter XIV

Chapter XV

Chapter XVI

Chapter XVII

CHAPTER XXIII

CHAPTER XXIV

TABLE OF APPENDICES

[1] All dates are in 1918.

CONTENTS

SKETCHES AND MAPS

SKETCHES

(*Bound in Volume*)

[1] All dates are in 1918.

MAPS

(*In Pocket*)

---

[1] All dates are in 1918.

LIST OF BOOKS

A.O.A. (Australian Official Account) : " Official History of Australia in the Great War 1914-18. Volume VI. The A.I.F. in France : May, 1918–Armistice " by Dr. C. E. W. Bean, M.A., Litt. D. (Australia : Angus & Robertson), published in 1942 in the interval between the compilation of the present volume and its being sent to press.

B.O.A. (Bavarian Official Account) : " Bayern im Grossen Krieg " (Munich : Verlag des Bayerischen Kriegsarchivs.)

A general account of the War in one volume with special reference to the part played by the Bavarians.

DAILLE : " La Bataille de Montdidier ". By Commandant M. Daille. (Paris : Berger-Levrault.)

The author was an instructor at the *Ecole de Guerre* ; his book describes the operations of the French First Army, with scant mention of the British.

F.O.A. (French Official Account) : " Les Armées françaises dans la Grande Guerre ". Ministère de la Guerre. État-Major de l'Armée. Service Historique. (Paris : Imprimerie Nationale.)

Tome VII, Volume I, covers the period dealt with in this volume.

GALLINI : " Les opérations de la 1ʳᵉ Armée française au 8 août 1918 ". By Lieut.-Colonel J. Gallini. (Paris : Charles-Lavauzelle.)

A useful compact account, with orders and maps.

GALLWITZ : " Erleben im Westen 1916-18 ". By General Max von Gallwitz. (Berlin : Mittler.)

The author was commander of the Group of Armies in the Verdun area, but his book throws a good deal of light on the campaign. He was one of the two generals summoned by the *Reich* Chancellor, Prince Max of Baden, at the end of. October to give their opinion on the state of the Army, the incident which led to Ludendorff's resignation.

GRASSET : " Montdidier, le 8 août 1918 à la 42ᵉ division ". By Colonel Grasset. (Paris : Berger-Levrault.)

The complete story of the French division next to the British (3rd Canadian Division) on the 8th August. It transpires that the two Allied divisional generals met, but as neither spoke nor understood the other's language and their staffs could only master a few words, their conferences, though cordial, were not very helpful and conversation was " painful " and carried out " mainly by signs ".

GRUSS : " Die deutschen Sturmbataillone im Weltkriege ". By H. Gruss. (Berlin : Junker und Dunnhaupt.)

An account of the German Storm Battalions published by the Military History Seminar of the Frederick-William University, Berlin.

KUHL : " Entstehung. Durchführung und Zusammenbruch der Offensive von 1918 ". By General von Kuhl. (Berlin : Deutscher Verlag.)

This is a most valuable source.

The author, the well-known Chief Staff Officer of General von Kluck in 1914, and later of Field-Marshal Crown Prince Rupprecht of Bavaria, was one of the three technical assistants of the *Reichstag* Commission which enquired into the causes of the loss of the War. His book contains the report which he made to the Commission, divided into five parts : The Relative Strengths, the Reinforcement and Supply of the Armies, the Decision to Attack, the Spring Offensives and the Defensive Battle in the Summer of 1918.

LOSSBERG : " Meine Tätigkeit im Weltkriege 1914-18 ". (Berlin : Mittler.) By General Fritz von Lossberg.

The author was Chief of the General Staff of Boehn's Group of Armies (*Second, Eighteenth* and *Ninth Armies*), which confronted the French First and British Fourth Armies from the 12th August onwards. A valuable and authoritative book. Lossberg was the protagonist of defence in depth.

LUDENDORFF : " My War Memories, 1914-18 ". By General Erich Ludendorff. (Hutchinson & Co.)

Translation of " Meine Kriegserinnerungen ".

MONOGRAPH : " Die Katastrophe des 8. August 1918 ". (Oldenburg : Stalling.)

" The Catastrophe of the 8th August 1918 ". One of the series of German official monographs on the War.

MORDACQ : " Le Ministère Clemenceau. Journal d'un témoin ". By General Mordacq. (Paris : Plon.)

General Mordacq was Chief of the Military Cabinet of M. Clemenceau, the President of the Council of Ministers and Minister of War in 1918. He seldom left M. Clemenceau's side and kept a full diary.

PERSHING : " My Experiences in the World War. " By John J. Pershing. Commander-in-Chief American Expeditionary Forces (Hodder & Stoughton.)

General Pershing's personal story founded on his dairies.

" REGT. No. . . . " These are references to the War histories of German regiments. The volumes vary in length and value : some give detailed accounts of the operations with extracts from the reminiscences of combatants ; others merely reproduce the official war dairies. Some of the latter type have been superseded by fuller accounts.

RUPPRECHT : " Mein Kriegstagebuch ". By Field-Marshal Crown Prince Rupprecht of Bavaria. (Munich : Deutscher National Verlag.)

A dairy full of interesting details kept by the commander of the Group of Armies (*Fourth, Seventeenth* and *Sixth*), which held the front from near Albert to the sea and thus faced the British Third, First and Second Armies and the Belgian Army.

SCHWARTE iii. : " Der deutsche Landkrieg ". Edited by Lieut.-General M. Schwarte. (Leipzig : Barth.)

A compendium of the War in 12 volumes. Volume III covers the operations on the Western Front from the time Hindenburg-Ludendorff took command until the Armistice, and contains extracts of operation orders and other useful matter.

SCHWERTFEGER: "Das Weltkriegsende". By Colonel B. Schwert
feger. (Potsdam : Athenaion.)

Colonel Schwertfeger, like General von Kuhl, was one of
the three technical assistants of the *Reichstag* Commission
which enquired into the causes of the loss of the War. His
book contains much valuable information.

WAR IN THE AIR: "The War in the Air". By H. A. Jones.
(Clarendon Press.)

The Official History of the part played by the Royal Air
Force.

Note :—" 1918 " Vols. I, II or III signifies " The Official
History of the Great War, Military Operations, France and
Belgium ". Volume I covers the period of the March
offensive to the 26th March, Volume II from that date to the
30th April, and Volume III, thence to the 6th August.

CALENDAR OF PRINCIPAL EVENTS

Mainly extracted from "Principal Events 1914–18" compiled by the Historical Section of the Committee of Imperial Defence, London. His Majesty's Stationery Office. 10s. 6d. net.

Western Theatre	Other Theatres	Naval Warfare and General Events
	AUGUST 1918	During this month 41 British merchant ships (gross tonnage, 145,721) were lost by enemy action.
8th. Battles of Amiens and Montdidier begin.		
11th. Battle of Amiens ends.		13th. Czecho-Slovaks declare war on Germany and are recognized by British Government as Allied nation.
15th. Battle of Montdidier ends.		15th. Last bombardment of Paris by long-range gun.
17th. Battle of Noyon begins.		
18th. British advance in Flanders begins.	18th. *Central Asia*: Merv taken by Bolsheviks.	
Action of Outtersteene Ridge.		
21st. Battle of Albert 1918 begins.		
22nd Battle of the Scarpe 1918 begins.		
	26th. *Caucasus*: Defence of Baku against the Turks begins.	
27th. Roye recaptured by the French. Germans begin retirement to the Somme line.	27th. Krasnovodsk (Caspian) occupied.	

Western Theatre	Other Theatres	Naval Warfare and General Events
29th. Bapaume recaptured. Noyon recaptured by the French. Battles of Albert 1918 and Noyon end. Conference of Maréchal Foch and the Allied Commanders-in-Chief.	AUGUST 1918—*continued*	
30th. Battle of the Scarpe 1918 ends. Bailleul recaptured. Second Battle of Bapaume begins.		
31st. Germans evacuate Mont Kemmel.		31st. British Naval attaché in Petrograd murdered.
1st. Péronne retaken. Mont St. Quentin captured.	SEPTEMBER 1918	During this month 48 British merchant ships (gross tonnage, 136,859) were sunk by enemy action.
2nd. Battle of Drocourt-Quéant (2nd–3rd). German retirement to the Canal du Nord and Hindenburg Position begins.		
3rd. Second Battle of Bapaume ends. Lens occupied.		
4th. Pursuit to the Hindenburg Position begins.		
6th. O.H.L. conference at Avesnes decides to fight on Hindenburg Position.		
9th. Ludendorff dismisses his strategic adviser, Col. Wetzell.		

Western Theatre	Other Theatres	Naval Warfare and General Events
	SEPTEMBER 1918—*continued*	
12th. Battle of Havrincourt. Battle of St. Mihiel (12th–13th).	15th. *Macedonia* : Battle of Dobro-polje (15th–16th). *Caucasus* : Baku evacuated.	15th. Austrian Government suggest "unofficial" peace conference. German Government makes peace offer to Belgium.
18th. Battle of Epéhy.	18th. *Macedonia* : Battle of Mona-stir-Doiran begins.	
19th. Approach to the Hindenburg Position continued to 26th.	19th. *Palestine* : Battles of Megiddo begin.	
	20th. *Palestine* : Nazareth and Beisan occupied.	
	22nd. *Macedonia* : Doiran occupied.	
	23rd. *Palestine* : Haifa, Acre and Es Salt occupied.	
	24th. *Macedonia* : Battle of Mona-stir-Doiran ends.	
	25th. *Palestine* : Battles of Megiddo end.	

CHAPTER I

THE PRELIMINARIES OF THE BATTLE OF AMIENS

(Maps 1, 2 ; Sketches 1, 2)[1]

On the 24th July, whilst the Second Battle of the Marne (18th July–6th August) was still in progress,[2] General Foch, who a fortnight later was to receive the rank and dignity of *Maréchal de France,* held an important conference. He summoned for the purpose to his headquarters at Bombon Château, near Melun, 25 miles south-east of Paris, the three Allied Commanders-in-Chief, General Pétain, General Pershing and Sir Douglas Haig. As a result of previous consultations with these coadjutors, he was now in a position to lay down the outline of the great counter-offensives which since the beginning of the year he had constantly borne in mind.[3] The Germans, who at the Marne in 1914 had offered to General Joffre the chance of almost re-enacting a " Cannae "—advocated as the crown of military art by their most recent war philosopher, General-Field-Marshal Graf Schlieffen—had now presented to the Generalissimo the opportunity so desired by their earlier theorist, General von Clausewitz : having exhausted themselves against the Allied defensive, they were ripe to be attacked and decisively defeated.[4]

General Foch, with the full support of his Government,[5] proposed a series of operations destined to free from interference three railways of vital importance for the future operations of the Allied Armies, which were imperilled by

---

[1] Map 1 issued with " 1918 " Vol. I, layered 1/100,000 should be used, if the battle is studied in detail ; otherwise the ground is shown sufficiently on End-paper A.

[2] Described in " 1918 " Vol. III. The German *Seventh Army* was being forced out of the salient (see Sketch 1) it had gained in the operations of 27th May–6th June, known as the offensive of the Chemin des Dames.

[3] See " 1918 " Vol. I, pp. 66, 70.

[4] " Begin with defence, end with offence. A quick powerful change- " over to the attack—the lightning stroke of retaliation—that is the most " brilliant act of the defence."—*Vom Kriege,* Tenth German edition, p. 356.

[5] During the preparations and operations in July and August M. Clemenceau constantly visited Maréchal Foch " in order to ensure " that he could give his whole time to his strategic task by aiding him " to overcome all difficulties raised by the Allied Governments and " generals ".—Mordacq ii, p. 137.

enemy salients made in the Allied front.[1] These lateral
railways, " lignes de rocade ", were essential for shifting
troops from one part of the front to another.[2] The northernmost of them, Paris–Châlons, was actually cut at Château
Thierry, where the enemy was in possession ; the next,
Paris–Avricourt, was endangered at two places by the
proximity of the St. Mihiel and the Château Thierry salients ;
Amiens, the junction between the Allies, was threatened by
the Montdidier salient and under fire. The first lines,
therefore, to be freed were—

> (1) The Paris–Avricourt railway in the Marne area,
> which passed ten miles south of Château Thierry. This
> would be effected by the fighting for the Château Thierry
> salient in the Second Battle of the Marne, in progress.

> (2) The Paris–Amiens railway. This was to be
> effected by an offensive of a combined French and
> British force, the French First Army and the British
> Fourth Army, in front of Amiens.

> (3) The Paris–Avricourt line in the Verdun area,
> where it was not 10 miles from St. Mihiel. This would
> be rendered secure by the reduction of the St. Mihiel
> salient, which General Pershing had in his mind as an
> American offensive.[3]

After these three operations, said General Foch, would
come others, to free the coal mining area in the north and
to drive the enemy from the neighbourhood of Calais and
Dunkirk.

The Germans continuing to fall back in the Château
Thierry salient, on the 28th July, after a second Conference
on the 26th at which Generals Debeney and Sir H. Rawlinson,
the commanders of the French First and British Fourth
Armies, who had already had a meeting to collaborate their
plans, were also present, General Foch issued the formal order
for the Amiens operations. This began—

> " 1. The object of the operations is to disengage
> " Amiens and the Paris–Amiens railway, also to defeat
> " and drive back the enemy established between the
> " Somme and the Avre.

---

[1] A translation of the whole memorandum is given in " 1918 " Vol. III,
Appendix XX.
[2] See Sketch 1.
[3] On 9th August the transfer of the American First Army from the
Marne to the St. Mihiel sector was begun by the shift of headquarters to
Neufchâteau (40 miles south of St. Mihiel).—Pershing, p. 540.

" 2. To do so, the offensive, covered in the north by
" the Somme, will be pushed as far as possible in the
" direction of Roye ".

The operation now envisaged differed only slightly from
that suggested to Sir Douglas Haig by General Sir H.
Rawlinson on the 5th July, after the successful attack
against Hamel, for which the Chief of the General Staff
had on the 13th instructed him to draft plans.[1] These the
commander of the Fourth Army had submitted in writing
on the 17th. They were based on the assumption that, in
addition to his present forces, the Australian Corps (less one
division) and the III Corps, he would receive as reinforcements the Canadian Corps, then in reserve, the 1st Australian
Division, which was still in the north, and the Cavalry
Corps. The inter-Allied junction being at a point a little
south of Villers Bretonneux, he proposed an advance of
about four miles, from the front between Villers Bretonneux
and the Somme,[2] protected by a flank in the French area
from Moreuil to the British right. He was anxious to
conduct the whole operation with British troops, and he
suggested the 10th August as the date.

Now, on the 28th, General Foch decided that the part of
the French First Army north of the Avre instead of merely
forming a flank, should take part in the advance and align
itself with the British, as well as providing for a flank ; but
he agreed that the inter-Allied boundary should be shifted
three miles (7,000 yards along the line of the trenches) to
the south, so that the Fourth Army's front would extend
across the Luce and the main portion of the initial attack
would be in General Rawlinson's hands. Further, to ensure
unity of command, he placed the whole French First Army[3]
under the orders of Sir Douglas Haig. He was anxious, in
view of the swift course which events on the Marne were
taking, that the date of the offensive should be hastened by
two days, so that the attack could be launched on the 8th.
General Rawlinson was informed by telephone at 6.45 p.m.
of the proposed change of date, which in spite of the forward
state of the plans, meant altering the times of arrival of

[1] See " 1918 " Vol. III, p. 311.
[2] See Map 1 and Sketch 2.
[3] From left to right XXXI, IX and X Corps, with the XXXVI in
reserve ; to these on 2nd August was added on the right the XXXV
from the Third Army.

reinforcements, putting " Herculean " labour into dumping ammunition, and general speeding up. After discussion of the time-table with a Staff officer from G.H.Q. who was sent to impress on him the urgency of the matter, General Rawlinson agreed to make Zero Day the 8th.

The essence of the plan was that the French XXXI Corps, the Canadian Corps and Australian Corps should first advance eastwards about four miles, guarded on the right by the remaining corps of the French First Army, so that the space between Avre and Somme should be filled.   The III Corps was to cover the left flank.

The distribution of the Allied troops by divisions on the 29th July, a date which it is convenient to take as both French and British situation maps for it are available, was as follows :—[1]

FRENCH ARMIES :

	Divisions in Line	Divisions in Reserve
Verdun and Eastwards :		
G.A.E. Seventh Army ..	9 (3 American, 2 Territorial)	2 (1 Territorial)
Eighth Army ..	10 (2 American, 1 Territorial)	5 (2 American)
Second Army ..	7	1 (Italian)
Between Verdun (exclusive) and the Oise :		
G.A.C. Fourth Army ..	6	4
Fifth Army ..	14 (2 British)	7 (1 Italian)
G.A.R. Sixth Army ..	7 (2 American)	8 (4 American)
Tenth Army ..	13 (1 British)	6 (1 British, 1 American)
North of the Oise :		
Third Army ..	9	3
First Army ..	9	3
	74 French 7 American 3 British	29 French 7 American 2 Italian 1 British

[1] See Map 2.

The 4 British divisions (15th, 34th, 51st and 62nd) of the XXII Corps (Lieut.-General Sir A. Godley) which had fought in the Second Battle of the Marne were about to be returned to the British area. The American First Army was about to be formed in the area of the French Sixth Army.[1]

BRITISH ARMIES :

		Divisions in Line	Divisions in Reserve
Fourth Army	Australian Corps.	3	2
	III.	2	1 (1 American)
Third Army	V. ..	2	2
	IV. ..	3	1 (1 American)
	VI. ..	3	1
First Army	Canadian	2	2
	VIII. ...	3	
	I. ..	3	
Fifth Army	XIII. ..	3	1
	XI. ..	2	1 (Portuguese)
Second Army	XV. ..	4 (1 Australian)	1
	X. ..	2	2
	XIX. ..	2	1 (1 American)
	II. ..	2	2 (1 American)
		36 British	12 British

[1] Besides the 14 American divisions with the French and 5 with the British, there were 8 others in France, and 2 more disembarking. The total of the American forces in France on 31st July was 54,224 officers and 1,114,838 enlisted men.—Pershing, p. 523.

Behind the British right was the IX Corps (consisting of the 18th and the cadre 66th Divisions). In the centre, behind the VIII Corps, was the XVII Corps (52nd and 56th and the 78th American Divisions) ; and behind the left, the VII Corps (consisting of the recently reconstituted 14th Division and the cadre 39th). In addition there were the Cavalry Corps (3 divisions), also behind the right, the 50th (reorganizing), 16th (just returned from the United Kingdom after reconstitution) and one Portuguese division ; but of these only one division of the IX Corps and the cavalry were in position as reserves for the forthcoming operation. To these, however, must be added the three divisions (21st, 32nd and 63rd) in reserve of the Fourth Army and the three in reserve of the French First Army (to which was moving one division of the French Third Army), a total reserve for the operation of eight divisions and the Cavalry Corps.

General Foch had no General Reserve, except the two French cavalry corps, as the rest had been used up in the Second Battle of the Marne ; but he considered that he had available to meet the enemy reserve of 67 divisions (60 according to British reckoning) :

10 American divisions (8 fresh) ;

4 Belgian divisions (all fresh) ;

21 British divisions (fresh or reconstituted) ;

38 French divisions (8 fresh or reconstituted) ;

2 Italian divisions ;

2 Portuguese divisions ;

a total of 77 (41 fresh or reconstituted), with 10 cavalry divisions (1 Belgian, 3 British, 6 French).[1]

The Intelligence returns for the 1st August showed a very different state of things on the enemy side to the returns of the 24th May, the count before the German offensive of the Chemin des Dames.

---

[1] F.O.A. vii. (i), p.163. How the total of 21 British divisions in reserve was arrived at is not clear : there were 14 in corps and Army reserve and 4 in rear areas. Perhaps the 4 in the XXII Corps which had been in the Second Battle of the Marne were included, and the 16th Division, which was arriving from the U.K., was not counted.

GERMAN DIVISIONS
24th May, 1918

	Divisions in Line	Divisions in Reserve	Total
Fourth Army	14	19	33
Sixth Army	16	8	24
Seventeenth Army	11	9	20
Second Army	13	20	33
Eighteenth Army	13	22	35
Ninth* Army	—	—	—
Seventh Army	8	9**	17
First Army	8	—	8
Third Army	7	1	8
Fifth Army	6	—	6
" C " Detachment	9	—	9
Nineteenth Army	4	1	5
" A " Detachment	5	—	5
" B " Detachment	5	—	5
Unlocated**	—	—	—
	119	89	208
Unfit	—	—	—

1st August, 1918***

	Divisions in Line	Divisions in Reserve	Total	Unfit
British-Belgian Front	11	11	22	3
	13	9	22	3
	11	5	16	3
	10	4	14	4
	11	4	15	3
	15	7	22	19
French Front	23	15	38	38
	11	—	11	7
	8	3	11	10
	5	—	5	—
	8	2	10	4
	6	—	6	4
	4	—	4	3
	5	—	5	5
	141	60	201	106
Unfit	78	28	106	—

* The *Ninth Army* was formed from the *Seventh.*
** Nine were unlocated at the time, but are counted as behind the *Seventh Army.*
*** The nearest date to 29th July available.

If a graphic be drawn from this table it will be seen that, neglecting the quiet sector of the front lying east of Verdun where the array of forces remained unchanged, the centre of gravity of the German forces had been shifted from the junction of the French and British fronts to the French left centre, and the reserves opposite the British had likewise been drawn eastwards and had been greatly reduced in strength. The total number of enemy divisions had dropped by 7 (in a few days it was to be 10) and of the 201 remaining, 106 were classed by the British Intelligence as temporarily " unfit " owing to the recent fighting, 15 were *Landwehr*, and 5 were of poor class. Strength and quality as a whole had both fallen off. On the 1st July the establishment of all German battalions had been reduced from 980 all ranks to 800. Fifty-four per cent. of the reinforcements in the first seven months of 1918 had been returned wounded, and 32 per cent. were lads of the 1919 class.

In artillery, too, the enemy had suffered. From April onwards British ammunition had been plentiful and each German battery when it was spotted had received two hundred rounds from 6-inch howitzers with gratifying results.[1]

The Royal Air Force had greatly added to the enemy's troubles. A captured order of the *XI Corps*, astride the Somme, dated the 21st July spoke of " the bloody losses recently caused by enemy air raids on billets and camps ". In the fortnight preceding the battle 188 tons of bombs were dropped by day and 96 (on 10 occasions) by night.

The local margin of superiority over the Germans was nevertheless very small ; for although the German reserves on the front selected for attack amounted to only 4 divisions, 25 divisions still remained in reserve in the north (9, however, reckoned " unfit "), some of which might be quickly shifted if the enemy obtained sufficient notice. The remains, too, of his " battering train " of guns, trench mortars and aeroplanes, used in each of his offensives, might still be a

---

[1] A captured order of Crown Prince Rupprecht's Group of Armies, dated 24th May, advised the use of alternative emplacements as a guard against " the occasional very heavy losses of material through enemy " counter-battery work ". Another order, signed by Ludendorff on 1st August, pointed out that " in round numbers " 13 per cent. of the German artillery taking part in active operations in the West had been completely destroyed by enemy fire in a single month (Not specified. In view of the French offensive it may have been July).

powerful factor. Surprise was the essence of Allied success.
To ensure as much initial secrecy as possible and limit
knowledge of the contemplated operation to as few persons
as possible, the preliminary arrangements were settled in
the Fourth Army by conferences of the principal officers
concerned, held at different places with small numbers at
first, increased only as time advanced. Sir Douglas Haig,
on his part, sent a personal letter to General Debeney to
explain that he refrained from meeting him in order not to
awaken suspicion. Both in the Fourth Army and the French
First Army the troops in the line were not to be acquainted
with the intended operation until 24 to 36 hours before zero
hour. The great problem was to conceal the assembly of
the additional troops and the accumulation of material.

On the 29th G.H.Q. issued to Generals Debeney and
Rawlinson by name as " personal and very secret ", the
formal operation order,[1] directing that the line Hangest-le-
Quesnel—Caix—Harbonnières—Méricourt, virtually the line
gained on the 8th August, should be seized as quickly as
possible and organized for defence. When this line had been
secured, the French First Army, with its right on the Avre,
was to " press the enemy in the direction of the Roye " [on
the great chausée leading south-east from Amiens], and the
Fourth Army, with its left on the Somme, similarly " press
" the enemy in the direction of Chaulnes [on the railway
" running E.S.E. from Amiens] ". The Amiens—Roye road
would at first form the Allied boundary. A short order was
sent by the Fourth Army to ten officers by name on the
31st, with a map showing the objectives and boundaries.[2]
It stated the corps which would be employed, allotted tank
brigades to them, and announced that further orders—as to
details—would be given in the form of instructions.

General Debeney also issued orders on the 31st to the
three corps commanders concerned only.[3] Omitting the
general outline, already known to them, the orders entered
into detail as to the exact localities of which the XXXI and
IX Corps were to make themselves masters on the first day,
even the divisions to be employed, and the action of these
corps and of the X Corps on the second day.

---

[1] Appendix II.   See Map 1 and Sketch 2.
[2] Appendix III.
[3] Appendix IV.

What General Rawlinson had in his mind was to repeat on a larger scale the well-planned and completely successful Hamel operation—that is the employment of as small a force of infantry as possible and the full use of tanks.[1] He proposed to engage, omitting the troops used for flank protection, nine divisions and 400 tanks, instead of 10 battalions and 60 tanks, as at Hamel.

The ground between the Avre and the Somme[2] was well suited to the use of tanks, being the great rolling plateau of the Santerre. Falling slightly from west to east, it was " a real billiard table " in the French area, according to one French author, but scooped by shallow depressions, leading towards the rivers, in the British.[3] It had a few large villages,[4] with strongly built houses, and here and there tiny woods ; but as the villages were in nearly every case enclosed by orchards and trees, they presented the appearance of woods, unless betrayed by a church steeple appearing above the foliage. The plateau is cut into by the valley of the Luce, whose course lies about two hundred feet below it, and although it has large bends was generally parallel to the line of the advance. A small stream in itself, only 4 to 9 yards wide and little more than knee-deep in August 1918, the Luce has pools and swamps, with belts of trees to a width of two or three hundred yards, along its course, so that it was not passable by formed bodies and vehicles except by causeways and bridges. The only available crossings in the Allied lines were those near Domart and Hourges, and to construct others would have " given away " the intended attack.

At its southern border the plateau blends into a swell of high ground, which near Moreuil, in the angle between the Luce and the Avre, overlooks the valleys of both streams and the plain to the north-east nearly as far as Villers Bretonneux. On the edges of the plateau towards both the Avre and the Somme the ground is cut by a series of deepish ravines descending into the broad flat valleys of these rivers,

---

[1] See " 1918 ", Vol. III, p.

[2] See End-paper A. Anyone who intends to study the operations closely should refer to Map 1 issued with " 1918 " Vol. I, which is on the 1: 100,000 scale and layered.

[3] Gallini, p. 52.

[4] Hangest had, pre-war, 1,396 inhabitants ; le Quesnel, 1,128 ; Plessier, 729 ; Demuin, 690 ; Mézières, 630 ; Domart, 630.

which, like the Luce, cut deep into the plain and have pools and marshes along their courses. The Avre has on the slopes of its right bank an almost uninterrupted belt of woods, and this in 1918 had been turned into a serious obstacle by the effects of shell-fire. Where the III Corps was to operate, between the Somme and the Ancre, the plateau is no more than a flat-topped ridge ; its slopes, too, to the rivers are broken by many spurs and re-entrants, which, though comparatively gentle on the northern side, are rough and abrupt on the southern, and unsuitable ground for tank operations. Here the long Chipilly spur gave the enemy good observation down the Somme valley.

The front of the German *Second Army* (General von der Marwitz),[1] which had been the centre Army in the great offensive of the 21st March 1918, exactly covered the proposed front of attack from the right of the French IX Corps near Hargicourt to the left of the British III Corps near Albert.

The *Second Army* consisted of 10 divisions in front line and 4 in reserve,[2] divided among three corps, the LI, XI and LIV. Of the ten, four by Intelligence reckoning were " unfit ".[3]

---

[1] He died in February, 1939, at the age of 82.

[2] On comparing the Intelligence Map of 1st August 1918 with the Monograph on 8th August issued in 1930, it was found that the total number, the names and the location of the divisions had been correctly ascertained, except that the *27th Division*, which arrived only on 3rd August, was not shown, the *54th*, which it relieved, being marked in its place.

[3] What General von der Marwitz thought of them is recorded in a report rendered to O.H.L. on 3rd August. Omitting the northernmost division (*233rd*), he stated that of the remaining 13 only two divisions were " fully battle fit ", five were fit for trench-warfare, three were only capable of defence on a quiet front, and three required relief.

The Monograph contends that this was an over-favourable estimate of the five noted as " fit for trench-warfare ", and of the three requiring a quiet front. Taking one of the former, it states that the rifle strength of the battalions of the three infantry regiments was 255, 286 and 404 ; and of one of the latter category, 183, 155 and 165. All were very short of officers, had long sick lists, and the reinforcements were untrained and " nearly entirely valueless ". The field artillery of the third category was also " completely fought-out ", the officers had lost influence over the men, and, owing to shortage of horses, the batteries were " incapable " of movement ".

These statements seem to be somewhat discounted by the report "early " in August " of General von Kuhl to Ludendorff (see Note at end of Chapter) ; but there is no doubt that many German divisions were of inferior quality owing to the withdrawal of their best men to join the " Storm " and machine-gun units.

The enemy defences, constructed on the high-water mark of the March offensive—except where the Germans had been pushed off it near Morlancourt and Dernancourt by the Australian Corps—consisted of little more than a front zone. North of the Somme there was only a single trench ; south of the Somme were three trenches, poorly wired, mostly with improvised chevaux de frise and coils of wire without pickets, and entirely lacking good shelters.[1] Behind the front system, according to air photographs, was neither Battle Zone nor Rear Zone, nothing more than the trenches of the old Amiens defences, a series of disconnected posts, with narrow trenches, dug in 1915 by the French, and now merely an additional trench of the Front Zone. About four miles behind this were the old Outer Amiens Defences, of front and support trenches, with good wire but of course sited on their eastern side. Between the two systems were a few small posts and length of trench dug in March 1918. The real strength of the defence, it was to be found, lay in the scattered machine guns, which were distributed in great depth, hidden in shell-holes and behind every piece of cover, but sometimes only concealed by the high corn.

Between the Outer Amiens Defence Line and the south-north course of the Somme (Voyennes to Péronne) eleven miles away there were no organized defences ; but near the river the ground was broken by shell craters, and seamed with the remains of trenches and wire, overgrown with grass and weeds, an obstacle to movement rather than a fortified zone, but still, as it was to prove, capable of defence by determined troops.

During this period of waiting the Commander-in-Chief received from the General Staff, War Office, a typewritten memorandum of 33 pages, dated 25th July, signed by Sir Henry Wilson, and headed " British Military Policy 1918–19 ". The G.H.Q. copy is endorsed by Sir Douglas Haig " Words ! " words ! words ! Lots of words ! and little else ".[2] It

---

[1] One account, " Regt. No. 148 " (*41st Division*), states that the trenches were not continuous, "only disconnected lengths giving cover " to the troops, in a few places to breast high ". The heavy artillery seems to have had deep dug-outs.

[2] It is printed in full as Appendix V.

was not helpful. It is sufficient here to point out that the Chief of·the Imperial General Staff did not contemplate the final offensive taking place before the 1st July 1919 and to give the summary of its conclusions :

" (i) At the earliest possible moment we must regain
" sufficient ground in front of the vital points in France
" to free us from anxiety, and enable us to make satis-
" factory preparations for our own offensive.

" (ii) Having done this we should husband our
" resources during the preparatory period, making
" arrangements so that by the end of this period we
" can concentrate the maximum forces in the West,
" equip them to the fullest extent with every mechanical
" auxiliary, and ensure them the most thorough training
" before making our supreme effort.   During this period
" a British reserve of 3 or 4 divisions should be stationed
" in Italy.

" (iii) Although our calculations must necessarily be
" based on many uncertain factors, we may reckon on
" a numerical superiority of 400,000 rifles by next July
" (1919) if things go reasonably well.   In view of this
" and other considerations, it would be unwise to defer
" the attempt to gain a decisive victory until 1920.   For
" purposes of calculation the 1st July 1919 should
" therefore be taken as the date by which all preparations
" are to be completed for the opening of the main
" offensive campaign.

" (iv) Beyond improving our position in Palestine by
" gaining possession of the Hejaz railway about Amman
" and consolidating our connection with the Arabs, no
" extensive operations in the subsidiary theatres should
" be undertaken during the preparatory period.   British
" formations in Macedonia should be replaced by Indian
" as fast as the latter can be provided and the troops
" thus liberated employed as seems best to further the
" main object in view."

An elaborate calculation by the C.I.G.S., received at G.H.Q. on the 15th August, put the expected Allied superiority on the 1st July 1919 at 624,000 instead of 473,000 as in the memorandum of the 25th July.

NOTE

The German Situation before the 8th August [1]

Ludendorff's plans after the evacuation of the Château Thierry salient by the *Seventh Army*, as set forth in an appreciation of the 2nd August, were given at length in the previous volume.[2] Briefly, they were that for a time the German Armies must stand on the defensive ; the Allies after their losses in the Second Battle of the Marne, were not likely to make a full-dress attack in the immediate future—a million Americans had certainly arrived, but " their small experience of war out-weighed the power of un- " strained nerves and the fresh offensive spirit of their strong and " splendidly equipped units ". Later on, he thought, full-dress attacks might be expected against the Lorraine front, the St. Mihiel salient, the Moronvillers position east of Reims, between the Oise and the Somme as far east as Soissons, and against the Kemmel front. The Amiens front except in so far as a small part was included between Soissons and the Somme, was not mentioned.

" Early in August " however, O.H.L. in addition to directing a gradual withdrawal in the plain of the Lys ordered the evacuation of the bridgeheads across the Ancre and the Avre (see Chapter II, p. [19 A]). At Ludendorff's special request however (Ludendorff, p. 679) General von Kuhl visited the *Second Army* " to discuss " once again the defensive measures on the line Moreuil—Albert ", that is the very front attacked on the 8th August. All that Kuhl judged necessary was " to relieve by fresh ones, two divisions that " had been a long time in line and seemed specially tired."

The last entry on the 7th August in the diary of Crown Prince Rupprecht, who was in command of the Group of Armies about to be attacked, was that according to prisoners' statements " a full-dress British attack, months in preparation, was intended between " Dickebusch and Meteren in the direction of Armentières ".

Ludendorff has declared as regards the *Second Army* sector :[3] " the divisional fronts were narrow, artillery plentiful and the " trench system organized in depth. All experience gained on the " 18th July had been acted upon. Only as regards position- " construction, the *Second Army* had not done as much, for " example, as the *Eighteenth* ". He had certainly issued instruc- tions ; but, ignoring the change which had come over part of the German Army in consequence of continuous heavy fighting in 1916-17-18, the failing discipline and blunted sense of respon- sibility even amongst officers—the beginning of the end—he had

---

[1] From the Monograph.
[2] " 1918 " Vol. III, p. 320.
[3] Ludendorff ii., p. 679.

not taken any steps to ensure that his wishes had been carried out. The Monograph (p. 26) furnishes an explanation : " maps were " sent in on which the Reserve Positions, switches, Artillery " Protection Positions, etc., shown in blue, looked very nice. " Actually, where these things should have been there were but " white tapes on the grass. Where get the labour to do the work ? " The greater part of the blue was eye-wash ". One officer said plainly " the great thing is to report. It doesn't matter so much " whether the positions are there as that the report goes in ".

In general, many captured documents spoke not only of lack of training but " the slow but steady deterioration of discipline ", and as early as June 1918 there were many deserters. After 1916, the year of Verdun and the Somme, the military value of the German officers and men had fallen faster than that of the French and British, whose natural fighting qualities now turned the scale.

CHAPTER II

THE PREPARATIONS FOR THE BATTLE OF AMIENS

(Map 1 ; Sketches 3, 4)

General Rawlinson's " General Instructions ", in continuation of his formal operation order of the 31st July, signed by his Chief General Staff Officer, Major-General A. A. Montgomery, were issued in parts between the 31st July and the 5th August.[1] They dealt, first, with " Secrecy " ; then with the readiness of reserves to move ; with artillery matters (the allotment of batteries and gun ammunition, barrages, counter-battery work, close support of infantry, etc.) ; tanks ; communications (light signals, pigeons, cables) ; issue of maps ; reservation and repair of roads; reliefs; policy after reaching objective (measures against counter-attacks) ; allotment of gas units ; strength and duties of the Royal Air Force and markings of machines ; and, finally, the bivouac areas, the line of advance and the mission of the cavalry.

Secrecy, naturally, was put first. As it would be impossible to conceal from a large number of junior administrative and transport officers and men the concentration of troops, guns, tanks and other apparatus in the back areas, and the accumulation of ammunition, in order to emphasize the necessity of secrecy, a small notice was printed with the heading " KEEP YOUR MOUTH SHUT ", issued to all ranks of all arms and services and ordered to be pasted into the " small book " carried by every officer and man.[2]

---

[1] They are printed for record in Appendix VI.

[2] " The success of any operation we carry out depends chiefly on surprise.

" DO NOT TALK.—When you know that your unit is making pre-
" parations for an attack, don't talk about them to men in other units,
" or to strangers, and keep your mouth shut, especially in public places.

" Do not be inquisitive about what other units are doing ; if you hear
" or see anything, keep it to yourself.

" If you hear anyone else talking about operations, stop him at once.
" THE SUCCESS OF THE OPERATIONS AND THE LIVES OF
" YOUR COMRADES DEPEND ON YOUR SILENCE.

" If you should ever have the misfortune to be taken prisoner, don't
" give the enemy any information beyond your rank and name. In
" answer to all other questions you need only say, ' I cannot answer '.
" He cannot compel you to give any other information. He may use
" threats. He will respect you if your courage, patriotism, and self-control
" do not fail. Every word you say may cause the death of one of your
" comrades.

" Either after or before you are openly examined, Germans, disguised
" as British officers or men, will be sent among you or will await you in
" the cages or quarters or hospital to which you are taken.

" Germans will be placed where they can overhear what you say without
" being seen by you.

" DO NOT BE TAKEN IN BY ANY OF THESE TRICKS."

The preparations were spoken of as the taking over more of the line from the French, with extra artillery to compensate for the weakness of the defenders. In the divisions in the line the word " raid " was used instead of " offensive " when this necessarily had to be mentioned.

The administrative control of civilians was facilitated by ·the fact that the town of Amiens had been evacuated in March. A " Forbidden Zone " had then been established in the Army area in which only a few inhabitants, who had to be in possession of passes, were allowed to remain under the supervision of the Assistant Provost Marshal with the assistance of the Intelligence Police and the French prévôté. A barrier line consisting of a chain of posts manned by the French prévôté prevented civilians entering this zone ; and the circulation of those permitted to be in it was reduced to a minimum in order, not only to prevent espionage, but also to facilitate the movements of troops.[1]

In general the instructions aimed at trying to persuade the enemy that normal conditions still continued. Normal artillery fire, active counter-battery work and harassing fire were to be maintained, but from positions other than the permanent emplacements of batteries; registration was to be carried out under cover of this fire, taking care to conceal the increase in the number of guns by never employing a large number at one time ; work on back lines was to go on ; on and after the 1st August all forward movement of troops and transport whether in front or in back areas was to take place by night ; aeroplanes were detailed to fly over the Army area and report if any unusual activity was noticeable ; newly arriving corps and divisions were not to open wireless stations until after Zero ; the number of reconnoitring officers was to be limited to the minimum compatible with efficiency.

The Fourth Army "Administrative Arrangements", a memorandum of 23 pages, issued over the signature of Major-General H. C. Holman, the Deputy Adjutant and Quartermaster-General, were particularly complete and summarized

---

[1] Similar arrangements were made for territory captured in the advance, with examining posts (including gendarmes and an interpreter) to sort up the inhabitants, evacuate them or issue passes. See details in Appendix VII, Section P.

the experience of four years of war.[1]   They give some idea
of the machinery at work in a battle in 1918. .They dealt
with subjects of : the railways, railheads, roads and canals ;[2]
the allotment of ammunition, and position of dumps and
refilling points ; and supplies (all units were to carry 3 days'
Iron Rations, and extra issues were made of solidified
alcohol, pea soup, Oxo and rum, while reserves of petrol and
lubricants were provided for the tank brigades).[3]

As regards water, a map was issued showing the initial
and forward water facilities ; sterilizers and water-carrying
lorries were allotted to corps, and locations suggested for
the sterilizers and water points in the forward areas.   For
Ordnance stores, the main gun park was established at Pont
Remy (on the railway 22 miles north-west of Amiens), but
an advanced park (containing 26 complete equipments of
the lighter guns with limbers, up to the 60-pdr. inclusive,
280 machine guns, besides spare parts) was to be formed at
Longeau (east of Amiens)[4] as soon as possible, a train being
kept ready loaded to be sent up as soon as circumstances
permitted ; and three ordnance workshops were allotted to
each corps (one only to the cavalry).   British labour companies employed on defences were to cease work on zero day
and be held ready to repair the forward roads, and detachments from traffic control squadrons and companies were
allotted to corps.

Under the medical arrangements two casualty clearing
stations (reinforced by extra surgical teams and nursing
sisters) were allotted to each corps for the sick and wounded,
together with motor ambulance convoys, advanced depôts
of medical stores and laboratories.   Three other casualty
clearing stations and a stationary hospital were detailed to
deal with gas, opthalmic, dental, nose ear and throat,

---

[1] They are printed in full in Appendix VII.   An account of the
Administrative establishments, machinery on the Lines of Communication
and bases behind the Armies : supply, medical, pay, ordnance. postal,
printing and stationery, canteens, social, press, graves registration, etc.,
will be found in " 1916 " Vol. I, Chapters V and VI.

[2] These subjects are summarized in Note I at the end of Chapter.

[3] " Fighting order " was worn by the infantry, that is the haversack
replaced the pack.   The load included 250 rounds of s.a. ammunition
(100 carried in bandoliers), gas mask, waterbottle, iron rations, entrenching
tool, 2 Mills bombs and 2 sandbags.   The Australians carried 2 water-
bottles.   A small number of shovels, picks, S.O.S. signals, wire cutters
and phosphorus grenades were distributed amongst the men.

[4] See Map 3 (railheads).

venereal and dysentery and N.Y.D. cases, and the sick in the back areas. Ten ambulance trains were provided.

Two stations were named to which remounts would be despatched by rail and other details as regards obtaining horses, and the veterinary collecting posts and evacuating stations were fixed. The location of the main and advanced " cages " for prisoners of war, and, in happy anticipation, an " overflow cage ", were also mentioned. After settling various domestic details, the final section dealt with the examination, evacuation and feeding of civilians in captured territory.

How far forward the immense administrative apparatus could be carried if the enemy fell back would depend on the rate at which the railways and roads could be repaired.

The corps issued orders similar in form to those of the Army, that is a formal operation order as warning, followed by detailed instructions, the Canadian Corps laying particular stress on the responsibility for the repair of bridges over the Luce and on priority of passage.

The first overt step in the operations was the taking over by the Australian Corps of 7,000 yards of frontage from the French.[1] The front in question was eventually to be the jumping-off place of the Canadians, but as they were not to come into the picture until later, the change would be unlikely to, and did not, provoke suspicion on the part of the enemy. An extension of front on the part of the Australians was not a probable preliminary of an offensive near Amiens ; it indicated rather a measure to free more French reserves for the Marne Battle. The change was effected by the III Corps, whose right was just north of Morlancourt, first taking over from the 5th Australian Division the $2\frac{1}{2}$ miles of front north of the Somme on the 30th July–1st August, with the 19th Division, sent up from G.H.Q. reserve in the IX Corps. The Australian 5th Division then went into reserve, and the 4th Australian Division, hitherto the reserve of the corps, was thus freed to be ready to take over the ground from the original right southwards to the new boundary.

Before leaving its old front the 5th Australian Division in the early morning of the 29th July carried out a very successful minor operation south of Morlancourt with two battalions of the 8th Brigade on a frontage of 4,000 yards.

[1] See Map 1 and Sketch 2.

The line was advanced about five hundred yards by what the Australians called "peaceful penetration", otherwise bold infiltration; 3 officers, 135 other ranks of the *107th Division* were captured, with 36 machine guns and 2 trench mortars; but the affair left a legacy of confused trenches and shell holes for the III Corps to take over. The retaliation at the time was slight and the local measures taken by the enemy to restore the situation were insignificant; his reply was to come on the 6th August at a most embarrassing moment.

The concealment of the move to the Fourth Army from the First Army front of the Canadian Corps, which had two divisions actually in the line, was a strategic problem of the utmost importance; for as the corps had hardly been engaged in the March and April fighting, its appearance in a new position would lead the Germans to expect an early offensive. Amongst his contemporaries who had faced him at manoeuvres General Rawlinson had the reputation for guile : " Rawly is a fox ", they said to themselves. On this occasion he fully justified this reputation. In order to mystify and mislead the enemy two Canadian battalions (the 4th Mounted Rifles and the 27th), two Canadian casualty clearing stations and the Canadian wireless section were moved at his request to the Second Army.[1] They were placed in the line opposite Kemmel Hill, lost on the 25th April, which, it was to be expected, would lead the Germans to imagine that the Second Army was preparing to recover that position.[2] The Royal Air Force, too, was ordered on the 27th July to occupy additional airfields in the Second Army area and steadily to increase activity until the 6th August; during the two days before the battle it was to exhibit great air activity on the fronts of the Third and First Armies. No Canadian troops were to be allowed to enter the zone of their battle position near Amiens until the day before Zero. The

---

[1] The battalions were told they were " to prepare the front for attack, " pending the arrival of the remainder of the Canadian Corps ".· They moved, according to one diary, without a written order " on pink signal " forms and faith " and, to their further bewilderment, in " strategic " trains ". The ruse was entirely successful. " On the German side " the insertion of Canadian troops in the line near Kemmel became "known, but not the shifting of the corps southwards." Monograph, p.19. See Note II at end of Chapter.

[2] The Canadian Corps Staff were at the time working out a scheme for a move to the Second Army area and the recapture of Mont Kemmel.

actual front here was not taken over from the three Australian battalions left in it until two hours before Zero. Finally, the divisions of the XVII Corps, the centre reserve, with a division from the VI Corps added to them, relieved the 2nd and 4th Canadian Divisions and took the place of the Canadian Corps in the First Army line.[1]

The moves of the reinforcements to the Fourth Army, except those of the cavalry, artillery and transport which marched by road, were carried out by rail and bus, cut straw from the fields being laid on the roads in and east of Amiens, and wheels wrapped round with ropes in order to deaden sound. Great activity, on the other hand, was exhibited by the wireless stations in the First and Second Army areas (including sending messages on the tank wave length, which was well known to the Germans) ; and by daylight false moves were carried out, and noise and dust created in order to convey the impression that a concentration of tanks was taking place near St. Pol (18 miles N.N.W. of Arras), a few machines being actually shown on a road on the heights near Notre Dame de Lorette.

The four divisions of the Canadian Corps (less the detachment sent to Kemmel which rejoined just before the battle) arrived in the Fourth Army area on the nights between 30th–31st July and the 3rd–4th August, their cantonments extending in the low ground from east of Amiens, near the junction of the Somme and the Ancre (3rd and 2nd Divisions) to the south-east, near Boves (1st Division) and south of Amiens (4th Division).

The Canadians were followed by the 1st Australian Division from the Hazebrouck front, where its place was taken by the 29th Division, in reserve to the XV Corps near Cassel. In addition, the 32nd Division, in reserve on the extreme left of the front at Proven (4 miles north-west of Poperinghe), whilst remaining at the special disposal of G.H.Q. was allotted to the Canadian Corps, and completed its assembly at Picquigny, west of Amiens, on the 7th. The three cavalry divisions, which had been collected in close billets west of Amiens, marched through the town that night (7th–8th) by a single pavé road, also used by tanks,

---

[1] On 4th August German O.H.L. notified the *Second Army* that " apparently two Canadian divisions had been relieved from their hitherto 'front position after a short tour ; particular attention should be given " to ascertain their whereabouts. . . . The front of the British Third " and Fourth Armies requires particular attention ".

which was sanded over to minimize noise and give the horses a good hold, and assembled in the angle between the Somme and Avre. On the previous night (6th–7th) the 1st, 2nd and 3rd Canadian Divisions had moved into the corps area, but did not relieve the 13th Australian Brigade which had been spread out to cover their front.

The Fourth Army [1] on the eve of the battle consisted of :

Canadian Corps: 1st*, 2nd, 3rd, 4th* Canadian and 32nd Divisions**.

Australian Corps : 1st*, 2nd, 3rd, 4th and 5th* Australian Divisions.

III Corps: 12th, 18th, 47th and 58th and American 33rd* Divisions.

IX Corps : Headquarters.

Cavalry Corps : 1st**, 2nd** and 3rd** Cavalry Divisions.

Between the 27th July and 10th August, for which dates returns are available, the " feeding " strength of the Fourth Army rose from 257,562 men and 54,323 animals to 441,588 men and 98,716 animals, the total strength of the B.E.F. being about 2,400,000 men and 420,000 animals.

In artillery, the Fourth Army was reinforced between the 29th July and the 6th August by ten Army field artillery brigades, the artillery of the 25th Division (whose infantry was being reconstituted at home) [2], and of the 5th Canadian Division (whose infantry had been used for drafts) ; and 13 heavy brigades and four siege batteries (less one section), drawn from the First, Second and Third Armies. The transfer was represented to the troops at large as the first stage of a rearrangement of the artillery.

The forward movement of this reinforcing artillery amid the already vast amount of traffic on the roads presented a

---

* Corps reserve ;
** Earmarked as G.H.Q. reserve, which also had available the 17th and 63rd Divisions (which went not to the Fourth but to the Third Army).

[1] Army Commander	-	General Sir H. S. Rawlinson, Bt.
Major-Gen. General Staff	Major-General A. A. Montgomery
D.A. & Q.M.G.	,,	H. C. Holman
Major-Gen. Royal Artillery	,,	C. E. D. Budworth
Chief Engineer	,,	R. U. H. Buckland

[2] The 25th Division artillery was allotted to the 12th Division, whose batteries had been left with the French First Army, but on 8th August were attached to 2nd Canadian Division.

complication of the road problem which was successfully solved, although the greater part of the heavy guns and ammunition lorries, besides tanks and armoured cars, had to use the same road out of Amiens to Roye at least as far as Longueau. The deployment of the artillery of the Canadian Corps had the special difficulty that the batteries had to share the Gentelles plateau (south-west of Villers Bretonneux) with the artillery of the French XXXI Corps. For the purposes of secrecy and surprise, the reinforcing artillery did not register in their battle positions, which were occupied under cover of night, but were to fire by the map.

The strength of the artillery at the disposal of the corps in addition to four anti-aircraft batteries was finally as follows :—

	Field Artillery Brigades					Heavy Artillery Brigades	6-inch Gun Batteries	12-inch Howitzer Batteries
		Mobile	*Mixed*	*8-inch*	*9.2-inch*	*Total*		
Canadian Corps ..	17	3	2	3	1	9[1]	3	1
Australian Corps ..	18*	2	2	3	2	9	4	1
III Corps	17	1	3**	3	1	8	3	1

*less a battery   **less a section

Total 1,242 field guns and howitzers, and 246 heavy and medium guns and howitzers, and 6 super-heavy howitzers,[2] but the Army total was 1,386 field guns and howitzers, and 684 heavy pieces, giving 29 yards per piece of the former and 59 per piece of the latter.[3]

The ammunition dumped at or near the gun positions amounted to (per piece) : 18-pdr., 600 rounds ; 4·5-inch howitzer, 500 ; 12-inch howitzer, 200 ; and the others, 400.[4]

The engineer units, in addition to those belonging to corps and divisions, comprised : gas (projector) companies, 3 (3)[5] ; gas (mortar), 2 (0) ; field, 1 (1) ; Army troops, 11 (11) ; siege, 2 (2) ; tunnelling, 7 (8) ; electrical and mechanical,

---

[1] Seven of these were " silent " until Zero.

[2] On 21st March 1918 the German *Second Army* of 21 divisions had 1,075 field guns, 696 heavy and 18 super-heavy. It was the weakest in artillery of the three Armies engaged in the March offensive. See " 1918 " Vol. I, p. 153.

[3] The French First Army (including the XXXV Corps) was better off as regards heavy artillery, possessing 780 field guns and 826 heavy and super-heavy, about 45 yards per field piece and 42 yards per heavy.

[4] The German supply on 21st March 1918 was larger : field guns, 800–1,000 ; heavies, 400–600 ; super-heavies, 200–325.

[5] The figures in brackets show the number with the Army at the beginning of July.

1 (1) ; boring section, 1 (1) ; Army workshop company, 1 (1) ; field survey battalion (with 5 sound ranging sections and 4 observation groups), 1 (1) ; anti-aircraft searchlight company, 1 (1), and sections, 5 (5) ; foreway company (tramways), 2 (1) ; barge filtration unit, 1 (0) ; advanced R.E. parks, 2 (0) ; forestry units, 3 (3) ; with an Army printing advanced section and advanced photographic section.

The Fourth Army Signal Company contained 4 airline sections, 2 cable sections, 1 light railway signal company, 1 signal construction company and 7 area signal detachments. In the pigeon service were 16 horse-drawn mobile lofts and 2 fixed lofts.

The Labour Corps units were 8 (4) group headquarters, 39 (26) labour companies ; 17 (4) area employment ; Indian, 3 (0) ; Chinese, 15 (0) ; non-combatant (conscientious objectors), 1.

The Army A.S.C. units were 2 pontoon parks (M.T.), 1 Army troops company (M.T.), 3 auxiliary companies (1 steam and 2 petrol), 1 water tank company, 2 mobile repair units, 1 workshop for anti-aircraft guns.

In the Medical Service were 7 motor ambulance convoys, 12 casualty clearing stations, 3 advanced depots of medical stores, 4 mobile laboratories, 2 mobile X-ray units, 1 mobile dental unit, 1 stationary hospital, 14 sanitary sections, and 7 sanitary squads. The veterinary service had 5 evacuation stations.

The Ordnance units were 4 mobile workshops (1 heavy, 1 medium, and 2 light), 1 Ordnance gun park and 1 officers' clothing depot.

The V Tank Brigade[1] was reinforced by the 2nd, 4th, 3rd (light tank) and 6th (light tank) Battalions, the 17th Armoured Car Company and four tank supply companies. The total was 342 heavy tanks, 72 whippets, as the light tanks were generally called, and 120 supply tanks, (66 for infantry and 54 for tank units' supply).[2] Their assembly was no easy matter, as not only had all movements to take place in darkness, but the machines had also to be hidden or camouflaged during daylight, and the noise of

---

[1] A brigade had an establishment of 3 battalions, each of 3 companies of 12 fighting tanks and 2 supply tanks.

[2] The maximum speed of the Mark V tank on good going ground was 5 miles per hour ; of the Mark V*, which was 6 feet longer in order to give more room to carry passengers and material, 4. For working speed this should be halved. The speed of the whippets, is dealt with later on.

their engines had to be drowned by keeping several aeroplanes flying along the line. On the night of the 6th–7th August the tanks were moved up in groups, mostly across country, to their preparatory positions about two or three miles behind the line. There during the following afternoon a chance shell struck a petrol-carrying tank of a supply company hidden in an orchard, and set it on fire. The flames and smoke attracted a bombardment in which all the 25 tanks of the company, and their loads, were destroyed. It was a very serious loss, but no other mishap occurred. On the next night, 7th–8th, the tanks were moved forward to their assembly positions, about a thousand yards behind the infantry starting line. They were deployed on the exact positions from which they were to advance next morning ; their routes were reconnoitred and marked, and obstacles on them removed.

The French First Army received two battalions of light tanks on the 6th August[1] ; but General Debeney judged them insufficient in number to employ in the attack. After a vain endeavour to obtain more from Sir Douglas Haig, he allotted them to the XXXI Corps, his left, with orders that they should be used with a second line division (153rd). It was subsequently arranged that four of the tanks allotted to the Canadian corps should co-operate with the left French division as soon as it came near Mezières.

The air squadrons normally with the Fourth Army and its corps were increased, and finally organized as the V Brigade (332 machines) and the IX Brigade (294 machines) ; with the III Brigade (136 machines), the I Brigade (19 machines) and X Brigade (19 machines), at hand and available. The machines numbered 110 corps aeroplanes, 376 fighters, 147 day bombers, 92 night bombers and 75 fighter reconnaissance aircraft, with 8 balloons.[2] One squadron was allotted to the Tank Corps.

The French also made a secret air concentration, the " Air Division " and other reinforcements being sent to the First Army, so that General Debeney had at his disposal 1,104 aircraft. This made an Allied total of 1,904. To these the German *Second Army*, even with about half the *Eighteenth* Army, could oppose only 365.

---

[1] Gallini, p. 29.
[2] See " War in the Air " VI, pp. 433–6.

Command of the air during the days of preparation was of the utmost importance in order to keep the enemy in ignorance of the concentration of troops and material. This was successfully secured, the weather on the whole being unfavourable for reconnaissance. On the 1st August visibility was good and the early morning of the 2nd was fine ; but between this latter date and the 7th when it was again fine after a ground mist in the early part of the day, the record is one of " rain and low clouds ", and fine only in the early morning of the 4th and 6th ; night flying was " impossible " on three nights.

The number of enemy planes which attempted long-distance reconnaissance was small ; the very few machines which crossed the line and operated in the forward area were dealt with by line patrols and anti-aircraft guns. A single indecisive combat was reported on the 5th and again on the 6th ; but 18 combats took place on the 7th, six decisive, one British machine being lost.[1]

From time to time the enemy had fired concentrations of gas into the Fourth Army area. In the week ending the 3rd August, gas shelling was at no time heavy ; only about 4,000 shell were noted, distributed on localities about $2\frac{1}{2}$ miles behind the front, mainly near Villers Bretonneux, with 225 casualties. On the morning of the 6th August between 3,000 and 4,000 rounds of mustard and lethal gas were fired into the Vaire–Corbie area ; but the casualties were light. On the night of the 7th–8th over 2,000 mustard gas shell were fired into the Méricourt (on Ancre) area and occasioned over five hundred casualties in the III Corps. In addition to the normal precautions, orders were issued to avoid the areas usually shelled with gas, and any German batteries which resorted to gas shelling were at once subjected to heavy counter-battery fire. On the night of the 7th–8th, immediately preceding the attack, when, naturally, the greatest anxiety prevailed, all available guns were specially authorized to open fire if the enemy began counter-preparations or opened a gas bombardment.

---

[1] The German report is that " 1st to 7th August only 37 flights were " possible, of which only 7 were photographic and watching flights. " On 2nd and 5th August the weather was impossible for flying ". In 8 [sic] air combats 1 German machine was shot down and 1 British machine forced to land. See also Note at end of Chapter I.

The signal to commence, for which the code word " Hell " was selected, was left to the judgment of the counter-battery staff officers of the various corps.

Statements of prisoners in this period seemed to indicate that the enemy expected an attack astride the Scarpe, whilst his own intentions were directed towards Vimy for an operation against the British as soon as the withdrawal to the Vesle, then in progress, was completed. Their replies as regards a Flanders attack were all negative. But four incidents which occurred in the five days preceding the 8th August caused no little anxiety as to whether the enemy had obtained or would obtain information regarding the actual impending offensive. In the early morning of the 3rd an Australian post near Hourges was captured and a sergeant and four men were taken prisoners ; but inquiries tended to show that the men of the post expected a long spell in the line and knew nothing of the offensive which was planned.[1]

During the afternoon of the same day, between Montdidier and Moreuil, on the front of the left wing of the French First Army, the enemy withdrew his forward troops across the Avre and Rivière des Doms, blowing up the bridges, and leaving only a few outposts west of Montdidier.[2] The retirement did not affect the French plans. The enemy similarly withdrew his front line west of the Ancre between Dernancourt and Aveluy Wood, opposite the left of the III Corps and his trenches were immediately occupied by British patrols.

On the 5th August the enemy began slowly withdrawing from the head of the salient won in the April Lys offensive between La Bassée and Kemmel,[3] and he continued the movement during the 6th and 7th to a total depth of nearly a mile. The width of the ground abandoned, about ten miles, corresponded with the front of the Fifth Army, which followed up with strong bodies of troops and took a few prisoners. As the German troops in the salient had been

---

[1] The capture of Australian prisoners seemed to the Germans to show that all was normal. A French corporal captured on the 5th–6th gave no more information than that he expected relief. Grasset, p. 37.

[2] This was merely a rectification of the front line, as it was judged undesirable for the forward troops in the then state of their morale to fight with a river close behind them. O.H.L. had agreed to small but indispensable salients being abandoned. Rupprecht, p. 426.

[3] See Sketch 1.

harassed by concentric fire, day and night, since they had taken possession, it was judged that the retirement was merely a local adjustment, to save wastage, and did not mean, unless carried further, any serious reduction of troops for use elsewhere.

The fourth incident was more serious.[1] Soon after dawn on the 6th, before the divisional reliefs consequent upon the extension of the III Corps front down to the Somme had been completed, the *27th (Württemberg) Division*, a good fighting division well-rested and with brand-new equipment, which had just relieved the *107th*, attacked on a 4,000-yard front, south of Morlancourt. The onslaught fell on the extreme left of the 58th Division, which was in the act of side-slipping, and on the right of the 18th Division, which was holding the position gained by the 5th Australian Division on the 29th July and was actually engaged in an inter-brigade relief. The Germans penetrated to a depth of eight hundred yards and according to their account " took " prisoner 5 officers and 231 other ranks of the 18th Division " and the 58th Division next to it on the right. None of " them said anything about an impending attack ".[2]

Next morning an attack by the 18th Division partially restored the situation and resulted in the capture of seventy prisoners. But the counter-attack, though it did not affect the general situation, had dislocated the III Corps plan to the extent of altering the infantry starting line, and consequently the artillery barrage calculations. What was more serious, it had tired out troops who were to be employed in the attack on the 8th. The bickering which continued on the 7th also caused the enemy to be more alert in the III Corps front than elsewhere.

On the 3rd August Sir Douglas Haig and his Chief of the General Staff travelled to Mouchy le Châtel (8 miles S.S.E. of Beauvais), whither General Foch and General Weygand came from Bombon to meet them. The Generalissimo was anxious that the Amiens operation should begin as soon as possible, as the Germans on the Marne front were falling back very

---

[1] See Map 1 and Sketch 2.

[2] Monograph, p. 40. The operation had no connection with any fear of an impending attack. The G.O.C. *Second Army* had judged a counter-attack necessary to put a stop to further advance near Morlancourt, on account of the good observation it would give over the Somme Valley and to the south of the river. The prisoners actually included some artillerymen engaged in establishing forward dumps of ammunition. They, like the infantrymen, divulged nothing.

quickly.[1] He was pleased and satisfied that the 8th had been fixed as the date. As regards the objectives, he wished that some place south of Chaulnes should be named. Sir Douglas Haig pointed out that he had given Ham, 15 miles beyond Chaulnes and across the river Somme.[2] With this General Foch was likewise satisfied. He was anxious that there should be no delay on the line Hangest—Méricourt, which, according to G.H.Q. orders, was to be put in a state of defence when it had been secured. It was pointed out to him that if this line were held Amiens would be freed from enemy gun-fire, and that preparations ought to be made to meet a counter-attack which might well be made to recover it : this, however, did not mean complete consolidation : the further advance on Roye–Chaulnes would be carried out as soon as the necessary fresh troops could move up. The Generalissimo then spoke of a possible extension of the French operations eastward to the Oise by engagement of the French Third Army, on the right of the First. Finally, he expressed the opinion that the Germans were breaking up. Sir Douglas Haig learnt that the reserves behind the ten front line divisions of the French First Army would be the 47th, 56th, 126th and 153rd, with the II Cavalry Corps. The similar reserves of the eight attacking divisions of the Fourth Army were the 1st and 4th Canadian Divisions, 1st and 5th Australian, the 32nd, and later the 17th Division with the Cavalry Corps. The American 33rd Division in the area was not at present available, as General Pershing did not wish it to to be employed in attack until fully trained.

When the Commander-in-Chief reached Montreuil after the conference he found a cipher telegram from the Chief of the Imperial General Staff, Sir Henry Wilson, marked " personal ". It suggested that they should exchange opinions by telegram marked in this manner which would not be seen by other persons in the War Office. Sir Douglas Haig regarded this as " an extraordinary proposal ", considering that it was impossible for a chief of the imperial

---

[1] Towards midday on 3rd, the French centre and left nearly reached the line of the Vesle between Fismes and Soissons. See " 1918 " Vol. III, p. 304. The four divisions of the British XXII Corps serving in the Marne area had already been released, and were beginning their return to the British area.

[2] Ham was not mentioned in the formal G.H.Q. order of 29th July, but it appears in that of 5th August (Appendix 7) and had been previously discussed.

general staff and a commander-in-chief in the field to exchange opinions on military matters in personal telegrams ; for it was the holders of the offices and not the individuals who were concerned.

On the 4th August, the fourth anniversary of the outbreak of war—by which day the Germans had completely evacuated the Château Thierry salient, the French advanced guards had reached the Vesle and the end of the Second Battle of the Marne was at hand—an open air United Service of Remembrance and Intercession was celebrated at G.H.Q. and at the various Army headquarters.

On the 5th an important conference was held by the Commander-in-Chief at Fourth Army headquarters at Flixecourt (13 miles north-west of Amiens). At this were present General Debeney, General Rawlinson and Lieut.-General Kavanagh (commanding the Cavalry Corps). Sir Douglas Haig first explained the more extended nature of the operations now contemplated by General Foch and the possible engagement of the French Third Army. In view of this, he thought that the Fourth Army orders of the 31st July[1] laid too much stress on reaching the old Amiens Defence Line as the final objective and repelling counter-attacks against it : the battle might develop into an operation of considerable magnitude ; provision should, in his opinion, therefore, be made for going farther, if surprise of the enemy was effected at the start. He told General Rawlinson—and his decision was embodied in a G.H.Q. operation order[2]—to arrange for an advance, as rapid as possible, to the old Amiens Defence Line, 5 to 7 miles away, which should be put into a state of defence ; he should not delay there, however, but forthwith push on reserves to capture the Roye–Chaulnes line, thrusting back the enemy in the direction of Ham so as to facilitate the action of the French Third Army from the front Noyon—Montdidier.

The Commander-in-Chief also directed that the Cavalry Corps, placed under General Rawlinson,[3] must be prepared to pass through anywhere between the river Somme and the Amiens—Roye road.[4] The 3rd Cavalry Division and a battalion of light whippet tanks had already been placed

---

[1] See Appendix III.
[2] Appendix VIII.
[3] See Appendix VI, section 13.
[4] The area south of this road would be under French artillery fire.

under the orders of the Canadian Corps. Sir Douglas Haig now ordered that a cavalry brigade, a battery R.H.A. and some whippet tanks should be placed at the disposal of the Australian Corps. These detachments were to continue with the two corps until they had passed through the infantry, when they were to revert to the Cavalry Corps.

Final orders in the sense of the Commander-in-Chief's directions were issued next day by the Fourth Army.[1] In order to carry them out :

the Cavalry Corps, as soon as it had accomplished its first mission—which was to gain possession of the old Amiens Defence Line between Hangest and the Amiens–Chaulnes railway, and hold it until relieved by the Canadian infantry—was to push forward with the least possible delay towards the line Roye–Chaulnes ;

the Canadian Corps, reinforced if necessary by fresh divisions, was to press on in support of the cavalry, keeping touch with the French on the right ;

the Australian Corps, pivoting on the Somme between Méricourt and Etinehem, was to swing its right forward to keep in touch with the advance of the Canadian Corps ;

the III Corps was to advance as soon as possible to reach the Amiens Outer Defence Line between Etinehem and Dernancourt, and consolidate it to form a defensive flank to the movement of the Fourth Army south of the Somme.[2]

The objectives (first, second and final) and boundaries were shown on a map.

At the Conference General Debeney also explained his plans in detail : [3] the corps of the First Army would be engaged successively from west to east, against the zone of the junction of the German *Second* and *Eighteenth Armies* ; his main attack would be made on the 9th from the south of Montdidier so as to join up with the Fourth Army in the direction of Roye.   He added that his II Cavalry Corps would probably follow in the track of the XXXV, his right corps.

---

[1] Appendix IX.
[2] It was arranged that the 47th Division, the northernmost of the III Corps north of the Ancre, should remain in position and keep the Germans around Albert quiet. It neutralized $1\frac{1}{2}$ divisions.
[3] See F.O.A. vii (ii), pp. 156, 157, 167.

On the same day, General Fayolle (G.A.R.) addressed a Note to Generals Debeney (whose First Army was under Sir Douglas Haig) and Humbert (Third Army) in which he said—[1]

" The rôle of the First Army is first and foremost to " flank and to cover the left [*sic*] of the British by " advancing between the Avre and the Amiens–Roye " road ; but the very direction of the left of the First " Army gives the battle in the French sector a far " greater task, which aims at—

" (1) forcing the evacuation of the Avre line,

" (2) the reoccupation of Montdidier,

" (3) forcing the evacuation of La Petite Suisse[2] by " manoeuvring to the north, or at least preparing for " this manoeuvre by occupying the line Roye–Rollot " [5 miles south-east of Montdidier].

" In consequence, the First Army should form two " masses of manoeuvre :

" 1. The principal one, already arranged for, debouch-" ing between the Avre and the Luce, taking the Avre " in reverse.

" 2. The other, the secondary one, debouching " between Montdidier and Rollot. This latter mass will " be formed by XXXV Corps reinforced by a division, " the 46th, from this date placed at the disposal of the " First Army, and, if events between the Vesle and the " Aisne permit, by a second fresh division.

" It is on this basis that the commander of the First " Army should enlarge his plan of attack.

" In order to facilitate its execution, the Third Army " has been directed to assemble on its left a mass of " heavy artillery intended to act against the massif of " Boulogne la Grasse,[3] and thus cover the right of the " XXXV Corps.

" This Army, in addition, should execute, in conjunc-" tion with the action of the XXXV Corps east of " Montdidier, a great coup de main with prospects of " exploitation, having for its first objective the long " ridge Méry[4]–Porte Farm.

---

[1] F.O.A. vii (i), Annexe 490.

[2] A wooded and broken hill region, 15–18 miles south-east of Montdidier between the Oise and its two right bank tributaries, the Matz and the Divette, opposite the right of the French Third Army.

[3] A wooded hilly area about 7 miles south-east of Montdidier.

[4] Seven miles S.S.E. of Montdidier.

" The action between Montdidier and the massif of
" Boulogne la Grasse will thus be in any case facilitated.
  " The commander of the First Army will send a report
" as soon as possible of the dispositions proposed as
" concerns the action of the XXXV Corps ".

In accordance with these instructions, General Debeney[1]
sent a secret instruction addressed personally to his corps
commanders which slightly modified the orders of the 31st
July.[2] He instructed the XXXI Corps merely to maintain
contact with the enemy ; the IX, X and XXXV, on the
contrary, were to carry on aggressive outpost activity in
order to attract the enemy's attention to the west and south :
the XXXI Corps, starting 45 minutes after Zero (which
would be communicated later), was given the direction of
Hangest, which was to be reached on the first day ; the
IX Corps, starting four hours after Zero, was to do no more
than make a semi-ellipse-shaped bite of two miles in depth
into the enemy's position so as to protect the right flank of
the XXXI.[3] The X. Corps, which was to advance as soon as
the situation permitted, was also to cover the right of the
XXXI, passing by the north of Montdidier : the XXXV
Corps was to prepare to attack south of Montdidier.

General Debeney issued an additional order on the 6th
which fixed the hours of attack of the XXXI and IX
Corps ; the X Corps was to open such artillery fire as was
" judged necessary " and the XXXV " demonstration fire ".
Parts of the second and third paragraphs are worthy of
record.[4] They are :

    " The attacks will be conducted with but one pre-
" occupation : to achieve the greatest rapidity in a
" succession of forward bounds.

    " Once the front is broken, the divisions must march
" against their objectives, in the prescribed direction.

    " Once an objective is captured, the attack against
" the next must be undertaken without delay.

    " ' Points d'appui ' will be taken by envelopment.

    " Alignment is not to be sought ; it is forbidden to
" wait for neighbouring divisions : liaison will be

---

[1] F.O.A. vii (i), Annexe 492.
[2] See Chapter I.
[3] See Map 1 and Sketch 4. The area is marked by Bois St. Hubert Plessier
—south edge of Bois de Genouville (just south of Moreuil).
[4] See F.O.A. vii (ii), Annexe 517.

" established by small detachments drawn from divisions
' in the second line.

*   *   *   *   *

" The attacks will be pushed on and continued until
" night ; from the very first day the troops must go
" very far ".

On the 6th August the 8th was formally fixed by G.H.Q.
as Zero Day, the hour being left to Generals Debeney and
Rawlinson to settle. The time chosen was 4.20 a.m., rather
more than one hour before sunrise, so that the tanks could
close up and the infantry battalions break the first line of
the enemy's defences under cover of darkness, and yet,
before they had gone many hundred yards, would have
sufficient light to keep direction. But as the French First
Army did not intend to employ tanks, its advance was timed
to begin forty minutes later (subsequently altered to forty-
five) than the British, in order that the enemy positions
opposite it might be subjected to a preparatory artillery
bombardment, with which the British intended to dispense,
because surprise was essential and the conditions were very
similar to those at Cambrai. That the enemy's position was
not strongly organized was felt to be an additional reason.

The artillery of the Fourth Army was broadly allotted two
tasks.[1] The first, to be carried out by about one third of its
guns, was at zero hour to form the creeping barrage.[2] The
second, in which all the remaining guns were to be employed,
was the bombardment of every known battery position and
such localities as were considered suitable as assembly places
for German reserves.

Special warning was given to the air forces not to bomb
or machine-gun the troops of their Allies, and the French
aircraft were further warned by General Debeney neither
to attack nor call for artillery fire on the main bodies of the
cavalry.[3]

The general instructions for the operations of the Royal
Air Force on the first day of battle were that :

at daybreak the day-bomber squadrons (147 aeroplanes), the fighter squadrons (376 aeroplanes) giving

---

[1] Details will be found in Appendix 4, para. 3 (G.S. General Instructions).

[2] The pace was first hundred yards, 3 minutes ; second, 5 minutes ;
next eight, 3 minutes each ; and then 4 minutes. A protective barrage
was to be maintained in front of the old Amiens Defence Line, until
Zero + 4 hours, when all barrages were to cease.

[3] F.O.A. vii (i), Annexe 516.

their support, were to attack enemy aerodromes on the Fourth Army front; in the evening they were to attack the railway stations at Péronne and Chaulnes, followed by the night bombers (92 aeroplanes). The fighter squadrons were to be ready to operate on the Fourth Army front, if the enemy air activity became important.

Fourth Army headquarters remained at Flixecourt, in the Somme valley on the Abbeville–Amiens road, 13 miles from Amiens, without an advanced headquarters. Sir Douglas Haig established his advanced headquarters in a G.H.Q. train, now taken into use, in a siding at Wiry, 11 miles south-west of Flixecourt, on the Longpré–Gamaches line.

NOTE I

Railheads, Railways and Road Movements

* (Map 3)

The Fourth (late Fifth) Army had lost every railhead in use before the German March offensive. Early in April the enlargement of eight existing stations and the construction of one new one had been put in hand. The lines in use in August 1918 are shown on Map 3. The Serqueux (45 miles south-west of Amiens)–Saleux–Amiens line forming with the Amiens–Flesselles–Canaples a convenient lateral, connected at Longueau junction east of Amiens, and the St. Roch avoiding line west of the city were both under regular shell fire.

The Fourth Army was based on Havre and Rouen, whence lines ran either via Serqueux, either to Amiens or to Longpré or via Gamaches to Longpré, which was the regulating station. A third line along the coast via Dieppe, Eu and Abbeville, was also available. For the advance the Amiens–Bréteuil line was in running order, with Boves station ready to be taken into use; the Amiens–Chaulnes line was repaired as far as Petit Blangy, with a siding repairable; the Amiens–Albert line was repaired as far as Heilly, with Corbie and Heilly station repairable. The Somme canal was open for barges as far as Lamotte Brébiere. There were plenty of roads in the Fourth Army area, even the tracks being hard and usable in summer time.

In the advance it was proposed that the Canadian Corps should repair the Amiens–Roye road, the Australian Corps the Amiens–Villiers Bretonneux and onwards, and the III Corps the Corbie–Sailly Lorette.

For the concentration movements of the troops added to the Fourth Army for the battle, first a forecast was made by G.H.Q. in tabular form, which indicated to the formations concerned the probable date of the move and the method, whether by rail (ordinary troop, tactical or strategic train, which affected the make up of the train)[1] or road.   In the former case the entraining and detraining stations were given.   A later notice for rail movements gave the hour of entrainment, the route to the station, and the rate of entrainment (number of trains per 24 hours).   For road movements, units were usually given a second warning—to be ready at 2 hours' notice from a certain hour—and a table of daily marches from billeting area to billeting area was issued.   The general principle was to move brigades and other bodies forward along the different roads from area to area[2] by stages on the different roads, in succession, at a day's march interval, until they reached the area of the Fourth Army which then took charge of them.   Thus on one march table is to be found :—

	Night of 31st July– 1st Aug.	Night of 1st–2nd Aug.	Night of 2nd–3rd Aug.	Night of 3rd–4th Aug.	Night of 4th–5th Aug.
Three Brigades, R.G.A.	Southern portion of Second Army area	Anvin area	Bernaville area	Fourth Army area	—
Two Brigades, R.G.A.	—	Second Army area	Anvin area	Bernaville area	Fourth Army area
Two Brigades, R.G.A.	—	—	Second Army area	Anvin area	Bernaville area

NOTE II

German Inaction Before the Battle

Although O.H.L. had calculated that the Allies had 80 divisions in reserve, of which 42 were fresh (Gallwitz ii., p. 344), it had no idea where they would be employed.

The taking over by the Australians of more front from the French was duly observed ; but as the British Fourth Army front was widened thereby, any offensive from it seemed precluded. The extension, indeed, appeared to confirm an O.H.L. appreciation of the 20th June. that " the British will not put in strong

---

[1] " Tactical trains " were kept in readiness to move infantry only short distances (15–30 miles), " Strategical trains " (as they were called) transported the units of a division complete. See " 1916 " Vol. I, p. 19.

[2] Each of these areas had a commandant and staff (area employment unit) and was organized to receive and accommodate troops.

" forces on their southern wing, but will, by preference, hold them in reserve behind the Flanders front and near Arras ". The *Second Army*, however, expected strong minor attacks near Villers Bretonneux.

Nothing could be learnt on the Amiens front by the air forces ; the Allies drove back the German fliers, and from the 26th June onwards " a strong air barrage over and beyond our [the German] " front line prevented any observation into their rear areas ". Some captured British flying officers stated on the 7th that a great attack was in preparation " between Dickebusch and Meteren in " the direction of Armentiéres " (Rupprecht ii., p. 431). From other prisoners no information was obtained.

" Only one sign of an impending attack was detected ; that was " noise caused by the transport of ammunition and other war " material to the dumps near the front line ". Some German troops claimed to have heard the noise of tanks approaching. This was attributed by the higher staffs to " phantoms of the imagin- " ation or nervousness ". But on the 3rd August—before any tanks had arrived near the front—the *Second Army* nevertheless reported " the traffic and sounds of motor engines noticed by the " troops make an impending tank attack from the Villers Breton- " neux sector seem possible ". No further measures, however, for defence against tanks were ordered.

The Summary of Information issued by Crown Prince Rupprecht's Group of Armies, giving the situation at 12 noon on the 6th August contains the note : " Results of reconnaissance : " about a hundred tanks observed on the road Ailly–Morisel " [Moreuil] ".[1]

But again nothing was done.

A German General Staff officer who was present in the *LI. Corps* has commented : " Not even a request [from the Army] to " keep a sharp look-out. We were anxious because anyone who " brings up a hundred tanks is not planning a joy-ride. The " Army Staff were astonishingly indifferent ". But the corps and divisional staffs also do not appear to have taken any special action, although they had reported that most of their troops were unreliable.

Ludendorff was evidently uneasy about the wave of defeatism which had evidently come over the German Armies : they were no longer " jauchzend " (shouting hurrah !), but, as is characteristic of the Teutonic races, had gone to the other extreme and were

---

[1] This was in the French XXXI Corps area. The two battalions of tanks (90 machines) allotted to it arrived, however, at Fouencamps (just south of Boves) by rail only on the night of the 6th-7th and did not leave that place until 1 a.m. on the 8th. The tanks seen must have been " phantoms of the imagination ".

4TH AUGUST

" zur Hölle betrübt " (depressed down to Hell).   On the 4th
August he issued an order of the day, which was soon after
captured.

" C.G.S. of the Field Army.
" Ia. No. 9670.op.

G.H.Q., 4-8-18
" I am under the impression that, in many quarters, the
" possibility of an enemy offensive is viewed with a certain degree
" of apprehension.   There is nothing to justify this apprehension,
" provided our troops are vigilant and do their duty.

" In all the open warfare operations in the course of their great
" offensive battle between the Marne and the Vesle, the French were
" only able to obtain one initial tactical success due to surprise,
" namely that of July 18th, and this success ought to have been
" denied them.   In the fighting which followed, the enemy in
" spite of his mass of artillery, was unable to obtain the slightest
" tactical advantage ; and yet, far from occupying prepared
" positions, our troops were fighting in open country and were
" merely holding the positions which they had chanced upon at
" the end of a day's battle.   All the enemy's attacks broke down
" with sanguinary losses.   It was not the enemy's tactical
" successes which caused our withdrawal, but the precarious state
" of our rearward communications.

" The French and British infantry generally fought with
" caution ; the Americans attacked more boldly but with less
" skill.   It is to the tanks that the enemy owes his success of the
" first day.   These, however, would not have been formidable if
" the infantry had not allowed itself to be surprised, and if the
" artillery had been sufficiently distributed in depth.   At the
" present moment, we occupy everywhere positions which have
" been very strongly fortified, and we have, I am convinced,
" effected a judicious organization in depth of the infantry and
" artillery.   Henceforward, we can await every hostile attack
" with the greater confidence.   As I have already explained, we
" should wish for nothing better than to see the enemy launch an
" offensive, which can but hasten the disintegration of his forces
[as had certainly been the case with the German forces].

" Commanders and men must be imbued with a bitter deter-
" mination to conquer, both in the defensive as well as in the
" offensive.   This is a consideration which must not be lost sight
" of during training.   Hence, we must not, in the present
" circumstances, neglect the organized defensive by devoting
" ourselves too exclusively to offensive tactics ; generally speaking,
" the organized defensive is the more difficult.   It is the latter, in
" fact, which imposes the greatest test upon the spirit of the troops.
" LUDENDORFF "

On the 8th August, the very day of attack, another memorandum from Ludendorff reached the German Armies (Gallwitz, ii. p. 342). " He expected surprise enemy attacks as the rule and " therefore made renewed demands for deep positions. The " forward zone should be so deep that tanks could not reach the " main line of resistance before it could be manned according to " plan, and resting troops and reserves deployed behind it for " counter-attack. Detailed instructions were given for the " disposal of the artillery in depth and its methods of fire. The " normal defence against assault by barrage fire was rejected . . . " It seldom fell in the right place, was too thin, began usually too " late, cost too much ammunition and endangered the infantry " when making a mobile defence ".

CHAPTER III

THE BATTLE OF AMIENS

FIRST DAY 8TH AUGUST 1918

THE CANADIAN CORPS

(Map 1 ; End-papers A, B ; Sketches 2, 3, 4)

The night of the 7th-8th August was a most anxious one for commanders and staffs, although all ranks were confident of victory and certain that the turn of the tide had come. The Germans seemed to suspect nothing. No enemy counter-preparations of any kind disturbed the completion of the British and French arrangements, except that one of the periodic gas bombardments and some sporadic H.E. shelling took place in the III Corps sector, as already mentioned. The hours of darkness were spent in moving the infantry of the attacking divisions into position. The night was moonless and fine ; but towards 3 a.m. a ground mist began to form in the river valleys, which gradually thickened and spread over the plateau, so that even when the sun rose it could not be seen, and at first visibility was little more than ten yards. These conditions made useful aeroplane work impossible, and, though one airman managed to fly up and down the line to screen the noise of the tanks, the squadrons of the Royal Air Force could not enter fully into the battle until after 9 a.m. The usual active counter-battery work and harassing fire were maintained until zero hour.

The divisions of the Canadian and Australian Corps were assembled in great depth. The distribution of the brigades varied slightly ; but the leading battalions were as a rule disposed in five waves, the last one composed of carriers, the others each of one company (less its carrying party). The first wave consisted of skirmishers (who helped to guide the tanks) in two lines thirty yards apart ; the second, third and fourth of small section columns in single file, thirty to sixty yards apart ; the allotted machine guns and trench mortars, and the brigade forward signal party were with the fourth wave. The waves were aligned on tapes, laid out under the protection of strong patrols, the front tape less than three hundred yards from the enemy. This distance was chosen, as No Man's Land averaged well over five hundred yards except in the III Corps area, where the opposing sides were in closer contact, so that with waves a hundred yards apart, the forming-up position might as far as possible be clear of the fall of the enemy's usual S.O.S. protective barrage. Tapes were also laid forward to guide the flanks of companies.

Behind came supporting battalions in larger groups in file, disposed diamond-wise. The deployment was not interfered with by the enemy except that about 3.30 a.m. a bombardment fell in the Bois l'Abbé area on parts of the 4th Canadian and of the 7th and 15th Australian Brigades for threequarters of an hour and drove them to shelter in trenches and shell-holes.

As zero hour approached the mist grew thicker, particularly in the Luce and Avre valleys ; it assisted to cover the launching of the attack—phosphorus bombs had been provided to be dropped from aeroplanes to conceal the advance of tanks, if necessary—but it did not clear completely until nearly 10 a.m. and embarrassed both the troops and the tanks in keeping direction and formation, and they made use of the sound of the barrage as a guide ; for they could not see the bursting shells unless they were dangerously close up. Under these conditions the attacking brigades became split up from the start into small groups and in most cases it was not until after 6.30 a.m. that they could be gathered into some semblance of order.

A few minutes before zero hour, 4.20 a.m., the tanks started from their assembly positions in order to be up with the front line when the barrage fell and the infantry advanced. Out of the total of 435 machines, 430 went into action.[1] It was five minutes or more after the barrage and bombardment opened before the enemy reply came down on the assembly places of the infantry, and the waves had by then moved forward. His fire was variously described as " very " wild and not very heavy " and " heavy " ; in any case it caused few losses and soon ceased, smothered by the British counter-batteries.

---

[1] Fuller (" Tanks in the Great War "), p. 223, says 415 fighting tanks out of 420.

The Canadian Corps[1] on the right, next to the French First Army, had been given a frontage of about seven thousand yards between the Amiens–Roye road and the Amiens–Chaulnes railway, both inclusive. It was new to the ground and had only arrived very recently, not having taken over the actual front line until two hours before Zero. Nevertheless the reconnaissance work had been well done and detailed plans made with great care.

Three of the Canadian divisions, the 3rd, 1st and 2nd, were disposed in the front line, with the 4th between three or four miles in rear, and the attached 32nd moving up from the west side of Amiens. On the right of the corps, as the French were going to launch their attack 45 minutes after the British,[2] was a so-called " Independent Force " under Brigadier-General Brutinel, the commander of the Canadian Machine Gun Corps. It consisted of the 1st and 2nd Canadian Motor Machine-Gun Brigades, the Canadian Cyclist Battalion and one section of medium trench mortars mounted on lorries. The task of this force was to pass through the 3rd Canadian Division and assure flank protection by making good the Amiens–Roye road between the second and third objectives.[3] It was, further, to support the cavalry should the latter be able to push beyond the third objective.

To keep close touch between the 3rd Canadian Division and the French an international liaison force was also organized. It contained a " section " of the 94th Regiment of the French 42nd Division with a machine gun, and a platoon of the 43rd Canadian Battalion, all under a French

---

[1] Corps Commander .. .. Lieut.-Gen. Sir A. W. Currie
    Br.-Gen. General Staff .. .. Br.-Gen. N. W. Webber
    Commander Royal Artillery .. Major-Gen. E. W. B. Morrison
    Commander Heavy Artillery .. Br.-Gen. R. H. Massie
    Chief Engineer .. .. .. Br.-Gen. W. B. Lindsay
    1st Canadian Division .. .. Major-Gen. A. C. Macdonell
    2nd Canadian Division .. .. Major-Gen. Sir H. E. Burstall
    3rd Canadian Division .. .. Major-Gen. L. J. Lipsett
    4th Canadian Division .. .. Major-Gen. Sir D. Watson
    Independent Force .. .. Br.-Gen. E. Brutinel
    32nd Division (G.H.Q. Reserve) Major-Gen. T. S. Lambert

[2] See Note at end of Chapter.
[3] See Map 1 and Sketch 2.

officer[1] and was to move first up the Andrea ravine and then on the Amiens–Roye Road.

The IV Tank Brigade (Br.-General E. B. Hankey) (1st, 4th, 5th and 14th Battalions, with Mark V machines) was attached to the Canadian Corps and No. 5 Squadron of the V Brigade, R.A.F. (Br.-General L. E. O. Charlton) was detailed to work with it. No. 8 Squadron was with the tanks, and No. 6 Squadron with the cavalry.

The task of the right of the 3rd Canadian Division, which had the 9th and 8th Brigades in front line, and the 5th Tank Battalion attached, was somewhat difficult, and it was not rendered easier by the fact that the French corps on its right would not advance at the same time.[2] It therefore was given a narrow frontage and had six field artillery brigades allotted to it for the barrage, whilst the 1st and 2nd Canadian Division had only four.[3] The first ground to be captured was intersected by the deep ravines which run from the plateau down to the Luce. Rifle Wood, just behind the enemy front trench, lay near the top of the gentle slope on the left (from the Canadian point of view) of one ravine; Hamon Wood and Jean Wood at the top of two other ravines; after these had been reached the ground ahead was level. The enemy trenches in front of Rifle Wood overlooked the small bridgehead across the Luce at Hourges; but, on

---

[1] A British liaison officer was also attached to the headquarters of the French 42nd Division and a French officer to the 3rd Canadian Division. Grasset, p. 35, however, relates that General Deville called on Major-General Lipsett on the 5th, but in spite of good will, " la conversation " est penible ", as neither general could speak or understand the other's language, and General Lipsett's G.S.O.1 only knew a few words of French.

[2] Opposed to the Canadian Corps was the greater part of the *225th Division*; the northern boundaries coincided, but the left of the German frontage extended a thousand yards into the French sector. As usual, each infantry regiment in the line had one battalion at the front, one in support, and one resting in the villages at the back of the sector. Behind the *225th* was the *1st Reserve Division* astride the Amiens–Roye road, east of le Quesnel; but owing to the direction of the German divisional boundaries, about N.W. by N., the support battalions of the *14th Bavarian Division*, and the resting battalions of the *1st Reserve Division*, though both these divisions faced the French, became involved in the fight with the right of the Canadian Corps.

[3] In addition, each division had one field artillery brigade for close support (these detailing a section to each infantry brigade) and a heavy brigade for bombardment; the remaining 6 heavy brigades and 4 siege batteries (long-range) were detailed for counter-battery work. Twelve 6-inch mortars on carriages accompanied the infantry and kept well up with them, one receiving a direct hit.

the other hand, the long slope up to them, being slightly convex a short advance from Hourges, would bring the attackers into dead ground. Major-General Lipsett therefore decided to crowd the 9th Brigade and one company of tanks into the bridgehead before Zero, when one battalion, deployed facing south-east, avoiding a frontal attack, would advance rapidly and turn Rifle Wood from the north and thus secure dead ground for manoeuvre. The rest of the brigade, drawn up facing north-east, would move along the south bank of the Luce under the edge of the plateau, one battalion to get in rear of the German defences in the Rifle Wood sector, whilst another made for Demuin and Courcelles.[1]

Of the two companies of the 5th Tank Battalion allotted to the 9th Canadian Brigade, B Company crossed the Luce by the bridge at Thennes, by permission of the French, and formed up along the Thennes–Hourges road, midway between the two villages ; A Company was spread along the Amiens–Roye road, with its head just short of the bridge over the Luce at Domart.

The 8th Canadian Brigade (less 2 battalions in divisional reserve), with C Company of the 5th Tank Battalion, which deployed on a line between Domart and Leopard Wood, was to capture Hangard and work along the northern bank of the Luce, turning any position which might be holding up the left of the 9th Canadian Brigade, and helping in any way possible the right of the 1st Canadian Division.

The 7th Canadian Brigade, with six tanks, was to pass through the 9th at the first objective, and, taking with it any tanks allotted to the latter which had not been put out of action, occupy the whole of the second objective in the divisional sector.

The tanks began moving forward at 4.8 a.m. and as they were travelling in second gear a faint hum only was audible at the front a thousand yards ahead ; but harassing fire was employed to cover this noise. Many shells of the enemy's counter-barrage fell, as expected, near Domart bridge, but made no direct hit and as the ground on each side was marshy their effect was small.

The attack of the 9th Canadian Brigade (Br.-General D. M. Ormond) was completely successful in spite of the fog and

---

[1] The Canadian and Australian brigades were still 4 battalions strong, against the British 3.

the cramped position from which it deployed. By 5.30 a.m. men of the 43rd Battalion were in Rifle Wood, although it was not until 7.30 a.m., after hard fighting, that the wood was cleared of machine-gun posts. Holland Wood to the south was taken by 7.10 a.m. and Vignette Wood, farther east, shortly afterwards. The battalion then occupied its first objective. The 116th Battalion, next on the left, had stiff fighting at first, its leading company losing all its officers and sixty other ranks ; but this company having overcome all resistance gave covering fire to the other three which attacked and captured Hamon Wood from the north and west. By 7.30 a.m. the 116th had occupied its first objective. The 58th Battalion, after overcoming resistance on the Rifle Wood–Hangard road by 5.20 a.m., pushed on against Demuin, which with the assistance of tanks was taken after considerable opposition by 6.30 a.m. ; Courcelles was cleared by 7.5 a.m. and the first objective occupied.[1]

The tanks did not have good luck and were handicapped, as for reasons of secrecy, detailed reconnaissances had not been permitted. The mist and battle smoke was so thick here and elsewhere that they could not see each other, nor the targets except for the flashes of discharge. Of the thirteen machines of B Company which had crossed the Luce at Thennes by 2.45 a.m., three were ditched in the mist en route to the front line and one was put out of action by gas fumes. One section had been detailed to assist the French near the international boundary ; of its four tanks one received a direct hit soon after leaving the position of deployment ; two were misdirected ; the fourth gave valuable assistance in clearing Villers aux Erables. The remaining five tanks of the company helped to clear the various small woods on the 9th Canadian Brigade front, and reached the first objective.

The machines of A Company, except for one, gave little but moral aid to the infantry. They had to cross the Luce at Domart bridge in single file, and about four minutes after Zero, the last tank when a hundred and fifty yards clear of the bridge received two direct hits. The barrage on the road being very heavy, the remaining 13 tanks were deployed and three became ditched in the swamp. Six other tanks

---

[1] For his gallant conduct on this day, until he was mortally wounded, Corporal H. G. B. Miner, 58th Battalion (2nd Central Ontario Regiment), was posthumously awarded the V.C.

received direct hits before reaching Hamon ; thus only six remained.[1]

The leading battalion, the 1/Canadian Mounted Rifles, of the 8th Canadian Brigade (Br.-General D. C. Draper) soon captured Hangard, and after stiff fighting reached the line Hangard cemetery–Cemetery Copse, where the 2/C.M.R. passed through it. Owing to the mist the leading eight tanks of C Company did not catch up until the infantry was in Hangard, where they helped to clear the village. They then passed on towards Demuin to secure a bridgehead there. The bridge, though kept under shrapnel fire until the last possible moment, was found to be blown up ; but by means of one of the " cribs " carried for the purpose, by 6.30 a.m. the tanks, including the second echelon of six, and the infantry had crossed. At this stage five tanks were out of action : two ditched, one hit and burnt out, one with seized gears and one with its entire crew gassed by fumes. After Demuin had been cleared of Germans little resistance was encountered except from isolated groups, and with the loss of one more tank, leaving eight, the first objective was reached. By 11 a.m. a bridgehead had been consolidated at Demuin and the divisional engineers had rendered the bridge passable for field artillery. The corps engineer units at once got to work repairing the roads.

The 7th Canadian Brigade (Br.-General H. M. Dyer), which was to pass through the 9th and 8th and occupy the second objective, about 2,500 yards from the first, on the whole frontage of the 3rd Canadian Division, was assembled north and north-west of Domart. At 5.20 a.m. it began to cross the Luce by foot-bridges thrown for the purpose on either side of the road bridge (which was reserved for horsemen and vehicles), and by 6.45 a.m. all four battalions were across and under shelter of the slopes near Rifle Wood. The advance was then continued in the mist without serious difficulties to the first objective. From this, accompanied by the 19 tanks available, the brigade started, according to plan, at 8.20 a.m. At that hour the barrage, which had halted in front of the first objective, ceased. Henceforward the advance of the three Canadian divisions was covered, when necessary, by the fire of the three field artillery brigades

---

[1] One tank was destroyed by a shell fired at 15 yards' range by a 5·9-inch howitzer. The whole German gun detachment as well as the men in the tank were killed by the explosion.

(II, V, and X) in close support, together with one 60-pdr. battery and one 6-inch howitzer (horse-drawn) battery per division.   By 12 noon, however, the rest of the field artillery had come up behind the second objective.

The R. Canadian Regiment, the R. Highlanders of Canada and 49th Battalion led the advance of the 7th Brigade, Brutinel's Independent Force co-operating on the right. The Germans offered a desperate but not a sustained resistance.   Wheelbarrow and Jean Woods were cleared with the help of tanks ; a platoon of the R. Canadian Regiment, noticing that the enemy was falling back from Mezières before the French attack, entered the eastern edge of the village and cut off part of the garrison.[1]   In the centre a German howitzer battery, firing point-blank from a depression a thousand yards east of Hamon Wood, was captured by a tank of A Company, with the assistance of two platoons of the R. Highlanders.   This tank, being unable to enter the wood on account of the size of the trees, had cruised round the northern edge, and behind the wood it had come on the flank of the battery, whose detachments it kept with their hands up until the infantry arrived.   A second howitzer battery was also taken by the same battalion.   A field battery was captured intact by an artillery patrol,[2] and turned on the enemy ; it soon after shot down a balloon in the act of rising.   The 49th Battalion encountered a good deal of resistance from machine guns in Cerfs Wood ; but between 10.20 and 11 a.m. the 7th Canadian Brigade was on its objective and consolidating.   The task of Major-General Lipsett's division was completed ; but only eight of its tanks remained.[3]

By this time a number of aeroplanes had come into action, dropping bombs on formed bodies of German troops, machine-gun posts, guns and transport on the roads, whilst others went on to bomb the railway stations and aerodromes.[4]

---

[1] See Note at end of Chapter.

[2] The artillery patrols were forward observation officer parties, consisting of 2 officers, with signallers and orderlies, for reconnaissance purposes.

[3] The tank records do not give the fate of the 11 which fell out between the first and second objectives, only the number which reached the second objective.

[4] " War in the Air " VI, pp. 437–46.

According to *Militär Wochenblatt* No. 6/1938, no damage was done at the aerodromes, as in the early morning all machines had been brought out of the tents and hangars, and scattered.

The initial attack of the 1st Canadian Division[1] was made by one brigade on an original frontage of just two miles, but gradually narrowing to one mile and three-quarters. The 3rd Brigade (Br.-General S. Tuxford), reinforced by a battalion from the 2nd Brigade, was to gain the first objective, where the 1st Brigade was to pass through it to the second ; the 2nd Brigade (less one battalion) was then to come up and continue on to the final objective. B and C Companies of the 4th Tank Battalion were to move ahead in the first advance, A coming up later in support.

The attack was carried out with 3 battalions (16th, 13th and 14th) in first line and two (5th and 15th) in support. The barrage was good except that it fell short on the 13th Battalion and caused thirty casualties. The 16th Battalion had a difficult task, as the contour of the ground near the Luce was broken and unsuitable for tanks ; but it pushed on and captured Aubercourt, where a tank gave assistance from the north, after a short resistance. Then, after laying hands on a regimental commander and all his staff in a quarry, it pushed on to the first objective. Twenty-one of the twenty-eight tanks (six being held in reserve and one ditched) reached the front line on the plateau and went ahead of the 13th and 14th Battalions. The Germans whom they encountered, demoralized by their looming up out of the mist, fled, many only half dressed. The enemy parties in the intervals between the tanks, however, though surprised, offered stout resistance to the on-coming infantry. Leaving these to be dealt with by the supports, the leading lines pushed on in the fog. Thus for a time fighting went on simultaneously all over the field.[2] Machine-gun nests in Hangard Wood caused considerable trouble, whilst one trench north of Aubercourt held up the attack for three-quarters of an hour, until Stokes mortars were brought up to bombard it. A nest of eight machine guns in shallow holes in the southern half of Morgemont Wood required the assistance of tanks to overcome it ; but a strongpoint on the eastern edge was captured by infantry alone. A general flight of the enemy on this front then took place and the

---

[1] It was opposed to the *117th Division*, the boundaries of both practically coinciding.

[2] For their very gallant conduct in capturing posts almost single-handed during this day Corporal H. J. Good, 13th Battalion (Quebec Regiment), and Private J. B. Croak of the same battalion who was killed, were awarded the V.C.

first objective wás reached soon after 8 a.m., a little late mainly in consequence of the fog. Of the tanks 12 only arrived, although the original 21 had been joined thirty minutes late by the machine which had been ditched. The 1st Canadian Brigade (Br.-General W. A. Griesbach), which had followed the 3rd, also lost a certain amount of time and it was ten to twenty minutes after 8.20 a.m., the appointed hour, by which time the mist was clearing off and the battlefield emerging into view, that the 2nd, 4th and 3rd Battalions moved forward, the 3rd having assembled barely half its strength. Their objective was a line parallel to the Luce from the western edge of Cayeux to within a quarter of a mile of the Caix–Guillaucourt road, and on the right the first part of the advance had to be made up the valley of the Luce and across its broken slopes, whilst on the left, on the plateau, several woods stood in the way. The battalions which had been joined by the six reserve tanks came at once under heavy fire, including direct artillery fire ; but they pressed on, the tanks rendering assistance to suppress enemy fire first from Ignaucourt and Cáncelette Wood, and later from Ruisseau Wood and Lemaire Wood (where two tanks were lost by field gun fire). Finally the enemy at 10.40 a.m., being reported from the air as on the run from the second objective, the tanks reached Cayeux ahead of the infantry, and took it. Thus the objective was occupied, with outposts pushed over the Luce, by 11 a.m. on the right and in the centre, and nearly one hour later on the left, on which flank the missing half battalion did not arrive until 10.25 a.m. Eleven of the eighteen tanks had survived.

The 2nd Canadian Division[1] had to start from a front nearly three thousand yards long, aslant to the line of advance ; but once started the width of its sector became less than a mile. Like the 1st Canadian Division, it deployed its brigades one behind the other : the 4th (Br.-General R. Rennie) to go to the first objective, the 5th (Br.-General J. M. Ross) to the second, and the 6th (Br.-General A. H. Bell) to the third ; but, unlike the 1st Division, each brigade used only two battalions instead of three in the front line,

---

[1] It was opposed by the southern half of the *41st Division*.

the other two following in support. One platoon was sent north of the railway to keep touch with the Australian Corps. Five sections of A and B Companies of the 14th Tank Battalion were allotted to the 4th Brigade ; these furnished 17 machines, 10 to be behind the right and 7, the left, C Company remaining in divisional reserve. Owing to the angle of the front to the line of attack the tanks for the left had an extra distance to go, and one was ditched on the way up. According to the battalion war diary : although the ground was hard and suitable, " all tanks more or less " lost direction and most, when the mist cleared, found " themselves in sectors other than their own. All tanks, " however, except two, were repeatedly in action ". There was hardly any need for them, as the barrage was " magnificent " and the 19th Battalion met with little resistance except from a strongpoint on the left ; and, with the 21st and two tanks in support, after some bomb fighting in the fog, entered Marcelcave south of the railway, the 7th Australian Brigade having occupied the northern part, as soon as the barrage of heavy guns on the village lifted at 6.23 a.m., and the tanks, which were shelling and machine-gunning the edge, ceased fire. The battalion reached the first objective by 7 a.m. The 18th Battalion encountered much machine-gun fire, particularly from Morgemont and Cancelette Woods ; but with the help of two tanks on the right, resistance was overcome and the first objective gained at 7.45 a.m. The tanks rallied behind Marcelcave. Three had received direct hits, two were ditched, one had broken down and in one the crew were overcome by gas fumes.

The 5th Canadian Brigade went through the 4th and advanced at 8.20 a.m., ten fresh tanks coming up from the rear echelon in three detachments and passing through the line a quarter of an hour later, followed by the ten others in support. Besides assisting in mopping up, here, as elsewhere, useful service was done by individual tanks as opportunity offered. The valley west of Wiencourt which runs south down to Cayeux was found to be full of enemy infantry and heavy guns ; but it was turned from the south by two tanks (one being hit and the other ditched, but both were able to go on firing), whilst other tanks cruised up and down the front of Snipe and Pierret Woods, raking them, and thus greatly facilitating the task of the infantry. An enemy assembly south of Wiencourt was broken up by a

single tank : the Germans stood their ground until it was
within 15 yards, but then broke and fled in all directions.
By 9.20 Wiencourt had been taken, and half an hour later,
with the help of nine whippets of the 6th Tank Battalion, six
of which attacked from the south and three from the north,
Guillaucourt also. The second objective was then gained
without further resistance. The tank losses of the 2nd
Canadian Division during this stage amounted to only four
(2 direct hits, 1 ditched, 1 broken down). The general
verdict was that the tanks had enabled a faster rate of
progress to be achieved than would otherwise have been
possible.

   Thus towards 11 a.m. the Canadian Corps had taken
possession of the entire second objective.[1]   The 4th Division,
passing through the 3rd, was timed to proceed to the third
objective at 12.5 p.m. ; but the hour at which the 1st and
2nd Divisions continued on was left to the commanders to
settle, taking into account the physical condition of the
troops. In the interval which would thus arise it had been
arranged that the 3rd Cavalry Division (Major-General
A. E. W. Harman) and the 3rd Battalion of the whippet
tanks should pass through the infantry and push on to the
third objective, a company of 16 whippets being sent with
each of the three cavalry brigades (6th, 7th and Canadian).
By this time the mist had cleared and the whole Santerre
plateau seen from the air was dotted with parties of infantry,
field artillery, cavalry and tanks moving forward. Staff
officers were galloping about, many riding horses in battle
for the first time, prisoners in formed companies marching
back with hardly more escort than the Canadian wounded
whom they were carrying, whilst overhead the planes of
the Royal Air Force were flying noisily to work. Indeed, at
this stage there was more noise of movement than of firing,
as the heavy batteries, almost wheel to wheel, with their
muzzles cocked up to the highest elevation, were no longer
in action ; for the infantry had gone so far that it was no
longer possible for them to shoot. About 10.30 a.m., as
Lieut.-General Currie was moving with his brigadier-general,
General Staff, from his headquarters in Dury, up the valley

---

[1] For the German account see Note at end of Chapter V.

from Boves to his advanced headquarters at Gentelles, he was able to feel assured that, except at isolated places, there seemed to be little resistance ; some parties of Germans were merely waiting under cover to surrender at the first opportunity, others were showing white flags, but, as in defeat in 1914, some of them opening fire when the Canadians came near to receive surrender. No enemy guns seemed to be firing and no co-ordinated defence was apparent ; many officers thought that armoured vehicles could have gone anywhere ; the 17th Armoured Car Company and armoured cars of the Canadian machine-gun brigades did so for a time. The attackers were soon, however, to encounter the German resting battalions and the divisions in reserve.

The corps aeroplane squadrons had already begun with considerable success to deal with the latter as they were marching up—by German accounts with far more success than appears in the British war diaries.[1]

With due measures for reconnaissance, the Canadian Cavalry Brigade (Br.-General R. W. Paterson) marched at 5.40 a.m. from Longueau to Cachy, followed by the other brigades of the 3rd Cavalry Division. Towards 8 a.m. they continued on to the valley east of Morgemont Wood, which still had Germans in it. When the leading troops arrived, scouts having found two passages at Ignaucourt, the brigades crossed the Luce there about 10.30 a.m. just as

---

[1] The Monograph, pp. 127, 131, 147, 175, 177, 178, 179, 183, 184, 192, contains many references to the air bombing and machine-gunning of the reserves, " unceasing air attacks ", " continuous air attacks which " . . . scattered the troops far and wide ", " a swarm of fliers which " came down and covered the whole assembly area of the regiment with " machine-gun bullets and bombs ", " lively attacks of numerous enemy " airmen ". On the branch railway west of Framerville (north-west of Harbonnières) a gun ammunition train was hit and exploded, there was " wild excitement among the retreating batteries, trains, etc." at the moment " 80–90 enemy planes appeared at most 300 feet above the " village to increase the confusion " and there was " a headlong [literally " headless] retreat of area-employment companies, trains, carriages and " motors ". Astride the Somme in the *43rd Reserve Division* area " under the effects of long-range fire and strong air attacks, baggage and " columns rushed eastwards in headlong confusion, some teams cut their " traces and galloped back in wild flight " ; the advance of the reserves " in the area of air attacks was slow " ; " the airmen worked over us " like madmen ", even late in the day " the air activity was enormous ; " the German airmen only appeared in the evening and then at last we " had rest ". The advance of the *119th Division* from the reserve suffered " several halts owing to air attack ".

the Canadian infantry were reaching the second objective, a few hundred yards farther on.

Moving to the south, the Canadian Cavalry Brigade made contact on the Amiens–Roye road with the armoured cars of Brutinel's Independent Force, which henceforward guarded the right flank. The brigade had already got touch of the French 42nd Division to the south, and entered Fresnoy, then almost empty, but subsequently reoccupied by the Germans.

Advancing through the infantry with fourteen whippets (2 having developed engine trouble), the Canadian Cavalry Brigade entered Beaucourt, but found it in course of evacuation and picked up about three hundred prisoners. The wood beyond, however, was strongly held by infantry and guns, and the brigade was unable to get near it ;[1] any attempt to approach le Quesnel, the ground in front of which was level and devoid of any sort of cover, also encountered very strong resistance, and came under fire from Fresnoy, which the French had not yet occupied.[2] Beaucourt Wood was not taken until infantry came up later ; Fresnoy not until 9.30 p.m., and le Quesnel remained at the close of the day in the enemy's hands.

Next on the left came the 7th Cavalry Brigade (Lieut.-Colonel E. Paterson acting). Its attached whippets failed to follow as ordered, as they could not keep up, and therefore gave no assistance to the brigade. The nominal speed of the whippets was 7 miles an hour ; but across country it was not more than half this. It was soon evident that when not under fire the cavalry was too fast for the whippets, and when under fire was unable to follow them. The result was a certain amount of mutual recrimination. Moving rapidly as machine-gun fire was opened on them from the south, the 7th Dragoon Guards, on the left, galloped and charged the Germans who were bringing machine guns to the southern border of Cayeux Wood, one squadron losing a large number of horses. Then whilst a troop gradually worked up the eastern border one squadron galloped through the wood, which it was able to do as the brushwood had been cut, and

---

[1] Beaucourt Wood happened to be held by the three resting battalions of the *192nd Division*, whose front was south of Moreuil in the French sector ; they were united as a composite regiment, known by the name of the senior officer, Major Bellmann.

[2] Le Quesnel and Fresnoy were defended by troops of the *1st Reserve Division*, which had been in reserve behind the former village.

captured 12 machine guns, a field battery and numerous prisoners. The 17th Lancers were sent up to hold the wood and with the help of K Battery R.H.A. a counter-attack was beaten off. The Inniskillings, on the right, detached a squadron against the north of Beaucourt Wood to assist the Canadian Cavalry Brigade, but were themselves unable to advance between the wood and Cayeux Wood.

At 1 p.m. Major-General Harman sent up the 1st Royals from the 6th Cavalry Brigade (Lieut.-Colonel F. H. D. C. Whitmore acting), his reserve, near Claude Wood, to the assistance of the 7th Cavalry Brigade, and forty minutes later ordered the latter brigade to go on and occupy the third objective, and the 6th (less one regiment) to take over the sector on the right originally assigned to the Canadian Cavalry Brigade. The second part of the order was subsequently cancelled and the 6th Cavalry Brigade took possession in support of the left of the 7th, and half its whippets went to assist the 11th Canadian Infantry Brigade. Meantime the 17th Lancers (7th Brigade) had made a rapid advance and by 2.35 p.m. had occupied the whole width of the sector allotted to its brigade on the reverse slope just short of the third objective. Mounted patrols sent eastwards a few hundred yards could see nothing and were not fired on; but all efforts to press nearer to le Quesnel failed, and the opportunity to envelop it was not accepted. The whippets which had failed to follow the 7th Brigade had moved southward to assist the attack on Beaucourt and Beaucourt Wood by the Canadian Cavalry Brigade and remained to help the 4th Canadian Division. The losses of this company amounted to seven; one tank destroyed and two disabled by shell fire and four by engine trouble.

The 9th Cavalry Brigade (Br.-General D'A. Legard) of the 1st Cavalry Division (Major-General R. L. Mullens) was detailed to work with the left Canadian division, and the 1st Cavalry Brigade (Br.-General H. S. Sewell) with the right Australian division. Moving *via* Villers Bretonneux and Marcelcave, at 11 a.m. the head of the 9th reached Guillaucourt. It had been preceded independently by the nine whippets of C Company, 6th Tank Battalion, which, after assisting the 5th Canadian Brigade to capture the village by attacking it from both north and south, had passed through the second objective at 10.15 a.m. and dispersed about four hundred of the enemy, who appeared about to counter-attack, but lost one machine by fire. Returning, the whippets supported the 9th Cavalry Brigade, which soon after its arrival at Guillaucourt received information brought to a report centre in the next village by an aeroplane (each whippet battalion had an attached aeroplane) that described the Germans on the run as far east as Rosières, four miles away and beyond the third objective. The 19th and 15th Hussars were sent forward at a gallop, covered by the fire of one whippet, and though the former regiment had to run the gauntlet of some machine-gun fire, fortunately ineffective, and of shell fire from the south, both regiments reached the third objective about 1 p.m., north of which they found the 1st Cavalry Brigade, whose adventures will be related in due course, already established. The remaining brigade of the 1st Cavalry Division, the 2nd (Br.-General A. Lawson), which had followed to Guillaucourt, was then ordered to fill the gap east of Caix between the 7th Cavalry Brigade and the 9th, which it was able to do. Thus except on the right near le Quesnel, the cavalry was in possesion of the third objective of the Canadian Corps and, having no orders from the Cavalry Corps to go farther, although Fourth Army orders clearly directed that the cavalry should push forward from the old Amiens Defence Line with the least possible delay, there the 3rd Cavalry Division stayed. The whippets had not given all the assistance which had been hoped; they had not arrived when the 3rd Cavalry Division had left the second objective, whereas they should have preceded its brigades, and their slowness in appearing when called up had already—except for the action of the nine which operated near Guillaucourt and of a section which dealt with the enemy machine guns along the edge of Beaucourt Wood to enable the 7th Cavalry Brigade to get on—led to the cavalry missing many fleeting opportunities ; but the whippets certainly gave confidence to the patrols which they accompanied. Light tanks and cavalry had never operated together before, never even dha enjoyed training exercise together. Experience in co-operation was evidently required.

The infantry of the 4th Canadian Division was to pass through the line of the 3rd at the second objective. It began moving forward at 5.20 a.m., 11th Brigade on the right, the 12th on the left and the 10th in reserve. They crossed the Luce by the footbridges at Domart and Demuin and after assembling on the dead ground south of the river moved to the Moreuil–Demuin road, the jumping off line, where they found that the thirty tanks of the 1st Tank Battalion, which had come by the Domart bridge, had already arrived. The brigade transport and attached artillery also followed across the Luce. All was ready at 10.30 a.m. but the advance was not made until 12.10 p.m.

A pause was made on the Mezières–Ignaucourt road until 1.30 p.m. in order to let the tanks, A, C, and B Companies in line, pass through, when the infantry followed them at a distance of about two hundred yards. The plan was that the tanks,[1] or at least some of them, should go straight on to the third objective, deposit infantry machine-gunners there, and then send back half their number to help forward the infantry. Ten tanks of A Company tried to reach le Quesnel, but nine received direct hits at 70 yards range from a field battery,[2] a thousand yards south of Beaucourt Wood, and all of them caught fire. Six tanks of B Company passing north of Beaucourt Wood reached the third objective, but on account of the situation on the right brought the machine-gunners back about fifteen hundred yards. Four tanks of B Company reached the third objective about 3.30 p.m. Of the 30 tanks only 11 rallied and only 5 were fit for fighting on the 9th.

Passing through the 3rd Canadian Division, the 11th Brigade (Br.-General V. W. Odlum) came in touch with the Canadian Cavalry Brigade and, like it, could at first make no progress against Beaucourt Wood, although Beaucourt village was held by the cavalry.[3] Two of the three tanks detailed to help the right battalion, the 54th, were soon on fire and the third disabled ; but assisted by the fire of the attached battery and of a captured German field battery manned by a patrol of the divisional artillery, the 54th and

---

[1] Mark V*, 6 feet longer than Mark V, and therefore a larger target.

[2] Two guns camouflaged with corn stooks faced the oncoming tanks. The other two were dug in, in a sunken road on the left of the tanks.

[3] Mainly on account of the fire of a German field battery recently brought up. This dangerous enemy had not been neutralized owing to the aeroplane which had been detailed to " spot " battery positions and point them out by firing Very lights on them, having been brought down by machine-gun fire.

102nd Battalions, with the support of the 75th, rushed the wood about 4.30 p.m. and after very stiff fighting established a line on the southern edge and down to the Amiens–Roye road. The Canadian Cavalry Brigade then went into reserve. Although about 3 p.m. the III Canadian Artillery Brigade came up to White House and at 5,000 yards range opened fire on le Quesnel, about 8 p.m. moving forward to Beaucourt, and an attached 6-inch howitzer battery also took part in the bombardment, any combination of artillery action in the afternoon was prevented by the damage done to the signal cables by tanks roaming about in search of targets. Otherwise in the later portion of the battle the tanks had earned general praise ; working independently they had overcome many machine-gun posts and small centres of resistance, and by their moral effect caused the surrender of many prisoners. The enemy still clung to le Quesnel and Fresnoy and thus stopped any further advance of the infantry.

The 12th Canadian Brigade (Br.-General J. H. MacBrien) after passing through the second objective was galled at first by fire from Beaucourt Wood ; but detaching one company to attack the northern edge, the 78th and 38th Battalions passed on, overcame isolated resistance and reached the line of the 7th Cavalry Brigade on the southern edge of the wood, south of Caix, about 4.45 p.m. The 72nd Battalion, in spite of heavy rifle and machine-gun fire from the south, then went through to the final objective, twelve miles from its starting point ; it also formed a defensive flank.[1] The 7th Cavalry Brigade was then withdrawn, but the 6th remained in the line with the 12th Canadian Brigade, the " isolated trees " being the point of junction with the 11th Brigade. The Independent Force held the Amiens–Roye road back to the White House. About 8.30 p.m. the enemy shelled the front line of the 6th Cavalry Brigade in the wood near the " isolated trees " and a counter-attack from Beaufort (east of le Quesnel) seemed imminent. An S.O.S. was sent up as a precaution to ascertain if the 4th Canadian Division batteries were in position ; but C Battery R.H.A. had its guns laid on the exits of the village and nothing developed.

---

[1] Lieut. J. E. Tait, M.C., 78th (Manitoba) Battalion, was posthumously awarded the V.C. for conspicuous bravery and initiative. He dealt with an enemy machine gun single-handed and, inspired by his example, his men rushed the position and took 12 machine guns. He was mortally wounded in repulsing a counter-attack later in the day.

The trouble of the cavalry that night was to find sufficient water, which could only be obtained from ponds and wells in the villages ; but other supplies, both to the cavalry and other troops arrived in the course of the night.

In the 1st Canadian Division, the 2nd Brigade (Br.-General F. O. W. Loomis) on a two-battalion front, left the second objective about noon. The 3rd Cavalry Division having cleared the enemy off, it met with no organized resistance and the 10th Battalion on the left reached the third objective at 1.15 p.m. and the 7th on the right did so at 2.35 p.m. The 4th Canadian Division, on the right of the 1st, not having then come up, steps were taken to guard that flank.

The 6th Brigade of the 2nd Canadian Division arrived at the first objective east of Marcelcave at 12.30 p.m. but was not ordered forward until 2.30 p.m. ; then the leading battalion was changed, so it was not until about 4.30 p.m. that the brigade left the second objective. It reached the third objective without incident, but could not establish contact with the Australian troops on its left.

The 2nd and 9th Cavalry Brigades were now relieved, the latter shooting down two out of a flight of low-flying German aeroplanes which passed over it soon afterwards.

As a result of the day's fighting the Canadian Corps had everywhere gained its final objective in the old Amiens Outer Defences except on the right. General Currie was making arrangements to complete his task by an early morning attack on le Quesnel. The divisional artillery had come up and was covering the line. Late in the evening the French occupied Fresnoy.[1] The corps had captured 114 officers, 4,919 other ranks and 161 guns, besides several hundred machine guns and other war material. Its losses amounted to about 3,500.[2]

The operations of the Royal Air Force in the afternoon will be dealt with as a whole at the end of the ground fighting on the 8th August ; it need only be said here that the orders for the bomber and fighter squadrons were changed and they were sent to attack the Somme bridges over which the Germans were retiring.

---

[1] See Note at end of Chapter.
[2] See Note I at end of Chapter VIII.

NOTE

THE FRENCH OPERATIONS ON THE 8th AUGUST[1] :

(Sketch 4)

The artillery of the French First Army opened fire at zero hour on its whole front, but the infantry did not at once advance. At 5.5 a.m. the XXXI Corps suddenly launched its attack.[2] The enemy who had already been seriously engaged with the British for three-quarters of an hour, was visibly upset by this unexpected extension of the battle. He did not succeed in checking the march of the 42nd and 37th Divisions, which passed on either side of the woods to the north-east of Moreuil. Between 9.30 and 10 a.m. the heads of these two divisions had reached the road Moreuil–Villers aux Erables, and the 153rd, which had followed, was preparing to insert itself between them[3]. On the right of the corps, the 66th Division punctually executed the operation laid down for it, entered Morisel, then captured Moreuil, after having enveloped it on the north and the south.

On the right of the XXXI Corps, after four hours less 20 minutes of a violent artillery duel, the IX Corps attacked the Avre front at 8 a.m. It had been able to throw footbridges over the river in the course of the night and during the artillery preparation, but the crossing of the river proved difficult, for the places selected were swept by enemy machine guns posted in Genouville Wood. One regiment of the 3rd Division managed to cross at Braches ; but only one battalion of the 15th Colonial Division succeeded in doing so south of la Neuville, and was soon forced to stop near the road Moreuil–Montdidier. Fortunately, the advance of the XXXI Corps on Morisel assisted the 15th Colonial Division and enabled it to force the passage of the Avre near Genouville Farm, which it captured about 11.30 a.m. To the west and south of Montdidier the X and XXXV Corps only showed great artillery activity.

During the afternoon the action was continued on the Santerre plateau. The XXXI Corps, thanks to the entry into the line of

---

[1] From F.O.A. vii (i), pp. 175–8.

[2] According to Grasset, pp. 83, 87, the 42nd Division at Zero (4.20 a.m.) advanced six hundred yards, and meeting with no opposition might have gone on, but by the barrage programme it had to wait until 5.23 a.m., at which hour the Canadians would be at Rifle Wood (they entered it at 5.30 a.m.). The 37th Division advanced at Zero + 45 minutes.

[3] According to Grasset, p. 110, the artillery had done its work so well that the Germans offered little resistance. On reaching its first objective at 7.30 a.m., the 42nd Division could have gone straight on but had to wait for the barrage. Touch was established with the Canadian line. The 42nd continued its advance at 7.43 a.m., but by 10 a.m. was held up just east of Villers aux Erables, and the barrage went on. The 153rd Division began to come into action at 10.15 a.m.

the 153rd Division with its two battalions of light tanks, captured
Mezières at 3 p.m. (of which the 3rd Canadian Division was
abreast soon after 11 a.m.).[1]

From left to right the 42nd, 153rd and 37th Divisions were
deployed from the south-east of Mezières to the north-west of
Plessier, while the 15th Colonial Division of the IX Corps had
nearly reached a point west of the latter village.

At 3.30 p.m., the commander of the First Army directed the
XXXI Corps to develop its success in the direction of Erches,
with Arvillers as the final objective to be obtained that evening.
He also began making arrangements for moving up his reserves,
the 47th and 56th Divisions behind the 15th Colonial and 3rd
Divisions, and the II Cavalry Corps (less the 6th Cavalry Division) towards St. Just en Chaussée (18 miles south of Moreuil).

After taking Mezières the XXXI Corps halted.[2]   But at
4.30 p.m., a great artillery preparation was begun and the three
divisions were ordered to continue their offensive that evening :
the 42nd Division against Arvillers, the 153rd against Hangest
and Erches, and the 37th against " Hill 97 between Arvillers
" and Saulchoy " [actually due west of Erches].   The XXXI
" Corps front must reach Arvillers this evening without fail ".

Operations were recommenced at 5.30 p.m. in front of Plessier,
and at 7.30 p.m., in front of Fresnoy.   But the enemy's resistance
stiffened and was too strong for any hope of reaching the objectives
laid down for the day.   Plessier was not taken until seven o'clock,
and Fresnoy not until 9.30 p.m. (that is more than five hours after
the 4th Canadian Division was abreast of it) ;   it was then too
late to go any farther.[3]

The IX Corps halted in the course of the afternoon about the
same time as the XXXI ; but as soon as the latter again advanced
the IX Corps followed its movements, and at night reached
the western and south-western edges of Plessier where liaison was
established with the XXXI Corps.

---

[1] Grasset, pp. 165–6, states that when Mezières was reached about
11 a.m. it was defended by machine guns ; the barrage was brought back
and fire ceased, and soon after 12 noon Mezières was discovered to be
deserted.

[2] Apparently because the barrage had ceased.   The 42nd Division went
on at 2 p.m. according to Grasset, whose times do not always accord with
those of the Official Account, but by 3.30 p.m., having by a misunderstanding declined Canadian help, was definitely held up in front of Fresnoy,
and Fresnoy not being taken, the 153rd Division delayed its attack
against Plessier and sent a regiment to help the 42nd.   Grasset, pp. 183–
196 and 210.

[3] The attack was made at 9.15 p.m. with the help of sections of light
tanks from south, west and east.   The northern party found the ground
" terribly strewn with khaki uniforms ".   No tanks were damaged in
this attack, but a company with the 153rd Division near Plessier had lost
13 out of 19 engaged.   Grasset, pp. 217–231 and 239.

CHAPTER IV.

THE BATTLE OF AMIENS—(continued)

FIRST DAY 8TH AUGUST, 1918—(continued)

THE AUSTRALIAN CORPS

(Map 1 ; End-paper A ; Sketch 5)

The frontage of the Australian Corps[1] extended from the Amiens–Chaulnes railway to the Somme, about seven thousand, five hundred yards.[2] The attack was to be made by four divisions. The 2nd and 3rd were to capture the first objective, three thousand yards away, running east of Lamotte and west of Cérisy. The 4th and 5th were to pass through them at 8.20 a.m. and take the second objective, five thousand yards farther ahead on the right, and three thousand on the left, running west of Harbonnières, east of Richmond Woods and then to Morcourt (inclusive). The same two divisions were subsequently to go on to the final objective, the old Amiens Defence Line. The 1st Australian Division, which had fought in front of Hazebrouck in the Battles of the Lys in April and had only just returned to the corps, completing concentration in the Fourth Army area on the 7th August, was kept in reserve. The V Tank Brigade (Br.-General A. Courage) containing the 2nd, 8th and 13th Battalions of Mark V Tanks, with the 15th Battalion (II Tank Brigade) of Mark V* tanks (carrying machine guns, Lewis guns and their crews) attached, and the 17th Armoured Car Battalion were allotted to the corps. The 1st Cavalry Brigade was to co-operate with it.

---

[1] Corps Commander .. .. Lieut.-General Sir John Monash
Br.-Gen. General Staff .. .. Br.-Gen. T. A. Blamey
Commander Royal Artillery .. Br.-Gen. W. A. Coxen
Commander Heavy Artillery .. Br.-Gen. L. D. Fraser
Chief Engineer .. .. .. Br.-Gen. C. H. Foott
1st Australian Division .. Major-Gen. T. W. Glasgow
2nd Australian Division .. Major-Gen. C. Rosenthal
3rd Australian Division .. Major-Gen. J. Gellibrand
4th Australian Division .. Major-Gen. E. G. Sinclair-
Maclagan
5th Australian Division .. Major-Gen. Sir J. J. Talbot
Hobbs
17th Division (G.H.Q. Reserve) Major-Gen. P. R. Robertson

[2] See Sketch 5.

61

Artillery support was provided by eighteen field artillery brigades, nine heavy brigades, four batteries of 6-inch guns and one 12-inch howitzer battery.[1] When the time should come for the 4th and 5th Australian Divisions to advance through the 2nd and 3rd, they were to be accompanied by their own divisional artillery, two Army brigades (VI Australian and XVI R.H.A.) and two 60-pdr batteries ; whilst six other field brigades were at the same time to take position to shell the second objective. No creeping barrage would be fired in this second phase, but aeroplanes would drop smoke bombs in front of the villages and other selected places where resistance seemed likely, and the heavy artillery was to continue firing on its distant targets.

Shortly before Zero (4.20 a.m.) the last echelon of the covering parties provided by the 6th and 10th Australian Brigades (Br.-Generals J. C. Robertson and W. R. McNicoll) withdrew and rejoined their brigades, which now became the reserves of the 2nd and 3rd Divisions. On account of the fog, the contact airmen of No. 3 (Australian) Squadron were not sent out.

The 2nd Australian Division sent forward its 7th and 5th Brigades (Br.-Generals E. A. Wisdom and E. F. Martin), preceded by 23 tanks (one having broken down) of the 2nd Battalion. The field artillery barrage was thick and accurate, and the tanks and infantry kept close to it. The 7th Australian Brigade, unlike the other brigades of the corps, which used only two battalions, attacked on a three-battalion frontage (26th, 28th and 27th Battalions). Except for the machine-gun posts, which the tanks as a rule quickly overcame, the resistance offered was feeble and the delays were few ; such as did occur were due to the mist, soon thickened as it was by battle smoke and dust, and to a belt of wire near the railway through which a gap could not at first be discovered.[2] The first objective was reached by 6.30 a.m.,

---

[1] Field artillery of the 1st, 2nd, 3rd, 4th and 5th Australian Divisions ; III (Aus.), VI (Aus.), XII (Aus.), XIV, XXIII, 189th, 298th Brigades R.F.A., and the XVI (Army) Brigade R.H.A.

R.G.A. Brigades : V, XIV and LXVIII (8-inch howitzer) ; VIII and LXIX (9·2-inch howitzer), LXXVII and XCIII (Mixed) ; IX and XXI (Mobile).

[2] Lieut. A. E. Gaby, 28th Battalion, who discovered a gap in the wire and attacked a machine-gun post, a company of fifty Germans with 4 machine guns surrendering to him, was awarded the V.C. : he was killed in action whilst again displaying conspicuous courage three days later, before he knew of the recognition of his gallant conduct.

that is about five minutes after the barrage moved off it. Consolidation was at once taken in hand ; but the enemy batteries and posts close in front were dealt with by the usual Australian practice of " peaceful penetration ".

The main difficulty of the 5th Australian Brigade (19th and 20th Battalions leading) was to keep direction, as the Roman Road lay athwart its path, being on the right when it started and on the left at the Inner Amiens Defence Line,[1] where the 17th and 18th Battalions were to pass through the leaders. Very little opposition was experienced, except about the double village of Warfusée—Lamotte, in the Cérisy valley ; this was rushed and the cellars were bombed ; two battalion headquarters were captured. By 7.10 a.m. the first objective had been reached. Nineteen tanks arrived there, two having struck land mines and two having received direct hits.

The 3rd Australian Division employed the 9th and 11th Brigades (Lieut.-Colonel J. E. C. Lord, acting and Br.-General J. H. Cannan). Of the 24 tanks of the 13th Battalion allotted to the division, all started and 18 arrived at the first objective. The divisional sector was next to the Somme, and the fog was so thick that visibility is said to have been limited to ten feet, and even less on the extreme left. The pace was therefore slower than expected, and the troops could not keep up with the barrage. This disadvantage was compensated for by the good work of the tanks in attacking strongpoints and small woods, and by the fact that in the fog the Germans could only fire blindly. The 33rd Battalion, on the right, found Accroche Wood, in the enemy front line, strongly garrisoned and full of machine guns ; but the attack was so little expected that the Germans had no time to offer resistance and surrendered with great readiness. The smaller Hazel Wood was also captured without much difficulty. The 35th Battalion, on the left, had heavy losses in officers ; but, aided by tanks, had no very strong opposition to overcome. Thus between 6.50 and 7.15 a.m. both battalions of the 9th Australian Brigade were on the first objective.

The 11th Australian Brigade had the thickest of the mist to contend with, and in places near the river encountered mud, weed and undergrowth. The 44th and 42nd Battalions

---

[1] For this see Map 1. The line passes just west of Warfusée.

led, the former, which had a wide front, being leap-frogged by the 41st on the ridge forming the western side of the Cérisy valley; the 42nd, on the Somme flats, had two platoons north of the canal (here south of the river), which seized the bridges as the advance progressed. Some hand-to-hand fighting occurred at the strongpoints and machine-gun posts; but, scared by the tanks and completely surprised and bewildered, the Germans surrendered in large numbers. A company on the left was on the first objective by 6. 10 a.m. and the rest had arrived by 7 a.m.

At this stage the total loss of the battalions engaged in the front line was less than a thousand, hardly a German shell had fallen since 5.40 a.m., and at least five field batteries, one battery of 4.2-inch guns and two 5.9-inch howitzers had been captured, with hundreds of prisoners.

In the suddenly clearing mist, at 8.20 a.m. punctually, although they had experienced some trouble in finding their place of assembly, the 5th and 4th Australian Divisions, in deep artillery formation, began to pass through the 2nd and 3rd. The 5th Division had 24 tanks of the 2nd and 13th Battalions and 18 of the 15th (Mark V*) attached to it, and the 4th Division had 24 of the 8th Battalion and 18 of the 15th. In addition, 12 cars of the 17th Armoured Car Company were allotted to the 5th, and by 7.40 a.m. they had arrived at Warfusée, towed over the broken roads by tanks. Any tanks remaining serviceable after the initial attack, and now rallying in Cérisy valley, were to assist. The 1st Cavalry Brigade and its whippets were by now assembled behind the original front line north of the Roman Road.

In front of the Australians there lay what appeared to be a great cultivated plain (Santerre); it had spurs projecting down to the Somme, and the tree-surrounded villages of Harbonnières and Bayonvillers standing out from it. The plain, however, is actually broken by three valleys which converge on Chipilly on the Somme,[1] the centre and longest of which extends almost to Harbonnières, whilst on the south side small valleys run down to the Luce from Wiencourt, Guillaucourt and Harbonnières.

The real resistance to the Australians in this phase of the battle came from the German artillery, for which there were good hidden positions in the heads of the valleys, but this

---

[1] See End–paper A.

did not stop them. When a machine-gun post gave trouble the infantry lay down whilst a tank tackled it ; in most cases the crews surrendered as the machine came near, or fled. Thus the advance was rapid.

The 5th Australian Division advanced with the 15th and 8th Brigades (Br.-Generals H. E. Elliott and E. Tivey) leading, and the 14th (Br.-General J. C. Stewart) in reserve. The 24 Mark V tanks preceded the infantry as far as the second objective, and were, towards the end, as much as three hundred yards ahead of it, and the 19 from the 2nd Australian Division followed the divisions in support.

In the 15th Australian Brigade, on emerging from the shelter taken against gun-fire, the 57th Battalion, on the right, encountered north-east of Marcelcave, a battery of 5.9-inch howitzers still in action and firing over open sights, and the 59th, on the left, also came under direct fire of a field battery ; in both cases the guns, with the aid of tanks, were captured, with the loss of one tank from howitzer fire. As 9 a.m. approached the advance had been so rapid that the battalions, as well as the tanks, had to halt to avoid running into the fire of their own heavy artillery, and suffered some casualties from short shooting of the supporting field artillery. About twenty minutes later the 1st Cavalry Brigade and the whippets passed through, moving south of Bayonvillers, and the Germans began to fall back in haste. The pace of the advance was again rapid, and the 60th Battalion, the right supporting battalion, was able to bring flanking fire against the enemy south of the railway in Pierret and Wiencourt, who was delaying the 5th Canadian Brigade. The 58th Battalion, the left support, with 6 tanks which had taken part in the first attack, mopped up Bayonvillers, shattered by the bombardment, which had been avoided by the leading battalions by passing south of it. By 9.55 a.m. a factory north of Guillaucourt had been taken, and by 10.20 a.m., ten minutes before time, the second objective was occupied by the 57th and 59th Battalions.

The 8th Australian Brigade had the 31st and 30th Battalions leading. As soon as the line of tanks topped the crest at the starting line, a German field battery which had been firing from half a mile away hit six in quick succession ; a seventh made straight for the guns, only to meet the same fate ; but a few minutes later the scouts of the 31st Battalion outflanked the battery, and the detachments, which were lying down in a beetroot field nearby, stood up and surrendered. Bayonvillers was to be passed on the north, but before the infantry was abreast of it, a 4·2-inch gun battery in the village knocked out three more tanks, leaving only two. A whippet tank at this instant turned aside and got behind the German battery, whereupon the gunners bolted. The 30th suffered some cross machine-gun fire from the valleys on the left, and this resistance led to the 32nd being sent into a gap which had arisen between the 31st and 30th. The posts were dealt with by the tanks and by rifle fire, and after an advance by rushes, the men of the 8th Australian Brigade, and of the 12th on its left, captured some hundreds of prisoners in the main Morecourt valley (Buchanan Wood marks its head), where the local reserves were sheltering. These Germans had no doubt been scared by the movement along the Roman Road about this time (9.30 a.m.), of the cars of the 17th Armoured Car Battalion, which fired into the valleys as they passed. The German batteries in front of the 8th Australian Brigade continued to fire, but when the advancing infantry line was about a thousand yards away could be seen to limber up and only a few of the teams were hit. The battalions were on the objective by 10.15 a.m., having captured at least three hundred and fifty prisoners.

The 4th Australian Division attacked through the 3rd with the 12th and 4th Brigades (Br.-Generals R. L. Leane and E. A. Drake-Brockman), the 13th (Br.-General S. C. E. Herring) being in reserve. The 46th and 45th Battalions of the 12th Australian Brigade had somewhat stiff fighting, the fire from the main Morecourt valley and the woods near it gradually increasing, and the broken nature of the ground preventing the tanks from giving much help, one actually rolling over whilst descending a slope. Fire from Lewis guns and the XVI Brigade R.H.A., pushed forward on the right to fire down the valley, enabled both battalions to clear it. They took 29 guns, many prisoners and booty; for the forward slope of the lower part was honeycombed with funk-holes for troops, and littered with huts, canteens and stores. Pressing on, the 12th Australian Brigade reached the second objective at 10.20 a.m.

The 4th Australian Brigade had to make a shorter advance than the others, but it had to cross the steep gullies between the spurs near the Somme and capture both Cérisy and

Morecourt, nestling among trees down by the river, the 15th
Battalion being specially detailed to deal with the former
village. From the moment of crossing the first objective at
8.20 a.m. the left of the brigade was constantly subjected to
fire from machine guns and artillery on the northern bank
of the Somme ; for, as will be seen, the III Corps had been
unable to press forward at the same pace as the Australians.
This fire became intense as the mist lifted and the day
advanced. The Germans at first swung round two guns on
Chipilly spur, and soon afterwards two other sections near
the village, previously engaged against the III Corps, at
times firing as fast as the detachments could load to enfilade
the left of the Australian Corps, and gradually more and
more guns were thus employed. The 13th Battalion, on the
right, with one tank, escaped this fire at this stage, and,
after much the same experience as the battalions of the 12th
Brigade on its right, on reaching the main Morecourt valley,
reaped a rich harvest of prisoners, food and delicacies and,
from a pay office, 25,000 Marks in notes. With barely a
pause the other slope was climbed, and though the troops
were now badly caught by the batteries north of the Somme,
they reached the objective there by 10 a.m.

The 14th and 15th Battalions, the latter with the special
task of capturing Cérisy, strongly opposed in front and
enfiladed from the north, made a desperate struggle to get
forward, supported by two guns each of the X Brigade
A.F.A., with the rest close behind. Of the six tanks
accompanying the 14th, all except one became casualties by
direct hits ; but they had helped to outflank the Germans
from the south, and with the remaining tank one company
of the 14th entered Morecourt from the west, where three
hundred prisoners were taken. Later two other companies
joined it, and by 10.20 a.m. here also the second objective
was gained.

The 15th Battalion had the assistance of six tanks, which
soon covered the short distance to the village, the detachments of two German field guns which had been firing down
the Hamel–Cérisy road making off.   In spite of machine-gun
fire from Chipilly, three companies of the battalion entered
and cleared the village, capturing several hundred Germans.
They then turned machine-gun fire on to the Chipilly guns,
with which the divisional artillery was now also dealing,
although it had been originally arranged that the Australian

and III Corps should fire only on their own side of the river, and earlier in the day proposals that the Australians should assist the III Corps by fire had been vetoed for this reason. Towards 1 p.m. heavy batteries also shelled Chipilly with good effect. In trying to reach the spur to the south-east of Cérisy all the tanks were knocked out, and the infantry found itself exposed to fire both from front and left flank, but nevertheless held on. The occupation of Morecourt by the 14th Battalion now, no doubt, had its effect ; for the Germans opposing the 15th Battalion drew off, and about 2 p.m. the canal bank south-east of Cérisy was occupied and junction made with the rest of the brigade.

The second Australian objective now being secured, it is a convenient opportunity to follow the operations of the 17th Armoured Car Battalion and of the 1st Cavalry Brigade, whose passages through the advancing line of the 5th Australian Division have been already noticed. They were able to break into the rear area of the enemy position beyond the main line of guns, in which transport and stragglers were on the move, and enjoyed a glorious hour, but only the main items of their adventures can be given here. The twelve cars,[1] after being delayed by running into British shelling directed on the retiring enemy near the Roman Road, reached the main Morecourt valley ahead of the infantry, and obtained splendid targets on the German troops massing in it, causing confused movements amongst them which called to mind the disturbance of an ant heap. Pushing eastwards,[2] the cars fired on the large dumps along the Roman Road near la Flaque, and captured and disabled a train. Two miles farther on some of them fired up and down the valley running from Herleville past Chuignes, which crosses the Roman Road there, scattering troops and transport. The road becoming blocked by press of vehicles trying to escape, the cars divided, half going southwards to Framerville and half northwards towards Proyart. At the former place some of a corps staff were surprised at a meal, and four officers captured (they were subsequently killed by a burst of machine-gun fire), and the village cleared.[3] The northern

---

[1] On a tourist chassis each had two turrets, each containing a machine gun ; the main body and engine were protected by thin steel plates.

[2] See Sketch 2.

[3] It was the advanced position of the *LI. Corps* staff. Plans of the Hindenburg Position were amongst the papers seized.

party of cars went to Chuignolles, hastening the flight of
many German detachments, and, throwing into confusion
long columns of German transport moving without any
precautions, returned to the Roman Road. The southern
party also returned to the Roman Road, and then both
parties patrolled the area east of the 5th Australian
Division's objective for some hours. By the end of the day
nine of the twelve cars were out of action, but they
required only slight repairs, not having encountered artillery
until the very last part of the advance, when a field gun
damaged one wheel each of two cars.

In the operations of the 1st Cavalry Brigade, the Queen's
Bays acted as advanced guard, and by 8.30 a.m. the two
leading squadrons, in close touch with the infantry, were
north and south of Bayonvillers.[1] Soon after 9 a.m. the
right squadron, passing through the infantry, came under
fire from Germans south of Harbonnières, who were escorting
some transport in the valley ; but two troops sent to charge
them captured or killed 46. No further advance, however,
could be made ; nor could the whippets which now came up
reach Harbonnières, which it had been their special task to
capture, or cross the road leading south from the village.
Three of the machines were lost, and, although further efforts
were made by both cavalry and whippets, they were still on
the same line when the Australian infantry began to arrive.

Meantime, at 10 a.m., the 5th Dragoon Guards, which,
with the 11th Hussars, formed the main body of the 1st
Cavalry Brigade, had been ordered, if resistance were not
too strong, to advance north of Harbonnières between the
village and Buchanan Wood, and reach the final objective,
the Outer Amiens Defence Line ; but it was not to go farther
than the Vauvillers–Framerville road, about a mile beyond
that line. The leading squadron, though fired at from
Harbonnières, raced for the Outer Defence Line, which it
found unoccupied. Seeing a train with a large railway gun,
set on fire by a bomb from a British aeroplane, as it was
trying to steam away from Proyart, it assisted the left
squadron in killing or capturing its occupants ; it then went
on, capturing three field batteries, to the Vauvillers road,
and, on being fired at from the village cemetery, dismounted
and came into action against the retreating Germans. The
left squadron, after the train episode, reached its final

[1] See Sketch 5.

objective between the Moulin de Vauvillers (where it captured a hospital) and Framerville ; but, turning south, met with resistance from a defended copse south of Vauvillers, and reduced by this time, by escorts for prisoners and casualties, to twenty men, fell back on the leading squadron, after putting some of the captured guns out of action on the way, and bringing back the artillerymen as prisoners. The third squadron, after crossing the Outer Defence Line behind the others, suffered considerable losses and fell back on it. The whole incident had lasted little more than an hour, and the regiment, on the arrival of the Australian infantry, withdrew into reserve north-east of Harbonnières. Shortly after noon, Major-General Mullens decided to move the 1st Cavalry Brigade south to assist the 9th Cavalry Brigade (with the Canadian Corps), which had not got so far forward. Attempts of the 5th Dragoon Guards and 11th Hussars to advance were checked for a time south of Harbonnières by fire ; but the former succeeded in joining the Queen's Bays near the Amiens–Chaulnes railway. Thus the 1st Cavalry Brigade was in position on the Outer Defence Line when, shortly after, the 9th Cavalry Brigade arrived on it south of the railway.

᛫ It had been intended that the Mark V* tanks (15th Tank Battalion), which had followed half a mile behind the leading brigades of the 5th Australian Division, should pass through them on the second objective, and deposit the machine guns and crews which they were carrying on the final objective as support to the cavalry. The advance of the 15th and 8th Australian Brigades had been so rapid that the tanks were not up when the infantry had arrived on the second objective, and the 57th and 59th Battalions of the 15th, not wishing that an opportunity should be missed, pushed on at once without waiting for them. Fire was coming from the valley south of Harbonnières, but this was brought to an end by the charge of two troops of the Queen's Bays, mentioned above, and towards 11 a.m. the two battalions had occupied a line from the railway to Harbonnières, and, with the help of a tank, had mopped up the village, where a number of baggage wagons, packed ready to move off, were seized. On its church tower the 59th Battalion hoisted the Australian flag. The 15th Australian Brigade then proceeded to occupy the Outer Defence Line, except on the right, where the Canadians were not yet up, and a flank was formed. No advance could be made by patrols towards Vauvillers (east of Harbonnières), as a nest of machine guns blocked the way, and a platoon which attempted to deal with it was nearly annihilated.

The 8th Australian Brigade, after a short wait, seeing fugitives streaming away down the Roman Road, pushed forward strong patrols from the second to the final objective, and, finding it empty except for a few stragglers, had occupied it by 11.30 a.m. The 5th Australian Division, except as above mentioned, had reached its objectives for the day. A heavy railway gun was then noticed in No Man's Land. Engineers of the 8th Australian Field Coy. went out, shunted the gun and its train, and drove them well inside the British lines.

Half an hour after the final objective was attained cavalry patrols, also a flare dropped by an aeroplane, gave warning that the enemy appeared to be gathering for counter-attack against the right. The Mark V* tanks with the machine-gun detachments, which had now arrived, and dismounted men of the Queen's Bays were sent to strengthen this part of the line ; but no actual enemy counter-attack took place, and about 1.15 p.m. the officer commanding the 57th Battalion sent messages to the units on its flanks asking them to co-operate in an advance to the Outer Defence Line. The 6th Canadian Brigade on the right could not help, as it was at this time still on the first objective east of Marcelcave,[1] although its advanced troops were near Guillaucourt, and, not ordered to advance until 2.30 p.m., it did not leave the second objective until 4.30 p.m. On the left, the 59th Battalion reported that, owing to the machine-gun nest east of Harbonnières, it could not make any move without the help of four tanks, and all its machines were out of action. So the idea of a small advance to complete the day's work of the 5th Australian Division was abandoned.

In the 4th Australian Division the advance from the second to the final objective, the Outer Defence Line, on the big spur which runs towards Méricourt, was to be carried out by two picked battalions, the 48th of the 12th Australian Brigade and the 16th of the 4th. Each was to be preceded by nine of the Mark V* tanks carrying machine guns and crews. Even before the 48th reached the

[1] See p. 24 f.n.

starting line beyond the main Morecourt valley it came under fire of two field guns, and had to extend, whilst the three tanks present were hit, and by 10.55 a.m., when the advance began, only three others had arrived. On the right, near the Roman road, the Outer Defence Line lay less than half a mile away, but on the left it was a full mile distant and the upper portion of the easternmost of the Morecourt valleys, carrying a partly-cut wheat crop, had to be crossed. The right company, therefore, reached its objective easily without opposition, but the centre and left, galled by fire from north of the Somme, where at least eight German batteries were now firing on the Australian flank, experienced stiff fighting and lost another tank. Owing to the haze it was judged dangerous to give artillery support ; so progress was difficult until a party of Germans in the forward trench put up their hands, when the rest were dealt with by envelopment, and by 12.10 p.m. the whole objective of the 12th Australian Brigade was in its possession.

Before the advance of the 16th Battalion, representing the 4th Australian Brigade, began with the object of forming a flank down to Méricourt (exclusive), information was received that Chipilly and all the objectives of the III Corps north of the Somme had been captured. This was by no means the case, and the Australians as they went forward now received fire, not only in flank but also from the rear. Four of the eight remaining passenger-carrying tanks had broken down before reaching the starting line, and the others, unable to climb the steep chalk slope ahead, were sent round by the road through Morecourt ; but then, after picking up seventy prisoners, they were able to mount the easier gradient to assist the left wing. Although Australian artillery had done much to smother German fire from the Chipilly area, the tanks were, however, soon all knocked out. The 16th Battalion, advancing in small groups under its own covering fire, notwithstanding the shells of the German artillery against its left rear, reached the Outer Defence Line about 12.30 p.m., capturing over two hundred Germans, and later adding to the score. Patrols found Méricourt full of the enemy, and, as Chipilly spur was still in his possession, the left flank was brought back about six hundred yards to connect with the 15th Battalion, which was holding the river bank near Morecourt.

In half a day's fighting, before 1.30 p.m., the Australian Corps had reached all the objectives assigned to it, except on the extreme flanks, where neither the Canadian Corps nor the III Corps was up. Its task was now to secure the second and third objectives against counter-attack, and this it set about doing. Armoured cars and cavalry had careered over the country in front of the final objective ; by 11 a.m. Lieut.-General Monash knew from contact aeroplanes that everywhere his troops were approaching the second objective. Both shortly before and shortly after mid-day messages were sent back by pigeon and telegraph that all was fairly clear, and it was possible to go farther. The casualties had been small, only about another thousand in reaching the second and third objectives ;[1] the captures amounted to 183 officers, 7,742 other ranks and 173 guns, besides hundreds of smaller trophies. Sufficient troops to continue the thrust were available. No further orders were, however, given either by General Rawlinson or Lieut.-General Monash. Nothing even was said to suggest that the Australian Corps should do what it could to assist the III Corps, which had not made the same progress as the others ; it was left to the Australian divisions by their own means and by receiving German fire to discover the situation on their northern flank. Misleading information sent from the III Corps had prevented Australian artillery aid being given early in the day, and it was not until about 11 a.m. that the 58th Division of the III Corps, through its Australian liaison officer, asked that Chipilly might be shelled. It was one of those cases in which it proved a mistake to have made a river line the boundary between two corps, and, as will be seen, the 3rd Australian Division was later sent to the north bank of the Somme, so that the whole valley came into the sector of the Australian Corps.

---

[1] See Note I at end of Chapter VIII.

CHAPTER V

THE BATTLE OF AMIENS (*continued*)

FIRST DAY 8TH AUGUST 1918 (*concluded*)

THE III CORPS AND THE RESULTS OF THE DAY

(Map 1 ; End-paper B, Sketches 2, 5)

The III Corps,[1] north of the Somme,[2] had the task of protecting the left flank of the Australians, keeping pace with their advance, and securing the high ground overlooking the passages of the Somme. General Rawlinson had originally settled that the corps should secure the line of the old Amiens Outer Defences between the Somme and the Ancre which, as it formed a refused flank running north-westwards towards Dernancourt on commanding heights, exactly answered requirements. But owing to the difficulties of the ground Lieut.-General Butler did not consider that the advance to this line could be completed on the first day. On the 8th therefore the III Corps, on the right, was to go no farther than the line of the Somme in the reach above Méricourt, which coincided with the line of the second objective of the Australian Corps, and, on the left, was to form a flank facing north, but south of Morlancourt. This village was to be " pinched out " next day by attacks from south and north. Although the III Corps had two successive objectives instead of three, and its role was more modest than that of the Canadians and Australians, it was unable to obtain the same large measure of progress.

The ground was certainly difficult. The long narrow plateau between Somme and Ancre with its sides, sloping sharply to the Somme and gently to the Ancre, indented by a series of short ravines, has already been mentioned. These ravines besides being a formidable obstacle to tanks and mounted troops provided the enemy with admirable

---

[1] Corps Commander .. .. .. Lieut.-Gen. Sir R. H. K. Butler
　　Br.-Gen. General Staff .. .. Br.-Gen. C. G. Fuller
　　Commander Royal Artillery .. Br.-Gen. C. M. Ross-Johnson
　　Commander Heavy Artillery .. Br.-Gen. A. E. J. Perkins
　　Chief Engineer .. .. .. Br.-Gen. A. Rolland
　　12th Division .. .. .. Major-Gen. H. W. Higginson
　　18th Division .. .. .. Major-Gen. R. P. Lee
　　47th Division .. .. .. Major-Gen. Sir G. F. Gorringe
　　58th Division .. .. .. Major-Gen. F. W. Ramsay
　　63rd Division (G.H.Q. Reserve) Major-Gen. C. E. Lawrie
　　American 33rd (Illinois) Division Major-Gen. G. Bell, Junr.

[2] See Sketch 5.

gun positions and assembly places for reserves, the more so as the high ground between them in the reaches between Corbie and Bray fell very steeply to the Somme, in places forming cliffs. Looking eastwards from the British front the ground rose gradually in a glacis-like slope for about five thousand yards and afforded innumerable and excellent machine-gun positions at all ranges, unhampered by woods then in thick foliage, which mostly lay in the ravines ; Malard Wood and Les Celestins behind it, and Gressaire Wood and its continuation the Bois de Taille, for instance, stand in the ravines running down to the Somme. Chipilly village lies at the mouth of another ravine at the foot of a long narrow spur, a dominating feature which projects into the Somme valley and, except northwards, offered splendid all-round observation, extending westwards as far as Corbie, 10,000 yards away, and giving views a long way behind the Fourth Army front line. Morlancourt, too, was in a ravine running down to the Ancre.

Ground, however, was not now the only trouble. All the divisions of the III Corps, from right to left the 58th, 18th, 12th and, beyond the Ancre, the 47th, had been in the line or in close reserve throughout the year ; all had suffered heavily in the March retreat, the 58th also having taken part in the Villers Bretonneux battle of the 24th-25th April, losing 3,530 of all ranks. Thus there was not only a shortage of experienced officers and n.c.os., but the ranks of the infantry units had been filled up with young recruits from home.

These convalescent divisions had not entered with great enthusiasm on the hard task of preparing a field of battle, in the hours of darkness and in bad weather. The reasons given them for the moves and reliefs had an unexpected effect. Believing that the French were not doing well on the Marne and that, bad omen, they were to take over more front, as the III Corps (with the 18th and 58th Divisions in it) had done before March 1918, the willing co-operation usually exhibited before an attack was absent. Then at 4.25 a.m. on the 6th August, before the reliefs consequent upon the extension of the Fourth Army front and the re-organization of the corps front had been completed, the *27th (Württemberg) Division,* as already mentioned, had attacked the southern half of the 18th Division and about four hundred yards of the left wing of the 58th. The troops fought splendidly and some of the ground was recovered on the 7th ; but as the principal parts in the offensive of the 8th had been assigned to the 58th and 18th Divisions, jumping off trenches had to be changed and barrages recalculated. Further, the 54th Brigade (18th Division) had suffered so many casualties that it was decided to substitute for it the 36th Brigade (12th Division) then in reserve, the 47th Division spreading out to relieve the 37th Brigade, which was north of the Ancre, so that it could relieve the 36th and become the divisional reserve. In compensation, the American 33rd Division (less 131st Regiment which was attached to the 58th Division) was placed at the disposal of the 47th Division.[1]

These final changes took place on the night of the 7th–8th which was very disturbed not only on account of movement but also of enemy shelling. The roads and river crossings in the Ancre valley and the Méricourt area received rafales of gas shell, so that the troops had to put on their gas masks, a terrible handicap in darkness and mist. The 36th Brigade marching up to replace the 54th had many casualties from gas, as did many of the field batteries, and as the gas hung about the crops and long grass, casualties continued from this cause throughout the day. The rear areas, too, were visited at regular intervals by bursts of high explosive, the last one only a few minutes before Zero, so that when the British barrage fell at 4.20 a.m. the Württembergers at first took it to be retaliation. Surprise was out of the question ; the enemy, actually of the same strength in divisions as the attackers, was ready and expecting a further attempt to recover all the ground lost on the 6th, and well disposed in depth with ample artillery support.[2]

---

[1] Companies of the 131st and 132nd Regiments had taken part with the Australians in the successful attack on Hamel on 4th July (see " 1918 " Vol. III, p. 202). The two infantry brigades, 65th and 66th, had then been in the line with the III and Australian Corps, but from 6th August both were attached to the III Corps.

[2] The front opposite the III Corps was held, south to north, by one regiment of the *43rd Reserve Division* ; one regiment of the *108th Division*, under the *43rd Reserve Division* (the *108th* was in the act of relieving the *43rd Reserve Division*, whose third regiment was south of the Somme) ; the *27th Division* (plus an infantry regiment and an artillery regiment of the *26th Reserve Division*, resting near Bapaume, and the artillery of the resting *107th* and *243rd Divisions*) ; the *54th Reserve Division* ; and the *233rd Division* ; that is 4 German divisions against 4 British. In reserve in the sector was the *243rd Division*. Four and a half of the battalions of the *43rd Reserve Division* had already been pulled out and 3 of these went back to help the *13th Division* south of the Somme.

The main attack was to be made by the 58th and 18th Divisions, in two phases. On reaching the first objective, about three thousand yards away, and after forming a defensive flank on the left a pause of about one hour was to be made until 6.30 a.m., when another line of brigades would pass through the first and proceed to the second objective. At the same time the 12th Division on the left would advance until abreast of Morlancourt and gain a footing on the steep convex slope of the ravine north and north-east of the village, so as, in conjunction with the main attack, to ensure its evacuation. In the first phase, in order to give the 58th Division a straight run at Malard Wood, its objective, Sailly Lorette in the Somme valley was to be captured by a battalion of the reserve brigade, and the 2/10th London (175th Brigade) was detailed for the purpose. No special arrangements were made as regards the village of Chipilly, which it was expected would be evacuated when the British appeared on the heights above it.

The artillery support of the main attack was provided by 350 field guns and howitzers[1]—one gun to 12 yards—firing a creeping barrage (first hundred yards in 2 minutes, but then slowing to 4 minutes, which proved too quick in Gressaire Wood), whilst the ravines were searched by a howitzer barrage which jumped from one line to another. To mark the position of the latter barrage a little smoke was fired in it. The counter-battery work was most effective and the enemy, as will be seen, was unable to get many of his guns away, whilst his accounts speak of all roads being shelled and all communication cables cut.

No cavalry and only one tank battalion, the 10th, with thirty-six Mark V machines and twelve supply tanks, was allotted to the III Corps, and from it C Company was sent to the 58th Division and A and B Companies to the 18th.

Although at 4 a.m. the enemy was shelling the back areas and his machine guns were going hard, punctually at 4.20 a.m. the troops moved forward close behind the barrage, in small groups at wide intervals followed by larger parties. Many of them arrived only just in time, as in the mist,

---

[1] The artillery of the 12th Division had been lent to the French for an attack on Morisel on 29th July and had not yet rejoined ; it was replaced by that of the 25th Division (reduced to cadre).

wearing gas masks, they had quite lost their bearings. Enemy shelling now almost ceased, hardly a shell was fired ; such resistance as was offered came mainly from machine guns ; the front position therefore was quickly taken and the stream of prisoners sent back made the III Corps realize that the war had taken a decided turn in its favour.

The 58th (2/1st London) Division (Major-General F. W. Ramsay) had sent forward the 174th Brigade (Br.-General A. Maxwell) which had the 6th and 7th London in front line and the 8th in reserve. After the capture of the front line, the opposition came mainly from the right, and the 6th London, with the help of one tank, had to fight the whole way to Malard Wood. But about 8 a.m. a line was established on the first objective, east of the wood. Parties of Germans, however, still remained in it and were not finally mopped up until afternoon had come. On account of the dense mist the tanks attached to the division were unable to follow the routes selected for them, or go forward with the infantry close behind the barrage. Ten had been ordered to assist the 174th Brigade, and two the 2/10th London (175th Brigade) ; these two and eight of the others appeared later and gave valuable assistance in mopping up.

Meantime, without the aid of the two tanks, which arrived ten minutes late, the 2/10th London had surprised the garrison of Sailly Lorette and by 6.30 a.m. had cleaned it up except for two machine-gun teams which held out in the church, until disposed of half-an-hour later with the help of a tank. The battalion then captured the quarry— from the machine guns in which the Australians had been suffering heavy casualties—and the sunken road beyond, against stiffening opposition, mainly from machine guns, only one field battery firing on it from Chipilly ridge. By 9.30 a.m. the 2/10th London had pushed forward a thousand yards farther, had captured 285 prisoners, 98 machine guns and 23 trench mortars, established liaison with the Australians, and gained a commanding position well up the spur north-east of Sailly Lorette with machine guns trained on Chipilly, 2,500 yards away.[1]

---

[1] According to Monograph, pp. 59, 62, the front line and support battalions in the *43rd Reserve Division* sector north of the Somme were "nearly entirely liquidated" and the commander decided to assemble all remaining men on the Chipilly spur. Four and a half batteries were left behind in the wood east of Malard Wood and three others had only one gun left between them, which, to save it, was buried.

The attack of the 18th (Eastern Division) (Major-General R. P. Lee) to the first objective was carried out by the 36th and 55th Brigades (Br.-Generals C. S. Owen and E. A. Wood). The former, having been lent from the 12th Division at short notice to replace the 54th, knew nothing of the ground except what could be learnt from the map ; it had been gassed and shelled in Heilly and on the Corbie–Bray road on the way up, but managed to arrive in time. Only the 7/R. Sussex and the 9/Royal Fusiliers attacked, as the 5/R. Berkshire was still retained in divisional reserve. The two battalions at once regained the rest of the ground lost on the 6th, but then became heavily engaged in what had been the old British front line. Meantime the 7/Queen's of the 55th Brigade, detailed to form the first part of the defensive flank (the 8/East Surrey and 7/Buffs being left holding the front line until required), encountered stout resistance from two battalions on the plateau,[1] which instead of waiting to be attacked in the mist came forward throwing stick grenades. The 7/Queen's soon lost the barrage. No tanks had arrived, and in the mist the fighting became a soldiers' battle, in which small parties of infantry co-operated as best they could. The situation, in consequence of the enemy's superior numbers, began to look serious. Lieut.-Colonel C. Bushell, V.C., D.S.O., the commanding officer, on realizing this, collected all available details, led them forward and drove the enemy out of the old front line.[2] Whilst making arrangements for the next advance Lieut.-Colonel Bushell was killed ; this was not known for some time, and as a consequence the leading battalions of the 36th and 55th Brigades remained where they were in the old front line.

The 36th Brigade was soon reinforced by the 10/Essex of the 53rd Brigade, which had been detailed to leap-frog it at the first objective, and the Essex, carrying with them the two battalions of the 36th, overcame all resistance and reached the first objective just as the barrage was lifting to go on to the second. No touch could be obtained on either

---

[1] Of the *120th* and *123rd Regiments* of the *27th Division*.

[2] Between 7 and 7.30 a.m. two thirds of the *III/123rd Regiment* and the *II* with *9/120th Regiment* had been swept away, and " infantry, " machine guns and trench mortars were fleeing to the rear in flocks ". Of the artillery of the *27th Division*, 3 batteries were silenced, 2 having all their guns unserviceable and one been reduced to a single gun. " With the other batteries it was much the same ". Monograph, pp. 63–7.

flank, but there was no time for delay; so the Essex after a short pause continued on. One party, only about eighty strong owing to the scattering of the men in the fog, reached the second objective immediately east of the Brickyard and by surprise captured two field batteries discovered on the north-west edge of Gressaire Wood, whose detachments, having settled down to breakfast, surrendered without a fight. By 8 a.m. the Essex party was well dug in but isolated. It was, however, shortly afterwards joined by three platoons of another battalion of the 53rd Brigade, the 7/R. West Kent, preceded by a tank, which like the Essex had passed through the front line under instructions of Lieut.-Colonel A. L. Richard (7/Buffs of the 55th Brigade), who had been put in charge of all the forward troops of the 55th when the death of Lieut.-Colonel Bushell became known. These platoons extended the flank to the left. The rest of their battalion, after driving off a considerable number of Germans who were to the north, by brigade orders held the first objective astride the Corbie–Bray road and eventually got in touch with the 10/Essex and the 7/Queen's.

The 8/R. Berkshire, the third battalion of the 53rd Brigade, which had followed the 10/Essex, met with some opposition on the flanks, but reached the first objective about 7.40 a.m. Getting in touch with the Essex and the 36th Brigade, it resumed its advance ; but the mist was clearing and about half a mile from the western edge of Gressaire Wood, the battalion was checked by fire from machine and field guns at point-blank range, so that after vain efforts to get forward a retirement was made to the first objective.

Thus the first objective had been secured piecemeal and after considerable delay, except on the right in the 58th Division sector. The 53rd Brigade (Br.-General M. G. H. Barker), which had duly passed through the 36th, had with two battalions formed the flank from the second objective to the first west of Gressaire Wood ; but, the mist lifting, it was seen that the third battalion on the right had failed to reach that wood and was back at the first objective.

The 18th Division had not received much assistance from its tanks ; the mist which favoured their approach hampered their activity during the morning, and little action took place in the afternoon. Of one company four tanks broke down before arrival at the starting point. Of the second company, four were held in reserve, one lost direction and joined the

12th Division, and two broke down. The others are said to have engaged any machine-gun posts which could be located. The reserve section went as far as the second objective. Seventeen of the 36 tanks rallied in the evening.

The 58th Division had also failed to reach the second objective. The 173rd Brigade (Br.-General C. E. Corkran), detailed for this operation, had followed the 174th closely, the 3rd and 2/4th London leading, and had passed through Malard Wood with it. As soon as the two battalions left the cover of the wood they came under very heavy fire, lost the barrage and were unable to advance. Possibly a few men got through ; for at 8.45 a.m. a report from a forward observing officer reached 58th Division headquarters that troops had reached the final objective, the eastern side of Chipilly ridge. This was confirmed from the air. Actually, the front line was back again on the first objective. Since the enemy in Chipilly was causing delay and heavy losses to the Australian troops south of the Somme, the 2/2nd London, the reserve of the 173rd Brigade was brought up, the brigade reorganized and arrangements were made at 1 p.m. for the renewal of the attack, under a fresh bombardment. Divisional headquarters now again received a report from the air that some British troops were already on the Chipilly spur, so the bombardment was cancelled and at 3 p.m. the 2/2nd London advanced, only to be received by a storm of bullets in front and cross fire from Chipilly village and Gressaire Wood. Receiving no support, the battalion fell back to the shelter of Malard Wood, where the 9/London (175th Brigade) had just arrived from the divisional reserve.

A further attempt to reach the eastern side of the Chipilly spur, under a rolling barrage and after a short bombardment, was arranged by the 175th Brigade (Br.-General W. Maxwell-Scott) for 7.30 p.m. ; but the battalions were farther back than supposed and nothing was effected. The 2/10th London, which was to co-operate, did advance from in front of Sailly Lorette under a field gun barrage which unfortunately fell fifteen hundred yards ahead. The leading parties were received by furious machine-gun fire from the western slopes of Chipilly spur, and, when they reached the road elbow north-west of the village, by similar fire from the front ; but they held their position until midnight when they were withdrawn.

The III Corps had felt more anxiety for the left, where the 10/Essex and 7/R. West Kent of the 53rd Brigade, which by this time had two tanks with them, had formed a flank between the first and second objectives, now not required as the second objective had not been reached, and very exposed. At 10.30 a.m. the 5/R. Berkshire (36th Brigade), in 18th Division reserve, was ordered to their assistance, and at 11.30 a.m. the 175th Brigade (less 2/10th London) was placed by the III Corps at the disposal of Major-General Lee. These measures were too late. The enemy had been dribbling troops and machine guns close up to the front of the Essex and R. West Kent and on either flank ; and two of his batteries had come into action at 500 yards' range on the western edge of Gressaire Wood. The two tanks were running out of petrol ; no reinforcements could be seen, and the Germans were working nearer and nearer. At 10.30 a.m. a retirement was therefore ordered. Begun at first with great steadiness, owing to the violence of the fire on the open plateau it soon lost all semblance of order and the men were told to scatter and get back as best they could.

Thus the main attack of the III Corps ended on the first objective. With well trained troops and more experienced company leaders it should have gained complete success.[1] The subsidiary attack north of it, carried out by the 35th Brigade of the 12th Division, although Br.-General B. Vincent was nearly blinded by gas and had to be invalided next day, achieved all that was required, an advance of nearly a thousand yards being made. The attack was launched at 6.20 a.m., two hours after Zero, with half the 1/1st Cambridgeshire, the 7/Norfolk and the 9/Essex in line and the rest of the Cambridgeshire in reserve. To deal with a possible counter-attack the 6/Queen's of the reserve brigade, the 37th, was attached.

Under a barrage fired by 48 field guns the centre and left battalions, in spite of the difficulties of mist and the wearing of gas masks, reached their objective, capturing 3 officers and 316 men.[2] But on the right, where the enemy was perhaps expecting an attack to retake the trenches lost by

---

[1] Monograph, p. 67 and elsewhere, comments on the lack of good British leaders in this sector.

[2] These would appear to belong to *III/123rd Regiment* and *I/124th Regiment* of the *27th Division* who were turned on both flanks and caught in rear by " four tanks " in front of Morlancourt. Monograph, p. 66.

the 18th Division on the 6th August, the two companies of the Cambridgeshire suffered heavy casualties, the enemy here also advancing to meet the attackers, throwing stick grenades.   So the companies were forced to lie down in the open short of the German position.   The other two companies having been brought up, a fresh advance was made at 12.25 p.m. after a ten minutes' bombardment by four batteries of the 169th (Army) Brigade R.F.A., and it was entirely successful.   Soon after this the tank " Ju Ju ", which had wandered from the 18th Division sector, appeared and was directed by the brigade to assist the infantry to mop up a pocket of the enemy south-east of Morlancourt. This operation was carried out and another batch of over three hundred prisoners taken.[1]

Towards evening a large body of Germans was seen approaching along the road east of Morlancourt, but it was scattered by the fire of the 18th Division artillery and of the machine-gun battalion.

The action of the air forces on the Army front during the afternoon remains to be mentioned.   From the first moment that airmen had been able to operate they had reported columns of enemy transport in retreat, and towards noon they added that the roads leading to the Somme crossings in rear of the *Second Army* were becoming crowded with retreating German troops and transport.   The interruption of traffic and closing of the ways by which fugitives could escape and reinforcements might come seemed to offer a reward well worth striving for ; it might lead to a capitulation.   No instructions on the subject from the Fourth Army or G.H.Q. can be found ; but towards noon Major-General Salmond cancelled, by telephone, all existing arrangements for bombing during the afternoon, and ordered instead attacks on the Somme bridges.[2]   These were to be bombed " as long as

---

[1] These would appear to have belonged to the *2nd* and *4th Companies* of the *124th Regiment* who were " taken in rear " Monograph, p. 66. The German compiler thinks that machine-gun nests alone prevented the British from entering Morlancourt.

[2] According to the recollection, in 1939, of Field-Marshal Sir Archibald Montgomery-Massingberd, who was Major-General, General Staff of the Fourth Army, the matter was settled between General Rawlinson and Major-General Salmond by telephone, they having several conversations during the day.   The only telegram on the subject is timed 4.15 p.m. (following one at 6.10 a.m.) from V Brigade to Fourth Army : " Bombing " targets Brie and St. Christ bridges, six machines for train bombing ".

" weather and light permit " and the fighter squadrons were to participate by dropping 25-lb. bombs.[1] The numerical superiority in favour of the British had, however, disappeared, and the orders led to a battle in the air in which the enemy forces increased from hour to hour.[2] Proximity to their aerodromes, too, gave the defenders an advantage of which they took the fullest advantage : " they went uninterruptedly " into the fight, landing only to load up with petrol and " ammunition, with occasional short rests. . . . That " the clouds were no more than from 1,200 to 2,400 feet up " limited the battle space in favour of the Germans ".[3] In the result, though 205 flights were made from the British aerodromes, no vital damage was done to the bridges,[4] forty-four aeroplanes were lost and fifty-two more wrecked or damaged and had to be struck off the strength. Some of them had been lost in the earlier attacks on aerodromes and on ground troops. The 8th August was an unlucky day for the R.A.F.[5]

The French " Division aerienne " did not take part in the battle on the 8th August, but received instructions at 4 p.m. to assist its First Army next day.[6]

The losses of the Fourth Army on the 8th August are not recorded separately ; they were, as the corps reports said, very small, as near as can be computed under nine thousand.[7]

[1] " War in the Air vi, p. 441.

[2] Soon after the 4.20 a.m. bombardment began the commander of the *Second Army* aeroplane squadrons warned the air forces on the whole front from Champagne to the sea that he might require help ; and then summoned it. The *Eighteenth* and *Seventeenth Armies* sent squadrons during the morning and about 1 p.m. the Richthofen squadron (under Captain Göring) arrived from the *Seventh Army*. *Militär Wochenblatt*, No. 6/1938.

[3] *Militär Wochenblatt*, No. 6/1938.

[4] The Fourth Army Intelligence at 8 p.m. telegraphed an air report : " North end of Péronne railway bridge demolished by our bombing. " Brie bridge damaged and traffic block caused. Direct hit south-west " end of Voyennes bridge, east [end ?] of Offoy railway bridge and line " at Voyennes and Bettencourt bridges destroyed ". Though the effect of air bombing on troop movements is frequently mentioned in the Monograph, no damage to bridges is recorded. Traffic was not interrupted.

[5] Thirty British machines were reported down in the *Second Army* area. The German losses have not been published. " The commander of the " *Second Army* air force had to deplore the crews of about twelve " machines ", says the Monograph. A life of " Hermann Göring ", p. 32, mentions that the Richthofen squadron lost within a short time 39 out of 50 machines and then 4 more.

[6] F.O.A. vii (i), pp. 180, 184 and Annexe 560.

[7] Cavalry Corps, 600 ; Canadian Corps, 3,500 ; Australian Corps, 3,000 ; III Corps, 1,700 : total, 8,800. See Note I at end of Chapter VIII.

The number of German prisoners who passed through the corps cages on the 8th was 281 officers and 12,134 other ranks (of twenty regiments of eight divisions) ; the French captured 150 officers and 3,200 other ranks (of four regiments of three different divisions) and nearly three hundred guns had been taken.[1]

The constant reports sent to General Rawlinson by the corps during the day and passed on to G.H.Q. had correctly reflected the situation, except that earlier messages from the III Corps had given hope of its final object being secured.

At 11.30 a.m. Sir Douglas Haig sent an officer to General Debeney to tell him of the situation and request him to send forward all his mounted troops to operate on the right of the British cavalry and extend the break in the enemy's front southwards by operating in rear of the Germans holding Montdidier. But General Debeney replied that his cavalry was not near at hand and the roads being blocked by infantry, it could not be got through earlier than the forenoon of the 9th. The Commander-in-Chief then motored to General Rawlinson's headquarters at Flixecourt. There he heard of the difficulties of the situation of the III Corps, but was told that Lieut.-General Butler had an adequate number of troops to deal with them. He directed General Rawlinson to continue operations on the orders already given him, which meant that after organizing his left strongly, and, if opportunity offered, advancing the line between Somme and Ancre to Bray–Albert, he was to push his offensive front to the line Roye–Chaulnes. His main effort was to be directed south-eastwards against Roye in order to help the French ; whilst the cavalry, working on the outer flank, should move on Roye–Chaulnes as soon as possible. Later in the day a formal G.H.Q. order was issued in this sense.[2] In the afternoon Sir Douglas Haig

---

[1] Lossberg, p. 354, states that General von der Marwitz told him on 11th August that the losses of the *Second Army* on the 8th had been very great, " about 700 officers and 27,000 men, over 400 guns and a great mass of machine guns and trench mortars ".

Two general results must not be overlooked : they were a general gain in morale and a recovery of the confidence of the troops in the Staff which had been shaken by the events of the closing months of 1917 and March 1918.

[2] Appendix X.

visited General Debeney at Conty (15 miles S.S.W. of
Amiens) and found him much distressed at the failure of
some of his troops. The Commander-in-Chief told him that
the British advance would clear his front, but that meantime
he must do his utmost to join hands with the British at
Roye, his cavalry being sent forward as soon as possible.
Towards 6 p.m. Maréchal Foch paid a visit to Sir Douglas
Haig and heard the good news of over 15,000 prisoners having
already been taken and of the better part of nine enemy
divisions having been identified and for the most part
" wiped out ". The Generalissimo was delighted and fully
concurred in all the arrangements made for the continuation
of the battle.

In the afternoon the Fourth Army Commander, accompanied only by an A.D.C., after ordering his three reserve
divisions to be moved forward : the 32nd, to around Domart,
behind the Canadian Corps, the 17th, to around Daours
(7 miles East of Amiens), behind the Australian Corps,
and the 63rd to Contay–Rubempré (10 miles N.N.E. of
Amiens), towards the III Corps, had motored to Canadian
Corps Advanced Headquarters at Gentelles (6 miles west of
Caix). Arriving there about 4 p.m., he found that Lieut.-
General Currie was out visiting divisional headquarters, so
he discussed with Br.-General Webber, the Br.-General,
General Staff, the plans for next day : the 4th Canadian
Division was to complete the capture of the right of the
objective, including le Quesnel, when the 32nd Division,
which he would release from Army reserve, would pass
through the 4th on a two-brigade front, and with the 1st and
2nd Canadian Divisions, on one-brigade fronts, continue
the advance. After General Rawlinson's conversation had,
been confirmed by a warning telegram from the Fourth
Army, sent to all corps, to the effect that the advance would
be continued next day, and that the 32nd Division was
placed at the disposal of the Canadian Corps, Lieut.-General
Currie on his return fixed the hour of advance at 5 a.m.
Orders to the above effect were on the point of being issued
about 6.30 p.m. by the Canadian Corps when a telegram was
received from the Fourth Army General Staff cancelling
the Army commander's release of the 32nd Division and
ordering Br.-General Webber to come to Dury (south of
Amiens and 8 miles from Gentelles) for a telephone conversation. The roads being hopelessly blocked by the 32nd

Division, then making for Domart in buses with the transport, following, by columns of prisoners and by lorries of all sorts, it was 8.30 p.m. before Br.-General Webber reached Dury and heard definitely from Major-General Montgomery on the telephone that the Canadian Corps could not have the 32nd Division.

Later reports had confirmed the absence of complete success on the flanks of the attack and brought to notice the heavy losses among the tanks and aeroplânes, which were put at 25 per cent. of number of tanks engaged,[1] and 13 per cent. of the total air strength of day-flying machines with the B.E.F. On the other hand, the human casualties had been few and there were other encouraging factors. Hope existed that Péronne railway bridge had been hit, and many German ammunition dumps could be seen on fire. The Amiens Outer Defence Line had been secured as an insurance against counter-attack. The success of the Canadian and Australian Corps had obviously been decisive. " When there are victories there are prisoners and captured " cannon ", as Moltke said in August 1914, and no doubt existed of the presence of these. So General Rawlinson felt no hesitation in issuing orders for the continuation of the advance next day ; but he did not yet feel justified in employing his second-line divisions.

There seemed no reason why Roye–Chaulnes, seven miles on, should not be reached without much effort, as the next organized German line was the old Hindenburg Position,[2] which ran from the Aisne, east of Soissons, in rear of La Fère and in front of St. Quentin and Cambrai, nearly thirty miles away.[3]

---

[1] Only 145 out of 415 were available for action next day.

[2] See End–paper B.

[3] See Appendix XI for the Fourth Army Orders. The time of issue is not marked or recorded, nor is the time of receipt noted in the diaries of the Canadian or the Australian or the III Corps. The time of issue would appear to be some hour in the early morning of the 9th ; for these corps had at 8.55 p.m., 11.40 p.m. and 10.15 p.m. on 8th respectively, issued preliminary orders for the continuation of the advance, no doubt based on the Fourth Army telegraphed warning order. Then at 4 a.m. the Canadian Corps, and at 5.50 a.m. the Cavalry Corps, issued orders in accordance with the Fourth Army written orders ; the diaries and orders of the Australian Corps (and its divisions) afford no clue as to time, except the diary of the 5th Division which at 6.55 a.m. received a message that " Scheme B " would come into force, Zero 11 a.m. Both the Canadian and the Australian Corps had, before the battle, prepared alternative schemes of advance from the Amiens Outer Defence Line.

The Br.-General, General Staff, of the Canadian Corps, an Imperial Officer, after being informed of all this, told Major-General Montgomery that the 3rd Canadian Division, bivouacked around Hamon Wood (south of Démuin), would have to be brought up and used again to undertake the rôle proposed for the 32nd Division, fresh orders would have to be got out, and, as the wires forward were none too reliable, these orders would have to go by despatch rider and motor car, so that in the congested state of the roads it would be impossible to maintain the 5 a.m. start.[1] Finally, 10 a.m. was fixed by Lieut.-General Currie and even this, as will be seen, proved optimistic. The 4th Canadian Division already had its instructions to attack le Quesnel at 4 a.m., but the final orders did not reach the other divisions of the Canadian Corps until the early hours of the 9th.

General Debeney's orders, issued at 9.30 p.m. on the 8th, which did not reach G.H.Q. until next morning, were framed merely to ensure that the British right was covered, not for exploiting the success.[2] The successive objectives of the XXXI Corps were to be Hangest, Arvillers and Erches, whilst the X and IX, echeloned back, were to cover its right ; the XXXV Corps, south of Montdidier, which was to have attacked, was now to " hold itself ready to attack " when it receives the order to do so ", and the cavalry was to " remain in the St. Just area and in that of Bonneuilles " Eaux ", that is over twenty miles from the Allied junction near le Quesnel.

NOTE

The Germans on the 8th August

(Map 1 ; Sketches 2, 4, 5.)

To quote the words of the official Monograph " As the sun set on " the 8th August on the battlefield the greatest defeat which the " German Army had suffered since the beginning of the War was " an accomplished fact. The position divisions between the Avre

---

[1] On the evening of 8th August the divisional advanced headquarters were (see Map 1) 1st, Stove Wood (north of Cayeux) ; 2nd, Pierret Wood (east of Marcelcave) ; 3rd, Domart quarry ; 4th, Demuin : respectively 6½, 6½, 2 and 4 miles in an air line from advanced corps headquarters in Gentelles.

[2] F.O.A. viii. (i), Appendix No. 561. See Sketch 4.

" and the Somme, which had been struck by the enemy attack
" were nearly completely annihilated. The troops in the front
" line north of the Somme had also suffered seriously, as also the
" reserve divisions thrown into the battle in the course of the day.
" The total loss of the formations employed in the *Second Army*
" area is estimated at 650 to 700 officers and 26,000 to 27,000
" other ranks.[1] More than 400 guns, besides a huge number of
" machine guns, trench mortars and other war material had been
" lost. . . . More than two-thirds of the total loss had
" surrendered as prisoners ".[2]

To take first the front line divisions, beginning with the opponents of the Canadian 3rd Division. " Except for a local fight at
" Mezières the fate of the *225th Division* was settled about 10 a.m.
" The entire position artillery was lost ; of the front line and
" support battalions practically nothing had come back ; and the
" resting battalions, thrown in piecemeal, had either been thrown
" back or had not got into action at all. Only two fragments were
" still in being, the already shaken Krause group [two engineer
" companies] south-east of Cayeux and three companies of
" *Reserve Regiment No. 18* just north of Beaucourt. Between
" these yawned a gap, completely unoccupied ".

The *117th Division*, opposite the 1st Canadian Division,
suffered such heavy artillery fire that the Canadians were upon
the front battalion, even into Marcelcave, before the troops could
get out of their shelters. Barrage fire was absent. Two of the
three regimental staffs were captured. Of one regiment only
" remnants " of two battalions got back, of another " only quite
few men ", of the third only " a small party [lit., small heap-let]
" remained ". The resting battalions were thrown in piecemeal
and after " considerable losses " were assembled east of the
Wiencourt valley, where shortly after 9 a.m., they were attacked
by tanks, aeroplanes and infantry, and suffered " extraordin-
" arily high losses ", barely escaping complete capture. In Marcelcave and Rosières there were explosions of ammunition dumps.
The destruction of guns by means of hand grenades and the stay
of batteries in action until the last round was fired are mentioned,
but not the loss of the entire artillery. Finally, the division is
described as " nearly quite shrunk to nothing, barely any infantry
" left ".

---

[1] A footnote states that " exact figures are not available, as the war
" diaries—as far as they exist—either do not give the casualties at all
" or do not give them separately for 8th August ". If, as usual, the
" total loss " does not include " wounded likely to recover within a
" reasonable time ", a percentage must be added for comparison with the
British casualties, probably not less than the normal 30 per cent. See
Note III at end of Chapter VIII.

[2] The total number of prisoners taken was about 15,000, less, not
more than two-thirds of 27,000.

The *41st Division* opposite Villers Bretonneux, astride the Amiens–Chaulnes railway, and therefore attacked by the 2nd Canadian and 2nd Australian Divisions suffered very heavily. " All the front and support battalions as well as the entire " artillery down to trifling remnants[1] had fallen a sacrifice to the " enemy. Of the reserves only seven infantry and three machine- " gun companies remained ".

An apologetic account is given of the *13th Division* opposite the 3rd Australian Division : the greater part of the defences shown on paper did not exist, it had only 27 out of its 36 field guns, 6 of which were early knocked out, and only 12 out of its 36 heavy howitzers ; of the 24 companies of the 6 forward and support battalions 13 were in the Forward Zone contrary to the defence theory, which made the front line the weakest. Of two regiments only a few men escaped, most of the others being taken prisoner ; of the third regiment only about fifty. The three resting batta-lions were directed to the western slope of the valley leading from Harbonnières to Morcourt ; the first was not up until after 8.30 a.m., when it was already under fire ; the second did not arrive until 9.30 a.m., and by 10 a.m., turned on both flanks and attacked from the air, " the situation was hopeless . . . . The " two battalions were broken and considerable parts surrounded " and had to lay down their arms ". The third and last battalion, with all the fugitives and the regimentally employed men and a battalion of the *43rd Reserve Division,* reached the next ridge by 12.30 p.m., its resistance was broken, and many prisoners were lost and a retirement made to the slopes of the valley between Proyart and Méricourt, where other reserve battalions of the *43rd Reserve Division* were waiting. All the artillery seems to have been lost, but the division received most valuable support from the guns on the Chipilly ridge.

By night a new defence line had been formed from near Plessier, opposite the French, to the Somme; it was held from South to North by *1st Reserve Division, Bellmann's Regiment, 119th Division,* remains of the *117th, 225th* and *41st Divisions, 109th Division, 107th Division,* remains of the *13th Division,* and *108th Division.*

As regards the divisions in second line : the *43rd Reserve* was caught in the act of being relieved by the *108th,* only 4½ battalions with artillery having been pulled out, some of which though exhausted were used to assist the *13th Division.* Six divisions lay in reserve within striking distance of the field. Only three were engaged during the day : the *119th,* which was east and south of Roye, the *1st Reserve,* astride the

---

[1] Three guns only escaped.

Amiens–Roye road between Roye and le Quesnel, and the *109th*, in an area extending from near Harbonnières about six miles eastward. The other three, all north of the Somme, were the *243rd* about six miles and more east of Albert ; the *107th*, south of Péronne ; and the *26th Reserve*, north-east of the *243rd*, in the *Seventeenth Army* area. These took so long to reach the field owing to not being ready and being delayed by air attacks and road blocks, that they only served to form a new line towards night. In addition to the divisions in reserve the three resting battalions of each division in the line were available.

The first action of General von Hofacker commanding the *LI. Corps* (front Contoire 10 miles northward to Marcelcave) was to lay hands on the resting battalions of the *14th Bavarian* and *192nd Divisions*, opposite the French, as he judged from the reports and noise of firing that the front of attack did not extend farther south than the left of the *225th Division* (opposite the Canadian right). He ordered the *14th Bavarian Division* to go to the south-west of Cayeux and Bellmann's regiment to stand ready in Beaucourt Wood. General von der Marwitz placed the *109th Division*, already alarmed, at his disposal at 5.30 a.m., with orders to assemble on its foremost troops near Harbonnières. A little earlier the *LI. Corps* begged the *III Corps*, on its left (south), to assemble the *1st Reserve Division* on the northern edge of the latter's sector ; this was immediately complied with and at 5.20 the *1st Reserve Division* sent forward counter-attack groups down the Amiens–Roye road towards Arvillers and Boucher, and later directed both to le Quesnel. The *Second Army* then made a request to the *Eighteenth Army*, immediately granted, for the services of the *119th Division*, and for it to be sent forward as soon as possible in the direction of Vrély (south-east of Caix). The *1st Reserve Division* about 8.30 a.m., was assembled with two regiments around le Quesnel and one east of Arvillers. It was directed to prepare to counter-attack, but at 9.46 a.m. was ordered to occupy the line Fresnoy–Beaucourt and went forward under lively artillery fire between 10.15 and 10.30 a.m., and was immediately attacked from the air.

Bellmann's composite regiment, in Beaucourt Wood, was also ordered to counter-attack, but was caught by fire both from the air and the ground whilst in the act of deploying.

A resting battalion of the *14th Bavarian Division* was driven through Beaucourt by the Canadian cavalry and joined Bellmann.

At this stage the *1st Reserve Division* came up ; and it sent one battalion to Bellmann, so that a line was formed from four hundred yards south of Fresnoy (from which a squadron of Canadian cavalry was driven) to the northern end of Beaucourt Wood. Then came the advance of the 4th Canadian Division and about 2.15 p.m. [*sic*] the defenders of Beaucourt Wood and the

line north of the Amiens–Roye road fell back slowly on le Quesnel-
Fresnoy remained in German hands until attacked later by the
French.

The *119th Division* got orders at 8.30 a.m. for its infantry to
travel by lorry and the artillery to march ; but as the troops were
out at training it was 10.30 a.m. before the first units started ;
they then found the roads blocked and were delayed by air
attacks, so that it was 2 p.m. before the first unit arrived at
Vrély and 7.30 p.m. before the last got to Warvillers (3 miles
south of Vrély). It was ordered to counter-attack in the sector
between the valley running from Beaufort to Caix and the Luce.
The troops had no maps and did not know the ground, and only
one regiment on the left went forward about 7.20 p.m. with little
artillery support, and without result. The last shots were fired
between 9 and 10 p.m. This no doubt was the preparation for
counter-attack noticed near Beaufort.   North of the Somme at
6.30 a.m., the *243rd Division* was ordered to Cappy and Bray,
about eight miles south, to block the Somme valley ; one regiment
and most of the artillery being with the *27th Division* in the line,
it was arranged to send to the *243rd*, an infantry regiment and a
field artillery brigade from the *26th Reserve Division*. The *243rd
Division* was not ready to march until six hours or more later,
was sent south of the Somme, and the head did not reach Proyart
until 5.30 p.m., and the tail Chuignes (three miles north-east of
Proyart) until 9 p.m.

The *107th Division* had been alarmed at 5 a.m. ; all its artillery
except three batteries were with the *27th Division*, so an Army
brigade was lent to it. It was then ordered to Foucaucourt on the
Amiens–St. Quentin road, about 12 miles from the centre of its
cantonments. At 1 p.m. it advanced, troubled only by aeroplanes
until three miles farther on it reached the line Framerville–
Proyart about a thousand yards from the old Amiens defences,
and came under lively artillery and machine-gun fire and then
stopped.

CHAPTER VI

THE BATTLE OF AMIENS (*continued*)

THE SECOND DAY 9TH AUGUST 1918

(Map 1 ; End-paper A, Sketch 6)

The 9th August, the second day of the battle, was a day of wasted opportunities, although it began well ; for le Quesnel,[1] which on the 8th had defied all attempts, was captured in an early morning attack by two battalions of the 11th Canadian Brigade (4th Canadian Division) assisted on the right by Brutinel's Independent Force. This action will be dealt with first.

The hour fixed for the assault was 4.30 a.m., and as the night was almost entirely peaceful, the British guns firing little and the German guns not at all, preparations met with no hindrances. A short preliminary bombardment was fired by the field artillery of the 3rd and 4th Canadian Divisions and two heavy brigades ; but the barrage did not open until ten minutes after zero hour owing to the failure of a despatch rider to find his way to the batteries. Difficulties of communication, now that the trench-warfare telephone system had been left behind, were harrassing not only the higher but also the smaller formations, and were to continue to be so in the semi-open warfare that was to follow. In spite of the exertions of the Signal Service, relay chains of runners, cyclists and horsemen established in some divisions could not compete in time and reliability with wires and cables, and when telephone lines were available it was forbidden to use them for operation orders or important messages for fear of being overheard by the enemy.

The 75th Canadian Battalion, which was to advance against le Quesnel from the north-west, moved forward punctually without the barrage, but covered by the fire of two motor machine-gun batteries ; the two leading companies of the 87th, which from the north were to work down the northern and eastern edges of the village, were late, the one five and the other eighty minutes, mainly owing to the difficulty of making their way in the dark through Beaucourt Wood, their place of assembly. The 75th soon

---

[1] See Map 1 and Sketch 6.

encountered heavy rifle and machine-gun fire from le Quesnel, but none as on the previous evening from Fresnoy, for the place was now in the hands of the French. Advancing rapidly, by 5.30 a.m. the battalion was in the village and after mopping it up, capturing in the process the effects of a divisional headquarters, continued on. Some severe fighting took place in the wood south of the village ; but the armoured car detachment coming up on the right and the 87th Battalion being now on the left, the Amiens Outer Defence Line, the final objective of the 8th August, was reached. It was soon discovered that one pocket of Germans had been left between the two battalions, and another north of le Quesnel. These were dealt with by bombers with the help of the five tanks of the 1st Tank Battalion which remained fit for action, but two of these tanks were now destroyed by an anti-tank gun.

The 4th Canadian Division then took over the Amiens Outer Defence Line from Caix (on the Luce) southwards and came into corps reserve, the 3rd Canadian Division moving into its place for the advance.

The day turned out to be fine, with excellent visibility, and observation balloons as well as aeroplanes were early sent up by both sides. Little could be seen of the enemy and no reinforcements could be observed on the roads. Cavalry patrols, on the other hand, on the fronts of the Canadian and Australian Corps reported that apparently the enemy had established a continuous line marked by the villages of Beaufort, Rosières, Vauvillers, Framerville and Méricourt. The German infantry had allowed the horsemen to come within four or five hundred yards and then had emptied a few saddles ; a cavalry advance was obviously impossible. The III Corps reported that the line still ran on to Morlancourt, with Chipilly held as an advanced post ; obviously no trench system likely to require a systematic bombardment or to impede determined infantry lay ahead. It had not yet been discovered that the enemy, owing to reinforcements, was in strength quite equal to the attackers. The number of German divisions available at short notice to support the Amiens front had been correctly forecast by the Intelligence Branch, but they had come on to the field many hours earlier than expected.[1]

---

[1] See Note II at end of Chapter.

Attacks on the Somme bridges had been continued by the Royal Air Force during the night, fifty aeroplanes dropping six tons of bombs, and operations were resumed at 5 a.m. to prevent reinforcements from arriving, with 50 fighters on escort and 74 fighters on patrol above to protect 30 bombers. Voyennes, Béthencourt and Falvy (6, 4½ and 3 miles, respectively, south of St. Christ),[1] and Brie, as well as the bridges at the two latter places, were attacked, also Feuillères and Cappy (4 and 7 miles respectively below Péronne). At the last named place the station was bombed. No damage of importance, however, was done anywhere. The air fighting though continuous was less costly than on the previous day, but 45 aeroplanes had to be written off. Thirty-four enemy planes and one balloon, at least, were sent down.

Of the 415 tanks which paraded on the 8th only 145 were now fit for action, and their casualties during the day amounted to 30 per cent. as against an estimated 25 (actually nearer 60) on the first day.

The ground fighting during the day was of a very disjointed nature ; the attacks of various divisions and brigades started at different times and under different conditions. Some of them were covered by artillery, some supported by tanks, whilst others were carried out by infantry unaided. The German defence was similarly very uneven and without any serious attempt at counter-attack. In the result only a bare three-miles advance, half the way to Roye–Chaulnes, was accomplished.

General Rawlinson's orders[2] directed the Fourth Army to advance and establish itself on the general line Roye–Chaulnes–Bray sur Somme–Dernancourt, whilst the French came up to Roye. The principal rôle was assigned to the Canadian Corps, whose objective was Roye–Hattencourt–Hallu. On the right the French and on the left the Australian Corps, with Lihons–Chuignolles as its objective, and the III Corps, directed to the line " east side of Etinehem–Dernancourt ") were to cover the flanks. It was left to Lieut.-Generals Currie and Butler to fix the hour of advance of their corps and to inform the Australian Corps. The former commander, we have seen, owing to the 32nd Division being

---

[1] See End-paper A.
[2] See Appendix XII.

withheld, had chosen 10 a.m., instead of 5 a.m. as at first settled. The III Corps had already arranged to continue operations against Chipilly ridge at dawn.

Lieut.-General Sir C. T. McM. Kavanagh had on the night of the 8th ordered the 2nd Cavalry Division (Major-General T. T. Pitman), then concentrated behind the left of the Canadian Corps at Guillaucourt, to push forward in the direction of Roye at daybreak, and the 1st Cavalry Division (Major-General R. L. Mullens), then in support of the Australian Corps, to take the direction of Chaulnes. Each division was to be accompanied by two companies of whippets. The 3rd Cavalry Division (on the right near Beaucourt), after relief by Canadian troops, was to fall back into reserve. At 5.30 a.m., after receipt of the Fourth Army orders which directed the cavalry to " operate on the right of the Fourth " Army in such a manner as to gain the objectives allotted " to the Canadian Corps and to facilitate the advance of the " French First Army ", Lieut.-General Kavanagh cancelled his previous orders and directed the 2nd and 1st Cavalry Divisions to support the infantry instead of preceding it to the line Roye–Chaulnes, concentrating as a preliminary : the 2nd Cavalry Division south of Caix and the 1st south of the wood between le Quesnel and Caix. These rendezvous were later changed to south of Guillaucourt (on the Amiens–Chaulnes railway) and east of Caix. As the cavalry—the brigades being allotted different sectors of the front—and the whippets attached to them followed the infantry, and did nothing independently, their action will be related in connection with the infantry operations.

The engineers, including the tunnellers, except when bridging was required, were chiefly employed on this day and on the following days in searching for and removing booby traps, on water supply, on improving roads and on erecting sign-boards.

By Canadian Corps orders, the 3rd, 1st and 2nd Canadian Divisions were to advance in two bounds to within striking distance of the objective named by the Fourth Army, the 3rd Division passing through the 4th after the latter's capture of le Quesnel. They were given respectively Folies, Beaufort–Warvillers, and Vrély–Rosières as their first objectives ; after securing these they were to continue on towards the line Andéchy (4 miles short of Roye)–Damery–Fouquescourt–Chilly–Lihons.

The advance of the 3rd Canadian Division was led by the 8th Canadian Brigade. This brigade, in expectation of moving down the Amiens–Roye road, had been ordered to assemble by 10 a.m. in the valley one mile north of Mezières ; but at 9.15 a.m., Major-General Lipsett gave Br.-General D. C. Draper instructions to move against Folies with two battalions, acting, with seven tanks of the 5th Tank Battalion, as advanced guard to the division. It was not until after 11 a.m. that the brigadier completed his reconnaissance, noon before his instructions were given out and after 2 p.m. before the 5th and 4th Canadian Mounted Rifles, after assembling on the western side of le Quesnel wood and village, respectively, had passed through these localities and had deployed on their eastern side—the village being heavily shelled by the enemy, although German posts, which had to be cleaned up, were still holding out on the eastern outskirts. Information had an hour earlier been received from Brutinel's Force, which was co-operating on the right, that the French south of the Amiens–Roye road were being held up by fire from the copse east of le Quesnel wood and the light railway north of it ; but on the left of the 3rd Canadian Division, the 1st was already advancing. With the assistance of two tanks and the fire of the 324th Siege Battery, the 5/C.M.R. in a very short time reached the copse and the light railway, beyond which the French, though assisted by two Canadian motor machine-gun batteries, were too weak to progress. By 4.20 p.m. the C.M.R. had cleared Germans out of the beetroot factory, a mile farther on, and entered the southern outskirts of Folies. Three-quarters of an hour later the French were reported to be in Arvillers.[1]

The 4/C.M.R., starting a little earlier than the 5th, with three tanks, encountered stiffer opposition and lost two of its tanks, but entered Folies at the same time as the 5/C.M.R., to find troops of the 1st Canadian Division had drifted there. For co-operation in the general advance, by brigade orders issued at 5.45 p.m., the two battalions went on, entered Bouchoir and occupied a trench lying eastward and northward of it. During the evening the 7th Canadian Brigade

---

[1] See Note I at end of Chapter.

was moved up in order to be ready to pass through the 8th and continue the advance next day.

The 5th Cavalry Brigade (Br.-General N. W. Haig), sent to the right flank, was unable to make any forward movement from le Quesnel until 3.30 p.m., when two advanced squadrons of the R. Scots Greys, with three whippets, moved to Folies, and two others, with four whippets, followed the infantry into Beaufort and beyond. Towards 6 p.m., learning from patrols that a gap existed between the left of the French just east of Arvillers and the right of the Canadian Corps, the first named two squadrons formed a defensive flank facing south, Brutinel's Force completing the connection with the French First Army.

In the 1st Canadian Division, its 1st Brigade was at 7.30 a.m. given verbal orders to capture the villages of Beaufort and Rouvroy, moving to the attack at 11 a.m. ; but as the artillery brigade which was to support the advance was not in position, zero hour was postponed until 1.15 p.m. About 1.45 p.m. the le Quesnel–Caix road was crossed by the 1st and 2nd Battalions under ever increasing machine-gun fire, particularly from trenches outside Beaufort Wood. The Germans were soon driven out, and then rapid progress was made by the use of short rushes, the Canadian infantry having had good training in open warfare. Folies on the right was reached and with the help of seven whippets, attached to the 3rd Cavalry Brigade, Beaufort was taken and passed through, and just before 4 p.m. Marmites Farm, a thousand yards beyond that village, was entered. Then the 2nd Battalion ran into very violent machine-gun fire and casualties became heavy. Nevertheless the 2nd Battalion and the 4th, which had passed through the 1st, still assisted by the whippets, which dealt with many machine guns, continued to advance until they reached a line of trenches four hundred yards west of Rouvroy, the enemy falling back to the wood bordering the village and to some high ground south of it. The attack was now held up and the whippets withdrew ; but at 5.40 p.m. Br.-General W. A. Griesbach put in his last battalion, the 3rd, with the 8th Hussars (3rd Cavalry Brigade) in support, in a determined effort to capture Rouvroy and conform to the result of the success of the 2nd Canadian Brigade on his left. Before the advance of the 3rd Battalion through the 2nd had begun, information came to brigade headquarters that three platoons of the 2nd Battalion had forced their way into Rouvroy. The 3rd was thereupon ordered to clear the village and relieve the 2nd. The 1st and 4th Battalions, still unable to advance, were directed to follow the 3rd, push eastwards and form a defensive right flank to connect with the 3rd Canadian Division east of Folies, all of which tasks were duly performed. The 8th Hussars which had sent a squadron round the southern side of Rouvroy, after suffering from an enemy barrage, were withdrawn with the rest of their brigade to west of Warvillers Wood.

The 2nd Brigade of the 1st Canadian Division was unable to advance before 1 p.m. The 7th and 10th Battalions in the line had been there during the night, so the 5th and 8th were to make the attack, side-slipping southwards to reach the narrow front, under a thousand yards, from which they were to jump off. They were to be supported by the 14th and 15th Battalions of the 3rd Canadian Brigade, then in reserve, which was to take over the 7th and 10th in place of its own pair as soon as the 2nd Canadian Division on the left had passed through the line.

The re-marshalling of the battalions took some time. Accordingly when, at 7.30 p.m., Br.-General F. O. W. Loomis received notice by telephone that Zero was 10 a.m. he represented his difficulties and obtained a postponement first to 11 a.m. and later to 1 p.m. The artillery did not receive notification of the second change and fired the 11 a.m. barrage ; so when the 5th and 8th Battalions moved off they did so without artillery support except from one battery on the left. They had at first no help from tanks, for the twelve machines of the 4th Tank Battalion told off to them were half an hour late ; but they soon caught up and subsequently did valuable service. In the later part of the attack two regiments of the 3rd Cavalry Brigade co-operated, and seven whippet tanks, sent by the 2nd Cavalry Brigade at 3.30 p.m., proved very useful in silencing machine guns.

No sooner did the 2nd Canadian Brigade—with a right flank guard as the 1st Brigade was not ready—begin its advance on Warvillers and Vrély over flat country covered by growing corn, than it encountered serious opposition, particularly from Hatchet Wood. This was overcome after a struggle and over three hundred prisoners and many machine guns were captured by the 8th Battalion.[1] Advancing by rushes, the 5th Battalion reached the enemy's front line, capturing twenty machine guns, and then halted half an hour for the 8th Battalion to come up.[2] An attempt by a squadron of the 16th Lancers (3rd Cavalry Brigade) to charge and round up a party of German machine-gunners holding out in a copse after the Canadian infantry had passed by, completely failed. When the advance was resumed Warvillers village and wood were captured about 4.30 p.m., though at the cost of heavy casualties. The 5th Lancers co-operated in the attack on the village ; but a squadron which was directed to encircle it from the north was held up by wire fences and stopped by machine-gun fire. Another halt was made for the troops on the flanks to come level, as the 8th Battalion had been checked in front of Vrély and had lost 14 officers and over four hundred other ranks. Then, towards dusk, with the help of the tanks and whippets, after many attempts, the two battalions reached the Rouvroy–Méharicourt road between those two places, obtained touch with troops on the right and left already in them, and during the night pushed outposts east of the road.

In the 2nd Canadian Division, the 5th and 6th Brigades were to attack side by side, the former, which had been in reserve during the night, coming up on the right of the 6th, which was in the line. Due notice was received that the advance would be resumed at 10 a.m. and of the postponement to 11 a.m. At the latter hour the deployment of the 5th Brigade had not been completed, the fifteen tanks of the 14th Tank Battalion allotted to it had not arrived, and Br.-General J. M. Ross[3] learnt from the 2nd Brigade on his right, that its advance would not take place until 1 p.m., so he waited. The 6th Brigade, however, protected on the left by the 5th Australian Division and covered by a thin

---

[1] For most conspicuous gallantry during the attack on Hatchet Wood Corporal F. C. Coppins and Private A. Brereton, 8th Canadian Battalion, were awarded the V.C.

[2] For most conspicuous gallantry during the attack by the 5th Canadian Battalion on this day Sergeant R. L. Zengel, M.M., was awarded the V.C.

[3] Br.-General Ross was wounded about 3 p.m. and succeeded by Br.-General T. L. Tremblay, who commanded the 5th Brigade until the end of the war.

barrage, moved punctually, its line of advance taking it across open fields raked by machine guns from front and flanks.   The 9th Cavalry Brigade was in support, but the allotted seven tanks of the 14th Tank Battalion did not appear to time, for, owing to the excellent observation enjoyed by the enemy from the rise on which Rosières stands, it had not been possible to assemble the tanks farther forward than fully twelve hundred yards in rear of the infantry.   Screened by smoke grenades, five machines, two having broken down, soon came up, and the 31st and 29th Battalions, followed by the 28th, reached the southern outskirts of Rosières about 1.30 p.m.   Very heavy fighting ensued in the village, the one tank which entered was put out of action, and it was not until 2.30 p.m. that the troops of the 31st Battalion were level with the centre of the village, the 29th having passed through the northern part, and two hours more before Rosières had been cleared of the enemy.   A fresh advance was then begun, the sugar factory taken and a line occupied beyond the Méharicourt–Rosières road.   Two companies of the 28th Battalion went on to the Méharicourt–Lihons road, but were later withdrawn.   Three more tanks had meantime been knocked out by direct gun fire, so that only one rallied.   At 4 p.m. the 9th Cavalry Brigade sent out a number of patrols, and moved forward.   Later it was used with the infantry to form an outpost line from Méharicourt to another sugar factory twelve hundred yards to the north, but it was relieved during the night.

The 5th Brigade, urged by the divisional commander, who feared for the right of the 6th Brigade, had not waited to complete its deployment.   At 11.45 a.m. one company had advanced, followed at 12.30 p.m. by three others, and at 1 p.m. by the remainder.   Fifteen tanks of the 14th Tank Battalion which were to work with the 5th Brigade arrived late, but did good service when they did appear.   The 2nd Cavalry Brigade followed the infantry, a squadron of the 9th Lancers being used to keep touch.   The 25th and 22nd Battalions, which led, encountered heavy machine-gun fire all the way, especially near Vrély and east of Méharicourt, and since moving over the open ground was certain to prove costly and in order to get at machine-gun nests from a flank, the companies worked along the ditches and sunken roads and in dead ground in small parties covered by Lewis-gun detachments. It was said by an artillery observer that the Canadians seemed to know exactly what to do, and how to do it.

By 3.15 p.m. the leading parties were through and east of Vrély and by 5.30 p.m. were consolidating a line five hundred yards east of Méharicourt, ahead of their neighbours, with whom touch was not established until 7.30 p.m.[1] The squadron of the 9th Lancers when near Méharicourt rode forward towards Fouquescourt, and seeing some German machine guns galloped to capture them ; but the country proved unsuited for mounted action, being on the edge of the devastated area and covered with trenches and wire and pitted with shell holes, so after suffering heavy casualties the squadron fell back. These machine guns and others were found and destroyed by six whippets of the 6th Tank Battalion which, however, lost two of their number hit by a field gun firing from near Fouquescourt. The rest of the 2nd Cavalry Brigade was used dismounted to fill gaps in the line, and later occupied a sector from the cross-roads north of Rouvroy to the south-west corner of Méharicourt until relieved by infantry during the night.

The Canadian Corps, its advance having been begun late, did not reach the objective. The difficulties of communication due to the sudden change from trench warfare to open warfare had been very great ; the frequent breakdowns were partly due to the troops, whose inexperience made them oblivious to the respect due to wires and cables lying on the ground, so that these were injured by tanks, vehicles, horsemen and marching columns. Owing to the heavy traffic on the few main roads available, Dury (3 miles south of Amiens)— Boves–Fresnoy–Roye for the Canadian Corps, Amiens– Villers Bretonneux–Brie for the Australian Corps, and Amiens–Corbie–Sailly le Sec–Bray for the III Corps, mounted orderlies, though slower than motor-cyclists, often proved the quicker in the end.

The 4th Canadian Division had been able to attack as ordered, without counter-order, at 4.30 p.m. and, as will be seen, the advance of a single battalion of the III Corps at 5.30 a.m. penetrated the German line ; so it may be fairly assumed that had not a counter-order been given as regards

---

[1] For most conspicuous gallantry on 8th and 9th August, 1918, Lieut. J. Brillant, M.C., 22nd Battalion, was awarded the V.C.

the employment of the 32nd Division, the general advance of the Canadian Corps could have begun at 5 a.m. as originally fixed by Lieut.-General Currie, or at any rate very soon after that hour. Even with the same delays as occurred in the execution of the 10 a.m. (postponed to 11 a.m.) advance, the divisions of the Canadian Corps would have been under way by 9 a.m., with a whole day instead of only an afternoon before them, and the enemy would have had less time to pull himself together and bring up reinforcements.

The rôle which the Australian Corps had to play and even its time of starting depended upon its neighbours. It had to cover the left of the Canadian Corps, and its own left was not to advance until the III Corps reached the edge of Bray. It seemed to Lieut.-General Monash that his left wing, the 4th Australian Division, next the Somme, would probably not be called on to push forward more of its troops than its extreme right flank ; but late at night on the 8th he gave his divisional commanders an outline of his plan for the advance of his right wing, the 5th Australian Division. The frontage of the Australian Corps, between the Amiens–Chaulnes railway, which runs E.S.E., and the east-west course of the Somme, would gradually widen as it progressed ; he therefore intended that the 1st Australian Division—which earlier in the day had been ordered forward to Hamel (north of the Amiens–Brie highway) and Aubigny (5 miles west of Hamel), where it arrived between dusk and midnight—should pass through the right wing of the 5th, and that, later in the day, the 2nd Australian Division would similarly relieve the left wing of the 5th.

This warning was followed about 2 a.m. on the 9th by an order to the effect that the attack would take place that day, but not before 10 a.m. : it allotted tanks : 14 of the 2nd Battalion to the 1st Australian Division ; 15 of the 15th Battalion, to the 2nd ; and 7 of the 8th Battalion to the 5th. The field artillery, four brigades each for the 1st, 4th and 5th Division sectors, was to be ready to open fire at 10 a.m.

The orders of the 1st Australian Division, whose head-quarters were in Villers Bretonneux, were not issued until 3.40 a.m., and then had to be sent out by car and motor-cyclist ; so that it was 8.45 a.m. before battalions were on the march to the rendezvous, Harbonnières, 10 miles to the south-east, on the other (southern) side of the Villers Bretonneux–Brie high road. Thus, although the Canadian Corps changed the zero hour from 10 a.m. to 11 a.m., it was certain by 9.30 a.m. that the 1st Australian Division could not be in position in time. The 15th Australian Brigade, the right wing of the 5th Australian Division, at the request of the 6th Canadian Brigade, agreed, with Major-General Hobbs's consent, to go forward and cover the Canadian flank. This was no light task, as the brigade had to engage without the fourteen tanks which had been assigned to the 1st Australian Division and without a barrage, with which that division had decided to dispense.

Very soon after crossing the old Amiens Defence Line the 60th and 58th Battalions, which led the advance, came under considerable shell fire, and were pinned to the ground by the intensity of the enemy's machine-gun fire. The succcess of the 6th Canadian Brigade, with four tanks, on the right, and the progress of the 8th Australian Brigade, the left of the 5th Australian Division, now attracted the attention of the Germans, and the loan of one tank from the Canadians assisted matters, so that the 15th Australian Brigade was able to make some headway.

The 8th Australian Brigade, delayed by shelling and the time taken to circulate orders, had attacked at 11.40 a.m. It thus lost the thin barrage arranged for 11 a.m. and the support of its six tanks, which, going forward at 11.15 a.m., had been knocked out one after the other by an anti-tank gun firing from a shed in Vauvillers. Nevertheless, the advance of the 29th Battalion, in conjunction with the 60th and 58th, went slowly on, with the assistance of aeroplanes diving at the enemy machine guns, and field guns shelling the rise behind the enemy's line over which reinforcements must come.   Shortly before 1 p.m. the battalions of the 1st and 2nd Australian Divisions, marching in small parties, began to come on to the field and assemble south and north of Harbonnières. The Germans opposite the 5th Australian Division thus menaced and their right flank turned by the 8th Australian Brigade, began to retire from a line of sunken huts and trenches which they had been holding opposite the 15th Australian Brigade.   An Australian charge completed their rout and gathered in three hundred prisoners and 21 machine guns ; whilst the 8th

Australian Brigade took Vauvillers and sent back an officer and 138 men as prisoners. The enemy was followed by fire, and parties started in pursuit ; but from a highway half a mile beyond Vauvillers strong opposition quickly blazed up. By this time, 1.45 p.m., the troops of the 1st Australian Division, headed by their tanks, began to pass through ; the 15th Australian Brigade, its task well fulfilled, was halted, and the second stage of the day's operation commenced.

The 2nd Australian Brigade (Br.-General J. Heane), with Lihons hill as objective, now led the advance with the 8th and 7th Battalions, without a barrage, the 3rd Brigade (Br.-General H. G. Bennett) following two miles behind. It was attacked by two German aeroplanes en route to the starting line without effect. Each battalion had attached to it two guns of C/189 Brigade R.F.A. and seven tanks. Throughout, the battalions encountered a slight amount of field-gun shelling, but the opposition came mainly from the left flank, as the 2nd Australian Division did not begin its attack through the 8th Australian Brigade until nearly three hours later. On the southern flank the Canadians had reached the outskirts of Rosières by 1.30 p.m. and were soon in possession of the village ; so little trouble was experienced on the right except from a strong party in Rosières station, where huge dumps of timber were accumulated ; but the defence was soon abandoned. By 3.30 p.m. the 2nd Australian Brigade had crossed two miles of bare, grassy plain, with another mile to go. Then shell fire gradually knocked out the tanks, but the infantry managed, at heavy cost, especially in officers, to reach the old trenches of 1916, some twelve hundred yards from Lihons, which was being shelled by the heavy artillery to prevent the arrival of reinforcements. Later the Australians were able to push half-way up the large flat hill on the reverse slope of which Lihons stands. The 7th and 8th Battalions had lost a third of their strength, and were therefore reinforced by two companies each from the 5th and 6th Battalions.

The 2nd Australian Division should have been ready at its rendezvous in the old Amiens Defence Line, just east of Harbonnières, by 11 a.m., but the issue of orders and other preparatory measures were not over until 1.30 p.m., and the hour of passing through the 8th Australian Brigade near

Vauvillers was then fixed for 4.30 p.m., it apparently being estimated that it would take until then to reach the front line, though actually the companies were there between 3.40 and 4 p.m., and were attacked whilst assembling by a dozen German aeroplanes. The 7th and 5th Brigades led, with Framerville as objective ; guns were to shell important points ahead of the attack, but no barrage would be fired. The thirteen tanks unfortunately proved to be of the long passenger-carrying type, no others being available. As in the case of the 1st Australian Division, the most dangerous opposition to the 2nd came from the left, where the 4th Australian Division stood fast. The presence of the 1st Australian Division about a third of a mile away on the right, discovered only during the course of the fighting, secured that flank. As soon as the attack was under way no doubt about the issue was possible : the Germans in front fled ; those in a stronger line behind rose and retired, the enemy gunfire ceased, and Framerville was taken with three hundred prisoners. By that time all the tanks but two had been hit, and one of these two broke down ; the thirteenth, however, after circling round, was able to proceed homewards to report that the line was beyond the objective. By 8.30 p.m. Lieut.-General Monash knew the general position of his front and that the day's objective had been nearly reached. The lack of co-ordination of the attacks, due to the uncertainty about the zero hour and to the slowness and difficulties of communication in semi-open warfare, had resulted in the Australian battalions suffering losses which need not have been incurred.

The fighting on the 8th August north of the Somme, following on the losses of the 18th and 58th Divisions in combat with the *27th (Württemberg) Division* on the 6th and 7th, had seriously depleted the ranks of the III Corps. During the evening of the 8th, therefore, Lieut.-General Butler sought permission of the Fourth Army to make use of the American 131st Regiment (33rd Division), as strong in infantry as a British brigade, which, although in corps reserve, could not be employed without reference to the Army.

Permission having been received, corps orders were issued at 10.15 p.m.

The 58th Division (with the American 131st Regiment attached) and the 12th Division were to attack at dawn, passing through, so as to include, the front of the 18th Division, which lay between them.

The 18th Division, opposite Gressaire Wood (which it had failed to capture and was full of guns covered by machine guns), was to return the 37th Brigade, now its reserve, to the 12th Division and withdraw the 36th Brigade, then in the line, as soon as the 58th and 12th Divisions had passed through ; the 53rd Brigade was to be in close support of the attacking divisions and the 55th in reserve (the 54th had already been sent back behind Albert for rest).

The 58th Division was to attack northwards and eastwards, so as to outflank Gressaire Wood, whilst, on its left, the 12th Division was to pinch out Morlancourt and go forward to the old Amiens Outer Defence Line. Twelve tanks of the 10th Tank Battalion were allotted to the 58th and eight to the 12th Division. Later, at 1.25 a.m. on the 9th, the 58th Division was ordered to detail a force to secure Chipilly and Chipilly spur as far north as the parallel of Etinehem. These localities formed a little fortress. The spur, extending into an acute southern bend of the Somme rises steeply on its southern and eastern sides from the marshes of the river, whilst its western side is protected by a narrow valley flanked by machine guns which fired up it from Chipilly village and down it from the shelter of Gressaire Wood. Along the path which ran northward from Chipilly below the western edge of the spur was a line of machine guns in concrete emplacements, and a second line was sited on the eastern side of the spur. Field guns in this village commanded the river bridge and the road approaches from the west.

Soon after the 1.25 a.m. order was issued it became certain that the 131st Regiment could not possibly be in position by dawn.[1] At 2.20 a.m., therefore, the general

---

[1] The 131st Regiment on 8th August was in the neighbourhood of Baizieux, a little under 3 miles due north of Heilly (north-west corner of Sketch 6) and somewhat farther by road. At 4.30 p.m. on that day it received orders from III Corps to move two battalions to Heilly and one battalion to Franvillers (between Baizieux and Heilly), where the regiment would be under the 58th Division in corps reserve. By

Continued at foot of next page.

attack was postponed until the afternoon ; but the 58th Division was to carry out the special attack upon Chipilly as arranged, notifying the left Australian division (4th) of the hour selected.

It had been expected that the Germans, having, according to Intelligence information, received reinforcements, would counter-attack, but they remained quiet—owing to the serious casualties they had sustained. After discussing the situation with his divisional commanders, Lieut.-General Butler about noon sent out verbal orders by telephone and at 1.15 p.m. written orders for the continuation of the attack, provisionally fixing 5 p.m. as zero hour. This, at 3 p.m., was altered to 5.30 p.m. in order to give time to recall the patrols which were out keeping touch with the Germans, who it was suspected were thinning their line. The objective was a line[1] from the cross roads north-west of Etinehem, along the high ground east of Morlancourt to Dernancourt, the northern portion only coinciding with the old Amiens Outer Defence Line.

The written orders of the 58th Division were issued at 1.30 p.m., with an addendum for the 173rd Brigade at 2.5 p.m.[2] ; but as a warning order had been sent out at noon officers of the 131st Regiment were already carrying out reconnaissances. The 174th, 173rd and 175th Brigades of the 58th Division were already in the line.

The 174th (less the 8/London to be attached to the 175th) without artillery support, but assisted by 3 tanks, was to

---

Continued from previous page.

8.45 p.m. the two battalions had reached Heilly, and at 10 p.m. the 58th Division telephoned orders for the regiment to move to a position astride the Corbie–Bray road 3,000 yards south of Heilly and facing east, ready to attack at dawn. These orders could not be carried out by the American troops owing to lack of time. After telephonic communication between the regimental commander and Major-General Ramsay, commanding the 58th Division, they were cancelled. The two battalions were sent through Vaux into a position of readiness in the valley separating that village from Sailly le Sec. The troops reached their destination, where the third battalion joined them, extremely exhausted, without rations, one battalion without Lewis guns and with only a hundred rounds of S.A.A. per man.

[1] The line shown as reached on Sketch 6.

[2] This early issue was accomplished by a General Staff officer dictating to a clerk who typed direct on to mimeograph wax sheets.

occupy Chipilly and the ridge north of it.[1] The 173rd was
to side-slip southwards to make room for the Americans and
cover their right flank. The American 131st Regiment, with
5 tanks of the 10th Tank Battalion, was to attack Gressaire
Wood with the 175th Brigade[2], with 5 tanks on its left. An
artillery barrage would open on the starting line at zero
hour on the front of the 131st Regiment and 175th Brigade
and, after 8 minutes' fire on the right and 20 minutes' on
the left, move forward at 100 yards in 4 minutes to the
objective, in front of which it would rest for one hour. By
request of the 174th Brigade, the 58th Division artillery
turned fire on to the southern part of Chipilly spur from
12.30 to 2.30 p.m., and bombarded the whole spur from
4 to 5 p.m.

At 4.15 p.m. the 6/London of the 174th Brigade, only
6 officers and 90 other ranks strong, advanced against
Chipilly. The 7/London furnished a patrol to protect its
left flank, but the rest of this battalion was to wait until
5.30 p.m. to join in the general attack, then making for the
south-eastern corner of Gressaire Wood. The 6/London was
immediately met by severe enfilade fire from Les Celestins,
the wood behind Malard Wood, and from the ridge above,
and could make no progress until two companies of the
2/10th London (175th Brigade, but attached to the 173rd),
which had nearly captured Chipilly on the previous day,
appeared on the left from the south-west corner of Malard
Wood, where it had remained since the previous night.

Though detailed as support to the 173rd Brigade, when
the artillery opened fire and no other troops appeared, the
officer commanding, being unaware of the postponement to
5.30 p.m., had decided to attack. Skilfully using steady
covering fire to keep down the enemy machine guns on the
terraces of the ridge, whilst some parties took advantage of
the cover of the steep sides of the valley, the 2/10th London
worked south-eastwards. The German machine-gun nests
just north of Chipilly gave great trouble, so the artillery
assistance was again requested.

[1] Conflicting reports had come in as regards Chipilly. One had come
from the Australian Corps that an Australian patrol (actually two n.c.os.
of the 1st Battalion) had entered the village (southern and western parts)
during the night and found it empty ; but in the early morning Lieut.-
Colonel C. B. Benson of the 6/London, after a personal reconnaissance,
reported Chipilly and the heights as fairly strongly held.

[2] This brigade was four battalions strong : less the 2/10th London but
plus the 8/London (174th) and 5/R. Berkshire (36th).

At this juncture having seen that the attack on Chipilly was held up, the 1st Australian Battalion sent over via Cérisy a patrol, under the two n.c.os. who had entered the village during the previous night and were certain that they could again reach it. Half a mile from Chipilly the patrol came in touch with the 2/10th London, which, under its guidance opening out to 12 paces, in spite of heavy fire from the ridge, entered the village. Under cover of a smoke screen now put down by the artillery, the Australians and Londoners pushed round the rear, or eastern side of the spur and rushed the machine-gun posts which had given so much trouble. K Company of the 3rd Battalion of the American 131st Regiment, which had offered assistance to the 2/10th London, now joined in, and by 8 p.m. a line had been established in front of Chipilly and across the high ground to the north-east. Two hundred prisoners (of whom the Australian patrol claimed eighty) were taken and 12 machine guns. Some of these guns were turned on such of the Germans as tried to escape across the Somme.[1]

In support of the right of the 58th Division, the 4th Australian Division sent three companies over the river.

The main attack of the III Corps at 5.30 p.m. encountered very determined resistance[2] and only at the cost of very severe casualties did the troops reach their objective. The barrage, though heavy, was unsatisfactory, as many of the shells destined for Chipilly ridge fell in the valley in front, and the enemy was thus not prevented from making full use of his machine guns to enfilade the advance.

The task of the 173rd Brigade was to cover the right of the attack, cross the ridge and reach the road from Chipilly to the south-eastern edge of Gressaire Wood. The brigade advanced punctually from Malard Wood with what remained of the 3rd, 2/4th and 2/2nd London in line ; but on reaching the Chipilly–Morlancourt road, five hundred yards ahead and attempting to descend into the ravine beyond, the three

[1] The 2/10th London gave the patrol of the 1st Australian Infantry Battalion, which was under C.Q.M.S. Hayes, written thanks for " their conspicuous bravery to-day and their magnificent work ".

[2] In addition to the *43rd Reserve, 27th, 54th Reserve* and *233rd Divisions* originally in the line facing the III Corps, the *108th* (in relief of the *43rd Reserve*) and *243rd Divisions* had come up, and one regiment had been sent from the *13th Division* south of the Somme.

battalions were held up, as the 2/2nd London had been on
the previous day, by cross fire on the slopes from Chipilly
and Gressaire Wood. It was not until the 6th and 2/10th
London had secured Chipilly about 8 p.m. that the survivors
of the 173rd Brigade were able to continue the advance, and
before 11 p.m., by using the bayonet, they had completely
occupied their objective, shortly after which Lieut.-Colonel
D. E. Sandars, 3/London, who had led them, was severely
wounded by a shell.

Some delay occurred in orders reaching the American
131st Regiment which was still in its position astride the
Corbie–Bray road, so that it did not start until nearly
4 p.m., with $3\frac{1}{2}$ miles to go. The men were full of enthusiasm,
marched at speed regardless of shells, and doubled the last
mile for fear of being late for the barrage, and they arrived
just in time. They had first to reach Malard Wood and then
deploy at a considerable angle to the front of the wood
so as to face the southern face of Gressaire Wood squarely.
To assist the alignment Major-General Ramsay arranged
for a smoke screen to be put down on the starting line. The
1st and 2nd battalions were in front line with the 3rd in
support, and they started punctually across the slope of the
side of the valley. They at once came under a hail of machine-
gun bullets from Gressaire Wood ; the fire was particularly
heavy on the right which was exposed to enfilade fire from
machine guns across the valley. A long fire fight ensued.
Regardless of losses the Americans persevered, taking nearly
two hours to cover rather less than a mile. After being
reinforced, the 1st Battalion by a company of the 3rd
Battalion, and the 2nd Battalion by the 7/London,[1] towards
8 p.m., at the same time as the 174th Brigade entered
Chipilly, the Americans were able to report that they had
reached their objective on the left and somewhat later, with
the 173rd Brigade, on the right, and that they were digging
in. In front of the combined attack the Germans had fallen
back, abandoning to the victors the dug-out headquarters
of the K.T.K. (battle troops commander) of the sector,
complete with telephone switchboard, orders and maps.

The front line of the 175th Brigade, on the left of the
Americans, was parallel to its objective 2,500 yards away ;
between lay level ground. Under cover of outposts the four

---

[1] This battalion went into action 17 officers and 360 other ranks strong
and came out with 3 and 60 ; and other battalions suffered similarly.

attacking battalions had early in the day been withdrawn from the line for assembly and rest in a ravine behind it. They attacked at 5.30 p.m. with the 12th and 8/London in front, the 5/R. Berkshire in support and the 9/London in reserve. Progress was slow, but by 8 p.m. the leading battalions were within five hundred yards of the objective. An hour later the 12/London was on its objective with the 9/London behind its right flank, and in touch with the American 131st Regiment. The 8/London got within a hundred yards of its objective ; but as it had suffered many casualties and was out of touch with the 12th, the 5/R. Berkshire was sent up in close support.

Reports of the evident final success had continued to come in ; so at 8.40 p.m. Major-General Ramsay gave orders that the American 131st Regiment and the 175th Brigade should send out strong patrols with machine guns to cover the consolidation of the line, whilst other patrols should discover whether the old Amiens Outer Line was occupied by the enemy or not : in the latter case outposts were to be established in it. These orders were followed by a message despatched at 11.15 p.m. that owing to successes farther south the enemy was reported to be retiring everywhere, and that the Army commander had ordered the Amiens Outer Line to be occupied without delay, and the 131st Regiment and the 175th Brigade to push on at once and seize it. Much opposition was encountered by the patrols from machine-gun and artillery fire and from snipers, but little else—for the Germans north of the Somme were retiring to the Etinehem–Méaulte line—and though the patrols were supported they were unable to reach the old Outer Defence Line. The 58th Division, however, reached its original objective.

No less than seventy guns and howitzers were found in Gressaire Wood—8-inch, 5·9-inch, 4·2-inch, 4·1-inch and 3·7-inch.

The 37th Brigade (Br.-General A. B. Incledon-Webber), with the 1/1st Cambridgeshire attached, was detailed to carry out the task of the 12th Division (Major-General H. W. Higginson) and on the 8th/9th it was assembled west of Morlancourt ready to pass through the 35th Brigade at 4.30 a.m. (at midnight the hour was changed to 5.30 p.m.). Notice of the postponement did not reach 37th Brigade

headquarters until its battalions were already on the move.
The 6/Buffs was to advance south of Morlancourt at 5.30 a.m.
and the 6/Queen's and 6/R. West Kent north of the village at
6.20 a.m., the 1/1st Cambridgeshire, with 3 tanks, being
assigned the duty of mopping it up. It was found possible to
stop the centre and left battalions, but not the Buffs who
went on and actually penetrated the German position just
south of Morlancourt. Being recalled they retired under cover
of an advanced platoon post without loss, bringing back one
prisoner and a machine gun. The incident would seem to
show that had the orders for a 4.30 a.m. advance been
maintained an easy success would have been achieved on
this front.

In the evening at 5.30 p.m. the attack was carried out
according to plan. The Buffs and the Queen's, in spite of
being covered by an artillery barrage, now encountered fierce
resistance ; although they got touch with the 175th Brigade
they did not quite reach the old Amiens Outer Defence line ;
the R. West Kent, however, on the left, established themselves in this objective.[1]

One of the tanks which were to assist the Cambridgeshire
showed itself fifteen minutes before Zero and was spotted by
the Germans ; " there was a metallic clang and flash of
flame " : it was knocked out by a field gun. Its premature
arrival was no doubt responsible for the enemy being ready
to meet the attack of the Buffs and the Queen's. Notwithstanding that all hope of surprise had disappeared, the
Cambridgeshire advanced at 5.30 p.m. without waiting for
the remaining tanks, which were late. Machine guns and
trench mortars in Morlancourt immediately opened fire ; but
the companies, though they had three hundred yards of fire-
swept zone to cross, rapidly advanced to the village. They
were heroically assisted by Company Sergt.-Major Betts
(killed on the 22nd August) who single-handed worked his
way to the rear of the defenders, and opened fire on them.
After clearing the village of Germans the Cambridgeshire
proceeded to the brigade objective. But only two platoons
being required to fill a gap on the right of the 6/Buffs, the
rest of the battalion was withdrawn. Thanks to good leading,
it had lost only 2 officers and ten other ranks.

---

[1] For most conspicuous gallantry near Morlancourt on this day Sergeant
T. J. Harris, 6/R. West Kent, was awarded the V.C., posthumously.

The III Corps had done better than on the 8th and had in the two days captured 100 officers and 2,860 other ranks and hit the enemy far harder than known at the time ; [1] but it was not yet abreast of the Australian Corps.

Though substantial progress had been made on the 9th August, the resistance offered had been far greater and the general results everywhere less than expected. Possibly, on general principles and in particular on account of the fog and the absence of substantial wire entanglements which might check the infantry, it would have been more profitable to have withheld all the cavalry divisions (not the corps mounted troops) and a large reserve of tanks until the afternoon of the first day or even the morning of the second. But the real causes of the limited success on the second day were the changes in orders and the consequent late start of the operations.   It was not a case like that of the second day of the Battle of Arras in 1917, when after a fine initial success organized defences with many belts of wire still remained to be overcome, and fresh *Eingreif* divisions were at hand to counter-attack ; on the 9th August the Canadian and Australian Corps had definitely broken through, and the German reinforcements were only " tired " divisions.   The day furnishes another example of the old saying " Order, counter-order, disorder ".

The number of prisoners taken by the British now numbered 387 officers and 15,516 other ranks with over two hundred guns, to which must be added 150 officers and 4,300 other ranks with over a hundred guns taken by the French.   Again severe losses of tanks had been suffered, half of those engaged being out of action ; the air losses, as already mentioned, had not been so heavy.

Sir Douglas Haig—like Maréchal Foch, as will be seen—not being satisfied with the progress made by the French First Army, had an interview with General Debeney about

---

[1] See Note II at end of Chapter.

4 p.m. on the 9th.[1] The latter reported that he had visited all his corps commanders in order to hasten up affairs. In view of the hard fighting north of the Somme and the extension of the battle front of the Fourth Army, so that the density of troops was not sufficient to meet a serious attack, Sir Douglas Haig asked the commander of the French First Army to include Roye and a frontage extending three miles north of it in his sector. This General Debeney declined to do, as it would upset his plans—he was thinking more about connection with the French on his right than the British on his left ; but he agreed to take over Roye and the village of Goyencourt to the north-west, which would give him room to envelop the town.

It was settled with Generals Debeney and Rawlinson that the advance should be continued next day.

All captured guns were removed that they might not be retaken by the enemy, as had happened in his counter-stroke at Cambrai.

NOTE I

THE FRENCH ON THE 9th AUGUST[2]

(Sketch 4)

The French offensive on the 9th in the words of Daille (p. 197) " had little life in it " (" *manque de souffle* "). He adds that " Ludendorff made the same observation ". This lack of offensive spirit in the First Army was noticed at the time by Maréchal Foch who, according to the French Official Account, " on two occasions " during the morning [of the 9th] reminded General Debeney : ' It " ' must be quite understood that the French First Army should " ' reach Roye as *soon as possible* and stretch out its hand to the " ' Third '. As long as this result is not obtained, no means of " ' achieving it should be neglected : ' *With this object in view* " ' *divisions should not at any cost be withdrawn* [the 42nd next the " ' Canadians had been withdrawn]. Those which cannot advance " ' should be leap-frogged, should join the Second Line and be " ' used in support until the result desired by the High Command " ' has been obtained . . . Therefore *push on quickly*, march " ' in force, . . . *send up supports* in rear with every man you " ' have until *achievement of the result* ' ". Finally, Maréchal Foch telephoned at 10.35 a.m. : " ' General Debeney must not lose

---

[1] An account of the French operations and General Foch's dissatisfaction is given in Note I.

[2] From F.O.A. vii (i) and Daille.

" ' sight of the fact that his wheeling wing is on the north side of
" ' the Avre, on the Roye road, in touch with the British Army
" ' and should be stronger ' . It is in that direction above all that
" he must act and therefore ' push forward the XXXI Corps,
" ' drums beating, on Roye, without losing a moment and pre-
" ' venting any delay or hesitation ' ". (F.O.A. vii. (i.), p. 182).

The four French divisions next to the British, from left to right,
the 126th (which had relieved the 42nd), the 153rd and the 37th of
the XXXI Corps and the 66th of the IX Corps, with the 47th and
the 56th Divisions in support, starting at 8 a.m. made an advance
of about 2½ miles, the 152nd Division of the X Corps on the right
connecting the new line to the old front. Thus a right flank
facing south-east was made for the Canadian Corps. The
advance, however, was slow : Hangest was not taken until
11 a.m., Contoire not until 1.30 p.m., and in the afternoon
" progress slowed down ", no doubt on account of the arrival of a
fresh German division, the *82nd Reserve*, at Arvillers ; but at
night after the British 5th Cavalry Brigade and Brutinel's
Force had filled the gap, as already narrated, the French caught
up the British Line and contact was established in front of
Bouchoir with the right of the Canadian Corps.

The XXXV Corps (169th and 133rd Divisions in front line,
with the 46th and the II Cavalry Corps in rear, received orders
during the morning (time not marked, but it was after news of the
capture of Hangest had reached General Debeney) to advance at
4 p.m. to attack Assainvillers and Faverolles, passing south of
Montdidier. The II Cavalry Corps was to follow the XXXV
Corps and be ready " to act on the rear of the German troops
" facing the French Third Army [on the right of the First]. " The
XXXV Corps drove a wedge about 2½ miles deep in the German
front. No opportunity occurred for the cavalry to act ; but the
" Division aerienne " bombarded Roye and two other railway
junctions and various road junctions.

The 60th and 166th Divisions in the line between the advances
of the XXXI and XXXV Corps did not attack.

NOTE II

The Germans on the 9th August[1]

(See Sketch 6)

To support the nine divisions (including the *108th* which was in
the act of relieving the *43rd Reserve*) originally in the line opposite
the Fourth Army on the morning of the 8th August, during the
8th and the night of the 8th–9th six more divisions, *1st Reserve,*

---

[1] From Schwarte and regimental histories.

the *119th*, *109th*, *107th*, *243rd* and *26th Reserve*, had been brought into the line.   During the 9th, three more divisions (*21st, 79th Reserve* and *5th Bavarian*) appeared on the British front and one (*82nd Reserve* from the *Eighteenth Army*) on the French front, which went into the line between Arvillers and Hangest.   The *21st* resting east of Cambrai, was alarmed at 8.45 a.m. on the 8th, took train in the afternoon and in the early morning of the 9th reached Péronne, whence it marched 11 miles south-west to Lihons.   The *79th Reserve*, similarly alarmed, travelled from Coucy le Château by bus and lorry to Réthonvillers (five miles east of Goyencourt,) where it began to arrive at dawn on the 9th. The *5th Bavarian*, resting in the Arras sector, left at 1 p.m. on the 8th by train and bus for Feuillières (four miles S.S.E. of Cappy) and then marched to Rosières where it was assembled by 3.15 p.m. on the 9th.   The remains of the *13th, 41st, 117th* and *225th Divisions* as well as the *43rd Reserve*, were gradually withdrawn.   This left four divisions which had been in the line on the morning of the 8th, all on the northern wing opposite the III Corps, three from reserve which had been partially engaged on the 8th, and six fresh divisions, a total of 13, to confront the four Canadian, five Australian, seven British (three in Second Line) and one partly trained American division.

Ludendorff was opposed to any withdrawal, even to the shortening of the line north of the Somme ; he was continually speaking on the telephone to the Group of Army headquarters, giving instructions as to the disposal of even battalions of the temporary divisions (Rupprecht ii, p. 435).

According to German accounts, the morning of the 9th passed quietly on the greater portion of the *Second Army* front ; but on the boundary between the *Second* and *Eighteenth Armies* there were violent attacks resulting in the loss of le Quesnel and Hangest. During the afternoon, fighting broke out again on the whole front between Morlancourt and the Avre.   The enemy met with success everywhere and the German line partly under compulsion and partly of its own free will fell back to Morlancourt–Proyart–Méharicourt–Rouvroy–Saulchoy (2 miles S.S.W. of Erches).   The urgent need of reinforcements on far-separated parts of the front necessitated the use on this day, and on the following days, of all divisions held in reserve, as well as of some specially brought up, often from a distance.   As the infantry, to gain time, travelled by lorry they frequently arrived without their fighting transport and without artillery, and the staffs without horses.   In the stress of circumstances the divisions had often to be thrown piecemeal into the battle, and even when sent in as a whole at once suffered such losses that their engagement according to plan was impossible. For the same reason favourable opportunities for delivering counter-attacks could not be utilised, and the few which took place were delivered after the psychological moment had passed. When on the 9th the first phase of the battle ended, the situation from the German point of view was unfavourable.

North of the Somme, the infantry had suffered very heavily— one regiment of the *27th Division* was down to 200 men (" Regt. No. 123 ", p. 144, two battalions in front line were reduced to 44 men in all)—and such complete confusion prevailed that orderly leading had become impossible (" Regt. No. 120 ", p. 110). So at night all troops were ordered back to the line Etinehem–Méaulte (" 27th Division ", p. 90).

Ignoring the afternoon advance of the French XXXV Corps, it is said that all indications tended to show that the enemy was about to attack the southern face of the German salient, Mont-didier–Noyon. So during the night of the 9th–10th the right flank of the *Eighteenth Army* was withdrawn about four miles to the line Etelfay–Onvillers–Marest [1] covered by rear guards. " It had to leave a lot of material behind " (Ludendorff, p. 682)—and the *Second Army* conformed by swinging back its left.

Late in the evening General von Hutier (*Eighteenth Army*) was summoned to Crown Prince Rupprecht's headquarters and told that his whole Army must retire, otherwise it would be outflanked on the north. Only after a long telephone discussion did Ludendorff agree that a withdrawal might be made to the line of the Matz–Ricquebourg . (11 miles south of Roye)—Conchy (seven miles S.S.W. of Roye)—l'Echelle (four miles west of Roye) (Rupprect, p. 436). This movement was carried out, the line being that to which the French First Army advanced on the 10th. Crown Prince Rupprecht adds that the retirement of the *Eighteenth Army* was none too soon.

The German communiqué was " laconic but said much. The " enemy had broken in south of the Somme on a broad front. " These fearful tidings caused a panic in Germany. And no less a " one among her Allies. The German military plenipotentiary at " Austro–Hungarian headquarters called up Ludendorff and told " him that the unrest in Vienna was great. Ludendorff did not " conceal the seriousness of his view. General von Cramon " begged him to consider ' the harmful effect that a short bleak " ' admission of a disaster had on our Allies, who saw in Germany " ' their only salvation. Such admissions did not help, they must " ' be toned down [literally beautified], if not on account of the " ' German public, then for the sake of our Allies ' ". (Bloem's " Der Weltkrieg " ii., pp. 227–8.)

---

[1] See Sketch 4.

CHAPTER VII

THE BATTLE OF AMIENS (*continued*)

THE THIRD DAY 10TH AUGUST 1918

(Map 1 ; End-papers A, B, Sketches 4, 7)

The air attacks on the Somme bridges were continued during the night of the 9th–10th August, when 106 aeroplanes dropped a total of 16½ tons of bombs. These attacks were repeated by night with decreasing intensity until the 13th–14th, and thereafter intermittently. " The bombing failed " to achieve its object. Some of the bridges suffered minor " damage, but not enough to make them unsafe for traffic ".[1] German night bombing on the 9th–10th was also directed against bridges, particularly those of the Luce, at Domart,[2] over which a mass of traffic was passing. No hit was obtained ; but one bomb fell amongst the horses of the field artillery of the 32nd Division, bivouacked east of Domart, which in consequence was delayed in going into action on the 10th. Otherwise, no inconvenience was caused, and the noise of the explosions hardly served to waken sleeping men tired after two days of battle.

The achievements of the 10th were disappointing ; the various attacks, as on the 9th, started at different times without co-ordination, on the misunderstanding that the operation was a pursuit, whereas the German resistance was stiffening. The advance made was small, a maximum of little over two miles on the Canadian Corps front. The French[3] did slightly better than on the 9th, bringing into action on the right of the First Army seven divisions of their Third Army, thus extending the line of battle by ten miles ; the First Army occupied Montdidier (which had been abandoned by the enemy), and as a whole came up nearly abreast of the Canadian Corps. Thus the battle front was increased to 35 miles, straight, from the French right at Chevincourt to the British left at Dernancourt, though, as it was slightly concave, its actual length was more. But, like the British, the French advance came to an end when it reached the new German position of resistance.

---

[1] " War in the Air " vi, p. 452.
[2] See Sketch 7.
[3] See Sketch 4.

The principal reason for this small success was that just ahead of the two French Armies, the Canadian Corps and the right of the Australian Corps lay the remains of the old Allied and German front lines of February 1917, prior to the enemy's retirement to the Hindenburg Line.[1] For a breadth of three miles the ground was pitted with shell holes and intersected by old trenches and belts of wire almost intact and hidden by long grass. These formed a physical obstacle to rapid advance and offered ideal positions to determined machine gunners.[2] The position to be attacked differed indeed little from those faced in normal trench warfare, except it was not backed up by a mass of batteries established in good emplacements and connected by a well protected telephone system. The delays on the 9th had enabled the Germans to bring up more reinforcements. Fourteen divisions additional to the original garrison at least, and two more were suspected, had been reported on the British front and ten more on the French.[3] Only one fresh British division, the 32nd, the cause of dispute on the evening of the 8th, had been brought into the line, having been placed at the Canadian Corps' disposal during the afternoon of the 9th.[4]

G.H.Q. orders for the 10th merely gave the same objectives to the French First Army and British Fourth Army as on the previous day : Roye–Chaulnes–Bray–Dernancourt. In the Fourth Army orders[5] General Rawlinson as before left it to the G.O.C. Canadian Corps to fix the time of advance (he made it 8 a.m.) and communicate it to his neighbours ; the Cavalry Corps, as before, was directed to operate on the right of the Fourth Army " in such a manner as to gain the " objectives allotted to the Canadian Corps and to facilitate " the advance of the French First Army " ; the 13th Tank Battalion, in Army reserve, was transferred to the Canadian Corps. A supplementary order[6] made the Corbie–Bray road,

---

[1] See End-paper B.

[2] There is no indication that the existence of this belt had been notified to the troops. Several battalion commanders state emphatically that it was not, and, as will be seen, the G.O.C. Cavalry Corps had the area reconnoitred for large cavalry movements.

[3] See, however, Note II at end of Chapter.

[4] The 32nd (New Army) Division came to France in November 1915. It had been engaged in the Battles of the Somme 1916, in the pursuit to the Hindenburg Line and coastal operations in 1917, and in March and April 1918 fought in the Third Army.

[5] Appendix XII.

[6] Appendix XIII.

instead of the Somme which had not proved satisfactory, the boundary between the Australian Corps and the III Corps from 8 a.m. on the 10th.   This meant that the Australians took over the sector of the 58th Division (which went into reserve) and with it the American 131st Regiment and the artillery on that front, that is the 58th Division Artillery, the V (Army) Brigade R.F.A. and the LI. Brigade R.G.A.   The American 66th Brigade headquarters, the 132nd Regiment and the 124th Machine Gun Battalion of the American 33rd Division were also to be transferred from the III to the Australian Corps as soon as possible.   The 58th Division (less artillery) later left the front for rest, the 47th (2nd London) Division from the Albert sector becoming the corps reserve, the 18th, from rest, replacing the 58th in front line.

General Debeney directed his Army to continue its operations, the XXXI Corps in the direction of Andechy and Roye, the X and XXXV Corps " pinching out " Montdidier and then facing east, the cavalry following the XXXV Corps.   General Fayolle (G.A.R.) decided that the time had come for the Third Army also to join in and push as far as possible.[1]

Ninety additional British fighting aeroplanes were brought into the battle on the 10th ; so that on this day the total concentration of single-seater fighters was 480, which represented seventy per cent. of the Royal Air Force fighter strength on the Western Front.   Many combats took place, which on the whole ended in favour of the British, with no great losses.[2]   The air bombing morning and evening was directed against the railway stations at Péronne and Equancourt (6 miles N.N.E. of Péronne) on the line to Bapaume.

During the evening of the 9th, the 1st and 2nd Cavalry Divisions had been relieved by infantry and, with the exception of advanced posts, withdrawn to join the 3rd in the neighbourhood of Caix and Cayeux.   They then passed into reserve, whilst, by orders issued at 11.55 p.m., Lieut.-General Kavanagh instructed the 3rd Cavalry Division to push forward patrols at 5 a.m. on the whole front of the Canadian Corps and to follow half an hour later with the main body

---

[1] See Note I at end of Chapter.
[2] " War in the Air " vi, pp. 452–3.

and as many whippet tanks as were available, to a position of readiness between le Quesnel and Caix. The 6th Cavalry Brigade took over the advanced posts of the 2nd Cavalry Division, and the 7th Cavalry Brigade those of the 1st Cavalry Division. At 5 a.m. the patrols moved out and the two brigades followed to a position 1½ miles west of Vrély, behind the left of the Canadian Corps, with the Canadian Cavalry Brigade in reserve. The cavalry patrols and special patrols detailed to report " on the suitability of " the ground up to and beyond the objective for the employ-" ment of cavalry moving fast in large numbers " sent back the correct information that the country was unsuitable, even impassable, for cavalry—unless dismounted—and also for whippet tanks, and that the infantry was progressing very slowly. So until afternoon, when the further cavalry action will be related, the division stood fast.

In the Canadian Corps, the 3rd, 1st and 2nd Divisions were to hold the line gained on the 9th and consolidate it to be held as the main line of resistance in case of a heavy counter-attack, whilst the 32nd Division and 4th Canadian Division, guarded on the right by Brutinel's Force, passed through at 8 a.m. to gain the line (of the railway) Roye–Hattencourt–Hallu.

The day was fine and hot, with a slight ground mist which persisted until after 8 a.m., thus favouring a concealed advance. As on the 9th, the operation began well. The 8th Canadian Brigade (3rd Canadian Division), on the right, by an early morning attack captured le Quesnoy, which had resisted all efforts on the previous day, just as the 11th Canadian Brigade had on that day laid its hands on le Quesnel. Assembled soon after midnight east of Bouchoir, the 2/Canadian Mounted Rifles had moved to a jumping off line about four hundred yards north and north-west of its objective, with machine-guns on its flanks. The advance took place at 4.20 a.m. with four tanks of the 5th Battalion following on each flank. The enemy's fire was heavy, and four tanks were knocked out ; but by 6.30 a.m. the Canadians had occupied le Quesnoy and an hour later were garrisoning the trench line on its eastern edge. The 1/Canadian Mounted Rifles followed the 2nd through the village, and, moving north-east, had by 9.15 a.m. occupied, as ordered, the old British front line trenches west and north-west of Parvillers.

For the general advance at 8 a.m. the 32nd Division Major-General T.S. Lambert[1]), which was in mass bivouac west of Beaucourt, 6 miles behind the front line, received orders by telephone at 8.15 p.m. on the 9th, followed by verbal instructions given at 9.15 p.m. to a General Staff officer of the division called to Corps headquarters, and again by written orders at 12.15 a.m.   The 96th and 97th Brigades (Br.-Generals A. C. Girdwood and J. R. M. Minshull-Ford), which were to lead, completed their approach in the ground mist without a hitch, although very few maps were available, and by zero hour were ready to cross the starting line behind the Canadian front line.   In support were the batteries of the 5th Canadian Division (not itself in France),   the LXXXVI (Mobile) Brigade R.G.A., and twenty tanks of the 4th and 5th Battalions.   Eight tanks, including four which had assisted in the early morning attack were allotted to each of the two attacking brigades and four kept in reserve.   The 32nd Division artillery, in consequence of the night bombing already mentioned, was late and did not come into action until 10.30 a.m.

The first part of the advance, although over open ground, was easy, as not only had the Canadians captured le Quesnoy, but the French on their right also had entered Erches. Then the old trench area was reached and heavy machine-gun fire encountered.   No co-operation came from the right or left, as the French in trying to move forward from Erches had lost heavily, and for the moment were unable to continue the attack, and the 4th Canadian Division, on the left, had not yet started. Br.-General Girdwood reinforced the 15th and 16/Lancashire Fusiliers with the 2/Manchester, and by 9.30 a.m. Wood 101 South (1,000 yards east of le Quesnoy), with two machine guns in it, was captured. Progress then became very slow ; but an hour later, the 96th Brigade had reached the cross-roads on the Roye highway to Andechy and Damery and the old German front line, although under very heavy fire from Square Wood, Middle Wood and Parvillers, and three or four tanks working ahead of the infantry had been destroyed by anti-tank gun fire.   In view of the situation on the right, Br.-General Girdwood sent an order to battalions to consolidate ; but before this could reach them they made another most determined

---

[1] He had received command in May, after commanding an infantry brigade in the 23rd Division.

advance, rushed and captured a German " pill-box " on the western edge of Square Wood and then the wood itself. The enemy at once shelled the wood and counter-attacked, and the battalions were forced back, Lieut.-Colonel H. K. Utterson (of the Dorsetshire Regiment), commanding the 15/Lancashire Fusiliers, being killed ; but they clung to the western strip of the wood and the pill-box, the line then, about 1.30 p.m., running northwards to Quarry Wood.

About 2 p.m. four tanks arrived and brigade orders were issued for the advance to be resumed against Damery Wood and village ; all four machines were, however, put out of action within ten minutes of crossing the old German front line.   Square Wood, though retaken, was lost again, and the final line remained as before.

The 97th Brigade, like the 96th, at first made good progress, delayed mainly by having to pass through gaps in two belts of wire of old back lines, on which machine guns were concentrated.   But soon the enemy was seen running back and the field and heavy artillery supporting, the 32nd Division was able to move forward from position to position. On approaching the old British front line, the 10/Argyll and Sutherland Highlanders, on the right, received heavy machine-gun fire ; the 5/Border Regiment (attached), on the left, reached this line, however, about 10 a.m., even got beyond it and obtained touch with the 1/Canadian Mounted Rifles, lying west of Parvillers, whilst on the left could now be seen men of the 10th Canadian Brigade advancing in extended order, with a field battery firing over them, and German infantry retiring in similar formation before them. Intact old German wire and machine-gun fire in front of Parvillers and Fouquescourt, although artillery fire was turned on these villages, prevented further advance, seven of the eight tanks working ahead of the infantry being put out of action by anti-tank gun fire.   It was past 11 a.m. before the Argyll reached the old British front line on which German gun-fire was now falling, and they could not get beyond it, though a few men did make their way through the wire in front of the old German line.

Varying reports of the course of the action had reached 32nd Division headquarters during the morning, and at one time it was believed that Parvillers had been captured.   At 3 p.m. the situation was thought to be that the 96th Brigade had been checked on a line running along the western edge of Square Wood and thence along the track which led to Parvillers (really the line ran to Quarry Wood), and that the 97th was held up on the western outskirts of Parvillers, and beyond this place was in the old German front line. Actually, except on the extreme right and left, the brigades had not been able to advance beyond the old British front line.

Major-General Lambert came to the conclusion that further progress could only be achieved by a properly combined attack supported by artillery and tanks. After visiting the two brigade headquarters, however, and learning of the stiffening of the enemy resistance, the severe casualties, and the small reserves—now only a portion of the reserve battalion of each brigade engaged—he decided that fresh troops and carefully planned artillery preparation were necessary. He reported in that sense to the Canadian Corps and ordered his troops to consolidate what had been won.

In the 4th Canadian Division the 10th and 12th Brigades were detailed to make the left attack. Each had attached to it, a machine-gun battery of eight guns, a field battery, a section of 4.5-inch howitzers, three 6-inch trench mortars, an engineer company and sixteen tanks.[1] The division in addition to its own field artillery had two Army brigades R.F.A. and a heavy mobile brigade R.G.A. attached.

In view of the trenches and obstacles in front, it was deemed that success would greatly depend on the tanks ; so as 8 a.m. approached, when, owing to delay in orders reaching tank headquarters, a sufficient number to warrant the launching of the attack had not arrived, the corps commander's consent to a postponement was obtained. Meantime, and until 11 a.m. Fouquescourt, Fransart and Maucourt were bombarded. It was not until 10.15 a.m. when 22 tanks were available, two hours after the advance of the 32nd Division, that the 44th, 46th, 72nd and 85th Battalions, with the 47th, 50th, 78th and 38th in support, and the tanks leading, crossed the starting line and went forward under a rolling barrage, which began when the front line was reached at 11 a.m.

The battalions of the 10th Canadian Brigade (Br.-General R. J. F. Hayter) encountered practically no resistance for the first thousand yards and until they reached the support

---

[1] Actually 10 tanks of the 1st and 3 of the 14th worked with the 10th Brigade and 12 of the 13th Battalion with the 12th.

trenches of the old British system. Then the enemy barrage came down and the attackers became involved in old trenches and wire. But the rolling barrage was excellent and the tanks were useful, only three of the ten with the brigade being put out of action ; so soon after 1 p.m. the 44th Canadian Battalion reached the old German front line west of Fouquescourt and an hour later the western edge of the village, whilst at 1.25 p.m. the 46th reported that it had reached its objective, a hundred yards east of the Fouques-court–Maucourt road, and was consolidating, that casualties had not been heavy, and that two field artillery brigades were moving forward to cover the advance to the final objective.

In the 12th Canadian Brigade also, in spite of opposition and enfilade fire from Lihons, the woods south-west of that village and the Lihons–Chaulnes ridge, a rapid advance of the 72nd and 85th Battalions had by 1.30 p.m. carried them through Maucourt and Chilly—where the tanks of the 13th Battalion, after dealing with many machine-gun posts, helped in the " mopping-up "—to the first objective, the old British front line beyond Chilly, a left defensive flank being formed in order to keep touch with the Australian troops.

The advanced German troops had been driven in, and a mile and a half of ground gained. Rumours of the de-moralization of the enemy began to circulate ; so at 2.25 p.m. the Cavalry Corps headquarters issued orders for the 3rd Cavalry Division to seize the high ground north of Roye, the 2nd to occupy Nesle (6¼ miles S.S.E. of Chaulnes) and the 1st to move to the low ground north-west of Warvillers behind the centre of the Canadian Corps. Little came of the attempted execution of these orders except casualties, as horsemen cannot charge entrenchments. The 3rd Cavalry Division sent the Canadian Cavalry Brigade along the Amiens–Roye road as the only feasible route, and at 3.30 p.m. it advanced through Bouchoir. A squadron of the Fort Garry Horse, the leading regiment, after passing through the 32nd Division found that Z Wood and Damery immedi-ately in front were still strongly held, so inclined to the right, crossed the Amiens–Roye road and, after galloping through a barrage and riding through wire and over trenches, captured Andechy, which contained a large supply depot ; but after handing it over to the French, who quickly

appeared, the squadron could make no further progress.[1]
The squadrons following tried to take Z Wood by a charge
along the Amiens–Roye road, but were shot down. A further
attempt was prevented by the intervention of an infantry
brigadier who represented that such action was suicidal.

The 4th Cavalry Brigade (Br.-General C. H. Rankin) of
the 2nd Cavalry Division advanced from Rouvroy, but was
driven back by fire from Fouquescourt, which was still in
the enemy's hands.

The ground and the situation were as unsuitable for
whippet tanks as for cavalry. The sixteen machines of the
3rd Tank Battalion did not come into action, but nevertheless
one was knocked out near Rouvroy by gun-fire. Seven
whippets of the 6th Battalion also came under this fire and
lost one ; the remaining six tried to force their way to
Parvillers over the old trench system ; all were ditched and
three received direct hits. The commanding officer of the
second detachment, after making a reconnaissance on foot,
decided that an advance was not practicable ; for in addition
to the obstacle of ground the Germans had two field guns in
Middle Wood and more in the outskirts of Parvillers which
could fire at point-blank range at the tanks as they advanced.
Only seven out of the fourteen whippets rallied in the
evening.

So far from the conditions being ripe for the employment
of cavalry and whippets, even in the second stage of the
infantry advance very slight progress was achieved. Under
a good barrage, the right of the 10th Canadian Brigade (parts
of the 44th and 47th Battalions) entered Fouquescourt, but
gun-fire was still falling on the village and led to a withdrawal.
By 4 p.m., however, the enemy was dribbling back. At this
moment two tanks of the 14th Battalion appeared, one was
surrounded by Germans and blown up, but in the wake of
the other the Canadians re-entered Fouquescourt and by
6 p.m. were in possession of it, although mopping up took
some little time longer. To get touch with the 32nd Division,
the right flank was extended round the village. On the left,
owing at first to enfilade fire from Fouquescourt, the 50th
Canadian Battalion, which had passed through the 46th,
was unable to reach its objective and did not do so until

---

[1] F.O.A. vii (i), p. 188, states that the XXXV Corps arrived " towards
" midday at Andechy and Guerbigny [south of Erches] ". Canadian
accounts record that it was 4 p.m. before the French arrived in Andechy.

the village had been captured. Later, at 7.40 p.m., a general advance of the 10th Canadian Brigade took place, supported by the eight remaining tanks. This, in spite of stiff opposition, by 8.45 p.m. had carried the left as far as the Roye–Hattencourt–Hallu railway and, on the right with gaps which had to be patrolled, extended to Fouquescourt.

The 12th Canadian Brigade, with the 8 remaining tanks (3 had been hit by artillery fire, or disabled by bombs, and one ditched in the old trenches, beyond recovery), sent its supporting battalions through the leaders, and although the old trench system hampered movement, the 78th entered Hallu about 2 p.m. well ahead of the 10th Brigade still held up at Fouquescourt ; the 38th, owing to fire from the front and from the Lihons–Chaulnes ridge, with difficulty reached the Chilly–Lihons road, where it lay pinned down by fire. About 3.30 p.m., whilst the brigade was thus scattered, a strong enemy detachment was seen advancing from the east and north-east against Chilly, still held by its captors, the 72nd Battalion. By short rushes the Germans in places came within fifteen yards of the line before being driven off with very heavy losses. At 7.30 p.m. they repeated the attack, trying to reach Chilly round the left flank of the 78th Battalion in Hallu.

The headquarters of this battalion were at the northern end of Chilly, and all its available personnel were put into the firing line, whilst another party of the battalion attacked the intruders in flank, so that they quickly drew off, again suffering heavily. Gaps were then filled, and during the night two companies of the 38th Battalion worked their way forward to complete the line between the 78th at Hallu and the Amiens–Chaulnes railway.

In the Australian Corps, Lieut.-General Monash ordered the 1st Australian Division to move to the attack of Lihons and Chaulnes at 8 a.m., the zero hour fixed by the Canadian Corps. The 2nd Australian Brigade handed over the left half of its front to the 3rd, which came up during the night from south of Harbonnières, but was not in position until a quarter of an hour before Zero, its deployment having been spotted by a low-flying German aeroplane which at once fired two white flares to indicate a target for the artillery. The 1st Australian Brigade (Br.-General I. G. Mackay), released from watching Chipilly by the 13th Brigade of the 4th Australian Division, came into reserve. No tanks were available, as the crews of those which had survived were tired out ; but a barrage was arranged in haste, to fall, at 7.45 a.m., seven hundred yards ahead of the presumed front line. The right battalion of the 2nd Australian Division was to guard the northern flank.

Warned by the aeroplane signal and by the barrage, which was too far ahead to be of any use, as soon as the 6th, 5th and 9th and 11th Battalions advanced, the 25th of the 2nd Australian Division conforming, the Germans received them with furious fire, and a very large number of company officers fell. A thousand yards west of Lihons, on the summit of the hill, lies a wood (Crépey Wood), an oblong of about five hundred yards' frontage and half that depth. A tangle of undergrowth with gaunt skeleton trees still standing, it was in the sector of the 9th Battalion, and around and in it the fiercest fighting of the day took place.

The first advance carried the Australians past the flanks of the wood but not into it. Posts were established on all sides of it, but all except those in the south were in the course of time swept away. On that flank the 4th Canadian Division did not start until 10.15 a.m., but the 12th Canadian Brigade sent forward one battalion to protect the right of the 2nd Australian Brigade. Over almost level ground, with occasional small buildings and copses and seamed with old trenches, the 6th and 5th Battalions of the latter brigade could make little further progress and lost heavily. Then the arrival of one tank and the progress of the Canadians somewhat eased the situation. The 9th Battalion meantime, aided by parts of the 5th and 10th Battalions (the latter from support) and the fire of two trench mortars brought up on mules, cleared Crépey Wood sector by sector, and the 11th and 25th Battalions, north of it, fought their way to the Lihons–Framerville road.

After several vain attempts during the afternoon to retake Crépey Wood, at 5.30 p.m. the Germans began to bombard it and then counter-attacked direct and northwards of it ; they entered the wood only to be driven out or slain. They then finally desisted, but their resistance in this quarter had delayed the 1st Australian Division, so that the right was nearly three miles behind the Canadian left.

North of the Somme some progress was made, the old Amiens Defence Line being reached on the whole front, and later when the 13th Australian Brigade came into action Etinehem was captured and the right was advanced almost to Bray.

During the night of the 9th–10th the 1st Battalion of the American 131st Regiment came up on the right of the 2nd, and shortly after 6 a.m., in accordance with orders issued by the 58th Division at 11.15 p.m. on the 9th, the two battalions pushed through the outlying portions of the woods (Bois de Tailles) in the Chipilly ravine. In spite of much opposition from snipers and from both artillery and machine guns, they continued on to the high ground beyond, so that by noon (10th August) the old Amiens Defence Line had been made good.[1]

The 175th Brigade of the 58th Division, still in the line, did not move so early or in such force as the Americans, and was more cautious, sending forward first only strong patrols and then one company of the 9/London. The reports which came back varied. Towards 11 a.m. the brigade heard that the patrols which had entered the Bois de Tailles on their front had been driven out of it by a heavy concentration of mustard gas and that the ravine was being shelled ; a few minutes later came information that the wood was clear of Germans, that the remaining three companies of the 9/London had entered it, but that advance to the Amiens Defence Line was prevented by gas backed by strong fire action. The 12th Division on the left also reported that the defence was too strong to be overcome without a regular attack with artillery and tanks, and that Major-General Higginson intended to organize one for 6 p.m. A combined attack of the 175th Brigade and the 12th Division was then arranged, the G.S.O.1 of the division coming over to Br.-General W. J. Maxwell-Scott's head-quarters at the brickyard behind Bois de Tailles for the

---

[1] For this Line see Sketch 6 or Map I.

purpose. But about 4.30 p.m. just as the latter officer was about to hold a conference with his commanding officers news reached him that the 9/London had at 2.10 p.m. occupied the major part of the Amiens Defence Line in the brigade sector and was in touch with the Americans on the right. Having passed on this information to the 12th Division Br.-General Maxwell-Scott sent up the 12/London and 5/R. Berkshire to the right and left of the 9/London, and they secured the rest of the line allotted to the brigade up to the light railway without opposition. Consolidation was easy, as the trenches of the old Amiens Defence Line were in fair condition and the Germans had left behind enormous dumps of wire, which were utilized to increase the existing belt on the eastern side.

The 37th Brigade (12th Division), with the 9/Essex (35th Brigade) and six tanks of the 10th Battalion and specially supported by the 169th (Army) Brigade R.F.A., made its attack at 6 p.m. across the flat top of the main ridge, with the 6/Buffs, 9/Essex and 6/Queen's in line. It was entirely successful, and a howitzer battery was captured; but a knoll, Hill 105, from which the principal resistance had come, remained in enemy hands. The trench running across the knoll was cleared by the tanks and entered by men of the 6/Buffs, who were unable, however, to retain it.

The attack of the 10th and 13th Australian Brigades on either bank of the Somme was specially planned by Lieut.-General Monash himself. It was intended that both brigades should break through at night (9.30 p.m. being selected) at one place, in the direction of Proyart (on the south side of the Somme, immediately south of Chuignolles) and Etinehem (on the north side), respectively, and then, turning inwards towards the river, roll up and cut off the Germans. A few tanks were allotted to each brigade, but more for the purpose of alarming the enemy by their noise than any other reason, for the experience of the use of tanks at night was very small. The artillery was not to fire on the front of attack except for intermittent bursts of the heavy batteries on Chuignes valley and the roads and bridges farther east.

The operations of the 10th Australian Brigade were a complete failure. The brigadier did not understand the purpose of the tanks, and they were put in the front of the column, and alarmed the enemy. The movement was discovered whilst the long drawn-out columns were still on the Roman Road, and shelling, bombing and machine-gun fire forced it to halt. Every time a tank moved there was a renewal of the fire, and eventually the attack was abandoned.

The attack of the 13th Australian Brigade was made against the Etinehem spur—a tactical feature, almost as important as the Chipilly spur, commanding the southern bank of the Somme. The 50th and 49th Battalions, which after marching up the Corbie–Bray road assembled astride the Chipilly–Bray and Corbie–Bray roads respectively, so as to pass by the right of the Americans. Each had one company as advanced guard. They were covered by the cross fire of machine guns. The four tanks of the 10th Tank Battalion available were ordered merely to move along the Corbie–Bray road making as much noise as possible, and then return.

Little resistance was encountered except for an occasional burst of machine-gun fire, and after sending up a flare which revealed the presence of the 50th Battalion the Germans ceased fire and retired rapidly, taking most of their guns with them. At the road junction about fifteen hundred yards west of Bray, the 50th Battalion turned south and occupied the Etinehem spur, but not quite as far as the tip, whilst the 49th formed on its left and established a defensive flank facing north along the Bray–Méaulte road, in touch with the American 131st Regiment in the Amiens Defence Line.

A company of the 51st Battalion detailed to mop up the village of Etinehem, which is tucked away in a small re-entrant, entered it at dawn on the 11th to find that it had been evacuated.[1]

It was obvious that the offensive was petering out on the whole front, like so many others before it, as the initial success had not been exploited with the necessary rapidity

---

[1] The history of the *27th Division*, pp. 91–2, admits that there was "sudden fear" and "the infantry was overcome by panic" and that the way into Bray stood open. ". . . The terrible night of the 10th–11th "August will remain for ever in the memories of all who took part".

and daring. General Rawlinson pushed the advance with caution from one good line to another, and did not urge infiltration. This hesitation to exploit recklessly can be understood ; for by this time the German defensive tactics were well known : the retirement of the advanced troops might be only a prelude to a heavy counter-attack by the *Eingreif* divisions stationed close at hand.

In view of the Amiens offensive possibly coming to a stop, or at any rate not going farther than Roye–Chaulnes–Bray–Dernancourt, on the morning of the 10th August Sir Douglas Haig, from his advanced headquarters at Wiry, sent a General Staff officer to General Horne (First Army) with instructions that he should complete the details of his plans, already in hand,[1] for the capture of La Bassée and the Aubers ridge in conjunction with an advance by the Third Army against Bapaume and of the Second Army against Kemmel. The situation had indeed developed exactly as Maréchal Foch had expected on the 2nd August, when after handing over the French First Army to the British Commander-in-Chief, he said, " Go as far as you can the first " day, go on again on the second, and again on the third, " before the enemy can concentrate his reserves. After that " you will certainly have to pause ; but you may succeed " in going so far that the enemy will have to clear out of " the Amiens salient. Renew the attack as soon as you can " and you may force him over the Somme ".[2]

At 11 a.m. Maréchal Foch arrived at Wiry, bringing with him a general directive which embodied his intentions as regards further operations. In translation—it hardly admits of summarizing—it was as follows : [3]

" I. The action of the British Fourth Army and the " French First Army should be continued eastwards in " the general direction of Ham [on the Somme], the right " of the British Fourth Army following the line Gruny " [3 miles N.N.E. of Roye]–Ham, the left of the French " First Army south of this line :

" The British Fourth Army will endeavour to reach " the Somme below Ham, in order to make preparations " for a crossing ; at the same time it will continue its " action astride that river in the reach Bray–Péronne ;

---

[1] " 1918 " Vol. III, p. 312. See Sketch 1.
[2] Recorded by Lieut.-General Sir John Du Cane.
[3] See Sketch I.

" the French First Army will support this advance
" with the road Ham–Guiscard [6 miles south of Ham]
" as its objective.

" II. From now onwards the march of the French
" Third Army will be directed on Lassigny–Noyon, in
" order to exploit the advance of the French First Army
" and clear the Montdidier area, and later the Noyon
" area, of the enemy :

" III. The attention of the Field-Marshal is drawn
" to the importance of making preparations as soon as
" possible for operations of the British Third Army in
" the general direction of Bapaume and Péronne, in
" order to break the enemy's front and exploit any with-
" drawal without delay ".

A discussion on the directive ensued. Maréchal Foch was
strongly in favour of pushing on to the line Noyon–Ham–
Péronne and securing the Somme bridgeheads, in other words,
for continuing the frontal attack and extending the battle
to the right. Sir Douglas Haig's plan, on the other hand,
was to make the main operation the proposed threat on the
left, by the British Third Army, against the right of the
Germans opposing the French First Army and the British
Fourth Army rather than to continue the frontal attack of
these latter Armies against stiffening opposition. He pointed
out the difficulty of carrying out the Maréchal's plan unless
the enemy was quite demoralized and the Somme could be
crossed at his heels, and he outlined his own proposals for
capturing the Aubers ridge and thus freeing the coal mine
area round Béthune, and for movements against Bapaume
and Monchy le Preux.[1] Maréchal Foch agreed that such
action was desirable, but thought that the advance east of
Amiens could be carried out at the same time as the operations farther north. This Sir Douglas Haig pointed out
would be possible only if the opposition on the present
battlefield did not increase, but he thought that this was
bound to happen as more German reserves had arrived ;
it would then become necessary to put into execution the
plan for the advance of the British left on Bapaume and
Monchy le Preux. Maréchal Foch, however, was confident
that the Germans were demoralized, since the French First

---

[1] Monchy le Preux was on high ground four and a half miles south-east
of Arras, and from it good observation could be obtained of the enemy's
position. It had been evacuated by the Third Army during the German
offensive of March 1918.

and Third Armies were not encountering serious resistance—
the Germans in front of them had in fact retired.[1] Sir
Douglas Haig, whilst not going so far as to believe in the
demoralization of all the German divisions, admitted that
some might be badly shaken and that a continued offensive
east of Amiens might drive the enemy considerably farther
back, since his resistance had not become so strong as to
preclude further advance.   After the interview, therefore,
he gave orders to the French First and to the British Fourth
and Third Armies in the sense of Maréchal Foch's directive.[2]
His instructions to the Third Army were that it should
" carry out raids and minor operations in order to ascertain
" the enemy's intentions on the Albert–Arras front, and take
" immediate advantage of any favourable situation which the
" main operations may create, and push advanced guards in
" the general direction of Bapaume ".   General Byng, on
the same day, issued orders for contact to be maintained
with the enemy by advanced guards (the defence outposts
and their reserves) should the enemy make any withdrawal.

General Pétain and General Fayolle on their part,[3] with
the road Soissons–Chaulnes as the first objective, ordered the
French Tenth Army to be prepared at short notice to extend
the battle to the right and follow the progress of the Third,
south of the Oise.   The French Third Army was to " press
" forward with the maximum of activity " on its whole front,
and the First after capturing Roye was to advance against
the Canal du Nord between Moyencourt and Bussy (the one
12 miles and the other 3 miles north of Noyon).   To ensure
that the commander of the Third Army need not trouble
his head about his right flank, his XVIII Corps, on the right,
was transferred to the Tenth Army.

In the afternoon Sir Douglas Haig visited Canadian Corps
headquarters, now moved forward to some dug-outs in a
little hill south-east of Demuin,[4] and explained what was
required to Lieut.-General Currie and to General Rawlinson
who had come there.   The commander of the Fourth Army
was opposed to further attack on his front.   When told it
was the wish of Maréchal Foch, he became almost insubordi-
nate and replied " Are you commanding the British Army

---

[1] Note II at the end of Chapter, compiled from German sources, shows
that Foch's view had some justification.
[2] See Appendix XIV.
[3] F.O.A. vii (i), pp. 190–1, Annexes 600 and 602.
[4] See Sketch 7.

" or is Maréchal Foch " ? While the discussion was proceeding a message arrived from the Cavalry Corps, timed
2.25 p.m., giving the information on which Lieut.-General
Kavanagh had sent his cavalry divisions forward—that the
enemy's opposition was diminishing—which seemed to settle
the question of advance. The Commander-in-Chief then
went on to visit the headquarters of the divisions of the
Canadian Corps, and towards 6 p.m., at le Quesnel, he heard
a different account of the situation from the 32nd Division.
Major-General Lambert had just returned from visiting his
brigades. His opinion was that the enemy's opposition had
stiffened : on the old battlefield ground the numerous
trenches and shell craters favoured delaying tactics : there
was much intact wire and there were many enemy machine
guns. Sir Douglas Haig came away more determined than
ever to press upon Maréchal Foch the value of an offensive
by the Third and First Armies, and this determination was
not lessened when he heard that the total number of prisoners
taken during the day by the Fourth Army was only just
over one thousand. As it was getting late, he decided to
postpone his visits to the Australian and III Corps until
next day.

Under date of the 10th August the French Intelligence
Branch handed to Maréchal Foch an appreciation of the
German situation.[1] It was considered that in view of the
Allied offensive the enemy would probably carry out further
retirements in order to establish himself on positions whose
flanks were not threatened and on which he could reorganize
his divisions.[2]

" It may be expected that the first retirement will be
" towards the Hindenburg Line, resting to the north on
" the Artois heights and to the south on the steep banks
" of the Aisne east of Soissons ; the second retirement
" would be to the general line of the Serre and the Aisne,
" called the Hunding–Brunhilde position ; the third to
" the position Hirson–Mézières–Sedan [not an official
" German position]. Thus the great salient formed by
" the enemy's front in the general direction of Paris

---

[1] See End-paper B.
[2] The appreciation is partly reproduced in the text, but given at
length in F.O.A. vii (i), Annexe 597.

" would be gradually reduced. These retirements would
" probably be accompanied by the abandonment of the
" St. Mihiel salient and later followed by retirement in
" Alsace to the line Strasbourg–Molsheim [*sic*],[1] but this,
" for both political and economic reasons, is not likely
" to be carried out except at the last extremity.

" The first retirement would lead to a shortening of
" the front by about twenty-five miles ; the second by
" about the same length ; the third would produce
" another diminution of some thirty-six miles : a total
" of 86 miles. The front to be held would thus fall from
" a total length of about 440 miles to about 350 miles,
" but the increase in the total number of the Allied
" divisions, the parallel increase of our reserves, and the
" possibility of our acting simultaneously in a greater
" number of sectors will force the enemy to maintain
" great density on the whole of the front, and thus he
" will be unable to hold thinly sectors like those of the
" Vosges are at the present moment. Taking into account
" all these general considerations, and on the supposition
" that the enemy must keep a certain co-efficient of
" density on the different parts of the front where he
" will have to provide reserves for a battle, it may be
" concluded as an approximate estimate that by the
" various retirements the German High Command will
" have at its disposal in reserve about a hundred
" divisions.

" This figure should be considered as a maximum, as
" it is based on the hypothesis that the total number of
" German divisions on the Western Front will remain
" 205. And one may reckon that this total will not be
" maintained owing to lack of reinforcements ; this will
" naturally lead the enemy to break up some of the
" divisions [by the time of the Armistice the number of
" German divisions on the Western Front had fallen to
" 184 plus 2 Austrian] ".

The conclusion therefore was drawn that the Allies might
be certain of retaining superiority in reserves.

---

[1] Molsheim is only 13 miles S.S.W. of Strasbourg. This Strasbourg-
Molsheim position, sometimes called the Breusch position (along the
river Breusch), was organized in peace time. Perhaps therefore
Strasbourg-Molsheim may be taken to mean the defences organized
before the war nside the German frontier.

NOTE I

The French on the 10th August

(Sketch 4)

The French First Army started early, at 5.30 a.m. after 30 minutes' artillery fire. " Its advance was greatly facilitated " by the fact that the enemy had retreated in the course of the night". The town of Montdidier was found completely destroyed. The enemy seemed " to be retreating on a wide front leaving " behind him only weak detachments". The G.O.C. XXXV Corps ordered his divisions to press on.   " It is no longer ", he said, " a case of methodical, slow and carefully mounted " attacks with a debauch of artillery fire, but of strong reconnais- " sances working by encirclement and pushing forward rapidly ". But the XXXI Corps on the left could not advance beyond Andechy ; and in the course of the afternoon the X and XXXV Corps " were compelled to halt in front of the old French trenches " of 1916 ".

The Third Army started even earlier, at 4.20 a.m., without any artillery preparation, its right division standing fast and the other six swinging forward with the right of the First Army and coming to a stop with it, the total advance of the wheeling flank being six miles. The outskirts of Roye were reached.[1]

NOTE II

The Germans on the 10th August

Further reinforcements reached the German front opposite the Fourth Army, drawn from the reserves of Armies lying to the north of the *Second Army*, the *Seventeenth Army* parting with a total of four, the *Sixth* with two and the *Fourth* with five ; whilst the *Eighteenth Army*, opposite to the French First Army, was strengthened by a total of three, drawn from the *Seventh* (two) and the *Ninth* (one) on its left. But in addition to the three divisions which had arrived on the 9th August, only four more, all warned on the morning of the 8th, actually reached the field ; they formed almost a complete new line from the Amiens–Roye road to Chaulnes, thus mainly in front of the Canadian Corps. These divisions were the *221st* (from the *Seventh Army*, Noyon area), which early took position astride the Amiens–Roye road near Bouchoir ; the *121st* (from the *Ninth Army*,

---

[1] The little town was not taken, as Map 21 in F.O.A. vii (i) shows.

Laon area) which was sent to the line Goyencourt–Hattencourt ;
the *Alpine Corps* (from the *Fourth Army*, Tourcoing area) which
arrived on the Hattencourt–Hallu front early on the morning
of the 10th ; and the *38th* (from the *Sixth Army*, Cambrai area)
which went to Chaulnes. Considerable delay occurred in the
transport. The *38th Division*, warned to be ready at 2 p.m.
on the 8th, did not begin to leave until 7.30 p.m., one infantry
regiment by lorry and two by train, and they did not reach
Chaulnes until the evening of the 9th. They found that " troops
" were falling back in disorderly flight, among them drunken
" Bavarians, who shouted to the *94th Regiment* ' What do you
" ' war-prolongers want ? If the enemy were only on the Rhine—
" ' the war would then be over ' ". (" Regt. No. 94 ", p. 265.)
To the *263rd Reserve Regiment* (*79th Reserve Division*), sent up
to take the place of the *1st Reserve Division*, which was " pouring
back ", some of its men shouted " We thought that we had set
" the thing going, now you asses are corking up the hole again "
(" Res. Regt. No. 263 ", pp. 193–4). The only news the staff
of the *38th Division* received was that there might be remains
of the *117th* and *119th Divisions* in front, but in any case there
was a wide gap between them which had to be filled. By early
morning of the 10th the division was in front of Chaulnes and the
gap filled. In Nesle, where part of the *Alpine Corps* detrained,
it found a chaos of scared men, loose horses and a confused block
of vehicles. " There was general excitement and fear of renewed
" air attacks. . . . In the early hours of the 10th August no
" one could give a clear idea of the actual position at the front ;
" no one knew anything about troops on right and left, or about
" the divisions in position, . . . individuals and all ranks in
" large parties were wandering wildly about, but soon for the
" most part finding their way to the rear, . . . only here and
" there were a few isolated batteries in soldierly array, ready to
" support the reinforcing troops." (" Das deutsche Alpenkorps
im Westen ", p. 54.) The staff of the supply depots had fled,
abandoning their stores (" Res. Regt. No. 263 ", p. 193).

Of the original divisions, five (the *43rd Reserve, 13th, 109th,*
117th and *225th*) had been or were on the point of being relieved.
At 8.15 a.m. the corps had ordered the *221st, 79th Reserve* and
119th Divisions, opposite the Canadian Corps, back to the line
Fresnoy–Hattencourt–Fonchette in two bounds ; but as the
121st Division, the *Alpine Corps* and *38th Division* had now
arrived behind them, at 10.30 a.m., the *Second Army* counter-
manded this and ordered the three divisions to remain in the line
Damery–Parvillers–Fouquescourt.

The effect of the three days' fighting on the German leaders
has been recorded in " Das Weltkriegsende ", pp. 90–1, by
Colonel B. Schwertfeger, who was one of the military technical

members of the *Reichstag* Commission which enquired into the loss of the War.   On the 11th, the Kaiser attended a meeting of the higher leaders at Avesnes, Hindenburg-Ludendorff's headquarters.   Ludendorff declared that a heavy defeat had been suffered, that the warlike spirit of some of the divisions left a good deal to be desired, and that, as quoted from the history of the *94th Regiment*, troops falling back had shouted to one division as it came up the words " Strike-breakers " and " War-prolongers ".   When the Kaiser and the Crown Prince suggested that too much had been asked of the troops, Ludendorff replied that the collapse of the *Second Army* on the 8th August could not be accounted for by the divisions being overtired.[1] He offered his resignation, but it was not accepted (Lossberg, p. 358).

The Kaiser then uttered the historic words " I see that we " must strike a balance.   We have nearly reached the limit " of our powers of resistance.   The war must be ended " (" Kaiser " und Revolution ", p. 43, by Major Niemann, who was in attendance on the Kaiser).   A meeting at Spa was arranged for the 13th.   Meantime it was hoped to hold a good, shortened front : Ribecourt (five miles south-west of Noyon and close to the Oise)— Roye–Albert.

Thus the collapse of Germany began not in the Navy, not in the Homeland, not in any of the sideshows, but on the Western Front in consequence of defeat in the field.[2]

The local commanders were in favour of retiring at once to the line of the Somme—Voyennes (west of Ham) to Péronne— extended on the south along the Canal du Nord to Noyon and on the north to Bapaume and Biache (in the Hindenburg Line east of Arras), for their men were worn out by fighting in shell holes or shell-trap villages to which supply was very difficult.   They were overruled, but the withdrawal mentioned was actually carried out at the end of the month.

---

[1] Crown Prince Rupprecht records of this period (ii, pp. 430 and 441) that the censor found in letters home such phrases as " It is time " that our Government got peace, more and more Americans are coming " out and we are having a foul time : too many hounds are the death " of the hare ".   " The war will end when the great capitalists have killed " us all ".   " You at home must strike, but make no mistake about it, " and raise revolution, then peace will come ".   " The air is literally " poisoned by British airmen, so that we cannot understand where the " newspapers get the stories of the heroic deeds of our aviators ".

Of four divisions it was reported that the attitude of the men was " bad " and they were " little reliable ".

[2] In the Balkans the battle which broke the German-Bulgarian front did not begin until 15th September ; in Palestine the final advance which broke the German-Turkish, not until 19th September, and in Italy the Battle of Vittorio Veneto, not until 24th October.

Colonel von Tschischwitz, the Chief of the General Staff of the defeated *Second Army* was removed, and partly no doubt that the blame for further defeat should not fall on either of the two Crown Princes, O.H.L. orders were given, to take effect on the 12th, that the two Armies engaged in the battle, the *Eighteenth* and the *Second* of Crown Prince Rupprecht's Group,[1] and the *Ninth Army* of the German Crown Prince's Group, east of the *Eighteenth*, should be formed into a new Group of Armies under General von Boehn, whose *Seventh Army* had made the Chemin des Dames offensive in May, with Major-General von Lossberg, who had been chief General Staff officer of the *Fourth Army* in the Lys offensive in April, as his chief of the staff.

---

[1] The *Eighteenth Army* had been transferred from the German Crown Prince's Group on 23rd July on account of the strain on the latter's staff after the French attack of the 18th. (Rupprecht ii, p. 426.)

CHAPTER VIII

THE BATTLE OF AMIENS—(*concluded*)

FOURTH AND CONCLUDING DAY 11TH AUGUST, 1918

(End-Paper A, Sketches 4, 8)

In accordance with Maréchal Foch's wishes and Sir Douglas Haig's orders, on the evening of the 10th August both General Debeney and General Rawlinson issued formal operation orders for " the continuation of the offensive ". Those of the French First Army[1] added to this definition of the intention : " the attacks will be resumed at dawn " ; fixed boundaries between corps, giving Bussy (north of Noyon) and Ham as the farthest points ;[2] directed the II Cavalry Corps to " seek opportunity to advance in front of " the infantry " ; and instructed all corps to reorganize their artillery.

General Rawlinson ordered the Fourth Army [3] " to press " on to the Somme between Ham (exclusive) and Péronne " and establish bridgeheads on the right bank of the river " ; north of the Somme a strong position on the general line then occupied was to be established and to be " held at all costs " as a defensive flank to the Fourth Army " ; the Cavalry Corps was to " assist " in the operations. Railheads had by now been pushed forward[4] ; Supply railheads were opened at Boves, Longueau and Corbie, an ammunition railhead at Petit Blangy and a field force canteen at Villers Bretonneux.

It was left, as on previous days, for the G.O.C. Canadian Corps to decide on the hour of advance, " which should be " as early as possible ". The hour fixed by Lieut.-General Currie was 4.20 a.m.

---

[1] F.O.A. vii. (ii), Annexe 605.
[2] For these places see End-paper B.
The orders of the G.A.R., which directed the Third Army to " push " the enemy actively on its whole front" and the Tenth Army to be prepared for its left to follow the progress of the Third, mentioned that the First Army " after taking Roye should advance to the Canal du Nord " which it will reach between Bussy and Moyencourt (south of Nesle) ".
[3] Appendix XV.
[4] See Map 3.

At dawn a ground mist again covered the battlefield, but the day gradually grew warmer and became dry and dusty. The French Third and First Armies, except near the junction of the latter with the British, where the gains were " fort " restreints " owing to " gros obstacles comme dans le " secteur britannique ", effected an advance on their whole front of about 1½ miles[1] ; the Canadian and Australian Corps, restrained early in the day by the Fourth Army headquarters, although nearly all the heavy artillery, 60-pdrs., 6-inch and 8-inch howitzers, was now up,[2] made little progress against the German defences, but were for good reasons not encouraged to press on.[3]   They were indeed, subjected to counter-attack ; to oppose their ten tired divisions the enemy had now on the Fourth Army front south of the Somme twelve untired divisions, nine of which had come into the battle since the morning of the 8th August and three were entirely fresh, besides some remnants of the original seven divisions in the line.   But nothing worse happened than that the left of the Canadian Corps, exposed as the Australians were not up in line with it, fell back a short distance.   No opportunity for the use of cavalry presented itself and in the course of the afternoon the three cavalry divisions, with the attached whippet tanks, were withdrawn, two to the neighbourhood of Amiens and the third to Ignaucourt–Cayeux, less one brigade which remained with the Australian Corps.

In the Canadian Corps, the 32nd and 4th Canadian Divisions were left in the line to make the attack, the 3rd, 1st and 2nd continuing to consolidate the old Amiens Defence Line ; these three divisions were, however, warned to be ready to pass through the leaders on the morning of the 12th. A good proportion of the batteries were well forward, the field artillery standing in the open, the heavy in depressions of the ground and such other cover as could be found.   All put up overhead camouflage screening.   Their difficulty in providing support was that the location of the enemy's

[1] See Sketch 4.
[2] The artillery at the disposal of the Fourth Army had not yet been reduced.   Four Army Brigades R.F.A. left it for the Third Army on 11th August.   The next transfer was on the 20th, when the VIII Brigade R.G.A. (9·2-inch howitzers) left.
[3] See Sketch 8.

F *

defence lines and the position of his guns were only vaguely known, not being marked on the maps as in trench warfare ; so no assistance could be given to the infantry except by rolling and standing barrages, and by firing on the villages and woods, and on such special targets as presented themselves to the observers, if information about them could be given to the batteries in sufficient time to be of value.

The 32nd Division was quite prepared to resume the attack ; for Major-General Lambert, who had already made divisional plans, had held a conference and given his formal orders at 11.30 p.m. before the corps written orders issued at 10.15 p.m. reached him at midnight. The zero hour originally fixed by the division had been 8.30 a.m. ; then it was found that neither the battalions nor the sixteen tanks of the 4th and 5th Battalions detailed to support them and hidden at Warvillers 4 miles away, could be ready even by 8.30 a.m., still less 4.20 a.m. as proposed by the corps, so 9.30 a.m. was finally selected.[1]

The 14th Brigade (Br.-General L. P. Evans), not engaged on the previous day, led the attack of the 32nd Division, with one company of the 96th Brigade and a battalion (less one company) of the 97th attached. The first objective was the line Damery Wood–Damery–Parvillers–La Chavatte. Damery and Parvillers, with the space between them, were not, however, to be attacked frontally, but kept under heavy artillery[2] and machine-gun fire, whilst the infantry pushed by them ; at Zero + 62 minutes when fire lifted from them, the two villages were to be assaulted from the flanks and rear.

The approach march was made and the forming up completed without detection ; but after that all went wrong. The French 126th Division when it attacked at 4.30 a.m. had failed to gain possession of Z Wood ; so the right flank was enfiladed ; the rolling barrage fired by three brigades of field artillery dropped, it was stated, five hundred instead of three hundred yards ahead of the starting line and thus left many German machine guns untouched ; a line of machine-guns in a ditch two hundred yards in front of Parvillers, in

---

[1] Notice of the change of hour was sent to the French 126th Division on the right ; but the message reporting the change of that division's headquarters miscarried, and the 32nd Division's notice was delivered at the vacated headquarters and did not arrive in time to stop the French, who unfortunately attacked early and were driven back.

[2] The number of brigades R.G.A., with howitzers and 60-pdrs., employed in the 32nd Division sector seems to have been 4. The Canadian Corps had a total of 7 plus 2 mobile brigades R.G.A.

particular, continued in undisturbed action ; German trench mortars, too, concealed in shell holes also fired without hindrance ; finally a belt of wire 30 to 50 feet deep and waist high held up the attackers. Twelve out of the sixteen tanks were quickly put out of action. Of the eight tanks of the 5th Battalion which arrived in time and were directed towards Damery, six were knocked out by direct hits, the other two entered and cleared Damery twice ; but the infantry, owing mainly to enfilade fire from north and south, could not take advantage of this. Of the eight tanks of the 4th Battalion directed towards Parvillers, which arrived late, three were put out of action by an anti-tank gun, three were badly ditched in the old defensive system, and the remaining two recognizing the impossibility of their task returned to their rendezvous.

Directly the 1/Dorsetshire, 5th/6th Royal Scots (14th Brigade) and 2/K.O.Y.L.I. (97th Brigade) advanced they came under very heavy fire all along the front, but by 11 a.m., with the help of the two tanks mentioned above, the Dorsetshire got within a hundred yards of Damery, but no farther. Near Parvillers no progress whatever could be made,[1] and the K.O.Y.L.I. could advance no more than two hundred yards towards La Chavatte.

At 10.5 a.m. the 32nd Division received a telephone message from the Canadian Corps to the effect that the Army commander—and he confirmed it later in the day— did not wish the attack to be pressed very strongly if it would entail heavy casualties. Major-General Lambert at once rode to the headquarters of the 14th and 97th Brigades and gave orders that the reserves were not to be used unless the situation showed good prospects. At 12.30 p.m. he received a second message directing him to consolidate the ground won unless more could be gained at small cost. Towards 1 p.m. he seemed to see an opportunity to exploit the advance made towards Damery, which place appeared to be weakly held, by putting in the reserve battalion, 15/Highland L.I., of the 14th Brigade. The enemy's fire did not, however, slacken, and Br.-General Evans, after communicating with divisional headquarters, refrained from further advance. Thus the total gain was a wedge of ground about a thousand yards deep, which had Damery (exclusive) at its apex.

[1] Parvillers was surrounded by " an old wired position ". " Res. Regt. " No 261 ", p. 105.

During the night the 32nd Division (less artillery) was relieved by the 3rd Canadian Division. The artillery support it had received had been insufficient for success in such difficult ground.[1]

Delay occurred in the start of the 10th and 12th Canadian Brigades, owing to their waiting until the gaps in their line had been filled before they advanced, and to the German artillery shelling their front heavily from early morning. Towards 10 a.m. this fire developed into a severe bombardment of the 10th Brigade front, and of the village of Hallu held by the 12th. Soon enemy infantry could be seen assembling in Hallu Wood, south of the village. An S.O.S. was signalled to the covering artillery, but failed to get through, and half an hour later the Germans launched an attack.[2] The left of the 10th Brigade (50th Battalion) was driven back slightly after inflicting considerable losses on the enemy, and Hallu was lost; but the 78th Battalion clung on to the railway embankment west of the village, supported on its left by two companies of the 38th. Just before 1 p.m., however, the commander of the 78th judged it advisable to fall back to a trench west of the railway.

The idea of retaking Hallu was entertained by Br.-General J. H. MacBrien, but in view of General Rawlinson's policy of not pushing the attack in the face of the strong opposition which had now developed, the idea was abandoned. By corps orders, too, the intended attack from the south on Chaulnes, in the Australian area, was cancelled and the line of the 12th Canadian Brigade withdrawn to the main line of defence east of Chilly. The Germans made no further effort to advance, and about 2 p.m. were driven out of Hallu by an artillery barrage. Later they made repeated attempts, continued until midnight, to break in and turn the left flank

---

[1] The casualties of the 32nd Division on 10th and 11th were officers: killed 26, wounded 49, missing 1; other ranks: 262, 1,312, 98; total 1,748.

[2] The attack was made by the newly arrived *Alpine Corps* (actually only of the establishment of a division) which had orders to take Hallu and Chilly. ("Das deutsche Alpencorps im Westen", p. 55, and "Res. Regt. No. 261", p. 107.) Low-flying British aeroplanes considerably embarrassed the Germans. ("Res. Regt. No. 262", p. 264.) As on 13th, although constantly kept up to establishment, the battalions of the *Alpine Corps* had "at best barely 300 fighters of all ranks" ("Alpencorps", p. 55) they must have suffered considerable loss on the 11th.

of the 12th Canadian Brigade by bombing up old trenches ; but although they got within fifteen yards they were repelled. After dark, as if expecting attack, they sent up flares and opened violent machine-gun fire, but did not attempt to advance.

In general, therefore, the Canadian Corps had gained a little ground on the right and lost some on the left, the retirement in that quarter bringing it in touch with the Australian right.

The Fourth Army orders issued on the night of the 10th had given as objective for the Australian Corps on the 11th the line of the Somme from St. Christ (inclusive) to Bray,[1] and it was to establish bridgeheads on the right bank. The Germans, however, were still offering strong resistance about Lihons–Chaulnes on the Australian right front, and before any question of advance to the Somme could be entertained this high ground must be captured. During the day Lihons (900 inhabitants) was secured and other progress made in the Australian centre and on the left.

At the close of the fighting on the 10th the Australian Corps had made plans for a dawn attack to reach a line running past the eastern edge of Lihons to the existing front near Avenue Cross on the Amiens–Brie highway, which had been mentioned as the third objective on the 9th.[2]

Major-General Glasgow, in the 1st Australian Division, continued to use the brigades (the 2nd and 3rd) in the line, still keeping the 1st in reserve. At 4 a.m., soon after the ground mist had formed—it did not clear until 10.30 a.m.— the 8th Battalion, with one company of the 7th, the leading unit of the 2nd Australian Brigade, moved forward ; three companies of the 10th and 12th Battalions, with the 11th Battalion of the 3rd Australian Brigade, starting from the western side of Crépey Wood, were a little later, a quarter of a mile to the left rear, both were covered by a barrage 500 yards ahead fired by four field artillery brigades, whilst throughout the operations the heavy batteries shelled Chaulnes (1,200 inhabitants) and Triangular Wood west of the village. Nine tanks of the 2nd Battalion were available,

---

[1] For these places see End-paper A.
[2] See Sketch 8.

and five were detailed to work just ahead of the 2nd Brigade and four of the 3rd Brigade, but had difficulties on account of the ground mist. Three of the latter four were an hour late ; the fourth and the other five arrived only a few minutes after time, and, following on, did good work in mopping up. Seven in all eventually had mechanical trouble, but none was reported as put out of action by the enemy.

The advance was very rapid, the enemy was surprised at breakfast, and his machine-gunners seemed flurried and mostly fired wildly over the heads of the Australians ; a few posts, however, were passed over in the mist and these caused much trouble for a time. By 6 a.m., or soon after, Lihons and Auger Wood, to the north-by-west of the village, had been cleared and the objective had been reached, although the news took two hours to reach brigade headquarters. Some time was required to fill a large gap between the two brigades and establish touch throughout, and as early as 6 a.m., after an enemy aeroplane had flown low over the line, Crépey and Auger Woods were deluged with gas, and the 12th Battalion was shelled with mustard gas at 1,200 yards' range. Then the Germans,[1] concealed by the mist, launched a sudden counter-attack against the left centre of the 11th Battalion, only to be three times repulsed with exceedingly heavy losses. About 8.30 a.m., also, a series of counter-attacks was made north of Auger Wood by part of a newly-arrived division,[2] and the Germans broke through the right of the 11th Battalion ; with the help of the 10th and a section of the brigade trench-mortar battery, they were thrown back after heavy fighting, and the objective regained. A protective barrage was put down and consolidation was then begun. A further enemy attack, about 1.20 p.m. by a battalion under a barrage, was stopped by machine-gun fire. During the rest of the day the Germans made frequent attempts to creep forward with bombs and machine guns up the complicated network of old trenches ; in some cases they reached the line, only to be killed. By 4 p.m. the objective of the 1st Australian Division round Lihons hill and northward was firmly held without any gaps of sufficient width to cause uneasiness. It was found that the right flank was now five hundred yards ahead of the Canadian left.

---

[1] The *5th Bavarian Division* was identified.
[2] The *38th*.

The 2nd Australian Division was to gain a line from the left of the 1st, round Rainecourt to the right flank of the 3rd, supposed to be at Avenue Cross.

The attack was made, simultaneously with the 1st Australian Division, by the 26th and 28th Battalions of the 7th Brigade and the 19th and 20th of the 5th. No tanks were available, but the brigades had the same command of artillery support as those of the 1st Australian Division. The enemy apparently had orders to retire slowly if attacked ; for the 26th Battalion encountered practically no resistance, and though the 28th came under machine-gun fire directly it started, it was not checked and was on its objective by 4.45 a.m. The 19th Battalion reported itself there at 5 a.m. ; the 20th was a little later, as it received fire not only from the front but also from Proyart to the north, which was still in the enemy's hands. In the sector of these two battalions he had replied to the barrage by turning 9·2-inch and 4·2-inch howitzers on to the village of Framerville and the orchard north-east of it, but this fire soon ceased. The 20th Battalion had to form a defensive left flank, as the 3rd Australian Division was short of Avenue Cross, a company of the 28th Battalion being sent up to help, and here a local counter-attack at 5.30 a.m. was repulsed. When the mist lifted the troops who were digging in the open were subjected to intense and deadly sniping, but as the day wore on enemy activity decreased and the 2nd Australian Division was able to settle down.

After the failure of its 10th Brigade to capture Proyart during the night of the 10th–11th, the 3rd Australian Division took no part in the 4 a.m. attack except by putting down a barrage on the German positions in front of the 5th Brigade of the 2nd Australian Division. This provoked some retaliation on, but did not move the two battalions of the 10th Brigade which were in the line.

North of the Somme nothing of importance happened. When day broke the 13th Australian Brigade was shelled from several directions, and a counter-attack was expected. It was noticed that the Germans were dribbling back to the unoccupied tip of Etinehem spur and digging in there, and later that they were re-entering Bray in some strength, they apparently having abandoned both localities during the night. Artillery was turned on these and they were evacuated afresh, but later re-occupied. To secure the line against attack from the south a small defensive flank was formed by two companies, one of the American 131st Regiment, and one of the 51st Australian Battalion. The right was still, however, badly exposed to German fire from behind Méricourt spur, south of the river. It was therefore arranged that the 11th Brigade of the 3rd Australian Division should capture the spur during the night and cut off the Germans. At 8.30 p.m., after Proyart had been bombarded in order to mislead the enemy, three companies, which had been dribbled into position in daylight, covered by a smoke screen, moved forward under a rolling barrage, strengthened on the flanks by machine-gun barrages; parallel barrages were simultaneously fired across the neck of the Méricourt peninsula, east of the village, and trench mortars kept the village under fire. The artillery fire did not seem very effective, although that of the trench mortars and machine guns was good; enemy machine guns took the attack both in front and in flank and it could proceed only by short rushes. At 9 p.m. the batteries ceased fire and a quarter of an hour later, by use of the bayonet, complete success was achieved and the river reached. Nearly two hundred prisoners of the *108th Division* were taken with material of every description; later two officers and seventy men, cut off in the woods, surrendered, and at 4.20 a.m. Méricourt, with eighty-four more, was captured.[1]

During the morning Sir Douglas Haig, continuing his tour of the front, visited Lieut.-General Monash at Australian Corps headquarters at Bertangles (5 miles north of Amiens) and learnt of the small losses so far sustained, less than a thousand men in each of the five divisions. General Byng (Third Army) arrived by appointment, and the Commander-in-Chief told him to be ready to attack in the direction of

---

[1] " Regt. No. 97 ", p. 73, states that orders had been received by the *108th Division* during the morning to evacuate the Méricourt position, but the operation could not be carried out by daylight. It was just about to be begun when the Australians broke through the *13th Division* (this division was represented by 2 regiments reduced to 2 battalions each, the third regiment, reduced to one composite battalion, having been withdrawn) on the left. The capture of a whole company is admitted. In the *13th Division*, " Regt. No. 13 ", p. 314, admits the capture of 2 companies after hand to hand fighting. " Regt. No. 15 ", p. 360, introduces tanks into the attacks!

Bapaume as soon as reinforcements reached him, with the object of outflanking the enemy's present battle-front. He then motored on a couple of miles to III Corps headquarters at Villers Bocage (7 miles north of Amiens), to find that Lieut.-General Butler was suffering from insomnia and that Lieut.-General Godley (XXII Corps) was going to act in his place for a fortnight. Later he saw the commanders of the five Australian divisions and then General Rawlinson at Villers Bretonneux.

Subsequently General Rawlinson held a conference with his corps commanders. He pointed out that all reports indicated that the Germans were offering increased resistance and that they had been able to bring up fresh troops and to reinforce their artillery : they were now holding the western edge of the area devastated partly by the battles of the Somme in 1916, partly by their retreat to the Hindenburg line in 1917, and partly by their offensive in the spring of 1918 : the country over which any further advance would have to be made was difficult for infantry and almost impossible for cavalry or for tanks : it was certain that the enemy had decided to make a stand west of the Somme, although whether this was in order to cover the withdrawal of the main forces to the eastern bank, or meant that he intended to occupy a line on the western bank to be defended to the utmost was not yet plain : three cavalry and thirteen infantry divisions with part of one American division had been engaged against twenty-four of the enemy's divisions,[1] and although casualties had been light in comparison to the number of prisoners taken, the troops had been continually on the move and subjected to great strain since the 8th August : tanks and their crews had suffered heavily, and it had not been possible to bring forward all the heavy artillery or to supply what was at the front with ammunition : moreover previous experience had shown that once the initial impetus of an offensive had been expended, and the enemy had been able to reorganize his defences, infantry attacks even when assisted by tanks became increasingly costly in casualties : artillery support, too, owing to the time required to bring forward the guns, diminished as the attack progressed, and it became increasingly difficult to co-ordinate attacks and prevent them from being made disjointedly and on narrow fronts : if casualties were to be

---

[1] Twenty-two not twenty-four would appear to be the total.

kept down it was essential for the infantry to advance on
a wide front, well supported by artillery and in close co-
operation with tanks : since these factors could not be
ensured, as he had no intention of trying to burst through
regardless of cost, with the approval of Sir Douglas Haig,
he had decided to discontinue the attack for the moment,
but corps might make local offensives in order to effect
minor improvements designed to obtain a good starting line
for the general attack when it was resumed—probably on
the 14th or 15th August. Orders to this effect were issued.[1]

Thus the Battle of Amiens came officially to an end. For
quite other reasons, the Battle of Montdidier, by which name
the simultaneous operations of the French First Army are
known, also ceased on the 11th. At 7.30 p.m. General
Debeney had issued orders for the continuation of the battle ;
but at 11 p.m. he postponed their execution until the 13th,
for at 12.15 p.m. " General Debeney who was under Field-
" Marshal Haig only from the tactical point of view, received
" orders from General Fayolle [G.A.R.] which modified the
" constitution of his Army. At the beginning of the battle
" on the 8th August the Army covered a front of 18 miles.
" Now this front was reduced by a third [by the gradual
" elimination of the enemy salient]. It had thus become
" necessary to withdraw a certain number of divisions, which
" would be placed either in the reserve of the G.A.R. or
" G.Q.G. This operation would absorb about a day to carry
" out ; so the continuation of the offensive against Roye,
" which as a matter of fact required preparation by powerful
" artillery action, originally fixed for the 12th was put off
" to the 13th ". It was then postponed by Sir Douglas
Haig's order to the 15th, then by General Debeney's request
to the 16th and finally to " une date ultérieure ".[2]
Maréchal Foch himself had begun to recognise the increased
opposition. Late at night, at 10 p.m. of the 11th, with
Generals Weygand and Desticker, he appeared at Sir Douglas
Haig's train. He still hoped that the British might reach
the Somme, but agreed to the objective being reduced to
the sector Ham–Brie (4 miles south of Péronne) ; and he
now begged that the Third Army might take the offensive

[1] See Appendix XVI.
[2] F.O.A., vii. (ii), pp. 195–6, 201, 209.

as soon as possible. The measures agreed upon are recorded in the Instruction which he sent next morning to General Pétain and Sir Douglas Haig. This gave a new orientation to the continuation of the operations.[1] The matter of most importance, it said, was to obtain the maximum result from the battle in progress and to exploit to the utmost the deep penetration obtained by the British Fourth Army and French First Army on the 8th, 9th and 10th August : in view of the resistance of the enemy, nothing could be gained by uniform pressure on the whole front : powerful concentrated attacks should be made against important points whose capture would particularly embarrass the German communications. He suggested two such points : (a) Roye, an important road centre, which should be attacked as soon as possible by the French First Army and the right of the British Fourth Army, the French Third Army supporting and exploiting this offensive to the south in order to clear the Noyon area of the enemy ; and (b) the Amiens–Brie highroad, which should be attacked without delay by the centre of the British Fourth Army from the area Lihons–Herleville (2½ miles north of Lihons) north-eastwards in order to reach, or at least keep it under effective field-gun fire : in conjunction with (b) the left of the British Fourth Army should advance eastwards to clear the enemy out of the angle of the Somme at Péronne.

Independently, however, of the frontal actions indicated above, Maréchal Foch considered that the results of the success could be increased to vast proportions by extending the wings of the present battle (a) north of the Somme by an attack of the British Third Army, as already suggested by Sir Douglas Haig, in the direction of Péronne–Bapaume, in order to outflank the enemy's defensive line on the Somme and compel him to make another, deeper, retirement ; (b) east of the Oise by an attack of the French Tenth Army in the direction of Chauny (half-way between Soissons and St. Quentin) and the high-road Soissons–Chauny,[2] in order to force the enemy to evacuate the hilly, wooded massif between Tergnier (7 miles north-east of Chauny) Guiscard and Noyon. An attack farther east would come later. Maréchal Foch concluded by asking the two commanders-in-chief to let him

---

[1] The Instruction, Annexe 631 in F.O.A, vii., (ii) is translated in Appendix XVII.
[2] See Sketches 12 and 1.

know how soon and in what strength the operations which he had outlined could be undertaken, bearing in mind that these must be launched as soon as possible and at the shortest possible intervals of time.

Early on the morning of the 12th, in accordance with Maréchal Foch's and his own intentions, Sir Douglas Haig issued a short formal order :

" The French First Army and British Fourth Army " will resume the attack on the 15th August " and gave as objective " the general line Roiglise [2 miles south- " east of Roye]–Chaulnes ".[1]

The great offensive of the 8th August had not produced all the material results expected, largely because the effect of the initial surprise had not been utilized to push the enemy over the devastated area near the old trench-warfare front.

That more was not achieved after the magnificent first effort of the Canadian and Australian Corps must be attributed partly to the complete success of the attack of the 5th Australian Division on the 29th July when on the point of leaving the Morlancourt area north of the Somme. The retaliation by a fresh first-class Württemberg division on the 6th August upset the preparations of the III Corps, reinforced the enemy opposed to it and prevented surprise on the 8th. The III Corps was therefore unable to advance at the pace of its sister corps in the Fourth Army, and in consequence the left of the Australian Corps was held up by and suffered heavy loss from enfilade fire from the north bank of the Somme.

The line of the Somme between Ham and Péronne and of the Canal du Nord, its continuation southwards to Noyon, had not been reached although the enemy losses had been heavy. The French had captured 259 officers and 11,114 other ranks and 259 guns[2] and the British, 439 officers and 18,061 other ranks and 240 guns, including one 9·2-inch, that is a total of 29,873 prisoners. The British casualties were about 20,000 for the four days of battle,[3] and those

---

[1] See Sketch 12.

[2] These figures are actually the figures for 6th to 15th August, but there were few captures between 11th and 15th.

[3] See Table in Note I at end of Chapter.

of the French First and Third Armies for ten days (6th to 15th August) 24,232. The total number of enemy human casualties may in the circumstances be estimated at least $2\frac{1}{2}$ times the number of prisoners, that is to say about 75,000 for the *Second Army*.[1] A far greater number of prisoners would have been secured had the advance of the Fourth Army been rendered easier by the French First and Tenth Armies moving forward simultaneously on the 8th, instead of piecemeal from left to right. The German *Eighteenth Army*, instead of being caught, fell back unhindered before the French in a well-timed retreat on the night of the 9th–10th.

The moral effect of the Allied victory was far greater than the material : for the first time both the German High Command and the men in the ranks admitted a defeat and that the greatest defeat in the War. And they never in the coming days were able to shake off the impression of the inevitableness of final collapse.

The halt for security's sake on the old Amiens Defence Line on the afternoon of the 8th, and the late start on the 9th—around 1 p.m. in the Canadian Corps and 11 a.m. in the Australian Corps—gave the enemy time to bring up reinforcing divisions to the Fourth Army front, from the rear and from the north, in the nick of time. Six fresh divisions appeared on the 8th, three on the 9th, and four on the 10th, so that in fresh divisions alone the defenders equalled the total number of the attackers, counting the one fresh division, the 32nd, put in on the third day. A line of fresh divisions sent through the tired ones in the early morning of the second day, judging by the effect of the 4.20 a.m. attack on le Quesnel, would have brought great results. But after four years' experience of the Western Front and of German defence tactics General Rawlinson's caution can well be forgiven.

A factor even more tiresome perhaps than the delay and caution was the nature of the ground in which the advance became involved. The new German divisions thrown hastily into battle as they arrived might well have been overrun in the open field, but the advance of the Fourth Army led it to the old front lines of the winter of 1916–17. Thus the enemy found well-wired and quite fightable trenches ready-made in the right place. What was the beginning of a pursuit

---

[1] See Note III at end of Chapter.

was thus transformed into trench-warfare, but without the usual array of artillery support, and General Rawlinson rightly called a halt.

The action of the tanks and the cavalry, though they won small triumphs, did not come up to expectation. Given that there were no great belts of wire to break down on the 8th August and that the morning fog though it favoured unseen approach hampered movement, the tanks might have achieved more important results had they been kept back until later in the day. They certainly saved many infantry lives and enabled the attack to go forward more quickly than it would without them ; but the work of clearing the enemy out of woods and villages, and of crushing machine guns, could have been done by trench mortars and accompanying artillery, as the Germans showed in March, 1918. It should be noticed that the percentage of tanks which were knocked out increased with each day, as the enemy artillery grew accustomed to them : it has been put at 25 per cent. on the 8th, 30 per cent. on the 9th and 50 per cent. on the 10th. The attempts to use cavalry as a mounted arm in direct attack before every enemy machine gun had been captured or silenced brought little profit in spite of the gallant efforts of the squadrons.

Since the War the Germans, to save their self-esteem as soldiers, have attributed their defeat to the massed attack of tanks. Even a well-informed and sober writer like General von Kuhl (Crown Prince Rupprecht's Chief of the Staff) stated to the Parliamentary Committee which enquired into the loss of the War that " Four hundred tanks of the Fourth " British Army in thick fog broke suddenly into the positions " of the *Second Army* ", and he asserted that " from now " onwards in all attacks of the year 1918 the tanks played " a decisive role ".[1] Dr. Helfferich, the Secretary of State, has written :[2] " With innumerable tanks the foe overran " our lines. Quite a number (*eine ganze Anzahl*) of the " staffs were surprised and taken prisoner by tanks far " behind the front line " and thus " the control of the battle " was handicapped." Readers of the narrative of the operations will see that this was far from the case—it is to be greatly regretted that no massed tank attack was made, not even planned, and that no attempt at a raid behind the

[1] Kuhl, p. 195.
[2] " Der Weltkreig " iii, pp. 440–1.

enemy lines was made except by the 17th Armoured Car Company. Even the moral effect was not so great as claimed ; for at least the German gunners stood up well at the shortest range to the approach of tanks. But a legend which persists to this day was created. Actually the infantry with machine guns was the instrument of success ; but its vital assistant was the artillery, which now provided with ample supplies of reliable ammunition, very different to that of July 1916,[1] had gained and continued to maintain to the end a definite ascendancy over the enemy's batteries.

The failure, with heavy loss of machines, of the massed air attack against the Somme bridges is of special interest to-day. The defending aircraft, though fewer in number, were effectively superior as, their aerodromes being nearby, they could be longer in the air of the battlefield than assailants coming from a distance ; and they could be, and were, quickly reinforced from adjoining fronts.

The staffs, of all formations great and small, had been trained in trench warfare period and, except for a very few old hands, had no experience of the difficulties of communication in, and the speed of open warfare. To this must be attributed many of the delays, which were aggravated by the heavy traffic on the roads when the supply apparatus of so many divisions and batteries had only a limited number of roads available, not enough to allow separate " up " and " down " routes. Interruption was also caused by the damage to wires and cables laid across country occasioned by the passage of tanks and parties of horsemen. The communication troubles might have been eased by the higher commanders moving up nearer to the troops ; Sir Douglas Haig brought his headquarters train abreast of Fourth Army headquarters, and Canadian Corps headquarters were twice moved forward ; but this appreciation of the changed circumstances was not general. In the advance of the old Army in 1914 to the Marne and from the Marne to the Aisne no such communication difficulties had occurred.

O.H.L. gave as reasons for the defeat of the *Second Army* :[2]

" (1) The troops were upset by tanks which broke " through in fog ;

---

[1] See " 1916 " Vol. I, p. 122.
[2] Gallwitz, ii, p. 340.

" (2) there were hardly any more positions and
" obstacles on which to fall back ;
    " (3) the resting battalions of the reserves of the
" higher leaders had not sufficient artillery to adapt the
" new form of artillery resistance to enemy troops and
" tanks which had broken through ".

NOTE I

THE CASUALTIES, 8th–11th AUGUST

The casualties after the 7th August are not recorded daily
by all formations ; the returns mostly cover the whole period
8th to 15th August, four days more than the actual battle. The
following are the figures available :

CAVALRY CORPS

		Officers			Other Ranks		
	Killed	Woun- ded	Miss- ing	Killed	Woun- ded-	Miss- ing	Total
1st Cavalry Division : (8th–13th August)	8	23	1	39	323	14	408
2nd Cavalry Division : Period ending noon 9th August)	–	2	–	2	17	7	28
3rd Cavalry Division : 7th-11th August)	7	24	1	45	305	69	451
	15	49	2	86	645	90	887

The loss in horses was 1,800

III CORPS

Casualties from noon 7th to noon 15th Aug.

		Officers			Other Ranks		
	Killed	Woun- ded	Miss- ing	Killed	Woun- ded	Miss- ing	Total
12th Division	.. 23	55	2	175	1,288	306	1,849
18th Division	.. 12	55	15	176	1,069	668[1]	1,995
58th Division	.. 23	84	4	264	1,597	434	2,406
	58	194	21	615	3,954	1,408	6,250

[1] Battalion diaries give a total of 792 for 8th.

CANADIAN CORPS

8th–11th AUGUST

(Compiled from statistics supplied by the Historical Section, Ministry of National Defence, Ottawa.)

	Officers			Other Ranks			
	Killed	Wounded	Taken Prisoner	Killed	Wounded	Taken Prisoner	Total
8th August ..	60	138	1	978	2,665	26	3,868
9th August ..	44	100	–	533	1,893	4	2,574
10th August ..	37	45	1	432	1,319	25	1,859
11th August ..	13	19	1	169	537	34	773
	154	302	3	2,112	6,414	89	9,074

AUSTRALIAN CORPS

8th–13th AUGUST

(Noon to noon)

(Extracted from A.O.A. vi, p. 684)

	Officers	Other Ranks	Total
1st Aust. Division ..	114	1,817	1,931
2nd ,, ..	75	1,220	1,295
3rd ,, ..	52	1,043	1,095
4th ,, ..	44	740	784
5th ,, ..	54	832	886
	339	5,652	5,991

The following details are from the diaries :—

	Officers			Other Ranks			
	Killed	Wounded	Missing	Killed	Wounded	Missing	Total
8th August ..	6	30	–	77	461	78	652
9th August ..	13	74	1	172	1,011	39	1,310
10th August ..	20	70	1	137	830	34	1,092
11th August ..	13	50	1	200	1,006	51	1,321
12th August ..	8	25	3	55	352	31	474
(To noon 13th)	60	249	6	641	3,660	233	4,849
13th August ..	5	22	1	144	758	98	1,028
	65	271	7	785	4,418	331	5,877

TOTAL CASUALTIES

Cavalry Corps ..	..	..	887
III Corps	..	..	6,250
Canadian Corps	..	..	9,074
Australian Corps	..	..	5,991
			22,202

NOTE II

THE FRENCH ON THE 11th AUGUST

(Sketch 4)

" The gains obtained by the [French] First Army in the course
" of the 11th August were very restricted " ; its advance encountered great obstacles. In the XXXI Corps, next to the British,
the 126th Division was " counter-attacked and driven back,
" involving in its retirement the 153rd Division on its right ".
At 5.30 p.m. the attack was renewed, but " on the whole day
" only a small advance was made by the XXXI Corps, about a
" thousand yards. It was still four thousand yards from Roye ".
The X Corps met with increasing resistance. The XXXI Corps,
" operating on difficult ground covered with old trenches, could
" only advance slowly ". The II Cavalry Corps was sent back to
the valley of the Avre.

The Third Army during the 11th continued to drive back
enemy rear guards, gaining a belt of ground varying from a
thousand to four thousand five hundred yards. " Although the
" enemy resistance became intensified on the whole front, the
" commander of the Third Army did not believe that he had
" more than rear guards in front of him ".

In the Tenth Army, General Mangin issued an order for an
advance on the 15th August. (F.O.A. vii. (ii.), Annexe 630).

NOTE III

THE GERMANS ON THE 11th AUGUST

(See End-paper B)

German accounts speak only of local fighting with varying
results on the front of the *Second Army*, both south and north of
the Somme, that is on the fronts of the French First and British
Fourth Armies ; but of continued violent attacks against the
Eighteenth Army by the French Third Army without much success
—the situation maps, however, show that the *Second Army*

was forced back from a thousand to four thousand five hundred yards beyond the line to which on the previous day Ludendorff had consented that a retirement should be made.

On his arrival at Avesnes, O.H.L. headquarters, Major-General von Lossberg, the newly appointed Chief of the Staff of Boehn's Group of Armies, was received by Ludendorff " who gave an " impression of very great despondency " (Lossberg, p. 352). He was informed that the situation of the *Second Army* was " very serious ". Strong enemy attacks were expected against the *Eighteenth Army* ; for the moment the front of the *Ninth Army*, opposite to the French Tenth Army, was quiet. The *Seventeenth Army*, next on the north of Boehn's Group, was in expectation of an attack, by the British Third Army, between Albert and Arras. " Nothing had been done to renovate the Hindenburg Position ".

Lossberg repeated a proposal which he had already made on the 19th July, that the Hindenburg Position (which formed a retrenchment to the present German salient, 36 miles behind it in the centre and intersecting the front near Vailly on the Aisne in the east and near Arras in the west) should forthwith be occupied and renovated by the reserve divisions which were arriving, and only the absolutely necessary reinforcements sent up to the battlefront.[1] His reason for advising this course was that the initiative had passed into the hands of the Allies, and that they had struck the German front at a very sensitive place. Ludendorff would not agree, and stuck to his decision to fight the battle out on the present line. He was opposed to voluntary retirements to shorten the line, because, although they economized divisions, they allowed the enemy to do the same and to accumulate reserves ; besides they had a bad effect on morale and encouraged the enemy (Kuhl, pp. 198–200). He ordered, however, that a new retrenchment on the line Noyon–Péronne–Combles (that is the Canal du Nord–Somme line) should be reconnoitred and constructed. He stuck to this decision also, although Lossberg pointed out that it would take a long time to reconnoitre and construct the position— and, as he points out, it was speedily overrun by the enemy. " Nothing was done about the renovation of the Hindenburg " Position ".

General von Lossberg adds that up to the 12th the whole of the divisions sent up to the front from the reserve were put into their places by O.H.L. ; after that date the divisions allotted to the Group of Armies had to be used to relieve worn-out divisions, and he prints in heavy type " Boehn's Group of Armies during the " whole of its existence never had any reserve at its own disposal ". (Lossberg, p. 355).

---

[1] In Kuhl, p. 198, it is stated that the back positions had fallen into neglect because in the winter 1917–18 every available man had been taken for the preparations for the spring offensive.

As regards the German casualties, the factor of $2\frac{1}{2}$ applied to compute the total losses from the number of prisoners captured, is derived from the figures supplied to Mr. Winston Churchill by the *Reichsarchiv* for the casualties July–November, 1918.[1] After deducting 10 per cent. from "missing and prisoners" for men temporarily absent the total loss was 750,947 out of which 313,081 were prisoners. This factor would make the total German casualties in the battle of Amiens about 75,000. This is probably under the mark as six divisions had been relieved and four more were on the point of being relieved, and had certainly lost 5,000 men apiece (e.g., the *13th Division* had five weak battalions left out of its nine) a total of 50,000, and the 27 other divisions in the battle (12 opposite the British, 15 opposite the French First and Third Armies) certainly averaged over a thousand casualties apiece. The total of 75,000 is more or less confirmed in another way by the statement made by the commander of the *Second Army* (see Lossberg, p. 354) that the losses of that Army on the 8th August alone were roughly 700 officers and 27,000 other ranks. Adding a half of this number for the 9th, a quarter each for the 10th and 11th, a total of 55,400 is reached. The *Eighteenth Army* certainly lost at least a third of this number, which makes a total for the two Armies of nearly 74,000.

On the face of it, the 8th August hardly seems to have deserved the fatal label of " the black day of the German Army " bestowed on it by General Ludendorff. In the anonymous " Kritik des Weltkrieges " (p. 238–9), however, it is explained what the First Quartermaster General had in his mind : after the battle divisional commanders and officers from the front were summoned to O.H.L. : from them he learnt that parties had surrendered to single horsemen and whole detachments to a few ranks : in some units the officers had lost all influence and had fled with their men. Ludendorff " drew the conclusion that the balance had finally " come to rest on the side of the Entente ". All thoughts of the offensive had to be laid aside and " he could no more even think " of long and successful resistance in the attrition of defensive " battles ".

---

[1] It may be noted as evidence of the German endeavour to minimize their losses that the total of " prisoners and missing ", including missing who later returned, is given as 347,867. In the period 18th July–11th November the French, Belgians and British actually took 385,500 !

CHAPTER IX

THE PAUSE BETWEEN THE BATTLE OF AMIENS

AND THE BATTLE OF ALBERT 1918

12TH–20TH AUGUST

(Sketch 9)

During the eight days which followed the 11th August no important action took place on the front of the British Fourth Army or of the French First and Third Armies on its right ; but south of the Somme,[1] by minor affairs which involved heavy fighting and provoked counter-attacks these Armies gained a zone, roughly the enemy's forward zone, which averaged about two thousand yards deep, all along the front ; and on the 18th the French Tenth Army, next on the right, joined in, and continuing on the 19th, made a similar advance of about two thousand yards ; but neither Lassigny nor Roye or Chaulnes was captured. Yet Ludendorff has written : " August 20th was another black day. " In some places the men could no longer stand the " tremendous artillery barrages and tank attacks ".[2]

To begin on the right of the Fourth Army, on the 12th August the 9th Canadian Brigade (of the 3rd Canadian Division which had relieved the 32nd Division) captured Quarry Wood[3] and Middle Wood, and closed in on Parvillers from both flanks. Middle Wood was recovered next day by the enemy, and some other ground lost ; but on the 14th, in a fight that lasted from 6 a.m. until after 11 p.m., the 7th Canadian Brigade, which had relieved the 9th, nearly reached Parvillers and, although counter-attacked, finally obtained possession of the village and of Middle, Blücher and Hermann Woods. It could not, however, approach Damery. On the 15th, after a feint attack combined with a flank attack, and a reconnaissance which located the enemy machine-gun nests, the whole of Damery and a considerable piece of the ground east

---

[1] See Sketch 9.
[2] Ludendorff, p. 694.
[3] For these localities see Sketch 8.

163

of the village were after fierce encounters cleared of the
enemy, whilst the French secured Damery Wood. Keeping
a heavy barrage on the village, at 1 p.m. and 3.30 p.m.
Germans, identified as belonging to the *121st Division*,
counter-attacked, some broke in at one place, but, thinking
themselves surrounded, surrendered freely in batches to the
number of one hundred and fifty. By 5 p.m. the fight was
over and Damery and Parvillers held. The French completed a successful day by capturing Z Wood about 6 p.m.
Strong patrols sent towards la Chavatte and Fransart
encountered such resistance as to show that the enemy there
was not retiring.

On the 16th the French " having noticed a certain weaken-
" ing of the enemy's resistance ",[1] by General Debeney's
orders attacked Goyencourt, and reached the western edge,
and also captured two villages south-west of Roye. Further
advances were made to bring the line abreast of Goyencourt.
The Canadians secured Fransart and woods south of it ; but
three attempts against la Chavatte failed, and efforts by
patrols to reach Fresnoy and a wood south of it were in vain,
as these places were in the German main position. On the
17th la Chavatte was captured by an enveloping attack ;
considerable bickering took place, and in the end attempts
to advance beyond la Chavatte and towards Hallu Wood and
village were abandoned.

The 18th August was a quiet day, but in the late afternoon
the position on the left of the corps was improved by the
11th Canadian Brigade pushing forward five hundred yards.
Under arrangements concerted with Maréchal Foch, to be
mentioned later, orders were issued on the 19th by the
Fourth Army for the Canadian Corps to hand back to the
French the line as far north as Lihons, that is the sector of the
front corresponding to that taken over from them for the
battle of the 8th August. The French XXXI and XXXV
Corps began the relief that night and it was completed by the
morning of the 27th. All heavy artillery covering the front
in question was left in position, pending further orders.

The Canadian Corps passed for the moment into G.H.Q.
reserve. Between the 8th and 19th August it had captured
9,203 prisoners and 162 guns. Its own losses had been well
under nine thousand,[2] and it had advanced in the first four

---

[1] F.O.A. vii (ii), p. 211.
[2] See Note I at end of Chapter VIII.

days, measuring from Domart to Chilly, over 15 miles. For gallantry in the hard fighting around Damery and Parvillers two Victoria Crosses were awarded to Canadians.[1]

In the Australian Corps the line was improved by resolute advances. On the 12th the 7th Australian Brigade filled up part of the re-entrant angle in the front at Meule Favre, east of Vauvillers, the 11th Battalion advancing to a line from the Rosières-Herleville road to the 5th Australian Brigade line east of Framerville. The 10th and 11th Australian Brigades, which now occupied the whole of the 3rd Australian Division front, by the skilful operations of a few parties lasting from 8.30 a.m. until nearly 9 p.m., without artillery support but under covering fire from rifles and Lewis guns, got possession of Proyart and a line beyond.[2] The 43rd Battalion (11th Brigade) also mopped up Méricourt, which had been cut off by the advance of the previous night.

At 1 a.m. on the 13th, whilst 4.5-inch howitzers shelled the river bank and heavy artillery bombarded Bray, three battalions of the 13th Australian Brigade (now with the 131st Regiment, U.S.A., organized into "Liaison Force" under Br.-General E. A. Wisdom of the 7th Australian Brigade) with an 18-pdr. battery turned the last Germans off the tip of Etinehem spur and advanced to the river bank. The Meule Favre re-entrant was further reduced by the 2nd Australian Division until the line on the 18th ran from Auger Wood (just north of Lihons) to Avenue Cross (on the Amiens–Brie highway). Other minor readjustments were carried out, not without resistance from the air as well as the ground.

---

[1] For most conspicuous gallantry during the counter-attack on 13th August Sergeant R. Spall, P.P.C.L.I., was awarded the V.C. posthumously.

For his great initiative and splendid example to his company on 12th August, Private T. Dineson, 42nd Battalion (Royal Highlanders of Canada), was awarded the V.C.

[2] Sergeant P.C. Statton, M.M., 40th Battalion, seeing that the right of the 37th Battalion on his immediate left was held up by machine-gun posts, armed only with a revolver captured two single-handed. The garrisons of the other two posts then retired. For this most conspicuous gallantry Sergeant Statton was awarded the V.C.

Measures were now taken to rest some of the Australian divisions : the 17th Division, from G.H.Q. reserve in the Australian Corps area, on the 13th relieved the 3rd Australian Division, which went into corps reserve. The 17th Division was itself relieved by the 5th Australian Division on the 18th, on which day the very weak 6th Australian Brigade (2nd Australian Division) advanced the line to Herleville, but after severe fighting with a fresh German division could not hold all its gains. On the 19th the 32nd Division took over the 2nd Australian Division's front on the right of the line, where it had gone in place of the 1st.

Between the 8th and the 15th August the Australian Corps had captured 8,767 prisoners and over a hundred guns.[1]

Soon after midday on the 12th General Pershing came to Sir Douglas Haig's advanced headquarters. The occasion seems to have been the receipt of information that Mr. Lloyd George had been endeavouring through political channels to arrange that a number of American divisions should remain with the British.[2] In view of the impending St. Mihiel operations and the national desire to form an American Army, he expressed himself anxious to recover at least three of the five American divisions in training with the British forces, adding that Maréchal Foch wished that he should make the request himself. Plain speaking had always been the feature of the intercourse between the two commanders-in-chief, and it was not lacking on this occasion. Sir Douglas Haig said clearly that as the British had trained and virtually equipped the divisions, they expected to have some use of them, and only parts of one, the 33rd, had been sent into battle ; he had in his mind their employment, with British troops, in an attack against Kemmel at the end of September. General Pershing whilst insisting on their return said that he would not claim them as long as the present battle was in progress, and the meeting ended with Haig saying " in his frank straightforward way : ' Pershing, " ' of course you shall have them, there can never be any " ' difference between us ' ".[3]

---

[1] For the casualties see Note 1 at end of Chapter VIII.

[2] Pershing, p. 545.

[3] Pershing, p. 545. Between 19th and 24th August the 33rd, 78th and 80th Divisions were withdrawn to join the American First Army ; this left the 27th and 30th with the British, and they remained to the end.

Subsequently the British Commander-in-Chief held a conference at Fourth Army headquarters at which were present General Rawlinson, General Debeney and General Byng (Third Army). He explained the situation to them and discussed the continuation of the operations on the 15th. But more important than this were his instructions to General Byng, which were embodied in a formal order issued next day.[1] Reinforced by four divisions, two cavalry divisions, several battalions of tanks, and additional artillery, the Third Army was to break into the enemy's position on about a four-mile front, 7 miles south of Arras, and then if possible push southwards in the direction of Péronne in order to outflank the forces opposing the Fourth Army. The breach might be widened northwards and the important observation point of Monchy le Preux recaptured. The 20th August was provisionally fixed as the date, but it depended upon railway movements. Sir Douglas Haig then informed Maréchal Foch in writing of the orders which he had given.

The commanders on the spot were against the continuance of the Amiens attack, at any rate without longer preparations than Zero on the 15th permitted. On the evening of the 13th General Debeney telephoned asking for a postponement of the attack until the morning of the 16th on the grounds that the Germans were now in a strongly prepared position, protected by much wire,[2] and that he was experiencing difficulty in getting up ammunition. General Pétain, too, it subsequently transpired, thought that the operations of the Tenth and Third Armies could not be resumed before the 16th. From Fourth Army headquarters came a hint that General Rawlinson considered that the attack would prove very costly; so Sir Douglas Haig summoned him to come to Wiry next morning. At a meeting at 10 a.m. on the 14th General Rawlinson exhibited photographs of the enemy defences on the front Roye–Chaulnes, and showed the Commander-in-Chief a letter from the G.O.C. Canadian Corps in which Lieut.-General Currie said that " to capture the position in question would " be a very costly matter " and that he " was opposed to " attempting it ". Sir Douglas Haig accordingly ordered

---

[1] Appendix XVIII.

[2] The German position in front of Roye captured in 1917 had been maintained in good order by the French, as a model to exhibit the enemy's methods to young officers and other ranks under instruction.

the date of the attack to be postponed, but he directed wire-cutting, counter-battery work and other preparations to be continued with vigour. He also directed General Rawlinson to arrange for III Corps in the sector between the Somme and the Ancre to " push on " to get possession of the Cappy crossing, four and a half miles above Etinehem, as soon as the pressure of the Third Army began to have effect.

An officer was sent to General Debeney with the aeroplane photographs and similar instructions. . He continued on by air to Maréchal Foch's headquarters at Bombon, carrying a letter from the Field-Marshal announcing the postpone-ment. In this it was stated that, in addition to the informa-tion on the photographs, the ground ahead was broken and difficult for tanks, that in the past 48 hours the enemy artillery fire had greatly increased and that at least sixteen German divisions were holding the position in front of Debeney's and Rawlinson's Armies.

Shortly after, at 11.45 a.m., the Third Army reported that the Germans (*Seventeenth Army*) were falling back on more than a six-mile front between the Ancre and Bucquoy (10 miles south of Arras) and were being vigorously followed up.[1]

Sir Douglas Haig's letter, sent by air to Maréchal Foch, brought a reply by return at 5.30 p.m. In view of the serious German resistance, he said he quite understood the necessity for effective artillery preparation ; but he could see no necessity for subordinating the date of the attack of the French First and British Fourth Armies to that of the British Third Army : " Very much to the contrary, the " attack of the First and Fourth Armies should be hastened " as much as possible, and followed as rapidly as possible by " that of the Third Army ". Not content with this Note, at 9.10 p.m. he sent a telegram in cipher through the French Mission at G.H.Q., marking it " very urgent ", to the effect that in view of the preparations made by General Debeney to attack on the 16th and of the success of his operation depending upon its being supported, as agreed, by a British offensive extending as far north as Hattencourt, he earnestly requested that the date arranged for the operation should be

---

[1] See Map 4 and Sketches 10 and 11.   This retirement, and a similar small one near Ypres, were only for the purpose of flattening out a salient ; it affected only the outpost zone, not the main line of resistance. See Ludendorff, pp. 689–90.

adhered to, and that the Fourth Army should be ordered to give the support unless it were utterly impossible for the troops of its right wing to do so ; if this were the case he begged to be informed at once.

A serious difference of opinion having thus arisen, the British Commander-in-Chief, determined to carry out the wishes of the Generalissimo unless in so doing he should imperil the British Armies. He re-examined the situation very carefully and at 10 a.m. on the 15th held a conference with the commanders of the First and Third Armies and of the Cavalry Corps. He learnt from General Byng that the Germans had continued to fall back opposite the centre of his front and that his troops had already entered Beaumont Hamel and Serre, and were in the western outskirts of Beaucourt and Bucquoy. Br.-General Cox, the head of the Intelligence Branch, reported that the enemy seemed to have only one division left in reserve on the Third Army front, Albert to Arras, and only ten in reserve fit to fight between the Oise and the sea. Sir Douglas Haig therefore directed that the Third Army should press on with Bapaume as its objective, even before the reinforcements promised should arrive, in order to prevent the enemy from destroying bridges and roads, and that the First Army should take advantage of the advance of the Third to attack and capture Orange Hill and Monchy le Preux (3 miles north-east of Neuville Vitasse). The Fourth Army was to continue its preparations south of the Somme and take advantage of any opportunities which might arise for gaining ground ; north of the Somme, in co-operation with the Third Army, it was to press the enemy and follow him up. A formal operation order embodying these decisions, which modified the instructions given to General Byng on the 13th,[1] was prepared and issued.[2]

At 3 p.m. Sir Douglas Haig, accompanied by Lieut.-General Lawrence, visited Maréchal Foch at his advanced headquarters at Sarcus (20 miles south-west of Amiens) and explained his plans and how the action of the Third Army had been accelerated. The Generalissimo pressed him to attack the Roye–Chaulnes position next day ;[3] but this he declined to do on account of the heavy casualties which it would involve if undertaken before the assault had been duly

---

[1] See Appendix XVIII.
[2] Appendix XIX.
[3] See Sketch 9.

prepared by heavy artillery, and he stated clearly that he was
responsible to his Government and his fellow countrymen for
the handling of his troops. Maréchal Foch gave way, and
admitted that the French First Army was short of ammunition and could not continue counter-battery work for more
than one day longer, so that the attack had either to be made
next day or be abandoned.

On his return to Wiry, the Commander-in-Chief wrote a
letter to Maréchal Foch, who had appeared to desire a
statement in writing, giving details of his plans with copies
of the orders and instructions which he had issued. He
stated that the British Fourth Army south of the Somme
was maintaining continual pressure, which would not be
relaxed ; that north of the Somme it would later co-operate
with the Third, and make every effort to gain ground ; that
the Third Army had already begun to press the enemy back
and the pressure would increase as the reinforcements
arrived ; and that the First Army would also attack, the
date depending upon the progress of the Third.

Before this statement was despatched, a letter arrived
from Maréchal Foch in which he put in writing his acceptance
of Sir Douglas Haig's view, saying :

" The reasons which you adduce appear to me to
" justify your modification of the course of action laid
" down in my Directive of the 12th August,[1] and I rely
" on the momentum which you will give to your attack
" north of the Somme to permit the active renewal of
" the thrust south of that river for the purpose of
" conquering the objectives which I indicated ".

In the concluding paragraph he withdrew the French
First Army from Sir Douglas Haig's control, ending his
letter with the compliment that

" the co-operation under your direction has given the
" most complete results in that the objects aimed at,
" the freeing of Amiens and the Amiens–Paris railway,
" are achieved, but as the operations therefore enter a
" new phase I consider that the best results will be
" attained by restoring the First Army to General
" Pétain's command ".

To General Pétain he wrote :

" I request you without delay to combine the opera-
" tions of your First, Third, and Tenth Armies with the

---

[1] See Chap. VIII and Appendix 16.

" object of freeing the region[1] Lassigny–Noyon–Forest
" of Carlepont (south of the Oise at Noyon) and at the
" same time to prepare for freeing the region Roye–
" Chauny–Soissons later on."

The formal transfer of command of General Debeney's
Army took place at 12 noon on the 16th. On the same day
Sir Douglas Haig received notice by private letter from
General Pershing that he would require three out of the
five American divisions under British command at the
earliest possible date in order to carry out a task assigned
to him by the Generalissimo. Having heard nothing from
Maréchal Foch on the subject, the Commander-in-Chief
wrote to him at once to enquire if the transfer should be
made, pointing out that if such were the case the length of
the British line must be reduced by the frontage of three
strong divisions, at least 18,000 yards ; otherwise he would
be unable to continue the operations which had been
projected.

On the 17th G.H.Q. received two telegrams from Maréchal
Foch. The first, timed 9.30 a.m., addressed also to G.Q.G.,
read that " the operations in preparation by the several
" Armies for the resumption of the forward movement should
" be pushed forward without delay, and launched as soon as
" the Armies are ready, at latest on the 20th August ".

The second telegram contained a formal operation order
addressed to the three commanders-in-chief. It directed the
despatch without delay of the American 33rd, 78th and 80th
Divisions to the American area. In compensation the
French First Army was to extend its front northward to the
region of Lihons[2] thus releasing the Canadian Corps. This
relief would be carried out as rapidly as possible ; but
Field-Marshal Haig was requested not to delay the release
of the American divisions until it had been completed. He
was also requested to leave behind all batteries in the
Canadian Corps area except those actually part of the
divisions.[3]

All these orders were forthwith carried out. As already
mentioned, the French First Army began the relief of the
Canadian Corps on the night of the 19th–20th August and

---

[1] See Frontispiece.
[2] See Sketch 9.
[3] The telegram is in F.O.A. vii (ii), Annexe 701.

completed it on the 27th, and between the 19th and 24th the three American divisions were withdrawn from the front and were by the 25th clear of the British area.[1]

Sunday, the 18th August, was marked by a visit of M. Clemenceau to the British front. The French Government had in the previous week decided to confer on Sir Douglas Haig their highest military honour, the " Médaille Militaire ", a decoration bestowed only on " other ranks " and commanders-in-chief. The French Premier was specially desirous not only to announce the award himself to the Field-Marshal but also to pin on the medal personally,[2] and he did so at Amiens in the presence of the British Ambassador, Lord Derby, and Maréchal Foch. He subsequently inspected the 7th Canadian Brigade and the captured guns.

On this day the 9th and 29th Divisions (Major-General H. H. Tudor and Br.-General H. H. S. Knox, acting) of the XV Corps (Lieut.-General Sir B. de Lisle) of the Second Army, at 11 a.m. carried out a very successful attack against Outtersteene ridge between Merris and Bailleul ; east of Hazebrouck.[3]

On the 19th Sir Douglas Haig, fearing that there might be in the Third Army a repetition of the loss of opportunities which had occurred in the Fourth Army, paid a visit to General Byng at his headquarters at Villers l'Hopital (23 miles west of Arras), and subsequently motored to the headquarters of the VI Corps (Lieut.-General Sir A. Haldane) and the IV Corps (Lieut.-General Sir M. Harper). The Commander-in-Chief expressed his dissatisfaction with the Third Army plan, which he thought was too limited : it aimed at no more than an advance of about six thousand yards in the centre, protected by defensive flanks, with exploitation by infantry advanced guards and tanks. The object, he pointed out, was to break the enemy's front, push on quickly to prevent bridges and roads from being destroyed and to gain Bapaume as soon as possible : the flanks would be secured by the simultaneous advance of the Fourth and First Armies. He ordered a cavalry regiment to be attached to each corps from the two cavalry divisions allotted to the

---

[1] American Order of Battle i, p. 227.
[2] Mordacq ii, p. 182.   The Chief of M. Clemenceau's Military Cabinet records " la grande sympathie, ou plus exactement la grande affection, qui " liait les deux hommes, le Maréchal Haig et M. Clemenceau ".
[3] Described in Chapter XXIX. See Sketch 7.

Third Army. The optimism of the Generalissimo and the British Commander-in-Chief seems to have been justified by the state of the German Army as disclosed in recent years.[1]

On his return to Advanced G.H.Q., Sir Douglas Haig informed Maréchal Foch that the Third Army's operation would be begun on the morning of the 21st : it could not take place earlier owing to delay in the arrival of tanks and other troops. An order was sent to the First Army directing General Horne, whilst continuing his preparations to attack Orange Hill and Monchy le Preux, to hold three divisions, and such tanks as were available, in readiness to exploit any success of the Third Army, or to reinforce it ; whilst on the morning of the 21st in order to deceive the enemy as to the frontage of attack of the Third Army, the First Army was to carry out a heavy bombardment of the enemy defences. The attack of the Fourth Army north of the Somme was fixed for the 22nd, south of the Somme for the 23rd.

On the 20th the French Tenth Army[2] attacked northwards with twelve divisions (only two of which had been rested) on a 12-mile front, from near Soissons to its left boundary on the Oise, and made an average advance of over three thousand yards. The extension of the great offensive to the right and left had begun : Ludendorff calls the 20th " another " black day. Again we had suffered heavy and irreplaceable " losses ".[3] The French Third and First Armies between the Tenth and British did not, however, advance. At 10 p.m. as an officer was leaving for G.H.Q., Maréchal Foch took the opportunity to send a letter to Sir Douglas Haig, telling him of the success of the Tenth Army : the enemy, he said, was shaken everywhere by the blows he had received and those blows must be repeated without loss of time : " I therefore count on the attack of your Third " Army, already postponed to the 21st, being launched that " day *with violence*, carrying forward with it the neighbouring " divisions of the First Army and the whole of the Fourth " Army. After your brilliant successes of the 8th, 9th and " 10th, any timidity on their part would hardly be justified " in view of the enemy's situation and the moral ascendency " you have gained over him ".

---

[1] See Note II at end of Chapter.
[2] See Sketch 12.
[3] Ludendorff, p. 694.

On the 5th August His Majesty King George V had begun a visit to his troops, and he remained until the 13th. During this period he inspected in succession portions of the Second, First, Third and Fifth Armies, besides the Tank Corps, transportation services and hospitals, and he visited the King of the Belgians. On the 12th he motored to the Canadian and Australian Corps in the battle area and invested Lieut.-General Sir Arthur Currie and Lieut.-General John Monash with the K.C.B., presented General J. Pershing with the G.C.B., General T. H. Bliss with the G.C.M.G., and General Debeney with the K.C.B. He also saw all the divisions of the III Corps on parade, including troops of the American 131st and 132nd Regiments which had served with them, to whom he presented a number of M.C.s. and M.M.s.

NOTE I

The French Movements 12th–20th August

(Sketch 9)

During the 12th to 20th August, the French Third and First Armies, like the British Fourth Army, were unable to make more than slight progress, and the Tenth only just began to get on the move.

The French Third Army attempted to advance on the 12th, but had little success. Renewed efforts on the 13th had no great results, and General Fayolle pointed out to General Humbert, the Army commander, that in trying to gain his objectives he must not lose sight of the necessity of " acting in conjunction and " simultaneously with the First Army ". Thereupon General Humbert postponed further action to the 15th, when both his corps, the XV and the XXIV, were to advance to limited objectives.

On the 14th, General Pétain, writing to Maréchal Foch in answer to the latter's letter of the 12th, reported that " the " offensive designed to capture the junction of roads at Roye " and to clear the country round Noyon would begin on the 16th ". Although Sir Douglas Haig had made arrangements to attack on the 15th with the French First and British Fourth Armies, General Pétain considered that the combined operations to be undertaken by the Tenth and Third Armies could not begin before the 16th : on that day the Third Army, in conjunction with the First Army, now restored to his command, would attack ; the former to free the country round Noyon, the latter to " make " its principal effort towards Laucourt and Goyencourt " (that is to outflank Roye on south and north). The Tenth Army would attack on the 17th " if the tanks, without which the launching of " the attack would be very difficult, arrived in time ".

As already explained, the offensive of the British Fourth Army was postponed. The XXXI Corps and X Corps of the French First Army made slight advances on the 15th.

In the afternoon of that day, General Debeney informed his corps commanders that the attack fixed for the 16th was postponed, and " on procédra seulement à des destructions method- " iques mais en réduisant la consommation des munitions " ; close contact was to be maintained with the enemy and the Army was to be ready to advance at once if he fell back.

On the morning of the 16th, as there had been signs during the night of a slight weakening of the German resistance, General Debeney instructed his corps commanders to keep in touch with the enemy and to push on towards their respective objectives as defined on the 10th August, but only " by sustained infiltration " supported by artillery and partial attacks ".

On the 17th the French First Army gained a little ground. The left of the Third Army, trying to act in conjunction with the First Army, made very little progress. The XXX and VII Corps, the centre of the Tenth Army, by 8 a.m. had reached some high ground which was to be a jumping-off place for the more important operations to follow.

On the 18th and 19th the Third and First Armies made only small advances. The latter was still delayed at Beauvraignes, which the Germans held strongly. For the 20th General Debeney gave the following objectives to his corps : XXXV Corps, Beauvraignes ; X Corps, Laucourt ; XXXI Corps, Roye. General Humbert (commanding Third Army) ordered his corps to organize the positions which they had reached. The Tenth Army also attacked on the 18th and 19th, and gained a certain amount of ground preparatory to the offensive of the 20th mentioned in the text.

At 11 p.m. on the 20th General Pétain, as a result of this success, telegraphed to the G.A.C. that the Sixth Army [1] as well as the Fifth should be ready to cross the Vesle—to which the Germans had been pressed back in the July offensive—at the first evidences of withdrawal and should keep on the heels of the retreating enemy.

---

[1] The Sixth Army was on the right of the Tenth, and the Fifth was behind it west of Reims. See Map 2.

NOTE II

The Germans During 12th–20th August

(Sketch 11)

On the 15th August, it was calculated by the Intelligence Branch that the state of the German Armies on the Western Front, excluding one Austro-Hungarian division and four dismounted cavalry divisions, was :—

Divisions

Army Groups	In Line		In Reserve		Total
	Fit	Unfit	Fit	Unfit	
Crown Prince Rupprecht's	28	6	9	2	45
Gen. von Boehn's	7	33	6	19	65
German Crown Prince's	6	21	4	29	60
Gen. von Gallwitz	6	6	2	–	14
Duke of Würtemburg's	1	13	2	1	17
	48	79	23	51	201
	127		74		

None was " unlocated ".   Of the unfit divisions 24 had been resting for 14 days or more ; the remainder had either been withdrawn recently or were of poor quality.   In the *Second Army* of 23 divisions opposite the British, nine were of this category, but only two really fresh.   Of the *Eighteenth Army* of 18 divisions opposite the French First and Third Armies, only two were really fresh, but only one was " unfit ".

Thus since the 8th August, the number of " unfit " had risen from 109 to 130, and in the next five days three more were to pass into this class.

On the 12th General von Boehn took over command of the *Ninth, Eighteenth* and *Second Armies*, with headquarters at le Cateau.   He, like his Chief Staff Officer, Major-General von Lossberg, failed to persuade Ludendorff that the best course of action was to send the available reserves to the Hindenburg Position to put it into a state of repair ; " for General Ludendorff, " in complete misapprehension of the serious situation at the " front, stuck to defending every yard of ground ".   General von Boehn, made aware by Lossberg of the " bad condition " of the fighting troops of the *Second Army*, visited the front every day ; but little could be done except to " send the relieving divisions, " which arrived in ever dwindling numbers, to the most threatened " front.   The foe, however, did not let go, engaged more and more " reserves [*sic*] and by the 18th August had pressed the *Eighteenth*

" and *Second Armies*, with constant heavy losses, back to the
" line south of Noyon—west of Roye–Lihons–west of Bray–
" Albert. On the 20th the enemy also attacked the *Ninth Army*
" with superior forces and threw it back in spite of the stoutest
" defence".

On the 13th and 14th two conferences took place. On the
evening of the 12th before the first of them, to Colonel von
Haeften, Ludendorff " without reserve disclosed the seriousness of
" the situation ". At 9 a.m. on the 13th Field-Marshal von Hindenburg appeared to enquire of Ludendorff what he should say at
the Conference at 10 a.m. with the *Reich* Chancellor and the
Foreign Secretary. He received the reply that the truth must be
told, and Ludendorff then proceeded to depict to him the seriousness of the situation just as he had to Haeften. (Schwertfeger, pp.
91-2.) At the meeting Ludendorff " explained that it was no
" longer possible to force the enemy to sue for peace by an
" offensive. The defensive alone could hardly achieve that
" object and so the termination of the War would have to be
" brought about by diplomacy". (Ludendorff, p. 686.)

But the First Quartermaster-General had already conceived
the idea of putting the blame on someone else ; for " the greater
" part of the rest of the talk was taken up with the complaints of
" O.H.L ; about the state of feeling in the Homeland and its
" reaction on the front; the weakening of the Government's
" authority; the too small support given to the generals com-
" manding Army corps districts ; the shortage of supplies, and the
"inadequate reinforcements ". (Schwertfeger, p. 92.). On the other
hand, Ludendorff would not abate his demands for the retention of
Belgium and a large share of Western Russia, though Admiral
von Hintze, the Foreign Secretary, demonstrated that the political
situation was " very serious : Austria-Hungary morally and
" materially exhausted, ready to collapse ; Turkey going her own
" way ", and Bulgaria " always making more demands " as " her
" army is exhausted ". Ludendorff thought these ideas were
" black pessimism ".

A difference of opinion exists as to whether or not anything
definite was settled at the Crown Council which took place next
day, presided over by Wilhelm II. Hindenburg, always an
optimist, expressed his hope that by the strategic defensive " it
" would be possible to succeed in remaining on French soil and
" finally thereby to subject the enemy to our will ". The Field-
Marshal already knew the opinion of some of the higher leaders
that the " defence in depth " of 1916 and 1917 required too many
troops to be practised in the latter half of 1918. Ludendorff
states that Hindenburg spoke thus only to cheer up those present.
The Kaiser said that " a suitable time must be chosen to come to
" an understanding with the enemy. The King of Spain and the

" Queen of the Netherlands are suitable channels ".   To this the Chancellor added "such a moment would be after the " next success in the West ".

Ludendorff states that "on the 14th His Majesty ordered " peace negotiations to be opened " (p. 689).   Others, including Colonel Schwertfeger, do not think that "a clear order " to take steps towards peace was given; but he himself states later (p. 103) that "Hintze as early as the 15th August, that is a day " after the Crown Council in Spa tried to open the way to negotia- " tion with the Queen of the Netherlands ".

The perturbation of the German authorities was further increased by the arrival in the afternoon of the 14th of Kaiser Carl of Austria, with his Foreign Minister, Count Burian, and his Chief of the General Staff, General von Arz. They found "an " atmosphere of gloom ".   Burian stated that their opinion was that "somehow or other the war must be ended as soon as " possible " ; he wished to make an appeal for peace "to all " at once.   When Ludendorff asked for Austrian divisions for the Western Front, Arz replied that his opinion was the Royal and Imperial Army could in no circumstances hold out over the winter. Nothing was settled.   Kaiser Carl left German O.H.L. after this, his last meeting with his brother Kaiser, "feeling " depressed, but satisfied in one respect, that at least he had " found basic agreement for the beginning of steps towards " peace ". (Austrian O.A. vii, p. 498.) But on his return to Vienna his anxieties were increased by learning from Tzar Ferdinand of Bulgaria, who was passing through, that he had begged and been refused help by the German High Command.

CHAPTER X

THE BATTLE OF ALBERT 1918 (¹)

21ST AUGUST

(Map 4 ; Sketches 10, 12²)

In view of the situation that the enemy in front of the French First Army (General Debeney) and British Fourth Army (General Sir Henry Rawlinson) was in a strongly entrenched old position, and that the co-operation of the French Third Army (General Humbert) on the right had so far produced no enveloping effect, it had been finally decided that the attack begun on the 8th August should now be extended on both wings as Maréchal Foch had always had in his mind to do. The French Tenth Army (General Mangin) and possibly the Sixth (General Degoutte) were therefore to join in on the right, whilst, on the left of the Fourth, the British Third Army (General Hon. Sir Julian Byng) and later the First Army (General Sir Henry Horne) were to attack in a south-easterly direction, so as to turn the line of the Somme south of Péronne and thus assist the further progress of the Armies which had made the original successful advance.

The French Tenth Army had come into the battle on the 20th, but the British Third Army, as has been seen, was not ready on that date ; so it had been settled that on the 21st the latter Army should launch a limited attack in order to gain the line of the Albert–Arras railway ;³ that the 22nd should be employed in preparations for a further advance by the Third Army and in bringing forward the left of the Fourth Army between the Somme and the Ancre ; and that on the 23rd the Third Army and the left wing of the Fourth

¹ The official Battle Nomenclature gives : " The Second Battles of the " Somme 1918 " 21st August–3rd September, with the subheadings " Battle " of Albert 1918 " 21st–23rd August, with the tactical incident of the capture of Chuignes 23rd August ; and " The Second Battle of " Bapaume " 31st August–3rd September, with the tactical incident of the capture of Mont St. Quentin, and the occupation of Péronne ; but the Somme title for 1918 has never come into use, being reserved for 1916, and the Battle of Albert did not end until the 29th August.

² Map 4 shows the operations of the Third and First Armies from the 21st August to the 3rd September ; Sketches 10, 14, 16 and 18 give them in detail by days.

³ See Map 4 and Sketch 10.

179

Army should deliver a full-dress attack, whilst the right wing of the Fourth Army south of the Somme pushed forward to cover the flank of the main operation, and, on the extreme left, the First Army took advantage of any withdrawal to follow up the enemy.

The Second Army (General Sir Herbert Plumer), which had 10 divisions in the line (two American and two second-line) and five in reserve, was to continue minor enterprises, in order to gain ground towards Mont Kemmel and keep the enemy in expectation of an attack against that place, which if he were compelled by the action of the other Armies to withdraw his reserves southward might actually materialize.[1]

The Third Army[2] consisted of three corps, the V, the IV and the VI. The first contained two divisions, the 21st and 38th. Each of the latter two, three divisions, the 37th, 42nd and N. Zealand in the IV Corps, and the Guards, 2nd and 59th in the VI Corps. Of the reserve divisions, one, the 17th, was sent to the V Corps, two, the 5th and 63rd, to the IV, and one, the 3rd, to the VI.[3] In Army reserve were two cavalry divisions and the 62nd Division.

Seven brigades R.F.A. and four brigades R.G.A. were transferred from the Fourth to the Third Army; so that after the redistribution the strength in artillery according to a G.H.Q. return was—

	18-*pdrs.* and 4·5-*hows.*	*Yards per piece*	*Heavy pieces*	*Yards per piece*
First Army	832	54	384	116
Second Army	792	46	426	103
Third Army[4]	828	43	466	76
Fourth Army	1,216	33	540	75
Fifth Army	496	47	166	140

The distribution of the five battalions of tanks (156 machines) will be given later.

[1] See Chapter XX.

[2] Major-General, General Staff, Major-General L. R. Vaughan; D.A. and Q.M.G., Major-General A. F. Sillem; G.O.C. R.A., Major-General A. E. Wardrop; Chief Engineer, Major-General W. A. Liddell.

[3] The 3rd, 21st and 59th had been engaged in both the March and April battles, the 37th and 38th in neither, the 5th in the April fighting and all the rest in March.

[4] A Third Army return gives 996 field-guns and 482 medium and heavy; of the latter 234 were 6-inch howitzers and 96 60-pdrs. The A. and Q. diaries, which give "arrivals" and "departures", do not serve to explain the discrepancy.

The fighting strength of the III Brigade R.A.F. (Br.-General C. A. H. Longcroft) was brought up to ten squadrons by the addition of two American and four British. One squadron was attached to each corps for attacks against land targets ; a second squadron was put at the special disposal of the Tank Corps commander (Major-General H. V. Elles) for low-flying attacks against anti-tank guns. Arrangements were made for a corps contact plane to fly along the front at fixed hours and call for flares to indicate the line reached.

The ground in front of the Third Army lay across the watershed between the Somme and the Scarpe, the highest part being in the south almost along the boundary with the Fourth Army ; it was broken by many cross spurs and valleys and on the north descended very gradually towards the Scarpe ; the upper valleys of the Ancre and the Sensée, which nearly meet near Achiet le Grand, are the principal depressions. The area had been covered with villages and small woods and orchards, but had been devastated in the German retirement in 1917. It lay between the battlefields of the Somme 1916 and Arras 1917. As will be seen from the names on the map, Pozières, Thiepval, Puisieux, it had on the extreme right formed the northern portion of the old Somme battlefield ; but north of this, though it had been traversed in the 1917 advance and the March 1918 retreat, the surface was regarded as favourable for tanks ; only near Croisilles and Bullecourt did it just touch the fringe of the Arras battlefield of the spring of 1917. The roads had been made passable for artillery and tanks by the pioneers, and complete arrangements provided for water supply by the engineers.

The thirteen divisions of the Third Army, 50 per cent. of whose infantry were said to be " boys ", who would do well if the first action in which they took part was a success, were faced by the eight southern divisions of the German *Seventeenth Army* (General von Below) with two divisions behind them in reserve.[1]

---

[1] The *Seventeenth Army* contained in all 13 divisions, three continuing the front northwards opposite the First Army. Of the eight divisions with which the Third Army was at first concerned only one (*4th Bavarian*) was rated first class, five were second class and two (*3rd Naval* and *234th*) third class. All except the *4th Bavarian*, which was in the April battle, had fought in the March offensive. The two divisions in reserve were ranked as second class and third class.

The same steps as in the Fourth Army before the 8th August were adopted to ensure secrecy, but no positive measures were taken to deceive. Only the General Staff and a few senior engineer officers had knowledge of General Byng's instructions. The enemy seemed unsuspicious ; he did carry out some gas shelling on the night of the 20th–21st but no more than normal ; but this cost the 23/Royal Fusiliers, which had to pass through it on the 21st on the way up, nearly four hundred gas casualties.[1] Several of the divisions of the Third Army had been given special training with tanks, behind the line. A feature of the Third Army arrangements was the leap-frogging of divisions ; some in the actual front line, or others after they had reached the first objective, were to be passed through by fresh divisions brought up in rear of them. Otherwise the plan resembled that of the Fourth Army : a fixed objective which would serve as a good defensive line being given ; when this had been secured exploitation with the assistance of cavalry and tanks might follow. No preliminary bombardment was to be fired, the barrages were to fall at Zero, 4.55 a.m.

General Byng's orders were issued on the 18th. The following is a summary :

1. The left of the IV and the right of VI Corps will on a date to be notified later make a surprise attack on the spur Ablainzevelle—Moyenneville as a preliminary operation.

2. If this attack is successful, the IV and VI Corps will exploit the success by pushing infantry and tanks through the line Irles—Bihucourt—Gomiecourt and thence northward along the Albert-Arras railway.

3. At the same time, the IV Corps will capture the remainder of the Serre—Miraumont ridge, including the Beauregard Dovecot.

4. The V Corps will be prepared to push across the Ancre in a south-easterly direction towards the Pozières ridge and prolong the right of the IV Corps.

5. For these operations the 5th Division is allotted to IV Corps and the 3rd Division to VI Corps.

---

[1] The attack of the 21st is said in German accounts to have been a surprise ; but it so happened that the *52nd Division*, resting in Flanders and one of the best German divisions, had been entrained at midday on the 20th and reaching Cambrai on the 21st was sent to the front.

6. Attention is drawn to the absolute necessity for preserving secrecy regarding the operation and for making the troops detailed for exploitation thoroughly mobile.

7. The 1st Cavalry Division, working directly under Army headquarters, will be prepared to take advantage of any opportunity which may present itself for passing through the exploiting troops and continuing the success in the direction of Bapaume.

8. The III Brigade R.A.F. will detail one fighting squadron[1] to work with the tanks on IV and VI Corps fronts against enemy anti-tank guns.

9. The I and II Tank Brigades are allotted to IV and VI Corps respectively. The areas of action allotted to the various types of tanks in the first day's action are :

Mark IV.   A line east of Logeast Wood to Moyenneville.

Mark V.   A line south-east of Achiet le Petit and Achiet le Grand, thence north along the railway.

Whippets.   Line Irles—Bihucourt—Ervillers (all inclusive).

Armoured cars.   The area Biefvillers (and towards Bapaume), Sapignies, Béhagnies and Ervillers.

Some gun-carrying tanks were allotted to both the IV and VI Corps.

Thus the main attack was to be carried out by the IV and VI Corps, the advance of the V Corps on the right depending on the measure of their success. It is therefore convenient to describe the operations from left to right.[2]

As a preliminary, it should be stated that in many divisions the infantry formation adopted had the object of keeping control in the hands of the few efficient officers rather than of tactical considerations. It became normal for the infantry to follow the barrage in groups at very wide intervals, but not in great depth. The artillery was by comparison highly efficient, and the infantry soldier came to rely more and more on the barrage (generally marked by some smoke shell), not only to prepare his way, but to guide him as well. The remarkable feature of the operations was their success in

---

[1] The second squadron already mentioned.
[2] They can perhaps be best understood by reading the German account first. See Note II at end of Chapter.

spite of the weakness of the battalions and their almost total
lack of training in open warfare. It might have been different
had the eighteen and nineteen year-old boys who filled the
ranks been subjected to a prolonged bombardment or forced
to retreat. Their discipline, however, was good, and they
had been well trained at home, although not in open warfare.
They were keen and physically fit, and, however tired, a
night's rest was certain to restore them.

The fighting conditions in this latter part of August
closely resembled open warfare. As the operations progressed, although the ground was seamed with old trenches,
the Germans did not occupy continuous lines, and thus there
was room for manœuvre. Their system of defence was to
hold the ground by fire, in depth, artillery and machine
guns furnishing not only the framework but also the
resistance. In these circumstances, the British artillery,
except in the attack of localities, could not support the
infantry either as closely or as quickly as in trench warfare :
information could not be passed back to the guns with telephone rapidity, and the machine gun is a very small target
which takes much time and ammunition to hit. Nor could
our own machine guns, owing to their flat trajectory, give
the support expected unless the lie of the ground permitted
overhead fire. Thus the extreme range of the barrage often
formed the limit of the infantry advance. In attacks
ordered at short notice, as most of them were, it was not
always practicable to employ the carefully calculated
trench-warfare type of creeping barrage, each battery firing
down a corridor, but good results were obtained by allotting
some of the batteries to particular brigades, even to
battalions.

Touch of the enemy was frequently lost ; the advance was
then carried out by " advanced guards " in each divisional
area and in bounds from line to line, with mounted men
reconnoitring to the front and on the flanks. The danger
of counter-attack was always present as the Germans still
had reserves in hand ; but when they were sent up they were
rarely used to fling back the attackers, being urgently
required to strengthen the front at weak places. Tanks, when
available, and low-flying aeroplanes gave valuable assistance,
but never brought about decisive results. A steady advance
rather than attempts at deep infiltration, even on a small
scale, was the general policy.

The formal orders of the VI Corps[1] (Lieut.-General Sir Aylmer Haldane) were issued on the 19th. The 59th Division (Major-General Sir R. D. Whigham) which held the left sector was not to take part in the main attack, but only to push forward patrols to test the strength of the enemy and gain ground if possible. The action of this division can be described in a few words : it established six posts, five without difficulty, on a line six hundred yards out and no counter-attack was made against it.

The assault was to be made by parts of the Guards and 2nd Divisions, the 3rd Guards Brigade on the left standing fast. The 2nd Guards Brigade (Br.-General B. N. Sergison-Brooke) was to advance through the 1st Guards and 5th Brigades which were in the line, and the 99th Brigade (Br.-General W. E. Ironside) through the 6th Brigade. Machine-gun companies were attached to the two brigades, 26 tanks of the 12th and 15th Battalions (of the II Tank Brigade under Br.-General A. Parker) to the Guards and 12 of the 12th Battalion to the 2nd Division, and the advance of the infantry was to be covered by seven and six brigades respectively of field artillery under Br.-Generals F. A. Wilson and G. H. Sanders, whilst three and two brigades, respectively, of heavy artillery, dealt with distant targets. This works out at no more than 70 guns per mile ; in addition, the Arras–Albert railway was to be enfiladed from the north of the corps area by long-range guns.

Three objectives were defined : the first from Moyenneville (inclusive) south-westwards to the corps boundary ; the second the Arras–Albert railway, which on the right ran in a cutting 10 feet deep but gradually decreasing in depth ; and the third from Moyenneville east of Gomiecourt to the corps boundary north of Bihucourt. For the move from the first objective the time was fixed as Zero + 90 minutes, when the leading brigades of the 3rd Division would pass through the 2nd Division ; but no advance was to be made from the second objective until cavalry, whippets and armoured cars had pushed through, when the divisions were to be prepared to exploit their success.

The field artillery was not to fire a continuous and creeping barrage except through the villages of Moyenneville and

---

[1] Br.-Gen. G.S., Br.-General R. H. Kearsley ; D.A. and Q.M.G., Br.-General J. B. G. Tulloch ; C.R.A., Br.-General J. G. Rotton ; C.H.A., Br.-General A. Ellershaw ; C.E., Br.-General R. N. Harvey.

Courcelles, but to form three standing barrages in succession : first on the slight ridge 500 to 1,000 yards short of the first objective, secondly on the first objective, and thirdly on a line from the north and west sides of Hamelincourt through Courcelles and along the ridge to the south-west of the latter place.

As zero hour approached a thick fog settled over the field of operations.[1] This had as one result that many of the tanks lost their way ; so that at the beginning of the advance only six tanks out of 18 reached the 1/Coldstream and the 1/Scots Guards, the leading battalions of the Guards, and none was seen or heard by the troops of the 3rd Division at the first objective, but those attached to the 23/Royal Fusiliers and the 1/R. Berkshire of the 99th Brigade (2nd Division) duly appeared.

The advance at 4.55 a.m. to the first objective was easily accomplished at small loss, resistance being offered only by a few machine-gun nests ; the great difficulty was keeping direction in a fog thickened by the smoke of the barrage. The movement was continued at 5.40 a.m. to the second objective, the 3/Grenadiers in the 2nd Guards Brigade passing through the two leading battalions and the 8th and 9th Brigades (Br.-Generals B. D. Fisher and H. C. Potter) of the 3rd Division through the 99th Brigade.[2] Tanks should have led the advance, but none arrived in time, although thirteen eventually reached the second objective and one tank which had strayed from the 9th Brigade assisted the 8th as it got near the railway line. The fog not only slowed up the advance so that the barrage was lost—which did not much matter as the enemy, though his machine-gun fire greatly increased, could not see to aim —but also made it difficult even for the infantry to keep direction and touch : the leading companies of the Grenadiers were in fact found behind the support companies, of which one platoon assisted by a tank was the first to reach the

---

[1] Some accounts give the visibility as only 10 yards or even 3 yards. Others say 30 or 40 yards. It no doubt varied in different places. The lifting of the fog is variously reported as having taken place at different times between 10 a.m. and 12 noon. After this the day became very hot.

[2] Each brigade had attached to it one section of a field company R.E. and one section of the 174th Tunnelling Company R.E. to examine dug-outs for booby traps.

railway,[1] which was occupied by 11.30 a.m. in the Guards sector. The 8th Brigade had made more rapid progress, the 7/King's Shropshire L.I. and the 1/R. Scots Fusiliers reaching the railway by 8.45 a.m. The 13/King's of the 9th Brigade, next to them on the right, arrived only 15 minutes later ; but the 1/Northumberland Fusiliers, on the right again, ran up against very strong opposition ; the left flank of the 63rd Division (IV Corps), next to it, also was being held up. The right wing of the Fusiliers faced by a forward slope, was unable to overcome the enemy's machine-gun fire and reach the railway, although the reserve battalion, the 4/Royal Fusiliers, was engaged to support it. Later in the day, as will be seen, the 63rd Division renewed the attack without success.[2]

Thus the VI Corps had secured the whole of its second objective—now known to have been the German main line of resistance—except about half a mile on the extreme right—and about twelve hundred prisoners. As the fog lifted and a hot sunny day followed, this line came under constant artillery and machine-gun fire, and no sign of enemy demoralization which could be exploited by tanks and cavalry was manifest.

No advance was made from the second objective. At 12.15 p.m. the Guards Division sent orders to the 2nd Guards Brigade not to go beyond the railway without tanks or cavalry, and none appeared. This, however, did not prevent the front line battalions from improving their positions by gaining ground locally, and during the night they pushed forward some five hundred yards beyond the railway to the western edge of Hamelincourt. In the 3rd Division sector the 6th Tank Battalion sent a patrol of whippets from Courcelles round Gomiecourt ; it returned safely but lost two machines by direct hits after recrossing the British line. The 2nd Cavalry Brigade (Br.-General A. Lawson) in the course of the morning moved up the 8th Hussars and 4th Dragoon Guards to a position between Courcelles and Logeast Wood. Both regiments sent out patrols, but no chance of successful cavalry action occurred, and at 7 p.m. the brigade was withdrawn with the loss of 98 men and 163 horses, without having had an opportunity of effecting anything.

---

[1] The platoon was led by 2nd Lieut. A. Duff Cooper, later Secretary of State for War.

[2] The reason will be found in Note II at end of Chapter.

In the IV Corps (Lieut.-General Sir G. M. Harper)[1] the attack was to be made by the three divisions in the line : the 37th (Major-General H. Bruce-Williams), the New Zealand (Major-General Sir A. H. Russell) and the 42nd (Major-General A. Solly-Flood). The objectives continued the line of those of the VI Corps, that is, the first was about a thousand yards away on the high ground east of Ablainze-velle–Bucquoy and thence ran by the eastern edge of Puisieux and Hill 140 (overlooking Miraumont and the Ancre valley) to the corps boundary. On the left the second objective was the railway line not quite as far south as Miraumont, but as it was nearly four miles away, an intermediate objective half-way was given ; and on the right a flank was to be formed overlooking the Ancre, in order to connect to the V Corps line. At the first objective the 63rd Division (Major-General C. E. Lawrie) and the 5th Division (Major-General J. Ponsonby) were to pass through the 37th to the second objective and eventually exploit the success to the third objective just east of Bihucourt and Irles.

The attack was to be covered by fifteen brigades of field and six (111 guns) of heavy artillery, but in this case a creeping barrage was to be fired, the 18-pdrs. using shrapnel up to a range of 5,500 yards and H.E. beyond this, and the 4·5-inch howitzers H.E. throughout.

The I Tank Brigade (Br.-General C.D'A.B.S. Baker-Carr) was allotted to the IV Corps and detailed 22 tanks of the 7th Battalion (Mark IV) to the 37th Division, and four to the 63rd and 5th Divisions (for the capture of Logeast Wood). The 10th Battalion (Mark V) was held back for the attack on the second and third objectives. Of the 3rd Battalion (Whippets) one company each was detailed to join the 63rd and 5th Divisions and the third company, with six armoured cars of the 17th Battalion, was reserved for exploitation. The tanks with the 37th Division were directed to keep close up to the barrage, the infantry following at fifty yards' distance, and the machines having been well hidden in woods a mile or less from the front, all but four arrived to time in spite of the fog. With their assistance, the 111th and 63rd Brigades (Br.-Generals S. G. Francis and E. L. Challenor), each with a battalion of the 112th Brigade

---

[1] B.G.G.S., Br.-General R. G. Parker ; D.A. and Q.M.G., Br.-General W. H. V. Darell ; C.R.A., Br.-General J. G. Geddes ; C.H.A., Br.-General T. E. Marshall ; C.E., Br.-General C. M. Carpenter.

(Br.-General A. E. Irvine) and two sections of machine guns attached, had little difficulty, in spite of a stout resistance by some machine-gun posts in Bucquoy, in reaching the first objective, taking 362 prisoners at a cost of only 194 casualties.

The New Zealand Division, which sent forward two battalions of the 3rd (Rifle) Brigade (Br.-General H. Hart), captured Puisieux by attacks through its northern and southern outskirts without much difficulty ; then, guided in the fog by the sound of firing, rushed the enemy machine-gun posts between the village and the first objective, and by 6 a.m. had secured this. The 42nd Division, in order to form a flank, attacked at Zero with the 125th Brigade (Br.-General H. Fargus), which employed the 1/5th Lancashire Fusiliers in front line, and 55 minutes later put in on the right the 127th Brigade (Br.-General Hon. A. M. Henley), which employed the 1/7th and 1/6th Manchester. No great difficulty was experienced in reaching the first objective.

The 63rd and 5th Divisions, which were to pass through the 37th, had left their places of assembly behind Bucquoy at Zero and began to cross the first objective punctually at 6.25 a.m., the fog, owing to its being thickened by the smoke of the battle, was denser even than at zero hour. To the intermediate objective they had the same artillery support as the 37th Division ; but beyond this line, which they were timed to reach at 7.37 a.m., the range was too great, and to cover the further advance the XXVII and XV Brigades R.F.A. of the 5th Division (C.R.A., Br.-General A. H. Hussey) were ordered to take positions west of Logeast Wood and east of Bucquoy ; they were not to fire a creeping barrage, but to exploit any opportunities for inflicting loss and to answer any calls for support. Their forward observing officers accompanied the leading infantry and later on sent back messages by signal lamps. The other field batteries were to move forward later, at 7.37 a.m., when the creeping barrage ceased ; but they were held up by shelling and by fire from low-flying aeroplanes, lost horses and did not reach their new positions in time to assist the advance of the two divisions from the intermediate position. Thus the artillery support was weak, and to this factor must be partly attributed the failure of the two divisions to reach their final objective.

In the front line were the 188th and 189th Brigades (Br.-Generals J. F. S. D. Coleridge and H. D. De Pree) of the 63rd Division and the 15th and 95th Brigades (Br.-Generals R. D. F. Oldman and C. B. Norton) of the 5th ; each brigade had attached to it one or two sections of a field company R.E. and a machine-gun company. The tanks of the I Tank Brigade were redistributed : for the capture of the intermediate objective 28 tanks (Mark IV, including 12 survivors of the first attack) of the 7th Battalion ; for the capture of the second and third objectives 24 tanks (Mark V) of the 10th Battalion, 24 whippets of the 3rd Battalion ; and for exploitation 12 more whippets, six armoured cars, and the 9th Cavalry Brigade (Br.-General D'A. Legard).

The intermediate line was reached along the whole front of the two divisions without great difficulty, except for the troubles of keeping touch and direction in the fog. The only serious opposition encountered was in and near Logeast Wood, which somewhat delayed the 63rd Division, so that it was not until about 9 a.m., after reorganization and change of leading battalions, that it left the intermediate line, where the 5th Division had arrived more than half an hour earlier. In the 188th Brigade sector serious resistance was offered by the enemy from Achiet le Grand and its cemetery, which the weak artillery support was unable to subdue, the 3rd Division on the left also, as we have seen, meeting with strong opposition. Heavy casualties were suffered in the advance in the lifting fog over open ground ; only one company of the Anson Battalion, on the left, managed to reach the second objective ; several tanks were knocked out by short-range artillery fire ; and the brigade had to fall back. The left of the 189th Brigade did no better ; but its right, the Hood Battalion, reached the second objective and about 11.30 a.m. joined up on the right with the 5th Division ; four tanks which had rendered great assistance were by then out of action. All further attempts of the 63rd Division to advance failed, the Hood Battalion was counter-attacked, and at night the advanced outer flanks of the division in the second objective were withdrawn to the general line of the centre held up in front of Achiet le Grand.

In the 5th Division, the 15th Brigade assisted by six tanks and guided in the fog by the straight road from Bucquoy, took Achiet le Petit about 8.30 a.m. after some resistance, overcome by the help of a captured battery of 5·9-inch howitzers. Though on leaving the village the fog suddenly lifted and machine-gun fire was received, the 1/Cheshire and

16/R. Warwickshire pressed on, reached the railway line, and about 9.30 a.m. gained a footing in the third objective on the high ground over a thousand yards beyond, reporting their success by pigeon. The 95th Brigade did not get so far. It met with considerable opposition when it attempted to advance beyond the intermediate line, so about noon Br.-General Norton sent up his reserve, the 12/Gloucestershire, to pass through the leaders. Although the barrage had been lost and no tanks were available, an advance, in which some of the 1/East Surrey took part, to a mile beyond the intermediate line was achieved over open undulating country, although the enemy was on rising ground ahead. A few parties actually reached the railway line, but they were unable to remain, and fell back to a line about a quarter of a mile west of it, forming a short defensive right flank as the front of the New Zealand and 42nd Divisions was some six hundred yards farther back.

Some tanks also reached the railway, but about 11 a.m. when the mist lifted, being within close range of enemy guns they were knocked out.[1]

As neither the 189th Brigade nor the 95th could come up level, both flanks of the 15th Brigade were exposed and it was counter-attacked and forced behind the railway, and eventually occupied a line between this and Achiet le Petit. The leading battalions of the New Zealand Division also had not been able to make much progress beyond the intermediate objective ; for when the fog lifted they found themselves in an exposed position swept by machine-gun fire and had to make a slight withdrawal. The 1/7th Lancashire Fusiliers and 1/7th and 1/6th Manchester which led the advance of the 42nd Division very nearly reached the flank position assigned to it, but not Beauregard Dovecot and the ground north of it. At 2 a.m. on the 22nd, however, a company of the 1/7th Lancashire Fusiliers captured the Dovecot, and repulsed a counter-attack.[2] But the position was untenable ; so the line was withdrawn three hundred yards and the Dovecot remained unoccupied by either side.

Thus though the IV Corps had made a good advance, the main attack of the 37th, 5th and 63rd Divisions, having

---

[1] The history (p. 409) of the *91st Reserve Regiment* (2nd Guard Reserve Division) claims that trench mortars and an anti-aircraft gun knocked out seven tanks as they crossed the ridge north-east of Achiet le Petit. Its *III Battalion* at the end of the day had only 30 men left.

[2] By a fresh division, the *52nd*.

gained three miles on a three-mile front and captured about fourteen hundred prisoners, it had not quite reached the Arras–Albert railway at any point.

The V Corps (Lieut.-General C. D. Shute)[1] had, as a preliminary operation in support of the IV Corps, to cross the Ancre. This river had been canalized at a higher level than the marshy floor of the valley, and the banks having been damaged by shelling, most of the valley, to a width of three hundred yards, was flooded and the main stream was indistinguishable ; in fact the Ancre had become a stretch of marsh and water covered by a tangle of fallen trees, branches and reeds, with wire—almost unnecessarily—added to make it a more difficult obstacle.

As defined in Lieut.-General Shute's order, the tasks of the V Corps were : (1) to prolong—by about a thousand yards—the right of the IV Corps to the Ancre near Beaucourt ; (2) to exploit any initial success by pushing across the Ancre between Hamel and Miraumont in a south-easterly direction ; and (3) to extend this footing later by crossing the Ancre between Hamel and the corps southern boundary. The first two operations were allotted to the 21st Division (Major-General D. G. M. Campbell), and it was to use strong battle-patrols for the second. In regard to the third, the 38th Division (Major-General T. A. Cubitt), also employing strong battle-patrols, was to feel for the enemy and push on if he showed signs of weakening. Should serious resistance be encountered, neither division was to be committed to a costly attack. Zero+50 minutes (5.45 a.m.) was made the starting time, and six field artillery brigades and the four brigades of corps heavy artillery were to support the two divisions. Ten per cent. of smoke shell was to be fired in the creeping barrage by the field guns.

The 62nd Brigade (Br.-General G. H. Gater) carried out the attack of the 21st Division north of the Ancre, with the 2/Lincolnshire[2] in front line. By 6.38 a.m., thanks to an

---

[1] Br.-Gen. G.S., Br.-General R. H. Mangles ; D.A. and Q.M.G., Br.-General H. M. de F. Montgomery ; C.R.A., Br.-General R. P. Benson ; C.H.A., Br.-General A. M. Tyler ; C.E., Br.-General A. G. Stevenson.

[2] This battalion had had a disturbed night. First it had to repel a heavy raid and then, two hours before the attack, endure in the dark an intense mustard gas bombardment which came down on " Y " Ravine running from Beaumont Hamel to the Ancre. About a hundred men were put out of action and many others affected.

intensive and accurate bombardment by artillery and Stokes mortars, Beaucourt was taken with 93 prisoners at the cost of only thirty casualties, and its capture reported by pigeon. The advance to the railway was then made, and the 1/Lincoln-shire passing through with the reserve of the 2nd, prolonged the line of the 42nd Division.

South of Beaucourt owing to machine-gun fire, which the field artillery of the 21st and 17th Divisions (the latter division was in reserve) was unable to smother, it was not until about 3.30 p.m. that two companies of the 12th/13th Northumberland Fusiliers (62nd Brigade) managed to cross the Ancre and establish themselves five hundred yards beyond it. It was not, however, until 8.30 p.m. that the 1/East Yorkshire of the 64th Brigade (Br.-General A. J. McCulloch), held back by corps direction, received instructions to cross, and not until 2 a.m. on the 22nd that one platoon got over, and it was subsequently counter-attacked and driven back. In the 110th Brigade (Br.-General H. R. Cumming) four companies of the 6th and 7/Leicestershire managed to slip across the Ancre in the morning fog, although they could not maintain themselves there when the fog lifted ; but during the night the passages had been improved by the 98th Field Company R.E. and the 6/Leicestershire was able to push patrols over.

In the 38th Division, on the right of the Army which had the support of only its own artillery (under Br.-General T. E. Topping), the experience was the same as in the 21st. Patrols of the 114th Brigade (Br.-General T. Rose Price) which attempted to cross the Ancre at four different places during the day had no success ; those of the 115th (Br.-General W. B. Hulke) managed in the fog to negotiate the water, but found the farther bank strongly held. On the following night, however, six sections of a company of the 14/Welch forded the river and established themselves in an unoccupied trench in Thiepval Wood, which they held until reinforced on the night of the 23rd/24th.

On the whole the operations of the Third Army on the 21st had resulted in a considerable gain of ground. During the afternoon it was decided by General Byng that, in consequence of the difficulties in crossing the Ancre, the

38th Division should wait until the Fourth Army had occupied Albert, which it was expected to do next day, when the division would be passed through that town. Where the second objective had not been reached the troops were very near to it. The fog had been favourable to the infantry, enabling them to get to close quarters with the enemy machine-gun posts before being seen and to outflank his defences, and with far fewer casualties than they would have suffered in fine weather. The fog may even be said to have been favourable to the tanks, though it caused some to be late and others to lose direction ; for when the fog lifted many were knocked out by enemy fire. Exploitation by cavalry and tanks beyond the infantry objectives was not found possible anywhere, for the enemy still held a line, though not a continuous one, and the stage of open warfare was very far from having been reached.

The success of the Third Army had been sufficient to warrant the renewal of the advance of the Fourth Army on the 22nd, as planned, with the expectation that both Armies would be able to push forward together on the 23rd. It was estimated that the enemy had 11 divisions in the line opposite them, with 37 available in reserve, of which 12 were fresh, seven tired, and seven had been smashed up on the 8th August.

NOTE I

THE FRENCH ON THE 21ST AUGUST

(Sketch 12)

On the 21st the French First Army, like the British Fourth Army next to it, did not move, but the Tenth and Third Armies made good progress on the whole 30-mile front from Soissons to beyond Lassigny, the Tenth Army to an average depth of three miles, in places nearly five, and the Third about half the average distance of its neighbour.

In the Tenth Army the I Corps and the XXX Corps, on the right, attacked eastwards and found the Germans well organized in strength and supported by powerful artillery which prevented occupation of the plateaux north of Soissons. The VII Corps made progress north-eastwards. The XVIII Corps, moving northward, reached the Oise, but was unable to cross it, its line running roughly along the south bank of the river. The Third Army, taking advantage of the advance on its right, pushed out reconnoitring forces all along its front.

NOTE II

THE GERMANS ON THE 21ST AUGUST[1]

(Sketch 10)

" At 5 a.m. on the 21st August a mighty rolling barrage in thick
" fog opened the fight between Hamel and Moyenneville. Soon
" after the British divisions and squadrons of tanks began to
" advance, and the German troops, according to plan, evacuated
" the 3,000 to 4,000 yards' wide forward zone. The enemy attack
" expended itself in the first stage and under the fire of the German
" batteries and machine guns, stuck fast at the Miraumont–
" Courcelles railway and at the Ancre." The *4th Bavarian Division*
had only been in the line three days and the instructions for the
planned retirement had not penetrated down to all the units of
the two regiments in the front line. " The battalions in the
" forward zone offered resistance west of Achiet le Petit, whilst
" the *2nd Guard Reserve Division*, on their right, had given way
" before a thrust from the north-west, and so they were cut off in
" the fog. But towards 11 a.m., as visibility improved, the
" companies of both regiments which had occupied the artillery
" protective position west and south-west of Achiet le Grand.
" attacked the British and drove them back to Achiet le Petit,
" taking a hundred prisoners. The enemy assault had been
" brought to a stop with heavy loss, without the employment of
" the reserves. Nevertheless, in the course of the day the *6th
" Bavarian Reserve Division* was ordered forward to Sapignies "
[2 miles east of Achiet le Grand].[2]

---

[1] From B.O.A., pp. 534–5.
[2] This division had been resting since 6th August near Cambrai.

CHAPTER XI

THE BATTLE OF ALBERT 1918—(*continued*)

22ND AUGUST

(Sketches 10, 12, 13, 14.)

The 22nd August was spent by the Third Army (General Hon. Sir J. Byng), much against the Commander-in-Chief's inclination, in making preparations for a further advance. It was disturbed by a German counter-attack made, however, under a complete misunderstanding of the situation. The left of the Fourth Army (General Sir H. Rawlinson) north of the Somme was engaged in driving the enemy from his salient Bray–Dernancourt–Albert[1] (inclusive). The backbone of this salient was the long ridge of high ground between the Somme and the Ancre which afforded the Germans good views over the valleys of those rivers. Until Albert was recaptured it was well nigh impossible for the right corps of the Third Army to cross the swamps of the Ancre and press forward with the rest of the Army.

The German line between the Somme at Bray and the town of Albert (inclusive) was held by four divisions, the *43rd Reserve*, the *27th*, the *54th Reserve* and the *233rd* with two, the *25th* (fresh) and the *13th* (tired) in reserve, the latter being early used to reinforce the *233rd*, and the former, as will be seen, to make a counter-attack farther north.

A warning order had been issued by the Fourth Army on the 19th August : the main attack involving an advance of about two miles on a four-mile front was to be carried out by the III Corps (Lieut.-General A. Godley), actually by the 47th and 12th Divisions, with the 18th swinging forward to protect the left, whilst the 3rd Australian Division covered the right. This distribution placed the right wing of the 12th Division astride the mile-wide top of the ridge, which broadened out to nearly two miles near the objective, where it was not narrowed by the Happy Valley on the south side nor on the north by the long Fricourt valley. The 3rd Australian Division and 47th Division had to work across the spurs leading to the Somme, the right of the 12th Division along the top of the ridge, and its left over the

---

[1] See Sketch 13.

spurs leading to the Ancre, with the 18th Division assigned to the low ground between Méaulte and Albert.

In view of the varying distances, more on the right than on the left, which the several divisions had to advance, an intermediate objective was fixed about a thousand yards from the final objective. On reaching it, the 3rd Australian Division would halt for sixty-six minutes in order to give time for the left of the 47th Division to arrive, when the general advance was to be resumed. Ten tanks (Mark V) of the IV Tank Brigade were to work with both the 47th and 12th Divisions and four with the 18th; if the final objective were captured the III Corps Cavalry (2 squadrons of the 1/1st Northumberland Hussars), a troop of Australian Light Horse and six whippet tanks of the 6th Tank Battalion were to be ready to exploit the success by seizing the high ground, two thousand yards ahead, between Great Bear Copse and Bois Français.

The 58th Division (Major-General F. W. Ramsay), the reserve of the III Corps, was to send one brigade to a position behind the 47th and 12th Divisions, and one as reserve to the 18th; the latter was to detail one brigade, with guns, engineers and machine guns attached, to keep touch with the right of the Third Army and if circumstances permitted, to move through Albert.[1] Four extra brigades of field artillery were allotted to each of the 47th and 12th Divisions[2] and two extra to the 3rd Australian and 58th; the 47th and 12th Divisions, in addition, had the support of about forty 60-pdrs. of the corps artillery.

There was to be no preliminary bombardment. The 3rd Australian, 47th and 12th Divisions were to follow a creeping barrage, with smoke shells in it in the proportion of one to 15, which would begin at 4.49 a.m., four minutes after Zero, three hundred yards in front of the jumping-off line, and then move at the rate of a hundred yards in four minutes to the final objective. In the case, however, of the Australians, the barrage would make a pause on the intermediate line; in the 18th Division, to allow for the difficulties of the ground, it would make three halts.

---

[1] Each division of the III Corps had been warned on the 15th to have such a composite brigade ready, as an advanced guard, to follow up the enemy.

[2] The artillery of the 47th Division was supporting the 18th Division. It had two brigades of the 50th Division Artillery, one brigade of the 18th and three Army Field Brigades.

The night of the 21st/22nd being fine, a large amount of bombing was carried out : a total of twelve tons of explosives was dropped on Cambrai railway station and hangars at the aerodromes of Moislains and Offoy ; sheds at Marcoing station (on the Bapaume–Cambrai line) were set on fire ; and the railway bridge at Aubigny au Bac over the Sensée was hit.   During the fighting on the 22nd the air bombing was mainly directed against the railways radiating from Cambrai towards the front ; it was stoutly resisted by the enemy fliers, so that much confused fighting took place, in which four German planes were shot down, two in flames, without loss of a machine.

The Germans were uneasy and evidently expecting attack on the 22nd,[1] and were assisted by the bright light of a waning moon.   The deployment was nevertheless successfully achieved, although from 10 p.m. on the 21st the enemy carried out harassing fire on the front and back areas, mainly with 4·2-inch H.E. and gas shells.   At 2.30 a.m. he opened a bombardment of the front line, his machine guns too being very active, and continued it until 3.40 a.m., by which time a mist had arisen.   The bombardment was resumed at 4 a.m., fortunately with lengthened range, so that very few casualties were suffered.   When the British barrage dropped at 4.45 a.m. the retaliation on the batteries firing it was prompt.

The 9th Australian Brigade (Br.-General H. A. Goddard) led the advance on the right northward of Bray.   The village was not attacked as it was strongly held and could better be dealt with when progress had been made to the north of it ; but the 3rd Australian Pioneer Battalion, which was put into the line to hold the Etinehem spur, made demonstration of attack and actually gained a little ground.   The 35th and 33rd Battalions reached the intermediate line without much difficulty, the 33rd capturing a battalion headquarters and forty men.[2]   The pause on the intermediate line enabled the enemy to set about reorganizing his infantry and correcting the range of his guns.   Although most of his fire fell in rear of the attackers, some gas shells dropped among them forcing them to wear gas masks, and when the advance was resumed at 6.43 a.m. the opposition had stiffened and there was much machine-gun fire from Bray.

---

[1] Prisoners captured said that they had been standing-to since midnight.
[2] Of the *124th Regiment 27th (Württemberg) Division.*

But the Australians reached the final objective in the valley north of the village about 8.15 a.m. and in spite of fire carried out consolidation.

The 47th (2nd London) Division (Major-General Sir G. F. Gorringe) sent forward the 141st Brigade (Br.-General W. F. Mildren), which had taken over the divisional front on the night of the 20th/21st. In mist and smoke it had to cross a valley and a spur before it could reach the Happy Valley, its objective. Owing to bad staff work and the insufficient training of the young troops in movements in darkness, smoke, and mist, the two leading battalions, 1/20th and 1/19th London, lost count of distance and though the Germans surrendered freely, the battalions halted considerably short of the intermediate objective—as much as half a mile short on the right.

The 142nd Brigade (Br.-General R. McDouall), which had followed a mile behind the 141st, now took up the attack with the 1/22nd, 1/23rd and 1/24th London in line. It at once met with strong opposition, and, having started too far back at the appointed time, from the mistaken line of the 141st, lost the barrage. When visibility improved and the 141st discovered its error and moved forward to the intermediate line, the enemy shelling had become so heavy that it was impossible to consolidate there. Meantime, soon after 8 a.m., the extreme right of the 1/22nd London had reached its objective, the Chalk Pit at the southern end of the Happy Valley, and established touch with the 33rd Australian Battalion ; but the rest of the brigade could not get within three hundred yards of the objective. The German artillerymen on the front were now firing over open-sights, whilst oblique gun fire came from Ceylon Wood to the south-east, and particularly fierce machine-gun fire from Hill 105, part of the objective ; thus all further movement became impossible. To make matters worse, a gap arose between the 142nd Brigade and the 35th Brigade (12th Division) which left the enemy free to enfilade the troops of both. Of the ten tanks allotted to the 47th Division, the four with the 141st Brigade, carrying entrenching tools, reached the intermediate objective ; but of the six with the 142nd, only one. This tank entered the Happy Valley and rounded up a number of Germans, but owing to engine trouble and casualties among the crew had then to be withdrawn.

The two squadrons of the 1/1st Northumberland Hussars which with six whippet tanks were to push on to the line Great Bear Copse–Bois Français as soon as the 47th Division reached the final objective, had assembled in the early morning west of Tailles Wood. Though their patrols had not returned, the cavalry rode forward at 7.45 a.m., but owing to mechanical trouble the whippets did not accompany them far. Coming up to the successful part of the 142nd Brigade, but without ascertaining from the brigadier whether the road was clear, the squadrons entered the Happy Valley from the south and headed for the high ground on the north-east, actually behind the German front line. As soon as the leading squadron topped the rise it was confronted by a wire fence and found itself under rifle and machine-gun fire at very short range and bombing from the air. Retirement was at once ordered, and the squadron, reduced to twenty-three men, rallied in a sunken road west of the southern end of the Happy Valley, where the second squadron joined it. The two then retired behind the line of the 47th Division, the various parts of which had no serious difficulty in maintaining themselves in the positions they had won.

The 12th (Eastern) Division (Major-General H. W. Higginson) sent forward the 35th Brigade (Br.-General A. T. Beckwith) and the 36th (Br.-General C. S. Owen). One battalion of the latter (the 5/R. Berkshire on the left) was detailed to clear Méaulte under a barrage (moving at the rate of a hundred yards in two minutes, twice as fast as the remainder of the barrage on the divisional front). In order to keep down the fire from a German trench running due south from the village until the divisional barrage arrived, fifty drums of burning oil were projected into it at Zero by " D " Special Company R.E. and it was specially shelled by heavy artillery and field-howitzers.

The 5/R. Berkshire, although its assembly was seriously interfered with by gas, with the help of four tanks which kept well up, and of one company of the 6/Northamptonshire (54th Brigade, 18th Division) which co-operated on the left, quickly overcame all resistance in Méaulte. In the mist two of the tanks nearly charged into two enemy field batteries, and did succeed in silencing one with gun fire and dispersing the detachments of the other with machine-gun fire.

The general infantry advance was made for the first few hundred yards in the traditional waves, but then, in spite of the mist, in small bodies of sections and platoons, with almost complete success. The main resistance came from machine guns in shell holes.

In the 35th Brigade, the intermediate objective, where a twenty minutes' pause was to be made, was reached in good time by the 1/1st Cambridgeshire and 7/Norfolk, and then the 9/Essex and 6/Buffs (37th Brigade) passed through them. The three tanks attached to the brigade were late owing to a gas bombardment, and only one was able to proceed beyond the intermediate objective and this turned back when the mist began to clear. Pursued by heavy fire as it passed back through the 9/Essex, it occasioned that battalion heavy losses. The Essex therefore, like the 142nd Brigade, were forced to halt a little short of the objective ; but the 6/Buffs, on their left, succeeded in reaching it and in capturing many prisoners and machine guns.

The 9/Royal Fusiliers and 7/R. Sussex of the 36th Brigade with three tanks, which arrived late but in time for mopping up, were equally successful and on the final objective before 8.30 a.m.

The brigades of the 18th (Eastern) Division (Major-General R. P. Lee), though the plan assigned them was no more than the formation of a defensive flank, had no easy task before them. The 54th Brigade (Br.-General L. W. de V. Sadleir-Jackson, who was wounded on this day) had to bring up bridging material and force the passage of the Ancre, there 14 feet in breadth and 6 feet deep, with wide, marshy edges much cut up by shell fire ; and the 55th Brigade (Br.-General E. A. Wood) had to fight its way through Albert, a fair-sized town, over half a mile deep and much knocked about, the eastern portion of which was very strongly held.

Progress was easier than had been expected, possibly because the opposing German division, the *233rd*, had been in the line since the 6th July and its supporting division, the *13th*, had been badly battered during the 8th–12th August and, after a short rest, had been hurriedly brought back to the line.

During the night of the 21st/22nd patrols from the 54th Brigade managed to cross the Ancre in spite of incessant fire ; light trestle bridges were brought forward by the engineers and by 2 a.m. parties of the 6/Northamptonshire and 11/Royal Fusiliers were across. In consequence, the barrage which was to have fallen at Zero on the eastern bank for ten minutes was now omitted and orders were given for it to open on its second line, the high ground east of Vivier Mill, at Zero instead of 5.15 a.m.

At 4.45 a.m. sixteen footbridges spanned the Ancre, and with few casualties the 6/Northamptonshire (less one company near Méaulte) and the whole of the 11/Royal Fusiliers were over the stream and ready to launch the attack from the Vivier Mill–Albert Road, which they did at 5.53 a.m. the appointed hour, accompanied by four tanks of the 4th Battalion, which did good service.

By 8 a.m. the 6/Northamptonshire had almost reached its final objective and was digging in. The 11/Royal Fusiliers met with more severe opposition and, galled by enfilade fire from Albert, lost heavily; it nevertheless established a line east of Bellevue Farm, about half a mile from its objective; unable to advance from this position at 10 a.m. it began to dig in with its left on Black Wood.

The 8/East Surrey (55th Brigade), detailed to clear Albert and make good along the narrow-gauge railway east of the town, was shelled in the brigade assembly area with gas and high-explosive; but, under a barrage, it began the task of mopping up the eastern half of Albert promptly at 5.45 a.m., the hour fixed. In the mist many of the enemy's posts were taken completely off their guard, and the East Surrey going on in order to profit by the enemy's disorder were by 9.20 a.m. on the appointed line. By 10 a.m. Albert was practically free of Germans. Owing to interruption of communications the 7/Buffs, which should have continued the advance, did not appear, but it reached the eastern edge of Albert soon after without suffering any casualties.

Some misleading messages, whence they emanated is not known, as to the position of the 54th Brigade, stating that Tara Hill to the north was in its possession, led to the artillery being instructed not to fire on the hill; but when the 7/Buffs attempted to advance from the East Surrey line, it received violent fire from the western slopes of Tara and suffered such losses that further progress was impossible; connection, however, was made with the 54th Brigade at Black Wood.

By 12 noon, therefore, although in the centre the 142nd and 35th Brigades were a few hundred yards short of the final objective, excellent progress had been made ; but the day was hot, the men exhausted and short of water, and a great deal of ammunition had been expended. The Germans, now the mist had lifted, had good observation over the field from the higher ground which it had been hoped the cavalry would secure, and from observation balloons ; it was impossible to get up supplies, or for the field artillery to move forward from its original positions, now out of range, to support the infantry, although the heavy guns, farther back, were brought forward. Signs of German movement had been reported during the morning and shortly after 1 p.m. observers with the 33rd Australian Battalion, the left wing of the 9th Australian Brigade, saw German infantry emerge from Caftet Wood, near Carnoy,[1] in artillery formation, preceded by a line of skirmishers, moving in the direction of the left flank of the 47th Division north of the Happy Valley.[2] This information was immediately sent back, but did not reach the 47th Division headquarters until 2.20 p.m. Meantime Major-General Gorringe had received reports from other sources that bodies of Germans were crossing the Bray–Fricourt road making for the junction of the 47th and 12th Divisions, and at 2 p.m. a German barrage to cover the movement had begun. It was obvious a counter-attack was being launched.

The line of the 142nd Brigade was very thin, about six hundred men spread over about two miles. Br.-General McDouall sent up two officers and 80 men with eight Lewis guns, part of an improvised brigade reserve, and called for a barrage from the supporting artillery, which could not be complied with owing to shortage of ammunition at the gun positions. The enemy was able to filter through the line, and the 1/23rd and 1/24th London, much reduced by heavy losses, fell back to the intermediate position, where the 141st Brigade was dug in. The enemy attack then spread southwards to the 1/22nd London and the 3rd Australian Division. Against the latter no progress whatever was made ; the 1/22nd London formed a defensive left flank, which was

---

[1] Where the *25th Division* was concentrated (Regimental history). Soon after the attack had developed the commander of the *X Corps* had given orders for a counter-attack and tor the *25th Division* to be moved forward to lead it. See Note II at end of Chapter.

[2] The objective was Hill 107, near the head of the valley.

eventually extended by two battalions of the 11th Australian Brigade and a battalion of the 140th Brigade sent up by Br.-General H. B. P. L. Kennedy. The resistance offered was sufficient to stop the Germans, who lost heavily, fell into complete confusion and at night withdrew from their advanced and salient position.[1]

At 6.25 p.m. Major-General Gorringe ordered Br.-General Kennedy (140th Brigade) to take charge of the situation, reinforcing the line with his own units if necessary, and during the night the line of the 47th Division was reorganized, without any interference from the enemy, with the 141st Brigade on the right and the 140th on the left.

When the retirement of the 142nd Brigade exposed the right of the 12th Division, the 9/Essex (35th Brigade) fell back about a third of a mile. Major-General Higginson ordered the 37th Brigade to safeguard the right flank, but the 35th Brigade managed to re-form its own line. Elsewhere on the 12th Division front the afternoon passed without incident. In the 18th Division the 2/Bedfordshire (54th Brigade) in the course of the afternoon passed through the 11/Royal Fusiliers, which was east of Bellevue Farm with its left on Black Wood, and captured the high ground beyond, thus prolonging the line of the 6/Northamptonshire on the final objective.

The left wing of the Fourth Army had fulfilled its task of obliterating the enemy salient between the Somme and the Ancre and of recapturing Albert.

The Third Army,[2] according to the G.H.Q. programme, was to stand fast on the 22nd whilst guns and troops were got into position for the continuation of the general advance next day. Some attacks were made on its divisions without success, the enemy failing to penetrate anywhere and leaving many prisoners in British hands. These attacks receive scant notice in the Third Army reports and would hardly be worth mentioning were it not that they were the outcome of a general offensive ordered by General von Below of

---

[1] See Note II at end of Chapter.
[2] See Sketch 10.

the *Seventeenth Army*.[1]   Under the misapprehension that the British had tried and failed to break through on the 21st " he believed that he could not better upset the hostile plans " than by an attack on a broad front next day.   The orders " were given in all haste ".   The result was extremely disappointing to him.[2]

In the V Corps, on the right, the 62nd Brigade of the 21st Division was attacked about 5 a.m.[3] and its extreme left driven back slightly, so a defensive flank was formed. Another attack at 7.30 a.m. got within thirty yards of the line, but was repulsed.   In the 110th (Br.-General H. R. Cumming) the sister brigade on the right, which was not attacked, two companies of the 6/Leicestershire crossed the Ancre north of St. Pierre Divion and, by bombing up trenches, got in touch with the forward companies of the 12th/13th Northumberland Fusiliers (62nd Brigade), already established across the stream.

In the IV Corps (42nd, New Zealand, 5th and 63rd Divisions) the enemy apparently intended to make a strong attack on the 42nd Division at 5 a.m. and fired a bombardment.   But the movement, organized in haste, miscarried. Parties drifted from north to south across the front of the 5th Division, which was also bombarded and half-heartedly attacked, although the short front of the New Zealand Division between the 42nd and 5th was left in peace.

A significant incident happened on the front of the 5th Division.   Two scouts of the 1/Devonshire (95th Brigade) had worked forward in the mist of the early morning to an old trench, which they found unoccupied.   Suddenly a crowd of Germans jumped into it.   The scouts opened fire with the surprising result that the whole party, 242 strong but not able to see how small was the number of their opponents, surrendered and were marched back by the two men.[4] About the same time, farther to the left, the 12/Gloucestershire of the same brigade sent out two platoons to the front

---

[1] B.O.A. p. 535.   One of the Army's two reserve divisions, the *6th Bavarian Reserve*, had been engaged on the 21st ; the other, the *40th*, was employed in the counter-offensive.

[2] See Note II at the end of Chapter for the German account.

[3] By part of the *40th Division*.

[4] Lance-Corporal G. Onions received the V.C. and his companion Private H. J. C. Eades the D.C.M.   The German party had been sent to attack the 42nd Division and had lost its way.

to enfilade the advancing enemy. They did so with such good effect that with assistance from troops of the 42nd Division they captured 180 Germans and five machine guns.

The 63rd Division easily repulsed the 5 a.m. attack and a more serious one which, beginning between 7 and 8 a.m., continued with intervals until 11 a.m., when a general enemy withdrawal took place. This offered one company of the machine-gun battalion excellent targets of which it took full advantage. About 1.15 p.m. the enemy attacked again, threatening especially the left of the division where there was a gap owing to a small success the enemy had achieved against the 9th Brigade (3rd Division) ; but this was filled by the 2/Royal Irish, who drove the enemy out of the trench he had taken.[1]

In the VI Corps the 8th Brigade, the left of the 3rd Division, was attacked at 5 a.m.,[2] as was the 2nd Guards Brigade, next to it ; but the Germans were everywhere repulsed with heavy loss. They did not advance again on this part of the front, although they continued shelling and machine-gun fire for the rest of the day. About 7 a.m., however, they fell on the 9th Brigade (on the right of the 8th) and succeeded in establishing themselves in a refused flank on its right. From this position of vantage, by trench mortar and machine-gun fire, they inflicted considerable casualties on the 9th and 8th Brigades, but could not dislodge them. The trench was retaken at 10 p.m. by the 1/North-umberland Fusiliers under cover of a trench-mortar barrage and sixty prisoners were captured.

Thus the German counter-offensive north of the Ancre had even less success than the attempt at one made south of the river.

Before noon on the 22nd, before the results of the day were known, G.H.Q. issued a short order directing that the attack of the Third Army should be resumed with the utmost vigour, the Fourth Army co-operating, as " the enemy is

---

[1] The *91st Reserve Regiment* (*2nd Guard Reserve Division* in the line) claims that one company reached the south-east corner of Logeast Wood ; but British accounts do not support this.

[2] By the *40th Division*.

" being pressed from the Scarpe to Soissons,[1] and it is
" essential in accordance with the general plan of operations
" that he should be attacked continuously and with the
" utmost determination ".

At 11.30 p.m. Sir Douglas Haig emphasized this order by
telegraphing to his Army commanders and the G.O.C.
Cavalry Corps instructions[2] (conversationally known as
" ginger ")—based on a memorandum received from
Maréchal Foch. They were requested to bring to the notice
of all subordinate leaders that the methods hitherto followed
with limited objectives when the Germans were strong were
not suited to the present weakened condition of their troops
and the disorganized state of their plans : the enemy had
not the means to deliver effective counter-attacks, or even
to hold continuous positions ; advance in regular lines and
step by step was no longer necessary ; each division should
press on even if its flanks were temporarily exposed, and
reinforcements should be directed on sectors where the
troops were gaining ground, not where they were checked ;
the most resolute offensive was everywhere desirable and
risks which a month before would have been criminal to
incur ought now to be taken as a duty.

On receipt of the order from G.H.Q. the headquarters of
the Fourth Army issued theirs of which the following is a
summary, fixing the objectives[3] :

(1) The portion of the Australian Corps north of the
Somme and the III Corps on its left were to exploit
their successes by a combined attack to be made at
4.45 a.m. on the 23rd to gain a line roughly one mile
ahead. This line ran along the eastern edge of the
Bray spur, due north to a point west of Billon Farm,
thence slightly north of west across the high ground to
the Bray–Fricourt road, and west of north along the
high ground to Becordel Bécourt and thence along Tara
Hill to the Albert–Bapaume road.

(2) South of the Somme the Australian Corps was to
carry out the operation to improve the position between
Lihons and the river, mentioned in the two Fourth
Army orders of the 19th August earlier in this chapter.
The line to be established ran north from the front line

---

[1] See Note I at the end of Chapter.
[2] Appendix XX.
[3] These orders were issued before the result of the German counter-
offensive during the afternoon of the 22nd was known. See Sketch 13.

just south of Herleville, crossed the Amiens–Brie road half a mile west of Foucaucourt, and, passing south of Chuignes and north of Chuignolles, rejoined the front line on the southern bank of the Somme ; if opportunity occurred, the sector of the line from Chuignes to the river was to be swung forward so as to run through that village due north across the high ground to the western outskirts of Cappy on the south bank of the Somme opposite the south-eastern end of the Bray spur.

The headquarters of the III Corps issued orders at 6.30 p.m. for an attack by the 47th, 12th, and 18th Divisions. A modification had to be made, however, on receipt at corps headquarters of information as to the result of the German counter-offensive during the afternoon. Lieut.-General Godley judged that the 47th Division, particularly the 142nd Brigade, would be unable to continue the attack.[1] He therefore determined to limit the offensive on the 23rd to his northern wing where, to enable the V Corps, the right of the Third Army, to make progress it was essential that the Tara Hill–Usna Hill ridge astride the Albert–Bapaume road should be captured. After a consultation between Major-General Lee, commanding the 18th Division on the left of the Fourth Army and Major-General Cubitt, commanding the 38th Division, the right division of the Third Army, it was decided that the 53rd Brigade (Br.-General M. G. H. Barker), of the 18th Division, which had been in reserve on the 22nd, and the 113th Brigade (Br.-General H. E. ap Rhys-Pryce), of the 38th Division, should make a combined attack early on the 23rd : the 53rd Brigade against Tara Hill, and the 113th Brigade, moving through Albert and north of the Albert–Bapaume road, against Usna Hill. In order to give these two brigades room in which to deploy east of Albert it was necessary for the 55th Brigade, then in the eastern outskirts, to secure the final objective, astride the highway, which it had been unable to reach during daylight. A night operation was therefore necessary. After preparation by all available artillery, trench mortars and machine guns from 7 to 11 p.m., the 7/Buffs (55th Brigade), covered by patrols, in spite of

---

[1] The 175th Bde., 58th Division from corps reserve was placed at the disposal of Major-General Sir G. F. Gorringe, commanding 47th Division, to enable him to relieve the 142nd Brigade.

its exertions during the day, advanced with great dash and by 2.30 a.m. (23rd) had secured the original final objective. All was thus ready for the main operation.

NOTE I

THE FRENCH ON THE 22nd AUGUST

(Sketch 12)

The French First Army, next to the British, again did not move. The right and centre of the Third Army advanced about 1½ miles and reached the line of the Divette ; the Tenth Army continued to make good progress on its whole front except on the extreme left, pushing eastwards about two miles. The enemy resistance opposite the Third and First Armies seemed to be increasing, and reserves, at least seven divisions, to be collected opposite the junction of the Third and First Armies.

NOTE II

THE GERMANS ON THE 22nd AUGUST

(Sketches 10 and 13)

The histories of the infantry regiments opposite the Fourth Army sector, as excuse for defeat, all speak of the severity of the rolling barrage : " it was not that it was directed on one line or " on a narrow zone and then moved forward, but from the very " beginning a zone more than a kilometre in depth was over- " whelmed with a perfect hail of shell " " *27th (Württemberg) Division.*"

As soon as it was certain that the British were going to attack, the regiments in the divisional reserve were brought forward close to the line. They had scarcely reached their new positions when the following corps order was received :
(Extract)

(1) The corps orders a counter-attack to be made with all available reserves.

(2) The main counter-attack will be made by the *25th Division* [then in reserve near Vaulx Vraucourt].

In addition to all its own troops it will have the *123rd Grenadier Regiment (27th Division)* placed at its disposal. It will drive the enemy from the high ground east of Poplar Hill[1] through our outpost line and past Morlancourt.

(3) The *54th Reserve, 233rd,* and *27th Divisions* [to the last of which the *43rd Reserve Division* was attached] will support the main counter-attack with all their available artillery.

---

[1] Poplar Hill is the point on Sketch 13 marked 107 on the main Bray–Albert road.

(4) The left boundary of the attack : Bronfay Farm—northern edge of Tailles Wood.

(5) The *27th Division* will attack and capture the high ground north of Etinehem, mop up the village and push on through Tailles and Gressaire Woods in touch with the *25th Division.*

The commander of the *27th Division*, however, decided that he could not attack for three reasons :

(*a*) he had no infantry reserves available in his own division after the *123rd Grenadiers* had been taken away ;

(*b*) he could not support an attack by the *203rd Reserve Regiment* (*43rd Reserve Division*) through Bray or an advance by the *202nd Reserve Regiment* (*43rd Reserve Division*) south of the village across the Somme, because his own artillery had been ordered mainly to support the attack of the *25th Division* by firing in the *54th Reserve Division's* sector ;

(*c*) the infantry regiments, both of his own division and of the *43rd Reserve Division*, had no longer the necessary strength to deliver an attack, although the regiments of the *43rd Reserve Division* were numerically a little stronger than those of the *27th Division.*

There was nothing to be done therefore but to await the effect of the counter-attack by the *25th Division*, which was fresh. But orders were given for the infantry of the *27th* and *43rd Reserve Divisions* to keep in touch with the advance of the left flank of the *25th Division*, which they did.

" The counter-attack by the *25th Division* did not take place " until the late hours of the afternoon. According to the first " messages and information it had been surprisingly successful. " It was rumoured that the division had reached Tailles Wood " and Morlancourt itself. These rumours reached O.H.L. also. " . . . But the truth was that the *25th Division* had not driven " the enemy back more than 500 metres at any point. It lost " heavily and its units fell into complete confusion ".

In the attempted advance of the *27th Division* the *124th Regiment* was completely shattered. The remnants were collected well behind the line. During the night the *120th Regiment*, and the *201st Regiment* (*43rd Reserve Division*) were, to some extent, able to reorganize their units.

The second reserve division, the *13th*, did no more than unsuccessfully reinforce the *233rd* in front of Albert.

What is known of the attempted counter-attack of the *40th Division* and others against the Third Army has been given in notes to the text.

CHAPTER XII

BATTLE OF ALBERT 1918 (*continued*)

23RD AUGUST

(Sketches 10, 12, 13, 14.)

On the 23rd August, a day of great heat, both the Fourth and Third Armies and the French Tenth Army continued the offensive.[1] The attack of the Fourth Army (General Sir H. Rawlinson) launched on the 22nd was extended to the south of the Somme. It had been intended that all its troops north of the river should continue their operations in conjunction ; but the German counter-offensive made against them during the afternoon of the 22nd had disarranged this plan ; only the northern (left) wing of the III Corps (Lieut.-General Sir A. Godley) was engaged, and this in crder to support the right of the Third Army. Although south of the Somme two divisions of the Fourth Army were opposed by four German, and north of it one division by two, on both banks the results of the day's fighting were very satisfactory, a wedge of ground two miles in mean depth on a frontage of over four miles being gained, the objectives reached and many prisoners and guns captured.

The Third Army (General Hon. Sir J. Byng)[2] was equally successful, on a larger scale, seven divisions, opposed by seven German, advancing two to four thousand yards on an eleven-mile frontage, capturing a number of villages and reaching their objectives with only one failure of importance, and driving the enemy from the last hold on his main line of resistance, the strongly entrenched Arras–Albert railway embankment and cutting.

At the junction of the Fourth and Third Armies, by a small operation, the Germans were driven farther from Albert.

The 23rd August was, in fact, disastrous for the Germans, as their own regimental accounts admit.[3] The German official summary of the day[4] hardly gives a true picture ; for, in spite of the divisional odds being actually against the

---

[1] See Sketch 13.
[2] See Sketch 10.
[3] See Note II at end of Chapter.
[4] B.O.A., p. 535.

British, it reads, " only step by step did the German troops,
" under pressure of superior force (*Uebermacht*) yield a few
" feet of ground ". Similar assertions are, however, made
for nearly every day of the " Allied Advance to Victory ".

The objective assigned by the Fourth Army to the
Australian Corps was the general line Herleville–Chuignes–
Froissy Beacon (near the Somme canal, at this spot 600 yards
or more from the river). To reach it Lieut.-General Sir J.
Monash decided to employ the 32nd Division (Major-General
T. S. Lambert) already in the line, and the 1st Australian
(Major-General T. W. Glasgow), which was to take over
from the 5th Australian Division, and carry out the operation
in three phases.

The objective in the first phase was the line Herleville–
Plateau Woods–Arcy Woods–Chuignolles, beyond which was
a long deep valley running from Herleville down to the
Somme. The enemy had been occupied since the 12th in
entrenching this line, which was on a rise of ground, and a
certain amount of resistance was to be expected, to overcome
which artillery and tanks must be used. The second objective
was a line along the western slopes of the Herleville valley
between Chuignolles and Chuignes, and, as no serious
opposition was likely, the attack was to be made by the
1st Australian Division without artillery support. The final
objective, if all went well, was the high ground east of the
valley above mentioned, the village of Chuignes (which is at
the bottom of a branch valley leading into the Herleville
valley) and a line just west of the Chuignes–Cappy road.

During the night of the 22nd/23rd the enemy opposite
the 32nd Division, which had to capture Herleville and the
line on either side of it, as on the two previous nights, was
restless. This symptom here and elsewhere at the front,
was not entirely due to the Royal Air Force which, the night
being fine with the moon shining in a clear sky, bombed
back areas, the railway junctions of Somain, Valenciennes
and Cambrai, and repeated this at daylight, also attacking
the villages used as billets, and troops and transport on the
roads opposite both the Fourth and Third Armies. As one
sign of uneasiness, the German high velocity guns and heavy
howitzers shelled roads and tracks leading to the front, and

paid special attention to the area between the villages of Harbonnières, Vauvillers and Framerville, but without occasioning casualties. Between 2 and 4 a.m., when the 96th and 97th Brigades (Br.-Generals A. C. Girdwood and J. R. M. Minshull-Ford) of the 32nd Division were lying out on the bare glacis slope in front of Herleville, at first, in strong moonlight, red and green lights were constantly sent up by the German front line, and bursts of gunfire followed. It was later discovered, however, from prisoners that the attackers had not been seen. Fortunately most of the shells went over and fell in a valley five hundred yards in rear, but shortly before zero hour a number of them found the left company of the 10/Argyll and Sutherland Highlanders, on the northern flank of the division, and caused the loss of all its officers and 70 per cent. of its men, so that it had to be relieved. Nevertheless, by 3.45 a.m., the forming up of all the front-line battalions had been accomplished.

No preliminary bombardment was fired ; the advance was covered by a creeping barrage (10 per cent. smoke, 45 H.E. and 45 shrapnel), which dropped two hundred yards ahead of the line at Zero, 4.45 a.m. In the case of the 32nd Division it was provided by six brigades of field artillery,[1] and of the 1st Australian, which had a wider frontage, by nine.[2] To mislead the enemy as to the extent of the attack, the artillery of the 4th Australian Division, on the right of the 32nd, also fired the barrage.

The corps heavy artillery, in addition to counter-battery and normal target fire, kept the Somme crossings at Cappy and Eclusier and the great Amiens–Brie–St. Quentin road under steady fire.

Fourteen tanks of the 10th Battalion were allotted to the 97th Brigade of the 32nd Division, which was to attack Herleville, and 12 each, of the 13th and 2nd Tank Battalions, to the two attacking Australian brigades.

The Royal Air Force gave considerable assistance with low-flying attacks in addition to its other activities, particularly in spotting and firing on guns and machine-gun nests. These were carried out on the Fourth Army front chiefly by No. 203 Squadron.

---

[1] 32nd and 2nd Australian Divisions and XIV and 189th (Army) Brigades R.F.A.

[2] 2nd and 5th Australian Divisions, V, XII, XXIII and 298th (Army) Brigades R.F.A., and XVI (Army) Brigade R.H.A.

It was dark at 4.45 a.m. when the advance began. The 96th Brigade, with the 4th Australian Brigade on its right, had only a short distance, some three hundred yards, to go, but considerable opposition was encountered by the 16th Australian Battalion and the 16/Lancashire Fusiliers, the enemy, except on the extreme right, fighting stubbornly with machine guns and bombs ; but the brigade objectives were reached and consolidated.[1]

The 97th Brigade sent the 2/K.O.Y.L.I. and 10/Argyll to the attack, each with six tanks, with the 1/5th Border Regiment in reserve. The tanks, eight with the leading companies and four with the supports, reached the infantry before the barrage made its first lift at 4.48 a.m., at which moment the reply of the enemy, not very heavy or accurate, began to fall. With valuable assistance from the tanks the two battalions, although they had to cross nasty open ground, went straight through to their objective, which they reached between 8.30 and 9 a.m. Clearing Herleville and passing over a maze of German trenches north of it, they killed and took prisoner many Germans, those in the village seeming bewildered ; a captured battalion commander told Br.-General Minshull-Ford, as excuse, that his men had only just come into the line and did not know it.

Four of the tanks remained in support of the 97th Brigade until 7.15 a.m., when they were withdrawn ; the other five still available, in accordance with orders, went to assist the 2nd Australian Brigade.[2]

A gap was discovered on the left of the 97th Brigade. The new left company of the Argyll had been ordered to keep touch with the Australians, and when the latter eased off to the left it had stuck to them ; coming under heavy machine-gun fire, it lost all its officers, all its sergeants save one, and about fifty men, and the rest joined the 6th Australian Battalion and remained with it all night. From behind the gap thus caused and particularly from Herleville Woods parties of Germans machine-gunned the main Argyll

---

[1] For his great gallantry, initiative and leadership, Lieut. L. D. McCarthy, 16th Australian Battalion, was awarded the V.C. With a small party, he cleared 700 yards of enemy trench almost single-handed, killing 20 Germans and capturing 40.

[2] Of the balance one had received a direct hit and was burnt out whilst on the objective, whilst another had mechanical trouble there ; the third broke down on the way to the objective. Both damaged machines were repaired.

line. They were dealt with by trench mortars and bombs, and the unpleasant situation gradually eliminated ; but it was not until towards 9 p.m. that the gap was filled by the Australians and a platoon of the 1/5th Border Regiment.

The K.O.Y.L.I. also received machine-gun fire from the left rear, and formed a defensive flank to meet a rumoured counter-attack from the Herleville valley, which did not, however, develop. No less than twelve bombing attacks, covered by machine-gun fire, were made up old trenches against the Yorkshire front. But all were repulsed, and when dusk fell, in conjunction with the 96th Brigade, posts were pushed four hundred yards forward.

During the night of the 21st/22nd the 2nd and 1st Australian Brigades (Br.-Generals J. Heane and I. G. Mackay), which were to lead the attack of the 1st Australian Division, had relieved the 14th and 15th Australian Brigades ; but battalions of the two latter were left in the front line, so that the enemy might have no inkling of the coming assault, and it was not until half an hour before zero hour that they were withdrawn.

The 2nd and 1st Australian Brigades attacked with the 6th and 5th and the 4th and 1st Battalions, respectively, and the other four in reserve. The 14th Australian Brigade (5th Division, Br.-General J. C. Stewart) was placed at the disposal of the 1st Australian Division for defensive purposes, if required.

The ground over which the 2nd Australian Brigade had to advance to the first objective was well adapted for defence, being intersected by deep gullies and sunken roads, besides old trenches, and dotted with woods, with the Herleville valley beyond it. Although at Zero the twelve tanks had not arrived, the infantry moved forward punctually under an excellent, evenly placed barrage. The enemy outpost line did not give much trouble ; but from the woods beyond opposition to the 6th Battalion was stiff, and the forward movement slowed down, with the result that the barrage was lost. The 5th Battalion encountered little resistance, except near St. Martin Woods, and this was overcome with some assistance from the 7th Battalion in support. By 5.15 a.m. heavy fighting in the 6th Battalion sector was in progress in St. Denis Wood No. 1 and the ground east of it. Half an hour later this wood was captured, but Germans still held out in the big St. Martin's Wood No. 4 and casualties became heavy, particularly amongst the officers. The tanks now arrived and rendered valuable assistance, one machine knocking out twenty machine guns in front of St. Martin's Wood No. 4 after a stubborn fight ; but the posts in the woods still held up the advance. A company commander of the supporting battalion, the 8th, grasping the situation, took forward his men, re-formed the 6th in dead ground and charged into and through the woods.[1] By 6.25 a.m. the groups in the front line were crossing the Herleville valley just east of the woods, and by 7 a.m. the right had reached the objective. The left was checked by fire from Plateau Wood No. 2 to the north. This wood was skilfully attacked from the rear, and by 7.30 a.m. the whole of the objective of the 2nd Australian Brigade had been attained, seven of the twelve tanks reaching it, and nine rallying after the action.

Fire was so intense that exploitation was out of the question. The situation, besides, was not satisfactory, owing to the gap on the right, already mentioned, between the 6th Battalion and the 32nd Division. At 10 a.m. a second company of the 8th Battalion was sent to mop up Herleville Wood, in which, it proved, many enemy snipers were hidden, and to close the gap. The company had fighting most of the way. Midday was past before it reached a sunken road close behind the front line from which it could flank the gap, and, as already mentioned, it was night before the gap was closed.

The 1st Australian Brigade, with its left on the Somme canal, had a more complicated task than the 2nd ; so it was to be carried out in three phases. The 4th and 1st Battalions led with the 3rd in support and the 2nd in reserve. Ahead, beyond the spur on which the front line stood, was the lower end of the Herleville valley, with branch valleys on either side of it, in which lay the villages of Chuignolles and Chuignes. Here, also, were many small woods.

The first objective was Arcy Woods–Chuignolles–Luc Wood, in order to form a defensive left flank commanding

---

[1] Lieut. W. D. Joynt, 8th Australian Battalion, was awarded the V.C. for his brilliant initiative and leadership on this occasion and subsequently, until he was badly wounded.

the lower end of the Herleville valley. At 4.45 a.m. eleven tanks moved through the front line and, following closely, the infantry made rapid progress and took prisoners in considerable numbers. By 5.45 a.m. the line was east of Matto Woods, and Chuignolles wood and village had been captured ; the left, after hard fighting and running into its own barrage, was actually some hundreds of yards beyond the objective. The second line companies of the 4th Battalion which had leap-frogged the original leaders were delayed by the pace of the barrage, but supported by two tanks and overhead machine-gun fire, they pressed through Arcy Woods, capturing a 15-inch gun in No. 2, and between 7 and 7.15 a.m. reported themselves on the first objective. Their attempts to push farther were at first unsuccessful. The position in Chuignes was obscure, but a patrol reported that the village itself was not occupied by the Germans, although they had many machine guns on the high ground north of it. Heavy machine-gun fire indeed was harassing the left flank, and, although this was overcome with the help of the 59th Battalion (5th Australian Division), attempts to enter Long Wood (north of the eastern end of Chuignolles) failed, and Luc Wood, west of it, also offered much resistance. With the help of the 10th Battalion (3rd Australian Brigade), which, at 6 a.m., had been ordered to guard the left flank, by 7.45 a.m., in spite of fire from Marly Woods, on the north-east, Long Wood had been cleared'and posts established on its eastern and northern edges, and by 9.15 a.m. Luc Wood also. An hour later the field artillery succeeded in overcoming the fire which had been harassing the left flank ever since the opening of the attack, and the 10th Battalion prolonged the line to the Somme. When the artillery barrage ceased at 7 a.m., and the tanks had no protection from it or from smoke, several received direct hits, and only six of the eleven rallied.

By the enterprise of the 1st Battalion in capturing Chuignolles and Long Wood, the second phase of the attack, with a line along the foot of the western slope of the valley between Chuignolles and Chuignes as objective, had become merged into the first phase. There remained the final task of capturing Chuignes and of establishing a line running north from that village across the high ground by Garenne Wood to the Somme, and the Germans were holding this in strength.

Major-General Glasgow decided therefore that an artillery barrage was necessary to cover the infantry advance. This was to be made at 2 p.m. by the 3rd Battalion (1st Australian Brigade), against Chuignes, and by the 3rd Australian Brigade, through the left of the line of the 1st Battalion, against the rest of the objective, defined as from the southern edge of Garenne Wood to the northern end of Marly Woods lying to the north-west. The 1st Battalion itself was to exploit its previous gains and push forward to a spur on the far side of Herleville valley, the lower part of which was full of coal and timber stacks and huts, and other similar spurs between it and the Marly Woods.

The 3rd Battalion crossed the valley under heavy field-gun and machine-gun fire, but as it approached Chuignes under a barrage the Germans retreated hurriedly, and the final objective east of the village was gained. By good use of ground the 1st Battalion, although it had barely half an hour's notice of the attack, by 3.30 p.m. had also reached its objective, dislodging the Germans, either shooting or capturing them as they tried to escape, and seizing an anti-tank gun which, since the early morning, had been causing much trouble.

The battalions of the 3rd Australian Brigade, which had been sheltering near St. Germains Wood, between Proyart and the Somme, since early morning, had suffered from shell fire and the consequent explosion of a dump, losing about one hundred and fifty men, before they advanced between 12.30 and 1 p.m. The 12th and 9th led with the 11th in support. No tanks were sent to the 3rd Australian Brigade. It had been intended that those which had accompanied the 1st should have assisted it, but this plan was abandoned, first because no suitable rallying point unexposed to direct enemy gun-fire could be found ; and, secondly, because the eastern slopes of the Herleville Valley near Chuignolles were almost precipitous and beyond the capabilities of the tanks.

After passing over the high ground west of Chuignolles the 12th Battalion was seen working down the gulley on the north side of the village ; it came under fire from machine guns still hidden in Long and Marly Woods, and was unable, by two hundred yards, to reach the jumping-off line alongside the 1st Battalion. The 9th had to pass through a barrage of 8-inch and gas shell which delayed and somewhat dis-organized it ; but, nevertheless, it arrived at the jumping-off line to time. The corps heavy artillery now opened fire against the defenders of the high ground, including those east of Bray, whence the advance could be enfiladed.

The 12th Battalion followed the barrage, fired by three field artillery brigades, which fell at first two hundred yards in front of the jumping-off line, as closely as it could. The Germans remaining in the woods were rapidly mopped up ; the heights overlooking Chuignolles from the east were rushed by the right wing of the 12th Battalion ; but sharp fighting at the top took place before the enemy fell back northwards to Garenne Wood, in which there were many machine guns. To avoid frontal assault which would have been costly, the wood was attacked from the north and south-east and soon captured with about seventy prisoners. To the left wing of the 12th and to the 9th Battalion less resistance was offered, but the 11th was nevertheless drawn into the battle. Two of its companies took the enemy in flank by surprise whilst the other two attacked Froissy Beacon from the canal side and thus determined the result. In little over an hour the 3rd Australian Brigade had secured its entire objective and thus completed the task of the Australian Corps, which on this day struck one of its hardest blows, according to plan. The enemy's artillery line had not, however, been reached and in consequence the Australians were exposed to severe shelling.

North of the Somme, the pioneer battalion of the 3rd Australian Division, seeing the retirement of the Germans near Froissy Beacon as a result of the attack of the 3rd Australian Brigade at 2.30 p.m., sent patrols and machine-gun detachments across the river in boats left by the enemy, and pushing over the swampy ground between the river and the canal inflicted considerable casualties. At 3.30 p.m. the battalion received orders from the 9th Australian Brigade to occupy Neuville and the area south of Bray (which was to be attacked during the night) enclosed between the river and the canal. Footbridges were thrown over the Somme and the canal near their junction south of Neuville, two companies were sent over, and by 8 p.m. the area had been mopped up with little opposition.

In the III Corps the 47th and 12th Divisions were not engaged in operations on this day, but the 18th Division co-operated with the attack of the 38th Division of the Third Army, as will be narrated in dealing with that Army.

On the evening of the 21st General Byng (Third Army) had issued orders for the extension to the left of the attack made that day.[1] His object was to gain a good departure position for an advance against the crescent-shaped Hamelincourt–Héninel[2] ridge, between the Sensée and the Cojeul, which was concave to the VI Corps front. He left it to Lieut.-General Haldane to select the objectives for the 23rd, and placed additional troops at his disposal. These were the 52nd, 56th and 57th (less a brigade) Divisions,[3] two Army Brigades R.F.A., three brigades R.G.A. and the III Tank Brigade (63 tanks) ; the 2nd Cavalry Brigade also would move into his area.

Sir Douglas Haig's order of the afternoon of the 22nd[4] obviously demanded something more than a partial and preliminary operation. General Byng, with the assistance of Lieut.-General Haldane, therefore elaborated a scheme for a more vigorous offensive, and proceeded with it to G.H.Q. There he had discussed it with Lieut.-General Lawrence, the Chief of the General Staff, and received approval.

The whole Third Army was to attack, the R.A.F. providing five squadrons for low-flying operations : No. 3, No. 17 American and Nos. 1, 54 and 73 of the headquarters IX Brigade, temporarily attached to the III Brigade ; whilst No. 73 was to co-operate with the tanks and make diving attacks on anti-aircraft batteries.[5]

As the enemy's position, Irles–Achiet le Grand opposite the IV Corps, in the centre of the Third Army, was exceedingly strong, to approach it frontally would have involved very heavy casualties. It was therefore decided to turn it on both flanks. The V Corps, on the right, linking up with the Fourth Army attack would turn the Thiepval position, opposite it on the bank of the Ancre, from the south and then push north-eastwards towards Pys (south of Irles).

---

[1] See Sketch 10.

[2] Héninel is two miles north-east of Henin, just off Sketch 10.

[3] The two former had been in the First Army (the 52nd previously in Palestine) ; the 57th came from the general reserve, it had not been engaged in the March–April offensives.

The VI Corps already contained the Guards, 2nd, 3rd and 59th Divisions. The reinforcements gave it a total of 564 field and 252 heavy guns.

[4] *See* p. 207.

[5] Neither the British nor the German regimental diaries give details of the place and time of the air-attacks.

The VI Corps, on the left of the IV, in addition to extending its left as already arranged, was to capture Gomiecourt (two miles north of Achiet le Grand and on high ground commanding that village) during the night of the 22nd/23rd, and after this village had been taken the IV Corps was to advance against the Irles–Achiet le Grand position. The VI Corps in conjunction with the IV Corps—at a time to be arranged between the two commanders—was to push forward eastwards from Gomiecourt towards Sapignies–Ervillers. Great importance therefore attached to the successful result of the operations against Gomiecourt and they will be dealt with first.

Lieut.-General Haldane selected the 3rd Division (Major-General C. J. Deverell), his earlier command, and seven brigades of field[1] and two brigades of heavy artillery,[2] to capture the village, supported by 12 tanks of the 7th and 12th Tank Battalions. If successful Major-General Deverell was to push eastward from Gomiecourt towards Béhagnies–Ervillers in order to overlook the Sensée valley. At a conference at 2 p.m. zero hour was made 3 a.m. but it was subsequently changed to 4 a.m., and even that hour gave little time for preparation. The 2nd Division (Major-General C. E. Pereira), in reserve, was to close up to the 3rd and be prepared to pass through it at about 11 a.m. to attack Béhagnies and Ervillers in conjunction with the attack of the IV Corps ; but it was to carry out the operation irrespective of the success or failure of the IV Corps. So sure did Lieut.-General Haldane feel of taking Gomiecourt and of taking it quickly that he fixed the hour for the general attack only 55 minutes later than that of the 3rd Division.

Under a creeping barrage, 75 per cent. shrapnel and 25 per cent. H.E., and a fixed barrage from 40 machine guns, the 76th Brigade (Br.-General C. L. Porter) moved forward on Gomiecourt, with the 8th on its left and the 3/Grenadiers (2nd Guards Brigade) guarding the latter's outer flank. Although some trouble occurred in taking up assembly positions owing to the presence of enemy parties which had

---

[1] 2nd and 3rd Division and XVIII, XXXIV and LXXVI (Army) Brigades.

[2] LXX and LXXXIV R.G.A. (21 guns) which were to fire on special targets, including Béhagnies and Ervillers.

penetrated the British line and were west of the Albert–
Arras railway, the start was punctual. Keeping close to
the barrage over the thousand yards of flat open ground
which had to be crossed, although the tanks had some
difficulty in crossing the railway and arrived late, the two
brigades were completely successful. Gomiecourt, with
300 prisoners, was taken by the 76th Brigade[1] by 5 a.m.,
eight tanks assisting in the " mopping up ". The 8th
Brigade[2] met with considerable resistance from machine-gun
nests ; but by 4.45 a.m. was on its objective north of
Gomiecourt. The four tanks with it obliterated several
machine-gun nests, and rounded up over a hundred prisoners ;
but three were then knocked out by direct hits of H.E. shell
and the crew of the fourth was disabled by anti-tank rifle
fire. At this stage, as the 76th Brigade had formed a right
defensive flank, the 9th Brigade on the right had no more
to do than clear out some machine-gun nests, in the process
of which it took a few prisoners.

The main attack of the VI Corps was made by the Guards,
56th and 52nd Divisions, the latter two passing through
the 59th. Its direction took it slantwise across the series
of spurs and valleys between the Sensée and the Scarpe,
which drop gently from the Artois plateau north-eastwards
down to the plain of Douai. The objective was a good
observation line about twelve hundred yards away, marked
by a point immediately east of Hamelincourt, Boyelles, and
Boiry Becquerelle, and rejoining the front line 800 yards
south-east of Mercatel. It was thus in a sector where little
or no attempt had been made to go forward on the 21st.
The advance was to be covered by a creeping barrage (84 per
cent. shrapnel and 16 per cent. smoke) fired by seventeen
brigades of field artillery, whilst 70 per cent. of the
seven brigades of heavy artillery were to be used on counter-
battery work and the rest to engage special centres including
Croisilles and Hénin. The 12th Tank ·Battalion was to
co-operate with the Guards Division, the 11th with the
56th, and the 9th with the 52nd.

---

[1] 2/Suffolk and 1/8th King's Own leading, 1/Gordons guarding right
flank and providing reserve. For the German account see Note II at end
of Chapter.
[2] 2/Royal Scots and 7/Shropshire L.I. leading.

The 2nd Guards Brigade led the attack of the Guards Division (Major-General G. P. T. Feilding), supported by five Army brigades of field artillery[1] and two heavy.[2] As we have seen, its right battalion, the 3/Grenadiers, was ordered to move forward at 4 a.m. to protect the left flank of the attack on Gomiecourt by the 3rd Division. Its left battalion,. the 1/Scots Guards, was to wait until 4.55 a.m., the hour of the main attack. In the interval it was caught by a heavy hostile barrage, no doubt provoked by the attack of the Grenadiers. Only three of the eight tanks (Mark IV) of the 12th Tank Battalion detailed to assist it appeared ; but after considerable opposition from machine guns the Scots Guards took their objective, Hamelincourt and many prisoners, and by 8 a.m. had established themselves on the eastern side and were in touch on the right with the 3/Grenadiers and on the left with the 56th Division.[3]

The attack of the 56th Division (Major-General Sir A. Hull) was carried out by the 168th Brigade (Br.-General G. G. Loch), with a battalion of the 167th, the 512th Field Company R.E., two companies of the 1/5th Cheshire (Pioneers) and one company and a section of the machine-gun battalion attached. Two companies (21 tanks) of the 11th Tank Battalion and three brigades of heavy artillery[4] supported it, and the barrage was fired by six brigades R.F.A.[5]

The first objective was the villages of Boyelles and Boiry Becquerelle ; after these had been secured, the brigade was to establish posts in a German reserve trench bearing the names of those villages, which ran obliquely to the line of the first objective and was 1,200 to 600 yards from it. The operation having to be initiated at very short notice, the artillery of the 56th and 57th Divisions had not had time to register nor the infantry to reconnoitre. The 168th Brigade and attached troops had marched eight miles north-east from the St. Amand area (11 miles W.N.W. of Achiet le Grand) to Blaireville during the afternoon of the 22nd and then three miles farther during the night to their forming-up positions behind the junction of the Guards and 59th Divisions ;

[1] XIV R.H.A. and LXXII, XCIII, 155th and 315th R.F.A.

[2] XXIX and LXX.

[3] See Note II at end of Chapter.

[4] XIII, XXII and LXIII R.G.A.

[5] Guards, 56th and 57th Divisions, under Br.-General R. J. G. Elkington, C.R.A. 56th Division.

subsequently much enemy gas shelling had to be endured by the brigade, so that respirators had to be worn for two hours.

In the attack the infantry of the 56th Division started at 5.7 a.m. after a 12-minute barrage begun at Zero. Complete success attended it ; although as usual the German machine gunners fought well, the nests and the villages succumbed quickly to outflanking movements. By 6 a.m. the Kensingtons (1/13th London) had reached their objective south of Boyelles ; the 1/4th London, assisted by three tanks, took the village, and the London Scottish captured Boiry Becquerelle. The battalions then proceeded to push out posts towards the German reserve trench.

The task of the 52nd Division (Major-General J. Hill) was to form the left flank from near Boiry Becquerelle back to the front line, passing through the 59th Division. Major-General Hill detailed for it the 156th Brigade (Br.-General A. H. Leggett) with one machine-gun company ; nine tanks of the 9th Battalion were allotted to it, and artillery support was given by six brigades R.F.A.[1] and two R.G.A.[2]

Here again there had been haste. On the 22nd the 52nd Division was in reserve, four or five miles west of Arras, and it was necessary to bring the 156th Brigade up to its assembly position by lorry ; but as there was much congestion on the roads, only by great exertions on the part of several staffs had the brigade managed to arrive in time to advance at zero hour.

The artillery barrage was very good and, possibly because the German main defence was farther back on Hénin Hill (a little over a mile east of Hénin on the Hamelincourt–Hénin ridge), not much opposition was offered notwithstanding that the tanks were late, although they caught up during the advance. By 6 a.m. the objective was in the hands of the 1/4th and 1/7th Royal Scots and the 1/7th Scottish Rifles, who had advanced in line, finding their own supports, and the ground was then cleared for some five hundred yards beyond the left flank.

At 9.25 a.m., informed of these various successes all along the line, Lieut-General Haldane issued orders for the Guards Division to advance across the Sensée to the higher ground

---

[1] Those of the 40th and 52nd Divisions and the V and 232nd (Army), under Br.-General C. E. Palmer, C.R.A. 40th Division. The infantry of the 40th Division was not employed, as it had recently been reconstituted with B.1 men.

[2] VIII and LXXXVIII.

beyond on the St. Léger ridge, on the south side of the
Sensée, and for the 56th and 52nd Divisions to conform.
The ensuing movements led to a considerable gain of ground,
but to a somewhat disjointed line being formed.

Major-General Feilding sent forward only the 1/Coldstream
(2nd Guards Brigade), with four machine guns, on the right.
It crossed the Albert–Arras railway at 11 a.m., and soon
came under an artillery barrage, but, pressing on, reached
the objective near Hally Copse about midday.   The centre
and left of the 2nd Guards Brigade also advanced but did
not cross the Sensée.   It was soon found that there were no
troops on either flank.   The gap on the left was never filled,
as the right of the 56th Division was held up on the Ervillers–
Boyelles road, though the rest of the division made progress.
The gap on the right was filled by sending up first two
companies of the 1/Scots Guards and then the 1/Grenadiers
(3rd Guards Brigade), which, however, about 6 p.m. had to
throw back a flank to get within a thousand yards of the
2nd Division in front of Ervillers.

The 2nd Division had closed up behind the 3rd, through
which it was to pass, 11 a.m. being given as the hour of
attack.   The 5th Brigade (Br.-General W. L. Osborn) had
Sapignies and Béhagnies as objectives and the 6th Brigade
(Br.-General F. G. Willan) Ervillers ; but they were to
consolidate a line at least two hundred yards beyond these
villages.   Three sections of machine guns were allotted to
each brigade, two to follow in rear as " guns of opportunity ".
The 99th Brigade (less a battalion) was ordered to protect
the right flank and get in touch with the 37th Division
(IV Corps) which would be attacking Bihucourt.

Nine whippets of the 6th Tank Battalion co-operated with
the 5th Brigade and six with the 6th.   The artillery support
was the same as previously for the 3rd Division ; but the
pace of the barrage, to suit the whippets, was calculated at
150 yards in two minutes, too fast for the infantry and too
slow, as it proved, for the whippets, which preceded the
infantry.   It was arranged that when the barrage reached
the three villages named as the objectives it should
pause long enough for the infantry to catch up.   Where
the whippets were able to co-operate success attended the
operation, but where, as in the case of the 5th Brigade,
the tanks failed to get on, the infantry was left not only
without their aid, but also without the barrage.

The ground to be traversed was devoid of cover. Three of the whippets leading the 5th Brigade were soon knocked out by a well-placed anti-tank gun, and four others sheered off to the south towards Bihucourt, so that only two which had crossed the railway farther north co-operated in the direct advance on Béhagnies. According to plan, the 5th Brigade was to skirt the northern edge of Gomiecourt and then *turn* south-east, the 2/Highland L.I. advancing on Béhagnies and the 24/Royal Fusiliers, following four hundred yards behind, on Sapignies. These battalions after passing through the enemy's artillery barrage came under intense machine-gun fire,[1] especially from the left from ground between the 5th and 6th Brigades, which the two whippets were unable to smother. The attack of the Highland L.I. was finally checked on a ridge a thousand yards short of Béhagnies, the Fusiliers then extending the line to the right.

The 6th Brigade fared better.[2] After advancing across the railway south of Courcelles, in spite of the enemy's barrage and machine-gun fire, with the assistance of the tanks (two out of the four being knocked out by direct hits) and some machine guns carried up to the railway on pack animals, the German nests were overcome, and the battalions were ready to assault Ervillers before the barrage had lifted off the village. Some stiff fighting took place in it ; but by 1 p.m. the whole of Ervillers had been taken and a line was then consolidated along its eastern edge.

On the right of the 5th Brigade the 99th Brigade, represented by the 1/K.R.R.C. and a composite company of the 23/Royal Fusiliers,[3] more than fulfilled its duty of flank guard. Receiving fire from the right whilst moving south-eastwards past the south of Gomiecourt, the K.R.R.C., then leading, detached two companies in that direction ; these, assisted by three of the whippets which had sheered away south from the 5th Brigade, took the Germans in rear and completely cleared the area, capturing 420 prisoners. The one and a quarter battalions of the 99th Brigade eventually took position, according to plan, in a sunken road between the 37th Division and the 5th Brigade.

---

[1] Lieut.-Colonel W. L. Brodie, V.C., commanding the 2/Highland L.I., was killed.

[2] 2/South Staffordshire and 1/King's in front line with the 1/K. Berkshire (99th Brigade) and 17/Royal Fusiliers in second line.

[3] This battalion had been reduced by gas casualties on 21st August to a fighting strength of 158.

At 2 p.m. Lieut.-General Haldane ordered the 2nd Division to press its attack and make every endeavour to occupy Mory (east of Ervillers). The enemy, however, was holding his front line in strength, and machine-gun fire stopped the advance of the 6th Brigade from Ervillers, so that it could not get up level with the Guards Division on the left ; it was evident the ground was too open for any attempt to be made before night.

At 8.40 a.m. Lieut.-General Haldane had given formal orders for the 56th Division, which had reached its first objective and according to its original instructions was to have exploited its success, to advance against the Boyelles and Boiry Reserve Trenches in conjunction with the Guards and 52nd Divisions. Patrols had already been pushed forward some five hundred yards by the Kensington and 1/4th London of the 168th Brigade, but owing to machine-gun fire from the left flank and left rear they had been forced to retire. As runners had great difficulty in reaching the battalions, and the latter no less in communicating forward to their companies, it was 1.20 p.m. before the line advanced. The Kensington, on the right, on leaving Boyelles were met by heavy machine-gun and artillery fire[1] and could not get within a thousand yards of the new objective ; the 1/4th London reached it without much opposition, the defenders of the trench surrendering ; the London Scottish, on the left, already had two platoons in Boiry Reserve Trench, but the completion of the conquest led to stiff fighting, the issue being determined by a flanking movement over the open. The defenders, 86 of all ranks, then surrendered. Thus the 56th Division had secured all but the right sector of its final objective.

The 52nd Division hearing that troops of the 56th Division were in Boiry Reserve Trench had earlier pushed the outposts of the 1/4th Royal Scots into the continuation of this trench north of the Cojeul, and similarly had on the left established touch with the 2nd Canadian Division of the XVII Corps.

Besides easing the task of the IV Corps, the operations of the VI Corps had resulted in a gain of ground of 2,000 to 3,000 yards along its whole front of 12,000 yards, and the artillery had been moved forward as the situation developed.

---

[1] Their commanding officer Lieut.-Colonel R. E F. Shaw was killed whilst reconnoitring.

The opposition had come almost entirely from machine-gun
nests and artillery, the German infantry putting up a poor
fight and surrendering freely when opportunity offered.

The IV Corps (Lieut.-General Sir M. Harper), on the right
of the VI Corps, like its neighbour, began the day with a
preliminary minor operation. The 42nd (East Lancashire)
Division and New Zealand Division were directed to capture,
by an attack at 2.30 a.m., Beauregard Dovecot to the
north-west of Miraumont, taken and lost on the 21st, and the
ridge north-east of it. This ground commanded the valley
traversed by the section of the Albert–Arras railway which
the IV Corps had been unable to reach on the 21st, although
the VI Corps had secured its portion. Covered by the
artillery of both divisions and of a brigade lent by the 5th
Division, the assault against the Dovecot and the ridge was
made by two companies each of the 1/10th Manchester, 1/8th
Lancashire Fusiliers and 1st N.Z. Rifle Brigade. After some
opposition from machine guns the entire objective was
reached without much difficulty, and prisoners and machine
guns captured. The right flank of the corps was thus made
secure, and the importance of the original task of the V
Corps—to turn the enemy flank in that area—had been
considerably lessened.

The main operation of the day for the IV Corps, to begin
at 11 a.m., was an attack of the 5th Division (Major-General
J. Ponsonby) and the 37th Division (Major-General
H. Bruce Williams). The latter during the night had relieved
the 63rd Division in the line, without, however, the outposts being changed. The 5th was to capture Irles and
the 37th Achiet le Grand and Bihucourt. The 42nd and
the New Zealand Divisions were to prolong the attack to
the right by clearing the enemy from the valley of the Ancre
down to Miraumont (exclusive). The main attack was
covered by eleven brigades of field artillery[1] and four brigades
of heavy,[2] supported by thirteen tanks of the I Brigade.

For the 5th Division the objective was a line running along
the eastern edge of Irles and thence towards Bihucourt. As
on the 21st the 95th and 15th Brigades (Br.-Generals C. B.

---

[1] Of the 5th (one brigade only), 37th, 62nd, 63rd and N.Z. Divisions
and XXVI and 293rd (Army) Brigades.
[2] XXXIV, LIV, LVI, XC.

Norton and R. D. F. Oldman) were sent forward. The seven tanks of the 7th Battalion were not ready in time enough to go into action, as repairs had to be executed and ammunition shifted from unfit to fit machines ; but a barrage from twenty machine guns was fired obliquely from the high ground south and south-west of Achiet le Petit.

The 12/Gloucestershire, on the right of the 95th Brigade, delayed by the deep railway cutting, lagged behind the artillery barrage, came under close machine-gun fire from the front and enfilade fire from the right, suffered heavy casualties, and was unable to advance beyond the ridge which overlooks Irles from the west. Though reinforced by small detachments during the afternoon, by 4 p.m. it had not captured the village. The 1/East Surrey, on its left, met with opposition only in places, and by 11.40 a.m. had taken its objective.

In the 15th Brigade the 16/R. Warwickshire, in spite of considerable casualties, also went straight on to its objective, arriving there five minutes after the 1/East Surrey. The 1/Bedfordshire had more resistance to encounter and three belts of wire to negotiate before reaching the railway ; it was delayed and lost many officers. Two tanks of the 10th Battalion which were working with the 37th Division then appeared and, knocking out a number of machine guns, enabled both the Bedfordshire and the 1/Essex (37th Division) to capture the railway cutting and eventually gain the final objective.

The 5th Division having thus been successful except on the right near Irles, Major-General Ponsonby decided to put in the 13th Brigade (Br.-General L. O. W. Jones) and to pass it through the front line to capture the village and exploit the morning's success on the whole front up to Loupart Wood, which lies east of Irles. An artillery barrage was arranged, many of the batteries having been moved forward during the day. But again no tanks were ready.

In spite of the short notice, all three battalions of the 13th Brigade, the 1/R. West Kent and 14th and 15/R. Warwickshire, advancing abreast, passed through the line punctually at 7.30 p.m. The situation in Irles was so uncertain that the village was left out in the barrage and only the right platoon of the West Kent passed through it ; but Lieut.-Colonel H. A. Colt, commanding the 12/Gloucester-shire, of his own initiative, organized an attack against the place and, going forward at the same time as the 13th Brigade with his battalion and its small reinforcements, captured Irles. All three battalions of the 13th Brigade reached their objectives and at night held the front line of the division.

In the New Zealand Division, on the right of the 5th Division, the 1st Battalion N.Z. Rifle Brigade duly went forward at 11 a.m. under a barrage fired by the II Brigade N.Z.F.A., and against some opposition established itself on a line facing Miraumont, four hundred yards from it, and in touch on either flank with the 42nd and 5th Divisions respectively. The village itself was not to be attacked until next day.

The 37th Division, on the left of the 5th, had as its first objective a trench about two hundred yards beyond Achiet le Grand and thence southwards, and had therefore to cross the railway and capture the village on its way. The second objective was the eastern edge of Bihucourt and thence a line running south-westwards towards Irles. Zero hour, as for the 5th Division, was 11 a.m. Five brigades of field artillery were available for the barrage[1] and five batteries of heavy artillery[2] to shell Achiet le Grand, Bihucourt, and the western exits of Biefvillers and Grévillers, beyond Bihucourt. The remainder of the heavy artillery was assigned to counter-battery work. Six tanks of the 10th Tank Battalion were to co-operate, particularly in taking Achiet le Grand and Bihucourt. It was the first time that the 37th Division had to work with tanks, and after much consideration Major-General Bruce Williams decided that as the tanks could assemble only some distance behind the line, they must make a running start and catch up the infantry in time to take the latter on for the attack on the railway, which they managed to do.

The 112th and 111th Brigades led the attack. The latter, with the 13/Rifle Brigade and 13/K.R.R.C. in line, led by their commanding officers carrying flags, met with complete success. The railway cutting, 30 feet deep, was stormed and Achiet le Grand, with the help of the 8/Somerset L.I.

---

[1] 37th and 63rd Divisions and the XXVIII Brigade of the 5th Division.
[2] Belonging to the XXXIV, LVI and XC Brigades R.G.A.

(from the 63rd Brigade, which was following the 111th), occupied and several hundred prisoners captured in the dug-outs with which the railway cutting was honeycombed. By 12.30 p.m. the first objective beyond the village was secured. The third battalion, the 10/Royal Fusiliers, passed through the line at 1.20 p.m. and, assisted by a fresh barrage, in spite of considerable opposition, took Bihucourt and the final objective.

The 112th Brigade (without any of its 1917 battalions thanks to the reorganization of the infantry into three-battalion brigades in January 1918), in spite of the success attained on its right (by the 15th Brigade) and left (by the 111th Brigade), though it began well, encountered consider-able difficulties. The 1/Essex on the right was held up by the defenders of a trench four hundred yards west of the railway and was not able to progress until about 1.40 p.m., when a tank arrived and firing along the trench enabled the battalion to advance and capture it. The railway cutting was shortly after, about 2 p.m., occupied without much trouble. The 13/Royal Fusiliers, on the left, also met with opposition at once from the brickworks west of Achiet le Grand. This was overcome by a flank attack, and the advance continued to the railway, where a stiff fight ensued. By pushing on small parties under covering fire of trench mortars, Lewis guns and rifles, the defenders were brought under enfilade fire and surrendered to the number of four hundred. The battalion then went on and came up to the right of the 111th Brigade on the first objective. The third battalion, the 1/1st Hertfordshire (full of new officers and men who did not know each other, under a recently arrived lieutenant-colonel), should have passed through the 13/Royal Fusiliers at 1.20 p.m., but it lost direction and, going too far to the south, struck the railway in the sector of the 1/Essex, with which it was held up. Both these battalions went over the railway shortly after 2 p.m., the Hertfordshire through the right of the 13/Royal Fusiliers ; but they fought independently, without of course the 1.20 p.m. barrage, and under machine-gun fire. Thus only the right of the Essex gained the second objective and got touch of the 15th Brigade, the line then bending back to run along the first objective on the left of the brigade. The gap on the left was filled by the 111th forming a right defensive flank along the southern edge of Bihucourt.

Meantime, at 1.5 p.m., the 37th Division had received orders from Lieut.-General Harper that if the objective were captured the success should be exploited by an advance to a line about a thousand yards beyond Irles and Bihucourt, in co-operation with the advance of the 5th Division, already related.   About 3 p.m. verbal orders, followed by written orders, were issued by Major-General Bruce-Williams for the 112th and 63rd Brigades, covered by a barrage, to pass through the line of the original second objective at 5.30 p.m., and after capturing the new objective to go on to Biefvillers.   This evening attack had no chance of success.   Both brigades were met by heavy fire.   In the 112th Brigade sector the barrage was put down 300 yards in front of the unreached second objective, given as the starting line, but actually 800 or 900 yards in front of the line from which the brigade started.   A large area with numerous machine guns in it was thus left untouched by fire.   After advancing about two hundred yards, the attackers returned to their starting line.   The 63rd Brigade, after covering rather more ground, also fell back, and further attempt was postponed until the early morning of the 24th.

The operations of the IV Corps had achieved considerable success and had resulted in the line being carried forward an average of over two thousand yards.   The strongly defended railway line, the German main line of resistance, which the *183rd, 4th Bavarian* and *2nd Guard Reserve Divisions* had orders to hold to the last, before which the corps had failed on the 21st, had been overrun, and the defended villages of Achiet le Grand, Bihucourt and Irles and numerous prisoners taken.[1]   The troops were considered to be in a condition to continue the attack next day ; so during the night the enemy communications were subjected to vigorous harassing fire from the heavy artillery.

In the V Corps (Lieut.-General C. D. Shute) no change of importance took place on the 23rd August in the situation of its left wing, the 21st Division.   The 50th Brigade (Br.-General G. Gwyn-Thomas) of the 17th Division pushed

---

[1] B.O.A., p. 535, says that " in the afternoon troops of the *6th Bavarian* " *Reserve Division* rallied the fragments (*Trümmer*) of the *2nd Guard* " *Reserve* and *4th Bavarian Divisions* ".   By the following morning the *40th* and *6th Bavarian Reserve Divisions* had taken their place in the line.

out patrols and gained some ground.   The principal event was the frontal attack at 4.45 a.m. of the 38th (Welsh) Division, in co-operation with the 18th Division (III Corps, Fourth Army) planned in order to drive the enemy farther from Albert and secure a line over Tara and Usna Hills (between which ran the boundary of the Fourth and Third Armies), along Rubber Trench down to the marshes of the Ancre south-east of Aveluy.   After the capture of this objective, an endeavour was to be made on the left to push on out of the Ancre valley to Crucifix Corner.

In the 18th Division sector, the 53rd Brigade[1] was employed with three battalions abreast, the 10/Essex, 7/R. West Kent and 7/Queen's (55th Brigade) aided by a divisional artillery barrage and by six tanks of the 1st Tank Battalion (which arrived a few minutes late, but did very good work without any loss).   Although the resistance was at first strong, the attack was completely successful, and by 6 a.m. the objective was secured.   On the right of the 53rd Brigade the 54th (Lieut.-Colonel A.E. Percival, acting vice Br.-General Sadleir-Jackson wounded), keeping up steady pressure during the day, advanced the line about a thousand yards.

The 113th Brigade, leading the attack of the 38th Division, sent forward the 13/R. Welch Fusiliers with the 14th and two tanks of the 1st Tank Battalion in support, covered by divisional artillery and machine-gun barrages.   Concentrating its attack on Usna Hill, when this was taken the enemy line was outflanked and 194 Germans surrendered. The 115th Brigade (Br.-General W. B. Hulke) then crossed the Ancre, secured Crucifix Corner and came up on the left of the 113th.

The 114th Brigade pushed some posts into Thiepval Wood, so as to keep touch with the 17th Division (Major-General P. R. Robertson).   This division, on the left of the 38th, on account of the difficulties of crossing the Ancre marshes did no more than advance the line of posts of the 50th Brigade, so as to reach the jumping-off position for the 24th.

This completed the initial operations north of the Somme. The Third Army had had a very successful day, gained a considerable amount of ground and taken over five thousand prisoners.   General Sir J. Byng ordered a further advance

---

[1] See Sketch 13 for this.

for the 24th August. This actually began before midnight of the 23rd/24th, but will be described under the events of the 24th. General Sir H. Rawlinson also intended that the Fourth Army should continue to push forward on the 24th, and that the III Corps should begin by a preliminary night operation. The German fighting troops, beaten in open encounter by inferior numbers—as is now known—were obviously discouraged and inclined either to run or surrender. It behoved to keep them in that frame of mind.

NOTE I

THE FRENCH ON THE 23rd AUGUST[1]

(Sketch 12)

The French achieved little on the 23rd August. General Fayolle directed General Debeney, if possible, to support the British operations with the left of the French First Army ; but this Army, " weakened and delayed by the extension [re-extension] of its front towards the north, was not yet in a condition to re-launch an attack." General Debeney, however, gave orders to accelerate the taking-over from the British so that it might be completed by 8 a.m. on the 25th.

In the French Third Army some units of the XV Corps crossed the Divette between Noyon and Lassigny and established themselves in the village of Evricourt on the northern bank.

The French Tenth Army on the 23rd began a new offensive on the extreme right of the battlefield, on the front Soissons–St. Mard (eight miles north of Soissons) ; but it realized "only insignificant gains " : the XXX Corps " failed completely " and " all " the efforts of the I Corps produced no better results. This " offensive being of the first importance, the French High Com-" mand decided to increase the resources of the Tenth Army "[2].

NOTE II

THE GERMANS ON THE 23rd AUGUST

The histories of the infantry regiments of the two German divisions, the *107th* and *21st*, upon which the main attack of the 1st Australian Division fell, make no concealment of the disaster

---

[1] From F.O.A. vii (i), pp. 242–3.

[2] A small gain made by the XVIII Corps, on the left wing of the Tenth Army, which is shown on the French Map No. 25, has no mention in the text.

of the 23rd August. To take the *107th Division*, the southern one, first, the *232nd Reserve Infantry Regiment* says : " the day was a " catastrophe for the regiment. It cost its old, good stock : All " three battalion staffs, all company commanders, all medical " officers, the greater part of the excellent telephone detachment, " and more than 600 men ; and in the period 8th to 22nd August " we had already lost 300 men. Only two officers and 42 other " ranks, mostly of the II Battalion, in addition to the regimental "staff, escaped ".

In the *21st Division*, the *80th Fusilier Regiment* says : " slight " fog still prevailed in the Somme valley when at 4.35 a.m. [*sic*] " violent fire fell on the front of the division. In a very short " time Chuignolles, Chuignes and the [Herleville] valley were " shrouded in thick smoke and vapour which soon prevented any " view. This hot fire had not lasted very long before, suddenly, " tanks which had been hidden by the morning mist and the " smoke of the guns appeared quite close to the main line of " resistance, followed by the assaulting British troops. In " several places the tanks broke in and a short, desperate fight " ensued. Crushed by the weight of hostile infantry, shot into " from the flanks and rear by the tanks, the defenders of the " main line of resistance succumbed to the enemy's superiority ".

The *65th Regiment* of the *185th Division*, which south of the *107th* faced the attack of the 97th Brigade (32nd Division) on the right flank, speaks of furious hand-to-hand fighting in Herleville and mentions a counter-attack made to regain the village during which a party got as far as the church before it had to fall back to the eastern edge. The regimental history thinks that the *185th Division*, and especially the *65th Regiment*, " shattered the " attempt made by the British with very strong forces [a brigade " against a division] to break through [the 97th Brigade had only " to form a flank] ". The regiment lost 395 of all ranks.

The history of the *243rd Division*, near the Somme, which was driven across the Herleville valley by the 3rd Australian Brigade, like most histories of German higher formations endeavours to conceal the truth, saying : " the attack broke down in front of the " second main line of resistance " ; but the regimental histories tell a different tale : " the second line of resistance" being described as " isolated shell-holes and scarcely discoverable little wooden " notice boards on short poles with the pretentious inscription " ' Second Main Line of Resistance ' ". (*478th Regiment*.) The *122nd Fusilier Regiment* says : " great anxiety was felt for the " II Battalion ; but very soon wounded and stragglers from other " units brought us the sad truth ; the battalion had been attacked " suddenly in the rear and then from both flanks. Then it had " been attacked frontally as well, and for the most part captured. " . . . In the evening about fifty men reported to the "regiment". As regards the II and III Battalions, "it was "really impossible to talk about companies. They were merely "weak platoons". The *479th Regiment* accounts for its defeat by saying that the British "drove in front of them German prisoners "who wore steel helmets, but who otherwise had taken off all "their equipment". It ends with the statement that "six "battalions, *II* and *III/479*, *II/87*, *III/80* and *I* and *III/148*, "were in the *479th's* sector ; but they were only wrecks, utterly "fought out. The *II/479th* in the evening of the 23rd had a "fighting strength of two weak companies, *III/479* of only one "weak company".

Of the Germans opposite the Third Army there is less information. It was the *2nd Guard Reserve Division* which was driven out of Gomiecourt and at night it had to be relieved. The *4th Bavarian Division*, south of it, was attacked in flank and rear. "The resistance of the division whose units had become much "disorganized in the previous fighting and already had lost "2,800 men, was by now exhausted ; it also was relieved".

The historian of the *234th Division* calls the 23rd August "the "black day of the *234th Division*". Its front extended from Gomiecourt through Ervillers to St. Leger. Following German methods the British (the 76th and 2nd Guards Brigades) broke in on both wings and killed or captured the greater part of the defenders : "the old *234th Division* was no more". The casualties of the infantry alone are given as 67 Officers (25 missing) and 2,339 other ranks (1,574 missing).

CHAPTER XIII

BATTLE OF ALBERT 1918—(*continued*)[1]

24TH AUGUST

(Sketches 13, 14)

Both the Fourth and the Third Armies continued the offensive on the 24th : the latter again made good progress eastwards ; the former, temporarily restricted to covering the right of the Third, improved its position north of the Somme. To use the words of the French Official History " the British successes were confirmed and accentuated ". The French Tenth Army continued to meet with very serious opposition and only one corps made ground, north-west of Soissons ; the Third and First Armies made preparations to resume their advance should the enemy show signs of commencing a retirement.[2]

The Fourth Army on the night of the 23rd/24th carried out the relief of the 10th Canadian Brigade (4th Canadian Division) ; so that the international boundary then ran a mile south of Chilly.[3] On the following night, in spite of much gas shelling by the enemy, the retaking over of the front held by the French before the 8th August offensive was completed by the relief of the 11th Canadian Brigade and the 12th Australian Brigade (4th Australian Division) ; the boundary then passed a little north of Lihons and the Canadian Corps was transferred to the First Army.

The weather during the 21st, 22nd and 23rd had been intensely hot, but on the 24th it became cloudy and cooler, with some rain and drizzle ; until about midday the clouds were so low and visability so poor that little assistance could be given by the R.A.F. to the infantry or the tanks either by fire or by spotting batteries and machine-gun nests ; the advance therefore was greatly hampered, as will be seen. During the afternoon, however, two squadrons attacked reserve German troops and transport on the roads, and bombing attacks were made on the railway stations of

---

[1] According to the official " Battles Nomenclature ", the Battles of Albert ended on the 23rd, and no name is provided for the fighting on the 24th and 25th, the Battle of the Scarpe beginning on the 26th.

[2] F.O.A. vii (i), p. 244. See Note I at end of Chapter.

[3] See Sketch 13.

Péronne and Velu (five miles east of Bapaume). A few new enemy divisions were identified on the British front on this day.

General Rawlinson's orders, issued on the afternoon of the 23rd, confirmed what had already been arranged : " to-night and early to-morrow the III Corps is pushing " forward to occupy the Green Line [the general line reached " on the 24th] and exploiting in the direction of the green " arrows [north-eastward]. If the advance meets with " success on the right a combined attack will be made by " the Australian Corps and III Corps at 4 p.m. to-morrow, " 24th August, with the line marked blue on attached map " as objective ".[1]

The 3rd Australian Division (Major-General J. Gellibrand) was to take an important part in the operations of the III Corps by attacking Bray ;

the 47th and 12th Divisions had to capture the final objective beyond the Happy Valley, which the corps had failed to gain on the 22nd except on the extreme 'left ;

the 18th Division, on the left again, in co-operation with the 38th Division (Third Army), was to push farther from Albert and secure Chapes spur, which runs from la Boisselle towards Bécourt, whilst the 38th Division took la Boisselle and Ovillers la Boisselle (a mile north of la Boisselle).

Of the corps reserve, the 58th Division, the 174th and 175th Brigades remained under the command of the 18th and 47th Divisions, respectively.

The three divisions of the III Corps in the line were to exploit any successes gained, and for this purpose each had allotted to it one squadron of the XXII Corps cavalry[2] and a company of the XXII Corps Cyclists.[3]

With the object of surprise, which was fully achieved, and in order to give the whole day for exploitation, all the attacks, including that of the Australians, were timed for

---

[1] Map not reproduced. As will be seen, the combined attack did not take place.

[2] A and B Squadrons 4th Australian Light Horse and one squadron Otago Mounted Rifles. The III Corps cavalry (1/1st Northumberland Hussars) was kept in reserve.

[3] Lieut.-General Sir A. Godley of the XXII Corps then resting was still commanding the III Corps during the absence through illness of Lieut.-General Sir R. Butler.

1 a.m., in order, the moon being a couple of days past full, to have the advantage of bright moonlight.   Creeping barrages were fired at zero hour after crash barrages of heavy artillery had been dropped at intervals on selected targets.

Three companies of the 40th Battalion, with one company of the 37th of the 10th Australian Brigade (Br.-General W. R. McNicoll) was sent against Bray, which lay about five hundred yards from the front line.   At Zero in bright moonlight a barrage was dropped on the western edge of the village and five minutes later crept forward through it, followed by a machine-gun barrage, with a flank barrage on the northern side, whilst all approaches were kept under machine-gun fire and part of the divisional artillery fired on selected positions east of Bray, in particular on the ridge just west of Ceylon Wood and the gully which runs towards Bray from the north-east.   One company was sent north and another south of the village to unite and establish posts on the objective five hundred yards beyond its eastern border ;   whilst a third company followed to attack and clear Bray and consolidate a position in support of the leading two. The fourth, in reserve, provided carrying parties to the front line.

The opposition was not serious and came solely from machine guns, and these were rushed.   In Bray a certain amount of fighting took place ;   but most of the garrison had evacuated it when the artillery barrage fell.   At the cost of three killed and 71 wounded ; 186 prisoners were captured, as well as three loaded trains on the railway sidings and dumps of ammunition and timber.   By 2.10 a.m. on the right and 2.50 a.m. on the left the final objective had been gained.   Connection was made on the right with the divisional pioneer battalion, though the bridge over the Somme river was found to be blown up, and on the left with the 37th Battalion which pushed forward posts north and north-east of Bray.

The attack of the 47th and 12th Divisions, under barrages which fell at Zero, with harassing fire on the enemy's centres of communication, was also successful.   The objective, on the far side of the Happy Valley, was reached promptly without serious opposition, except on the right wing of the 12th where, and in consequence on the left flank of the 47th, the situation for some hours gave reason for anxiety, and the objective was not attained until after 6 p.m.[1]

In the 47th Division, in order to cover the assembly of the 175th Brigade (Br.-General H. W. Cobham, 58th Division) and the 140th Brigade which were to attack, the 141st was ordered to establish a line of posts a hundred yards west of the main Bray–Albert road. The operation was well carried out by parties of the 18th and 1/20th London, which worked their way silently behind the German line of posts and surrounded and captured them before the garrisons could resist.

To assist the 175th Brigade in dealing with the Happy Valley, for which purpose two companies of the 2/10th London, the reserve battalion, had been specially attached to the attacking battalions, the 1/15th London (140th Brigade), then holding the line at the southern end of the valley, was to move up it, clearing out the enemy, but on arrival at the northern end rejoin its own brigade. After dawn, to deal with any stray Germans left in the valley, five tanks of the 1st Tank Battalion—they arrived about 4.45 a.m.—were to enter it, three from the southern and two from the northern end, and complete the mopping up and then help in checking any counter-attacks which might be launched.

The 12th, 9th, 1/17th and 21/London[2], in the front line of the two brigades, had little difficulty in reaching their objective, indeed, owing to the confusion of trenches, in some cases went beyond it, although crossing the Happy Valley was made unpleasant by the enemy dropping heavy shells into it, no doubt thinking that tanks were massed there. As indication that the precautions taken were not unnecessary, it may be added that when the 1/15th London moved up the valley it captured over three hundred prisoners.

On the left of the 47th Division, the 37th and 36th Brigades (Br.-Generals A. B. Incledon Webber and C. S. Owen) of the 12th Division, with the 6/R. West Kent, 6/Queen's, 7/R. Sussex and 5/R. Berkshire in front line, encountered great opposition from machine guns and, on the right, from

---

[1] See Note II at end of Chapter.
[2] The former 1/21st London, the 2/21st had been disbanded on 27th May.

two strongpoints. These prevented the advance of the 6/R. West Kent and the right of the 6/Queen's, although the rest of the line reached the objective. A dangerous gap therefore came into existence between the 47th and 12th Divisions. The 21/London, on the left of the former, organized a defensive flank ; but casualties grew heavy, and attempts to take the nearer of the strongpoints, close to " Pear Tree ", by bombing failed. At 4 a.m. the 37th Brigade gave orders for the infantry to dig in and not to press the attack, as the artillery was to shell the two strongpoints. Meanwhile the enemy was reinforced and his resistance stiffened. Shell fire increased, the ground was swept by bullets, and the defensive flank of the 21/London was so hammered by trench mortars from the " Pear Tree " strongpoint, that two companies of the 1/15 London had to be sent to reinforce it. The morning was cloudy and dark and the situation became threatening, even the objective already gained by the 47th Division and the left of the 12th was retained only with difficulty. Three tanks of the 1st Tank Battalion were at 7.30 a.m. placed at the disposal of the 37th Brigade to support the 6/R. West Kent in an attack on the two strongpoints. This did not take place until 1.30 p.m. and was unsuccessful, two tanks being disabled, whilst the guns of the third jammed. The Germans several times showed a disposition to counter-attack, but nothing materialized, a major concentration of troops being spotted from the air and broken up by artillery fire.

At 2 p.m. General Rawlinson, in view of the situation, cancelled the combined attack which was to have been made by the Australian and III Corps at 4 p.m.

For nearly three hours after the failure of the attempt of the tanks and the R. West Kent a fire fight went on, no attempt being made by the units on either flank, which had successfully reached their objectives, to envelop the strongpoints and surround them. Then about 6 p.m. the Germans made a small counter-attack—it was designed to cover a withdrawal—and shortly afterwards the 140th Brigade reported that the enemy had evacuated the southernmost of the two strongpoints. The retirement from both was confirmed by patrols, and the 6/R. West Kent and the right company of the 6/Queen's then went forward and occupied the objective and completed the line of the III Corps. The stout defence of one regiment the *115th* of the fresh *25th Division* had upset the second part of the Fourth Army's plan.[1]

The main task of the 18th Division was to capture Chapes spur, between Sausage and Avoca valleys, in co-operation with the 38th Division (Third Army) on its left, which was to take la Boisselle. At 1 a.m., under a barrage, it sent forward the 7/R. West Kent and the 8/R. Berkshire, the 10/Essex, the right and third battalion of the 53rd Brigade, and the 54th Brigade remaining in the line but sending out patrols. The attack proved successful, and contact was made on the left with the 16/R. Welch Fusiliers of the 113th Brigade, which had meantime captured la Boisselle; but the attempts to secure a continuous divisional line were for many hours foiled by two obstacles : first, Bécourt Wood, which was strongly held, and, secondly, the la Boisselle crater (blown by the British on the 1st July, 1916), four hundred yards south of the village, also strongly occupied. The wood was gradually cleared by patrols, but the crater required an organized attack which was launched at 8 p.m. under cover of a Stokes mortar bombardment when over two hundred prisoners were taken.

General Byng's orders for the continuation of the advance of the Third Army eastward on the 24th were issued at 5.35 p.m. on the 23rd : [2]

The V Corps was to push forward eastwards towards Rocquigny and Morval, about eight miles ahead south of Bapaume, as soon as possible, clearing up any Germans left between the southern Army boundary and the Ancre ;

the IV Corps was directed on Rocquigny (exclusive) and Lagnicourt (three miles E.S.E. of Vaulx Vraucourt) ;

the VI Corps, on Quéant (four miles north-east of Vaulx-Vraucourt) and Vis en Artois ;

the 1st and 2nd Cavalry Divisions were to take advantage of any opportunity to push through and exploit the success of the infantry.

[1] See Note II at end of Chapter.
[2] See Sketch 14.

likely that had the 64th Brigade gone straight on to its original final objective, it might well have met with disaster.

The reason for the non-appearance of the 17th Division on the immediate right of the 21st was that, after a magnificent start, it had gone astray. The 50th Brigade was detailed to lead its attack with one machine-gun company, one section 78th Field Company R.E., and one section 175th Tunnelling Company R.E. to search for booby traps, attached; it was covered by the divisional artillery and sixteen guns of the LXII Brigade R.G.A. under the C.R.A., Br.-General P. Wheatley. In front line were the 10/West Yorkshire and the 6/Dorsetshire. Starting from three hundred yards west of the Thiepval–Grandcourt road, the West Yorkshire took the Stuff and Schwaben Redoubts, which had so stoutly resisted British attacks in 1916, pushed through the ruins of Thiepval and reached the final objective beyond the village by 3.30 a.m., one company having passed through the British barrage and attacked the enemy in rear, capturing 120 prisoners. Only three platoons of the Dorsetshire reached the objective and at 4.5 a.m. the 7/East Yorkshire was sent up to pass through the Dorsetshire and carry the attack to the objective, which it duly did.

The brigade was then ordered to continue the advance on (the ruins of) Courcelette, starting at 9 a.m. But instead of going due east, owing to lack of landmarks, the West Yorkshire and Dorsetshire wandered south-east towards heaps of rubble and brickdust where Pozières had stood. The brigade staff, sitting on the western slopes of the Ancre in communication with the division, could see the mistake being made by the Dorsetshire and tried but failed to correct it by sending a message by flag. A mounted staff officer was then despatched, but he was too late to remedy the mistake; and when, to prevent further mishaps, the brigade staff crossed the Ancre, touch with divisional headquarters was lost.

Unaware of the swing of the 50th Brigade to the southeast the 52nd (Br.-General W. Allason), ordered to follow it in its attack against Courcelette, kept the right direction. On arriving within a thousand yards of that village it discovered that the 50th was not in front and the enemy was in possession; so a line of battle outposts was formed and later touch with the 50th obtained.

Pozières, which was in the enemy line of resistance, was taken by the 50th Brigade about 4 p.m. The Germans were not disposed to lose such an important site and, after bombardment, twice counter-attacked heavily. They were repulsed with the help of a single 18-pdr. which was got up ; but as the right was badly exposed to enfilade fire a slight retirement in the village was ordered by the two battalion commanders, the line consolidated, and touch gained at last on the right with the 114th Brigade (38th Division).

Although the 52nd and 110th Brigades had been sent up to the inner flanks of the 17th and 21st Divisions, the gap between them, in which lay Courcelette hidden in a minor depression, remained with the village still held by the enemy. Notwithstanding this, at 5 p.m. Major-General Campbell issued orders for an advance by the 110th Brigade, covered by one brigade of artillery, eastward on le Sars ; for the 62nd to concentrate slightly ahead of the present position of the 110th ; and for the 64th to reorganize in a ravine behind its present position. The 6/Leicestershire (110th Brigade) lost direction and was late, and the 1/Wiltshire went forward alone at 8 p.m. Its advance over devastated country in the dark was no easy matter ; but the battalion reached its objective west of le Sars and was then far ahead of any other troops ; the 6/Leicestershire, on the left, when it came up, did not advance so far, although it reached and passed Pys. The ground all round the 110th Brigade was held by the enemy who was strongly established in D'Estremont Farm (just south of le Sars) ; brigade head-quarters actually found themselves behind the foremost German troops and had some difficulty in slipping away. But the brigade held on in its advanced position, delighted as the night progressed to find troops of the 127th Brigade (42nd Division) on its left.

The operations of the two wings of the 38th Division, the right division of the V Corps, remain to be told, and con-tinuing the narrative from north to south the left attack by the 114th Brigade, starting from Thiepval Wood, will be taken first, with the preliminary remark that each of the three brigades of the division had a machine-gun company and a section of the 178th Tunnelling Company attached to it, and that five bridges across the Ancre were to be repaired or constructed by the 123rd and 151st Field Companies R.E. between Aveluy and St. Pierre Divion.

To reach the starting line, which was held by the 13/ Welch, the 14th and 15/Welch had to cross the Ancre which runs there in two channels. The 15th found a bridge ready, but that for the 14th had not been completed and the men had to wade the Ancre in the dark with the water up to their chests, with the result that only one company reached Thiepval Wood by zero hour and the machine and Lewis guns were an hour and a half behind time. At 1 a.m., under a barrage fired by four field batteries and twelve guns of the XXXV Brigade R.G.A., the companies present, with very little opposition, for fire was mainly directed—too late— on the river crossings, reached their objective, nearly two miles from the starting point, and formed up alongside the first position of the 50th Brigade.

In the right attack by the 113th and 115th Brigades, two battalions of the former, the 16th and 14/R. Welch Fusiliers and the 17th of the latter brigade, led the advance at 1 a.m. La Boisselle was then taken without much difficulty ; in the centre the old mine crater and a few strongpoints caused some delay before they were captured with a hundred prisoners ; but on the left a trench in front of Ovillers stopped progress and thus gave the enemy opportunity to fire into that flank. The 10/S. Wales Borderers (115th Brigade) which had been " mopping up ", was sent to the left, but was stopped by fire from a northern continuation of the same trench that was holding up the 17/R. Welch Fusiliers. Farther to the left again the 2/R. Welch Fusiliers, however, successfully cleared the area about Authuille Wood, taking about two hundred prisoners and 17 machine guns.

The battalions of the 38th Division had thus attained all their objectives except Ovillers. The V Corps therefore directed Major-General Cubitt to " pinch out " the village. He ordered an advance to begin at 4 p.m. :

> the 113th Brigade on Contalmaison in conjunction with the 18th Division on its right, which was attacking the la Boisselle crater,
>
> the 114th on Pozières, and
>
> the 115th, in the centre, not to move direct on Ovillers but past it on the higher ground to the north.

No movement was made before 5.30 p.m. and then enemy machine guns made the operation a very slow one. The 113th Brigade was checked in front of Contalmaison ; but the Germans in Ovillers, being turned on the north by the 115th Brigade, abandoned that stronghold, and about 10 p.m. the ruins were found to be clear of them. The 114th Brigade discovered that Pozières was already in possession of the 17th Division and therefore halted on the Ovillers–Courcelette road. By a somewhat belated adoption of the too rarely applied principle of envelopment, and by pushing forward on the flanks of stubborn resistance, the 38th Division had reached all its objectives and taken 634 prisoners.

The operations of the V Corps on the 24th may therefore be classed as very successful ; the audacity of some of them had been rewarded ; la Boisselle, Ovillers, Pozières, Thiepval, and Grandcourt had fallen ; and considerable ground had been won. A wide gap around Courcelette certainly existed between the 17th and 21st Divisions ; but the enemy did not appear to be in a position or in a condition to take advantage of it.

In the IV Corps, whose centre and left were well forward but whose right was hanging back blocked by Miraumont, Lieut.-General Harper had issued orders for :

the 42nd Division, aided by the night attack of the 64th Brigade on the high ground to the south-east already narrated, to take Miraumont and the high ground to the east between that village and Pys ;

the New Zealand Division to pass through the 5th, which was facing Loupart Wood and Grévillers, and take those localities ;

the 5th Division to advance south-eastwards in order to cover the right of the New Zealanders and form a defensive right flank on the line Irles–Loupart Wood, so as to connect with the 42nd Division ;

the 37th Division, to push through Biefvillers, about two thousand yards ahead, and gain touch with the right of the VI Corps ;

the 63rd Division, to remain in reserve about Bucquoy and Ablainzevelle, in the old front line of the 21st August.

As ultimate objectives which it was hoped to reach, Warlencourt, le Barque, Thilloy, Bapaume and Favreuil were mentioned.

Instructions were given for divisions to push forward guns and batteries in close support of the infantry and, in addition to the artillery and tank support of the previous days, the New Zealand Division was to have the services of the XXVI (Army) Brigade R.F.A., all available guns of the 5th Division and the XC Brigade R.G.A., thirteen tanks Mark IV of the 7th Battalion and a company of whippets.

Patrols of the 42nd Division which tried to enter Miraumont during the night of the 23rd/24th were held off by machine-gun fire. In the morning hours, however, after McCulloch's brigade had established itself on the high ground to the south-east, resistance in the southern part of the village weakened ; so that between 10 a.m. and noon the 127th (Manchester) Brigade (Br.-General Hon. A. M. Henley) was able to pass through it without much fighting, cross the Ancre, there 15 to 30 feet wide but fordable in places, and get touch with the 21st Division. In the northern part of Miraumont stronger opposition was offered ; but the 126th (East Lancashire) Brigade (Br.-General G. H. Wedgwood), attacking at 1.50 p.m., after two and a half hours' struggle, succeeded in clearing the whole village and taking 540 prisoners, a battery of 5·9-inch howitzers and some 4·2-inch guns.

At 4.30 p.m., Major-General Solly-Flood issued orders for the advance to be continued first to Pys and then to Warlencourt, both in the upper valley of the Ancre ; but the movement did not begin until about 8 p.m. The former village was reached without difficulty, but Warlencourt proved to be a honeycomb of machine guns ; so after reconnaissance the 127th Brigade withdrew about three-quarters of a mile to a good position in touch with the 21st Division on the right ; the 126th Brigade withdrew likewise to the south-east corner of Loupart Wood, where it established contact on the left with the 5th Division.

The New Zealand Division, with the 1st N.Z. Brigade (Br.-General C. W. Melvill) leading, accompanied by eight tanks and three whippets, went forward at 4.30 a.m. with the 2nd N.Z. Brigade (Br.-General R. Young), with five tanks and a company of whippets, in support about three thousand yards in rear, ready to push through as soon as Loupart Wood, Grévillers and a quarry north of the latter place had been reached. The day was cloudy at zero hour and still rather dark, as already mentioned, but machine guns were employed to clear the way, and as no artillery barrage had been fired it was some time before the enemy noticed the advance. He then offered a stout resistance and it was not until midday that the 1/Wellington, assisted by four tanks, had taken the whole of Loupart Wood. The 2/K.O.S.B. (5th Division) which had followed took a machine-gun post at the south-west corner of the wood and formed a defensive flank along its southern edge as arranged. The 2/Auckland with two of the four tanks, the others having broken down, advancing on both sides of Grévillers and then " mopping " it up from the rear, had by 6 a.m. taken the greater part of the village and by 9 a.m. had entirely cleared it ; but as at that hour fire was still coming from Loupart Wood the battalion was unable to advance beyond Grévillers.

News had reached the 2nd N.Z. Brigade about 8 a.m. that the 1st was held up by fire from Loupart Wood, but had reached the edge of Grévillers ; Br.-General Young therefore sent forward only two of his four battalions, the 2/Otago and 2/Canterbury, on the left of the brigade, to pass north of Grévillers. The former battalion captured a line of trenches four hundred yards east of Grévillers and one company and the 2/Canterbury with eight tanks pushed on. They found Biefvillers abandoned, and in spite of meeting a heavy artillery barrage as they crossed a crest which knocked out four tanks and killed Lieut.-Colonel W. S. Pennycook of the Otago, they nearly reached Avesnes, a suburb of Bapaume. There, however, they could not stay, as the left was exposed to very heavy fire, and they withdrew to the trenches east of Grévillers held by the Otago. A fresh advance in conjunction with the 63rd Division was ordered for 7.30 p.m. ; but, as will be seen, it did not take place. In the evening therefore the line of the N.Z. Division ran east of Loupart Wood and Grévillers to Biefvillers and the 13th Brigade of the 5th Division formed the right defensive flank ; the other two brigades of that division were kept in reserve by Major-General Ponsonby.

The 63rd Brigade of the 37th Division received a telephone message only at 12.15 a.m. that it was to attack Biefvillers at 4.30 a.m. The brigade-major barely succeeded in delivering orders to the battalions in time for the movement to begin at the appointed hour, but it was impossible to organize much artillery support. The 8/Lincolnshire, on the left, was held up by machine-gun fire and could not advance very far ; but the 8/Somerset L.I. on the right with the assistance of two tanks and the co-operation on the right of the New Zealanders, though Lieut.-Colonel J. H. M. Hardyman was killed, succeeded in entering Biefvillers about 6 a.m. The village was then so heavily bombarded that the battalion had to evacuate it and occupy a position west of it, the 4/Middlesex being brought up to form a defensive left flank. The Germans, however, did not reoccupy Biefvillers and later, as already mentioned, it was found empty by the 2/N.Z. Brigade.

Shortly before noon, when only part of Miraumont had been taken and there seemed little chance of the 42nd Division pushing any farther, Lieut.-General Harper sent Br.-General R. G. Parker, General Staff, to 63rd Division headquarters at Hénu (nine miles west of Bucquoy) to order Major-General Lawrie, whose troops were then on the move forward to Achiet le Petit and Logeast Wood behind the 37th Division, to change direction south-east and march to the area north-west of Loupart Wood and Grévillers behind the New Zealand Division. Thence he was to advance south-east in touch with the New Zealanders on the left, who also received corps orders to move forward at the same time, with the right flank refused, to le Barque–Thilloy on the southern edge of the corps area, there to join with the front of the V Corps.

At a conference at 3.30 p.m. at his new headquarters near Bucquoy Major-General Lawrie gave out and explained his orders, fixing 7.30 p.m. as the hour for leaving the concentration area. The 188th and 189th Brigades were to advance in echelon assisted by eight tanks, with the 190th (Br.-General W. B. Lesslie) in support behind the right. The first-named brigade was in position by 6.45 ·p.m., but the 189th was delayed by traffic congestion in the area behind the battle front, which it had to cross diagonally, also by aeroplane attack and by gas shelling. Br.-General DePree, who had ridden forward with his battalion commanders to reconnoitre, was met by heavy fire from the trenches beyond Loupart Wood, and every evidence was apparent that the enemy, as far south as Warlencourt opposite the 21st Division, was holding strongly to his ground. The tanks had not arrived, the battalions could not be in position before 7.15 p.m., little time was available to explain that the operation was an attack, not a mere advance; so Br.-General DePree, as the senior officer on the spot, at once cancelled the operation, informed the 188th Brigade and reported to divisional headquarters. The 188th Brigade and the New Zealand Division were already on the move and the artillery had opened fire; but with some difficulty the advance was stopped before it had gone very far. Major-General Lawrie did not approve of the decision and relieved Br.-General DePree of his command, and ordered the attack to be made at 5 a.m. on the 25th.[1] Patrols sent out during the night from the 188th and 189th Brigades met with strong opposition soon after leaving their lines.

This ended a disappointing day for the IV Corps. Except on the extreme right where the fall of Miraumont, thanks to the V Corps sending the 64th Brigade to the heights south-east of the village during the night of the 23rd/24th, had enabled the 42nd Division to come forward, the progress made had been small, but the objectives of the 24th were to be gained next day.

In the VI Corps, reports of the successful actions on the 23rd had come in slowly, and it was 8.33 p.m. on that day before the formal orders for the continuance of the advance at 7 a.m. to a line about four miles ahead, were sent out. The 62nd Division was brought into action, but no other addition of any fresh troops to the corps was made.

The 2nd Division was directed on Vaulx Vraucourt;

the Guards Division on Ecoust St. Mein;

the 56th Division on Croisilles, so as to take the defences of Hénin Hill from the south;

---

[1] After enquiry Br.-General DePree was on 5th September given command of the 115th Brigade and later promoted to major-general. The G.O.C. of the 63rd Division was relieved of his command and not further employed.

the 52nd Division (Major-General J. Hill) was to conform to the advance of the left of the 56th ; the
Canadian Corps (First Army), next on the left, had been
ordered similarly to conform to the 52nd ;

the 62nd Division (Major-General W. P. Braithwaite),
in reserve, to move forward during the morning and
relieve the 3rd Division on the railway east of Courcelles ;

the 3rd Division, after relief, to sideslip northwards
close behind the Guards Division.

The outstanding feature of the ground over which the VI
Corps had to operate was the series of long, gently sloping
spurs which stretch out mainly in a north-easterly direction
from the Artois Plateau, the valleys between them furrowed
by the upper, northern course of the Sensée stream, which
rising near Sapignies passes by Mory to St. Léger and
Croisilles ; the general aspect, however, was that of a great
rolling plain.

The 2nd Division ordered the 99th and 5th Brigades to
send patrols across the valley in front of them towards
Sapignies Switch (which ran north-east from the east of
Achiet le Grand to Béhagnies) and Béhagnies, and the 6th
Brigade to push forward to Mory Copse on the ridge north
of Mory village which itself lies in a depression. This brigade
after a little progress was held up by fire, and the patrols of
the other two found their objectives strongly held. At
9.30 a.m. Major-General Pereira held a conference with his
brigade commanders, with the result that Br.-General
Ironside was ordered to lead the 99th Brigade (plus the
1/King's of the 6th Brigade) from the right wing to the left,
and, under a divisional creeping barrage, and assisted by
nine tanks of the 9th Battalion and machine guns, to attack
Mory Copse ridge from the valley north-east of Ervillers at
3.30 p.m. With one check, caused by heavy machine-gun
fire, the 1/R. Berkshire, with six tanks, reinforced by two
companies of the 1/King's, went forward, took the objective
and joined up with the right of the Guards Division ; but
the enemy still remained in Mory village.

It had been arranged that if the attack on Mory Copse
was successful the 6th Brigade should attack the ridge
between Béhagnies and Mory ; but the 17/Royal Fusiliers,

which it sent forward at 5.5 p.m., came under enfilade fire from Mory, was forced to come to a halt and then dug in facing the village.

At night the 6th and 99th Brigades were relieved by the 187th Brigade of the 62nd Division, but the 5th remained in the line with orders to capture Sapignies and Béhagnies at all costs on the morning of the 25th.

The Guards Division detailed the 3rd Guards Brigade (Br.-General G. B. S. Follett) to make the attack at 7 a.m. It had the XIV and 155th (Army) Brigades R.F.A. in close support and two companies of machine guns attached, whilst the remainder of the artillery with the division, under Br.-General F. A. Wilson, fired the barrage. The advance was made on either side of the Sensée valley to St. Léger, the 1/Grenadier Guards and 2/Scots Guards to the south and the 1/Welsh Guards to the north, with Ecoust St. Mein and the high ground east of Bullecourt, over four miles away, as objectives. The divisions on either side not yet being abreast of the Guards, good prospect of reaching the objectives was not apparent.

On account of thick wire in front, and intense machine-gun fire from Mory Copse (until reached by the 2nd Division late in the afternoon) and from the little valley running north-eastwards down to Ecoust St. Mein, the 1/Grenadiers, which suffered 150 casualties, was unable to advance very far. The 2/Scots Guards, after beginning well and taking more than a hundred prisoners, was similarly brought to a standstill south of St. Léger, although parties working through that village in vain tried to take the enemy's position in flank. The 1/Welsh Guards met with opposition from the outset, but, overcoming many machine-gun posts, reached the trench, called St. Léger Reserve, which ran north and south past the eastern edge of St. Léger. The day therefore closed with the three battalions of the 3rd Guards Brigade in line but separated, although finally touch was gained with the divisions on either side when these came up.

The attack of the 56th Division, with Summit Trench (a northern extension of St. Léger Reserve) 2,500 yards away as its first objective, was carried out at 7 a.m. by the 167th Brigade (Br.-General G. H. B. Freeth) with one company of machine guns attached, supported by its own divisional artillery as well as that of the Guards and 57th Divisions and the XIII, XXII and LXIII Brigades R.G.A. Twelve tanks of the 11th Battalion were to co-operate but only ten appeared.

The 167th Brigade, having relieved the 168th during the night, advanced with the 1/8th and 1/7th Middlesex and 1/1st London in line under a good barrage, preceded by the tanks. The resistance, chiefly from machine-gun posts, was not very severe and by 10 a.m. the whole of the first objective had been taken. Summit Trench was covered by a low ridge from fire from Croisilles and any attempt to advance over this ridge met with intense fire and, as has been seen, the Guards on the right were also held up. The old trench systems of 1916 and 1917 north and north-east of Croisilles had been named as the second objective, in order, in conjunction with the Guards Division, to envelop that village. As an outlyer of the Hindenburg Line, it was known to be very strongly wired and held. Without the help of the Guards it seemed hopeless to make the attempt ; but during the afternoon an airman reported that there was a tank in Croisilles—it turned out later to be a broken down lorry— so orders were given by the division for the attack to be continued at 7.30 p.m. with the two tanks still available. Lieut.-Colonel C. H. Pank of the 1/8th Middlesex, who carried out a reconnaissance, telephoned to the brigade and the division that the ground ahead was broken and well wired, and that unless the German machine-gun fire could be subdued the attack was unlikely to succeed. The battalions were nevertheless ordered to proceed. The barrage was not very strong, as some batteries were on the move forward and could not take part ; not only heavy machine-gun fire but also gun fire flared up ; the two tanks were soon put *hors de combat*, one having its roof blown in by a trench mortar shell and the other being rendered untenable by a phosphorus bomb thrown on to it. Some of the leading troops managed to go forward as much as five hundred yards ; but the fire was too severe and the attack failed. The 167th Brigade then consolidated Summit Trench.

The 52nd Division had sent the 157th Brigade (Br.-General C. D. Hamilton-Moore), with the 156th in echelon on its left rear, to attack at the same hour as the 56th Division advanced. It had the same artillery support as on the previous day. Hénin was taken without difficulty by the 1/6th and 1/5th Highland L.I. of the 157th and the lower slopes of Hénin Hill (on the Hamelincourt–Héninel ridge), the first objectives, were reached by 9 a.m., where the 1/7th Royal Scots and 1/7th Scottish Rifles (156th Brigade) came up on the left. The two brigades were now faced by the main Hindenburg Position, and the 52nd Division should have waited until the 56th, on its right, fixed the Zero for the next advance.[1] The 157th Brigade, however, pressed on up Hénin Hill and ran into the fire of the British heavy artillery which was bombarding the Hindenburg Position. Communications being cut, it was some time before this fire could be stopped and before a fresh assault by the two Highland L.I. battalions could be arranged for 3.45 p.m. They then went forward under a light barrage, but were unable to cross the uncut wire, which was well defended by machine-gun and trench mortar fire. Finally the attack was stopped by order of the brigade, and the line of the first objectives, the lower slopes of Hénin Hill–Hénin, reoccupied. The left flank had been greatly strengthened by the capture by the 2nd Canadian Division of Neuville Vitasse on the high ground north of Hénin Hill.

The enemy opposition throughout the day had been offered almost entirely by scattered machine guns. The riflemen seemed to have no desire to fight. Many of the machine guns, as later discovered, were a hundred to a hundred and fifty yards ahead of the main line, outside any wire, skilfully concealed by camouflage on wire netting. Unless these guns happened to be struck by the barrage, they were able to remain in action all day. Thus it was that night and early morning attacks in poor visibility had succeeded and daylight advances had failed. Advance in a general line after dawn favoured the enemy's machine-gun tactics which were best countered by stalking under good covering fire by small parties suitably equipped with machine guns, trench mortars, demolition charges, smoke producers, rifle-grenades and bombs. On the German side the engineer companies were

[1] The Hindenburg Position (see End—paper B, " German Retirements " and Map 4) ran from near Vailly on the Aisne past St. Quentin by Quéant (just off Sketch 14, being three miles south-east of Bullecourt) north-westwards to the Scarpe in front of Arras. The Wotan Line, which crossed it at Quéant, cut off a smaller part of the front mostly north of the Hindenburg Position, from Sailly Saillisel northwards to Quéant and in front of Armentières ; the portion north of Quéant was known to the British as the Drocourt–Quéant Line.

specially trained to take the lead in this kind of work,[1] but on the British side they almost entirely engaged on road repairs and water supply, for which the enemy used forced civilian, even prisoner of war, labour.

NOTE I

THE FRENCH ON THE 24TH AUGUST

(Sketch 12)

The account of the 24th August in F.O.A. is short, for little happened. The French First and Third Armies prepared to resume their advance in conformity with the instructions of General Fayolle : " The case must be envisaged when the progress of the " British Armies on the north and the advance to be expected of " the Tenth and Sixth Armies on the east ensure a withdrawal of " the enemy. In this eventuality all arrangements ought to be " made for an energetic and violent pursuit, ready to be launched " at the first indication of retirement ". The First Army, as already noticed, completed the relief of the Canadian troops up to the north of Chilly, and of the 4th Australian Division in the Lihons area.

The Tenth Army continued to find the enemy was resisting strongly between the Ailette and the Aisne ; on the 24th, only the I. Corps managed to make a small advance. The account then passes on to the 25th.

NOTE II

THE GERMANS ON THE 24th AUGUST

(Sketch 13)

The histories are available for the units of three of the five German divisions (the sixth, the *13th*, was moved northwards) opposing the left wing of the Fourth Army north of the Somme, formed by the 3rd Australian Division and the 47th, 12th and 18th Divisions of the III. Corps. It will be noticed that the accounts of the fighting mention four lines of resistance, to the last of which, east of Suzanne—west of Maricourt—east of Montauban, the Germans retired at the end of the day.

---

[1] See Gruss's " Die deutschen Sturm-battaillone im Weltkriege. Aufbau und Verwendung ".

The history of the *120th Württemburg Regiment (27th Division)* opposite the 47th Division, in the south, says of the fighting on and after the 22nd August :

" What took place on these days in the deep valley between
" the high ground at Bray, Suzanne and Maricourt could no
" longer be called a battle. The hostile brigades rolled forward
" behind a mighty curtain of fire and thoroughly smothered
" the very mixed up German combatants, who had to defend
" themselves simultaneously against infantry, squadrons of
" tanks, cavalry, and aircraft. What did it matter if here
" and there our guns blew up a tank, if our machine guns shot
" an attacking cavalry detachment to pieces, if our fighter
" aeroplanes shot down several hostile machines ? The
" enemy filled the gaps in the twinkling of an eye, but the
" brave body of Württembergers and their helpers got weaker
" hour by hour. . . . When on the 25th August the regimental
" commander on orders from the division assembled the
" regiment near Curlu [2¼ miles north-east of Suzanne] he
" saw before him just one company not quite at war estab-
" lishment strength, that is to say two hundred and fifty
" souls [instead of 3,000] amongst whom were only a few
" officers ".

The northern boundary of the *25th Division (115th, 116th and 117th Regiments)* was a line joining the southern edges of Fricourt —Mametz—Montauban, and the southern boundary one running from Bronfay Farm to the southern edge of Maricourt : that is, it faced the 12th Division (the *54th Reserve Division* was presumably north of the *25th* : it did not go out of the line until the 25th August).

" The *116th Regiment* held the sector on the left of the
" *115th Regiment*. . . . Suddenly at 12.50 a.m. there broke out
" an extraordinarily heavy bombardment along the whole
" front, and about half-an-hour later the enemy made a
" general attack. . . . On the right flank Nos. 2 and 4 com-
" panies were overrun . . . only a few got away. The greater
" part of the companies on the left flank were also lost. . . .
" The front of the regiment was rolled up from the north
" [this would seem to have been by the 21/London], and the
" enemy, moving down a hollow [? Happy Valley], thrust
" against the right flank of the *III. Battalion*. . . . On the left
" flank the British got in rear of Nos. 7 and 8 Companies at
" the point of junction between the *116th* and *117th Regi-*
" *ments* and cut off their retreat [this might be the operation
" of the 1/15th London up the Happy Valley]. Here too
" almost everything was lost. . . . With extraordinary
" rapidity and with greatly superior numbers [two British
" battalions against three German] the enemy then turned

"from this point against the *III. Battalion*, now attacked
"from two directions. Nos. 11 and 12 Companies were
"overpowered after hard and close fighting. Both sides lost
"heavily. . . . Part of No. 9 Company was also overrun. . . .
"The main line of resistance was lost and with it the greater
"portion of the regiment. The second main line of resistance
"could not be held any longer owing to threats of encirclement
"from the north ; so orders were given to withdraw to the
"third line of resistance. The remainder of the *III. Battalion*
"occupied the east edge of Carnoy, and what had been saved
"of *I. Battalion* formed the outposts ".

But events in the *Seventeenth Army* sector (to the north) compelled the division to withdraw farther to the east, and at 9 p.m.
the movement, code-name " Sunset ", began. The new line of
resistance held by the *II.* and *III. Battalions* ran from Bazentin le
Grand (5 miles north of Suzanne) to Suzanne.

The history of the *115th Regiment,* which apparently occupied
the two strongpoints which held up the right of the 37th Brigade,
says :

"The whole divisional sector was bombarded by guns of
"all calibres for half-an-hour. About 2 a.m. the British
"advanced to the assault against the regiment in thick
"masses. . . . By 4.30 a.m. the enemy's attack had been
"broken. . . . An hour later there was a second attack in
"force. . . . The losses that the enemy suffered as he fell back
"were bloody [these attacks were made by one battalion,
"the 6/R. West Kent and the right of another, the
"6/Queen's]. When he realized that he could not break
"through here with his artillery and infantry, he pushed
"forward his tanks in strong squadrons [3 tanks] in the third
"attack of the day, at 3.30 p.m. This also failed. . . . By
"4.30 p.m. the whole battle zone was again firmly in the
"regiment's possession. . . . Our neighbours on the right and
"left [*27th* and the *54th Reserve Divisions*] had not fought so
"fortunately, and as both flanks seemed to be threatened . . .
"the division gave orders to fall back during the night to
"the fourth line of resistance, which ran from the west edge
"of Montauban, half-way between Carnoy and Maricourt ".

The history of the *15th Regiment* (*13th Division*), which after
assisting the *233rd Division* on the previous days was on the 24th
re-engaged a little farther north near the Bazentins (Sketch 14),
apparently north of the *83rd* mentioned below, says :

"As regards rest the night of the 23rd-24th August was
"soon over. As early as 1 a.m. a British barrage resounded,
"and shortly afterwards an attack was made against the
"*233rd Division* and against the *83rd* [this division had just
"relieved the *3rd Naval Division* north of Albert] and

" *25th Divisions* on its right and left.   North of Bécourt the
" enemy succeeded in gaining a considerable amount of
" ground so that la Boisselle and even Pozières were
" captured.   The regiment lost heavily in casualties and
" prisoners and had to withdraw. . . . The troops were
" completely exhausted by the great heat of the day ".

The eight German divisions originally opposite the thirteen of
the Third Army had been reinforced by no less than nine[1] : as
we have just seen, by the *13th Division* and the *83rd* ; by the
52nd, which went to the Miraumont sector on the 22nd ; by the
111th, which came up on the 24th to Favreuil (a mile north of
Bapaume) ; by the *40th*, which on the 22nd entered the line near
Courcelles (between Ablainzevelle and Ervillers) ;   by the
16th Bavarian (said to be 2,000 infantry short) which, coming
up on the morning of the 24th, was just in time to support the
183rd Division after it had been hustled out of Grévillers by the
New Zealand Division ; by the *52nd Reserve Division*, which
according to B.O.A. (p. 536) was in the act of relieving the
183rd Division on the morning of the 24th ; by the *6th Bavarian
Reserve Division*, which had reinforced the front near Biefvillers
and northwards and was driven out of it ; and by the *220th*, also
put in between Biefvillers and Ervillers.

The regimental histories available give a picture of complete
confusion ; the troops of the *6th Bavarian Reserve Division* were,
for instance, " thrown piecemeal into the fight and into the
" mix-up of the units of two other divisions " ; but the arrival
of the various reinforcements managed to stop the British at
critical places.   " Res. Regt., No. 91 " (*2nd Guard Reserve
Division*), p. 417, states that when the division was withdrawn on
the evening of the 24th, the regiment had only 64 men left, and the
two other regiments 300 and 100 respectively.   Over 2,000
prisoners of this division were taken 21st–24th August.

---

[1] The mentions of these are all taken from regimental histories and
B.O.A. and confirmed by " Histories of the two hundred and fifty one
divisions of the German Army which participated in the War ".   The
list may not be exhaustive.

CHAPTER XIV

BATTLE OF ALBERT 1918—(*continued*)

THIRD ARMY

25TH AUGUST ([1])

(Sketches 13, 14)

For the continuation of the operations G.H.Q. on the afternoon of the 24th issued the following orders, which, being short, are transcribed verbatim :

The Third Army will continue to press the enemy, advancing in the general direction of the line Manancourt [8 miles south of Bapaume]–Quéant [12 miles south-east of Arras, due north of Manancourt].[2]

The Fourth Army, operating astride the Somme, will continue to protect the right of the Third Army.

The First Army will be prepared to attack the enemy south of the Scarpe at short notice, in co-operation with the advance of the Third Army. The chief object of this attack will be to pierce the Drocourt–Quéant line[3]. and subsequently to operate in a south-easterly direction against the right flank of the enemy's troops opposed to the Third Army.

To enable the First Army to carry out its task, the following additional troops are placed at its disposal :

(*a*) Cavalry Corps (less 2nd Cavalry Division) ;

(*b*) Canadian Corps (4 divisions) ;

(*c*) 4th Division ;

(*d*) Tanks (to be notified later).

The dividing lines between Armies for purposes of communications are shown on the attached map.[4]

---

[1] In the Fourth Army the operations of 25th August were continued into the 26th ; on the 26th the First Army began to come into the picture on the left of the Third. It has therefore been thought best to deal first with the Third Army on the 25th, next with its right flank guard the Fourth Army, on the 25th and 26th, and then with the Third and First Armies on the 26th, whose action 26th to 30th bears the official name of the Battle of the Scarpe.

[2] See Sketch 14.

[3] It ran from the Hindenburg Line near Quéant northward across the Scarpe to Drocourt (10 miles north-east of Arras), roughly up the right margin of Sketch 14 from abreast of Bullecourt. It is shown in Sketch 18.

[4] Not reproduced.

G.H.Q. also issued special instructions with regard to the employment of cavalry : in view of the possible rapid disintegration of the enemy's forces and in the hope of obtaining strategic results when a favourable situation arose, the bulk of the cavalry was to be kept together as a corps and handled by one commander : the only detachments permitted were to be about one troop to each division, and about one regiment to each corps.

The enemy north of the Somme having fallen back three miles during the night to the line marked[1] by Suzanne–Maricourt–Montauban–the Bazentins, though still holding fast north of this, resistance to the Fourth Army was weak, so that in conjunction with the Third Army it was able to gain a little ground somewhat easily during the 25th. The right and centre of the Third Army also made good progress ; but its left, now confronted by the Hindenburg Line, stood fast as it was necessary that some preparations should be made before its attack. South of the Somme the Australian Corps had no more to do than improve its position and prepare for a further advance. The French First Army on its right did not move.

FOURTH ARMY

In the Fourth Army, General Sir H. Rawlinson had on the previous day given instructions, in addition to those regarding the exploitation of success, that the Australian and III. Corps should at once form small groups of 60-pdrs. (horse-drawn) and 6-inch guns (steam-tractor drawn) to be pushed forward boldly, " leap-frogging " each other, for the purpose of keeping the enemy's communications under fire. He pointed out that the roads by which the enemy could withdraw his guns were limited in number ; these roads and the bridges over the Somme behind the enemy should therefore be kept under fire and, in addition, certain localities, Villers Carbonnel and Barleux (both on the western side of the north-south reach of the Somme), Péronne, and, north of Péronne, Clery, le Forest and Combles : in shelling the roads only shrapnel or H.E. with the rapid action 106 fuzes was to be used—in order not to damage too seriously those which would be required for use later on. He added that

---

[1] See Sketch 13

the loss or destruction of our guns as a result of bold action was of minor importance in comparison with the harm which could be caused to the enemy: the long-range heavy howitzers were to be moved forward before other howitzers, and the fire of the 12-inch and 14-inch guns was to be directed on Péronne until further orders. Owing to the infantry brigadiers not knowing of these instructions to the artillery, they in some cases stopped the groups of 60-pdrs. and 6-inch guns firing in fear of the shells dropping amongst their men. The infantry seldom had to complain of lack of artillery support, though the batteries often received their orders for the many dawn attacks only as light was fading on the previous evening, and in the dark had to advance to new battle positions over new country, lay out lines of fire and re-establish communication with the infantry. The embarrassment caused to the Germans by long-range fire is very evident from the regimental histories of units and divisions sent up as reinforcements and reliefs. It was not until these histories became available that the full extent of the disorganization and demoralization of the German troops by the 25th/26th August was realized; it was greater than G.H.Q. believed. In these books it will be found that on the enemy's side " the days were spent in bloody fighting " with an ever and again on-storming enemy, and the nights " passed without sleep in retirements to new lines "; [1] infantry regiments (equivalents of British brigades) were " reduced to fought-out battalions "; divisions were " hopelessly intermixed "; they were ordered to retire to escape capture, and several were withdrawn altogether owing to heavy casualties; all counter-attacks failed; " indubit-" able defeat " was experienced and, as will be related in due course, the German leaders found themselves forced to order a general retirement. [2]

The air force was busy during the night of the 24th/25th; the railway junctions at Somain (13 miles north of Cambrai), Cambrai, Douai and Valenciennes, through which lines passed to the battle-front, were the main targets; but bombs were dropped on billets and troops, and on transport on the roads in the area behind that front. The Germans made fewer flights, but attacked Boulogne and the aerodrome at Bertangles (5 miles north of Amiens). In retaliation, the

---

[1] " Leib Regiment No. 115."

[2] See Note at end of Chapter and Note II at end of Chapter XV.

day bombers of the headquarters IX. Brigade were given German aerodromes as objectives on the 25th, and bombed those of Étreux (south-east of Le Cateau) and Mont d'Origny (near Guise), both about thirty miles behind the battlefield. The corps squadrons, by contact and artillery patrols, kept touch with the advance, not only making machine-gun attacks on artillery by diving, but also signalling a large number of fleeting targets, and directing gunfire on single batteries and even small concentrations of troops.

General Sir Julian Byng's orders for the continuation of the general advance of the Third Army on the 25th were issued at 7.53 p.m. on the previous evening. No zero hour was fixed ; but by the light of a bright moon three days past full all the corps made early starts, zero hour varying from 2.30 a.m. to 9 a.m., with 3.30 a.m. for the units of the VI. Corps, which had been warned at all costs to capture by a night attack Sapignies and Béhagnies, which had held up the advance of the 2nd Division, since the afternoon of the 23rd. To a great extent, the operations were treated as being of the character of advanced-guard actions against a somewhat demoralized enemy, who, as in the retreat of March 1917, held on for a time in the hope of inflicting heavy losses before retiring from position to position back to the Hindenburg Line ; in some orders, indeed, the operations were called " the pursuit ".

The V. Corps was to advance about four miles, to Flers–Gueudecourt, and then onward another four miles so as to obtain touch with the IV. Corps on the left at Riencourt les Bapaume (2 miles south-east of Bapaume). It was then to push cavalry along all the roads to the east ;

the IV. Corps was to advance through Bapaume to the line Riencourt les Bapaume–Beugnâtre ; there, as it was nearer the Hindenburg Line (which passed north-westwards by Bullecourt and Crosilles) than the V. Corps, it was to re-organize in depth and patrol all roads to the east ;

the VI. Corps, after capturing Sapignies, Behagnies and Mory by night attack, was to continue the advance with its right and centre about two miles to Vaulx

Vraucourt–Ecoust St. Mein (only 2,000 yards from Bullecourt in the Hindenburg Line), so as to come abreast of the IV. Corps ; but the left flank was to be maintained at Hénin Hill for the present.

At 8 a.m. on the 25th the XVII. Corps, which had on the 23rd handed over the right sector of the First Army to the Canadian Corps, and now contained only the 59th Division, out of the line, was to be transferred to the Third Army. The 52nd and 56th Divisions and their frontages were also to pass at that hour from the command of the VI. Corps (which contained six divisions) to the XVII.[1]

The V. Corps orders directed that " the pursuit " should be resumed at the earliest possible moment, and continued with the greatest rapidity and determination, giving the enemy no time to recover.

The 8th Hussars (9th Cavalry Brigade, 1st Cavalry Division), allotted as corps cavalry, then at Contay (7 miles west of Albert), was to advance as early as possible and exploit along all roads leading eastwards ; but no opportunity occurred for its employment ;

the 38th Division was to advance on Flers ;

the 17th Division, on Gueudecourt, a strong force of machine guns from both divisions being sent to High Wood (south-west of Flers) when captured ;

the 21st Division, on Beaulencourt, to obtain touch with the IV. Corps.

Major-General Cubitt selected 2.30 a.m. as zero hour, and sent all three brigades of the 38th Division forward in line, each with a brigade of field artillery attached to provide a barrage. Their first objective was the ridge east of Contalmaison (still in enemy hands), along the north edge of Mametz Wood, the wood and village of Bazentin le Petit, and High Wood.

The 113th Brigade took Contalmaison, which had been bombarded by heavy artillery during the night, without much opposition, and reached the first objective by 5 a.m. ; the advance, in semi-darkness and mist, had led to many pockets of Germans being overlooked, with the result that

---

[1] The artillery of the 40th, 52nd, 56th and 57th Divisions, the V. and 232nd (Army) Brigades R.F.A., and the VIII., XIII., LXVI. and LXXXVIII. Brigades R.G.A. were also transferred.

brigade headquarters were nearly caught by an enemy company, which itself was captured by a company of the 13/R. Welch Fusiliers.

The 115th Brigade, similarly, met with little opposition, and quickly occupied its objectives between Mametz Wood and Bazentin le Petit wood, later extending its left to include the village of Bazentin le Petit.

The 114th Brigade had during the earlier part of the night advanced through Pozières without much opposition and relieved the 50th Brigade (17th Division). But when it attempted to go on without artillery support it could not, in consequence of machine-gun fire, get any farther than the Contalmaison–Martinpuich road, fifteen hundred yards short of the 115th Brigade in Bazentin le Petit.

In the afternoon, touch having been established with the 18th Division (Fourth Army) south-west of Mametz Wood, the 113th Brigade sent the 16/R. Welch Fusiliers through the wood, where the 38th Division had fought in July 1916, and, after some opposition, it reached the eastern edge. In the late evening the enemy made a determined but unsuccessful counter-attack on the 10/South Wales Borderers of the 115th Brigade in Bazentin le Petit. Otherwise the position of the 38th Division remained unchanged.[1]

Major-General Robertson gave orders for the 17th Division to advance at 4 a.m. ; with, as first objective, a line running east of Martinpuich and then turning north-west to cross the Albert–Bapaume road half-way between Courcelette and Le Sars. The 50th Brigade, relieved by the 114th Brigade, became the reserve ; the 51st (Br.-General R. M. Dudgeon) was to come up on the left of the 52nd in the line north of Pozières, and then the two brigades, supported by the LXXIX. and LXXVIII. Brigades R.F.A. respectively, were to move forward together. To reach the starting line about a mile west of Courcelette, the 51st Brigade, warned only at 10 p.m., had to make a night march of more than two miles from the eastern bank of the Ancre opposite Hamel ; but, in spite of the dense mist which prevailed about dawn, it arrived in good time.

---

[1] Both brigade and battalion war diaries give the position of the 114th Brigade as on the Contalmaison–Martinpuich road ; but the histories of the 38th Division and of the Welch Regiment put it on the Bazentin le Petit–Martinpuich road.

The 52nd Brigade took Martinpuich after some opposition, the 12/Manchester encircling it from the south and the 10/Lancashire Fusiliers from the north. Beyond the village further advance was stopped by machine-gun fire, especially from the direction of High Wood to the south-east, which field artillery fire could not suppress, and during the afternoon the enemy established himself on the higher ground in this direction, only five hundred yards from Martinpuich. No touch could be got of the 38th Division to the south, for its 114th Brigade was held up on the Albert–Martinpuich road, so a defensive right flank was formed south of Martinpuich by the 10/West Yorkshire, of the reserve brigade, sent up for the purpose.

The 51st Brigade met with little opposition in Courcelette, and by 11 a.m. had reached a position between Martinpuich and Le Sars ; here its right experienced the same oblique machine-gun fire from the south-east as had the 52nd Brigade ; but its left was able to make further progress, and by evening the outer flank was little short of Eaucourt l'Abbaye.   The general advance of the 17th Division amounted therefore to about one mile and a quarter.

For the 21st Division, Major-General Campbell planned a series of " leap frog " advances, to begin at 6 a.m.   At that hour the 62nd Brigade, which was in second line, was to pass through the 110th and, under a barrage, advance north-eastwards to the line (eastern edge of) Eaucourt l'Abbaye–le Barque (on the left divisional boundary).   As soon as this line was made good the 110th Brigade was to pass through it and later the 62nd again take the lead.

When the 1/Lincolnshire and 12th/13th Northumberland Fusiliers of the 62nd, led by Br.-General Gater himself, moved forward, compasses had to be used until a distant German balloon showed above the ground mist.   The two battalions had hardly left the line of the 110th Brigade before they were struck by machine-gun fire from the high ground north of le Sars, were checked and lost the barrage.   They were unable to move forward till 11 a.m., by which time two light trench mortars had been brought up to crush the machine guns, and a company of the 2/Lincolnshire, the reserve, moving by a concealed route, had turned the enemy's flank north of le Sars.   Then the brigade took Le Sars and the Butte de Warlencourt, a large isolated

mound between the two villages, which had offered so much
resistance in 1916, capturing a large party of Germans there,
and reaching the objective except on the right. Connection
was then made on the left in the southern part of le Barque
with the 63rd Division already established there ; [1] on the
right owing to the weakness of the brigade there was a gap
of nearly a thousand yards to the 17th Division, covered by
Eaucourt l'Abbaye ; so at 2 p.m. the 110th Brigade was
diverted and sent to fill the space just in time, as the enemy,
taking advantage of the gap, had initiated a counter-attack.
He was repulsed, but two battalions of the 110th Brigade
were retained in position in the gap, and no further progress
of the 21st Division took place on this day.

The three divisions of the V Corps had made substantial
progress, although they had not reached the distant objectives suggested for them ; Contalmaison, Pozières, Bazentin
le Petit, Martinpuich, Courcelette and Le Sars had been
taken ; but between Bazentin le Petit and Martinpuich a
gap existed, faced by High Wood still strongly held by the
enemy.[2]

Lieut.-General Harper fixed 5 a.m. as the hour of advance
of the IV Corps with the line Riencourt les Bapaume–
Beugnâtre, two miles beyond Bapaume, as the objective for
the 63rd, New Zealand and 37th Divisions ; the 42nd
Division, in the line, after they had passed through it, would
become the right reserve, and the 5th, only one of whose
brigades had been employed on the previous day to form a
right defensive flank, the left reserve.[3]

After the cancellation of the attack of the 63rd Division
on the evening of the 24th, Major-General Lawrie, in accordance with corps orders, had directed that the advance should

---

[1] The *3rd Naval Division*, which was in the line near Authuille on
21st August, but had been shifted northwards near Warlencourt, was
" outflanked on the left and driven back with heavy losses ".   B.O.A.,
p. 526.

[2] Ludendorff, pp. 692–3, says that " the situation there [in the shell-
" hole area of the Somme battlefield east of Albert] was extremely critical
" about 25th August ".

[3] Brigades of heavy artillery were affiliated to divisions : LIV and LVI
to the 63rd, XC to the New Zealand, XXXIV to the 37th ; the LVII
and XCII, long-range gun brigades, covered the whole corps front and
fired on distant roads and villages, and co-operated with the divisions
when required.

be resumed—the New Zealand Division now co-operating on the left—at 5 a.m. on the 25th. The 189th and 188th Brigades (Commander W. M. le C. Egerton, acting) and Br.-General J. F. S. D. Coleridge) were to capture le Barque and Thilloy, and then go straight on to Riencourt les Bapaume. The 190th Brigade was to follow in support, ready to meet any development to the south. The tanks which were to have co-operated on the previous evening had gone back to their base and did not take part in the operations of the 25th.

Under a barrage, the Hood and Hawke Battalions of the 189th Brigade advanced through Loupart Wood ; but on debouching from it in the mist they came under machine-gun fire from the south-east, and both lost their commanding officers (Lieut.-Commander S. H. Fish and Commander S. G. Jones). The machine guns were silenced by Lewis-gun fire and the advance, reinforced by the Drake Battalion, was continued past the southern end of le Barque (it lies, with Ligny Thilloy, on the upper course of the Ancre) to the road to Bazentin le Petit, which was reached at 11 a.m. after a five-hours' struggle. The 21st Division was not yet up on the right, and on the left Thilloy, which stands out at the end of a flat spur projecting into the Ancre valley, was in the enemy's possession. The advance of the 189th Brigade then came to a stop.

The 188th Brigade, with the 1/Royal Marines, Anson Battalion and 2/Royal Irish in line, met with little opposition for the first mile up to the Albert–Bapaume road ; then it encountered machine-gun fire ; but nevertheless the Marines took le Barque and entered the western part of Ligny Thilloy, and the leading men of the other two battalions entered Thilloy about 7.50 a.m.[1] Behind Thilloy were two German battalions in reserve and, well aided by guns and machine guns, they counter-attacked and by 9 a.m. had recovered the village.[2] The line of the 188th Brigade was then established along the eastern edge of le Barque, and thence northward to the Albert–Bapaume road, touch being established with the troops on both flanks.

---

[1] All German accounts (e.g. B.O.A., p. 536) say with tanks, but this was not the case.

[2] The counter-attack was made by the *11th Bavarian Regiment* and the *I/21st Bavarian Reserve Regiment*, supported by the three batteries of the *8th Bavarian Field Artillery Regiment*, all of the *16th Bavarian Division* which had arrived on the 24th. See Note at end of Chapter.

K *

Between 3 and 4 p.m. the enemy made a strong counter-attack against le Barque, advancing in the open under a barrage ; but this was met by such heavy fire from guns, machine guns and rifles that it was completely broken up.[1] A counter-attack, made in heavy rain about 9 p.m. north of Thilloy, met with the same fate.[2]

The 1st New Zealand Brigade at Grévillers, was ordered by Major-General Russell to co-operate with the 63rd Division by advancing at 5 a.m. to a line extending from the northern end of Thilloy along the Thilloy–Bapaume road. The 2nd New Zealand Brigade, on the left, its outer flank protected by the 37th Division which was at Bihucourt not so far forward, was to advance to a line east of Avesnes (near Bapaume) and along the Bapaume–Sapignies road as far as " The Monument ".[3] The 1st N.Z. Brigade, relying on surprise and speed over easy open country, had no barrage ; but three artillery brigades fired one for the 2nd N.Z. Brigade, which also had the assistance of eight Mark V tanks of the 10th Battalion and 15 whippets of the 3rd Battalion.

Complete success attended the attack of the New Zealanders. In the 1st Brigade, the 2/Wellington reached the cross-roads a thousand yards N.N.W. of Thilloy, and then, capturing Avesnes, extended its left along the Thilloy–Bapaume road to join up with the 2nd Brigade. In the 2nd Brigade the 1/Canterbury, with the Mark V tanks, and the 1/Otago met with stubborn resistance from machine guns, but were able to deal with them in the fog, and by 7 a.m. were close up to Bapaume and thence lay along the Sapignies road to the Monument. The fog now began to thin, further progress became impossible ; even when, about 9 a.m., the whippets came forward they could not, in the face of heavy fire, go beyond the firing line. At 6.30 p.m., by divisional order, however, the 1/Otago co-operated with the 37th Division in an advance, as will be narrated below.

To the 37th Division, which was to cover the left flank of the N.Z. Division, the objective assigned was a line running aslant from about a mile west of Favreuil to half a mile

---

[1] This counter-attack was made by the *44th Reserve Division*, brought up from 3 months' rest " in place of the *3rd Naval Division* ".

[2] Apparently made by the *16th Bavarian Division*.

[3] A commemorative monument, a mile north of the town, of the Battle of Bapaume in 1871.

west of Sapignies. This line lay across two spurs (on the easternmost of which is the Monument), with a col between them, commanding the Mory valley. Major-General Bruce Williams detailed the 63rd and 111th Brigades to lead, starting at 5 a.m. from Bihucourt, that is simultaneously with the New Zealand Division, but one hour and a half after the 2nd Division on the left was to attack Sapignies.

At first the advance of the 4/Middlesex and 8/Lincolnshire of the 63rd Brigade, and the 13/Rifle Brigade and 13/K.R.R.C. of the 111th, did not make much progress ; but as soon as the mist cleared they pushed ahead and were on the objectives about 7 a.m. Thence the 63rd Brigade went on to the Bapaume–Sapignies road to the left of the New Zealanders and into the southern end of Sapignies where, about 8 a.m., it got in touch with the troops of the 2nd Division who had taken the village.

At 3.15 p.m., by corps direction, Major-General Bruce Williams, after consultation with Major-General Russell of the New Zealand Division, issued orders for an attack on Favreuil at 6.30 p.m. in conjunction with the left of the New Zealand Division and the right of the 62nd (which, as will be seen, had relieved the 2nd Division). The 62nd Division was prevented from co-operating by a German counter-attack, and the operation was carried out by the 1/Otago and the 111th Brigade under a barrage of both heavy and field artillery. The New Zealanders captured Monument Wood and the southern part of Favreuil without special difficulty ; but an enemy barrage came down on the 13/Rifle Brigade and 13/K.R.R.C. as they were making ready, so opportunely that it was suspected that the divisional telegraph message ordering the attack must have been tapped. The ground was flat and open, and strong opposition came from a trench west of Favreuil ; the 13/Rifle Brigade turned this trench from the south, capturing a hundred and fifty Germans, and then pushed on to the village and got in touch with the 1/Otago. The 10/Royal Fusiliers, in support, making use of a covered approach, came up on the left of the 13/K.R.R.C., which was exposed owing to the absence of the 62nd Division, and turned the enemy's flank in the trench from the north, so that here also the German garrison surrendered. The northern end of Favreuil was not, however, cleared until night had come on, when touch was gained with the 62nd Division.[1] During the night the 37th Division was relieved by the 5th.

The IV Corps, on this fifth day of the advance, in spite of two fresh enemy divisions[2] having been brought up against it, had progressed well over a mile and in places nearly three miles. The strong opposition encountered at Thilloy from one fresh division and another nearly fresh, which had come into the battle on the previous day only, had prevented much progress on the right, and Favreuil, being defended by another fresh division, could not be taken until late in the evening.

In the VI Corps, the 2nd Division was detailed by Lieut.-General Haldane to capture Sapignies and Béhagnies by a night attack at 3.30 a.m. Both villages are on the lower slopes of a long spur enclosed by two source branches of the Sensée. Mory, north of them, was left for a later operation. Major-General Pereira selected his 5th Brigade for the task, and during the night the 187th Brigade (62nd Division) took over the left sector of the 2nd Division in front of Ervillers in order to free the 6th and 99th Brigades to strengthen the reserve. The 186th Brigade (62nd Division) was ordered by the corps to act as support to the 5th Brigade.

Under a creeping barrage fired by seven brigades of field artillery, after bombardment of the villages by the heavy artillery,[3] two battalions, the 24/Royal Fusiliers and the 2/Highland L.I., with three sections of machine guns and

---

[1] The barrage and opposition encountered near Favreuil at 6.30 p.m. was to a great extent due to the fact that the attack of the New Zealand and 37th Divisions almost coincided with a German counter-attack ordered to be made at 6 p.m., after one hour's bombardment, by the *36th* (from rest near Laon), the *40th Division* (originally in reserve) and the *111th* (it had arrived on the field at 1 p.m. only from rest since the 17th, after being in a quiet sector). The object of this movement was to retake Sapignies, Béhagnies and Mory. (" Regt. No. 134 ", p. 79). The *6th Bavarian Reserve Division* which had been turned out of Sapignies and Béhagnies, should have taken part (" Regt. No. 174 ", p. 134), but was not in a fit state to do so. It was the *111th Division* which opposed the 111th Brigade at Favreuil, and the *40th* and part of the *36th*, the 62nd Division. For the disastrous results of this counter-attack, which is said to have been crushed by artillery fire, see Note at end of Chapter.

[2] The *36th* and *44th Reserve*.

[3] Artillery of the 2nd and 3rd Divisions, and XVIII., XXXIV. and LXXVI. (Army) Brigades R.F.A., and LX. and LXXXIV. Brigades R.G.A.

one whippet tank, attacked Béhagnies ; they were completely successful and established a line three hundred yards beyond the village.   Starting one hour later, the 2/Oxford L.I. followed the Royal Fusiliers past the south side of Béhagnies and then attacked Sapignies from the north, capturing it entirely after some resistance by 7.15 a.m.   The complete success of the 5th Brigade was a good augury for the day.[1]

In the general advance at 9 a.m. the 62nd Division, after relieving the 2nd, was given Vaulx Vraucourt and its northern extension Vraucourt as objectives ; the Guards Division, Ecoust St. Mein with its south extension Longatte, only a mile from the Hindenburg Line ; the 56th and 52nd were to begin the attack on this line, but as they and their sector were transferred to the XVII. Corps at 8 a.m. on the 25th, the account of what happened to them will be given later.

In the 62nd Division, the 187th Brigade (Br.-General A. J. Reddie), its left wing, had, as already mentioned, taken over the Ervillers sector, and the 186th (Br.-General J. L. G. Burnett) which had followed the 5th Brigade (2nd Division), in support, was to pass through it after Sapignies and Béhagnies had been captured.   The two brigades, covered by the same artillery which had earlier supported the 5th Brigade, were given as first objective the portion of the flat ridge between Mory and Vaulx Vraucourt beyond the Sensée valley in which Mory lies, and the continuation of this high ground southward towards Beugnâtre.

Considerable opposition was offered to the 5/Duke of Wellington's, which led the advance of the 186th Brigade through the 5th Brigade ; but by 10.30 a.m. it had nearly reached the Favreuil–Mory road, some mile and a half ahead. Here it came under enfilade fire from both these villages, which were still in the hands of the enemy, and very little further progress could be made.   About 5 p.m. the Germans put down an intense artillery barrage, and at 6.15 p.m.— that is just before the brigades of the 62nd Division should have gone forward in conjunction with those of the 37th Division on the right—their infantry advanced in counter-attack.[2]   The main thrust coming from the direction of Favreuil, the right company of the Duke's was drawn back

---

[1] The front attacked was held by the *6th Bavarian Reserve Division.* " Bav. Res. Regt. No. 16 " (p. 332), which held the front, says that " few " came back living from the murderous close fighting ".

[2] See footnote, p. 274.

to meet the onslaught.` But the Germans would not face the artillery and rifle fire which was loosed upon them—as their own accounts admit—and drifted back. By 8 p.m. all the original line was reoccupied by the Duke's and touch gained with the 37th Division, which by this time was in occupation of Favreuil.

In the 187th Brigade, the 5/K.O.Y.L.I. and the 2/4th York & Lancaster, after relieving the 6th and 99th Brigades of the 2nd Division during the night, were to make the attack, the one south and through Mory and the other north of that village. The change-over took longer than was expected, and about 6 a.m. Br.-General Reddie informed the 62nd Division that he did not consider it possible to advance at 9 a.m. Major-General Braithwaite told him to fix his own hour ; so he ordered a conference of his battalion commanders at the headquarters of the 5/K.O.Y.L.I. for 7 a.m., intending to make 10.30 a.m. zero hour. The message to attend did not reach the commanding officer of the York & Lancaster until 8.30 a.m., such are the uncertainties of communication on the battlefield. He at once started to comply, but, as he had not been told that the attack had been postponed, left instructions for his battalion to carry on. The 2/4th York & Lancaster, though without the artillery barrage it expected, began to advance at 9 a.m., and all Br.-General Reddie could do when he heard of this, it being too late to stop the battalion, was to order the 5/K.O.Y.L.I. to support the attack by advancing as soon as possible, and his third battalion, the 2/4th K.O.Y.L.I., to be ready to push through the York & Lancaster in the later stages of the movement.

The last-named battalion was received with machine-gun fire ; but, in spite of casualties and lack of a barrage, it pushed on about a quarter of a mile before it came to a standstill. Towards 10 a.m. the 5/K.O.Y.L.I. went forward through and south of Mory, also without a barrage, and the 2/4th moved out in support of the York & Lancaster. The situation then remained stationary till about 5 p,m, when, as farther south, the Germans[1] began a bombardment and then counter-attacked. They met with little success, only driving back the right company of the York & Lancaster ; the 2/4th K.O.Y.L.I. promptly intervened and, carrying the

---

[1] The *40th Division* and part of the *36th*.

York & Lancaster company with it, charged with the bayonet and regained the whole line, even advanced slightly beyond it, whilst the retiring enemy came under an artillery barrage and suffered further heavy losses. During the night the 5/K.O.Y.L.I. sent forward patrols unhindered to a road about three-quarters of a mile east of Mory, so that its front was some two thousand yards ahead of the 186th Brigade on the right and a thousand ahead of the other two battalions of the 187th Brigade near Mory Copse.

In the Guards Division, the 3rd Guards Brigade was to continue the advance it had led on the previous day, with Longatte–Ecoust St. Mein as objective, and Mory Copse north of the village, the copse being now included within the divisional boundary. The division was to be covered as before by seven brigades of field artillery and two of heavy. A company of the 9th Tank Battalion was detailed to co-operate, and it was laid down that except for patrols, villages were not to be entered by the infantry, but left to the tanks.

As in the other divisions of the Corps, 9 a.m. was made the zero hour ; but by some misunderstanding the 3rd Guards Brigade went forward at 4.30 a.m., and therefore without support on either flank.[1]

On the right, the 1st Grenadier Guards, with three tanks, at first made good progress in the thick mist, but eventually came under fire from an old trench, " Banks Trench ", about a mile from the starting line, with flat, open ground in front of it. When the mist lifted two tanks were knocked out and the battalion received machine-gun fire from both front and flanks. After hanging on for some time, it was ordered to

---

[1] Br.-General G. B. S. Follett was killed in action a month later, on 27th September, before he had furnished an explanation. His brigade-major had been taken ill with appendicitis on the evening of the 24th, so some confusion may have arisen. Br.-General Follett, it seems, spoke on the telephone to his battalion commanders, and, in view of the danger of the enemy listening in, is reported by one of them and by the commander of an artillery brigade to have said " zero hour will be at—you know " how many lives a cat has ? " " Yes ! ", and was then understood to say " well, halve that ". It is suggested that he really said and " a " half on that ", which would have made Zero 9.30 a.m. Br.-General Follett may have decided to start at that hour and not at 9 a.m., or have thought that 9.30 a.m. was the corps zero hour. A more likely explanation is that the brigadier may have heard that the 2nd Division was attacking Sapignies at 4.30 a.m. The brigade orders as regards zero hour were not confirmed in writing.

retire to a trench north-east of Mory Copse, and later in the
day extended its line to the north.[1]

The 2nd Scots Guards, south of St. Léger, with one tank,
was also held up close to Banks Trench ; the 1/Welsh Guards,
without any tanks, north of St. Léger, after rushing some
advanced posts with the bayonet, ran into uncut wire and
was withdrawn to its starting line. At night the 3rd Guards
Brigade was relieved by the 1st.

Thus on this fifth day of the battle, the VI. Corps had
made good progress except on the extreme left near the
Hindenburg Line.

The XVII. Corps (Lieut.-General Sir Charles Fergusson),
as already mentioned, took over the 56th and 52nd Divisions
from the VI. Corps at 8 a.m.   These divisions had been
ordered to begin the attack on the Hindenburg Line ; but
Major-General Hull (56th Division) pointed out that it was
strongly held and well wired, and that without tanks, which
were not available, success could not be expected. He was
therefore instructed to do no more than capture Croisilles
and a trench beyond it in the valley of the Sensée, so as to
get up level with the expected advance of the Guards on
the right and the position of the 52nd Division on the left.
Patrols of the 56th Division came at once under machine-gun
fire, and no progress was made. Thus the XVII. Corps did
not change its position on the 25th.

On the whole, therefore, the Third Army had achieved a
considerable advance with the V. and IV. Corps, less with
the VI. and none with the XVII. That any progress was
made is remarkable, as its original thirteen divisions had not
been reinforced, whilst the German eight divisions originally
in front line had been supported by no less than eleven fresh
ones, whose efforts to restore the situation by counter-attack
had been completely liquidated.

---

[1] " Regt. No. 5 ", p. 384, of the newly-arrived *36th Division* claims to
have repelled the attack of the 1/Grenadier Guards and killed or taken
prisoner a party of fifty which approached in the mist. It also mentions
the destruction of two tanks. It adds that towards midday the fighting
died down, and then passes to the counter-attack already mentioned.

NOTE

THE GERMANS ON THE 25TH AUGUST OPPOSITE THE THIRD ARMY

The regimental and divisional histories for this period plainly disclose the state of disorganization into which the German troops had fallen. Two more fresh divisions had been thrown into the battle, making a total of eleven divisions, at least, brought up to reinforce the original eight in the line. These two were[1] the *36th* (brought from rest to Bapaume on the 24th) and the *44th Reserve* (from rest to Martinpuich on the 25th).

To quote the Bavarian Official Account :

" On the 25th August the British continued their attacks
" on both sides of Bapaume with particular determination.
" In the sector of the *6th Bavarian Reserve Division,* Sapignies,
" south of Béhagnies, was lost. In vain was the *111th Division*
" brought up on both sides of Favreuil from second line to
" remedy the damage. In the end, this village also became
" the prize of a stronger enemy [not stronger in numbers :
" one British brigade and one New Zealand battalion against
" two German divisions]. At night the *6th Bavarian Reserve*
" *Division,* hopelessly mixed up with troops of the *111th* and
" *220th Divisions,* lay on the Beugnatre–Bapaume road."

" South-east of Bapaume near Warlencourt, the British
" in the early morning had overrun the *3rd Naval Division,*
" which had been put in on the left of the *16th Bavarian*
" *Division,* and the *14th Bavarian Regiment,* which had held
" out against all frontal attacks, was outflanked on the left
" and driven back with heavy losses to the Albert–Bapaume
" high road. Soon after, British tanks broke into Thilloy,
" but it was re-captured by a battalion of the *21st Bavarian*
" *Reserve Regiment,* well supported by an *Abteilung* of the
" *8th Bavarian Field Artillery Regiment.* [No tanks were
" used in this quarter ; Thilloy was taken by parties of the
" 63rd Division, which were driven out by machine-gun and
" field-gun fire.] Major-General von Möhl (*16th Bavarian*
" *Division*) had already given orders for a general counter-
" attack in the direction of Grévillers. Only towards mid-
" day was any relief felt, when the *44th Reserve Division,* in
" place of the *3rd Naval Division,* regained possession of the
" eastern part of Ligny Thilloy and the high ground east of
" Eaucourt l'Abbaye [these localities had not been in British
" possession. The counter-attack of the fresh *44th Reserve*
" *Division* was repulsed by the 110th Brigade (21st Division)
" and the 189th Brigade (63rd Division)]. Meanwhile, the
" troops of the *16th Bavarian Division* had pressed forward

---

[1] For the other nine see Note II to Chapter IV.

" again to the high road west of Thilloy and, although they
" lost a little ground again, they resisted all further assaults."

" Regiment No. 5 ", p. 384, (*36th Division*) makes long excuses
for the failure of the counter-attack by the *36th*, *40th* and *111th*
Divisions : " Scarcely had the bombardment opened before the
" troops were overwhelmed by a devastating barrage of the enemy
" guns.   It rolled unceasingly for two hours.   Then the British
" sprang up.   In places they are three deep and their fire scatters
" the thin line."

" Regiment No. 134 " (*40th Division*) says the counter-attack
" was drenched with fearful artillery fire and flooded back under
" heavy losses ".

" Regiment No. 73 " (*111th Division*) adds that " 18 British
" aeroplanes flew over and reported the advance, and all approach
" roads and cross-roads were under artillery fire ;   about 8 p.m.
" the British attacked [the only attack was made by one company
" of the 5/Duke of Wellington's (62nd Division) to regain a little
" lost ground] and the units of the division were ordered to retire
" in order to avoid being taken prisoner.   It had been an
" indubitable defeat."

CHAPTER XV

BATTLE OF ALBERT 1918—(*continued*)

FOURTH ARMY

25TH–26TH AUGUST

(Sketches 12, 13)

The Fourth Army operation orders, issued in the evening of the 24th, directed the execution at 2.30 a.m. next day of the second phase of the attack which should have taken place at 4 p.m. but had been postponed in view of the opposition offered at the junction of the 47th and 12th Divisions of the III. Corps. The objective was a line two thousand yards ahead,[1] from a copse north of the Somme opposite Cappy northward three miles to Caftet Wood, thence it ran back north-west along the road towards Fricourt to rejoin the front line at the junction of the 12th and 18th Divisions. Should the 18th Division be able to advance eastwards in touch with the 38th Division (Third Army), the refused left flank of the 12th Division along the Fricourt road would be shortened or might entirely disappear. The objective line crossed the highest part of the long sinuous ridge between the Somme and the Ancre and ran down the long spur which stretches southward from it towards Cappy and the short spur northwards towards Fricourt.

In a telegram sent out at 8.25 p.m. on the 24th, General Rawlinson pointed out to his corps commanders that the Germans were showing more and more plainly that they were becoming more and more demoralized—as was becoming obvious to the fighting troops : they must therefore be given no rest and every advantage taken of the moonlight to press on : if the operations north of the Somme in the early morning of the 25th were successful, they should be exploited with the utmost energy, and Maricourt and Mametz, on either side of Caftet Wood, occupied : south of the river, every opportunity should be taken by the Australian Corps to advance along the Somme towards Péronne. This telegram led to the divisions of the III. Corps being ordered to send forward advanced guards of all arms as soon as the final objective was secured. It was not known until the

---

[1] See Sketch 13.

fighting was in progress that the enemy opposite the Fourth
Army had been reinforced by three divisions, all opposite
the III. Corps.[1]

The 3rd Australian Division (Major-General J. Gellibrand)
and the 58th, 12th and 18th Divisions (Major-Generals F. W.
Ramsay, H. W. Higginson and R. P. Lee) of the III. Corps
(Lieut.-General Sir A. J. Godley) carried out the attack.
The general result will be understood more readily if the
operations of the centre, that is the 58th and 12th Divisions,
of the III. Corps, are narrated first.

In the 58th Division (whose staff had taken over from the
47th at 10.45 a.m. on the 24th), the 175th and 140th Brigades,
which had carried out the first phase of the attack on the
previous day under the 47th Division, were entrusted with
the execution of the postponed second phase. The men were
very tired when at dusk in a silence unbroken by any firing
they moved to the new position of assembly on the slopes
of the valleys which penetrated deeply into the main ridge
on either side ; there they extended and lay down. Touch
was obtained with the units on either flank, rations were
issued and compass bearings taken. Then, except for a few
sentries and patrols, all slept until a few minutes before zero
hour. It had been intended that six tanks should have given
assistance on the top of the ridge, but none, owing to overhaul
being necessary, were available.

The sky was clear and the moon bright at 2.30 a.m. (25th) ;
but half an hour later it became cloudy and soon a dense
fog came down in the Somme Valley. The excellent artillery
barrage, however, served to guide the advance, which was
carried out in extended lines. Only stragglers and deserters
were encountered, as the enemy had withdrawn ; so by
6.30 a.m. the brigades had reached the objective, some two
thousand yards from the enemy's new line, and were
consolidating.

The 173rd Brigade had followed in close support behind
the 175th and 140th Brigades. At 5.45 a.m. Br.-General
C. E. Corkran received divisional orders that if these brigades
reached the objective without gaining touch with the enemy,
he was to pass through them and, with the LXXXVI. Brigade
R.F.A. and a squadron of the Northumberland Hussars,
form an advanced guard and move on Maricourt, passing
north of Billon Wood (which lies on the east side of Billon

---

[1] See Note I at end of Chapter.

Farm). He detailed the 2/4th London, with one troop of the Hussars, a section of artillery, and a section of machine guns, as his vanguard, and at 8.30 a.m. it got under way, by which time the fog had cleared considerably. Within half an hour this vanguard was in contact with the enemy who, mainly by fire from a ridge west of Billon Wood, resisted stubbornly. Br.-General Corkran ordered the 2/4th London to attack the wood, supported by the 2/2nd, with the 3rd in reserve. By 1 p.m.[1] the greater part of the wood had been captured, but not the eastern and northern borders. At 2.40 p.m., whilst the 2/4th London was still trying to clear the wood, he directed the 2/2nd on the left to move north of it, giving both battalions the Suzanne–Carnoy road, beyond, as their objective. Owing to the heat of the day, a Sunday, which had now become fine and sunny, and the fatigue of the men, the movement was not launched until 4.30 p.m. After hard fighting it met with considerable success ; the two battalions reached a salient about half a mile from Maricourt,[2] formed by two roads. But as Maricourt (in the new German line) was strongly held, and Carnoy on the left flank was also still in enemy hands, no further progress could be made. A violent thunderstorm had arisen towards 8 p.m., and rain was now falling heavily and continued until 10 p.m., so that everybody was very uncomfortable.

The 37th and 36th Brigades, which also had led the advance of the 12th Division on the previous day, had the same experience as the brigades of the 58th Division : they reached their objective, practically without opposition, about the same time, although the fog was thicker than to the south, with visibility put at fifty yards. By 7.15 a.m. the division was informed that prisoners stated the Germans had fallen back to the Suzanne line, and between 9 and 11 a.m. that patrols had been unable to gain touch with the enemy west of the Caftet–Fricourt road, half a mile to the front.

Major-General Higginson at 7.15 a.m. had, like the 58th Division, detailed an advanced guard, the 35th Brigade ; but in this case it was to do no more than assemble in a valley south of Fricourt ready to move forward as soon as

---

[1] At midday the 140th Brigade was withdrawn from loan to the 58th Division and reverted to its own, the 47th.

[2] Shown on Sketch 13.

the XXII. Corps mounted troops[1] had made good the Carnoy–Montauban ridge. These were sent forward at 7.45 a.m., and soon encountered opposition. At 11.35 a.m. Major-General Higginson, who already knew that the 18th Division on his left was in Fricourt, received information that about a hundred Germans had been located on the high ground west of Montauban, 2 miles away, and forty minutes later that a few of the enemy were still in Mametz, under a mile to the east of Fricourt ; so he ordered the 35th Brigade forward and the 37th to extend its front to the left to include that of the 36th, which was then to assemble astride the cross roads just south-west of Fricourt. Owing to the usual delays, it was not until 3.15 p.m. that the 35th Brigade left the valley south of Fricourt, moving, with the 1/1st Cambridgeshire and 7/Norfolk leading, against the Carnoy–Montauban ridge. They were received by a heavy barrage and by machine-gun fire from Germans holding the ground west of Carnoy—east of Mametz. Fighting their way forward in the heat of the August afternoon, with determination over the many old trenches which seamed this area, by dusk they reached a line through the south-western edge of Carnoy almost due north to the divisional boundary on the Mametz–Montauban road, where a post was rushed. The left of the 35th Brigade was now in advance of the 18th Division's right. In the thunderstorm it pushed posts to within a hundred yards of the summit of its objective, the Carnoy–Montauban ridge, machine-gun fire preventing further progress.

The duty assigned to the 18th Division was to thrust as far eastward as possible without getting too deeply involved. Major-General Lee at 2.30 a.m., sent forward the 54th Brigade (Lieut.-Colonel J. A. Tyler, acting) and before it the Germans fell back, apparently demoralized by attack in a fog. In the face of ever-weakening opposition further advance was made, so that by 10 a.m. the divisional line ran through Fricourt northwards to the cemetery south of Contalmaison on the boundary with the Third Army.

The 55th Brigade, with a troop of the Otago Mounted Rifles, one company of the XXII. Corps cyclists, two Army brigades R.F.A., a section of the 92nd Field Company R.E.

---

[1] See p. 238 (f.n. 2).

and two machine-gun companies, had been detailed as advanced guard for the further operations. It was not, however, to take over this new duty until it reached a north-south line through the eastern edge of Montauban ; it was then to push eastwards to Guillemont, two and a half miles farther. Orders to this effect reached the 54th Brigade at 8.40 a.m., but the 55th did not receive them until about 10 a.m., at which hour Major-General Lee himself arrived at brigade headquarters in Bécourt Château, where he remained until 5 p.m. The brigade's orders were not issued for another hour, and it then advanced to the line gained by the 54th Brigade, where it was to take over the left of the line and await reports from the divisional mounted troops.

As soon as the first report from the cavalry had come to hand about 12.30 p.m., showing that the Germans ahead in the valley north of Mametz (Caterpillar Valley) and Mametz Wood were maintaining their positions, four field batteries were brought up east of Bécourt Wood and, under their fire, the advance was resumed by both brigades. Progress was very slow, and not until nightfall did the 11/Royal Fusiliers (54th Brigade), 7/Buffs and 8/East Surrey (55th) reach a line from the eastern edge of Mametz due north across Caterpillar Valley to a little short of the western edge of Mametz Wood, where they established touch with the 38th Division on its northern edge.

On the whole therefore the divisions of the III. Corps had advanced well over two miles and were in contact with the new German position.

Turning now to the 3rd Australian Division, on the right of the III. Corps, its troops had in front of them not only the long spur already mentioned, but also the village of Suzanne, on the edge of the Somme, with the valleys from it running right up to Maricourt, and, beyond, the Frise loop of the Somme river[1] with very steep slopes, almost cliffs, on its north side. Major-General Gellibrand had as objective for the 2.30 a.m. attack the line on the long spur, which overlooks Suzanne, with Ceylon Wood on the western slopes of the valley below.

---

[1] The canal cut off this loop.

The 10th and 11th Australian Brigades (Br.-Generals W. R. McNicoll and J. H. Cannan), each with a field artillery brigade attached to deal with fleeting targets, attacked from the eastern outskirts of Bray under a creeping barrage ; the guns of the Australian Corps south of the Somme co-operated by placing an enfilade barrage on three sides of the objective spur. Very little resistance was encountered and the enemy's retaliation was weak and scattered ; the 37th, 39th, 44th and 43rd Battalions reached the objective, the right of which rested on the Somme, in little over an hour, mopped up Ceylon Wood and hastened to consolidate before daylight under a protective barrage which, after a time, was changed to harassing fire. Meantime the 40th Battalion, wearing gas masks on account of the heavy concentration of gas, drove off enemy machine-gunners who had escaped notice in the fog, cleared the Somme peninsula between Bray and Suzanne, and established a bridge-head opposite Cappy.

Shortly before 9 a.m. Major-General Gellibrand issued orders for the continuation of the advance at 1 p.m. These reached the 10th Brigade at 9 a.m., but the 11th not until 11.30 a.m. The northern end of Ceylon Wood instead of the southern and thence to south-east of Billon Wood now became the boundary with the 58th Division, this extension to the left being ordered because the Frise loop of the Somme would narrow the front on the right. An advance was not, however, to materialize. About 10 a.m., when the fog lifted, the Australians were subjected to such heavy and accurate gun-fire from the direction of Suzanne and Maricourt that the men on the forward slope of the ridge had to be withdrawn and any advance by the left of the Australian Corps was prevented. The feature of the German defence was the fire of single field guns and groups of machine guns hidden in the many small woods and copses with which the valleys northward of Suzanne were dotted. Throughout the day conflicting information reached Major-General Gellibrand about these copses ; reports of capture were soon succeeded by others of heavy machine-gun fire coming from the same localities. Any attempt, too, to return to the crest of the ridge which had been the original objective was met by a withering fire of guns and machine guns. Further advance was therefore postponed until 3 p.m. ; but at that hour the 58th Division was not yet in complete possession of Billon Wood on the left—its final attack was not launched until

4.30 p.m.—so the Australian advance was again postponed until dark, 8 p.m. being fixed.

South of the Somme as soon as information reached the 1st Australian Division that the enemy on the northern bank was retiring, patrols were sent out by the 1st and 2nd Australian Brigades. Except on the right considerable opposition was encountered, and no great effort was made to drive the enemy back until 4 p.m. and then only by bombing up old communication trenches ; but by night-fall a line on the eastern edges of Lapin and Olympus Woods to Cappy (exclusive) had been occupied and touch established with the 3rd Australian Division across the Somme.

In the continuation of the operations north of the Somme the thunderstorm and heavy rain greatly increased the difficulties of the night advance of the 3rd Australian Division and III Corps. The movement of the former was to be in three bounds : first to the western edge of Suzanne, second to the eastern edge, and third to a north-south line about seven hundred yards east of the village, running a little short of western edges of a line of copses lying above Vaux, with outposts beyond.

The 39th Battalion, which led the advance of the 10th Australian Brigade to capture the first two lines, did not receive the orders until 8.40 p.m. It moved forward at 9.20 p.m., but rain and darkness, loss of touch with the 11th Brigade and machine-gun fire made its progress slow. By 5 a.m. (26th), however, it had dug and occupied a series of posts along the first line with patrols pushed into Suzanne.

At 8.30 a.m. (26th) the 39th Battalion resumed the advance against increasing machine-gun fire to the second line. Moving in small bodies, the battalion quickly reached and occupied it by posts in the same way as the first line, utilizing German trenches as far as possible. The enemy's artillery, which hitherto had been very quiet, soon began to fire on this position and continued to do so heavily all day.

The 37th Battalion now passed through to climb the ridge in front which overlooked the Somme ; it received machine-gun fire from a wood on the left, but attacked and cleared it, and continued to advance to the third line, having considerable hand-to-hand fighting on the way. In retiring from the line towards Vaux Wood (overlooking Vaux from

the west) the Germans suffered many casualties, so by
1.15 p.m. the wood had been completely occupied. In the
evening a small operation of the 40th Battalion, on the right
of the brigade, took it forward almost to the western edge
of a wood abreast of Eclusier. After this preliminary an
order from the division, given at 7 p.m., to occupy the whole
of the Suzanne–Vaux peninsula was carried out at 3 a.m.
(27th) by the 38th and 37th Battalions without opposition,
as the enemy, after blowing up the bridges at Eclusier and
Vaux, had withdrawn.

In the 11th Australian Brigade the 44th and 43rd
Battalions, starting at 9 p.m. and 10.15 p.m. (on the 25th)
respectively, reached the first objective about an hour and
a half later. Both battalions came under the fire of machine-
gun posts, which were promptly attacked by the flanks and
captured. The 43rd then went to a position half way to
the second line, but failed to regain touch of the 58th
Division.

At 8 a.m. (26th) the two battalions received orders to
occupy the third objective, the left to establish outposts well
out on that flank ; but it was not till about 1 p.m. that they
were able to advance. They encountered direct machine-gun
and artillery fire over open sights ; but every advantage was
taken of the great amount of natural cover on the slopes
leading to the top of the spur ; so that by 2.30 p.m. the
whole of the 44th Battalion had reached the third line.
Owing to fire from the north, it was not until dusk before
the 43rd arrived there, making contact on the right with the
44th, and making its left secure. At 8 p.m. orders were
received for the 37th, the 44th and the 41st (passing through
the 43rd) Battalions to secure the line Vaux–north-east
corner of Vaux Wood, and thence north-westwards to the
Suzanne–Maricourt road and north towards Maricourt. A
start was made at 1 a.m. (27th), and by 2.50 a.m. the new
line had been gained[1] and touch regained with the 58th
Division.

Major-General F. W. Ramsay (58th Division) at 1.30 p.m.
(25th), soon after the 175th and 173rd Brigades had obtained
a footing in Billon Wood, gave orders for the 174th Brigade,
then in reserve in the Happy Valley, to relieve the 175th,
and as soon as the relief was completed to push forward with

[1] See Sketch 13.

the 173rd ; but the orders did not reach Br.-General A. Maxwell until 6 p.m.[1] The final instructions were for the brigade to push through on the right of the 173rd, which had edged rather too much to the left. The 174th started at 7 p.m. without waiting for rations and water, the men tired by the heat and worn by the occasional shelling of Happy Valley, which was resumed as the brigade moved off. The 7/London led as advanced guard. The storm and rain soon broke and it became pitch dark, the battalion ran into shell fire and Major H. W. Priestley, commanding the 8/London, was wounded by a fragment of shell and was carried from the field, although this did not become known to his company commanders for some time. No one knew the ground, which was broken by the heads of the several valleys, touch was lost for a time between the battalions, and it was nearly midnight before Billon Wood, a little over two miles from the starting place, was reached. A line east of the wood was then occupied in contact on the right, after some delay, with the Australians south of the wood, and on the left with the 173rd, whose right battalion was subsequently relieved.

At 1.30 a.m. the 174th Brigade issued orders for the further advance at 4 a.m. under a barrage which would cover both the 174th and 173rd and open on the German trench along the Suzanne–Maricourt road over fifteen hundred yards from Billon Wood. This road marks the sole of the valley which falls from Maricourt to Suzanne ; on reaching it the brigade would rest half an hour before moving forward again. These orders did not reach the battalions until 2.15 a.m.

The 7th and 8/London, or at any rate parts of them, moved forward shortly after 4 a.m. down the slopes of the valley and encountered machine guns which had escaped destruction, as the barrage had fallen behind them. There was some confusion in the dark, and the 8th, at first in support, soon came up with the 7th. Progress was slow and difficult and the casualties were considerable ; it was not therefore until 9 a.m. (26th) that parties were established on a line along a crest overlooking the Suzanne–Maricourt road, where the 43rd Australian Battalion did not appear until later. Any advance beyond this point was for the moment impossible ;

[1] There is no explanation of the delay ; possibly the orders were not sent out until the attack of the 173rd Brigade at 4.30 p.m. had been launched. It was the custom of the 58th Division at this period whenever a divisional order was issued to send a junior staff officer to make sure that it was, if possible, being carried out.

for the slopes of the next spur were studded with machine guns, and the right flank was in the air. The enemy made frequent attempts to envelop on this side, which were frustrated by a defensive flank. The advance of the Australians in the afternoon eventually made the right secure.

The 173rd Brigade also had gone forward at 4 a.m. with the 3/London leading and the 2/2nd in support. After encountering the same difficulties as the 174th it had by 9.30 a.m. reached a line along the western side of Maricourt ; some of the 3/London actually entered the village, but were unable to remain there. Owing to enemy fire, it was not until the afternoon that touch on the right with the 174th Brigade was gained. In view of a possible counter-attack, the 2/4th London, in reserve at Great Bear, was sent forward with instructions to deny the high ground north of Billon Wood to the enemy ; but no further change in the situation of the 58th Division took place.

In the 12th Division it had been Major-General Higginson's intention when, on the 25th, he pulled out the 36th Brigade and placed it in reserve, that it should next morning pass through the 35th Brigade and take over the duties of advanced guard to the division. In view, however, of the resistance offered to the 35th during the afternoon a formal attack, supported by as much artillery as possible, became necessary. Three objectives were defined : first, the crest of the Carnoy–Montauban spur, which is marked by the road between these villages ; second, the road running north from Maricourt and passing half a mile east of Montauban ; third, a spur a mile farther east and the high ground to the north of it ; a total advance of about three miles. Some difficulty occurred in calculating the barrage, as the position of the most advanced troops of the 35th Brigade was not known, and it was not possible to arrange that it should conform with the barrage of the 58th Division. It was finally settled that no artillery fire should fall in the 12th Division zone within two hundred yards of the southern divisional boundary, which ran south of Carnoy and north of Maricourt. Thus it happened that divisional orders were not ready until 11 p.m. and it was after midnight before the officer carrying them reached Br.-General C. S. Owen (36th Brigade), and nearly 2 a.m. on that wet dark night before he could collect his battalion commanders and give them verbal orders for the 4 a.m. attack, and then there were three miles to march to the starting point. Further delay took place in consequence of the late arrival of the pack mules with reserve small arms ammunition, and of shelling which forced the battalions to leave the road and march across wire and trenches on a compass bearing, the later part of the way in single file.

Thus the 5/R. Berkshire and 7/R. Sussex were unable to arrive at the starting line in time to move off before 4.45 a.m. and 4.30 a.m., respectively, and lost the barrage—which in any case dropped too far ahead, nearly fifteen hundred yards, to be of any use. Both at once came under machine-gun fire. The Berkshire managed to reach the first objective, then suffered severe casualties and could advance no farther, but established touch with the 58th Division on the right. The Sussex, which had a longer distance to go, were held up in the valley in front of the first objective. The Germans spotting the gap between the battalions, after two attempts, rushed the left flank of the Berkshire and cut off half a platoon, but were then driven off by a machine gun and desisted from further effort. The left of the Sussex near some old mine craters were also in danger ; this was overcome by bombing, in which parties of the 1/1st Cambridgeshire (35th Brigade) took part. Until 3 p.m. little change occurred in the situation, when the Sussex reported that the Germans were retiring. Patrols were sent out to keep touch with them, and the capture of Montauban by the 18th Division on the left about 4.30 p.m. enabled the 7/R. Sussex and then the 5/R. Berkshire to advance. Thus by nightfall the line of the 36th Brigade ran from a copse north-west of Maricourt almost due north to the divisional boundary short of Montauban ; that is between the first and second objectives of the day.

To come now to the 18th Division, the left of the Fourth Army : between 8 and 10 p.m. on the 25th, the German positions west of Montauban had been heavily shelled by the divisional artillery. On account of rain and darkness, little more could be done during the night ; but as soon as it became light Br.-General E. A. Wood (55th Brigade) sent forward the two troops (of the Otago Mounted Rifles and Northumberland Hussars) attached to his brigade. By 8 a.m. (26th) it was found that the enemy was retiring eastward of Mametz Wood and that fire from the spur south-west of Montauban was slackening. The cavalry was therefore recalled and the 11/Royal Fusiliers (54th Brigade) with the 7/Buffs and 8/East Surrey ordered to push on with all speed.

The advance of the 38th Division (Third Army) on the left facilitating progress, by 9.30 a.m. Mametz Wood was completely cleared, and by midday, against stiffening opposition, the leading troops were three hundred yards east of Marlborough Wood, north of Montauban. Throughout the early afternoon the artillery continued to shell the village and the enemy position near it, whilst machine guns in Marlborough Wood swept the wide open ridge on which it stood. The capture of Montauban was effected about 4.30 p.m. by a well-handled composite company of the Buffs, consisting entirely of very young soldiers, which took sixty prisoners. The leading troops of the 11/Royal Fusiliers entered the village immediately afterwards from the south-west. By 6 p.m. the line of the 54th and 55th Brigades ran northwards from the eastern edge of Montauban, mentioned in divisional orders of the previous day as the place where an advanced guard should be organized. Br.-General Wood therefore decided to exploit his success by sending forward his reserve, the 7/Queen's, then in Caterpillar Valley between Mametz and Marlborough Woods. A new situation, however, had at once to be dealt with, as the Germans counter-attacked the 8/East Surrey on the left, across the front from the shelter of the shallow valley a thousand yards behind Montauban, in which lies Bernafay Wood, and it was not until 8.30 p.m. that they were dispersed. The 7/Queen's had meantime arrived and was sent in pursuit. It reached the western edge of Bernafay Wood about 9.30 p.m. ; but the wood was found to be strongly held and the battalion was withdrawn.

Preparations were taken in hand in all three divisions of the III Corps for an early advance next day.

It had become more than usually obvious during the 26th that the staffs and the regimental officers had by no means shaken themselves clear of the methods of command to which they had become accustomed in the long years of trench warfare. More initiative, for instance, was now required of battalion and company commanders in taking advantage of opportunities and of assisting their neighbours ; the Staff officers, on their part, should have been constantly at the front, not for the purpose of interference, but to assist the regimental officer with information about neighbouring units, by obtaining artillery support and reinforcements, and by taking measures to fill dangerous gaps between units and formations.   To the old officers of the original B.E.F. the methods of open warfare in 1918 appeared to be the earnest striving of small units each " on its own " rather than the team-work to which they had been accustomed.

It remains to relate the advance of the brigades of the Australian Corps, the right wing of the Army, south of the Somme.   During the night of the 25th–26th the enemy again shelled the line of the 2nd Australian Brigade with gas, not so heavily as before, but combined with a good deal of indiscriminate bombardment.   This expenditure of ammunition, in conjunction with other signs, seemed to indicate that a retirement was in contemplation—as indeed was the case—but only a short one to conform with the movement north of the Somme.

The principal advance was made by the 3rd Australian Brigade (Br.-General H. G. Bennett) next to the river.   It put the 11th and 10th Battalions in front line, which moved forward at 6 a.m. under the barrage, first after clearing Cappy to a line a thousand yards forward on the left, but a somewhat less distance on the right, whilst machine guns on the left covered the large area in the bend of the Somme. The Germans had retired to a line from north-east of Fontaine les Cappy, to a point nearly half a mile south-east of Eclusier on the Somme canal ; they made little resistance, and that chiefly by machine-gun fire, except on the left, where though an orchard held on the line gained was soon captured, one wood fell only after a hard struggle.

After rest and food the advance was resumed at 10.30 a.m. By this time the fog had cleared and the enemy artillery, which had so far taken little part became very active and progress could be made only slowly by groups working forward from cover to cover.   By 2 p.m. the 11th Battalion had, with artillery support, arrived just west of Fontaine les Cappy, whence its line ran north to the 10th Battalion, whilst on the right it was in touch with the 1st Australian

Brigade. This brigade, making use of patrols, in conjunction with the 3rd had gradually swung forward pivoting on the latter's right. The right of the 10th Battalion advanced slowly like the 11th ; the left with the support of oblique fire from two batteries of horse artillery in action near Olympus Wood got forward more rapidly, but had a stiff fight for another wood before the Germans were put to flight and retired to a third wood. This also was taken and cleared by 6 p.m. ; but, owing to its position in a valley, the line was established west of it, and it was kept clear by patrols. The right of the forces north of the Somme was now well secured.

NOTE I

The French on the 25th and 26th August

(Sketch 12)

On the 25th August the left wing of the I Corps and the entire XXX Corps of the French Tenth Army made a little ground against the German flank north of Soissons. The Third and First Armies, nearest the British, did not move, but made preparations to resume the advance in accordance with General Fayolle's instructions issued at 10 p.m. on this day. In these he pointed out that neither Army as it stood was ready to undertake a general offensive (" offensive d'ensemble ") : " both Armies must nevertheless prepare and carry out, by means of heavy concentration of fire, local actions designed to improve their positions : in any case they must be absolutely ready to smash any German attack . . . : moreover, it was necessary to bear in mind the time when the progress of the British Armies on the north and the advance which the Sixth and Tenth Armies were expected to make eastwards would cause the Germans to withdraw : with this object in view, very close touch must be kept with the forces on either flank . . . : in short, all preparations must be made for energetic and resolute pursuit, to be executed at the first sign of retirement."

On the 26th in the French First Army, the 126th Division of the XXXI Corps at 4.50 a.m. attacked Fresnoy les Roye (3 miles north of Roye) and the trenches west and north of the village, which stood on a knoll and gave good observation. It was in possession of all its objectives by 7 a.m. To complete this success, at 1 p.m. the 126th was put in again with the 47th Division and gained some ground on the ridge to the south of Fresnoy ; and at 4 p.m. the 56th Division attacked St. Mard (on the Avre, south-west of Roye), and after a lively struggle, captured it.

The Third Army and the left wing of the Tenth " limited themselves to observing the enemy " ; the XXX Corps of the right wing of the Tenth made a little progress.

NOTE II

THE GERMANS ON THE 25TH AND 26TH AUGUST OPPOSITE THE FOURTH ARMY

(Sketch 13)

Three fresh divisions and one tired one, at least, reinforced the German front opposite the Fourth Army during the 25th and 26th. They were the *2nd Guard* and the *225th*, which came into action on the 25th at Dompierre, south of the Somme, and east of Albert respectively ; the *87th*, which arrived early on the 26th and was sent north of the *225th* ; and the *117th*, which, after having been opposite the Canadian Corps on the 8th, had been given a short rest and then put in near Maricourt on the 26th.

A few details from the regimental histories are of interest : The *13th Regiment* (*13th Division*) formed a battalion about two hundred strong, with four heavy machine guns from its three battalions for use as reserve in case of emergency. At 2.45 p.m. on the 25th this battalion was sent forward to fill a gap in the line of the *233rd Division* east of Albert. It occupied a position with two companies in what was known as the fourth main line of resistance from west of Bazentin le Grand (a mile north-east of Mametz Wood) southward, with the other two companies on outpost in touch on the right with the *347th Regiment* (*87th Division*), and, on the left, with the *217th Reserve Regiment* (*225th Division*). Just after 6 a.m. on the 26th the two forward companies were overwhelmed (by the 54th Brigade apparently). The two companies in the main line counter-attacked, but later had to swing back the right flank because the enemy had penetrated deeply there. Then, as touch on right and left had been lost, a further retirement was made to the high ground west of Longueval (2 miles east of Mametz Wood). The strength of the battalion by now had dwindled to sixty. The new main line of resistance ran from Longueval to Guillemont ($\frac{1}{2}$ mile south of Guinchy).

The history of the *115th Body Guard Regiment* (*25th Division*) says that during the night of the 24th–25th the regiment withdrew to the fourth main line of resistance, which here ran from a point half-way between Carnoy and Maricourt to the west edge of Montauban. The retreat was unnoticed by the enemy, who bombarded the empty positions in the early morning and then gradually felt his way forward towards the new line. During the late afternoon parties reconnoitring towards the valley through which the light railway ran west of Carnoy were repulsed. On the 26th the regiment had sharp fighting, and during the afternoon the line was withdrawn to the western edge of Bernafay Wood (east of Montauban) and Maricourt : it was possible to do this during daylight owing to the cover afforded by the maze of old trenches.

The history of the *27th Division* states that during the night of the 24th–25th the division fell back through a line held by troops of the *157th Regiment* (*117th Division*) at the disposal of the *27th Division* and of the *43rd Reserve Division*, which ran from east of Billon Wood to east of Suzanne. On the 25th the *157th Regiment* was forced back to the Maricourt–Suzanne Road, and the remainder of the *117th Division* was put at the disposal of the *27th Division*.

South of the Somme, the *122nd Fusilier Regiment* of the *243rd* (*Württemberg*) *Division* was holding the line just west of Foucaucourt, on the Amiens–Brie road :

" The enemy tried by every method to work forward close
" to the front, especially by night, and there were some stiff
" bomb fights. Even if one's own front was quiet, that of
" one's neighbour was seething. Consequently we were
" everlastingly on the *qui vive* and in a perpetual state of
" being alarmed and standing to. Nearly all the available
" effectives were required for reconnaissance and outpost
" duties. Company commanders had to exercise much skill
" to enable them to give their men at any rate the sleep that
" was necessary for them. Every morning it could be seen
" that the enemy had got closer. Losses weakened the
" already small companies . . . "

The history of the *479th Regiment* of the same division says that at 1.30 a.m. on the 25th, by order of the *42nd Brigade* (*21st Division*), which had command of this part of the line, the bridges in Cappy were to be blown up, but at two of them the explosive failed to detonate.

" By the evening of the 25th, II and III/*479* were only frag-
" ments without any fighting value. . . . From the 26th August
" onwards included in the effectives of these two battalions were
" men recovered from influenza, light duty men, or N.C.O.s and
" men recalled from first and second line transport."

Shortly after 11 p.m. on the 25th orders were received by the troops under the *21st Division* to fall back to the line : Somme Canal 500 yards east of Eclusier—cross-roads 700 yards south-east of Eclusier and thence southwards. These movements had been completed by daylight. " The *479th Regiment* was now only as " strong as a fought-out battalion."

CHAPTER XVI

The Battle of the Scarpe 1918
Third and First Armies
26th August

(Sketch 14)

On the 15th August G.H.Q. had given instructions to General Sir Henry Horne, commanding the First Army,[1] to make preparations at once with a view to being ready to take advantage of any withdrawal of the enemy by following him up and pressing him in the direction of Monchy le Preux,[2] or, if conditions were favourable, by delivering an attack on Orange Hill and Monchy le Preux. Two days later, General Horne submitted plans for an attack by three divisions between the southern boundary of the First Army and the Scarpe. The prospect of soon taking part in a major operation did not, however, prevent the First Army from initiating some local operations designed to hold the enemy to his ground. Thus, on the night of the 18th/19th August, a slight advance was made by troops of the 57th Division (XVII. Corps) south of Feuchy (on the Scarpe, due east of Arras) ; on the night of the 20th/21st, the 51st Division (then in the XVII. Corps), north of the Scarpe, advanced its line about a quarter of a mile and drove the enemy out of Fampoux ; and on the 24th and 25th the same division gained some more ground between Fampoux and Gavrelle.

On the afternoon of the 24th G.H.Q. issued the operation orders, already given,[3] for the continuation of the advance by the Third Army, guarded on its right by the Fourth, whilst the First Army was to co-operate on its left. The rôle assigned to the First was to pierce the Drocourt–Quéant Line[4] on its front and subsequently to swing south-east to

[1] Major-Gen. General Staff, W. H. Anderson ; D.A. and Q.M.G., Major-General A. W. Peck ; C.R.A., Major-General E. W. Alexander ; C.E., Major-General E. H. de V. Atkinson.
    The First Army at this time consisted of the XVII. Corps (5 divisions), the VIII. (4 divisions), the I. (3 divisions) and the XXII. (1 division) ; the XVII. Corps staff, with 1 division, was subsequently transferred to the Third Army, and the First Army received the Canadian Corps (4 divisions) from the Fourth Army on the conclusion of the first phase of 8th August operations.

[2] See Sketch 14.

[3] See p. 263.

[5] This ran, roughly, up the right margin of Sketch 14 from Bullecourt northwards. See Map 4.

297

operate against the right of the enemy troops opposing the Third Army. The 26th August was fixed for the combined movement of the two Armies, but only the right wing of the First Army, now the Canadian Corps (2nd and 3rd Canadian and 51st Divisions in the line, with the 15th in reserve), with part of the VIII. Corps on its left, was to take part ; and the extreme left, on both sides of the La Bassée canal, was also to advance.

The I. Brigade R.A.F. (Br.-General D. le G. Pitcher), with 13 squadrons, was available to co-operate with the First Army.

As a preliminary step, on the 23rd August the right of the 2nd Canadian Division, in co-operation with the 52nd Division, the left of the Third Army, made a small advance against Neuville Vitasse, at the junction of the Third and First Armies, and on the 24th took most of the village, which overlooks the Wancourt valley, and a sugar factory south of it.

The Third Army orders for the 26th were simple : the three corps on the right were to continue their advance eastwards, whilst the left corps, inclined south-eastwards in conjunction with the right of the First Army :

the V. Corps was to secure Flers and make junction with the IV. Corps at Riencourt les Bapaume, three miles ahead ;

the IV. Corps was to capture Bapaume and Favreuil and then reorganize in depth with advanced guards ready for a further advance ;

the VI. Corps was to capture Mory and assist the XVII. Corps in taking Croisilles, and then occupy a position east of Mory, ready for another advance ;

the XVII. Corps was to capture Croisilles in co-operation with the VI. Corps, and, on the left, north of the Cojeul, co-operate with the Canadian Corps, attacking south-eastward along both sides of the Hindenburg Position.

The First Army ordered the Canadian Corps, working in co-operation with the XVII. Corps, first

to capture Chapel and Orange Hills, two miles ahead, . and then exploit the situation east and south-east towards the line Wancourt–Guémappe–Monchy le Preux.

The forward boundary of the Third and First Armies was changed during the day from west-east to a line running E.S.E., in order to assist the advance of the Fourth Army and suit the new development. The Third Army did not make much progress, the country being seamed with the trenches of the Somme battles of previous years, but the Canadian Corps achieved important success.

The orders given by Lieut.-General C. D. Shute to the divisions of the V. Corps were, to keep good touch with each other :

> 38th Division to clear the Bazentin woods of the enemy, advance on Longueval and capture High Wood ;
> 17th Division to move on Flers ;
> 21st Division to advance to the road Factory Corner (north of Flers)–Ligny Thilloy ;
> the 6th Carabiniers (corps cavalry regiment), which did not arrive until midday, to cover the corps front as far as ground permitted, and particularly to assist the right brigade of the 38th Division.

No Army zero hour was fixed, but it was well understood that an early start should be made. Some brigades, however, owing to the late issue of divisional orders—between 1 a.m. and 2 a.m.—and further delay in orders reaching them, and the violent thunderstorm of the night of the 25th/26th, were not able to start as early as was intended.

The V. Corps met with stiff resistance from machine guns, the fire of which became more and more severe as the light improved.

In the 38th Division (Major-General T. A. Cubitt) the 113th Brigade (Br.-General H. E. ap Rhys Pryce), starting at 4 a.m. under a creeping barrage and well supported by machine guns, after engaging the 13/R. Welch Fusiliers, with the other two battalions in close support, took Bazentin le Grand soon after 7 a.m., the 14/R. Welch Fusiliers, brought up on the left, pushing on almost to the outskirts of Longueval. There about 5 p.m., its flanks being exposed, it was counter-attacked and, as a result, withdrawn to the general line about five hundred yards east of Bazentin le Grand. The right had meantime been reinforced by the Carabiniers, dismounted, who got in touch on that flank with the 18th Division (Fourth Army), which had taken Montauban (south of Bazentin le Grand) and completely cleared Mametz Wood.

The 115th Brigade (Br.-General W. B. Hulke) had not been able to start until after 6 a.m., but had then cleared the high ground north of Bazentin le Grand, thus assisting the 113th Brigade in the capture of the village ; then manoeuvring the 10/S. Wales Borderers south and the 17/R. Welch Fusiliers north of High Wood, it captured that wood about 12.30 p.m. and established a line on the high ground east of it.

The 17th Division (Major-General P. R. Robertson) made zero hour 5 a.m., and arranged to carry out its advance with the 52nd and 51st Brigades (Br.-Generals W. Allason and R. M. Dudgeon) in two bounds, first to the High Wood—le Barque road. In spite of a good barrage, the 52nd Brigade could make little progress before 10 a.m., when the position on the long ridge between it and its objective, whose defenders were holding it up, was captured by an outflanking movement from the south initiated by the 12/Manchester. The road was reached about 11 a.m., and in the afternoon the advance continued to a position about seven hundred yards west of Flers.

The 51st Brigade also met with considerable opposition and did not reach the High Wood—le Barque road until after midday. The left could make no further progress ; but about 7 p.m. the right was able to come up almost abreast of the 52nd Brigade. It was then decided by Major-General Robertson that the 50th Brigade should at 1.30 a.m. on the 27th pass through the other two and attack Flers.

The 21st Division (Major-General D. G. M. Campbell) made hardly any progress. The 64th Brigade (Lieut.-Colonel C. E. R. Holroyd-Smyth, acting) was ordered to advance at 5.30 a.m. from its position in reserve west of le Sars and pass through the 62nd Brigade, with the road Flers—Ligny Thilloy as its first objective, beyond which it was not to go without divisional orders. The 110th Brigade, on the right, was to remain in position until the left of the 17th Division had passed through it, when it was to assemble in reserve north of Eaucourt l'Abbaye. The 64th Brigade had two miles to march before it reached the front line and, being delayed by the difficulties of the way, lost the barrage, and was at once checked ; the third battalion, the 1/East Yorkshire, which, reinforced, went forward nearly half a mile and got within a hundred and fifty yards of the objective, but could not remain there ; so at the end of the day the outpost line was only about three hundred yards in front of the morning position of the 62nd Brigade.

The right and centre of the IV. Corps (Lieut.-General Sir G. M. Harper) made no progress on the 26th August ; for Thilloy and Bapaume were still strongly held, and three tired British divisions were attacking nine German, four of which were comparatively, and three quite, fresh, but another so battered that it had to be withdrawn during the night of the 26th/27th.[1] Nevertheless, the left wing carried the encirclement of Bapaume on the north a stage further and took Beugnâtre on the north of the town.

By corps orders, the capture of Bapaume was the principal object, and 6.30 a.m. was made zero hour.

The 63rd Division (Major-General C. E. Lawrie) was to capture or contain Thilloy and then advance until abreast of Riencourt les Bapaume, south-east of Bapaume ;

the New Zealand Division, to capture Bapaume and the high ground east of it ;

the 5th Division (which was to relieve the 37th), to co-operate on the left and exploit towards Beugnâtre.

The other divisions were to keep in close touch of, and synchronize their attacks with those of the New Zealand Division.

A great concentration of machine guns in the Thilloy area, in spite of good artillery support, prevented the progress of the 63rd Division against two good enemy divisions. The 189th Brigade (Commander W. M. Egerton), on the right,

---

[1] No less than five of the German reinforcing divisions, the *6th Bavarian, 16th Bavarian, 36th, 111th* and *220th,* had already been sent to the sector opposite the IV. Corps, in addition to the original two, the *4th Bavarian* and *183rd,* and two more (see Note at end of Chapter) appeared on the field during the day, the *12th Reserve* going to Thilloy, and the *23rd* to Beugnâtre.

was unable to move, and though the 188th Brigade (Br.-General J. F. S. D. Coleridge) managed to reach the north-western outskirts of the village by a short advance, it was enfiladed on the left and had to fall back again.

The New Zealand Division (Major-General Sir A. H. Russell) did not make a direct attack on Bapaume : the 1st Brigade was to encircle the town by the south, and the 3rd (Rifle) Brigade, passing through the 2nd Brigade, by the north. No creeping barrage was provided, but a battery of artillery was allotted to each battalion. Like the 63rd Division, the 1st New Zealand Brigade (Br.-General C. W. Melvill) encountered such heavy fire that it could not get forward. Northward of Bapaume, in conjunction with the 5th Division, the 3rd New Zealand Brigade (Br.-General H. Hart), with three battalions on a 2,500-yard front, in spite of enfilade machine-gun fire from buildings in the out-skirts of the town on the right and from Beugnâtre on the left, reached the Bapaume–Beugnâtre road, nearly five hundred yards ahead ; but there it was checked. At 3 p.m. Br.-General Hart gave orders for a further advance at 6 p.m., when the 5th Division was to capture Beugnâtre, and for patrols to be sent into Bapaume—which place they attempted to enter in vain. Good progress, nearly five hundred yards, was, however, made by the 3rd New Zealand Brigade round the north of Bapaume, until the machine guns on the outskirts inflicted so many casualties that its right was forced to fall back a little to the line of the Bapaume–Cambrai railway, still leaving the town enveloped on the north.

The 13th Brigade (Br.-General L. O. W. Jones) of the 5th Division (Major-General J. Ponsonby), detailed to relieve the 111th Brigade of the 37th Division in the line, cover the New Zealand left and move on Beugnâtre, had, in the pouring rain and darkness, great difficulty in reaching its jumping-off position in time ; for the fighting near Favreuil had not died down until after darkness fell, and the position of the troops of the 111th Brigade was imperfectly known. By 6.30 a.m., however, the 2/K.O.S.B., which was to lead the advance, was ready to do so. The battalion was soon held up by machine-gun fire of the two enemy divisions in the sector. For the 6 p.m. advance, in co-operation with the 3rd New Zealand (Rifle) Brigade, an artillery barrage was arranged by telephone, and machine-gun fire, direct, enfilade and overhead, provided. The operation was entirely successful : Beugnâtre was taken—the defending German divisions being withdrawn with very heavy loss—a line established two hundrĕd yards beyond the village, and touch gained with the divisions on either side.

As the VI Corps was so close to the Hindenburg Position, the main idea in the orders of Lieut.-General Sir A. Haldane was to keep touch with the enemy ; but

the 62nd Division (Major-General W. P. Braithwaite) was directed to try and establish itself in some old trenches about fifteen hundred yards west of Vraucourt;[1] and

the Guards Division (Major-General G. P. T. Feilding) to take a trench which was a continuation of the objective of the 62nd Division, first running north-westwards and then along the eastern edge of St. Léger Wood.

The 187th Brigade (Br.-General A. J. Reddie), in the centre, was well ahead of the rest of the 62nd Division, and therefore waited until the 186th on its right should come up. It was not until 9 a.m., after three hours' advance under a fairly heavy enemy fire, that the latter brigade drew evel, and no further movement was possible until evening, when the 186th and the 5/K.O.Y.L.I., the right of the 187th, worked themselves forward to the left flank of the 5th Division (V Corps) after its 6 p.m. attack. The left of the 187th was to have advanced in co-operation with the Guards Division, but as the attack of the latter was postponed, it remained where it was.

In view of the previous heavy exertions of the Guards Division and the expectation that the attack of the XVII and Canadian Corps south-eastwards athwart its front would clear the enemy away, Lieut.-General Haldane on the morning of the 26th had sanctioned the postponement of the Guards' attack until the following day. Actually it was found that the Germans had evacuated St. Léger Wood,

[1] This line was not reached until the 30th.

so that the 1st Guards Brigade was in the afternoon able to establish posts along the eastern edge, which had been its objective.

Thus the VI Corps gained ground both on its right and left wings.

The task of the XVII Corps (Lieut.-General Sir C. Fergusson)[1] was two-fold. Its right, the 56th Division (Major-General Sir C. P. A. Hull), was, in co-operation with the left of the VI Corps, to capture Croisilles, lying in the valley of the Sensée, an outwork of the Hindenburg Position, and a tough nut to crack, as experience in 1917 had proved. The left of the corps, the 52nd Division (Major-General J. Hill), was to co-operate with the Canadian Corps, moving south-eastwards down the Hindenburg Position. Two brigades of heavy artillery were allotted to each division, whilst a fifth was to bombard the section of the position affected. Zero hour was 3 a.m.

The 167th Brigade (Br.-General G. H. B. Freeth) of the 56th Division found uncut wire in front of the western edge of Croisilles, and came under heavy machine-gun fire ; so, as the co-operation of the Guards had been cancelled, it then stood fast. Even patrols sent out in the evening could not go very far.

The 52nd Division fared better. Its instructions were for its left wing to pivot on St. Martin, in the centre of its front, which would bring it into the valley of the Cojeul ; it was then to establish itself on the ridge beyond and get touch west of Wancourt with the Canadian Corps. As soon as this had been achieved the division was to co-operate with the Canadians in mopping up the triangular pocket which would be left behind between Wancourt and Neuville Vitasse, and advance in conjunction with the Canadians south-eastwards.[2]

The 155th Brigade (Br.-General J. Forbes-Robertson), then in divisional reserve, with a machine-gun company, was to pass through the 156th, then holding the left of the line,

[1] Br.-Gen. General Staff, Br.-Gen.W. D. Wright ; D.A. & Q.M.G., Br.-General R. F. A. Hobbs ; C.R.A., Br.-General E. H. Willis ; C.H.A., Br.-General N. G. Barron ; C.E., Br.-General W. D, Waghorn.

[2] The readjustment of the Army boundary between the 52nd Division and the Canadian Corps will be seen on Map 4 and Sketch 14.

and carry out the required operation. A strong creeping barrage, with one gun for each ten yards of front, was arranged by the C.R.A. (Br.-General A. D. Musgrave).

The attack on the flank of the Hindenburg Position, led by the 1/5th and 1/4th R. Scots Fusiliers in the darkness before dawn, was carried out according to plan and was completely successful, with comparatively few casualties. Touch was duly gained with the Canadian Corps west of Wancourt.[1]

The second part of the operation, the advance along the Hindenburg Position, was begun at 3 p.m., in co-operation with the 2nd Canadian Division. The 1/4th K.O.S.B. passed through the two leading battalions, crossed the Cojeul, which was only six feet wide and dry, south of Héninel, and without much difficulty occupied the northern end of Hénin Hill, which, though not conspicuous or steep, is the highest ground in the vicinity. The 1/5th R. Scots Fusiliers prolonged the line to the left, with the 1/7th Royal Scots (156th Brigade) beyond it to fill the gap between the left of the 52nd Division and the Canadian Corps.

The Canadian Corps (Lieut.-General Sir A. W. Currie), consisting of two Canadian divisions,[2] the 51st Division, and the artillery of the 15th, 16th and 39th Divisions,[3] arranged for the attack between Neuville Vitasse and the Scarpe, a four mile frontage. It was to be made in two phases by

---

[1] The *39th Division* was almost exactly holding the front attacked by the 155th Brigade, Hénin Hill to Wancourt, both inclusive, with south to north, the *126th, 172nd* and *132nd Regiments* in line. The regimental histories of the first and last, which are available, attribute their crushing defeat this day—by very inferior numbers—to the previous destruction of the defences by bombardment, to the fury (*Urgewalt*) of the barrage, to their own artillery dropping its barrage on them, to the use of artificial smoke (" Regt. No. 126 "), and to gas and tanks (" Regt. No. 132 ") ; the front battalion of the *132nd* was reduced to 76 of all ranks. " An " orderly retirement by echelons was impossible ", and the division lost 1,300 prisoners.

[2] The two others, the 1st and 4th, were on 26th August on their way from the Fourth to the First Army, the 1st arriving on the 27th, and the 4th on the 29th.

[3] The 15th Division had been relieved by the 2nd Canadian on the nights of 22nd/23rd and 23rd/24th August when the Canadian Corps took over from the XVII but left its artillery in the line. The 16th Division (less artillery) had gone to England to be reconstituted, but returned to France on 27th July ; its artillery brigades rejoined it on 7th September. The 39th was a cadre division.

the 2nd and 3rd Canadian Divisions (Major-Generals H. E. Burstall and L. J. Lipsett) side by side, with a third phase of exploitation.[1] The first objective, from left to right, ran due south from the Scarpe at Fampoux along a line of trenches to a point about five hundred yards beyond the Arras–Cambrai road, where it turned back westward to a point north of Neuville Vitasse, so as to form a defensive flank facing south. As soon as this line was gained, the 2nd Canadian Division was to send troops from the point where its line turned from south to west to work down a trench, to join up with the 52nd Division west of Wancourt, and, as already mentioned, to cut off the Germans in the area between Wancourt and Neuville Vitasse.

The second objective was about a mile and a half from the first, and ran, beyond the Cojeul, half a mile east of Wancourt and just west of Guémappe and Monchy le Preux, northward to the Scarpe.

The 51st Division (Major-General G. T. C. Carter-Campbell), north of the Scarpe, was given no defined objective, but was to be ready to exploit any success south of the river by pushing out patrols.

One company of nine tanks of the III Brigade was allotted to each attacking Canadian division ; but, as it turned out, the machines could not arrive until two hours after daylight, that is about 5.30 a.m. For the creeping barrage, the 4·5-inch howitzers were to fire 200 yards in front of the 18-pdr. barrage, and the heavy guns, 600 yards. Zero, as in the XVII Corps, was made 3 a.m.

The weather, with low clouds and rain during the night, was unfavourable for distant bombing operations : but in the area of the battle from 6.50 a.m. onwards No. 5 and 52 Squadrons, allotted to the Canadian Corps, flying at about two hundred feet, kept touch with the advance, whilst four more squadrons, also flying low, attacked ahead of it. The total cost of these measures was three pilots wounded, one plane missing and four wrecked.

---

[1] The total artillery, excluding that of the 51st Division, was 14 brigades of field (including those of the 2nd and 3rd Canadian, 15th, 16th and 39th Divisions and three Army brigades) and nine of heavy artillery (XIX, XLII, XLVIII, L, LIII, LXXVIII, LXXXI and XCI R.G.A., and II Canadian H.A.). Two brigades of heavy guns were allotted to each of the two attacking Canadian divisions, the rest being retained for counter-battery work. The batteries supporting the 2nd Canadian Division were under the C.R.A., Br.-General H. A. Panet, and those with the 3rd under Br.-General J. S. Stewart.

The ground in front of the two Canadian divisions was irregular and complicated, being cut by the valley of the Cojeul and its subsidiaries, and by the various small valleys leading northward to the Scarpe and eastward to the Sensée ; but it is dominated by the long and twisting ridge that leads from Thilloy les Mofflaines (south-east of Arras) via Chapel and Orange Hills round to Monchy le Preux. Under an excellent barrage, however, a most successful advance was made in the dark to the first objective. At first little resistance was encountered, but machine-gun fire, as usual, soon began to open and sharp fighting took place before the objective trench was reached.

The 2nd Canadian Division sent forward the 6th Canadian Brigade (Br.-General A. H. Bell) to form the right defensive flank, and the 4th (Br.-General R. Rennie) to capture Chapel Hill, a machine-gun barrage being fired by the 2nd Canadian Machine-Gun Battalion (less companies allotted to the brigades) and the 1st Canadian Motor Machine-Gun Brigade. After the first objective had been secured, about 6.30 a.m., in the 6th Brigade two companies of the 27th Battalion and the 28th Battalion on their right moved southward and mopped up the whole area down to the boundary with the 52nd Division without much opposition. The 4th Canadian Brigade, though it had some difficulty with machine-gun posts and had to use rifle grenades, and in one case a tank, to overcome resistance, went straight on from the first objective to the second, which was captured by 7.30 a.m.

In the 3rd Canadian Division the attack was entrusted to the 8th Canadian Brigade (Br.-General D. C. Draper). It also pushed forward over Orange Hill to the second objective with little pause, the two support battalions passing through the leaders. They then went on and captured the valuable observatory marked by the ruins of Monchy le Preux.

About 11 a.m. divisional orders were received by the 6th and 4th Canadian Brigades to continue the attack in a south-easterly direction, with new boundaries, the 6th to attack the high ground across the Cojeul south-east of Wancourt, and the 4th to advance between Wancourt and the Arras–Cambrai road. At the same time in the 3rd Canadian Division the 7th Canadian Brigade (Br.-General H. M. Dyer), which had followed in support, was to pass through the 8th, and with the eight tanks which had now arrived exploit its success. About half of the field artillery and some 6-inch howitzers were moved forward to support the advance and provide a barrage.

The 6th Canadian Brigade sent two battalions forward at 4.30 p.m. The enemy opened fire with machine guns, but this was ineffective until the battalions topped the slope out of the Cojeul valley and there found uncut wire. They were unable to make progress over the ridge between the Cojeul and the Scarpe, suffered considerable casualties and were held up for the rest of the day; but they obtained touch with the 52nd Division on the right. As soon as the situation became clear, Br.-General Bell ordered a night attack, without artillery support, in order to reach a trench, five hundred yards away on the eastern side of the ridge. This attack, carried out at 4.30 a.m. on the 27th, was entirely successful, the trench and its southern continuation being occupied.

The principal task of the 4th Canadian Brigade was the capture of Guémappe, which lies in the valley of the Cojeul south of a longish spur running south from the twisting ridge of Monchy le Preux (already in Canadian hands), so that the attackers had to descend into and cross a considerable depression. For this operation the 18th Canadian Battalion was brought up from support about noon to pass through the 21st, which with the 20th had made the morning attack. At first machine-gun fire proved heavy, but it was gradually overcome with the assistance of artillery, and about 5 p.m., after considerable opposition, the 18th Battalion took Guémappe and later established a line three hundred yards beyond it. At 7.45 p.m. the 20th Battalion, under an artillery barrage and with hardly any opposition, advanced and came up on the left level with the 18th.

Meantime the 7th Canadian Brigade of the 3rd Canadian Division, about 11 a.m. had passed through the 8th, with the Royal Canadian Regiment and Princess Patricia's Canadian L.I. leading. They were able to advance nearly a thousand yards, but were then stopped by fire from the front and from both flanks and all four tanks accompanying them were knocked out by shell-fire ; for Guémappe on the south and Pelves (on the Scarpe) on the north were still in the enemy's hands. The divisional boundary on the south having been extended to the Arras–Cambrai road, Br.-General Dyer sent up the 42nd Canadian Battalion to the right flank to clear the ground between the new boundary and Monchy le Preux; but before the 42nd got up level with the Royal Canadians some sharp fighting took place in the maze of trenches south of the village. No further progress was attempted, as the division was already beyond its objectives. To make its new position secure, the 49th Battalion was brought up behind the left flank.

In view of the 51st Division having possibly to take part in the operations on the 26th in the event of the offensive of the Canadian divisions south of the Scarpe turning out a success, Major-General Carter-Campbell had in a warning order defined the objectives to be reached. The first two each entailed an advance of about half a mile; but should a substantial success be achieved by the Canadians, a further advance of another half mile might be made to Greenland Hill, a knoll with gentle slopes and a flat top, the highest ground in the neighbourhood, commanding good observation to the east.

When, about 8.30 a.m., news was received at Canadian Corps headquarters of the capture of Monchy le Preux by the 3rd Canadian Division, the 51st Division was ordered to attack. The 152nd and 153rd Brigades (Br.-Generals W. H. E. Segrave and W. Green) advanced against the first objective at 10.30 a.m., covered by a barrage fired by the 16th and 51st Division artillery, under the C.R.A. of the 51st Division, Br.-General L. C. L. Oldfield.[1]

Little opposition was offered and the first objective was taken about midday. The attack was not continued until 7 p.m., when the second objective was reached without difficulty. In order to get abreast of the 3rd Canadian Division, the advance was then resumed and reached Roeux, on the Scarpe, and the western slope of Greenland Hill, whence the line was carried on by the 154th Brigade (Br.-General K. G. Buchanan), which had protected the left during the day and now formed a north defensive flank facing Gavrelle.

Next on the left, during the night of the 26th/27th, the 8th Division (Major-General W. C. G. Heneker) (VIII Corps)

---

[1] After firing the barrage for the 3rd Canadian Division, the services of the 16th Division artillery and the 256th (Army) Brigade R.F.A. were placed at the disposal of the 51st Division.

sent out patrols which occupied the enemy's front line and part of his support line, advancing an average depth of a thousand yards on a front of four thousand yards.

The extension northward of the Allied offensive by the First Army had a very great success. On the night of the 26th/27th the preliminaries of a retirement by the Germans were begun, and in this case it was not a voluntary one.

The decision to fall back affected not only the Arras–Somme front, but the Lys salient as well. The Second Army had made various small advances from the 18th August onwards ; but on the night of the 29th/30th the enemy began an extensive retirement on the whole Lys front and, as will be related, by the evening of the 6th September the Lys salient disappeared.[1]

NOTE

THE GERMANS ON THE 26TH AUGUST, OPPOSITE THE THIRD AND FIRST ARMIES, AND THEIR DECISION TO CARRY OUT A RETIREMENT

(Map 4, Sketch 11)

On the 26th, four more divisions are mentioned in German accounts as being brought up from rest near Douai to reinforce the most threatened sectors : (1) the *12th Reserve*, first to a position behind Bapaume (which was held by the *220th*) and then south-westwards to the right flank of the *16th Bavarian Division*, which was defending Thilloy ; (2) the *23rd Division* (which soon lost 700 prisoners) to the north-east of Beugnâtre, the *6th Bavarian Reserve Division*, which had been turned out of the village, being withdrawn into second line " after again (*sic*) losing in a few days " 35 officers and 1,900 men "[2] ; (3) the *7th (Dismounted) Cavalry Division* to Ecoust ; and (4) the *35th Division* to Monchy le Preux.

Of the troops facing the Canadians very little information is available except that they were subject to " the sharpest " pressure " and retired " step by step before the never ceasing " infiltration [the word used indicates holeboring] of the enemy ".

" Meantime the High Command had come to the decision to " abandon to the enemy the devastated battle area north and " west of the Somme ". (B.O.A., p. 537.)

---

[1] See Chapter XXI.
[2] The previous occasion seems to have been in the Chemin des Dames offensive of 27th May, in which it had " suffered heavily " on 28th May, and had " severe losses " on 1st June. It was relieved on 15th June and, after two months' rest, had returned to the front only on 23rd August.

According to General von Kuhl's official report to the
Reichstag Committee of Enquiry into the Loss of the War, the
question of a voluntary retirement to the Hindenburg Position
had been debated for some days, such a movement being regarded
as much better than being compelled to retire with heavy losses :
 " O.H.L. could not, however, bring itself to such a
" decision. As already mentioned, General Ludendorff had
" told the Kaiser he would not give up an inch of ground
" without a determined struggle. On the 4th August, before
" the breach made by the Allies on the 8th, O.H.L. had given
" instructions to the Groups of Armies to strengthen their
" present positions ".
 " The views of the Staffs of the Groups of Armies on the
" question of standing fast or retiring were different[1]. In a
" written report of the 11th August Gallwitz's Army Group
" [Verdun area][2] pointed out that in face of the further
" heavy enemy attacks to be expected, an obstinate resistance
" as adopted in 1916 and 1917 would result in great expendi-
" ture of effectives. On this account it would be fatal to
" limit ourselves to the pure defensive ; well-planned
" counter-attacks must be undertaken, principally against
" the flanks of the enemy's offensive. ' If we feel that we
" ' have the power to change the situation, we shall achieve
" ' this quicker if we put into practice the accepted mobile
" ' form of warfare, not mainly by defence repeated in one
" ' back position after another, but in the forward direction
" ' by large-scale counter-attack '.
 " The Staff of the German Crown Prince's Group of
" Armies [east of Verdun to short of Amiens], on the
" contrary, had towards the end of August come to the view
" that we were thrown on the defensive for good and all.
" In a letter (to General Ludendorff) on the 26th August, it
" was said that we must, in any case, reckon on the long
" continuation of the enemy offensive, and with strong
" fresh attacks against strategically or politically important
" sectors of the front. To the large-scale offensive plan of

---

[1] In his statement to the Reichstag Committee Kuhl gives only the
views of Gallwitz's and the German Crown Prince's Groups of Armies.
Elsewhere, General von Kuhl (p. 198), for Crown Prince Rupprecht's
Group of Armies (the Prince himself was on sick leave from 13th August
until into September, after an attack of influenza) says " after 8th August
" the right military course was the withdrawal of the Armies into the
" Hindenburg Position ".
Colonel-General von Boehn, " in view of the general situation, held
" that a retirement on the front of his Group of Armies [*Eighteenth, Second*
" and *Seventeenth Armies* holding from the Oise to beyond Arras opposite
" the French Third and First Armies and the British Fourth, Third and
" First (right wing) Armies] was indicated ". (Schwarte iii, p. 552.)
[2] See Map 2.

" the enemy ' we must oppose well-thought-out defensive
" ' measures. . . . The enemy has naturally the intention
" ' of destroying our reserves. We can escape this only by
" ' accepting attack solely where the ground offers favourable
" ' conditions for defence. When this condition is not
" ' present, we must retire sector by sector according to a
" ' definite plan. This retirement according to plan is only
" ' a temporary expedient. It must find its end in a strong
" ' permanent position[1], which offers favourable conditions
" ' for a stubborn defence, and by a wide-reaching shortening
" ' admits such economy of strength as to allow the pulling
" ' out of strong reserves. This permanent position must be
" ' so far removed from the present battlefield that, even
" ' after weeks of indecisive fighting there will still be
" ' sufficient elbow room for a retirement according to
" ' plan ' ".

The permanent positions recommended by the German Crown
Prince for the Groups of Armies of Crown Prince Rupprecht and
Boehn were : those held before the beginning of the spring
offensive and the Hindenburg Position ; for the Group of Armies
of the German Crown Prince, the Hunding-Brunhild-Argonne
Position (behind the Serre, Souche and upper Aisne).

In his answer of the 27th August, General Ludendorff, in
general, completely concurred in these remarks, but added :
" I regard, in any case, the retirement into the jumping-off
" positions of last March—the Hindenburg Position—as the very
" farthest we can go in consideration of the unfavourable rein-
" forcement situation ".

General von Kuhl remarks in his report that " the necessity of
" transporting back the huge amount of material collected in
" the course of years behind the Armies militated against a rapid
" withdrawal. This factor had, however, to take second place
" to tactical and strategical requirements. Finally, in spite of
" the slow, measured retirement, enormous masses of military
" apparatus had to be left behind ".

" Further, the retirement could on no account be carried out
" so fast that it did not leave time for the thorough destruction
" of the railways. Any possibility of the enemy following up
" quickly must be removed ".

To the later-made suggestion that the German Armies, after
the August fighting, should have retired at once to the Antwerp–
Meuse position, General von Kuhl replies that, in addition to the
above reasons against a rapid retirement, the work on this position
had not in August even been begun, and that the railway system

---

[1] *Dauerstellung*, not a " permanent fortification " but a position which
can be held " for the duration ".

became less and less convenient with every phase of the retirement, and that it would not have been possible to provide behind the Antwerp–Meuse position, even by field railways, the facilities to which the troops were accustomed.

On the 26th orders were issued for the retirement on the night of the 27th–28th of the *Second* and *Eighteenth Armies* (opposite the French Third and First Armies and the British Fourth Army) to a shorter line from Noyon along the east bank of the canal to Nesle, and thence along the Somme to the north-west of Péronne ; the left of the *Seventeenth Army* (opposite the British Third Army) was to conform, swinging back to Le Transloy–Vraucourt, abandoning Bapaume. This movement would leave the German Armies 15 to 20 miles in front of the Hindenburg Position, except in the north near Arras where it joined the front position. According to Ludendorff (p. 695) the line was selected because it offered a good obstacle against tanks. He says the retirement was carried out " about the night of the 26th–27th August ".

General von Lossberg (p. 355), with greater honesty than Ludendorff and Kuhl, admits that immediately after the 25th August the combined attacks on a broad front of the French and British " drove the *Seventeenth, Second* and *Eighteenth Armies* " back to the line south of Lens–east of Hénin–east of Bapaume " –east of Combles-Péronne–course of the Somme to west " of Ham–east of Noyon ".

CHAPTER XVII

THE BATTLE OF ALBERT 1918—(*concluded*)

THE BATTLE OF THE SCARPE 1918—(*continued*)

FOURTH, THIRD AND FIRST ARMIES

27TH–29TH AUGUST

THE GERMAN RETIREMENT TO THE SOMME LINE

(Sketches 11, 12, 15, 16)

During the three days following the 26th August the retirement of the German *Eighteenth, Second* and *Seventeenth* Armies[1] to a position behind the south-north course of the Somme between Ham and Péronne and a continuation of this line southwards to near Noyon and northwards to near Croisilles, was in progress. The movement was more marked in the southern and centre sectors, doubtless to avoid envelopment by the French, than in the north, where it pivoted opposite Arras on the end of the Drocourt–Quéant Line (Wotan Position). One symptom of retirement was that the enemy air force became more active, especially against horse and transport lines. The machine gun remained the backbone of the defence. A feature of the German operations was the method used in the withdrawal of the artillery. This was preceded by an intense bombardment, for the double purpose of holding off the attackers and of using up the ammunition dumped near the guns; the actual withdrawal of the field guns was covered by the increased fire of the high velocity and heavy guns, and so alternately. Further, a tactical trick employed, of which the British had already become aware, was to leave behind single field guns and sections in action in woods and copses to assist the retirement of the infantry and delay pursuit. Sometimes trench mortars kept up fire for these purposes after the field guns had got away, and a number of them, in consequence, were captured. The undulating country, particularly near and north of the Somme, singularly favoured late withdrawals both of infantry and guns. South of the Somme the enemy abandoned a good deal of material, and on both banks every day brought a fair haul of prisoners.

---

[1] See Sketch 11.

Steady progress in these circumstances was made by the Fourth and Third Armies and the right of the First, which was more pronounced on the right than on the left, where the First Army had the Drocourt–Quéant Switch in front of it. In liaison with the Fourth Army, the left of the French First Army began to advance on the 27th.

The general policy now ruling the situation may be understood from correspondence which passed between Maréchal Foch and the British and American Commanders-in-Chief about this time. On the 25th August the Generalissimo wrote a personal letter to Sir Douglas Haig couched in very friendly terms, yet containing some advice with a little dash of criticism about the steady advance in line. It ran :

" Your affairs are going very well. I can only applaud
" the resolute manner in which you are carrying them
" out, giving the enemy no respite, at the same time
" always increasing the breadth of the attack. It is this
" progressive widening of the offensive, *of an offensive*
" *reinforced from behind* and pushed strongly ahead
" against wisely chosen objectives, without worrying
" about keeping alignment or maintaining too close
" touch, which will give us the greatest results with the
" least casualties. It is unnecessary to tell you that
" General Pétain's Armies are about to continue their
" advance in the same manner ".

In his reply on the 27th Sir Douglas Haig cordially thanked the Maréchal for his kind letter and then, turning to business, gently hinted that others might be urged to do a little more. He first explained what he had in his mind : that the situation between the Somme and the Scarpe seemed to be developing very satisfactorily : that, while he was maintaining an active offensive on the whole of this front, he was specially strong immediately south of the Scarpe[1]—where he had the whole Canadian Corps—in order to pierce the Drocourt–Quéant line and reach Marquion (at the crossing of the Canal du Nord by the Arras–Cambrai road, 14 miles from Arras), which seemed to be the area whence the German *Seventeenth Army*, whose left extended down to Morval,[2] received its supplies. He was, however, strongly of opinion

---

[1] See Map 4.

[2] Morval is 5 miles south of Bapaume : the right of the *Seventeenth Army* was at Hénin Lietard, 3 miles N.N.E. of Drocourt.

it was desirable that American divisions should take an active share in the battle without delay and ventured to suggest for the Maréchal's consideration that the distribution of these divisions should be such as to enable a convèrgent movement to be carried out against Mezières[1] from the south, St. Quentin and Cambrai : the direction of his own attacks would bring him to Cambrai, provided the pressure on the remainder of the front was kept up.

Maréchal Foch had not overlooked the employment of the American troops, and some hint of this may have reached British G.H.Q. On the 23rd he had written to General Pershing[2] that, in view of the certainty of the Allies having to provide for a struggle of long duration and increasing extent, it would be necessary to make use of every trained American division : in this connection it was desirable that the two American divisions (27th and 30th) now behind the British front should be placed at the disposal of Field-Marshal Haig to co-operate in the next British attacks, just as the American 28th, 32nd and 77th Divisions were already taking part in the operations of the G.A.R. : further, the two American divisions in the Vosges sector (37th and 29th) might be relieved by others recently landed, so as to free them for a more active rôle. At a conference next day at Maréchal Foch's headquarters, General Pershing made it clear that there was " complete agreement as regards the general " plan of the operations of the American Army and the " organization of command." It was then decided (1) that from the 31st August the two American divisions in the British zone could be employed in offensive operations by Sir Douglas Haig, provided that in principle they were under the orders of an American corps commander (the G.O.C. II Corps was available); and (2) that from the 9th September two American divisions, in addition to the fourteen ear-marked for the St. Mihiel operation, should be ready to move to take part, according to circumstances, in either the operations of the French Armies or those of the American Army.[3]

---

[1] See Sketch 1.

[2] F.O.A. vii (i), p. 237.

[3] The general lines of the St. Mihiel operation (in French histories often called the Woevre operation) had been settled between Maréchal Foch and Generals Pershing and Pétain during 17th–19th August, and the assembly of the troops to form the American First Army began on the 21st.

Continuing his correspondence with Sir Douglas Haig, Maréchal Foch wrote on the 28th : " I well know that your " troops are continuing to advance with determination and " that the enemy is retiring in disorder. Keep the same " attitude as you describe ; continue your pursuit ". He added that the final objectives indicated by Sir Douglas Haig were those which he himself had in mind, and towards which he was directing the operations of the Allied Armies : these were actually being mounted in the different sectors, each in its own style and at dates close to one another : the distribution of the American divisions must depend on the development of the situation : for the moment it was important to press on as strongly and as far as possible.

On the following day (29th) at a conference at Mouchy le Chatel, Maréchal Foch, somewhat in contradiction of his letter, expressed his agreement with Sir Douglas Haig as regards the employment of the American troops, and the British Commander-in-Chief understood him to say that General Pershing would be given Mezières as an objective instead of St. Mihiel, the latter attack being cancelled. This, however, was not the case, as is now clear from the fact that an attack against St. Mihiel was carried out, from the Note addressed on the 30th by the Generalissimo to General Pershing,[1] and from the explanation given in his Memoirs.[2] The St. Mihiel operation was, he told General Pershing, to be reduced in scope, it was to free the Paris–Avricourt railway from interference by shell-fire by a northward advance ; but this was not to go so far as previously arranged, in order to leave larger forces available for the later " principal operations in the direction of Mezières ". He had in fact, adopted the plan of a convergent attack of all forces available suggested by Sir Douglas Haig.

FOURTH ARMY

To return to the operations :[3] on the right wing of the Fourth Army, the Australian Corps (Lieut.-General Sir J. Monash) had in the line the 32nd Division (Major-General T. S. Lambert), and the 5th and 2nd Australian Divisions

---

[1] Appendix XXI. See also Note III at end of Chapter.
[2] Vol. ii, pp. 200–202.
[3] See Sketch 15.

(Major-Generals Sir J. T. Talbot Hobbs and C. Rosenthal), which had relieved the 1st Australian Division during the night of the 26th–27th. Each Australian division had one brigade, the 8th and the 6th, in front line, and the 32nd Division had two, the 96th and 14th.

The German artillery was fairly active in the night between 11 p.m. and 1 a.m. against the centre of the 32nd Division front, a little mustard gas being used. Frequent patrols were sent out in expectation of detecting signs of retreat, as low clouds and rain hindered air observation. At 3.30 a.m. a patrol of the 2/Manchester (96th Brigade) discovered that the enemy's front trenches were empty. A quarter of an hour later, however, he opened a concentration of artillery on the front of the 14th Brigade which lasted until 5 a.m. and prevented a reconnaissance supported by artillery fire which was to have been made by that brigade. After occupying the abandoned trenches about 5.30 a.m. the 96th Brigade went forward at 7.30 a.m., but the French on its right refused to move until the morning mist had dispersed. In consequence of the enemy's artillery fire it was not until later that the 14th could do so, and the opposition to this brigade was always greater than to the 96th. But the defence everywhere was stout, and the fire from the machine guns and artillery heavy. Vermandovillers was nevertheless taken and, aided in the afternoon by the progress of the Australians on the left, a general advance of over two thousand yards was achieved.

The 8th and 6th Australian Brigades, having come into the line during the night, did not advance as early as the 32nd Division, though at dawn a copse in front of Fontaine les Cappy was discovered to be unoccupied, and a post near it was rushed. The advance was carried out in the favourite Australian way by strong fighting patrols. In consequence of information from the 32nd Division and the French on its right that the enemy was carrying out a withdrawal, more decisive measures were then ordered. When however, Foucaucourt was found to be strongly held with machine guns it was bombarded at 1 p.m. as a preliminary to a planned attack. Owing to short notice, however, the effect of the fire was lost, and it was 3.15 p.m. before the 30th Battalion, working up old trenches, after advance over the open had proved hopeless, enveloped the village, which was taken with 35 prisoners and 16 machine guns about 6 p.m. On its eastern edge the Australians were so pounded with shell that it was thought the enemy was firing away his dumps previous to retirement. On the rest of the line the resistance encountered was of the same character as opposite the 32nd Division, and about the same amount of progress was achieved.

Owing to the northward bend of the Somme opposite Frise, the direction of the further advance of the 3rd Australian Division (Major-General J. Gellibrand) and the III. Corps (Lieut.-General Sir A. Godley), north of the river, had to be changed from eastwards to nearly north-eastwards. The right wing, therefore, the 10th Australian Brigade and all but the left battalion of the 11th, was to stand fast for the present. On the 27th, 4.55 a.m. being fixed by the III. Corps as zero hour, the 41st Battalion (11th Australian Brigade) alone went forward, under a barrage, for the purpose of guarding the right flank of the 58th Division, the right wing of the III. Corps, by advancing to a line through Fargny Mill, just north of the Frise bend of the Somme. This, by 8 a.m., it had successfully accomplished but it had great difficulty in maintaining its position.[1]

The general objective given to the divisions of the III. Corps by Lieut.-General Godley was a line which began at the Chapeau de Gendarme Wood, north of Fargny Mill, and ran northwards to include Hardecourt aux Bois and Trônes Wood. All attacks were to be carried out under creeping barrages followed by a standing barrage for a short time after the objective was reached. Zero hour was 4.55 a.m., as in the 3rd Australian Division.

The 58th Division (Major-General F. W. Ramsay) sent forward the 174th and 173rd Brigades (Br.-Generals A. Maxwell and C. E. Corkran), giving them as first objective the system of trenches, about fifteen hundred yards away, running from Fargny Mill past the eastern edge of Maricourt Wood. It had been arranged between the two divisions that the 3rd Australian Division should attack Fargny Wood, actually just within the 58th Division area ; when, later,

---

[1] Lce.-Corporal B. S. Gordon, of the 41st Australian Battalion, was awarded the V.C. for outstanding gallantry on the 26th and 27th. Practically single-handed he captured 63 Germans and 6 machine guns.

the Australian Corps decided against this plan, no troops of the 58th were immediately available to deal with the wood, and although the 174th Brigade received fire from the northern edge and a small party occupied a trench facing it, evening had come before the wood could be cleared, a few prisoners being taken in it. Meanwhile the advance of the right of the brigade had been held up some three hundred yards from the objective, and the left wing, in error, halted in a trench short of its destination. These difficulties were soon overcome, and the objective was reached; then, however, the fire from the old German reserve line beyond was so strong that no further advance could be made. The 173rd Brigade had immediate success, and Maricourt village and wood were quickly captured; but beyond this, for the same reason as the 174th, it could not go.

Major-General Higginson gave the 37th Brigade (Br.-General A. B. Incledon-Webber), which was to lead the attack of the 12th Division, the Maricourt–Longueval road as its first objective, a box barrage being placed round the brickyard at the southern end of Bernafay Wood for twenty minutes to assist its envelopment. The first reports which came from the leading battalions were misleading; they had, it was said, passed the first objective and were at Hardecourt aux Bois on the final line. It was later discovered that they were west and slightly north-west of Favière Wood, which, in the devastated state of both localities, except for the distance passed over and its topographical situation in a valley, might well have been Hardecourt. The corps cavalry was sent up to exploit the supposed situation, but, after ascertaining the true state of affairs, reported that barbed wire, shell-holes and trenches made the ground impossible for mounted action. Meantime, German fire from Favière Wood and from trenches north-east of it forced the right of the 37th Brigade to fall back a couple of hundred yards to an existing trench, whilst later reconnaissance showed that on the left the British line ran from the north-west corner of Favière Wood to the vicinity of the captured brickyard, with posts pushed forward between Favière and Bernafay Woods. Earlier, soon after 9 a.m., in view of the troubles of the 18th Division on the left in Trônes Wood, the 35th Brigade (Br.-General A. T. Beckwith), was ordered up towards that flank to the Maricourt–Longueval road, and the 36th Brigade (Br.-General C. S. Owen), warned to be ready to support it ; but no necessity to employ them arose.

Shortly after 1 p.m. the 37th Brigade made preparations to co-operate with the 18th Division in an advance the latter proposed to make at 4 p.m. This movement was, however, cancelled an hour later, and the brigade was directed to swing its left forward to connect with the 18th Division east of Bernafay Wood. A direct advance over the open could not be carried out owing to the severity of the enemy fire, but it was found possible to filter men gradually into Favière Wood. About 5 p.m. a warning message was received that the 18th Division would make its attack to gain the eastern edge of Trônes Wood at 7 p.m. The 37th Brigade made ready to keep touch ; but though the 18th Division gained a success little change took place in the position of the brigade, and at 9 p.m. its line still ran as in the morning, with posts out towards Maltz Horn Farm. These posts, and those in Favière Wood, were withdrawn during the night in order to leave the ground clear for next day's barrage.

In the 18th Division (Major-General R. P. Lee), the 53rd Brigade (Br.-General M. G. H. Barker), after a day's rest, was brought up again on the evening of the 25th to carry out the attack on Trônes Wood—which the division had attacked from the south in the Battles of the Somme 1916—and, incidentally, capture Bernafay Wood. The orders given to it were first to secure the northern portion of Trônes Wood and then turn southwards, the barrage being adjusted accordingly ; they were, however, based on the erroneous information that Longueval Village and Delville Wood (both now without trees), lying on higher ground to the north, were, or soon would be, in British hands. Actually, the 38th Division had on the 26th halted short of these localities and did not gain possession of them until the 29th. Thus it happened, as on the right, the 12th Division's line was well in rear of the 18th's, that both flanks of the latter's advance were exposed to enemy fire.

The 7/R. West Kent and the 8/R. Berkshire, which had pushed close up to the barrage, suffering some loss from it, easily drove in the enemy outposts. The former battalion moved along the stream and light railway in the valley between Montauban and Longueval ridge, which run past the northern border of Bernafay Wood ; it then faced south, and, after waiting for the change of direction of the barrage from eastwards to southwards, cleared the wood without difficulty and occupied the line between its southern edge and Trônes Wood. The R. Berkshire which, moving eastwards, had to clear the northern half of Trônes Wood, under the first barrage, so that the southern movement of the two battalions should be simultaneous, soon came under heavy enfilade fire from Waterlot Farm to the north-east, and the two left companies were held up on the road which runs north from Bernafay Wood. The right companies, keeping up with the barrage, in spite of mounting casualties, reached the western edge of Trônes Wood, and there the company in support turned, as provided in its orders, to clear the southern part of the wood, and actually got astride of the wood along the light railway line. This move, however, left only a few men of the other company to complete the journey to the eastern edge. Those of them who reached there were counter-attacked from Waterlot Farm and, though they checked the enemy, they had to fall back west of the wood in order to avoid enfilade fire from Longueval and Delville Wood. The company on the railway in the wood also had to retire to the western edge, where it joined on to the line of the West Kent. It was now about 7 a.m. and two companies of the 10/Essex were hurried forward to assist the 8/R. Berkshire. Although Trônes Wood was under bombardment of the British heavy artillery, about 8 a.m. the Germans made a strong counter-attack through the southern portion towards the junction of the West Kent and the Berkshire. The western edge of the wood was now lost ; but the West Kent held on to the southern edge of Bernafay Wood, and a new line was formed along its eastern edge. An immediate counter-attack with the aid of the 12th Division was abandoned as impracticable, but preparations were taken in hand to execute one at 7 p.m. under the leadership of Lieut.-Colonel T. M. Banks (10/Essex, but commanding the 8/R. Berkshire). It was made by two companies of the 10/Essex and one of the 8/R. Berkshire against the southern half of Trônes Wood, after the wood had been bombarded by artillery of all calibres for half an hour. A company of the West Kent followed in rear to re-establish the line between the southern faces of the two woods, and four guns of the divisional artillery came up to give close support. The leading troops, creeping up close to the barrage, surprised the enemy, and in the hand-to-hand fighting which ensued over fifty Germans were killed and 73, with 20 machine guns, captured. This success completed the general advance of the Fourth Army on the 27th.

THIRD ARMY

The orders issued to the Third Army[1] simply entailed a continuance of the movement of the V., IV. and VI. Corps eastwards, and of the XVII. Corps, on their left, south-eastwards astride the Hindenburg Position, in co-operation with the Canadian Corps of the First Army. It was notified that the use of tanks should be kept to the absolute minimum, so as to give them time to refit and re-organize for the next big advance.[2] But it became very obvious that the divisions were tiring, and that fresh troops were required if the advance was to be carried on with vigour. The enemy's defence was fiercer than ever, owing to reinforcements having arrived and to instructions having been given to his troops to hold on in order to cover the removal of material. Without tanks tired infantry could not be expected to accomplish anything decisive against it. The staffs, too, were certainly tiring, and co-ordination of the divisional efforts on this day was woefully lacking.

Lieut.-General Shute of the V. Corps decided on making only a limited advance of about four thousand yards, so as to reach Morval, $3\frac{1}{2}$ miles ahead, and the ridge extending northwards from it. Small progress was made, and the line named was not gained until the 29th. No zero hour was fixed by the corps, and the divisions began to move at various times, the 38th on the right at 4 a.m., the 17th at 1 a.m. and the 21st at 9 a.m. After a short advance machine-gun fire, fiercer than ever owing to the arrival of new German divisions on the previous days, paralysed all attempts at movement. In the 38th Division sector, Longueval and Delville Wood were full of machine guns, which, even in the half-light of dawn, found their targets, and the only battalion which crossed the Longueval–Flers road had to fall back. In the afternoon the 122nd Brigade

---

[1] See Sketch 16.
[2] See Note I at end of Chapter XVIII.

R.F.A., galloping by sections through an enemy heavy-gun barrage, came up in close support behind the morning front line without loss of a gun, though seven teams received hits, and assisted in repulsing an enemy counter-attack. In the 17th Division Flers was taken during the night by the 50th Brigade (Br.-General G. Gwyn-Thomas), but later the line had to be withdrawn west of the village.

When the 64th Brigade of the 21st Division advanced at 9 a.m. it was held up by enfilade machine-gun fire from Ligny Thilloy and the slopes east of it, and the 63rd Division (IV. Corps), on the left, which was to have attacked the village, did not appear to be moving. The situation was duly reported to divisional headquarters and a junior staff officer was sent to the headquarters of the 63rd Division. Through some misunderstanding he brought back the information that an attack would take place at 11 a.m., as it did, but only in the form of strong patrols behind a barrage. Major-General Campbell thereupon cancelled the orders already given for the 110th Brigade to press the attack by passing through the 64th. This advance was actually in progress and prevented from continuing only by Staff officers running forward to stop it. The 64th Brigade was then instructed to send out patrols to make good a farm half a mile away, and the road for four hundred yards on each side of it, and then push on to the ridge a thousand yards ahead ; but they could not get within two hundred yards of the road. Thus the divisions of the V. Corps had not reached even the limited objectives assigned to them, and Longueval and Flers were still in the enemy's hands.

The IV. Corps made no progress whatever ; for the Thilloy sector was strongly held.[1] After an hour's bombardment by all available howitzers, field and heavy, the 190th Brigade (63rd Division), under a barrage, but without support from the divisions on either side, except from some patrols of the New Zealand Division, attacked Thilloy at 11 a.m. and, in the face of machine-gun fire, could make little progress. In a second attempt at 6 p.m., after a slightly longer bombardment, a few men penetrated into Thilloy, but could not hold on there. The 190th Brigade eventually dug in two or three hundred yards ahead of its starting point.

---

[1] The *12th Reserve Division* had on the 26th reinforced the *16th Bavarian Division*, which itself had only come into the battle on the 24th.

The New Zealand Division had been ordered to continue the encirclement of Bapaume ; but the town was still so strongly defended that it was considered advisable to confine any action against it to bombardment and to watching for signs of weakening. Patrols sent out during the attack of the 63rd Division on the right were heavily fired on, and could not go very far.

The 5th Division had been given Beugnâtre as its objective —if still in the enemy's possession. As the village had been taken on the previous evening, the division made no advance.

In the VI. Corps, after providing for the bombardment of the villages just behind the German front, the gist of Lieut.-General Haldane's orders to his leading divisions was that they should take every opportunity to gain ground if the enemy showed signs of weakening as a result of the enveloping movement of the XVII. and Canadian Corps farther north ; but no such signs were apparent, and the fighting resembled that of the autumn days on the Somme in 1916. At 7 a.m. the 62nd Division sent the 186th and 187th Brigades forward. The former used patrols and the latter four companies which, under a very good barrage, made some headway and consolidated a line about six or seven hundred yards from their starting point ; but the patrols accomplished nothing. The 1st Guards Brigade sent forward two battalions (2/Grenadier and 2/Coldstream Guards) at 7 a.m., the LXXIV. and LXXV. Brigades R.F.A. being used in close support, and the 1/Irish Guards later brought up to reinforce. On the right and left some progress was made, parties reaching a trench (Banks Trench) which ran south-eastwards from St. Leger Wood, but later having to withdraw. About 180 prisoners were taken, but casualties were heavy. As the 56th Division (XVII. Corps) did not advance until 9.30 a.m., the Guards' left flank was exposed and had to be withdrawn. In the evening, however, the left advanced again and occupied the northern end of Banks Trench, taking about a hundred prisoners.

The tasks allotted by the XVII. Corps (Lieut.-General Sir Charles Fergusson) were : 56th Division to maintain pressure on Croisilles—which the artillery of the 52nd also bombarded—and for the 52nd to continue its advance south-eastwards down the Hindenburg front line in conjunction with the Canadian Corps.

The situation north of Croisilles not being known until very late, although a warning message had been sent out at 4.50 p.m. on the 26th, it was 3 a.m. before the 56th Division issued definite orders for the 167th Brigade (Br.-General G. H. B. Freeth) to remain facing Croisilles, and for the 169th (Br.-General E. S. de E. Coke), to advance north of the village. The latter was to cross the valley of the Sensée, in which Croisilles lies, after making good as first objective the road on the slopes west of it, and push on to the second objective, the Hindenburg front line, over the stream which lay athwart its course. Beyond the stream it was to make connection with the 52nd Division. The barrage began at 9.20 a.m. and moved forward at 9.36 a.m. This late start proved a grave handicap to the operations of the right wing of the First Army. The 169th Brigade sent forward three companies : that on the right was stopped by enfilade machine-gun fire from Croisilles after going a quarter of a mile, the other two were able to advance nearly a mile to a line of trenches north of the village, where they were stopped by uncut wire and fire from the front. Later in the day, when news came that the 52nd Division had captured Fontaine lez Croisilles, to the north-east, the leading companies were reinforced and, making use of trenches, the 169th Brigade reached its second objective.

The 52nd Division also, for the same reason as the 56th, was unable to issue orders until 3.5 a.m. Major-General Hill had intended that the 155th Brigade, on the right, should advance first and clear the enemy off the Hindenburg Position as far as a cross trench half a mile away, before the main attack at 10 a.m., when the 157th and 156th Brigades (Br.-Generals C. D. Hamilton-Moore and A. H. Leggett) would advance, with Fontaine lez Croisilles as objective. The 155th Brigade's order went astray, so that the preliminary operation was not carried out, with the result that there was a gap between the 56th and 52nd Divisions, and the right flank of the 157th Brigade, which had to cross Henin Hill, suffered considerable casualties from enfilade fire. Under a good barrage both brigades, however, after an advance of over two miles, reached their objective beyond the Sensée ; but they were unable to go very far beyond it. At night the 57th Division relieved the 52nd.

FIRST ARMY

General Horne's formal orders were issued at 7.10 p.m. on the 26th : the Canadian Corps was to continue its advance : north of the Scarpe a defensive flank was to be formed : if the Drocourt–Quéant Line was found to be held in force, the corps was to be prepared to attack it on the 28th (at 3.15 p.m. on the 27th this date was postponed to the 30th), and for this purpose the 4th Division would be transferred from the Army reserve to the Canadian Corps at midnight 26th/27th.

Lieut.-General Currie gave as first objective for the 2nd and 3rd Canadian Divisions a line of high ground beyond the Sensée from Fontaine lez Croisilles (exclusive) to Vis en Artois and thence turned back to Boiry Notre Dame, about two miles ahead, with the left wing slightly bent back. This line was successfully gained by the right and centre, but not quite reached by the left.

Eight tanks were allotted to each division, but the 14th Tank Battalion could produce only four, and two of these were soon knocked out. The arrangements for co-operation of the Royal Air Force were as on the previous day and, though the weather conditions were always difficult, low-flying attacks were continued, and during the day some 650 bombs dropped and 47,500 rounds of machine-gun ammunition fired, many at troops in the battle area. The heavy artillery allotted to the divisions supported the infantry advance, and when the limit of the field artillery barrage was reached, a proportion of the field batteries limbered up and went forward to new positions.

Zero hour was made 4.55 a.m., but changed to 10 a.m. for the right division, in order to fit in with that of the 52nd Division on its right. The 2nd Canadian Division sent forward its 5th and 4th Brigades (the former passing through the 6th). The barrage being good, a rapid advance was made to the Sensée, still little more than a ditch and, in spite of considerable fire, the valley was crossed ; but the barrage could not cover the infantry very far beyond this and when it ceased the enemy's fire became so heavy that infantry could not advance more than five or six hundred yards from the stream. A bridgehead was therefore formed on the left in Vis en Artois, where the Arras–Cambrai road crosses the Sensée.

The 3rd Canadian Division employed the 9th Brigade (Br.-General D. M. Ormond), which sent forward the 52nd and 58th Battalions at 4.55 a.m., with the 116th in support ; the 43rd, on the extreme right, was to wait until 10 a.m., the hour at which the 2nd Canadian Division attacked. The eight tanks, which duly appeared, were heavily shelled when they advanced with the infantry, and were either knocked out or incapacitated. At first a little progress was made ; Bois du Vert was taken, and Bois du Sart, taken, lost and re-taken. The 116th Battalion, passing through the 52nd, tried to reach Boiry Notre Dame, but met with heavy fire from the village and from the right flank. Such was the situation when, about midday, the 43rd Battalion came up level on the right. A heavy concentration of artillery was now put down in Boiry Notre Dame, and at 1 p.m. the 116th Battalion again advanced ; but, after making considerable headway, had to fall back ; for Pelves, on the left, was still in enemy hands, and was, with its good field of fire, a thorn-in-the-flesh on that flank. No other movement was made except by the 43rd Battalion, which went forward and got touch of the 2nd Canadian Division in Vis en Artois. At night, the 8th Canadian Brigade took over the right sector of the wide-stretched front of the 9th as far as the Cojeul stream.

North of the Scarpe, in the 51st Division the 153rd Brigade was to make the principal attack at 10 a.m. against Greenland Hill, a knoll little more than thirty feet above the ground around it, the 152nd and 154th on either side conforming. At first all went well ; the 1/7th Gordon Highlanders and 1/6th Black Watch went over the hill, but they were counter-attacked up trenches on the right and the day ended with the brigade back at its starting point on the right, but a quarter of a mile ahead of it on the left.

In the belief that Greenland Hill had been captured, the 152nd Brigade sent a battalion forward at 2.30 p.m. to form a defensive flank; it was met by machine-gun fire, but gained about five hundred yards. On the left, the 154th found Gavrelle unoccupied and took up a line of posts east of it. About 5 p.m. the enemy re-took these posts, but he was driven out of them and the line re-established. The right and left wings of the 51st Division had therefore gained a little ground.

Of the troops of the Third and First Armies engaged on the 27th, the Canadian Corps had enjoyed the most successful day. It was to repeat its success next day, when the Australian Corps also was to make a fine advance.

FOURTH ARMY[1]

At 8.20 p.m. on the 27th the Fourth Army by telegram issued orders for further advance :

" Australian and III Corps will continue to press " back the enemy's rear guards. Australian Corps will " be directed on Péronne and will maintain touch with " the French First Army on its right. III Corps will " be directed on Bouchavesnes [4 miles north of Péronne] " and St. Pierre Vaast Wood, and will maintain touch " with the Third Army on its left ".

The advance of the Fourth Army on the 28th and the following day was more marked than that of the other Armies, because the enemy retirement behind the Somme line was a wheel pivoting on Quéant at the southern end of the Drocourt–Quéant Line, opposite to which stood the XVII Corps (Third Army) and Canadian Corps (First Army), and which the Germans intended to retain.

In the Australian Corps south of the Somme the brigades in the line were to continue to advance. The night of the 27th–28th was dark, and in the morning a ground mist formed, so that the German rear guards managed to slip off unobserved. An attempt made to steal ground near the river, towards Frise, at 2.40 a.m. was frustrated by the enemy ; but otherwise patrols operating during the night could not establish contact, and a party sent out by the 2nd Australian Division to the Sugar Factory south-west of Dompierre, which returned at 3.30 a.m., reported the place

---

[1] See Sketch 15.

clear but occasional fire from positions seven hundred yards further east. All the divisions resumed the advance early, but not quite simultaneously, and they experienced a most exhausting day, as the ground over which they had to advance was a maze of old trenches and wire. Low clouds and the ground mist prevented long distance bombing.

The 96th and 14th Brigades of the 32nd Division, the right of the Australian Corps, started at 5 a.m. and advanced a mile and a half unopposed to the line from Ablaincourt (inclusive) northwards towards Déniecourt along the front of Chateau Park and Soyecourt Wood. After a pause the advance was resumed, and again without opposition ; by between 11 a.m. and 12 noon it had progressed nearly three miles to a line from Marchelepot, where the left of the French First Army had arrived, roughly north to Berny en Santerre. There touch was gained with the enemy, but only light machine-gun fire received. Shortly after 1 p.m. a message, sent out at 11 a.m., was received from divisional head-quarters, that Major-General Lambert intended to obtain observation over the Somme valley with the 96th and 14th Brigades that evening, and that the 97th would move up east of Vermandovillers in readiness to push forward during the night. The men were very tired, resistance to further advance was encountered, including both heavy artillery and machine-gun barrages, but the two brigades were able to reach and consolidate under fire a line about $3\frac{1}{2}$ miles from the Somme fixed by a 5 p.m. divisional order in modification of that issued at 11 a.m.

The Australians encountered more opposition than had the 32nd Division. Their operations began early on the 28th and ended only in the early morning of the 29th ; for in the course of the afternoon Lieut.-General Monash, in the hopes of hustling the Germans to the Somme and capturing at least the bridges, ordered aggressive patrols. In the 8th Brigade, followed by the 15th, the 30th Battalion, starting at 6 a.m., and making eastward for Brie, on the Somme, immediately got touch of the Germans, who, however, turned out to be mounted on bicycles with machine guns attached, and were able to withdraw before the Australians could close with them. The 32nd Battalion, advancing an hour later, met opposition from long-range fire of machine guns ; but, in spite of the difficulties of the broken ground, reached a line through Fay, a mile ahead, about 9 a.m. It then pressed on to a line through Loge's Copse, where it was held up for a time by heavy fire, whilst by 2.30 p.m. the 30th on the right passed through the ruins of Estrées, on the Amiens–Brie highway, more than a 2-mile advance. A pause then took place for the 31st and 29th Battalions to pass through ; the former arrived at 5.30 p.m., but the latter did not appear, so the 32nd went on once more. By 9 p.m. this battalion had captured Assevillers, taking a few prisoners ;[1] but it was midnight before the 31st got to the western outskirts of Belloy, later found unoccupied, with the enemy in Park Woods, beyond it.

The 6th Australian Brigade, making for Halle and Mont St. Quentin, north of Péronne, employed three battalions in the front line ; for its frontage, owing to the bend of the Somme, would increase as it progressed. The 24th Battalion began to advance shortly after 5 a.m., and by 10 a.m. had gained an oblique line, with its right seven hundred yards north-west of Assevillers, and its left bent back towards Becquincourt, when machine-gun fire from the former village and artillery from Herbecourt stopped any advance except by reconnoitring patrols until after dark. At 9.30 p.m., after Assevillers had been captured by the 32nd Battalion, the 24th went forward again, and by 1.50 a.m. (29th) had reached a line running north from the outskirts of the village.

The centre battalion, the 22nd, had sent forward two companies at 6.30 a.m. A few Germans in Dompierre, on the right, made a little show of resistance, but the village was mopped up, and by 11 a.m. an advance of two miles had been made, and the line was then a thousand yards from the Assevillers–Herbecourt road. The enemy's resistance now became considerable, and he made several counter-attacks ; but by 1 p.m. the line had been advanced another five hundred yards. Little change took place before 7 p.m., when brigade orders were received that Herbecourt was to be captured by the 21st Battalion on the left, and that the 22nd should occupy the line of trenches running along the road south of the village, with a view to obtaining a good jumping-off line for next day. Patrols reported that the enemy had fallen back, and by 4 a.m. (29th) the objectives had been gained.

---

[1] Of the *2nd Guard Division.*

The 21st Battalion had begun to advance at 4.30 a.m. (28th), and by 10 a.m. had covered two thousand yards, its right just west of Green Wood, its left east of Cow Wood, with the flank turned back to face Frise. Strong fire coming from this village and from trenches west of Mereaucourt Wood, at 3.25 p.m., after a quarter of an hour's field artillery bombardment, these two localities were attacked by a company of the 23rd, attached to the 21st, and by four platoons of the latter battalion. Frise offered little resistance, for, as will be seen, Australians from the north bank of the Somme had already approached it from the west ; so the enemy in the Mereaucourt trenches was quickly overcome, 50 prisoners, 15 machine guns and 3 light trench mortars being taken, and the left of the line extended to the Somme. At 9 p.m. the 23rd Battalion and the 18th Battalion (5th Australian Brigade) relieved the 21st. Patrols sent out encountered only slight machine-gun fire, and at midnight, after a short burst of artillery fire on Herbecourt, the advance was resumed without hindrance, the village occupied and the line continued east of Mereaucourt Wood, which was mopped up during the night, to Feuillières on the Somme. There also the enemy had fallen back.

North of the Somme, the 3rd Australian Division and the III Corps were to make only a short advance of about a mile to a line northward from Curlu (inclusive), by Hardecourt aux Bois and Maltz Horn Farm to Trônes Wood. Zero hour was 4.55 a.m., and the usual creeping barrage was provided at that hour. The 9th Australian Brigade, which had relieved the 11th during the night, sent the 35th Battalion forward at 5.5 a.m., and it made good progress, a heavy German bombardment of one hundred and fifty rounds a minute falling behind it. By 5.50 a.m. it had, in spite of machine-gun resistance, occupied an intermediate objective, and two hours later its patrols were on the final objective. Owing to the good observation possessed by the enemy from the heights above Cléry at the bend of the Somme, very little change of position was possible during the day ; but after the 35th Battalion had got beyond Curlu, two companies of the 38th Battalion (10th Australian Brigade) were sent through the village to fill the gap between the Somme and the right of the 9th Brigade. They found Curlu had not been cleared, but after stiff fighting overcame all resistance. Another company, about 7.30 a.m., crossed the Somme after hasty repairs to the damaged German bridges, in order to take possession of the bend of the river between Vaux and Curlu and reach the canal bank west of Frise. It was specially noted that, although the German machine-gunners fought as stoutly as ever, the men had a feeling that the enemy's power of resistance was weakening. To accelerate any tendency to retire, a number of selected areas and points and the defile of Cléry through which the withdrawal of the enemy artillery must take place were shelled during the afternoon.

The 58th Division of the III Corps put in the 174th and 173rd Brigades again. Neither had much difficulty in reaching their objectives, only Bois d'en Haut, south of Hardecourt, offering much resistance ; but during daylight even patrols could not go beyond the objective.

The 12th Division used the 36th and 35th Brigades to storm the Hardecourt aux Bois–Maltz Horn Farm ridge. A deep and fairly steep valley lay in front of it, so that the 12th Machine Gun Battalion was able to bring direct overhead fire to bear for a considerable time whilst the battalions were advancing, a material aid to their progress. Keeping close up to the artillery barrage, the 9/Royal Fusiliers (36th Brigade)[1] and 1/1st Cambridgeshire and 9/Essex (35th Brigade) pushed on, capturing prisoners and machine guns, and bayoneting the detachments at their posts. Considerable fighting took place in Hardecourt, so that it was not until 11 a.m. that the Fusiliers could report they were on the objective ; the Cambridgeshire and Essex had gained theirs by 8.30 a.m. During the afternoon the Germans shelled the Hardecourt ridge and the valley west of it heavily and machine-gunned the forward slopes, making further movement impossible ;[2] but by 8 p.m. this fire had died down.

On the left flank, the 18th Division did no more than establish touch with the 12th near Maltz Horn Farm. The III Corps had achieved what had been ordered and no

[1] This battalion had 350 recruits of the age 18½ to 19½ in its ranks, who had been in France only a week.

[2] Lieut.-Colonel E. T. Saint, of the 1/1st Cambridgeshire, was mortally wounded.

more. On the whole front of the Fourth Army evident signs
of retreat had been found,. material abandoned, including
field guns, and a few cross roads blown up. Besides prisoners,
a complete map of the German water supply on its front
had been picked up, which was of great value, as the watering
of horses was a difficult problem, some of them having to
be sent back several miles to reach water. In a memorandum
issued on the 28th, General Rawlinson drew attention to
the skilful use of single guns and sections by the enemy,
already mentioned, which could be countered by similar
action. He added that the period of open warfare had
arrived, when the fire both of heavy and field guns would
have largely to be controlled by direct observation and
employed on the initiative of subordinate commanders.
During the morning the Fourth Army was informed by
G.H.Q. that the 74th (Yeomanry) Division, brought from
Egypt, was being entrained from the Fifth Army area, and
should be stationed in the III Corps area as G.H.Q. reserve.
It arrived next day.

THIRD ARMY [1]

At 1 p.m. on the 27th, General Byng issued orders for the
continuance of the attack on the 28th in the same direction,
eastward, but south-eastward for the XVII Corps as on the
27th : the V and IV Corps were to be prepared for the
possibility of the enemy attempting to evacuate Bapaume
during the night. Later the commanders of the V, IV and
VI Corps were told of the rumours of a German retirement
mentioned by prisoners, and directed to see that steps were
taken to ensure that the enemy did not withdraw unmolested,
but that if on the 28th he was found to be still holding his
position in strength, the day, pending the result of the
turning movement by the XVII and Canadian Corps, was
to be devoted to rest and to bombardment of points of
resistance and lines of approach.

Thus, for the greater part of the Third Army, the 28th
August was a day of comparative quiet, and only small
advances were made : the 38th Division (V Corps) found
Longueval evacuated after it had been bombarded, and

---

[1] See Sketch 16.

occupied its eastern edge. Banks Trench (running south-eastwards from St. Leger Wood) was also found to be evacuated, and about midday it was occupied by the extreme left of the 62nd Division and by the Guards Division which later pushed on nearly half a mile.

The XVII Corps took Croisilles and advanced about two thousand yards. Lieut.-General Fergusson's orders were for the 56th Division to move south-eastwards towards the Bullecourt area, and the 57th towards Riencourt and Hende-court, and for all 8-inch howitzer, 6-inch howitzer and 60-pdr. batteries to be brought up to positions from which they could bombard the Drocourt–Quéant Line and to be ready to open fire at 3.30 a.m. on the 30th.

After consultation between the divisional and brigade staffs, zero hour was made 12.30 p.m., half an hour after the German midday meal time. The battalions were by now very weak, and some reliefs were carried out.[1] In the 56th Division the 167th Brigade, in relief of the 168th opposite Croisilles, was to push through the village if it was evacuated and occupy the ridge south-east of it. Patrols during the night found that it was still held ; but at 8 a.m. they reported that it appeared to be abandoned. The 1/8th Middlesex was sent forward and met with strong opposition on the eastern edge ; but this was overcome in the course of the afternoon, and a trench on the objective ridge occupied.

The advance south-eastwards on Bullecourt was entrusted to the 169th Brigade, with the 168th in support and for the protection of the left flank. The movement was covered by a creeping barrage fired by four brigades of artillery,[2] and led by the 1/16th London (Queen's Westminster Rifles). This battalion immediately came under machine-gun fire, and found deep uncut wire in front of it, as the spaces between the trenches of the Hindenburg Position were wired by longitudinal belts. Swerving away to the left, the battalion lost direction and arrived in front of Hendecourt in the 57th Division area, instead of Bullecourt. Despite heavy casualties, three companies established themselves in the village, where a few parties from the 57th Division joined them. Although without support on either flank and

---

[1] The weakest seems to have been the 1/2nd London, which mustered 11 officers and 193 other ranks, of whom 35 belonged to battalion head-quarters.

[2] The 56th and 57th Division artillery (280th, 281st, 285th and 286th Brigades R.F.A.).

shot at from three sides, they hung on until 5.30 p.m., when, much reduced in numbers, they fell back to a trench five hundred yards north-west of Hendecourt, where they found a line organized and held by troops of the 57th Division. The 1/2nd and 1/5th London, which were in support of the 1/16th, had divided. The two left companies of both battalions followed the Queen's Westminster towards Hendecourt, and eventually joined them in their final position north-west of the village. The right companies moved correctly on Bullecourt and met with much opposition, Germans emerging from dug-outs after the barrage had passed over them. In the labyrinth of trenches and wired areas progress was slow ; the 1/4th London and two companies of the 1/13th London (Kensington) of the 168th Brigade, with light trench mortars, were sent up to reinforce ; but not until 7.30 p.m. was a line of trenches twelve hundred yards short of Bullecourt taken and consolidated by the troops of the two brigades, and touch obtained on the right with the 167th Brigade in front of Croisilles, and on the left with the 57th Division. The 56th Division thus ended the day with the greater part of its troops facing Bullecourt, but with the equivalent of two battalions on the 57th Division front facing Hendecourt.

The 172nd Brigade (Br.-General G. C. B. Paynter), which led the advance of the 57th Division (Major-General R. W. R. Barnes), was given as first objective a trench about five or six hundred yards short of the Bullecourt–Hendecourt road, mentioned above as the one to which part of the 56th Division retired. It advanced under a barrage fired by six brigades of field artillery, whilst two brigades of heavy artillery shelled the objective.[1] This was taken after considerable opposition by the 1/9th King's and 2/4th South Lancashire ; parties of both battalions then penetrated into Hendecourt, where they found the troops of the 56th Division which had gone astray, and later withdrew with them to the first objective, which became the limit of the day's advance. The XVII Corps was thus left astride the Hindenburg Position, with a gap in its front, the bulk of the 56th Division facing Bullecourt, and the 57th, with some of the 56th Division opposite Hendecourt.

---

[1] The 40th and 52nd Division artillery, V and 432nd (Army) Brigades R.F.A., with VIII and LXXXVIII Brigades R.G.A..

FIRST ARMY [1]

The First Army's orders to the Canadian Corps for the 28th were curiously worded : it was to continue the advance on Cagnicourt–Dury–Etaing and be prepared to attack the Drocourt–Quéant Line on the 30th, although the places above named were beyond it. Lieut.-General Currie gave the 2nd and 3rd Canadian Divisions as first objective a line of trenches about twelve hundred yards to the front, and about two miles short of the Drocourt–Quéant Line, the Army objective being given as the second. The 51st Division was to conform, with Plouvain–Greenland Hill as objective. No tanks were available. Zero hour was the same as in the XVII Corps, 12.30 p.m., and the artillery fire was similar.

The 5th and 4th Canadian Brigades which led the advance of the 2nd Canadian Division went well at first, but, after about a thousand yards or more had been covered, were checked by uncut wire and fire from the strongly held trenches which had been indicated as the first objective ; only a short length of them was taken by the right of the 5th Brigade. A line was eventually established in shell-holes about four or five hundred yards short of the German position. During the ensuing night, the 1st Canadian Division, under the difficulties of darkness and uncertainty as to the exact position, relieved the 2nd.

The 3rd Canadian Division (Major-General L. J. Lipsett) had greater success, and broke the German line. Its front had on the evening of the 27th been divided between its three brigades, 8th, 9th and 7th. They were given different zero hours, so that the whole of the field artillery (five brigades) should be available for the attack of the 9th Canadian Brigade, which was in the centre on the line between the Cojeul and the Bois du Sart. The 7th Canadian Brigade led off at 5 a.m., when it took Pelves. The 9th (with one battalion of the 8th attached) attacked at 11 a.m., when the 4th Canadian Mounted Rifles and the 52nd Battalion took the first objective and advanced beyond it to the western edge of Boiry Notre Dame and the road running south from it. The 58th Battalion then passed through and cleared up the village, and with the 42nd and P.P.C.L.I. of

---

[1] See Sketch 16.

the 7th Brigade by 3 p.m. had captured the high ground north of it, and Jigsaw Wood, and joined up with the 49th in Pelves.

The 8th Canadian Brigade on the right advanced at 12.30 p.m., the corps zero hour. The 43rd Battalion and 5th Mounted Rifles had previously been somewhat heavily shelled owing, no doubt, to the earlier movement of the 9th Canadian Brigade, and they, like the 56th and 57th Divisions, met with considerable opposition ; but they succeeded in rushing the enemy's front line and reaching the western part of Remy and the wood north of it. At night the 3rd Canadian Division was relieved by the 4th (British) Division with Brutinel's machine gun and cyclist force attached.

The 51st Division, on the left of the Canadians, did not attack on the 28th, but made preparations to capture Greenland Hill next day. Farther north, the 8th Division had patrol fighting and lost a little ground in and south of Oppy.

The 29th August brought almost a repetition of the operations of the previous day. During the night of the 28th–29th the Germans south of the Somme[1] fell back an average of four miles to the farther bank of the river ; north of the Somme they also retired, but a shorter distance, two thousand to four thousand five hundred yards, abandoning Bapaume, to a strong line Péronne–Morval–Le Transloy–Frémicourt (east of Bapaume). The Fourth Army and the right wing of the Third were therefore able to make considerable advances without much opposition. North of Bapaume, however, the enemy still held his line, and less progress was made. The weather improved, so that the headquarters IX Brigade day-bombing squadrons, heavily escorted, were able to drop bombs on Cambrai and Valenciennes station, but failed to reach Somain junction (14 miles north of Cambrai).

---

[1] See Sketches 11, 15 and 16.

FOURTH ARMY

On the right of the Fourth Army,[1] by the orders of the 32nd Division, the 96th and 14th Brigades were on the 29th to continue the advance and gain observation of the crossings over the Somme, for which purpose the high ground east of Misery was mentioned as being of importance : if patrols were found in any strength, the main bodies were not to be committed to an attack, but small rear guards and machine-gun posts were to be dealt with as during the past two days : the advance was to begin at 7 a.m. or earlier, at the discretion of the brigade commanders.

Towards dawn on the 29th patrols reported that the enemy seemed to have retired, and those sent out at dawn were unable to gain touch with him. The leading battalions of the 96th Brigade started at 6.15 a.m., those of the 14th at 7 a.m., and they were able to push patrols right up to the Somme. On the western bank only a few mounted men with a field gun were seen galloping down a street in Cizancourt. All bridges were reported to be destroyed, and at 4 p.m. Major-General Lambert ordered preparations to be made for crossing the river next day. His orders were later cancelled, as the corps commander, Lieut.-General Monash, had a plan for driving the enemy from his river line other than by frontal attack, as will be narrated later. The consolidation of the line gained by the 32nd Division was therefore taken in hand.

The Australian divisions started earlier than the 32nd, the 5th at 5.20 a.m. and the 2nd at 5 a.m. The 8th Australian Brigade, still leading the advance of the 5th Australian Division, by 6.30 a.m. reached the site of Villers Carbonnel without opposition. Prisoners taken there stated that a retirement was being made to the eastern bank of the Somme, but that resistance would be met at Eterpigny, held as a bridgehead on the western bank. This proved more or less to be the case. On the left, after Barleux, a mile and a half from the river, had been reached, heavy machine-gun fire was received from Eterpigny and the ground north-west of it, so that on the left flank the advance had to be carried on by dribbling the men forward by twos and threes. The enemy was, however, driven from his bridgehead, and blew up the main bridge, but whilst in the act of crossing the bridge

---
[1] See Sketch 15.

over the canalized river half a mile north of Eterpigny, was caught by machine and Lewis gun fire. A company of the 29th Battalion crossed by the same bridge, but could not make its way over the marshes and watercourses beyond, as the footbridges had been destroyed and short-range fire was opened on it. Elsewhere, owing to fire from the eastern bank, it was not possible to do more than establish posts along the river bank, and these suffered from continuous machine-gun fire and sniping for the remainder of the day, though artillery fire decreased. Nevertheless Br.-General Elliott (15th Australian Brigade), after a personal reconnaissance, made preparations to force a passage at Brie.

The 6th and 5th Brigades led the advance of the 2nd Australian Division. At 7.30 a.m., after Flaucourt had been reached and a position had been occupied half a mile beyond it, the 7th Brigade passed through the 6th, with Doingt (east of Péronne) and the trenches south-east of Péronne as its objective. The left was temporarily checked by machine-gun fire ; but the enemy detachments, on being outflanked, with others nearer the river, retired at speed across the Somme canal, which here is some way from the river, the bridge at Feuillères that they used being blown up after they had crossed. Biaches was captured by 9.30 a.m., in spite of fire from Mont St. Quentin (north of Péronne) and villages on the far side of the Somme, which barraged the slopes down to the river directly the Australians appeared. Only the railway bridge north of la Chapellette was found undestroyed, but fire was turned on it for two and a half hours by the German artillery and four separate explosions were heard. As had been the case farther south, posts were established along the western bank of the canal, the gap between the 7th and 5th Brigades being filled by the 6th.

The 5th Australian Brigade had the trenches immediately east and south-east of Mont St. Quentin as its objective, the dry Canal du Nord, west of Péronne, and the causeway at Cléry being suggested as points of crossing the Somme. Three companies of the 18th Battalion managed to pass the canal near a lock at the southern end of Cléry, the enemy having failed to destroy a light bridge on floats ; but machine guns raked the area beyond enclosed by the course of the Somme and further progress could not be made here. Elsewhere no point of passage could be found, as the only other intact bridge, near the entry of the Canal du Nord, led to a narrow causeway over a quarter-mile wide marsh. At 2.30 p.m., therefore, it was decided that until dark and pending the capture of Cléry by the 3rd Australian Division north of the Somme, no attempts at crossing should be made ; for, in view of the situation, Lieut.-General Monash had changed his plan.

North of the Somme the 10th and 9th Brigades of the 3rd Australian Division sent out patrols early, and it soon became manifest that the enemy had made at any rate a slight retirement. By midday patrols of the 38th Battalion (10th Australian Brigade), working over the ends of the spurs which descend to the Somme, had reached and passed Hem, whilst as early as 7 a.m. the 34th Battalion (9th Brigade) had formed a line through Summit Copse, where a left defensive flank was formed, as the 58th Division was not yet up. The infantry was by now weak in strength and very tired after its continuous operations ; but Major-General Gellibrand, learning from an air report that the divisions south of the Somme were $2\frac{1}{2}$ miles ahead, directed his brigadiers to push on. About midday Br.-General McNicoll (10th Australian Brigade) gave orders for the 38th Battalion, guarded on the left by the 40th, to attack with the object of gaining, first, a line of trenches about a quarter of a mile east of Howitzer Wood, and, secondly, the long high spur north of Cléry. " A " Squadron of the 13th Australian Light Horse was sent forward to try and seize Hill 110, a knoll on this spur ; but directly its patrols moved forward the enemy's artillery and machine-gun fire opened, and it was left to the 9th Brigade to capture the hill. Meantime, the troops of the 10th Australian Brigade had reached their original objective, but could make no further progress until 5 p.m., when, after half an hour's artillery fire, they advanced against Cléry and captured it, so that, by 10 p.m., their line ran from the centre of the village north-west to the 9th Australian Brigade. The 34th Battalion of this brigade had not gone forward until 4 p.m. After establishing touch with the 10th Australian Brigade at Howitzer Wood, it had reached Hill 110 at 5.40 p.m., where it captured 75 Germans, after killing thirty or forty, with the loss of seven of all ranks wounded. As the 58th Division was still in rear, a long defensive flank was again formed.

Lieut.-General Godley's orders to the III Corps for the 29th had been for—

the 58th and 12th Divisions to gain ground by means of patrols wherever possible, but not to attack ;

the 18th to swing forward its left to keep touch with the right of the Third Army ;

the 47th was to take over from the 12th, in preparation for an attack next day.

In consequence of their patrols reporting the unusual quietness of the enemy and of the statements of prisoners that a withdrawal was intended, the right and centre divisions took other measures, and co-operation was lacking.

The 58th Division sent forward an advanced guard of the 175th Brigade (Br.-General H. W. Cobham), to which the 1/4th Suffolk (Pioneers) was attached, to support the patrols and establish a line about twelve hundred yards ahead, with a view to keeping touch of the enemy without fighting ; at 1.20 p.m., by direction of the division, the advanced guard was ordered forward another mile to Maurepas and to the trenches along the road southward from this village towards Cléry ; touch to be assured with the 3rd Australian Division at Junction Wood. This line was to be occupied by 9 p.m., and field artillery moved over the open in broad daylight in readiness to support the operation. As it turned out, the line named, when it was reached, was well behind the general front formed by the divisions on either side of the 58th.

The 12th Division similarly sent forward an advanced guard of the 37th Brigade and attached troops of all arms, which included the corps cavalry and a company of cyclists. It indicated three lines to be made good in succession. Between 12.30 and 1 p.m. patrols reached Maurepas in the first objective, from which a few machine guns still in action hastily withdrew ; the 6/Buffs and 6/Queen's passed through the patrols soon after, the former capturing 2 officers and sixty other ranks in the village. By 5 p.m. it became clear that the Germans were on the line le Forest–Savernake Wood, the second objective ; the 6/R. West Kent came up on the left and by 8.15 p.m. this line was secured. Large dumps of 5·9-inch shell were discovered, and parties searching the wood had to wear gas masks, as the enemy had exploded a dump of gas shell in it. The last two hundred yards of the advance had been in the face of short-range artillery fire, and further progress was judged too difficult to attempt. The 58th Division was not up on the right, but patrols discovered that the Australians were on Hill 110.

In the 18th Division, the 54th Brigade with attached troops had taken over the front of the division during the night. At 3.30 a.m. Br.-General Tyler was informed by the division that the 38th Division (Third Army) was attacking at 5.15 a.m., and that he was to take every opportunity to push forward. Strong patrols sent out at 5.15 a.m. encountered no opposition, and by 7 a.m. they were east of the ruins of Guillemont. At 9 a.m. Major-General Lee gave instructions for a general advance to the Rancourt–Bapaume road in three bounds, the divisional artillery sending up batteries in close support. By 10 a.m., after slight opposition, the 54th Brigade line ran from Falfemont Farm northwards. In the further advance it was found these troops could not remain in Combles ; lying in low ground, the village was not only being shelled but also under machine-gun fire from the north, where the Germans still held Morval, and from the high ground to the south ; but by 5 p.m. a line was established on either side of Combles. As the Germans appeared to intend to make a stand in front of Rancourt, further operations were suspended.

THIRD ARMY[1]

The Third Army orders for the 29th were issued as early as 1.18 p.m. on the previous day.

The V and IV Corps and the right wing of the VI were to take advantage of any weakening of the enemy's front to push their advanced guards eastward towards the objective given in the orders of the 26th, that is the north–south line east of Bapaume marked by Le Transloy–Vaulx Vraucourt ;

the left wing of the VI Corps was to keep pace with the turning movement of the XVII Corps ;

the XVII Corps was still directed south-eastward on Quéant.

In consequence of the German retirement, the V and IV Corps were able to advance two to four thousand yards without much opposition.

---

[1] See Sketch 16.

Of the divisions of the V Corps, whose zero hour was 5.30 a.m., the barrage commencing at 5.15 a.m., the 38th Division had the special objective of the high ground east of Ginchy, turning Longueval (not captured when the orders were issued) and Delville Wood by the south. Its 113th Brigade met with scarcely any opposition and reached the objective by 9 a.m. ; the 115th Brigade, starting a quarter of an hour later, passed north of Delville Wood, which was left to the 114th Brigade to mop up, and was as successful as the 113th. When, however, in the evening at 6 p.m. the 113th with the 115th on its left advanced again to attack Morval, the position was found strongly held, and it halted in touch with the left of the Fourth Army, a little short of the village on the road between Combles and Lesboeufs, the latter village being taken by the 115th.

The 51st Brigade of the 17th Division, starting at 6.15 a.m., occupied Flers and Gueudecourt with very little opposition, and continued on to a ridge about fifteen hundred yards beyond the latter village ; two companies of the 7/Border Regiment actually went nearly another mile to the outskirts of Le Transloy in the new German line ; but, being unsupported on either flank, they were withdrawn after dark to the general line of the corps.

On receiving news of the unopposed advance of the 38th Division at 9.20 a.m., the 21st Division gave orders for the 110th Brigade (Br.-General H. R. Cumming) to push forward. Two hours later it advanced, encountering very little opposition until it had covered about three thousand yards ; then it was stopped by frontal machine-gun fire from Beaulencourt. The V Corps, therefore, had reached a north-south line through and including Lesboeufs.

The enemy in the early morning of the 29th evacuated Ligny Thilloy, Thilloy and Bapaume, before which his superior numbers had delayed the IV Corps for four days. The 126th and 127th Brigades (Br.-Generals G. H. Wedgwood and Hon. A. M. Henley) of the 42nd Division, passing through the 63rd division, went forward about 9 a.m. and advanced a thousand yards beyond Thilloy with no opposition except from shelling. From this line, by order of the division, the 126th Brigade went on alone, and, in spite of fire, by evening had reached, and on the left crossed, the Beaulencourt–Bapaume road ; but an attempt at 7.30 p.m. of the right failed to capture Riencourt, in the new German position, the approaches to which were very exposed.

The New Zealand Division about 8.30 a.m. advanced through Bapaume, then met with varying resistance, but by the afternoon was level with the 21st Division.

The 5th Division sent out patrols ; but as these could make no progress on account of machine-gun fire, a regular attack under a barrage was arranged for 5.30 p.m., in conjunction with the 186th Brigade of the 62nd Division, on the left, which seized a trench to protect that flank. After considerable resistance, a good position six hundred yards from the starting line was reached.[1]

Thus the IV Corps was established in line close to the new German position, with its right nearly a mile ahead of the left of the V Corps.

In the VI Corps, besides co-operating in the attack by the 5th Division, the 62nd Division, in order to obtain a

---

[1] The trench attack of the 186th Brigade was made by the 5/Duke of Wellington's, and is a good example of such an operation. The objective was a stretch of 1,300 yards of the old British line of 1917, consisting of front and support trenches about 250 yards apart, which ran roughly west and east at right angles to the line held by the battalion, so that the attack had to be made along them ; they were roughly parallel to each other, but converged and joined at the eastern end of the objective. A smoke barrage was put down on the northern (left) side of the north trench to screen the operation from observation. A creeping barrage, extending to 300 yards on each side of the trenches, advanced at the rate of 100 yards in 4 minutes. One company was employed, with another in close support and under the orders of the commander of the attacking company. The leaders were two bombing parties of 9 men each, one to work down each trench. Keeping pace with the bombers, a Lewis gun with 4 men worked along each side of each trench over the open to deal with enemy getting out of the trench, and to keep heads low. About 150 yards in rear the remainder of the leading company followed, working as two platoons, one down each trench and dropping section posts on the way as flank guards. The support company provided 4 Lewis-gun teams moving across the open 100 yards in rear of the leading company, and about 50 yards north and south of each trench. The remainder of the support company followed with one platoon moving down each trench. The enemy at first put up a stiff fight in the trenches, but the cross-fire from Lewis guns disorganized his bombers and enabled the attackers to use the bayonet, with which they proved superior. Enemy posts dotted about between the trenches were dealt with by the support company. By 6.30 p.m. the whole objective had been taken. Casualties were slight. Of the enemy, 35 were killed and 93 taken prisoner. One trench mortar and 15 machine guns were captured.

better jumping-off line for an attack against Vaulx Vraucourt, made some small attacks about 2 p.m., by which the
left of the 186th and the 185th Brigades advanced their line.

The operations of the 3rd Division (Major-General C. J.
Deverell), which had relieved the Guards Division, were
confined to patrol action, and without meeting much
opposition the 76th Brigade (Br.-General C. L. Porter)
succeeded in advancing its line an average of two thousand
yards to within about six hundred yards of the enemy's
new position.

The XVII Corps was ahead of its neighbours on either
flank. It had originally been intended that the 56th Division
should continue its attack against Bullecourt in the early
morning of the 29th. The troops of the three brigades at the
close of the 28th had, however, become so mixed together,
even with those of the 57th Division, and so divided, that it
would have been impossible to reorganize them and get them
into their jumping-off positions in the dark. Zero hour was
therefore put at 1 p.m., and even then the 169th Brigade
was still short of half its available strength. It was found
that the enemy had evacuated the ground west of Bullecourt,
so, thanks to the network of trenches in it, units of the
168th and 169th Brigades were able to take position during
the morning in a line within three hundred yards of the
village.

Under a barrage fired by the same artillery as on the 28th,
the London Scottish (168th Brigade) took the ruins of
Bullecourt against considerable opposition, and occupied
trenches on its southern and eastern sides, and the Kensington, though foiled by a redoubt at the station south of the
village, reached the Ecoust St. Mein road. The 169th
Brigade could collect only 325 men in time to make the
attack; but, it duly supported the left of the London
Scottish. At night the 167th Brigade relieved both the
brigades in the line.

In the 57th Division doubt existed as to the exact position
of the front line of the 172nd Brigade, through which the
170th was to pass in order to attack Riencourt and Hendecourt. It was therefore decided that the barrage should drop

a thousand yards ahead of the jumping-off line of the 170th Brigade and remain on the opening line for 45 minutes in order to give time for the infantry to come up to it. But it turned out that no men whatever of the 172nd were in front of the main line, and the 2/5th King's Own and the 2/4th L. North Lancashire, advancing over flat, open ground, met with strong opposition directly they started. Yet both battalions took their objectives, although they could not retain them. The King's Own entered Riencourt about 3 p.m., and for five hours held out, a thousand yards ahead of all other troops, and only withdrew when nearly surrounded. The L. North Lancashire captured Hendecourt, but in the early hours of the 30th were withdrawn to its western edge.

First Army

In the right wing of the First Army, the 29th August was chiefly a day of preparation for the attack on the Drocourt–Quéant Line. The cutting of lanes in its wire by all available 6-inch howitzers was begun.

In the Canadian Corps, Lieut.-General Currie ordered :
> the 1st Canadian (Major-General A. C. Macdonnell) and the British 4th Division (Major-General T. G. Matheson), to undertake such minor operations as might be required to secure the best jumping-off position ;
> the 51st Division to operate with a view to gaining Greenland Hill and the spur south-east of Plouvain.

The 1st Canadian Division made no advance. In the 4th Division, the 10th and 11th Brigades (Br.-Generals J. Greene and T. S. H. Wade), supported by the fire of nine field artillery brigades,[1] crossed the Sensée at 10 a.m. with very little opposition, and took Remy and Haucourt. Brutinel's Detachment also advanced a little.

The 154th Brigade of the 51st Division, under a barrage fired by its own artillery and that of the 16th Division, starting at 6.30 a.m., captured Greenland Hill by 8 a.m., and by evening the 152nd had come up on its right, and was within a quarter of a mile of Plouvain.

---

[1] 4th, 3rd Canadian and 5th Canadian Division, and the VIII, LII and 126th (Army) Brigades R.F.A.

At 12 noon on the 29th the Staff of the XXII Corps (Lieut.-General Sir W. P. Braithwaite)[1] returned to the line and took over from the Canadian Corps the front held by the 51st Division between the Scarpe and Gavrelle (exclusive), and during the following night the 11th Division (placed under the XXII Corps), relieved Brutinel's Detachment (attached to the 4th Division) of its sector immediately south of the Scarpe as far as Boiry Notre Dame, so that the XXII Corps front extended from this latter village to Gavrelle (exclusive).

The stage was now set for driving the enemy from the Somme line and breaking the Drocourt–Quéant Line.

It has often been asked why Ludendorff called the 8th August "the black day of the German Army". The defeat was not decisive. It would have been truer if he had said that "August was the black month of the German nation". It was the decline in morale of the army and the nation rather than in the fighting powers of the troops after the change of fortune which occurred in August, which was decisive. After the victory of Caporetto and the dictated treaties of Brest Litovsk (3 March 1918) and Bukarest (7 May 1918), the whole German nation was certain of victory. Its deception in August was all the greater because of the simulacra of victories presented by the creation of great salients in March, April and May and the arrival in Germany of tens of thousands of prisoners ; by the close approach to Amiens and Hazebrouck ; and by the spectacular collapse of the French at the Chemin des Dames. The Battles of the Matz and the Battle for Reims brought the first doubts. It was, it has been said, not the mere bad news of retirements in August, but, as regards the Army, the huge gaps in the ranks from casualties and desertions and, as regards the rear services and the public, the sight of innumerable trains of dead and dying, evacuated during August from the hospitals of Northern France, Belgium and Alsace-Lorraine which struck terror in all hearts. " For fifteen " days the public saw the stations blocked and the lines " encumbered with endless hospital trains and cattle trucks

---

[1] He took over on 28th August vice Sir A. Godley, who was commanding the III Corps, and was succeeded in the 62nd Division by Major-General Sir R. D. Whigham, lately Deputy Chief of the Imperial General Staff, this post being filled by Major-General Sir C. Harington.

" packed with wounded. . . . The Kaiser, the Ministers,
" the political parties, the newspapers, the people, the
" military chiefs, abandoned themselves to destiny, van-
" quished in advance in their hearts "

NOTE I

THE FRENCH 27TH–29TH AUGUST

(From F.O.A. vii (i))

(Sketch 12)

The experience of the French First Army in this period was
much the same as that of the British Fourth Army. The French
Third Army joined in the advance on the 28th ; the Tenth,
although outflanking the German line opposing the First and
Third, hardly moved.

" On the 27th, in liaison with the right of the British Fourth
" Army, the French First Army widened its front of attack ; the
" XXXV Corps took Crapeaumesnil (4 miles south of Roye) ;
" the X Corps, Laucourt (3 miles S.S.W. of Roye) ; and the
" XXXVI Corps, the Roye–Chaulnes railway ". At 9.30 a.m.
General Debeney (French First Army) telephoned orders for an
active pursuit of the retreating enemy ; and at 10 a.m. the XXXI
Corps took Roye. At 11 a.m. General Fayolle (G.A.R.) directed
the Third and First Armies to follow up the enemy " without
giving him breathing space, but not to play his game, that is to
" say, avoid useless losses ". For this purpose, the advanced
guards were to be supported by the maximum amount of field
artillery, whilst, at the same time, heavy artillery should carry
out long-distance shelling : strongpoints were not to be attacked
frontally but outflanked ; rapid progress was to be made wherever
opposition weakened. The First Army " keeping contact with
" the right of the British Army, would advance its right and
" centre in the general direction of Ham ". The Third Army was
" to manoeuvre by its left in the general direction of Guiscard
" (6 miles N.N.E. of Noyon), with the object of turning by the
" north the hilly country bordering the left bank of the river
" Divette [which flows eastward into the Oise below Noyon] ".

The Germans fell back rapidly. At midday General Debeney
ordered his corps commanders to push on their cavalry to keep
close touch. He gave new objectives to be reached that very
evening, which ran north and south through Nesle. By evening,
however, the First Army had been checked considerably short of
this line.

The Third Army made preparations to carry out the orders given during the morning of the 27th by General Fayolle for the XV Corps to move along the Oise Valley to try and take Noyon. But it did not try to advance.

The Tenth Army only made a very slight advance in the centre.

On the 28th the First Army made an advance of five miles, took Chaulnes and pushed on to Nesle. By the end of the day the outpost line ran roughly north and south on the east of that town, and joined the British at Marchelepot. General Debeney made preparations to force the passage of the Canal du Nord (roughly Noyon to Nesle) without delay and before strong forces could oppose him—" if the enemy holds on to the Canal du Nord, the " passage will be forced with the aid of artillery. The main " objective will be the Languevoisin–Voyennes ridge [the former " place is 1½ miles south-east of Nesle, and from it the ridge runs " eastward to the Somme ; thus, it is astride the canal], which " the XXXI Corps will attack from the west, and the XXXVI " from the north ". If no resistance was encountered on the canal, the XXXI Corps was to push across it, and the XXXVI Corps to take the Languevoisin–Voyennes ridge.[1]

The Third Army also made a big advance, and the XV and XXXIV Corps encircled Noyon on south and north-west. General Humbert gave orders for the attack to be resumed at 5 a.m. on the 29th, after a short artillery bombardment. The XV Corps was to outflank Noyon in conjunction with the 38th Division, the left of the Tenth Army, and not make a frontal attack ; the XXXIV Corps was to push on as fast as possible to Guiscard, as this would put the Germans in a nasty position if they delayed in Noyon.

On the 29th the enemy opposite the First Army took position on the line of the Somme and of the Canal du Nord, and the Army closed up to this water-line without crossing it.

The Third Army had hard fighting and did not make much progress, but Noyon was taken.

The I, XXX and VII Corps of the Tenth Army attacked at 5.15 a.m., as ordered. The Germans had brought up reinforcements, and the fire of machine and anti-tank guns caused serious losses, but by evening a little progress had been made. The left of the Army helped the Third Army near Noyon.

The French regard " The Third Battle of Picardy ", begun on the 8th August, as coming to an end on the 29th. According to

---

[1] F.O.A. says that the operations on the Canal du Nord were hampered and delayed by the First Army having at this juncture to return to the British four siege batteries which had been left provisionally in the former Canadian Corps zone.

F.O.A. vii. (i.), pp. 256–7, the losses of the First, Third and Tenth Armies had been :

	Officers	Other Ranks
Killed	423	9,110
Wounded	1,640	66,795
Missing	59	7,369

and these Armies had captured 633 officers, 30,820 other ranks and 890 guns. The total loss in the period of all the French Armies had been 2,390 officers and 97,306 other ranks killed, wounded. and missing.

NOTE II

THE GERMANS 27TH–29TH AUGUST

The histories of the German divisions and units opposing the Fourth Army contain a repetition of fights and withdrawals. Extracts from a few are given here as indicating the resolution of the subordinate leaders in spite of the state of confusion existing.

By the early morning of the 27th August the *I and Fusilier (III)* Battalions of the *Kaiser Francis Guard Grenadier Regiment No. 2 (2nd Guard Division)*, opposite the left of the British Fourth Army, were at Falfemont Farm (about half-way between Maurepas and Guillemont).[1] The *II Battalion* had been placed at the disposal of the *49th Brigade (25th Division)* for garrisoning the new main line of resistance, which ran Longueval–Bernafay Wood–Maricourt.

" Shortly after the battalions had reached the farm there
" was a new and strong hostile attack. Groups of the most
" diverse detachments of troops in thick masses streamed
" leaderless to the rear past the regiment's assembly position.
" It was thought that the British must already be east of
" Trônes Wood and in Ginchy. To restore the situation, the
" regimental commander, after consultation with the officer
" commanding the *115th Regiment (25th Division)*, decided to
" push forward with his *I Battalion* against the wood, and
" with the *Fusilier Battalion* against Guillemont. As some
" brave men of the *18th Regiment (41st Division)* were
" still hanging on to the edge of Trônes Wood, we soon
" succeeded in getting a firm grip of it. But there was
" violent fighting, in which *No. 10 Company* attacked from
" Guillemont, which had been quickly captured, before the
" enemy was completely driven out.[2] Only weak parties

---

[1] See Sketch 15.
[2] The British were not in possession of Guillemont

" reached Bernafay Wood and were unable to stay there.
" By about 8.30 a.m. the *Fusilier Battalion* (less *No. 10*
" *Company*) and portions of *345th Regiment* (*87th Division*)
" held the north-west edge of Guillemont, but without proper
" contact northwards ; the *I Battalion* was at the west edge
" of Trônes Wood; and between them *No. 10 Company*.
" Parts of the *25th Division* held Knackers Yard Hill ;[1] the
" *II Battalion* had found itself compelled, after violent
" fighting, to fall back to Favière Wood, as the front line on
" either flank had been lost and our own artillery was
" directing annihilating fire on to it. . . . North of Guillemont
" it was ascertained during the afternoon that the enemy
" was making fresh preparations for attack.   There were
" violent outbursts of fire against the *I Battalion's* position.
" About 6 p.m. a heavy bombardment began and lasted for
" 45 minutes.   The assault from west and north followed.
" Nos. *3, 1* and *2 Companies* held the west edge of Trônes
" Wood, but *No. 4 Company*, on the extreme right flank, was
" outflanked and, in spite of the most determined resistance,
" overcome.   *Nos. 2* and *1 Companies* were now attacked in
" rear.   After strenuous hand-to-hand fighting in which there
" were many casualties, Trônes Wood had to be evacuated.
" Only *No. 3 Company*, from the south corner, was able to
" fall back in an orderly manner to the northern part of
" Knackers Yard Hill.   From the remainder of the battalion
" about forty men rallied at the battle headquarters south-
" east of Trônes Wood and formed a strongpoint. . . ."
    " On the morning of the 27th the *122nd Fusilier Regiment*
" (*243rd Division*) was on a front of three kilometres on either
" side of the Amiens–Brie road [the boundary between the
" British 32nd and 5th Australian Divisions] west of Foucau-
" court.   As on previous days, the enemy worked forward
" energetically towards the weakly-held line.   The countless
" communication trenches and shell-holes gave him good
" cover for this purpose. His artillery fire increased, and
" was particularly heavy on Foucaucourt ".   About 4 p.m.
there was an attack which was repulsed, and another shortly
afterwards, also repulsed.   The third attack was successful, only
fifteen men from one company getting away.
    " Slowly, step by step, the regiment fell back towards the
" second main line of resistance about five hundred metres
" east of Foucaucourt, and by dusk it was established
" there. . . . The small remnant of the regiment left after
" the hard fight of the previous week was played out. . . .
" Other troops were in the same condition.   The higher
" command therefore planned to interpose during the night

---

[1] A hill eight hundred yards north of Hardecourt aux Bois.

" of the 27th–28th a considerable distance between us and
" the enemy in order to gain time to prepare an energetic
" defence. The new defence line ran about six kilometres
" east of the former position of the line Villers Carbonnel–
" Barleux–Flaucourt. The regiment fell back to this position
" on a wide front about 10 p.m."; and then went into
reserve.

The history of the *27th Division*, which was on the north bank
of the Somme, opposite the 3rd Australian Division remarks:
" Seldom has a divisional general had command of such a remark-
" able number of infantry brigades and regiments as General von
" Maur in the last days of August, 1918. On the 28th the number
" rose to 4 infantry brigade staffs and parts of 15 different regi-
" ments from five divisions ". The losses of the division in
August 1918 were 20 officers and 298 other ranks killed,
75 officers and 1,610 other ranks wounded.

Of the divisions opposite the Third and First Armies there is
little information, except that on the 27th four more divisions
were brought up : the *58th* to Bullecourt in the XVII Corps area,
and the *16th*, *20th* and *26th Reserve* to the Canadian Corps front ;
and on the 27th–28th the *4th Ersatz* also to this front. The total
reinforcements sent to the battle front of the Third and First
Armies since the 6th August thus amounted to not less than
23 divisions.

NOTE III

THE AMERICAN PLANS

(End-paper B)

The Note addressed by Maréchal Foch to General Pershing on
the 30th August had been discussed by the latter with General
Pétain on the 31st. The Note envisaged (from east to west)
(1) the reduced St. Mihiel operation by 8 to 9 American divisions,
and (2) " an offensive astride the Aisne covered on the east by the
" Meuse in the general direction of Mezières, comprising (*a*) an
" attack between the Meuse and the Argonne[1] by the French
" Second Army reinforced by 4 to 6 American divisions, to be
" prepared at once and launched as soon as possible after the
" St. Mihiel offensive ; (*b*) a Franco-American attack to be made
" between the Argonne and the Souain road [between Chalons
" and Mezières] also to be prepared at once so that it can be

---

[1] The Meuse passes through Verdun ; the Argonne lies 13 miles west
of Verdun and is about 10 miles across.

" launched a few days after the preceding one.   It will be executed " on the right by an American Army astride the Aisne, and on " the left by the French Fourth Army ".

This plan meant that the American Armies would be mixed up with the French : from right to left : French Eighth Army, American St. Mihiel Army, French Second Army reinforced by 4 to 6 American divisions, an American Army astride the Aisne, and the French Fourth Army.

On the 31st General Pershing wrote to Maréchal Foch : " there " is one thing that must not be done and that is to disperse the " American forces among the Allied Armies. . . . I do insist that " the American Army must be employed as a whole, either east " of the Argonne or west of the Argonne, and not four or five " divisions here and six or seven there ".[1]

At a conference between Maréchal Foch and General Pershing on the 2nd September " there was considerable sparring ", but it was agreed that the American Army should operate as a whole under its own commander on the Meuse–Argonne front, and that this sector, about ninety miles long, including certain French divisions left in it, should be under General Pershing's command. To give time to assemble the American Army on this front after the St. Mihiel attack, the launching of the second offensive was postponed from the 15th to the 25th September.

---

[1] Pershing Experiences, p. 574.

CHAPTER XVIII

THE BATTLE OF THE SCARPE 1918—(*concluded*) AND THE BATTLE OF PÉRONNE–BAPAUME[1]

CAPTURE OF MONT ST. QUENTIN AND OCCUPATION OF PÉRONNE

30TH AUGUST–1ST SEPTEMBER

(Sketches 17, 18, 19)

After his return from the conference of Commanders-in-Chief held on the 29th by Maréchal Foch, Sir Douglas Haig, acting on the Generalissimo's words " continue the pursuit ", issued the following order to the commanders of the First, Third and Fourth Armies :

" The First Army will deliver an attack against the " Drocourt-Quéant Line[2] south of the river Scarpe on " a date to be notified hereafter, and will exploit any " success gained. Such exploitation will be carried out " with a view to securing a front and flank on the " general line Bourlon Wood [5 miles east of Quéant], " Arleux [8 miles north of Bourlon] and the Sensée river " above Arleux, mounted detachments being despatched " at once to reconnoitre the approaches between Cambrai " [4 miles east of Bourlon] and Bouchain [7 miles N.N.E. " of Cambrai].

" The intention is then to direct the Cavalry Corps " south-eastwards so as to operate against the com- " munications of the hostile troops opposing the Third " and Fourth Armies.[3]

" The Third and Fourth Armies will co-operate by " vigorous action with the object of holding the enemy " on their respective fronts. The Third Army will at " the same time push energetically on its left in close " co-operation with the First Army.

---

[1] According to the Official Nomenclature Committee, the Battle of the Scarpe terminates on 30th August, that of Bapaume (Second Battle)—Péronne–Bapaume is a more appropriate name—covers 31st August–3rd September, and that of the Drocourt-Quéant Line, 2nd–3rd September.

[2] See Sketch 16.

[3] The tank situation was very poor owing to the heavy losses. See Note I at end of Chapter.

" The Third Army is to be directed on the general
" line Le Catelet–Marcoing [that is E.S.E. to a north-
" south line south of Cambrai 16 miles ahead] ; the
" Fourth Army on the general line St. Quentin (exclu-
" sive)–Le Catelet [that is eastwards to a north-south
" line south of the Third Army] ".

Operations were therefore continued on the 30th.

The main feature of the ground north of the Somme[1] over
which the left of the Fourth Army and the Third Army were
to operate was the low broad ridge near their boundary line,
marked by Morval and Sailly Saillisel, which beginning at
Thiepval (8 miles west of Morval) although, broken by the
valley of the Tortille (in which is the Canal du Nord) and
minor valleys, continues eastward for over 10 miles. The
rest of the ground may fairly be described as nearly flat.

Throughout the period dealt with in this chapter the
weather was good, though cold in the morning, and favourable for flying, except on the 30th August, when heavy cloud
interfered with long-distance flights. Bombing attacks were
made both by day and by night, and low-flying attacks
continued, but on a reduced scale.

Fourth Army

On the right, in the right wing of the Fourth Army, it
had been hoped that by following close on the enemy's heels
a crossing of the Somme might have been effected before he
had time to destroy the bridges ; but this hope had proved
delusive, and at the close of the 29th August the line of the
Australian Corps (less the 3rd Australian Division on the
north bank of the Somme at Cléry, 3 miles north-west of
Péronne) ran along the west bank of the Somme from its
boundary with the French First Army south of St. Christ,
past Péronne to opposite Cléry. The river in this reach was
a formidable obstacle, which had in the previous March
checked the Germans for three days until the line was turned
on both flanks. It was in fact a marsh over a thousand
yards in width, studded with many small islets overgrown
with rushes through which the stream threaded its way by

---

[1] See Sketch 17.

numerous channels ; the marshy parts were waist deep and the water channels too deep to be waded ; along the western side runs the canal. To cross this reach and the canal a very large number of bridges would be required,[1] and it was evident that the enemy had destroyed some of them. Ultimately it was ascertained that every bridge had been blown to pieces. To force a passage by frontal attack would inevitably cost heavy casualties and great expenditure of ammunition, besides requiring bridging material and time. Lieut.-General Monash had for some time been considering a plan to turn the river line from the north. As the 3rd Australian Division was on the northern bank west of Péronne, the Australian Corps had for some time been working astride the river, restoring the passages behind it as it progressed, and it was therefore in a position to manoeuvre. To explain his plan, Lieut.-General Monash assembled a conference of his divisional commanders at 2.30 p.m. on the 29th at 2nd Australian Division head-quarters. He proposed as a first step to capture Mont St. Quentin, a wide-spreading hill with the ruins of a village on it, lying at the end of a spur in the angle between the Somme and the Canal du Nord, a mile north of Péronne and over 140 feet above the town, with command of both the south-north and east-west reaches of the Somme. As the slopes of the hill were glacis-like, devoid of cover and defended by several lines of wire entanglement, it would have to be taken by surprise. The capture of Péronne would follow, and the line of the river would then be turned. To provide troops for the attack, the 32nd Division was to relieve the 5th Australian Division down to Lamire Farm (less than two miles south of Péronne), thus giving it a frontage of four and a half miles to hold defensively. The 5th Australian Division would occupy two and a quarter miles down to Biaches, just below Péronne, and the 2nd Australian Division two and a half miles down to the bridge at Ommiécourt, nearly opposite Cléry. The sector of the 3rd Australian Division, a short one, little over a mile, was to remain unchanged. All three Australian divisions were to advance eastwards, each being given an immediate and an ultimate objective :

---

[1] The so-called Brie bridge, on the main Amiens–St. Quentin road, in reality consisted of a causeway with eight separate bridges at irregular intervals.

5th Australian Division: the forcing of a crossing at the Péronne bridges ; if these were destroyed, it was to follow the 2nd Australian Division and make for the high ground south of Péronne, between the Somme and the Cologne. Ultimate objective, the wooded spur east of Péronne.

2nd Australian Division : the bridgehead at Halle (north of Biaches) ; then Mont St. Quentin.

3rd Australian Division : the high ground north-east of Cléry (a ridge runs north-eastward from Cléry, Bouchavesnes lying in a valley on its western slope) ; then a spur to the east overlooking Moislains.

During the night of the 29th–30th the engineers of the 32nd Division made bridges for infantry in file at three places on the Somme canal, and before dawn both the 97th and 14th Brigades had patrols on the eastern bank. They were received by machine-gun fire from some high ground about five hundred yards east of the canal, and were withdrawn by noon, having fulfilled the duty required by the corps commander of demonstrating and of confirming the presence of the enemy. The 8th Australian Brigade (5th Australian Division) was active throughout the day in reconnoitring the east side of the canal, which was found to be strongly held. On relief by the 32nd Division this brigade went into reserve.

In the 2nd Australian Division's sector, two bridges were thrown over the canal between Lamire Farm and la Chapellette, and about 7 a.m. the 26th Battalion of the 7th Australian Brigade crossed by them, but was unable to go farther owing to the marshes and depth of water in the streams, and so returned. In the evening the 7th Brigade was relieved by the 15th between Lamire Farm and Biaches. Earlier in the morning two companies of the 18th Battalion of the 5th Australian Brigade had tried to cross the Somme by the Ommiécourt causeway, as the brigade was to co-operate with the 3rd Australian Division ; but this passage had been partly destroyed, and was defended by enemy parties in the eastern part of Cléry, which had changed hands several times during the night. The 19th Battalion also failed to cross at Halle. The battalions of the 5th Australian Brigade were therefore withdrawn from their exposed position on the river bank, in full view of the enemy, to the west of

Feuillières ; but, moving off again at 10.30 a.m., they crossed the canal and river at that place, the passages having been repaired during the 29th, and occupied trenches on the western outskirts of Cléry. Little artillery support could be given, owing to the difficulty of getting guns across the Somme. The village and trenches to the east and north were therefore systematically mopped up, rifle grenades to dislodge the defenders and Lewis guns to catch them as they fled being the principal means used, and by 9 p.m. the 20th Battalion was on the high ground to the south-east. Subsequently the 17th Battalion came up on its right, thus occupying the ground east of Ommiécourt. Meantime this village, which the enemy had re-occupied, was found at 5 p.m. by a patrol of the 19th Battalion to be evacuated, and repairs to the causeway were taken in hand. A passage with a bridgehead had thus been secured.

The 10th and 9th Brigades of the 3rd Australian Division, north of the Somme, had hard fighting. Tired as they were, they were to push on north-eastwards in the early hours of the 30th—they started between 2 and 3 a.m.—in order, with an intermediate halt, to reach a line through Cléry Copse and Road Wood to the south-west corner of Marrières Wood ; the 5th Australian Brigade, from south of the river, was to come up on the right, which it was unable to do, as we have seen, until late at night. Some progress was at first made by the 10th and 9th Brigades, but the enemy was found to be strongly established on the objective, covered by nests of machine guns and snipers, and he repeatedly counter-attacked, particularly in the eastern part of Cléry. Finally, about 6.30 a.m., as the 5th Australian Brigade, which should have been on the right, was not across, and as on the left, though this flank was covered by patrols of the 13th Australian Light Horse, the 58th Division had not yet advanced, it was decided to wait for darkness before attempting to gain further ground.

The 58th Division had not on the previous night come up abreast of the 3rd Australian Division. Its 175th Brigade, with its attached troops of all arms, was still retained as divisional advanced guard ; the vanguard, consisting of the Northumberland Hussars and cyclists, with two field and two machine guns, went forward at 5.30 a.m. Shortly before

9 a.m. it was in touch with the halted 9th Australian Brigade about a thousand yards east of Hill 110 (1 mile north of Cléry). No further advance by mounted troops being possible, at 10.30 a.m. the infantry were sent forward under bursts of field artillery fire, and by 1 p.m. had occupied the crest west of Marrières Wood without any opposition except desultory shelling. Further progress was not attempted owing to heavy fire from machine guns and trench mortars; a line was dug on the reverse slope, and tentative arrangements were made for a night attack; but these were superseded at 9.45 p.m. by divisional orders that the 174th Brigade would attack at 5.10 a.m. on the 31st.

In the next sector the infantry brigades of the 47th Division (Major-General Sir G. Gorringe) were to relieve those of the 12th Division during the night of the 29th-30th August; but owing to the retirement of the enemy this change could not be carried out as planned, and it was arranged that the 142nd Brigade, to which mounted troops, artillery and machine guns had been attached, should, as advanced guard, pass through the line of the 12th Division at 6 a.m., the remainder of the division following. Actually, at the named hour the 142nd Brigade, realizing that a deliberate attack was necessary, sent forward two battalions with the third in support, under a barrage. By 9 a.m. the 1/24th London on the right, having met with only slight opposition, although the 1/22nd London on the left came under considerable machine-gun fire from the north-east, had captured Hill 150 (2 miles north of Cléry), taken over a hundred prisoners, two field guns and a number of machine guns and had reached a line from the western side of Marrières Wood—where later the left of the 58th Division arrived—north-north-westward to near Priez Farm. A fresh German division having been brought up, thus making a total of seven opposing the III Corps, although the counter-attack it made was feeble and hardly reached the advanced posts, no more progress could be made.[1]

The 18th Division sent a battalion of the 54th Brigade forward at 5.15 a.m., on its right south of Combles, after a quarter of an hour's opening barrage; but owing to Priez Farm being strongly held, very little progress could be made.

---

[1] The *232nd Division*, after a 28-hour railway journey, from Montmédy.

The events of the morning made it clear that the Germans intended to make at least a temporary stand on the line of the Somme as far north as Péronne and along the high ground Mont St. Quentin–Frégicourt–Morval. This has a series of spurs projecting south-westwards, which formed bastions to the line, with shallow valleys between them; Bussu (north-east of Péronne), Feuillaucourt, Bouchavesnes and Rancourt lying in these valleys. The southern part of the ridge was particularly favourable for defence, low scrub, ditches and quarries providing excellent cover and concealment for machine guns. For the first time since the 22nd August instead of the enemy's guns being dispersed for delaying action, they seemed to be grouped together once more for vigorous defence.[1] General Rawlinson had come to the decision to turn the enemy's position along the Somme by an eastward advance of the III Corps, north of Péronne and the Cologne, across the Canal du Nord (R. Tortille) to the line of heights marked by Buire Wood–Templeux le Fosse–Nurlu ; it was to be protected on the right by the Australian Corps. When, therefore, in the afternoon, Lieut.-General Monash put forward his plan for capturing Mont St. Quentin, although General Rawlinson considered it over-bold to attempt with so weak a force, he found that he had anticipated his Army commander's wishes, and, in some respects, had already carried out the orders which he received later during the evening.[2]

THIRD ARMY[3]

Before receiving G.H.Q. orders, General Byng had instructed the V and IV Corps to press the enemy's rear guards energetically on the 30th, both corps being given a direction a little south of east, to the line Manancourt–Ytres–Vélu, that is practically the Canal du Nord ; the VI Corps was to take advantage of any weakening of the enemy to push abreast of the above line to Beaumetz–Lagnicourt ;

---

[1] It is now known that the Germans hoped to hold this line and the Drocourt–Quéant Line for the winter. The instructions for defence issued by the *119th Division*, back in the line after a short rest and in the St. Christ sector of the Somme, are given in Note IV at end of Chapter.

[2] Appendix XXII.

[3] See Sketch 18.

the XVII Corps was to continue to co-operate with the Canadian Corps. On the arrival of the G.H.Q. orders, at 10.45 p.m. the Third Army issued further instructions giving the more distant objectives to be attained after the Drocourt–Quéant Line had been broken, emphasizing the importance of assisting the Canadian Corps in the task, and specially directing the XVII Corps to help with all the artillery at its disposal and push forward its left as soon as the Canadian Corps had broken the Line with a view to turning Quéant from the north. The VI Corps was to endeavour to gain a position from which it could attack the Hindenburg Position east of Quéant from the south.

In the V Corps there was no intention to press the attack and only slight progress was made : the enemy had a strong line and evidently meant to hold it. An advance on Morval by the 114th Brigade (38th Division) at 5.30 a.m. without a barrage was at once checked, and Br.-General Hulke (115th Brigade) was wounded. The 51st Brigade (17th Division) similarly failed against le Transloy, and patrols sent out three times by the 21st Division, after bombardments, found Beaulencourt strongly held.

The IV Corps on the other hand, with 5 a.m. as zero hour, made a considerable advance against severe opposition ; it took Bancourt and Frémicourt, established a good jumping-off line for attack against Beugny, and during the night captured Riencourt.

The 126th Brigade of the 42nd Division could at first make no impression on Riencourt, although the 1/5th East Lancashire, making use of old trenches, was able to close in from the north. A further attack was made at 7 p.m. by the 1/10th Manchester, which, although checked at first, cleared the village and established a line east of it.

In the New Zealand Division, two brigades attacked with 4 tanks of the 10th Battalion following. The 1st Brigade advanced against Bancourt. In spite of considerable machine gun fire, the village was taken. The left then went on about half a mile, but the right suffered many casualties by fire from Riencourt and had to form a defensive flank. It was not until the attack of the 42nd Division at 7 p.m. eased the situation that the right wing was able to make a little further progress.

The New Zealand 3rd (Rifle) Brigade moved against Frémicourt, passing north and south of it, leaving the mopping up to be done later. After clearing the railway cutting to the north-east, with the assistance of one tank, it established itself on a ridge six hundred yards east of the village. Here, being without support on either side, it was subjected to sustained fire and had to be withdrawn to a trench two hundred yards behind the crest, where it got in touch with the 1st New Zealand Brigade and the 5th Division.

This latter formation sent forward the 95th Brigade, under an artillery barrage, supported by seven tanks of the 7th Battalion (of which four were knocked out by enemy fire). In spite of machine-gun fire, the first objective, part of the Ytres–Beugny line, an old British " Army line ", six hundred yards west of Beugny, was captured and small parties penetrated into Beugny. The right, however, was unable to go on from the first objective owing to fire from Frémicourt, not then completely in the hands of the New Zealanders, and the left was therefore brought back.

The orders of the VI Corps were for the 62nd and 3rd Divisions to clear Vaulx Vraucourt, Ecoust St. Mein and Longatte at dawn—5 a.m. was the agreed divisional zero hour—if these localities had not already been captured. Ten tanks of the 15th Battalion were allotted to the 62nd Division, whose 186th and 185th Brigades (Br.-Generals J. L. G. Burnett and Viscount Hampden), advancing under a barrage, took and retained Vraucourt, but after penetrating to the eastern edge of Vaulx Vraucourt, were forced to withdraw. At the end of the day, therefore, the 62nd Division's front ran west of Vaulx Vraucourt and east of Vraucourt, with a gap between the brigades.

In the 3rd Division, the 76th Brigade sent the 1/Gordon Highlanders and 2/Suffolk to attack, under a barrage, after the villages of Ecoust and Longatte had been bombarded. Keeping close to the barrage, the left battalion suffering some casualties from it, the brigade secured the objectives. No sooner, however, had the 2/Suffolk captured the two villages than, instead of the 56th Division, enemy troops appeared on the left ; for the Germans had counter-attacked at Bullecourt and driven out the 167th Brigade. Assailed on this flank by heavy trench-mortar and machine-gun fire and then counter-attacked, the Suffolk had to fight their way back, with a loss of half their numbers, to a trench on the western side of Ecoust. Of the four villages attacked by the VI Corps, all therefore had been taken, but only one, Vraucourt, retained.

The XVII Corps had on the evening of the 29th issued orders that the next day was to be devoted to consolidation, with patrolling ; but the 56th Division, on the right, was to take advantage of any opportunity afforded by the attack of the VI Corps. The enemy, however, took the offensive. The 167th Brigade (Br.-General G. H. B. Freeth) had no sooner relieved the other two brigades of the 56th Division in the front line, when, about 5.30 a.m., it was attacked by a fresh German division ; [1] the officers and men of the two companies of the 1/London in Bullecourt were nearly all killed, wounded or taken prisoner. Efforts to recover the village by bombing along a trench on its southern edge were unsuccessful. The 7/Middlesex, to the north, was also attacked and driven back ; so when at night the 168th Brigade took over it found that the divisional line was still west of Bullecourt.

An attack against the 57th Division had come about 12.30 p.m., striking the open left flank of the 170th Brigade (Br.-General G. F. Boyd), but was repulsed. At night, however, it was decided to draw back the divisional line slightly, as its flanks were open, to trenches about four hundred yards west of Hendecourt, where touch was gained with the divisions on either side.

FIRST ARMY

During the 30th the 1st Canadian Division, the right of the Canadian Corps, with the co-operation of low-flying aeroplanes, made a very successful attack on the Vis en Artois Switch, and achieved a general advance of nearly two miles, coming up level with the 57th Division on its right ; the 4th Division took Eterpigny ; and Brutinel's

---

[1] The *7th (Dismounted) Cavalry Division.* Except for 3 days in the line, it had been resting since the end of May.

Force pushed forward a little. The re-entrant near Vis en Artois was thus straightened out and more progress made towards establishing a good jumping-off line for the attack against the Drocourt–Quéant Line, the wire of which the 6-inch howitzers continued cutting.

The attack of the 1st Canadian Division on the Vis en Artois Switch was carried out by the 1st Canadian Brigade (Br.-General W. A. Griesbach), and exceedingly well planned. It was made at 4.40 a.m. from two directions : by the 1st and 2nd Battalions from the southern end of the divisional front north-eastward on a 1,700-yard front, and by the 3rd Battalion through the 3rd Canadian Brigade eastward up communication trenches from the northern end of the front. The two attacks were covered by separate barrages—which, as they converged, required specially careful calculation—fired by nine brigades of field artillery and three of heavy.[1] Thus the plan had the advantages of attack from one unexpected direction, and of taking in enfilade the defenders of the German front opposite the 3rd Canadian Brigade. It was assumed in preparing it that Hendecourt on the right was in the hands of the 57th Division, but as the 170th Brigade had been withdrawn from the village late on the 29th, fire from this direction caused casualties to the 1st Canadian Battalion whilst it was forming up and during the first part of the advance. All, however, went well with the right attack. On the left, the frontal attack of the 3rd Battalion met with little resistance at first, but hard fighting occurred in the taking of the actual objective trenches. This was not over until 7 a.m., by which time the battalion was up in line with the others and had touch on the left with the 2nd Canadian Brigade (Br.-General F. O. W. Loomis). Heavy enemy shell-fire was then opened and interfered with consolidation, and at 11.45 a.m. an enemy attack pushed back part of the 1st Battalion ; but the lost ground was recovered by an immediate counter-attack well supported by artillery. In the afternoon the 4th Battalion, after driving back German parties, filled by a line of posts the gap between the 57th and 1st Canadian Divisions—which had arisen on account of the convergent attacks of the 1st and 2nd Battalions—and thus completed the new front.

---

[1] Those of the 15th, 39th, 1st and 2nd Canadian Divisions, and the 282nd (Army) Brigade R.F.A., under Br.-General H. C. Thacker, C.R.A. 1st Canadian Division, and the XLVIII., LXXVIII. and XCI. R.G.A

The advance of the 4th Division was not made until 4 p.m. in the afternoon, and, as the enemy had apparently seen the centre battalions moving into assembly positions in the morning, casualties from shell-fire were suffered before the attack began. The first part of the advance, except on the extreme right, was over, or rather through, swampy ground near the Sensée, water in places being up to men's waists ; but the resistance of the enemy's machine gunners and infantry was not very strong. The 2/Duke of Wellington's of the 10th Brigade (Br.-General J. Greene) took St. Servins Farm, about six hundred yards ahead, and the 1/R. Warwickshire some higher ground north of it ; but at night as it was much exposed to fire the farm was evacuated, and a position in a trench behind it occupied. The 1/Rifle Brigade of the 11th Brigade (Br.-General T. S. H. Wade) took and retained Eterpigny, the 1/Somerset L.I. working through Eterpigny Wood and coming up on the left. Brutinel's Force made an advance in the evening, and was then relieved by the 33rd Brigade of the 11th Division. The Sensée river thus became the boundary between the 4th and the 11th Divisions. Farther to the north, the 51st Division (now in the XXII Corps) advanced its line about five hundred yards and occupied Plouvain, which was found to be evacuated.

FOURTH ARMY[1]

On the 31st August the Australian and III Corps increased their advantage north of the Somme, the 5th Australian Brigade, by a magnificent feat of arms, obtaining a footing on Mont St. Quentin ; but elsewhere on the Fourth Army front and in the Third and First Armies no events of major importance took place. All the attacks were made early, and as the night was pitch-dark some difficulties occurred in forming up the troops.

The 32nd Division remained west of the Somme canal ; but four footbridges over this were completed and arrangements made, unless the opposition proved strong, to attempt a crossing during the night of the 31st August–1st September, in order to assist the Australian attack farther north.

---

[1] See Sketch 17.

In the 5th and 2nd Australian Divisions the situation before dawn was that the 15th Australian Brigade of the former held the angle of the river opposite Péronne, with the 8th and 14th in reserve ; the 5th of the latter, joined by its fourth battalion in the early morning, had secured on the previous day a bridgehead east of Cléry by the restored passage at Ommiécourt, the 7th and 6th still being on the southern bank.   The enemy forces confronting the Australians north of the Somme were considerable portions of no less than five divisions, with, in addition, two regiments of the *2nd Guard Division,* holding the Mont St. Quentin sector.[1]   At 5 a.m. the 5th Australian Brigade, only 70 officers and 1,250 other ranks strong, with the 17th and 20th Battalions abreast and the 19th following,[2] supported by five brigades of field artillery and four of heavy, moved against three objectives : the trenches between Anvil Wood and Mont St. Quentin village, the village itself and Feuillau-court.   They were undisturbed during assembly except by a little machine-gun fire from Park Wood to the right front, which was quickly suppressed.   Time did not permit of the usual form of barrage, so concentrations of fire by a pro-gramme based on the expected rate of advance were ordered, but the first fell nearly one mile ahead.   Two machine-gun companies were attached to the brigade ; they also did not attempt to fire a barrage, but one or two sectors were allotted to battalions, the other guns being used to strengthen weak points and fill gaps.

The attack was a complete surprise, and the centre and left battalions reached their objectives, Mont St. Quentin village and Feuillaucourt ; but the right, after a good advance, was checked by field guns and machine-gun fire from Anvil Wood, an aerodrome just north of it and St. Denis to the north-east ; on the left, too, the 3rd Australian Division was not up.   Taking advantage of the exposure of the advanced troops, at 7 a.m. the Germans, counter-attacking from two directions, drove back the 17th Battalion, which had two companies lying east of Mont St. Quentin village, to trenches just west of the Péronne–Bouchavesnes road.[3]   From this position repeated bombing attacks failed

---

[1] See Note III at end of Chapter.

[2] The actual attack was made by 550 men with 200 in support.   They took over 700 prisoners.

[3] This counter-attack, according to B.O.A., p. 540, was carried out by troops of the *2nd Guard, 38th* and *185th Divisions.*   See Note III at end of Chapter.

to dislodge the 17th. About 9 a.m. one company of the reserve battalion, the 18th, was sent up to reinforce the junction of the 17th and 20th, and two companies to the right wing held up in front of Anvil Wood. During the afternoon the exposed left flank of the 20th at Feuillaucourt was taken in enfilade from the north by gun and machine-gun fire, and this battalion was also withdrawn west of the Péronne–Bouchavesnes road. Meantime, in order to exploit the success of the 5th Australian Brigade, Lieut.-General Monash ordered more troops from the south to the north bank of the Somme. About noon, the 6th Australian Brigade crossed by a temporary bridge at Buscourt (below Ommiécourt), with the object of passing through the 5th Brigade and of extending its line towards Péronne ; marching through Cléry at 4 p.m., it moved south-eastwards on Halle and Park Wood. Although on reaching these localities its advanced guard was received by machine-gun fire, it continued on, and cleared and occupied a trench (Florina Trench), lying about five hundred yards beyond. One company pressed on to St. Radégonde, but was unable to remain there and returned to Florina Trench, which remained the limit of the advance of the 6th Australian Brigade ; it had been unable to get abreast of the right of the 5th, which meantime had not only retained its gains so boldly won, but had improved its position, so that it was over twelve hundred yards ahead.

The 14th Australian Brigade, followed by the 7th, was also brought across the river, using the passage at Buscourt, as that at Ommiécourt was under intense fire. In spite of the area east of Cléry and the banks of the Somme south of it being under constant shelling from the north-east, the brigade, with half of the 7th, proceeding in Indian file under shelter of the steep bank, with very few casualties, by evening had reached its place of assembly in a valley east of Cléry, where two brigades of field artillery joined it.

The 10th and 9th Brigades of the 3rd Australian Division, which were to capture the high ground south of Bouchavesnes just west of the Péronne–Bouchavesnes road, over two thousand yards away, had advanced at 5.45 a.m., under a barrage somewhat thin at first, forty-five minutes after the 5th Australian Brigade on their right. In spite of machine-gun fire from Road Wood, by working along old trenches, they reached the crest of the ridge, but were unable to establish themselves beyond, although they captured a number of field guns.[1] Later, the 10th Brigade was driven back a little by the same enemy counter-attack as had retaken Mont St. Quentin village. At the end of the day, however, the three Australian divisions had considerably increased the area of the bridgehead west of Péronne and were in possession of a vital pivot north of the town.

The attack of the III Corps was made by the 58th and 47th Divisions under creeping barrages at 5.10 a.m. and 5.30 a.m., respectively, that is slightly before the 3rd Australian Division advanced. The assembly of the troops presented great difficulties in the pitch-dark night, as the country was almost destitute of land marks. In the 58th Division, the 174th Brigade, passing through the 175th for the purpose, had to capture Marrières Wood and reach the Péronne–Bouchavesnes road ; the 47th Division had merely to swing forward, pivoting on its northern flank. Marrières Wood lies in a valley bottom and extends well up the slopes on either side ; it was known to be strongly held. The 6th and 8/London, with the 7th in support,[2] reached the far edge of the wood without difficulty ; for although the German artillery opened a severe counter-barrage, the infantry quickly abandoned the wood and retired to the high ground three hundred yards beyond. A party of the 6/London had now to be sent to the right to clear Road Wood, from which fire was being received, as the Australians, who could not be seen advancing, had not yet reached it, and, that accomplished, the 174th Brigade went on. The right was able to push on beyond its objective, the Péronne–Bouchavesnes road ; the left, on reaching the edge of the flat spur east of Marrières Wood, found that this commanded the valley behind the right wing, and, fearing to lose possession of the spur, and all its company commanders having fallen, went no farther. Nearly four hundred prisoners, two 4·2-inch howitzers, two field guns, a few trench mortars and many machine guns had been captured.

---

[1] Private G. Cartwright, 33rd Battalion, 9th Australian Brigade, received the V.C. Single-handed, under machine-gun fire, he captured a machine gun, killing 3 of the crew and capturing 9.

[2] Their strength was low, the 6/London numbering only 9 officers (3 lent by the 7/London) and 344 other ranks (53 of battalion headquarters), and the other battalions of the brigade were little better off.

The 47th Division detailed the 141st and 142nd Brigades (Br.-Generals W. F. Mildren and R. McDouall) to éxecute the forward wheel required of it up to the line from Hill 145 to opposite Priez Farm. By " peaceful penetration " during the night, the left, the 1/23rd London (142nd Brigade), reached its objective, and at 5.10 a.m. reported Priez Farm still held with a large number of machine guns. When the right, the 141st Brigade, advanced at 5.30 a.m. its attack went well and it gained touch with the 174th Brigade. But there was now a gap between the two brigades, and about 11 a.m. a battalion of a fresh German division[1] counter-attacked towards its left from the direction of Rancourt, and was repulsed only after close fighting. Three similar attacks during the afternoon were likewise repulsed.

The 18th Division did not advance on the 31st August. The enemy in front being in strength, it was decided to wait until next day, when the Third Army would be able to co-operate by making an attack on Morval.

THIRD ARMY ([2])

No fresh orders were issued by the Third Army for the 31st. By the V and the IV Corps no advance was undertaken ; but there was considerable artillery fire on both sides. In the VI Corps an attempt on the right to capture Vaulx Vraucourt failed, but on the left Ecoust St. Mein and Longatte were taken a second time, and in the XVII Corps the greater part of Bullecourt was also recovered from the enemy.

The New Zealand Division of the IV Corps was attacked by enemy infantry about 6 a.m. after a short bombardment, and it was driven back three to five hundred yards. A small enemy party also penetrated between the New Zealanders and the 5th Division ; but the ground was recovered and later an attack on the centre of the 5th Division was repulsed.[3]

---

[1] The *14th Reserve*. It had been in rest for six weeks.

[2] See Sketch 18.

[3] An account of the counter-attack is given in the histories of the *102nd Royal Saxon Grenadiers* and the *108th R. Saxon Rifles* of the *12th Division*, which, with the *12th Pioneer Battalion* and a regiment of the *4th Bavarian Division*, took part. The operation order is given in

Continued at foot of next page.

First Army

As part of the 1st Canadian Division's new front in the Vis en Artois switch was at right angles to the Drocourt–Quéant Line, the orders of the First Army for the Canadian Corps were to continue the advance and make the necessary adjustment, so as to be in position for an attack on the Drocourt–Quéant Line on the 2nd September ; the XXII Corps was to improve its defensive position, so as to control the crossings over the Trinquis river.

At 5 a.m. the 8th Canadian Battalion (2nd Canadian Brigade) advanced north-eastwards under a barrage and speedily captured two lines of trenches which faced east. To join on to this new line the 10th Brigade (4th Division) sent forward the 2/Duke of Wellington's at 2.30 p.m. over flat open ground to attack the farm six hundred yards ahead (St. Servin's Farm), which had been taken and evacuated on the previous day, and it gained a footing in the small wood which surrounded the farm. The Germans counter-attacked at 6 p.m. and recovered this ; but at 8.45 p.m. the 2/Duke of Wellington's retook the wood, captured the farm and established a line five hundred yards beyond, the 2/Seaforth coming up level on the left. Some reliefs were carried out during the night, and the order of Canadian brigades then became 3rd, 2nd and 12th.

In the XXII Corps on the 31st, the 11th Division pushed forward alone up to the Trinquis river, Hamblain les Prés being found evacuated, with scarcely any opposition except from artillery.

During the 1st September[1] good progress was made, and the Germans were driven with heavy losses from a line on which they undoubtedly meant to make a long stand. In the Fourth Army the Australian Corps occupied the whole of Péronne except a detached suburb, and captured the enemy's positions on and north of Mont St. Quentin ; still

---

Continued from previous page.

" Regt. No. 108 ", p. 251. The object was to recover the Frémicourt line. There was a 5-minute bombardment, 4.30 to 4.35 a.m. Six tanks were to have taken part, but did not arrive in time : they only got as far as Beugny where, in the dark, one of them knocked down a house and caused 30 German casualties. " The retirement was difficult and costly " : the battalions of the *108th Regiment* were reduced to two companies each.

The third regiment of the *12th Division, No. 100*, which did not take part, had already been reduced to one battalion of three companies.

[1] See Sketch 19.

farther north, the III Corps drove him from the strongly held heights between Bouchavesnes and Morval ; the corps of the Third Army[1] all gained ground, the VI, at last, taking Vaulx Vraucourt ; and in the First Army the Canadian Corps closed up to within assaulting distance of the southern half of the Drocourt–Quéant Line. If this link between the Hindenburg Position and the Lens defences to the north could be broken through, important results might ensue.

The situation along the Somme[2] remained unchanged : attempts made by the 32nd Division to cross the canal during the night of the 31st August–1st September were frustrated by the enemy destroying one bridge by shell-fire and another by a mine, and their reconstruction had to be abandoned owing to machine-gun fire.[3]

The originally low strength of the 5th Australian Brigade had been much reduced by the fighting round Mont St. Quentin, so Major-General C. Rosenthal (2nd Australian Division) decided that the 6th Australian Brigade (Br.-General J. C. Robertson), which had come up in rear of the 5th and had one battalion in Florina Trench in front of Halle, should relieve it during the night and complete the capture. He arranged with Major-General Sir J. T. Talbot Hobbs (5th Australian Division) that the 14th Australian Brigade (Br.-General J. C. Stewart), then in a valley east of Cléry, should take over Florina Trench and attack simultaneously in order to clear the area west of Péronne and capture the town. Four brigades of field artillery south of the Somme were available to support the attack of the 5th Australian Division, and three brigades south of the river and five north of it that of the 2nd ; each division had also one brigade of heavy artillery. As on the previous day, the artillery support took the form of concentration of fire on selected targets— with thirty minutes' fire before Zero—instead of a creeping barrage, to arrange which time did not permit. These various matters were not settled until nearly midnight ; so, in order to give time for orders to reach the troops, 6 a.m. was made zero hour—although an earlier start would have been preferred—and even this hour was only possible because the

---

[1] See Sketch 18.
[2] See Sketch 19.
[3] The *Alpine Corps*, which had been withdrawn from the line, was assembled in support near Falvy (4 miles south of Brie).

commander of the 6th Australian Brigade had foreseen that the projected operation might be one of those required of him, and had warned his officers during the afternoon. It so happened that two fresh German divisions, brought up to relieve two tired ones, met the attack of the 6th and 14th Australian Brigades.[1]

The troops had considerable trouble in reaching their jumping-off positions in time, as the 14th Australian Brigade found a pocket of Germans in Florina Trench, and the advanced patrols of the 6th as it came up encountered opposition from German posts ; but both brigades moved off simultaneously at 6 a.m. in misty drizzling rain, literally tore down the wire entanglements which they encountered, and got the enemy on the run. By 6.45 a.m., in spite of enfilade machine-gun fire, the 54th Battalion (14th Australian Brigade) had cleared St. Radégonde village and wood, and reached the wide wet ditch which enclosed Péronne. The main bridge in the causeway over it had been blown up ; but, under fire from the houses, although many of the garrison remained in cellars and dugouts, the battalion crossed the wet ditch on the débris of the road bridge and by a footbridge farther to the north ; by 8.40 a.m. it was in the centre of the town. Mopping up was then taken in hand, and very soon most of Péronne, with the exception of the isolated north-east suburb, was in Australian hands. Connection was established at another causeway south of the town with the 15th Australian Brigade, the 59th Battalion of which, led by Br.-General H. E. Elliott in person, had crossed the Somme by the ruins of the railway bridge, whilst, farther north, the 58th and 57th had closed up to the moat. On the left, the 53rd Battalion of the 14th Brigade, after some initial fighting on the starting line, met considerable opposition from Anvil Wood, and was hampered in overcoming it by fire from the localities immediately north of Péronne. This opposition a party of three men silenced by turning against it a captured field gun. By 7 a.m. Anvil Wood was cleared and the cemetery north-east of it captured ; but attempts to advance farther were checked by machine-gun fire from the ramparts of Péronne (the 54th Battalion not yet being in possession of the town) and from the north-eastern suburb. Uncertain what success the 6th Australian

---

[1] These were the *2nd Guard* and *38th*.   See Note III at end of Chapter.

Brigade had gained, the 14th now halted ; it did not use its 56th Battalion, and even reduced the number of troops in Péronne.

In the attack of the 6th Australian Brigade, as the position of the foremost troops of the 5th, through which it had to pass, was not accurately known, the artillery bombardment was directed on targets east of the Péronne–Bouchavesnes road. This had the result that the 23rd and 24th Battalions had to advance without artillery support about a thousand yards over ground in which parties of the enemy were still offering resistance. Progress, however, was made by use of the old trenches and by rushing from shell-hole to shell-hole. The right reached the trench system in front of Mont St. Quentin village, in which parties of the 5th Australian Brigade were found ; the left, leaving Feuillaucourt on its left flank, crossed the Péronne–Bouchavesnes road. There, owing to the intensity of the enemy's fire, it had to halt. The 21st Battalion was brought up to reinforce the 23rd, and then from 1 to 1.30 p.m. Mont St. Quentin village was bombarded by every available trench mortar and howitzer. This ended, the attack was renewed on the whole front, when, in spite of the stout defence by fresh troops, the village was captured, and an irresistible charge carried the 21st and 23rd Battalions through it and beyond St. Quentin Wood, on the eastern edge of which a line was established. Simultaneously the 24th Battalion, on the left, had reached its objective, a trench five hundred yards south-west of Allaines. The casualties had been heavy, orders for further advance were cancelled, and the 7th Australian Brigade was directed to pass through the line at dawn.[1]

---

[1] For the brilliant feat of arms of capturing a strongly defended and important tactical point against greatly superior numbers (see Note III at end of Chapter), several V.C.s were awarded : to Private W. M. Currey, 53rd Battalion, for capturing a field gun (later used against the enemy) and later a strongpoint ; to Corporal A. C. Hall, 54th Battalion, for capturing a machine-gun post, shooting 4 and capturing 9 of the occupants with 2 guns, and later leading successful parties to mop up similar posts ; to Corporal A. H. Buckley, 54th Battalion, for rushing a post with one companion only, shooting 4 and taking 22 prisoners. Later he was killed trying to cross the footbridge over the Péronne moat in order to reach a machine-gun post ; to Sergeant A. D. Lowerson, 21st Battalion, who, after displaying high courage and tactical skill, as culmination of a series of gallant actions, led a party of 7 men to storm a post, taking 12 machine guns and 30 prisoners ; he was severely wounded in the thigh, but continued at duty until all was secure ; to Private R. Mactier, 23rd Battalion, posthumously, " for the greatest bravery and
Continued at foot of next page.

On the left of the troops attacking Mont St. Quentin, the 3rd Australian Division had, in relief of the exhausted 9th and 10th Brigades, sent its 11th Brigade (43rd, 41st and 42nd Battalions) forward at 5 a.m. to seize the high ground between Bouchavesnes and the Tortille near Allaines. The barrage was thin, as the gunners were as worn out as the infantry, but steady progress was made against strong resistance by advancing up the trenches as well as over the open ; terrific fire from the front and from Allaines on the right flank then drove the Australians to ground short of the first of their two objectives, in touch with the 2nd Australian Division on the right, and half a mile behind the 58th Division on the left. Four hundred prisoners, 5 field guns and 15 machine guns had been taken by the 11th Australian Brigade.[1]

Lieut.-General Godley's orders for the 1st September directed an attack along the whole front of the III Corps at 5.30 a.m., after thirty minutes' artillery fire, under a creeping barrage. The first objective was the high ground Bouchavesnes–Rancourt, and then, if this were gained, the next rise, which overlooks the Tortille valley and is marked by l'Epine de Malassise (a knoll)—the western side of Moislain Wood (which lies on the south-western slope of a valley running down to Moislains)—the western edge of St. Pierre Vaast Wood (which is higher up the same valley). In the 58th Division, the 173rd Brigade, after two days' rest in reserve, was brought forward to pass through the 174th, which was to remain in front of Marrières Wood ; it had some difficulty in marching up through the congestion of traffic on the roads and tracks in the forward area, but completed its assembly in time. The enemy's artillery promptly replied to the creeping barrage, and strong opposition was encountered from machine-gun posts and the

Continued from previous page.
" devotion to duty " ; to Lieut. E. T. Towner, M.C., 2nd Australian Machine-Gun Battalion, who was in charge of 4 Vickers guns : he dashed ahead alone to capture a machine gun, shooting the crew with his revolver and turning the gun on the enemy caused the surrender of 25 men. After a series of valuable actions, he suffered a gaping scalp wound through his helmet, but remained at duty for another 30 hours.

[1] A V.C. was awarded to Lance-Corporal L. C. Weathers, 43rd Battalion, who, as leader of a bombing party, located a large body of Germans in a trench, attacked it, went back for more bombs and assistance, and with 3 men brought about the surrender of 180 Germans with 3 machine guns.

defenders of the western edge of Bouchavesnes ; but the attack, carried through to the second objective, which was reached at 10 a.m., was completely successful, 325 prisoners, 8 field guns and numerous machine guns being taken. Further advance was postponed, as it entailed movement down the slopes to the Tortille in full view of the enemy, and the divisions on either side were not yet up.

The 47th Division continued the attack with the 141st and 140th Brigades, which were directed against the trench systems west of Moislain Wood and of St. Pierre Vaast Wood, respectively. The former brigade, in spite of heavy casualties, reached its objective except on the extreme left ; the right of the 140th failed to get to St. Pierre Vaast Wood trenches. Thus a gap occurred between the two brigades, and in this was an enemy post with several machine guns, which could not be smothered by the Stokes mortar and rifle fire employed against it. A smaller gap in the centre of the 140th Brigade was, however, filled, and Rancourt mopped up by the support battalion, a number of prisoners and a complete dressing station being captured.

The 55th Brigade (Br.-General E. A. Wood), around Combles, detailed to make the attack of the 18th Division, had a difficult task before it to reach its objective, the western edge of St. Pierre Vaast Wood. From Combles a valley in the high ground runs up north-eastward to Sailly Saillisel, with Frégicourt lying on its southern slope and Haie Wood on its sole, and this valley is completely commanded by the high ground around the ruins of Morval. In order to evade enfilade fire from this position of vantage, Major-General Lee arranged that one battalion (8/East Surrey) should move under cover of the near side of the spur which forms the southern side of the valley, past Priez Farm and the northern outskirts of Rancourt, and then make direct for St. Pierre Vaast Wood ; a second battalion (7/Buffs) was to follow the first and eventually form on its left. To assist, on the right, one company of the 1/23rd London and the trench mortar battery of the 142nd Brigade (47th Division) would, in co-operation with a company from the 8/East Surrey, capture Priez Farm which lay almost on the divisional boundary, and, on the left, the 38th Division (Third Army) would form a smoke screen on the Morval side of the valley.

Priez Farm, though it seems to have escaped the barrage, was taken in due course ; but about a hundred of the enemy, with two machine guns, ran out of the building and put up resistance on the higher ground north of it. This party was rushed at 1 p.m. after a hurricane bombardment by the Stokes mortar battery, and 80 prisoners were captured. A second company of the 8/East Surrey, advancing south of the farm, mopped up the area north-east of Rancourt, whilst the remaining two companies pushed on and gained the objective. The 7/Buffs, following them, had to make a considerable detour to avoid the fire of the machine guns then in action north of Priez Farm, and was not able to report arrival on the objective until 11.15 a.m. The third battalion of the 55th Brigade, the 7/Queen's, following the path of the Buffs to a point between Priez Farm and Rancourt, turned north and by 2.30 p.m. had mopped up the area between the old front line, now held by the 54th Brigade, and the edge of St. Pierre Vaast Wood, the new front line ; the Queen's also cleared Frégicourt and Haie Wood, and secured over seven hundred prisoners.

About midday Major-General Lee, in consultation with Major-General Cubitt (38th Division), decided on an evening attack on Sailly Saillisel in the 38th Division area, which, as will be seen, a morning attack had failed to reach. In this attack the 55th Brigade (reinforced by a battalion of the 53rd) was to advance north-eastwards, whilst the 113th Brigade of the 38th Division attacked eastwards. The operation was carried out at 7 p.m. under converging creeping barrages, and was entirely successful ; by 10 p.m. the eastern outskirts of the village had been occupied. The 1st September had brought gains to the Fourth Army along its whole line north of the Somme.

THIRD ARMY[1]

The Third and First Armies had also made progress : the V Corps had done so on both wings, capturing not only Sailly Saillisel, as just mentioned, but Morval and Beaulen-court, although le Transloy still held out ; the right and centre of the IV Corps gained a little ground, which placed it in a better position for the attack which was to come on the 2nd; the VI Corps took Vaulx Vraucourt and also pushed forward its left level with the centre and right; the XVII Corps made a general advance, pushing forward a thousand yards beyond Bullecourt and finally taking both Riencourt lez Cagnicourt and Hendecourt.

After a conference with the divisional commanders of the V Corps, it was decided by Lieut.-General Shute to bring pressure on the enemy by attacking first on the north: the 21st Division against Beaulencourt at 2 a.m., and the 38th against Morval at 4.45 a.m.; afterwards, at 5.40 a.m., all three divisions were to attack: the 38th against Sailly Saillisel, the 17th against le Transloy and the 21st against a sugar factory 500 yards north of the latter place.

To put the earliest operation first: taking advantage of Riencourt les Bapaume being in the hands of the 42nd Division, the attack against Beaulencourt was made from the north. The 110th Brigade (1/Wiltshire and 6/Leicestershire in front line), advancing in the dark under a slow barrage moving at the rate of a hundred yards in six minutes, fired by two brigades of field artillery, took the enemy completely by surprise, captured 126 prisoners at the cost of 5 killed and 50 wounded, and established a line two hundred yards beyond the village on its southern and eastern sides.

The 114th Brigade of the 38th Division attacked Morval at 4.45 a.m. under a barrage of three brigades of artillery,[1] with all three battalions in front line, and after some fighting duly occupied the village. The 113th Brigade, which had followed up the attack, then relieved the 114th and completed the mopping up. The two early attacks had thus been entirely successful.

In the 5.40 a.m. attack—the 18th Division (Fourth Army) on the right, moving at practically the same time—the third brigade of the 38th Division, the 115th (17th and 2/R. Welch Fusiliers in front line) advanced E.S.E. from Lesboeufs, on the left of the divisional front, under a barrage fired by the same three brigades of field artillery as had covered the 114th Brigade. Between it and Sailly Saillisel lay open ground, every part of which was visible from le Transloy. The advance, however, went well until the Combles–le

---

[1] One of the 38th Division and both those of the 62nd.

Transloy road was passed, when fire was received both from the front and from the left. No further progress was made, and soon after 7 a.m. a counter-attack struck the left flank and forced the 2/R. Welch Fusiliers nearly back to Morval. This situation was relieved by two companies of the 10/South Wales Borderers (the brigade reserve) being sent to the left flank; they attacked with success, captured prisoners and machine guns and got touch with the 17th Division half a mile south of le Transloy. How the 113th Brigade at 7 p.m. co-operated with the 55th Brigade (18th Division) and took its objective, Sailly Saillisel, has already been related. It had been a long and hard day for the 38th Division.

As a preliminary to the 5.40 a.m. operation against le Transloy, for which the 17th Division detailed the 52nd Brigade, a company (10/Lancashire Fusiliers) was sent at midnight to capture the cemetery which lies about five hundred yards south-west of the village. In the darkness the company lost direction, so the attack miscarried. Another attempt was made at 4.20 a.m.; but the company was shelled with gas, which made the men sneeze and so disclose their presence; machine-gun fire was opened on them and the attack had to be abandoned.

The 52nd Brigade had further ill-luck when it started for the 5.40 a.m. attack, under a barrage fired by the divisional artillery, with the intention of pushing forward south and north of le Transloy and so of isolating it. The commander of the 51st Brigade, through which the 52nd had to pass, had gone out reconnoitring and, coming under short-range machine-gun fire from the German main position and his brigade-major being wounded, he had stayed with him and had not returned with the information which had been expected. By mistake, too, the starting line was placed too far in advance of the 51st Brigade line. The 9/Duke of Wellington's was stopped by fire after going only two hundred and fifty yards; the 10/Lancashire Fusiliers went farther; but, as the 21st Division on the left was unable to take the sugar factory, south of le Transloy, the Fusiliers had to fall back; and the 12/Manchester, which was to have come down on le Transloy from the north when the sugar factory had been secured, ran into machine-gun fire from it, and was therefore stopped. Further attacks on le Transloy were postponed until next day.

It was subsequently learnt that the 21st Division had not attacked the sugar factory ; the single company detailed for the operation having failed to reach the forming-up line.

The orders of the IV Corps did no more than direct the bombardment of enemy points of resistance ; but advantage was to be taken of any opportunity to advance eastwards. The New Zealand Division, in the centre, arranged for an attack to be made at 4.55 a.m. by its 1st and 3rd Brigades in order to gain some higher ground about five hundred yards in front of their position. Under a barrage fired by seven brigades of field artillery[1] both brigades attained their objective ; but the right battalion, being on a forward slope and exposed to fire from the neighbourhood of Villers au Flos to the south-east, was, in the afternoon, withdrawn behind the crest. The 42nd Division on the right pushed forward the left of its line to get touch with the New Zealand Division, and similarly the 5th Division on the left of that division, sent forward one company to capture a trench and join up with it.

The instructions given by the VI Corps were for the divisions in the line to establish themselves on a good jumping-off line for future operations, and this they succeeded in doing. The 185th Brigade of the 62nd Division, with the help of two tanks (one of which became ditched and caught fire), started at 6 a.m. under a barrage, and cleared Vaulx Vraucourt by an attack from south to north ; but machine guns on the ridge east of the village prevented any further advance in that direction. On the extreme left of the corps front, the 9th Brigade (3rd Division) made some progress in the morning towards getting up level with the 76th Brigade, and completed its task by an attack at 6 p.m.

The XVII Corps made a general advance of from a thousand to two thousand five hundred yards in two attacks,

---

[1] Three of the N.Z. Division, 317th (63rd Division), XXVII (5th Division) ; XXVI and 293rd (Army).

with zero hours at 4.50 a.m. and 6.5 p.m., respectively. The 155th Brigade of the 52nd Division, which had relieved the troops of the 56th Division during the night, was not ready at 4.50 a.m. and could not follow the barrage,[1] but by patrol fighting the brigade gained a satisfactory assembly position east of Bullecourt for the evening attack. The 171st Brigade (8/King's and 2 companies of the 2/7th King's in front line) of the 57th Division duly advanced in the half-light at 4.50 a.m.—the 1st Canadian Division on the left also doing so—against Hendecourt, and trenches south of it. Considerable resistance was encountered on the objectives ; hand-to-hand fighting took place in the trenches before they were secured by the 8/King's about 6.30 a.m., and it was 8.30 a.m. before the 2/7th King's was established in the enemy trench on the far side of Hendecourt.

The evening attack of the 52nd and 57th Division was carried out by the same two brigades, supported by the same artillery. It was completely successful in reaching its objective, the north-south ridge beyond Riencourt lez Cagnicourt and of capturing prisoners, except on the right flank. On this side there was a gap of almost a thousand yards' width to the left of the 3rd Division, and the 155th Brigade suffered severely from enfilade machine-gun fire, so that the 1/4th K.O.S.B., after losing 150 men, could go no farther than a trench a thousand yards south-east of Bullecourt, half-way to its objective. A company of the reserve battalion was brought up to make the right secure.

FIRST ARMY

At 1.25 p.m. on the 31st August, with the purpose of gaining a better position for the Canadian Corps' attack against the Drocourt–Quéant Line, Lieut.-General Currie issued orders for the 1st Canadian Division to capture Hendecourt Chateau and the Crow's Nest (a strongpoint on a prominent knoll north of the chateau), operating in conjunction with the 57th Division (XVII Corps) on the

---

[1] Fired for the 52nd Division by the artillery of the 40th and 56th Divisions and the 232nd (Army) Brigade R.F.A. ; and for the 57th. by the artillery of the 52nd Division, the 286th Brigade of the 57th Division and the V (Army) Brigade R.F.A.

right, which, as already related, was attacking Hendecourt village at 4.50 a.m. on the 1st September. It was most important to take the two localities in question before the main attack was launched on the 2nd September; for, if well defended, they might hold up the whole affair from the outset, besides continuing to command Hendecourt village, in the XVII Corps area, at short range. The arrangements for the combined attack had to be made somewhat hurriedly, but everything went according to plan. The other divisions in the front line of the corps, the 4th Canadian and 4th (British), were to push up level with the 1st Canadian.

The attack on the chateau and the strongpoint was carried out successfully by the 15th and 14th Battalions of the 3rd Canadian Brigade (Br.-General G. S. Tuxford) under a barrage fired by the divisional artillery, and both localities were taken and held in spite of counter-attacks.

At the same time the 5th Battalion of the 2nd Canadian Brigade, covered by the 39th Division artillery, attacked south-eastward along part of the Vis en Artois Switch in order to come up on the left of the 3rd Canadian Brigade. It met with strong opposition from the outset and had many casualties, but, reinforced by the supports, it succeeded, and by 10 a.m. was in touch with the front line of the 3rd Canadian Brigade. About 11.30 a.m. the enemy counter-attacked and drove the left of the battalion back, but it advanced again, and by 2 p.m. had recovered the ground which it had lost and was fully established again on its objective.

In the 4th Canadian Division (Major-General D. Watson), the 12th Canadian Brigade (Br.-General J. H. MacBrien), which held the front line in place of the left brigade of the 1st Canadian Division, was, with pauses, engaged in attack and counter-attack throughout the day. Some progress was made during the morning in getting up to a position level with the 1st Canadian Division; at 11.30 a.m. the German counter-attack against the 2nd Canadian Brigade also struck the right of the 12th, but was met by attack and repulsed. Fighting, however, continued, with the result that by evening the right of the brigade had established outposts about a thousand yards ahead of the morning line in touch with the 2nd Canadian Brigade. The left made an attack at 8.40 p.m., in co-operation with the right of the 10th

Brigade of the 4th (British) Division, in order to reach a better jumping-off line; but the enemy was found too strong, and the attempt failed.

The general result of the Canadian Corps operations on the 1st September had therefore been the gain of a good assembly position on the right and in the centre in front of the Drocourt–Quéant Line, with little change on the left. Wire-cutting had been continued, the corps heavy artillery being reinforced by the XXIX, XL and LXXVII Brigades R.G.A.

The 4th (British) Division had been so weakened by the casualties of the last few days that on the evening of the 31st it was considered not strong enough to attack on more than a one-brigade front; so during the night of the 1st–2nd September, fire preventing the operation taking place earlier, the 10th Canadian Brigade took over the frontage of the 10th (British) Brigade, leaving only the 11th (British) to represent the 4th (British) Division in the front line.

In the sectors of the XXII and VIII Corps there was no change in the situation.

By the evening of the 1st September, therefore, the inner wings of the Third and First Armies were within assaulting distance of the Drocourt–Quéant Line, and the Australian Corps, by capturing Mont St. Quentin, had turned the German line along the Somme. At this juncture Sir Douglas Haig received the following telegram from General Sir Henry Wilson, the Chief of the Imperial General Staff, sent off on the previous day, and marked " personal " :

" Just a word of caution in regard to incurring heavy
" losses in attacks on Hindenburg Line as opposed to
" losses when driving the enemy back to that line. I do
" not mean to say that you have incurred such losses,
" but I know the War Cabinet would become anxious
" if we received heavy punishment in attacking the
" Hindenburg Line without success. Wilson ".[1]

---

[1] The French (see F.O.A. vii (i), p. 288) also spoke of the Drocourt–Quéant Line as " The Hindenburg Position between Drocourt and Quéant ".

NOTE I

SITUATION AS REGARDS TANKS AND CREWS,
31ST AUGUST, 1918, 7 P.M.*

Battalion	Fighting machines on charge	Fighting machines fit	Fighting crews	Remarks
No. 1	16	16	26	Mark V Star
No. 2	18	17	25	Mark V
No. 3	18	13	29	Medium A
No. 4	26	26	30	Mark V
No. 5	Nil	Nil	13	Mark V
No. 6	21	16	32	Medium A
No. 7	25	17	36	Mark IV
No. 8	18	15	29	Mark V
No. 9	24	24	24	Mark V
No. 10	14	4	18	Mark V
No. 11	22	20	27	Mark V Star
No. 12	32	24	37	Mark IV
No. 13	20	18	27	Mark V
No. 14	24	16	25	Mark V
No. 15	23	22	27	Mark V Star
No. 17 (A.C.) ..	12	11	15	Armoured Cars
No. 1 G.C. ..	18	16	22	Includes 4 Tank Tenders
No. 2 G.C. ..	16	14	16	Includes 2 Tank Tenders
No. 1 T.S. Coy. ..	14	13	18	Supply Tanks
No. 2 T.S. Coy. ..	24	24	24	Supply Tanks
No. 3 T.S. Coy. ..	16	16	16	Supply Tanks
No. 4 T.S. Coy. ..	19	19	19	Supply Tanks
No. 5 T.S. Coy. ..	22	17	22	Supply Tanks

	G.C.	Supply Tanks	Mark V	Mark V Star	Whippets	Mark IV fighting
Machines fit for issue—						
Fourth Army Area ..	Nil	Nil	8	1	Nil	Nil
Third Army Area ..	Nil	Nil	Nil	Nil	Nil	Nil
Unfit machines still at salvage—						
Fourth Army Area ..	15	28	150	32	18	8
Third Army Area ..	2	30	23	14	35	4
Machines salved and sent to depot today ..	Nil	Nil	Nil	Nil	Nil	Nil
Machines fit for issue at Central Stores ..	Nil	15†	Nil	Nil	2	43

* A.C.=Armoured car; G.C.=Gun carrying; T.S.=Tank supply; T.T.=Tank tender.

† Includes Mark IV Supply Tanks with T.T. Gear.

Note.—The 16th Tank Battalion did not land in France until 10th or 11th September, 1918.

The 301st American Tank Battalion was not apparently in action till 29th September, 1918.

Gun-carrying tanks had either one 60-pdr., 5-inch gun or one 6-inch howitzer.

In an unsigned and undated memorandum (G.59/4) in War Diary Tank Corps, August, 1918, it is stated :

The total number of tanks actually engaged 8th–31st August (14 days' fighting) was 1,184.

The fighting strength of the Tank Corps on 8th August was approximately 7,200 of all ranks with 500 semi-trained reinforcements.

Fighting tanks on strength of battalions on 8th August, 630.

NOTE II

The French Operations, 30th August–1st September

It will be seen from the sketch map[1] that very little ground was gained by the French First and Third Armies during the 30th August–1st September, only small bites being made into the German front ; but the centre of the Tenth Army, north of Soissons, advanced nearly three miles.

NOTE III

The Germans, 30th August–1st September

(Sketches 19 and 20)

Summing up, General Schwarte (" Der grosse Krieg ", Vol. III, p. 553) says :

" The fighting which lasted from the 30th August until the
" German retirement to the Siegfried [Hindenburg] Position
" brings to a conclusion the fourth period of the battles.
" During the four days 30th August–2nd September the
" Allied Powers attacked unceasingly on a front of approxi-
" mately ninety miles from Arras to Soissons. They were in
" a position to keep on throwing fresh and well-rested
" divisions into the battle [only the 74th Division arrived,
" and was not employed]. The development of air fighting
" was great, and low-flying aeroplanes in large numbers took
" part in the attacks. . . . On the 31st the battle continued

---

[1] Sketch 20. Reduced from Map 27 in F.O.A. vii (ii). The gains made each day are shown by the dates on the lines.

" without interruption.   On this day also the progress
" between the Scarpe and Combles was not worth mentioning.
". . . On both sides of the Somme were bitter fights with
" varying results.   Between the Somme and the Oise the
" attacker could achieve no success.   On the 1st September
" fighting continued, but little change occurred."

The regimental accounts hardly bear out this summary.

No1th of the Somme on the 30th August opposing the five
divisions of the left wing of the Fourth Army were, from south to
north, the *185th, 14th Bavarian, 21st, 41st, 117th, 232nd, 14th
Reserve* and *87th*, with the *2nd Guard Division* in second line
behind Bouchavesnes ; but the divisions were much mixed up ;
besides the jumble of units in the front line, regiments of fresh
divisions had been handed to other divisions as reinforcements,
one regiment (*4th Guard Grenadiers*) of the *2nd Guard Division*
being on the night of the 29th–30th thrust into the line south of
Bouchavesnes to bolster up the *21st Division*, the remains of the
41st together with the *117th Division* being withdrawn.   A fresh
division, the *38th*, on the night of the 31st August–1st September
relieved the *21st*.   Such reliefs do not mean that all tired troops
were pulled out, only that a fresh staff took charge, and the
troops were gradually sorted out.

In general, the failure of the defence is attributed to low
effectives, some regiments " entered the fighting exhausted and
" below establishment " (" Regt. No. 80 "), and to the British
attacks by surprise without preliminary bombardment.   The
history of the *4th Guard Grenadiers* mentions that before the
regiment reached the front " some of the troops to be relieved
" had made off."   Communication failed ; an order on the 31st
for a general counter-attack at 7 p.m. did not reach regiments
until 8 p.m.

According to " Garde Gren. Regt. No. 2 " (*2nd Guard Division*),
the instructions given at 3 p.m. on the 30th were " the Army has
" given orders that in no circumstances must the enemy be
" allowed to advance beyond the line Halle-Bouchavesnes [which
" covered Péronne and Mont St. Quentin.] "

As regards the loss of Mont St. Quentin, according to " Guard
Gren. Regt. No. 1 " (*2nd Guard Division*) this regiment defended
Mont St. Quentin village on the 31st August, but was relieved
during the night by a regiment of the *38th Division* (not before
known to have been in the Péronne sector), and shifted north of
the village.   A sketch shows it in the line from the northern edge
of Mont St. Quentin to Feuillaucourt (inclusive), with the *2nd*
and *4th Regiments* beyond it.

" Regt. No. 96 " (*38th Division*) states that the division came
up from rest on the 31st August, according to B.O.A. (p. 540)
relieving the *14th Bavarian Division* which had been reduced to

700 rifles. It took over the front from the north edge of Péronne to Mont St. Quentin inclusive. Four companies of the *96th Regiment* and two of the *94th* were in the village and were attacked by the French (*sic*) and forced to leave it by a turning attack from the north. South of the *38th Division* was the *185th Division,* holding with a mixed body of troops of the *14th Bavarian, 38th* and *185th Divisions* the elbow of the Somme from La Chapellette to St. Radégonde. " Regt. No. 65 " (*185th Division*), p. 346, gives some highly interesting details of the fighting : " the " Australians stormed forward in thick lines, any gaps in which " were at once filled by supports in rear." Péronne was gassed (*sic*) and its streets swept with shell. The 15th Australian Brigade crossed the Somme mixed up with Germans, so that fire could not be directed on them . " Guard Gren. Regt. No. 4 " (p. 259) adds another lie that the Australians " killed all the wounded.'

NOTE IV

Translation of a Captured Document

119 Inf. Div.[1]   *Div. H.Q.*

  I. a No. 4056   *Secret*   29.8.18.

Instructions for the Conduct of the Defence in Winter Positions

Fighting will be conducted for the retention of the main line of resistance. All available effectives will be employed for this purpose, with the exception of an emergency garrison in the artillery protective line, which must not be employed forward of this line.

In the main line of resistance, the defence must be organized in such a manner as to ensure, by means of infantry and machine-gun fire, the prevention of a crossing of the Somme Valley by the enemy. Single machine guns (including heavy machine guns) must be pushed forward in front of the main line of resistance to the river bank, so as to have undisputed command of the river, especially at favourable crossing places (machine guns on the banks). The machine guns in the river bank emplacements must be permanently manned, but should only open fire in the event of a hostile attack. Shell-proof emplacements are not necessary ; the chief requisite is adequate concealment.

Patrols must be pushed forward into the Somme Valley by night, in order to obtain early intimation of any attempt on the part of the enemy to cross the river. Attempts by the enemy to

---

[1] This division came to the Misery–Licourt sector (west of St. Christ on the Somme) on the 27/28th August.

effect a crossing are to be expected. By skilful patrolling it should be possible to annihilate any hostile detachments which may attempt to reconnoitre the conditions of the river valley with a view to effecting a crossing, and to bring in prisoners from them.

The troops must on no account allow themselves to be lulled into a sense of security by the fact that the Somme forms an obstacle to the possibilities of an enemy advance. A determined enemy will carry out an attack at this point simply for the reason that it is least expected.

The enemy must be prevented from gaining a foothold on the eastern bank of the Somme at all costs. Demolition detachments must be sent out each night until the bridges have been thoroughly destroyed, and the remaining portions removed. Portions which cannot be reached must be destroyed by medium *Minenwerfer* fire.

CHAPTER XIX

THE BATTLES OF BAPAUME AND THE DROCOURT–QUÉANT LINE

2ND SEPTEMBER 1918

(Sketches 18, 19, 20)

Unperturbed by the discouraging telegram from the Chief of the Imperial General Staff received on the eve of the assault on the Drocourt–Quéant Position,[1] Sir Douglas Haig made no change in his plans nor in his orders and did not communicate General Wilson's misgivings to his Army commanders. He was duly rewarded with success.

Along the Somme,[2] south of Péronne, on the 2nd September activity was slight both in the French and in the British sectors, and no change took place ; attempts by Australian patrols to cross at La Chapellette were stopped by fire. On the whole French front[3] only the left of the Tenth Army near Soissons gained any ground. North of the Somme all the corps of the Fourth and Third Armies made good progress, the Canadian Corps of the First Army broke the D–Q Position and, as a result, about midday, the Germans, driven from the line they meant to hold for the winter and with the northern flank of the Somme line menaced, decided on a withdrawal of about fifteen miles to the front occupied before the March offensive.

FOURTH ARMY[4]

Lieut.-General Monash would have preferred to pause for a day in order to bring forward more artillery and give his tired troops a rest ; on the other hand, Lieut.-General Godley had a new and fresh division, the 74th, to put in, and it was of course desirable to keep the Germans on the move. It was therefore agreed that the Australian and III. Corps should, without further preparation, continue their advance,

---

[1] Henceforward in this chapter abbreviated to D–Q Position.
Though like the Hindenburg Position, it was usually spoken of as a "Line", it was a position of several lines, as will be seen.
[2] See Sketch 19.
[3] See Sketch 20.
[4] See Sketch 19.

the former to the spurs, marked by Doingt, Bussu and Aizecourt le Haut, which jut out from the portion of the main ridge lying in the area marked by Lieramont and Nurlu. Thus protected on the right, the III. Corps was to advance to cross the Canal du Nord (river Tortille), storm the Nurlu heights and secure the high ground south of them.[1]

During the night of the 1st/2nd September the Australian Corps passed the bulk of its field and heavy artillery over the Somme and the whole of the 15th Australian Brigade (5th Australian Division) crossed by the causeway south of Péronne to the support of the 14th which was in the town.

The 5th Australian Division (Major-General Sir J. J. Talbot Hobbs) was to complete the capture of Péronne and its suburbs and take St. Denis Wood (east of the village of that name) after a bombardment from 5.30 a.m. to 6 a.m., when the artillery would lift to more distant targets. Unaware that the infantry of the 2nd Australian Division was starting at 5.30 a.m., the 15th and 14th Australian Brigades did not move forward until 6 a.m. The bombardment was late and ragged, and it provoked very heavy retaliation which was maintained throughout the attack. In spite of this and of a fierce defence from behind cover of the ramparts and houses of the north-eastern suburb, and of fire from the village of .St. Denis, the Germans (portions of four divisions) were cleared out of the suburbs by 10 a.m. The marshes of the Cologne on the Flamicourt side prevented further progress eastward, but by the afternoon, after a pause for the 2nd Australian Division to drive the Germans from the Mont St. Quentin ridge, the St. Denis–Mont St. Quentin road was reached and a line occupied just short of it.

In the 2nd Australian Division (Major-General C. Rosenthal), its 7th Brigade (Br.-General E. A. Wisdom) attacked, through the 6th, north-east of Mont St. Quentin, at 5.30 a.m. on a three-battalion frontage, the fourth battalion being divided to guard the flanks. It was supported, as had been the case on the previous days, by a series of standing barrages put down by the field artillery, whilst the heavy batteries bombarded the two Allaines and other selected localities. The task of the division was to guard the right of the III.

---

[1] For a description of the canal see Note II at the end of Chapter XX.

Corps by extending a defensive flank from the southern end of Mont St. Quentin to Aizecourt le Haut, beyond which the III. Corps would provide its own protection. The right battalion almost immediately encountered heavy machine-gun fire, as the troops of the 5th Australian Division had not yet started ; on the left, the 74th Division of the III. Corps, though it also advanced at 5.30 a.m., was not making the progress expected, so a gap arose on that side. Defensive flanks were therefore formed as the centre progressed. The brigade experienced very stiff fighting, but eventually by working up trenches and by rushing from trench to trench captured both Allaines and Haut Allaines, and took toll of the enemy[1] retreating eastward in confusion over flat country. The attackers then continued on towards the objective, the trenches near Aizecourt le Haut. As the right of the III. Corps was not up, the final positions of the 7th Australian Brigade took the form of a salient covering the two Allaines. To render it secure, additional machine guns were sent up, the troops were well distributed in depth, and at dusk a battalion of the 11th Australian Brigade (detailed for mopping up duties, whose front had been taken over by the III. Corps) filled the gap between the 7th Australian Brigade and the III. Corps ; the battalion established a post on the canal, north of Haut Allaines, and cleared the enemy out of the trenches near the canal. Besides inflicting heavy losses, the 7th Australian Brigade had captured over two hundred prisoners, 93 machine guns and 8 trench mortars.

In the III. Corps, the 74th, 47th and 18th Divisions were all to advance. During the night of the 1st/2nd September the 74th Division (Major-General E. S. Girdwood), brought from Palestine, which had reached the Fourth Army area by train only a few hours earlier, had relieved the 58th Division under considerable difficulties, as many of the guides became casualties and some of the trenches allotted to it appeared to be occupied by both British and Germans. A line through a point two hundred yards north of Moislains was made the left divisional boundary, and on the right the new division took over most of the frontage of the 11th

---

[1] Mainly *38th Division.*

Australian Brigade, and the rest of it was to be absorbed as the advance proceeded. The 229th Brigade (Br.-General R. Hoare), which led the advance with the 230th (Br.-General A. A. Kennedy) in support, and the 231st (Br.-General C. E. Heathcote) in reserve, the 47th Division covering the left, had first to turn the enemy out of the trench selected as the starting line ; for it turned out that it had not been captured on the previous evening by the 3rd Australian Division, as supposed ; the enemy, too, had during the night pushed some machine-gun posts well forward, within the barrage line and they had to be cleared away before the infantry advance could begin ; thus the start was late, the protection of the barrage[1] was lost and, owing to the amount of wire and old trenches to be negotiated, the infantry were unable to catch it up ; but they moved as fast as possible and soon crossed the Canal du Nord.

Receiving enfilade fire from Allaines, not yet in Australian hands, the right, the 12/Somerset L.I., turned aside, attacked the village, took seventy prisoners, and then resumed its proper direction north-eastward. The left flank of the other leading battalion, the 14/Black Watch, hugged the canal, making for Moislains, which lay ahead and would, it had been hoped, from the direction of advance only require mopping up ; but now machine-gun fire was opened from the village, and was also received on the right flank, already in the outskirts of Aizecourt le Haut ; it struck even the right rear, whilst field-gun fire plastered the front. The two companies of the 16/Devonshire, the brigade reserve, detailed for mopping-up, were therefore sent to attack Moislains, but only gained a footing in the outskirts at heavy cost. At this juncture, about 10 a.m., the Germans counter-attacked the 229th Brigade from the east and north-east, and forced its battalions back to the canal.[2] This being an unfavourable position, badly overlooked, a retirement was made back to the starting line, during which troops of the 140th Brigade of the 47th Division, detailed to form the left defensive flank

---

[1] Fired by the brigades of the 58th Division (290th and 291st) and the LXXXVI. and 104th (Army) Brigades R.F.A. The divisional brigades, the XLIV. and 117th, were to go forward when the limit of range of the others was reached.

[2] The counter-attack, according to B.O.A., p. 540, was made by the *Alpine Corps*, which had arrived on 1st September, hastily brought back from the Somme " to stiffen the shaky front and revive the worn-out " troops ".

and moving in rear of the 229th Brigade, became intermingled with it. Meantime, one of the battalions of the supporting brigade, the 16/R. Sussex, under heavy shelling, had reached Haut Allaines and got touch with the 2nd Australian Division ; but the 229th Brigade now lay half a mile away to the north-west, and it was not until 5.30 p.m., when a company of the 15/Suffolk (230th Brigade) came up, that this gap was closed.

At 7.40 p.m. Major-General Girdwood ordered the 230th and 229th Brigades to advance their outpost line at dusk to the forward slope of the Tortille valley and relieve all troops of the 47th Division south of the interdivisional boundary. This operation was carried out with difficulty, and then, by arrangement with the 2nd Australian Division, orders were given for all troops of the 230th Brigade which were south of the canal to be withdrawn ; but the message reached the 16/Sussex so late that, as a daylight relief was impossible, it remained in the line until 1 a.m. on the 4th September. The 74th Division was unfortunate in its first fight in France in being not only handicapped by a bad start, but also in meeting the *Alpine Corps* of picked troops, after it had been told that it had only a beaten division in front of it which would make no stand. The incident showed once more that experience gained in outside theatres was insufficient training for the Western Front ; never, as one of its Staff officers said, had the division encountered such artillery fire.

In the 47th Division, whilst the 140th Brigade on the right, as already mentioned, was to maintain connection with the 74th Division, the 142nd, attacking through the 141st, was to capture the trenches along the south-western edge of Vaux Wood and their extension southwards towards Moislains. Losing touch of the 229th Brigade (74th Division) which it should have followed—the runners, the only means of communication, suffered many casualties—the 140th Brigade passed through Moislains Wood and moved down the forward slope towards Moislains. The 1/17th and 1/15th London, with much reduced numbers, which were leading, came under heavy artillery and machine-gun fire, but, though the battalions had no barrage to cover them, they reached a trench overlooking Moislains. It was soon discovered that

Germans were not only in the village, but also in the northern part of the trench which the Londoners had occupied, and in another to the left rear ; and soon afterwards, just as the 229th Brigade fell back carrying some of the 140th men with it, counter-attacks developed against the right front and left rear. Though the enemy movement across the open was stopped, bombing attacks up trenches against the left flank continued well into the afternoon, and, owing to the shortage of bombs with which to reply, were checked with difficulty and caused serious losses until the German parties were mopped up by the 18/London (141st Brigade, now in reserve).

For half an hour before the 142nd Brigade started at 5.30 a.m. to pass through the 141st on the western edge of St. Pierre Vaast Wood, the enemy maintained a heavy barrage, and throughout the advance over ground cut up by old trenches and shell-holes offered strong opposition.[1] Nevertheless, the brigade had a successful day. The 1/22nd London, on the right, reached a trench N.N.E. of Moislains, the northern part of the trench which the 140th had occupied; in the gap between the two brigades were several parties of Germans, those who, as above related, were using bombs against the 140th, and were not mopped up for some time. On the left, the 1/24th London managed to cut off a large party of Germans in dug-outs a little west of the south-west edge of St. Pierre Vaast Wood ; two officers and sixty men were captured, most of the rest making good their escape into the wood, where they stampeded some of their own defenders. The battalion was then able to reach the south-western edge of Vaux Wood, as intended, with its left bent back towards Lonely Copse. This defensive flank was extended during the afternoon by the 1/4th R. Welch Fusiliers (Pioneers), which previously had cleared the southern portion (south of a line through Lonely Copse) of St. Pierre Vaast Wood by working from north to south. Besides many prisoners, a battery of field guns was captured.

Farther north, the 53rd Brigade of the 18th Division was to clear St. Pierre Vaast Wood north of the 47th Division

---

[1] For conspicuous gallantry in rushing machine guns which were holding up the advance, Private J. Harvey (1/22nd London) was awarded the V.C. He was a company cook ; but every available man from the transport lines had been brought up.

sector and capture Government Farm beyond the northern corner. After the batteries had fired a twenty minutes' bombardment on the enemy front line, the 8/R. Berkshire and 10/Essex advanced at 5.50 a.m. under a creeping barrage which in the course of time became a series of standing barrages. The Berkshire first formed along the track through the northern part of the wood which led to Government Farm, and south of it a standing barrage was put down for a time ; a patrol was then pushed about five hundred yards down the eastern edge of the wood, picking up isolated German machine-gun posts, which fought feebly, so that no casualties were suffered. Two companies were next sent southward into the wood, where they captured 3 officers and 95 other ranks. The hostile shelling from guns of all calibres now became exceedingly heavy, many of the guns being in Vaux Wood and firing at close range. The complete clearing of the wood, which had a thick undergrowth, took therefore a long time and was not accomplished until the 4/R. Welch Fusiliers, had dealt with the southern portion. Definite and satisfactory touch was not, however, established with that division until next morning. The 10/Essex on the left met with inconsiderable opposition, but its progress was impeded by the thickness of the under-growth. The objective trench north-east of the wood was secured, but the heap of ruins known as Government Farm, round which a standing barrage was put down, was not actually occupied. A counter-attack a little farther north under a machine-gun barrage was repulsed by the 7/R. West Kent, the third battalion of the brigade.

After the success of the 53rd Brigade, the 141st was withdrawn from the western edge of St. Pierre Vaast Wood to reorganize. The 140th Brigade, reduced to no more than about seven hundred rifles, which, after its many days' fighting, had been detailed only to follow up a successful advance, and now found itself, unwarned, in the front line, was also relieved to rest and refit, the 74th Division extending northwards and the 142nd Brigade southwards to occupy the vacated front facing Moislains. The two brigades of the 47th Division left the line feeling that however severe their losses had been they had not been in vain and that the end was approaching.

FIRST ARMY[1]

As the success of the operations north of the Somme on the 2nd September depended on the Canadian Corps, the advance of the XVII. Corps, the left of the Third Army, being entirely dependent upon it, the narrative of the First Army will be given before that of the Third Army, whose movements will then be described from left to right.

The D.-Q. Position now to be attacked consisted of a front system and a support system, each with two lines of trenches provided with concrete shelters and machine-gun posts, and very heavily wired. The front line was mainly on the crest or on a forward slope, the support system on a reverse slope. It was without the depth of the Hindenburg Position ; but the Buissy Switch, connecting with the Hindenburg Support, served as a retrenchment.

The orders of the First Army (General Sir H. S. Horne) for the attack were issued at 7.45 p.m. on the 31st August :

" 1. Canadian Corps, with III. Brigade Tank Corps,
" 1 regiment of cavalry and 17th Armoured Car Battalion
" attached, will attack the D.-Q. Line on the 2nd
" September. Success will be exploited by pushing
" forward rapidly to seize the crossings over the Canal
" du Nord between Sains lez Marquion and Palluel
" inclusive, and the high ground [just beyond the canal]
" Deligny Mill–Oisy le Verger. Zero hour will be
" notified later [it was made 5 a.m.].

" 2. XVII. Corps, Third Army, is co-operating in the
" attack, and after the line has been forced, is intended
" to operate south-east on Quéant.

" 3. XXII. Corps will secure the left flank of the
" attack by holding the crossings over the Trinquis
" Brook, and will exercise pressure on the enemy with
" advanced troops. The commanders of the XXII. and
" Canadian Corps will direct special attention to the
" necessity for close touch between their troops at the
" boundary of their respective corps. R.A. XXII. Corps
" will be employed to assist the operations of the
" Canadian Corps by engaging hostile batteries which
" can fire on the left flank of the attack, and by blocking
" the crossings over the Scarpe river between Biache

---

[1] See Sketch 18.

" St. Vaast and Brebières [4 miles below Biache] with
" its fire.

" 4. VIII. Corps will continue to exercise pressure on
" the enemy with advanced troops, and will employ all
" available artillery to engage hostile batteries which
" can fire on the left flank of the Canadian attack.

" 5. Cavalry Corps will be held at 4 hours' notice to
" move, from zero hour on day of attack.

" 6. 1. Brigade R.A.F. will assist the attack according
" to arrangements made direct with the Canadian
" Corps ".

Lieut.-General Currie's orders were issued early on the
morning of the 31st.   The attack was to be carried out by
the 1st and 4th Canadian and 4th (British) Divisions,
with the 1st (British) Division and Brutinel's Independent
Force in reserve.   The general idea of the operations was
to break through the D.–Q. Position astride the Arras–
Marquion road and then swing outwards, rolling up the
lines to north and south.   The reserves of the two flank
divisions were therefore to be concentrated behind their
inner flanks.

The first objective was the line Cagnicourt–Dury–high
ground south of Etaing, beyond the D.–Q. Support System.
This having been gained, the advance was to be resumed at
Zero+3 hours to the second objective, the high ground west
of and overlooking the Canal du Nord and the Sensée,
marked roughly by Sains lez Marquion–Baralle–east of
Ecourt St. Quentin–Récourt, and thence, turning westwards,
back to the first objective south of Etaing.   Two further
objectives were mentioned, but, as the canal was not crossed,
need not be defined here.

Two companies of Mark V. tanks were allotted to each of
the three attacking divisions, and during the night of the
1st/2nd September the noise of their assembly was drowned
by aeroplanes flying over the area.   Their task was to aid
the infantry to reach and mop up the D.–Q. front system,
and they were to start early enough, before Zero if necessary,
to ensure that as many tanks as possible reached the first
line of enemy wire ahead of the infantry.   They were not to
go beyond the first objective except on the flanks, where
they might be used to mop up the Buissy Switch on the right
and Etaing on the left.

The artillery support, under Major-General E. W. B. Morrison, C.R.A. of the Canadian Corps, was provided by twenty brigades of field artillery[1] and eleven of heavy.[2]

The night-bomber squadrons of the I. and III. Brigades R.A.F. during the night of the 1st/2nd September attacked the defended villages on the left flank, Saudemont, Ecourt St. Quentin and Palluel, billeting areas and aerodromes. On the day of attack, No. 8 Squadron co-operated with the tanks, No. 73 dealt with anti-tank guns, No. 6 co-operated with the cavalry, and Nos. 5 and 52 with the attacking divisions. The day-bombers of the IX. Brigade, escorted by fighter squadrons, between 6.30 and 9 a.m. attacked the stations of Douai (7 miles north of Palluel), Aubigny au Bac (where the Cambrai–Douai railway crosses the Sensée), Marquion and Valenciennes, and certain bridges over the Sensée. Low-flying fighters of No. 54, 64, 208 and 209 Squadrons of the I. Brigade were given as main objectives various villages already in the heavy artillery programme, as a complement to it, and detailed a few planes to attack trains. Offensive patrols of No. 40 and 22 Squadrons gave protection to the low-flying craft and the armoured car force, and attacked kite balloons.[3]

The 3rd and 2nd Canadian Brigades led the attack south-eastwards of the 1st Canadian Division (Major-General A. C. Macdonell), each with three batteries of machine guns (24) and one composite company of tanks of the 14th Battalion attached. The 1st Canadian Brigade (Br.-General W. A. Griesbach), in reserve at first, was to pass through the 3rd and 2nd after the capture of the Buissy Switch (which lay between the first and second objectives) and take Buissy and Baralle.

---

[1] Those of the 1st, 2nd, 3rd, 4th and 5th Canadian Divisions, 4th, 15th and 39th Divisions, and the LII., 126th, 282nd and VIII. Canadian (Army) Brigades. Seven were allotted to the 1st Canadian Division, eight to the 4th, and five to the 4th (British) Division.

[2] XCI., LXXVιII. and L. Brigades R.G.A. were affiliated to the three attacking divisions; XIX., XXIX., XLII., XLVIII1., LIII., LXXVII. and LXXX1. did counter-battery work and fired on the bridges over the Canal du Nord and the Sensée; XL. remained directly under the C.H.A. (Br.-General R. H. Massie).

[3] For details see " War in the Air " vi., pp. 492–5.

At 5 a.m. the 3rd Canadian Brigade sent forward the 16th and 13th Battalions on a 1,600-yard frontage preceded by eight tanks. The enemy's artillery fire was light and did not cause many casualties, although here and elsewhere some of the wire had to be cut by hand, the tanks providing smoke to cover the workers. In general the obstacle, though thick, was sufficiently cut or trampled down. After a short resistance to the Canadian charge, the Germans surrendered in great numbers and the two trenches of the front system of the D.–Q. Position were taken. Continuing on without the tanks, the 13th Battalion captured the support system ; but intense machine-gun fire from the right, where the 57th Division was not yet up, now struck the 16th Battalion after it had gone about two hundred yards, and checked it. Under this fire, Lieut.-Colonel C. W. Peck, after vainly trying to get assistance from the tanks, which were engaged in mopping up, arranged for as many machine guns as possible to be brought forward to sweep the ridge which was the source of the hostile fire, and after a struggle of nearly an hour, the 16th was able to proceed and reach the support system.[1] Neither here nor elsewhere did the elaborate German defences of the D.–Q. Position, with an excellent field of fire, give the trouble that had been expected.

Between 8 and 9 a.m. the 15th and 14th Battalions of the 3rd Canadian Brigade passed through the 16th and 13th and continued the advance. They were now beyond the help of the artillery barrage and of the six remaining tanks, which had orders to go no farther than the first objective ; so, against considerable opposition, the attack was carried on by platoon and section rushes under rifle and machine-gun fire. The 15th, its right flank protected by some of the 16th Battalion, and later by the 3rd Battalion (1st Canadian Brigade), took Bois de Bouche, and by 1.30 p.m. reached the Quéant–Marquion railway, where its flank guard joined it.

The 14th Battalion had meantime taken Cagnicourt with hardly any casualties, the Germans surrendering in their dug-outs. The Bois de Loison was then overrun, and about 11.15 a.m. the battalion was in the Buissy Switch ; but here the enemy did not at once collapse, and fighting in this part of the Switch continued until nightfall.

---

[1] Lieut.-Colonel Peck was awarded the V.C. " for most conspicuous bravery and skilful leading when in attack under intense fire ".

The 2nd Canadian Brigade, on the left of the 3rd, attacked with its 7th Battalion and four tanks on a thousand-yard front, with the 10th Battalion and three tanks in support. In spite of the good barrage, the 7th almost at once came under fire of advanced machine-gun posts. These were gradually mastered, and with the tanks in front doing excellent work, the battalion assaulted and took the forward system of the D.–Q. Position ; seven tanks assisting, the support system and the northern end of the Buissy Switch were then taken without great difficulty, large numbers of the enemy surrendering.

At 8 a.m. the 10th Battalion passed through the 7th. Here also the attack was now beyond the barrage zone, and by 8.45 a.m. five tanks had been knocked out, and the advance, slightly downhill, was stopped by machine-gun fire. Assistance was then obtained from a field battery, sent forward for the purpose of dealing with nests of resistance, and from several captured German guns and machine guns, and the infantry again went on, working round the flanks of the opposition rather than attacking frontally. In Villers lez Cagnicourt, just east of the Buissy Switch, a long broadside village lying across a depression, the enemy offered stubborn resistance, so the attack had to proceed methodically ; but between 4 and 5 p.m. the whole of the village was in Canadian hands, and a line established on the road which ran through its eastern edge.[1] Here a halt was made whilst an artillery barrage was arranged to cover a further advance of about a thousand yards, which was made at 6 p.m. The Germans in the Buissy Switch south of Villers lez Cagnicourt made a very good defence, and it was not until 11 p.m., after hand-to-hand fighting, that this trench was taken and a line consolidated beyond it.[2] The 8th Battalion now came up on the left flank of the 10th, took over the northern sector of the outposts and formed a defensive flank along the Arras–Marquion road in touch with the

---

[1] Sergeant A. G. Knight, 10th Canadian Battalion, was awarded a posthumous Victoria Cross for conspicuous gallantry at Villers lez Cagnicourt, where on three separate occasions he charged parties of the enemy single-handed.

[2] The *1st Guard Reserve Division*, which had been in reserve since 25th August, after losing 2,400 in prisoners alone in the 8th August and subsequent fighting, had, on 1st/2nd September taken over the Buissy Switch. The *2nd Guard Reserve Regiment* held Villers lez Cagnicourt, which, according to a sketch in its history, had three lines of defence, and it lost 10 officers and 556 other ranks. The *1st Guard Reserve Regiment*, on its left (south) lost 31 and 615.

4th Canadian Division. The day's fighting of the 1st Canadian Division had thus resulted in the capture of the two systems of the D.-Q. Position, the first objective, and some progress across the Buissy Switch towards the second beyond the canal.

The 4th Canadian Division (Major-General Sir D. Watson) attacked with its 12th and 10th Brigades (Br.-Generals J. H. MacBrien and R. J. F. Hayter), twenty-five tanks of the 9th Battalion and nine of the 11th Battalion co-operating. Behind the artillery barrage, the divisional machine-gun battalion (less 24 guns) contributed overhead fire. The 11th Canadian Brigade (Br.-General V. W. Odlum), with the remaining 24 machine guns, was to pass through the other two brigades at the first objective. When at 5 a.m. the 72nd, 38th and 85th Battalions of the 12th Canadian Brigade advanced, each on a five-hundred yard front, the twenty-two tanks allotted to this brigade had not arrived, and some opposition was experienced from enemy outposts, some of which were so close to the jumping-off line as to be untouched by the barrage.[1] Then, aided by the tanks, the D–Q front and support systems were taken without great difficulty ; in places the Germans fought stoutly and three tanks were lost, whilst in others they were eager to surrender. The advance was then continued across a shallow valley ; but as soon as the three battalions reached the crest of the ridge beyond they came under fire of machine guns sited in depth out of reach of the artillery barrage ; they suffered severe casualties and found a sunken road which runs south from Dury strongly held ; so the attack was checked a little short of the first objective.

The 10th Canadian Brigade, with the 47th and 50th Battalions in front line and eleven tanks, had much the same experience as the 12th. Both systems of the D–Q Position were overrun and many prisoners taken. Leaving the tanks, the 46th Battalion then pushed through to attack Dury, another broadside village ; machine-gun fire was received from the right, but the position whence it came was outflanked and captured, and Dury was then occupied without much opposition.

---

[1] All three battalions reported that the tanks did not advance with the infantry at zero hour, but caught up afterwards. The O.C. 9th Tank Battalion claims that the tanks crossed the front line in advance of the infantry, and that 23 out of 25 reached the objective.

The two brigades of the 4th Canadian Division had thus reached, or nearly reached, their first objective very quickly, and at 8 a.m. the second phase of their attack opened. The 78th Battalion of the 12th Canadian Brigade and the 44th Battalion of the 10th, with the 11th Canadian Brigade (54th, 75th and 87th Battalions in front) between them, were to pass through the line. They suffered many casualties from fire during their approach march, and the advance had then to be made without barrage or tanks, and had no more shell support than one battery attached to each brigade and the brigade light trench mortars could afford. The 78th Battalion was not able to advance very much beyond the line already held ; the 11th Canadian Brigade, after hard fighting, drove the defenders from the sunken road south of Dury, but was unable to advance beyond the D–Q Position. Thus, the general result was that the 4th Canadian Division had reached its first objective, but, without artillery support, was not able to proceed farther.

The 4th (British) Division had only the 12th Brigade (Br.-General E. A. Fagan) in the line, with a frontage of fifteen hundred yards, but there were available to support it five brigades of field artillery, a battery of 8-inch howitzers and three batteries of 6-inch, nine tanks of the 11th Battalion, and 48 machine guns of the 4th and 11th Machine-Gun Battalions. The tanks found it impossible to come up behind the 12th Brigade owing to marshy ground ; they therefore went round by the north and caught up with the infantry in the D–Q front system. The 2/Essex and 1/King's Own led the advance. They were to avoid the village of Etaing, on the Sensée, to the left front at the northern end of the D–Q Position and it was to be taken from the south by the tanks after the D–Q front system had been secured ; it gave trouble to the left flank throughout the advance, as did also Prospect Farm south of it. By some mistake the tanks attacked Etaing Wood on a spur, half-a-mile south of the village, instead of Etaing itself, and thus did not stop the enfilade fire. Frontal resistance except from outposts which had escaped the barrage, was, however, insignificant, and the Essex and King's Own took both the D–Q systems with comparatively light casualties, and reached the first objective, where the 2/Lancashire Fusiliers reinforced them. At 8 a.m., in the second phase of the operation, the 11th Brigade passed through the 12th ; but it came under machine-gun fire from the left rear, from Prospect Farm and its vicinity. Some progress was made on the right, but eventually the troops fell back to the second trench of the D–Q Support System. Later in the day Prospect Farm was taken by a company of the 1/King's Own (12th Brigade) ; but well placed machine guns in Etaing Wood, north of the farm, barred further progress towards Etaing, and no assistance was rendered by the XXII. Corps, next on the left, except by the fire of artillery and machine guns on the D–Q System. At night, therefore, the 11th and 12th Brigades, somewhat intermixed, held the D–Q Support System with the left flank bent back through Prospect Farm south of Etaing.

The D–Q Position had been broken through everywhere where it had been attacked by the Canadian Corps, and, except on the extreme left, the line established well beyond it.

THIRD ARMY

The Third Army orders for the operations of the 2nd September, based on those of G.H.Q. of the 29th August for the attack on the D–Q Position,[1] were issued on the 31st and ran as follows :

" On the date on which the First Army attacks the " D–Q Line [subsequently fixed as the 2nd September] :

" 1. (a) V. Corps will complete the capture of Sailly " Saillisel and le Transloy, if not already in our hands " [the former was taken on the 1st September], and will " push forward with vigour towards Manancourt and " Etricourt [on the Canal du Nord about 4 miles away].

" (b) IV. Corps will capture Haplincourt and Beugny " and will push forward vigorously towards Ytres and " Vélu [the former on the Canal du Nord].

" (c) VI. Corps will capture Morchies and Lagnicourt " [2 miles ahead] and will push forward vigorously " towards Beaumetz [south-east of Morchies].

" 2. All Mark V tanks will be held in Army reserve " from receipt of this order and will not be available " during these operations.

---

[1] Given at the beginning of Chapter XVIII.

" 3. Zero hour for the operations ordered in paragraph
" 1 will be fixed by corps.
" 4. XVII. Corps will co-operate with the attack of
" the Canadian Corps, as arranged ".[1]

The orders of the XVII. Corps (Lieut.-General Sir C.
Fergusson), on the left of the Canadian Corps, had been
issued on the evening of the 31st August, and the preliminary
movement contemplated in them, the capture of Riencourt
lez Cagnicourt and the ground south of it, had been carried
out on the 1st September. The next objective included the
southernmost part of the D–Q Position. No tanks being
available, a frontal attack was not to be made against it,
but if the Canadian Corps was successful in breaking the
line, the left division (57th) of the XVII. Corps was to pass
through it on the immediate right of the Canadians and
then turn southwards and mop up the front facing the corps.
The right division (52nd) would be directed to conform. If
all went well, a third objective was to be tackled at once ;
it was the piece of the Hindenburg Position west of Quéant
and a line running north-eastward from that village to the
Bois de Bouche, where junction would be made with the
Canadian front ; the 63rd Division (transferred from the IV.
Corps on the 31st August) was then to pass through the 57th
and exploit the success by advancing on Inchy (on the
Canal du Nord) along the higher ground north of Quéant.
The ground over which the XVII. Corps was now operating
had been the scene of fighting in April 1917, when, however,
the British faced Inchy–Pronville–Quéant–Bullecourt, look-
ing northwards.

During the night of the 1st/2nd September No. 102
Squadron R.A.F. bombed villages behind the German line,
whilst low-flying aeroplanes co-operated in the attack, and
No. 12 Squadron which found the contact patrols for the
XVII. Corps kept it informed of the progress of the Canadian
Corps, on which its advance depended.

Zero hour was 5 a.m., and the first barrage, fired for the
corps by five brigades of field artillery,[2] was a flank protection
for the Canadian Corps, with 15 per cent. of smoke, 45
shrapnel and 40 H.E., and, according to plan, no infantry
advance was made. At Zero+84 minutes this barrage

---

[1] This refers to the instructions given on 31st August (see p. 600).
[2] Those of the 52nd and 57th Divisions and the V. (Army) Brigade R.F.A.

ceased, and the batteries (except those of the 286th Brigade of the 57th Division, which were to be held in readiness to advance) switched their fire on to an approximately east and west line across the D–Q Position two hundred yards south of the divisional boundary with the Canadian Corps. Six minutes later the barrage moved southward and covered the advance of the 172nd Brigade down the D–Q front system.   Half an hour earlier, that is at 6 a.m., the seven brigades of heavy artillery[1] ceased counter-battery work, and concentrated until 7.15 a.m. on the ground ahead, that is to say the triangle between the two branches of the southern end of the D–Q front system, on the Hindenburg Position north-west of Quéant, and on Quéant and other selected localities.   The 2/4th S. Lancashire and 1/R. Munster Fusiliers, after advancing on a one-company front behind the Canadian right, followed the barrage down the forks of the D–Q front system, covered on the right by the fire of the 57th Machine Gun Battalion.   Though there was some opposition, they were completely successful in capturing both branches.   Subsequently the R. Munster Fusiliers pushed forward to the third objective, about a thousand yards east of the eastern branch.

From his observation post, Br.-General Leggett, whose 156th Brigade, passing through the 155th Brigade, was, under a barrage, to lead the attack of the 52nd Division, was able to see the early success of the 57th Division, and on reporting it received, at 7.45 a.m., orders by telephone from Major-General Hill to advance at 8.45 a.m.   The 1/7th Scottish Rifles and 1/4th Royal Scots easily pushed along and took the first thirteen hundred yards of the Hindenburg Front Line as far as the D–Q front line.   After this the right and centre were held up by uncut wire, and the Germans seemed inclined to stand ; they were outflanked and enfiladed by the left, and by 3 p.m. the whole line as far as the outskirts of Quéant was taken.   The 1/7th Royal Scots, in reserve, then appeared and during the evening occupied the Hindenburg Support Line up to the Quéant–Cagnicourt road.

Meantime, the 1/4th R. Scots Fusiliers of the 155th Brigade had followed the right of the 156th ; at 5 p.m. it entered the Hindenburg Front Position and established itself on the right to beyond the Hirondelle stream, but not

---

[1] VIII., XIII., XXII., LIV., LXII., LXVI. and LXXXVIII. R.G.A.

far enough south to connect with the front line of the 3rd Division, which lay to the south-west. Patrols sent out during the night found Quéant evacuated.

The advance of the 63rd Division (Major-General C. A. Blacklock since the 30th August) was also dependent on the success of the 57th Division (Major-General R. W. R. Barnes), and the order for it to move at 8.10 a.m. was given by the corps commander an hour earlier. Its operations on this day were more of the nature of open warfare than of trench attacks. The 188th Brigade (Br.-General J. F. S. D. Coleridge), which had concentrated behind Hendecourt by 7.30 a.m., was entrusted with the attack. It was to pass through the 57th Division and make for the Quéant–Marquion railway between the Hindenburg Support Line and the right of the Canadian Corps. No barrage was available until after 9.30 a.m., as all the batteries were supporting the 57th and 52nd Divisions ; so the first part of the advance by the 2/Royal Irish and 1/Royal Marines was made by the use of infantry weapons and machine guns only, and it was checked by machine-gun fire from the as yet untaken Hindenburg Support and D–Q Support Lines. Artillery and machine-gun assistance was arranged, the Anson Battalion reinforced the centre, and at 1 p.m. the 188th Brigade went forward again and reached the Quéant–Buissy road a little short of its objective. The attached Drake Battalion (189th Brigade) was then brought up on the left, and at 6.15 p.m. it advanced southward towards Pronville ; it cleared the enemy from the long ridge in front of the 188th Brigade, broke through the Hindenburg Support Line and reached the Quéant–Inchy road. The Hood and Hawke Battalions (189th Brigade) were also placed at Br.-General Coleridge's disposal, and at 6.50 p.m. he ordered them to attack Inchy at dusk. They had difficulty in getting into position, and it was quite dark before the advance began. The two battalions were met by machine-gun fire, and, after going some distance, fell back to the railway line, which had been the day's objective. The Drake Battalion remained isolated east of Pronville.[1]

The general line of the XVII. Corps, therefore, extended westward from the Canadian right, excluding Quéant, to within a thousand yards of the 3rd Division (VI. Corps).

---

[1] The commanding officer, Commander D. M. W. Beak, was awarded the V.C. for his courage and leadership during this period.

The only part of the objectives of the corps not taken was at the extreme end of the left flank, but the encirclement of Quéant and Pronville from the higher ground north and east of these villages had been begun.

The VI. Corps (Lieut.-General Sir A. Haldane), which had a series of narrow spurs and valleys in front of it, had met with strong resistance, and did not capture the line Morchies–Lagnicourt, the objective named in Third Army orders ; a subsidiary objective, given in corps orders, 2,000 yards short of it, entailing an advance of about twelve hundred yards, was, however, secured. The 3rd and 62nd Divisions attacked at 5.30 a.m. with a company of Mark IV. tanks of the 12th Tank Battalion attached to each, whilst one company of whippets of the 6th Tank Battalion remained under corps orders. Only 18 hours' warning had been given to the tank commanders, so they could not arrange a practice with the infantry, and could do little more than give the officers concerned an address on co-operation with tanks. The ground in front, reported to be good going and dry, turned out to be stiff clay, with numerous deep sunken roads and high banks, impassable for tanks, and as even the starting lines for the 2nd September had been in the hands of the enemy on the 1st September there was little opportunity to reconnoitre.

The 8th Brigade (Br.-General B. D. Fisher) led the advance of the 3rd Division, all three battalions in line, assisted by nine tanks and covered by the fire of seven brigades of field artillery and two of heavy,[1] and two machine-gun companies. The barrage was excellent, and at first good progress was made. The outskirts of Lagnicourt were nearly reached and Noreuil was taken. Four tanks were knocked out whilst in motion, one received a direct hit whilst stationary, two were ditched and one broke its trail twice. Thus seven remained derelict on the field, and only two rallied. There seems to have been lack of co-operation between them and the infantry.[2] The right battalion came under very heavy

---

[1] Of the 3rd and Guards Divisions, XIV., LXXII. and 155th (Army) Brigades R.F.A., and XXXIX. and LXX. Brigades R.G.A.

[2] Accounts differ as to this. The infantry diaries record : 7/Shropshire L.I., on right, " tanks did good work until knocked out " ; 2/Royal Scots, in centre, " two tanks co-operated but could not climb the steep slope

Continued at foot of next page.

enfilade fire and fell back to a trench south-west of Noreuil ; the other two could get no farther than an extension of the same trench east of Noreuil.[1] Such was the situation about 10 a.m.[2] At 1 p.m. a message was received that the 62nd Division, on the right, had been counter-attacked, and that the enemy was within twelve hundred yards of Vaulx Vraucourt. The Shropshire were ordered to form a defensive flank on this side, the 2/Suffolk (76th Brigade, but at the disposal of the 8th) taking their place on the right of the Royal Scots. Later, as the enemy resistance seemed to slacken, two whippets co-operating, a very slight advance to better trenches was made.

The 62nd Division (Major-General Sir R. D. Whigham) sent the 187th Brigade (Br.-General A. J. Reddie), with the 9/Durham L.I. (Pioneers) attached, to attack through the two brigades in the line. The creeping barrage was fired by seven brigades of field artillery, and support was given by two brigades of heavy artillery,[3] eight tanks of the 12th Tank Battalion and two companies of machine guns. The IV. Corps, on the right of the VI., had attacked at 5.15 a.m., a quarter of an hour before VI. Corps Zero, part of the barrage beginning at 5.6 a.m., which perhaps led to the enemy being aroused ; for he put down a barrage on the 62nd Division's front before the three battalions of the 187th Brigade, the 2/4th and 5/K.O.Y.L.I. and 2/4th York & Lancaster, had started in line. The casualties were not at first heavy, and by 6.50 a.m., with the help of the tanks,

---

Continued from previous page.
" east of Noreuil " ; 1/R. Scots Fusiliers, on the left, " the tanks were " of no use ". The accounts of the II. Tank Brigade, the 12th Tank Battalion and tank officers concerned are to the effect that the infantry was 40 minutes late in starting (all the infantry divisions say the start was made at zero hour), and that the tanks advanced alone, with aeroplanes too far aloft to be protective, and that the enemy's observation balloons were left unmolested.

[1] Practically the line shown on Sketch 18 as that reached during the day.

[2] Nearly all the officers having become casualties, Lieut.-Colonel R. A. West, of the North Irish Horse, commanding the 6th Tank Battalion, who had ridden forward to reconnoitre, took charge and rode up and down with his orderly, encouraging the men, thereby drawing fire, as some of them complained, until he was killed. He was posthumously awarded the V.C. Since 8th August he had already gained the M.C. and a bar to the D.S.O.

[3] Those of the 2nd Division Artillery, and XVIII., XXXIV., LXXVI., XCIII. and 315th (Army) Brigades R.F.A. ; LX. and LXXXIV. Brigades R.G.A.

six of the eight being knocked out by anti-tank rifles, the right had reached the Beugny–Vaulx Vraucourt road, and the left had taken Vaulx Wood (east of Vaulx Vraucourt). Ten minutes later the enemy counter-attacked the left of the brigade with artillery support and recaptured the wood and ground north of it. The lost ground was recovered by an attack of the 9/Durham L.I. (Pioneers) at 2.30 p.m., and the position gained was held. At night the 62nd Division was relieved by the 2nd.

The orders of the IV. Corps (Lieut.-General Sir M. Harper) directed the 5th Division, on the left, to capture Beugny and Delsaux Farm (south of it) and the low ridge beyond them, and the 42nd, on the right, to capture Villers au Flos, the New Zealand Division, in the centre, conforming to their advance, with exploitation if possible. All the objectives were attained, except that Beugny, though surrounded on three sides, was not actually occupied.

In the 5th Division (Major-General J. Ponsonby), the 15th Brigade (Br.-General R. D. F. Oldman), with four tanks (one of which was knocked out) and a machine-gun company attached, passed through the 95th at 5.15 a.m. covered by a barrage found by four brigades of field artillery,[1] whilst the XXXIV. Brigade R.G.A. bombarded the objective localities. The 1/Norfolk, on the right, took Delsaux Farm without difficulty ; the 1/Cheshire, though caught by an enemy barrage some minutes before starting, forced its way into Beugny and half-way through the village. About 1 p.m. the Germans counter-attacked and penetrated into the gap between the 5th and the New Zealand Divisions ; but, reinforced by two companies of the 1/Bedfordshire, the Norfolk repulsed them ; the Cheshire withdrew their line to the western edge of Beugny, but elsewhere held their ground.[2]

The advance of the 2nd New Zealand Brigade (Br.-General R. Young) was covered by a barrage fired by two brigades (II. and III.) of its own artillery and the XC. Brigade R.G.A. The 2/Otago and 1/Canterbury, embarrassed by machine-gun fire from a well-defended trench and a derelict tank were

---

[1] Two of its own and one each of the 37th and 63rd Divisions.
[2] The counter-attack was made by the *49th Division*, which had been on quiet fronts or at rest for all 1918.

checked ; but by further successive attacks at 1 and 6 p.m., reached their place in the line in touch with the divisions on either flank.

The attack of the 42nd Division (Major-General A. Solly Flood) was made by the 127th Brigade (Br.-General Hon. A. M. Henley), with four tanks (two developed mechanical -trouble and the other two arrived after Zero, but later gave assistance), and two and a half machine-gun companies attached, under a barrage fired by five brigades of field artillery[1] and supported by the LVI. Brigade R.G.A.   As the line held by the 42nd Division was not so far to the front as that of the New Zealand Division, in order to prevent accidents, the barrage was to be dropped four hundred yards ahead, instead of the usual two or two-fifty, to enable the infantry to close up and advance at 5.15 a.m. abreast of the New Zealanders.   At 9.45 p.m. on the previous evening, with a view to assisting the advance to the starting line, the 42nd Division gave orders for the barrage to begin at Zero—9 minutes, with the result, as we have seen, that the enemy was aroused and dropped barrages on other divisions near by before their troops left their jumping-off lines.

The 1/6th Manchester, on the left, went right through to the northern part of Villers au Flos in just less than one hour ; but until the New Zealanders came abreast after their 1 p.m. attack, the Manchester were much troubled by fire from the left.   The 1/5th Manchester, which had the main part of the village to take, suffered enfilade fire from the right.   A particularly tiresome post was dealt with by two field guns attached to the battalion and a low-flying aeroplane of the No. 59 Squadron, and surrendered about 11 a.m., and soon after this the advance of the 21st Division entirely cleared the right flank.   The two battalions, with valuable assistance from the 127th Light Trench Mortar Battery, then completed the capture of Villers au Flos, and went on to their final objective about seven hundred yards beyond.

The V. Corps (Lieut.-General C. D. Shute) continued to engage its 21st, 17th and 38th Divisions, the main business being to take le Transloy.

---

[1] Those of the division, one each from the 37th, 63rd and New Zealand Divisions.

The 21st (Major-General D. G. M. Campbell) was ordered to carry out at 2 a.m. the capture of the Sugar Factory north of the village, which it had failed to attempt on the previous day, and this was achieved by the 7/Leicestershire (110th Brigade) under a barrage. The factory was retaken by enemy counter-attack about 4.30 a.m., but regained at 7 a.m. and held.

In the 5.15 a.m. attack, when the division had the objective of a copse (Lubda Copse), south of Villers au Flos, the 1/East Yorkshire (64th Brigade), detailed to take it, was at first held up by heavy fire from the le Transloy sugar factory, which had just been retaken by the enemy ; but when the factory was regained by the 110th Brigade, the advance was resumed and Lubda Copse occupied about 11.30 a.m.

The 17th Division (Major-General P. R. Robertson) was to capture le Transloy, after it had been bombarded during the night by seven batteries of heavy artillery. The village lay at the head of a shallow valley, with nearly level ground, on which Rocquigny stood, beyond it. It was to be surrounded by an advance of one brigade (52nd) south and one brigade (50th) north of it, which were to join forces beyond. The southern attack by the 12/Manchester and 9/Duke of Wellington's, starting at 5 a.m. from the right of the divisional front and working E.N.E., succeeded, in spite of machine-gun fire against the right flank, in establishing the Manchester on the Sailly Saillisel road to the south-east of le Transloy, and at 7 a.m. Major-General Robertson ordered the 50th Brigade (Br.-General G. Gwyn-Thomas) to send one battalion round the north of the village to get touch of the 21st Division and then work down the road from Villers au Flos to join up with the 52nd Brigade. One company only of the 7/East Yorkshire carried out the operation ; it met with very slight resistance and gained contact soon after midday. But by this time le Transloy had been evacuated by the enemy, and the 6/Dorsetshire (50th Brigade), which mopped it up, found " more than 30 machine guns and trench mortars, " but only two Germans ".

Divisional orders were now given for the 52nd Brigade, under an artillery barrage, to proceed at 5 p.m. to the second objective, the ridge about a mile south-east of le Transloy. This operation also met with little opposition and was completely successful. At 4 p.m. the V. Corps ordered that Rocquigny should be attacked, and at 5 p.m. the 50th Brigade was detailed by the 17th Division to undertake the task at 8 p.m. under a barrage, whilst at the same time the 52nd Brigade was to advance to the Rocquigny–Saillisel road.

The partly completed Wotan Line ran from Sailly Saillisel in the south, in front of Rocquigny, by Haplincourt, east of Beugny, by Lagnicourt to Quéant, and stout resistance was possible ; but the movements ordered were successfully executed. Rocquigny, where a very large store of soda water was found, was taken without much opposition by 10 p.m., and a trench beyond it, weakly held, was occupied. The 52nd Brigade joined up with the right of the 50th in this trench, with its right flank thrown back in an endeavour to gain touch with the 38th Division.

The 38th Division had not been able to advance. After the capture of Sailly Saillisel on the previous evening, its front line had been nearly two miles ahead of its left-hand neighbour, so Major-General Cubitt waited until 2.15 p.m. when he knew that the 17th Division had taken le Transloy and was going on, before ordering any advance. The 115th Brigade was then directed to pass through the 113th at 5 p.m., the hour at which the 52nd Brigade (17th Division) had been ordered to advance from le Transloy. Meantime Sailly Saillisel had been very severely shelled by the enemy ; the battalions of the 115th Brigade were heavily fired on before they reached their forming-up position on the eastern outskirts of the village, missed the barrage and never got going. This was an unlucky ending to a day when there had been so much success on the left wing of the corps, and on which the D–Q Position had been broken and a further retirement forced on the Germans.

It was obvious that in anything like open warfare the Imperial forces had the upper hand of the German legions, even with inferior numbers, and that their artillery was definitely superior and better supplied with ammunition. Machine-gun nests and previously entrenched positions still offered difficulties and caused loss of time, but the 2nd September had shown that they could be overcome. There was among the older hands a certain amount of surprise, even bewilderment, at the easy successes ; for in a few days the Armies had at small cost traversed well-known areas which in 1916 had taken months of arduous toil and heavy casualties to cross, whilst in 1917 initial successes had not led to very much serious progress.

NOTE I

The French on the 2nd September

(Sketch 20)

The French First Army on the 2nd September, " owing to the " stout resistance of the enemy", made slight progress, and that at one place only, east of Nesle.   The Third Army " spent the " 2nd in making preparation for an operation towards Guiscard". The Tenth Army attacked at 2 p.m. and gained ground eastwards on a seven-mile front north of Soissons.

NOTE II

The Germans on the 2nd September

(Maps 4 and 2)

The breaking of the D-Q Position had immediate effect : O.H.L. recognized defeat.   About mid-day[1] they issued orders for retirement behind the Sensée and the Canal du Nord and, farther south, to the Hindenburg Position, beginning that very night. The movement in the north was to pivot on the Scarpe near Etaing, but the new line was to run eastwards along the north bank of the Sensée to near 'Arleux, whence it went southwards behind the Canal du Nord, west of Bourlon Wood, to pick up the Hindenburg front line near Marcoing.   In the retirement, the *Seventeenth Army*[2] on the right, holding from near Combles (Fourth Army area) to the D-Q Position, was to move first on the night of the 2nd/3rd September, and the *Second* south of it, on the night of the 3rd/4th. The *Eighteenth* and the *Ninth*, farther south again, were to follow in succession, and the movement was to be completed by the 9th. Thus near St. Quentin the retirement amounted to 13 miles and near La Fère to 18, and the whole great salient won in March 1918 was to be abandoned.

---

[1] According to General von Zwehl in "Die Schlachten im Sommer " 1918 ", p. 27.   Ludendorff (p. 696) says " shortly after 2 p.m.".

[2] For the position of the German Armies see Map 2.

At the same time orders were given to complete the evacuation of the Lys salient won in April, 1918 : " the ground conquered by " the *Fourth* and *Sixth Armies* fell again into the possession of the British without fighting " (Lossberg, p. 35).[1]

According to regimental histories, the orders did not reach battalions of the *Seventeenth Army* until about midnight, but " by " the morning of the 3rd September the centre and left wing of " the Army [the right, which extended northward nearly to Lens, " had not to move] had occupied the new position Havrincourt– " Marquion–Arleux–Sailly en Ostrevent." (B.O.A., p. 352).

As far as can be discovered at present, the portion of the D–Q Position attacked by the 57th, 1st Canadian, 4th Canadian and 4th Divisions was held from south to north by at least seven German divisions : the *22nd* (which, after rest, since 3rd August, had just relieved the *36th*), the *7th Dismounted Cavalry* (mentioned in "Regt. No. 82 "—*22nd Division*—p. 128), *12th Reserve*, the *16th*, *2nd Guard Reserve* (Dury sector, according to "Regt. No. 77") and *20th*, with the *1st Guard Reserve* in Villiers lez Cagnicourt.

On this day Crown Prince Rupprecht, who was returning to the front from sick leave, recorded in his diary (p. 439) " In " Nürnberg the inscription on a troop train was to be read : " ' Slaughter cattle for Wilhelm & Sons '. Public feeling, for that " matter, is not only very bad in Bavaria, but also in North " Germany."

---

[1] Ludendorff (p. 694) says that the order was given " during the last " days of August ", but not carried out until the 2nd September (p. 698). An account of the retirement will be given in a later chapter.

CHAPTER XX

THE GERMAN RETIREMENT

THE ADVANCE TO THE CANAL DU NORD

3RD SEPTEMBER 1918

(Sketches 18, 19, 20)

The German retirement, begun on the night of the 2nd/3rd September in consequence of the breaking of the Drocourt–Quéant Position by the Canadian Corps and the turning of the Somme line by the capture of Péronne and Mont St. Quentin by the Australian Corps, was carried out in echelon from the right (north); it is convenient, therefore, to describe the British operations from north to south.[1]

The night was very dark, and it was dawn before it was discovered that on the front of the Canadian Corps and southwards to the V. Corps inclusive, the enemy had withdrawn. It had been intended to resume the attack on the 3rd all along the line north of the Somme, and the three Armies had instructed their subordinate formations to that effect.

FIRST ARMY

The orders of the First Army, issued at 8.15 p.m. on the 2nd, were:

" XVII. Corps, on left of Third Army, is continuing
" movement to-morrow to encircle Quéant and Pronville
" from the north.

" Canadian Corps will continue advance to-morrow
" on the Canal du Nord between Sains lez Marquion and
" Palluel, and will secure the high ground east of
" Récourt and east of Etaing, which will be held as
" defensive flank covering approaches over the Sensée
" river from the north-east.

" XXII. Corps will continue to hold defensive flank
" from Etaing (exclusive) to Railway Copse (exclusive),
" securing the crossings over the Trinquis river.

" Cavalry will be held at six-hours' notice ".

[1] See Sketch 18.

415

Lieut.-General Currie gave orders to the Canadian Corps in the above sense at 6 p.m. ; but during the evening the divisional commanders, after consultation with their brigadiers, reported to him the severe casualties which had been suffered and the many difficulties which confronted a further advance without adequate preparation. He communicated these view to the First Army and received authority to cancel the Army operation orders. Instead of a general advance close touch was to be kept with the enemy, and he was to be followed up at once if he began to withdraw ; but Etaing, on the left flank, was to be captured. Fresh orders were therefore issued at 12.20 a.m. on the 3rd. Later, when it was found that the enemy had disappeared during the night and retired over the Canal du Nord, all three divisions were able to advance up to, and in some cases beyond, the second objective of the previous day.

In the 4th (British) Division, the left formation of the Canadian Corps, it was noticed early in the morning that movement drew no fire, and patrols found that the enemy had withdrawn. At 5 a.m. the 12th Brigade attacked and took Etaing, from which most of the Germans had already withdrawn. At 7 a.m. the 11th Brigade went forward to the ridge north-east of Récourt and its spur down to Lécluse (inclusive) without opposition except fire from the northern bank of the Sensée, whose course here is a wide expanse of marsh and pools, where the enemy seemed established. No further movement therefore was made, and at night the 4th Division was relieved by the 1st (Major-General E. P. Strickland).

The two leading brigades of the 4th Canadian Division began their advance at 8 a.m. The general instructions of the corps were to make good the high ground commanding the Canal du Nord and secure bridgeheads beyond it. Soon after came a report from an aeroplane of No. 5 Squadron, which had flown at 300 feet over the battlefield, that there were no German troops west of the canal. The patrols of the 10th Canadian Brigade, on the left, found no enemy, but when, in the course of the morning, the 44th and 46th Battalions went forward they drew fairly heavy artillery fire ; they nevertheless reached the long knoll between Ecourt St. Quentin and Récourt, and faced north so as to form a defensive flank. Patrols reported the bridges over the

Sensée demolished and the causeway leading to Palluel blocked by an enemy post.

The 102nd, 54th and 87th Battalions of the 11th Canadian Brigade made a gradual advance of about three miles against some opposition from machine-gun fire to the ground over-looking the Canal du Nord ; but all attempts to push right up to the canal were stopped by artillery and machine-gun fire.   Patrols sent forward at night found the bridges destroyed ; those of the 102nd Battalion located a party of the enemy still on the west bank near Lock Wood (north-west of Marquion).   Its report came in only just before dawn on the 4th ; an immediate attack was launched by the 102nd Battalion, which succeeded, though at rather heavy cost, in driving the enemy over the canal and establishing a post on the railway which here crossed it.

The 2nd and 1st Canadian Brigades of the 1st Canadian Division also went forward to the canal, at 11.30 a.m. and 1.30 p.m., respectively, as they were already nearer to it than the 4th Canadian Division had been in its night position. Directly they began to move down the forward slopes they encountered the same resistance as their neighbours had experienced and also found the bridges destroyed.   The 8th and 10th Battalions of the 2nd Canadian Brigade and the 2nd and 4th Battalions of the 1st at the expense of many casualties reached the canal bank opposite Sains lez Marquion, however, between 5 p.m. and 6.30 p.m.   During the night they were slightly withdrawn, so that an artillery barrage could, if required, be put down on the canal.

THIRD ARMY

The Third Army orders for the 3rd September, issued at 4.50 p.m. on the 2nd, were for its right wing, the V., IV. and right of the VI. Corps, to
> " maintain firm and steady pressure on the enemy
> " rear guards and take advantage of any opportunity
> " for advancing " ;
the left of the VI. Corps was to " complete the capture
> " of Lagnicourt and of the high ground north thereof
> " overlooking Quéant, in conjunction with the XVII.
> " Corps " :

the XVII. Corps was "to continue operations for "encircling and capturing Quéant and Pronville from "the north".

Air reconnaissance on the morning of the 3rd discovered the retirement of the enemy on the fronts of the V., IV. and VI. Corps, and at 10.8 a.m. General Byng ordered these corps to "pursue the enemy with properly constituted "advanced guards of all arms", and to reorganize in depth without delay; the XVII. Corps was to advance to the Canal du Nord and "secure the eastern exits of Inchy, "Tadpole Copse (south of Inchy) and reconnoitre towards "Moeuvres".

This task was allotted by the XVII. Corps to the 63rd Division, covered by the artillery of the 52nd and 57th Divisions; the 57th Division, no longer holding any part of the front line, was withdrawn into reserve. The 189th Brigade[1] was sent forward, the 188th following in support. Quéant and Pronville were found evacuated; but, like the Canadians, the troops of the XVII. Corps encountered artillery and machine-gun fire as they approached the canal, and, later, infantry fire; for as the stretch of the unfinished canal here had no water in it, the enemy was still holding the western bank. The Drake Battalion, moving from its isolated position near Pronville, took Tadpole Copse during the afternoon, and later advanced towards Moeuvres: the Hawke Battalion by 1 p.m. cleared the Hindenburg Support Line against considerable opposition, and by midday the Hood Battalion had captured Inchy. During the night unsuccessful attempts were made, the corps cyclists co-operating, to seize the bridges on the two roads leading to Sains Lez Marquion and the bridge east of Moeuvres; the latter village was still strongly held, and later found to be well provided with dug-outs and cellars.

Meanwhile, in the 52nd Division, the right of the XVII. Corps, the 155th Brigade had worked along the Hindenburg front system to a point south of Quéant, and the 157th had then advanced south through Quéant and Pronville east of the 155th, without opposition, eventually reaching Tadpole Copse, now the right of the 63rd Division. Being thus squeezed out, the 52nd Division was, like the 57th, withdrawn into corps reserve.

---

[1] Still temporarily under Commander W. M. le C. Egerton, until the arrival in the evening of Br.-General B. J. Curling.

The VI. Corps made an advance of nearly six miles until it came up against the Havrincourt–Moeuvres sector of the Hindenburg Position, here reinforced by the Canal du Nord. Lieut.-General Haldane had issued orders for an attack at 5.20 a.m. by the Guards and 2nd Divisions, assisted by four Mark IV. tanks and six whippets against the Morchies–Lagnicourt–Quéant ridge. As suspected might be the case, no opposition was encountered and the objective was occupied by 6.30 a.m. The two divisions with, right to left the 6th, 99th, 2nd Guards and 3rd Guards Brigades leading, then continued their advance without serious opposition. By 10 a.m. it was evident to the corps commander that the Germans had retired and he gave instructions to both divisions to follow them up, each forming an advanced guard. Major-General Pereira, going up to the joint headquarters of the 99th and 6th Brigades, at 11.30 a.m. ordered forward the latter brigade with a squadron of Oxfordshire Hussars and six whippets. It was 1 p.m. before the Hussars and whippets moved off, but by 2.20 p.m. they had reached the line Hermies–Demicourt, overlooking the valley beyond which lay the Hindenburg Position two thousand yards away. The infantry followed, sustaining a few casualties from shell-fire, and by evening were on the line ordered.

The Guards Division went forward to the line Boursies–Pronville (exclusive), which it reached during the afternoon, the 2nd Guards Brigade occupying the old British line which ran in front of Boursies and then north-eastwards, and the 3rd a position along the large spur which extends towards Inchy. From this line the 2nd Guards Brigade was to have gone on as advanced guard : but any forward movement entailed descending the slopes to the canal under severe fire, and so no further advance was made.

The IV. Corps had intended to do no more on the 3rd than capture Beugny, which the 5th Division had surrounded on three sides, and to consolidate its gains. When Beugny was attacked at 5.20 a.m. it was found to be evacuated, and at 7.30 a.m. patrols of the 2nd New Zealand and 127th Brigades reported Haplincourt and Barastre similarly empty. Lieut.-General Harper therefore, at 8.30 a.m. issued orders for the line of the railway Ytres–Bertincourt–Vélu to be made good, with advanced troops on the line of the canal, which on the front of the 42nd and New Zealand Divisions ran in a tunnel. The Germans had abandoned defence of the canal south of Havrincourt, where it bends to the east, and had gone back to the Hindenburg Position; so the advance of the 5th Division, led by the 15th Brigade, was made without any opposition to beyond the railway. At night it was relieved by the 37th Division.

The 2nd New Zealand Brigade met with some slight resistance at Ruyaulcourt, on the hill above the canal tunnel, but brushed it aside and by evening had established a line east of the village across the line of the canal and in touch with the 15th Brigade on the left. In the 42nd Division, the 125th Brigade (Br.-General H. Fargus), with one troop of the Royal Scots Greys, attacked through the 127th Brigade, and by 9 p.m. reached its objective, the trench system east of Ytres, and therefore did not get touch of the 2nd New Zealand Brigade.

The V. Corps had intended that the 17th and 38th Divisions should, if possible, advance to the canal on the 3rd. The 21st Division, squeezed out by the narrowing of the front, became the corps reserve. The 50th, 113th and 115th Brigades were already moving forward when, at 10.15 a.m., Lieut.-General Shute ordered the divisions to organize advanced guards and push on, the corps cavalry (The Carabiniers) to regain touch with the enemy, and at 11.45 a.m. the corps heavy artillery to come up to the Saillisel–Bapaume road so as to fire on the canal. The cavalry reached Sailly Saillisel, whence the brigades of the 38th Division had started, at 1.30 p.m. and sent two squadrons forward. Moving in front of the infantry, they tried to cross the canal, but were stopped by fire and withdrawn when the infantry came up. By 3.30 p.m. the 50th Brigade had reached the line of Etricourt–Ytres railway, but could go no farther on account of fire from the eastern bank of the canal.[1]

In the 38th Division, the 114th Brigade, as advanced guard, about 5 p.m. passed through the 113th and 115th, but also could go no farther than the slopes overlooking the canal.

---

[1] The German *Second Army*, whose junction with the *Seventeenth* was near Havrincourt, had not yet begun its withdrawal to the Hindenburg Position, which took place on the night of the 3rd/4th.

For the Fourth Army the 3rd September was a day of rest and preparation for forcing a passage of the Somme, except that after the enemy's withdrawal farther north had been reported, the 53rd Brigade (18th Division), next to the Third Army, occupied Vaux Wood and established a line overlooking Manancourt on the Canal du Nord. An attempt by fighting patrols to occupy Riverside Wood failed in the face of heavy opposition. Elsewhere there was very little activity ; patrols of the 32nd Division were unable to cross the Somme owing to the vigilance of the enemy, and the work of preparing bridges could proceed only at night.

At 8.45 p.m. General Rawlinson sent a memorandum to his corps commanders which indicated that he was disinclined to attack the well-entrenched Nurlu position opposite his left, and would only make a feint of doing so ; his intention was to force a passage of the Somme at St. Christ, which should open a passage at Brie, whilst a turning attack was being made from Péronne.

On the same day G.H.Q. issued the following order :

" The successful operations carried out by the British " Armies since the 8th August have forced the enemy " to withdraw practically along the whole British front. " The principle on which Army commanders will now " operate will be to press the enemy with advanced " guards with the object of driving the enemy's rear " guards and outposts, and ascertaining his dispositions.

" No deliberate operation on a large scale will be " undertaken for the present. Troops will, as far as " possible, be rested, our resources conserved, and our " communications improved with a view to the resump- " tion of a vigorous offensive in the near future, in " conjunction with an operation to be carried out on " a large scale by our Allies.

" In accordance with the above, Army commanders " will draw as many divisions as possible into reserve " for rest and training ".

This order, although it did not prevent a continuation of the advance, put an end for a short time to organized attacks on a large scale, and thus closed the second period of the Advance to Victory which began on the 21st August, when

---

[1] See Sketch 19.

first the Third Army and then, on the 26th, the right of the First Army, joined in the offensive opened by the Fourth Army on the 8th August. During this period the Fourth Army, acting as right flank guard to the main operation, had advanced from the Lihons–Albert line to the Somme, 7 miles on the right in touch with the French, and 14 miles on the left ; the Third Army had advanced on the average 15 miles, and the First Army 12 miles, their operations ending with the storming of the Drocourt–Quéant Position and the approach to the line of the Canal du Nord. Twice had the German High Command ordered retirements : first, on the 26th August, to the Somme line and a continuation of it northward to Bapaume and the Drocourt–Quéant Position and, secondly, on the 2nd September, to the Hindenburg Position between Vailly on the Aisne and Vimy. Incidentally, the British successes in the Somme area had forced the Germans to evacuate the Lys salient. At least nineteen additional German divisions had been thrown in on the front of the Fourth Army, and at least seventeen on that of the Third Army and the Canadian Corps of the First Army. These enemy reinforcements were about the same in number as the total of the British divisions which they sought to stop. Counting the German divisions originally in the line, many certainly of poor quality, the Fourth Army had gained its successes with sixteen divisions against thirty-three, and the Third Army and Canadian Corps with eighteen against at least another thirty-three.

Whenever the British obtained a marked success the Germans retreated before advantage could be taken of it ; the effect of the advance of the Third Army, which G.H.Q. hoped would result in it being in a position to roll up the forces in front of the Fourth Army, was lost in this way.

In the circumstances of the comparative numbers of the opposing forces, Sir Douglas Haig having no large reserves to draw upon to relieve tired divisions or meet a counter-stroke, while the enemy still had some forty divisions in reserve, the prospects of exploiting a break-through, even if one could have been achieved, were exceeding small. The French, who had reserves and on the 14th September were able to economize the whole Third Army owing to the shortening of the line by the converging advance, did not make the effort which was possible with their superior numbers.

In explanation of German failure the Bavarian Official History[1] sums up the state of the German troops as follows :

" In the course of August the enemy had not succeeded
" in breaking through anywhere between Soissons and
" Arras. But the German front ached and groaned in
" every joint under the increasing blows delivered with
" ever fresh and increasing force (*sic*). Heavy losses in
" men, horses and material had been suffered, and the
" expenditure of man-power had reached terrifying
" proportions. The German divisions just melted away.
" Reinforcements, in spite of demands and entreaties,
" were not forthcoming. Only by breaking up further
" divisions [ten in August[2]] and regiments in the field
" could the gap be more or less filled. The number of
" companies in a battalion was reduced to three. The
" general and continuing crisis in the situation made it
" impossible to afford units the necessary rest and
" change, or even let them have their baggage trains up
" occasionally. The rations remained meagre and
" unvaried. In these circumstances, the troops deterio-
" rated both spiritually and physically. For the most
" part they were worn out [literally burnt-out cinders] ".

The Fourth Army took 12,414 prisoners, and the Third and First Armies, 33,827.

Its casualties in the second period had been :

	Killed	Wounded	Missing	Total
Officers ..	211	1,271	51	1,533
Other ranks ..	3,052	28,666	479	32,197

Those of the Third Army and the First Army (Canadian Corps only) up to the 3rd September were 2,661 officers and 53,055 other ranks, total 55,716.

It has been difficult in the narrative to give sufficient prominence to the work of the artillery, to whose support the success of the infantry was largely due. The following figures will give some idea of the scale of that support, and incident-ally of the labour involved in forwarding ammunition to the front, which was fully realized by the artillery commanders,

---

[1] p. 541.
[2] Kuhl, p. 208.
[3] Arrived at by deducting the losses in the Battle of Amiens from the total of the month of August.

so that not a round was wastefully expended. During the month of August in the Fourth Army the 18-pdrs. fired 1,532,545 rounds ; the 60-pdrs. 297,252 ; 6-inch guns, 20,576 : howitzers, 4·5-inch, 374,105 ; 6-inch, 442,964 ; 8-inch, 61,137 ; 9·2-inch, 38,516 ; 12-inch, 2,019. Between the 21st August and 3rd September, the artillery of the VI. Corps of the Third Army fired : field artillery, 804,929 rounds ; medium and heavy artillery, 201,753 rounds.

The railheads had not been much advanced.[1] In the Fourth Army those for the Australian Corps were at and around Villers Bretonneux and Corbie ; for the III. Corps, at and near Albert : that is 18 miles to 13 miles behind the front. Those of the Third and First Armies[2] were on the Albert–Arras railway, about 12 miles behind the front, from Miraumont northwards.

NOTE I

The French on 3rd September

(Sketch 20)

The French First Army " obtained no important result ", gaining only a tiny scrap of ground near Guiscard. The Third Army " allowed its tired troops to rest holding themselves ready to " follow up the enemy if the general conditions of the battle forced " him to retire ". The left centre of the Tenth Army made further progress eastwards.

NOTE II

The Canal du Nord

(End-paper B)

The Canal du Nord extends from the Oise Canal near Noyon on the south to the Somme near Voyennes, where it joins the Somme Canal, which then forms the waterway to Péronne and westward. At Péronne the Canal du Nord recommences and goes northward to reach the Sensée near Palluel, whence it is continued on to Douai by the Sensée Canal. The canal was under construction when war broke out in 1914, large stretches of it were dry, the excavation had not everywhere been made to its

---

[1] See Map 3.
[2] See Map 4.

full depth and the revetment had only been completed in certain parts. The canal remains in this derelict condition to the present day (1939).

The British Armies in September, 1918, were only concerned with the northern stretch— about thirty miles long—between the Somme and the Sensée. Its width and depth in this reach vary in different places. Its average width may be taken as 30 to 40 yards, and the average depth of the whole excavation in those parts where it had been completed as 30 to 40 feet, though in places where it passes through higher ground in cuttings it is as much as 60 feet deep.

Taking the canal from right to left,[1] south of the Manancourt–Nurlu road, near the junction of the Fourth and Third Armies, the canal bed was dry except for a quick-running little stream, 6 feet wide which formed no obstacle. North of this road there was water in the canal, evidently deep enough to form a serious obstacle, for the 38th Division troops crossing at Etricourt had to use the débris of a bridge to crawl over.[2] The canal first follows the valley of the Tortille to near its source and, 300 yards south of Vallulart, a mile north of Etricourt, enters a tunnel about 5,000 yards long, by which it passes through the watershed of the Somme and the Schelde, coming out of the tunnel again north of Ruyaulcourt. There was thus a stretch of nearly three miles where the canal ran underground, and this formed a weak point in the German defensive line. Troops of the IV. Corps, in fact, passed beyond the canal here on the 3rd September.

From the northern end of the tunnel the canal runs in a cutting down to a small tributary of the Schelde, called the Grand Ravin, whose valley it follows eastward as far as the northern end of Havrincourt Wood. There was water in the canal in the tunnel and round its eastern curve to a point south of Hermies, where there was a dam which was the beginning of a long dry stretch. From Havrincourt Wood the canal leaves the Grand Ravin and turns northward again, running in a deep cutting, revetted with brick, through the watershed of the Schelde and the Sensée, till, about fifteen hundred yards south of Moeuvres, it reaches one of the sources of the Agache and runs down the valley of this little stream for the rest of its course to its junction with the Sensée. During a great part of its passage through this watershed, the canal, though dry, formed a serious obstacle, owing to the depth of the cutting and the steepness of the brick revetment. This revetment continues to Moeuvres, though the depth of the excavation here is little more than 20 feet. Between Moeuvres and Inchy the revetment ceases (though it re-appears again farther north), and at Inchy the canal is only half-dug and is easily

---

[1] See Sketches 17 and 18.
[2] See Chapter XXII.

passable. The canal was still dry up to a lock 500 yards north of the bridge at Inchy. From this lock northwards there was again water in the canal up to its junction with the Sensée.

To sum up, the Canal du Nord had water in it from the southern boundary of the Third Army at Manancourt past Etricourt and through the tunnel to a point south of Hermies. From here there was a long dry stretch extending for nearly $7\frac{1}{2}$ miles to 500 yards north of Inchy. From here to the northern end of the canal at its junction with the Sensée it again had water in it. Of the dry stretch of the canal, 10,500 yards was in the Third Army area, and 2,500 in the First Army area.

CHAPTER XXI

THE OPERATIONS IN FLANDERS
5TH AUGUST–7TH SEPTEMBER 1918

THE ACTION OF OUTTERSTEENE RIDGE

(Sketches 21, 22)

It has already been mentioned[1] that at the beginning of August the Germans made several small withdrawals in order to rectify their front line, one of them being from the head of the salient won in the April (or Lys) offensive between Béthune and Bailleul. Ludendorff's plan for finishing off the war, after his Reims attack of the 15th July, by an offensive, of which the code name was " Hagen ", against the British in Flanders[2], had been frustrated by the French–American–British counter-attack of the 18th July in the Soissons area. This offensive in the north had been in preparation since the beginning of May, and its date finally fixed for the beginning of August ; but on the 20th July owing to events near Soissons the German front in the Flanders sector was placed on the defensive,[3] and Crown Prince Rupprecht, who was in command of the Group of Armies from near Albert to the sea, was given permission to evacuate unimportant salients.

At this time[4] the front of the British left wing, the Fifth and Second Armies, ran from 3 miles north of the La Bassée canal to just north of Ypres, whence the Belgian Army continued the line. The front from the canal was held by the left corps, I. (Lieut.-General Sir A. Holland) of the First Army (General Sir H. Horne),[5] the XIII. and XI. Corps (Lieut.-Generals Sir T. Morland and Sir R. Haking) of the Fifth Army (General Sir W. Birdwood),[6] and the XV., X.,

---

[1] See pp. 27–8.
[2] See " 1918 " Vol. III, pp. 250–2.
[3] Kuhl, p. 188.
[4] See Sketch 21.
[5] Divisions in the corps will be found on Sketch 21.
[6] Major-Gen. General Staff, Major-General C. B. B. White ; D.A. and Q.M.G., Major-General P. O. Hambro ; G.O.C.-R.A., Major-General C. C. van Straubenzee ; C. E., Major-General P. G. Grant.

As the frontage decreased the 3rd Division left the XIII. Corps on 13th August, and the 4th Division on 25th August. The 5th Division left the XI. Corps on 13th August, and the 59th Division replaced the 74th between 26th and 28th August.

XIX. and II. Corps (Lieut.-Generals Sir B. de Lisle, R. B. Stephens, Sir H. Watts and Sir C. Jacob) of the Second Army (General Sir H. Plumer), which included two American divisions (27th and 30th).[1]

All the British divisions of the Second and Fifth Armies had taken part in heavy fighting during the early part of the year and were regarded as not so forward in their recovery as those of the First, Third and Fourth Armies.

The preparations of the enemy had been very carefully watched, complete air photographs being obtained week by week ; and as the same formations, with the same staffs and same intelligence organization had remained on the front since the battle in April, any change in the German situation had been at once noticed. Early in June, when an attack seemed imminent, a systematic destruction of the enemy's establishments by bombardment was begun, and harassing fire had since been ceaselessly employed.

Information of the reduction of the large German reserves opposite the front in Flanders in order to feed the battle in the Soissons area had been obtained by the Intelligence Branch, and the gradual cessation of enemy offensive preparations was soon noticed. In an instruction dated 31st July the Fifth Army gave warning of the possibility of a withdrawal by the enemy to shorten his line, and dwelt on the importance of getting early information of any indication of such action, so that his retirement could be hindered. Constant patrolling and raids were to be undertaken and plans of action to be considered should either information of the enemy's intended withdrawal be received or should he succeed in effecting his withdrawal.

The gist of the instructions issued by the two corps was that in the advance patrols were to be pushed forward from one tactical locality to the next, supported by other troops whose duty it would be to consolidate the ground won. Should the advance be a long one, brigade and divisional reserves, covered by advanced guards, might be pushed

---

[1] The 35th Division was transferred from the XIII. to the II. Corps on 1st September. Between 28th and 30th August the 34th Division joined the XIX. Corps. The 6th Division left the corps on 1st September, and the American 27th Division on 4th September. On 17th August the 14th Division joined the II. Corps. On 27th August the 33rd and 49th Division left it. Between 28th and 30th August the 34th Division was transferred to the XIX. Corps. On 1st September the American 30th Division left and the 35th Division joined the corps.

through the patrols to accelerate the movement. The immediate objectives to be gained were given out. In the case of the XIII. Corps they were roughly all localities within a thousand yards of the front line ; in that of the XI. Corps, certain localities from five to nine hundred yards from the front line. Battalion and company commanders were not to wait for orders, but to act on their own initiative directly they discovered that the enemy was withdrawing. Every means was to be taken to send news of progress as frequently as possible both to the rear and to the flanks. The artillery was to be on the alert to support the advance and to change its S.O.S. lines.

The first withdrawal of the enemy took place on the night of the 4th/5th August.[1] Patrols discovered in the morning that he had evacuated about six hundred yards of his outpost line in Pacaut Wood, near the La Bassée canal, about the centre of the Fifth Army sector, and his empty posts were occupied by troops of the XIII. Corps. On the following day the XI. Corps was similarly able to push forward on both banks of the Clarence river. The enemy's retirement was continued on the 7th and 8th, and was followed up, the front abandoned extending southwards towards Locon and northwards to the edge of Calonne. On the 7th August the Fifth Army issued a further order directing corps to ascertain the extent of the enemy's withdrawal by means of small forces of all arms, to take precautions against ambushes, ruses and booby traps, and to provide against possible destruction of roads and bridges behind the advancing troops by delay-action charges. But on the 9th August considerable opposition was encountered, so that by the evening of that day the Fifth Army line ran in front of Locon, Pacaut Wood and Calonne, a total advance of nearly two miles. The enemy's resistance now stiffened, and between the 10th and 17th August the Fifth Army made only slight progress. Staff officers reported that the troops were somewhat sticky in following up the withdrawal, and that nearly everybody seemed to have forgotten how to use a rifle.

Meanwhile on the night of the 8th/9th August the Second Army[2] made attempts to advance, under instructions from

---

[1] See Note at end of Chapter.

[2] Major-Gen. General Staff, Major-General J, S. J. Percy ; D.A. and Q.M.G., Major-General A. A. Chichester ; G.O.C.–R.A., Major-General C. R. Buckle ; C. E., Major-General Sir F. M. Glubb.

General Plumer that the main object in case of an enemy withdrawal should be to exert continuous pressure upon his retiring forces, acting vigorously against his rear guards and thus hampering his choice of defensive lines, whilst making his retirement as costly as possible. The XV. Corps established posts in advance of its line south of Vieux Berquin, and the XIX. Corps pushed forward towards Kemmel, repelling a counter-attack on the morning of the 10th. During the night of the 11th/12th the XV. Corps gained a little ground east of Vieux Berquin and south of Meteren, and took the northern part of the former village; but a counter-attack on the evening of the 12th drove in some of the newly established posts. Between the 13th and 17th hard fighting took place on the XV. Corps front, but the capture of Vieux Berquin was completed and an advance made east of Meteren.

Any forward movement of the XV. Corps[1] was likely to be hampered by the enemy being in possession of Outtersteene Ridge,[2] which, though little more than a hundred and twenty feet above sea level, gave him good observation over the low-lying country round, of which the general level was sixty to seventy feet, and it was the last piece of high ground in this neighbourhood still in German possession. On the 10th August Lieut.-General de Lisle had instructed the 9th Division (Major-General H. H. Tudor) to make preparation to attack the ridge, and on the 14th August he held a conference to settle the final details. The operations were marked by the same care which had distinguished the 9th Division's successful attack of Meteren a month earlier.[3]

Against a direct attack from the west Outtersteene Ridge was guarded by the Meteren Becque, a muddy stream ten feet wide and not easily passable under fire; but as it approaches Meteren it turns eastwards and passed through the British line, which there inclined southwards, and this circumstance presented a means of avoiding the obstacle by attacking from the north.

The main operation[4] was therefore to be carried out by a

---

[1] B.G.G.S., Br.-Gen. H. H. S. Knox; D.A. & Q.M.G., Br.-Gen. G. R. Freeth; C.R.A., Br.-Gen. B. R. Kirwan; C.H.A., Br.-Gen. C. W. Collingwood; C.E., Br.-Gen. C. W. Singer. Br.-Gen. G. H. N. Jackson was acting as B.G.G.S., from 12th–25th August.

[2] See Sketch 22.

[3] See " 1918 " Vol. III, p. 209 *et seq.*

[4] For 9th Division operation order, see Appendix XXIII.

brigade of the 9th Division north of the bend of the Meteren Becque, which was to advance southwards under a creeping barrage, with its right on the stream. It was to be supported by a small party of the 29th Division (Br.-General H. H. S. Knox, temporarily) astride the stream. The first objective was to include Belle Croix Farm and Hoegenacker Mill,[1] about a thousand yards ahead and near the top of the ridge ; that attained, the attackers were at Zero + 46 minutes to extend about five hundred yards to the south and take Terrapin House, after which the flank was to be extended westward back to the old line at Gerbedoen Farm. Then the 29th Division was to advance across the Meteren Becque and take Outtersteene village. A feature of the opening operation was the barrage : the first round was to be entirely smoke, and after this 25 per cent. smoke, advancing 50 yards per minute, halting as a protective barrage 200 yards beyond the first objective until the advance was resumed.[2]

At the same time a brigade of the 36th Division artillery, on the left flank, was to put down a smoke barrage to hide the attack from enemy observation from Bailleul (3 miles to the north-east), and four artillery brigades with the 29th Division[3] were to co-operate on the right, one brigade firing the creeping barrage, another an enfilade barrage and the other two placing a rolling barrage from right to left across the front of the 9th Division. Six brigades of the XV. Corps heavy artillery, with a total of 57 guns and howitzers, were to bombard special points and put down a final protective barrage.[4] Four companies of machine guns of the 9th and 29th Battalions were to fire enfilade and creeping barrages, and one section of machine guns was attached to each of the attacking battalions of the 9th Division.

Zero was made 11 a.m. on the 18th August in the hope of catching the enemy off his guard, which was actually realized. The danger attaching to the late hour was that the attacking

---

[1] The official name of the action is Outtersteene Ridge, but it was known to the troops engaged as that of Hoegenacker Mill.

[2] It was to be fired by five brigades of field artillery, the L. and LI. (9th Division), and CXIII., CXIX. and CLXXXVI. (Army) Brigades, one firing in enfilade (that is across the front), all under the C.R.A. of the 9th Division, Br.-General A. R. Wainewright.

[3] XV. R.H.A. and XVII. (29th Division) and LXIV. and CLXXIV. (Army) Brigades, also temporarily under the command of the C.R.A. 9th Division.

[4] I., X., XXXIII., XXXVI., XLV., LXIV. Brigades R.G.A. under Br.-General C. W. Collingwood, C.H.A. XV. Corps.

infantry would have to be assembled in the trenches before daylight, and their presence might be noticed by enemy aeroplanes. To conceal the men, the trenches, as at Meteren on the 19th July, were covered with cocoa matting, with a black band painted on to represent the shadow. In the first instance it had been decided that the barrage should be put down at Zero − 1 minute and the infantry should advance at Zero + 3 minutes ; but on the 16th August, two days before the date fixed for the operation, a German document was captured giving the lessons drawn from the attack against Meteren : the British success was attributed to the use of smoke, and it was ordered that as soon as a smoke-barrage was seen, the British front line should be bombarded by artillery and swept by machine-gun fire. A change was therefore necessary, and it was ordered that the barrage should begin at Zero + 1 minute, and that the infantry should leave their trenches after counting ten from the opening of fire.

The 9th Division attack was carried out by the 27th Brigade (Br.-General W. D. Croft), after a rehearsal whilst it was in reserve. The line was formed by the 6/K.O.S.B., 11/Royal Scots, and 9/Scottish Rifles (less 2 companies) attached from the South African Brigade. The assembly of the troops was undisturbed. Each battalion advanced on a two-company frontage, each company on a two-platoon frontage, with the first wave in extended order and the rest in file. It was a baking-hot day, but the men; according to an eye-witness, " went over like a pack of hounds and " were consequently difficult to stop, it must be admitted " a good fault ". The Scottish Borderers, nearest the Becque, met with considerable opposition, but the other two battalions, advancing very rapidly, encountered very little, the Germans being taken by surprise, and all three, together with the detachment from the 29th Division, which consisted of two companies of the 1/K.O.S.B. (87th Brigade, under the temporary command of Lieut.-Colonel G. T. Raikes, 2/South Wales Borderers), and two platoons of the 1/2nd Monmouthshire (Pioneers), reached the first objective up to time. The advance to the final objective was equally successful, its capture, soon after midday, being signalled by firing blue smoke rifle grenades, and, for the notice of the R.A.F. patrols, red flares. The remaining two companies of the 1/K.O.S.B. had, during the last movement, swung their left forward to the Meteren Becque, pivoting on Gerbedoen Farm, so a flank was formed from the farm to Terrapin House.

Reconnoitring patrols were now sent out by the 1/K.O.S.B., and by the 2/South Wales Borderers on its right, and a company from the 1/Border Regiment (the reserve battalion of the 87th Brigade) passed through Outtersteene and dug in south of the village. After this, a general advance was made by the 87th Brigade, and by about 1.30 p.m. it was consolidating a line from near the Albert crossing on the Hazebrouck–Armentières railway, passing in front of Outtersteene, to Terrapin House. The 1/Border Regiment (less one company) was still kept in reserve, but machine guns were sent up to reinforce the thin infantry line. To secure the right flank, the 86th Brigade (Br.-General G. R. H. Cheape), according to plan, detailed two companies of the 2/Royal Fusiliers to capture Lyndé Farm and " The Trucks " (a number of railway trucks on a siding filled with ballast and shingle, and used as machine-gun positions), and eventually to push forward to the Vieux Berquin–Outtersteene road. Creeping up to assaulting distance, the companies attacked at 12.50 p.m. after a trench-mortar bombardment only, as all the divisional artillery was required for the 87th Brigade operation. The preparation was insufficient, and most of the enemy machine guns in the objectives, ditches and shell-holes proved to be still in action ; so the brigadier, to avoid useless sacrifice of life, stopped the attack. To safeguard the flank, the 29th Division ordered the 88th Brigade to place a battalion at the disposal of the 87th, and in consequence the 2/Hampshire took over the line of the railway from Albert crossing to the Meteren Becque, the 2/South Wales Borderers closing to the left.[1]

Next day, by an attack at 5 p.m. of the inner brigades of the 31st and 29th Divisions, the 12/Norfolk (94th Brigade, Br.-General A. Symons) and the 2/Royal Fusiliers (86th Brigade), under a barrage fired by three artillery brigades each of the 31st and 29th Divisions[2], in less than an hour

---

[1] The British casualties for the day were 671 ; the number of German prisoners taken, 697. For the German account see Note at end of Chapter.
[2] XXVIII., CLXV. and CLXX. of the 31st, and XV. R.H.A., XVII. and LXIV. of the 29th Division.

and a half gained the whole of the objectives of the 18th
August ; not only were Lyndé Farm and The Trucks
captured, but also the Vieux Berquin–Outtersteene road was
reached.[1]

As a consequence of this success, which might portend the
envelopment of the German Merville salient, the enemy on
the 19th/20th August began a fresh withdrawal on the Fifth
Army front opposite the left division of the XIII. Corps
and the whole of the XI. Corps front ; so that by the evening
of the 23rd the British line ran from Le Touret on the
La Bassée canal through Les Lobes, a mile to the east of
Merville and through Neuf Berquin to Meteren. During the
same day in the Second Army the inner flanks of the XV. and
X. Corps attacked and made a little progress towards Bailleul
and Dranoutre.

Between the 23rd and 28th only small advances were made,
but the fires and demolitions observed in the enemy lines
and the belts of wire being erected behind the existing front
pointed to his stand being only temporary. Although G.H.Q.
instructions issued on the 22nd[2] urged a most resolute
offensive and the taking of risks, the enemy's defences in
the north were still too strong for hasty operations. Indeed,
on the morning of the 24th the Germans counter-attacked,
unsuccessfully, against Dranoutre ridge. On the same day
the troops of the I. Corps attacked and took the mine craters
immediately east of Givenchy.

On the 29th the Germans resumed their retirement in front
of the Fifth Army, simultaneously with their withdrawal to
the Somme Line in front of the Third and Fourth Armies
farther south. On the 30th the movement extended to the
right wing of the Second Army. By the 1st September the
left of the First Army had begun to make some progress ;
by the evening of the 4th, the Fifth Army had reached the
old British line from near Neuve Chapelle to Bac St. Maur.
On the Second Army front on the 30th August Bailleul was
found evacuated ; on the 31st, Kemmel Hill and Vierstraat
were occupied, and the American 30th Division (II. Corps)
took Voormezeele ; on the 1st September the XV. Corps
reached Steenwerck and Neuve Eglise. Resistance then
stiffened a little ; but Wulverghem was taken on the 2nd,
Nieppe on the 3rd, and, after a first attempt had failed owing

[1] Casualties, 228 ; prisoners, 160.
[2] See pp. 206–7.

to thick wire and marshy ground, Ploegsteert village was captured by the 29th Division, with 244 prisoners on the evening of the 4th, and also Hill 63, overlooking it. Almost simultaneously, just to the north, the enemy drove back the outpost line of the X. Corps half a mile in the Douve valley, and he continued this counter-attack next morning. The ground lost was recovered by an attack under an artillery barrage on the 6th. Although the enemy had abandoned the Lys salient, he evidently meant to hold on to Messines Ridge, and having reached his old front of 1915 with the advantage of being in possession of Armentières, evidently meant to stand there. Some small advances were made during the next three weeks, but no material change took place. Two large discharges of gas were launched : on the night of the 10th/11th September, from 379 projectors in the Ypres sector, and at 10.30 p.m. on the 23rd, from 197 projectors near Ploegsteert ; there were frequent raids with small gains of ground, and captures of prisoners, the enemy also displaying considerable counter-activity.

In this interval preparations were made for the great offensive of the 28th September. The withdrawal of the Germans had rendered unnecessary the two attacks from the Festubert–Robecq line and against Mont Kemmel mentioned by Maréchal (then General) Foch in his Directive No. 3 of the 20th May,[1] but by the 2nd September it appeared to him that the time was ripe for widening the Allied front of attack by launching an offensive in Flanders, an operation which Sir Douglas Haig had begun to discuss with the Belgian G.H.Q. a week earlier. These discussions, orders and preparations will be described in due course in dealing with that offensive.[2]

---

[1] See " 1918 " Vol. III, p. 23.

[2] Casualties during the period 5th August–7th September were :

First Army	I. Corps,		..	..	894
Fifth Army	{ XIII. Corps, 2,432 { XI. Corps, 2,765 }		..	..	5,197
Second Army	XV. Corps, 4,832 X. Corps, 2,392 XIX. Corps, *2,867 II. Corps, **346		..	..	10,437
	Total	..	..	..	.. 16,528

Continued at foot of next page.

NOTE I

THE GERMANS IN FLANDERS

5TH AUGUST–7TH SEPTEMBER

(Sketches 21, 22)

On the 5th August, 1918, the Germans had 16 divisions in the line from the La Bassée canal to Ypres (exclusive), with about twenty in reserve. As the Lys salient was gradually evacuated the number in front line fell to 9, and the reserves to about 8, the rest being shifted southwards to meet the attack of the British Fourth, Third and First Armies.

The withdrawal of the enemy on the night of the 4th/5th August from the salient near the La Bassée canal does not seem to have been entirely voluntary, but due to raids and patrol activity. " Res. Regt. No. 51 " (p. 250) says " the front line battalions " of the *12th Reserve Division* had to be withdrawn before the " attack of superior forces to the new outpost line " ; and " Res. " Regt. No. 102 " (*23rd Reserve Division*) (p. 186) has " our " sectors were repeatedly attacked by superior forces and " withdrew fighting to the Green Line."

The Outtersteene sector, attacked on the 18th August, was held from the Hazebrouck–Armentières railway to 600 yards south of Bailleul by the *4th* and *12th Divisions*, the former with the *39th Reserve Regiment* (*13th Reserve Division*) attached, with the *52nd Division* to the south. Each division had three battalions in front line. Surprise and the breaking of the main line of resistance are admitted ; as the front had been so quiet, no action was expected, and patrols sent out during the previous night discovered nothing suspicious. A counter-attack, unmentioned in the British diaries, was made at 5 p.m. by three reserve battalions. One battalion of the *49th Regiment* (*4th Division*) was destroyed in the action, only 29 men returning ; the *62nd Regiment* (*12th Division*) lost two entire companies.

Continued from previous page.

The total number of prisoners taken was :

I. Corps ..	..	..	..	..	84
Fifth Army	..	..	..	..	408
Second Army	..	..	..	..	1,790
					2,282

The number of German killed and wounded is not available.

* Does not include the American 27th Division, whose losses are not known.

** Includes the American 30th Division.

CHAPTER XXII

The Pursuit to the Hindenburg Position

4th–11th September 1918

(Sketches 19, 20, 23, 24, 25, 26, 27)

Although it was suspected on the 3rd September that the Germans on the front of the Third Army had begun another retirement, no definite signs of such a movement had been reported. On the Somme they were standing fast. If they intended to retreat, it was clear they meant to offer as much resistance as possible, and that their rear guards, for the most part scattered field guns with escorts and machine guns, had received orders to hang on as long as they could. Owing to this attitude and the fatigue of the troops, which necessitated a number of reliefs, very little happened on the 4th September.

Fourth Army[1]

On the 4th September the Fourth Army made only a small advance on the left. To begin on the right : patrols of the 32nd Division (Major-General T. S. Lambert), under the Australian Corps, which tried to reach the eastern bank of the Somme were unable to do so. The rest of the Australian Corps made preparations for the continuation of the offensive. At night the 2nd Australian Division, which had done such strenuous work, was relieved, so that it might have several weeks' rest ; the 5th Australian Division (Major-General Sir J. T. Talbot Hobbs) and the 74th Division (Major-General E. S. Girdwood) (III. Corps) extended inwards to fill its frontage, and the other divisions of the III. Corps, by side-stepping southwards, took over a little more ground.

The magnificent successes of the Australian divisions had not been attained without heavy infantry casualties, so that the battalions were down to 350 and often less. Mr. Hughes, the Australian Premier, who was in London, was inclined to insist that he must be consulted before the divisions were employed again, and, furthermore, that arrangements must be made to grant the men " home leave ". His feelings of

---

[1] Sketches 19 and 23.

anxiety were greatly mollified by the fact of the successes ; but the necessity for rest was borne in mind, and, as will be seen, the Australian divisions were gradually withdrawn.[1]

In the III. Corps, Lieut.-General Godley, on the night of the 3rd, issued orders for the divisions to press the enemy and hinder his retirement ; wire-cutting in front of the trenches on the Templeux la Fosse–Nurlu ridge was to be begun forthwith, and a bombardment of these villages and of Aizecourt le Haut, as soon as possible. During the 4th a short general forward movement took place, and the Canal du Nord was crossed ; the 74th Division came up abreast of the apex of the Haut Allaines salient of the Australian Corps. Patrols of the 47th Division (Major-General Sir G. F. Gorringe) early in the morning found Moislains unoccupied except for a few German stragglers, but had to face stiff opposition from machine-gun posts in forcing the passage of the canal during the afternoon. In view of the further advance ordered for next day, Br.-General R. McDouall (142nd Brigade, holding the front of the 47th Division) endeavoured to gain as much ground as possible during the night, and crossed the canal on his whole front, and his patrols pushed a mile beyond it ; but the enemy's resistance ' was strong. Major-General Gorringe therefore decided that the 142nd Brigade troops should be withdrawn to a line only a little east of the canal, in order to permit of a barrage being fired to cover the advance next day.

A few parties did not receive this order and remained out until the 141st Brigade (Br.-General W. F. Mildren) passed through, taking refuge in German dug-outs during the barrage, and suffering no casualties from it. The 55th and 53rd Brigade (Br.-Generals E. A. Wood and M. G. H. Barker) of the 18th Division found Riverside Wood, on the lower slopes of the Nurlu ridge, still very strongly held ; but after the 38th Division (Third Army) on the left had captured Manancourt, the hostile resistance weakened, the canal was crossed, and, after some fighting, the wood was occupied.

---

[1] The casualties 31st August–2nd September had been :

				Officers	Other Ranks
2nd Australian Division		..	..	84	1,286
3rd	,,	,,	.. ..	43	554
5th	,,	,,	(2 brigades)	64	1,066

Between 24th and 30th August, the 3rd Australian Division had lost 1,200 men.

THIRD ARMY[1]

On the 4th September the Third Army made an advance of from twelve hundred to two thousand yards ; on the right and in the centre it crossed the Canal du Nord, and on the left it closed up to the Hindenburg Position.

General Byng's orders for this day were for the advance to be continued : when the German main line of resistance was located, the advanced guards were to engage it closely, but to refrain from large-scale attacks until he ordered them and they could be properly organized : if opportunity offered, bridgeheads were to be established across the Canal du Nord and the Sensée canal.

The V. Corps (Lieut.-General C. D. Shute), which now had the 38th and 17th Divisions in the line and the 21st in reserve, gave as first objective the Equancourt system of trenches. These covered a deep gap leading to Fins in the ridge which runs northward from Nurlu towards Neuville Bourjonval. Between Manancourt and Etricourt, in the 38th Division sector, the canal had water in it, and was forty yards wide, but the 114th Brigade (Br.-General T. R. C. Price) succeeded in forcing crossings, the 14/Welch at Manancourt and the 13/Welch at Etricourt,[2] and by 5.30 p.m. both battalions, covered at first by the lie of the ground from fire from Equancourt, were able to establish a line five to eight hundred yards beyond the canal. Further progress was stopped by the Equancourt defences, on which field artillery fire did not seem to have made much impression.

The 50th Brigade (Br.-General G. Gwyn-Thomas) crossed the canal on the whole front of the 17th Division. At 8 a.m. it sent its left battalion, the 10/West Yorkshire, over the

---

[1] Sketch 24.

[2] The History of the 38th Division, p. 59, gives the following description of the crossing : " The enemy had machine guns on the bank, but not " covering the actual water ; noticing this, Major Hobbs (13/Welch) " rushed a platoon down to an old trench on the near bank, from which " a ditch led down towards the débris of the Etricourt road bridge ; here " the platoon engaged the attention of the nearest machine gun, while " one section crawled down the ditch across the fallen bridge and up the " far bank ; crawling on their stomachs, this section advanced to within " charging distance of the nearest machine gun, then leapt up and " bayoneted the gunners ; they were quickly joined by the remainder " of the platoon, and a bridgehead was formed which enabled the " remainder of the company (under Captain Beecham, M.C.) to cross.

" Similar action took place at Manancourt, where a company of the " 14/Welch Regiment, led by Major J. A. Daniel, D.S.O., M.C., 15/Welch " (attached to the 14/Welch), crossed, and each of these battalions had " thus one company across at 11.30 a.m."

hill under which the canal tunnel lies, and through Vallulart Wood. The attack against the latter was much facilitated by the fire of a gun of the LXXVII. Brigade R.F.A., brought up within a hundred and fifty yards of the front line. At 10 a.m. the 7/East Yorkshire was able to force a passage of the canal to the south of the wood, and came abreast of the West Yorkshire. Both battalions then attempted to advance south-eastward against the Equancourt defences ; but, like the 114th Brigade, they were stopped by fire.

The IV. Corps (Lieut.-General Sir G. M. Harper) starting at 7 a.m., with the 5th Division in reserve, also crossed the canal on its whole front, except on the extreme left at the northern end of Havrincourt Wood, where the canal turns towards the Hindenburg Position. It had been hoped to reach a north-south line beyond Havrincourt Wood, which was to be turned from the north and the south ; but, as the official policy was merely to keep touch with the enemy rear guards and not engage in large-scale operations if strong opposition was encountered, such action was abandoned. Each of the three divisions in the line, the 42nd, New Zealand, and 37th, sent forward a brigade, with artillery, engineers and machine guns attached. The 125th Brigade (Br.-General H. Fargus) of the 42nd Division, astride the hill over the tunnel, after swinging its left forward about two thousand yards, was held up by fire from Neuville Bourjonval. It was not until 7 p.m. that two companies of the 1/5th Lancashire Fusiliers, in co-operation with a company from the 2nd New Zealand Brigade, attacked the village under an artillery barrage and took the northern portion, and this ended the day's operations.

The 2nd New Zealand Brigade (Br.-General R. Young) itself gained about a mile on the left against steady opposition from machine guns, and arrived within five hundred yards of Havrincourt Wood ; but the right, starting only twelve hundred yards from the wood, at once received heavy fire in front and from Neuville Bourjonval on the right, and, although it co-operated in the evening attack on that village, made little progress.

In the 37th Division, the 112th Brigade (Br.-General A. E. Irvine), whose extreme right was already across the canal, completed the passage except on the extreme left, making a good advance of fifteen hundred yards on the right and over three thousand on the left, in spite of machine-gun fire, and it managed to enter the north-western corner of Havrincourt Wood.

The VI. Corps (Lieut.-General Sir A. Haldane), now within two thousand yards of the Hindenburg Position, had its seven thousand yards frontage divided between the 2nd and Guards Divisions, with the 3rd and 62nd in reserve. The two attacking divisions employed the 6th Brigade (Br.-General F. G. Willan) and the 3rd Guards Brigade (Br.General G. B. S. Follett), which advanced at 5 a.m. to secure the line of the canal with its bridges intact, locate the enemy's main line of resistance east of the canal, and, if it was not strongly held, occupy it by patrols. Both brigades were able to advance more than half-way to the Hindenburg Position, the front zone of which was mainly west of the canal. An attack by the Guards at 6.30 p.m., under a barrage, failed to carry them to the German front line ; and another by the 6th Brigade at 10 p.m. was equally unable to capture " The Spoil Heap ",[1] which blocked the way, but no doubt caused its evacuation later in the night.

The 189th Brigade (Br.-General B. J. Curling) of the 63rd Division, holding the reduced frontage of the XVII. Corps, on the west bank of the canal, made no advance, but had some close fighting. It took and lost the canal bridge in the centre of its front, lost and re-took the north-eastern part of Inchy, and entered and was turned out of Moeuvres.

FIRST ARMY[2]

In the First Army (Canadian, XXII., VIII. and I. Corps) patrols sent out on the whole front of the Canadian Corps on the morning of the 4th, found all the crossings of the Canal du Nord and the Sensée strongly held. It was evident that the line of the canal could not be forced except by an organized attack in force, and, as this was for the moment forbidden, General Horne, at 6.15 p.m., issued the following order :

---

[1] This had already been contended for in the Battles of Arras 1917 (see " 1917 " Vol. I, p. 371) and became famous in the Battle of Cambrai 1917.

[2] Sketch 18.

" Canadian Corps will maintain touch with the enemy
" along the Canal du Nord and will mop up any pockets
" of the enemy remaining west of the canal between
" Sains lez Marquion and Palluel (inclusive). Area south
" of Sensée river between Palluel and Etaing will be
" cleared by troops of 1st (British) Division. Canadian
" Corps, after transfer of 1st (British) Division to XXII.
" Corps, will reorganize in depth ".

No important operation was undertaken by the Canadian,
XXII. and VIII. Corps during the period 4th to 26th
September, when this volume ends ; much artillery fire and
patrol activity took place, and endeavour was made to induce
the enemy to believe that a great attack was impending ;
but no material change occurred in the situation of these
three corps.

The operations of the I. Corps (Lieut.-General Sir A.
Holland) during August and the first week in September,
already narrated,[1] had been in co-operation with the Fifth
Army on its left. The connection was recognized by the
transfer of the corps to the Fifth Army at 12 noon on the
19th September. Before this, between the 8th and 19th
September, a further short advance had been made.[2] On
the 11th September the 15th (Scottish) Division (Major-
General H. L. Reed) took the Quarries west of Cité Ste Elie
and held them against the counter-attacks made during the
next few days. On the 11th the 16th (Irish) Division (Major-
General A. B. Ritchie) also attacked and took the line of
the railway west of Auchy lez la Bassée, was then driven
off by counter-attack, but advanced again and re-took it,
and on the 13th captured Auchy and Fosse 8, south of it.
North of the canal, on the 14th, the 55th Division (Major-
General Sir H. Jeudwine) took Rue des Marais and entered
Violaines, and on the 17th made a further advance, seizing
some trenches immediately north of the canal.

Thus in the First, as in the Fifth and Second Armies, for
the remainder of the period dealt with in this volume, there
is nothing of major importance to record ; only the Third
and Fourth Armies continued to advance, following up the
enemy's retirement.

---

[1] Chapter XXI.
[2] See Sketch 25.

On the 4th September Maréchal Foch at a conference at Mouchy le Châtel handed personally to Sir Douglas Haig a Directive, dated the previous day, copies of which had already been sent to Generals Pershing and Pétain. He first had to inform the British Commander-in-Chief that in an interview with General Diaz (Chief of the General Staff of the Italian Army) on the 3rd he had learnt that "the "eventuality of an immediate offensive co-operation of the "Italian Armies must unfortunately be put aside"—the Italian offensive did not begin until the 24th October, three weeks after the appeal of the German Government to President Wilson for an armistice.

The Directive did little more than put on paper what had been settled with General Pershing on the 2nd September. It ran :[1]

"At the moment the Allied offensive is developing "with success from the Scarpe to the Aisne, forcing the "enemy to retire on the whole of this front.

"To widen and increase this offensive, all the Allied "forces must be brought into the battle, without delay, "following converging directions from favourable parts "of the front.

"With this object :

"1. The British Armies, supported by the left of the "French, will continue to attack in the general direction "of Cambrai and St. Quentin.

"2. The centre of the French Armies will continue "its action to throw the enemy beyond the Aisne and "the Ailette.

"3. The American Army will carry out the following "operations :

"(a) The offensive arranged in Woeuvre [St. Mihiel] "reduced to reaching the line Vigneuilles–Thiaucourt– "Regniéville [the base of the St. Mihiel salient], which "will be sufficient to achieve the results desired : the "freeing of the Paris–Avricourt railway, and the gain of "a satisfactory base for future operations.

"This attack is to be launched as soon as possible "in order to leave no respite to the enemy, at latest on "the 10th September [it began on the 12th September].

---

[1] See End-paper B.

" (b) An offensive in the general direction of Mezières,
" as strong and violent as possible, covered on the east
" by the Meuse, and supported on the left by an attack
" of the French Fourth Army.

" This latter offensive is to be mounted with the
" greatest speed, so that it can be launched at latest
" 20th–25th September [it began on the 26th September].
" Its objective in the first place will be by working on
" either side of the Argonne (around Apremont) to
" throw the enemy back on the line Stenay–le Chesne–
" Attigny [this east-west line runs from the Meuse
" westwards to the point where the Aisne near Vouziers
" changes its course from northwards to westward] ;
" then to reach the Mezières area, manoeuvring east-
" ward[1] in order to overcome the resistance on the
" Aisne ".

FOURTH ARMY[2]

During the 5th, 6th and 7th September the Fourth Army
made good progress, advancing with energy all along its front
against the retreating German *Second Army*. Against the
Seventeenth Army, whose northern wing was already anchored
in the Hindenburg Position, the Third Army, forbidden for
the moment to organize a great attack, could do no more
than swing forward its right and centre, keeping pace with
the left of the Fourth Army.

On the evening of the 4th the information received by
the Fourth Army showed that the enemy was retiring on
the front of the Third Army and the right of the First Army,
and on portions of the French front east of Noyon, and
appeared to be withdrawing on the front of the III. Corps.
Sir Douglas Haig was in favour of a leisurely pursuit in order
to afford the troops a little rest and give time for the American
and French offensives planned by Maréchal Foch to be
prepared, before he attacked the Hindenburg Position ; but
orders were issued by General Rawlinson, at 10.45 p.m. by
telegram, for the Australian and III. Corps to follow up

---

[1] " par l'est " in the original. The south–north course of the Aisne on
the west of the Argonne must be meant.
[2] Sketch 23.

energetically with strong advanced guards to prevent roads and railways being destroyed. Lieut.-General Monash was prepared for such an operation, and had issued orders so as to have three divisions in the line, the 3rd Australian Division (Major-General J. Gellibrand), taking over the left of the corps front, and the two others side-stepping to the right to make room for it. The 32nd Division would then hold as far as to the Brie–Mons en Chaussée road (exclusive), the 5th Australian Division up to an east-west line through Cartigny (3 miles E.S.E. of Péronne), and the 3rd Australian Division to the boundary with the III. Corps, a line passing through the southernmost point of Bussu Wood. The new arrangement could not be effective at once, and was not an accomplished fact until the 7th September, although the 3rd Australian Division took over a small piece of the front on the 5th. The advance, it was ordered, was not to be delayed on that account, and each division was to form an advanced guard of an infantry brigade with artillery attached and advance by a series of bounds in co-operation with the French XXXVI. Corps on the right and the V. Corps on the left.

In accordance with these instructions, although the Germans (now known to be strong rear guards) were still defending the crossings of the Somme, the 97th and 14th Brigades (Br.-Generals J. R. M. Minshull-Ford and L. P. Evans)[1] of the 32nd Division set about trying to force a passage. At 5 a.m. (5th September) Lieutenant T. W. Hepburn of the 15/Highland L.I. (14th Brigade) managed to cross just south of Eterpigny (a mile north of Brie), by a path through the marshes, and push a considerable way eastward without encountering any enemy. He then returned and led his company over ; a second followed, and then the rest of the battalion, which, after some fighting, reached the spur a mile north-east of Brie and took position on it, capturing 54 prisoners and 9 machine guns. At 10.30 a.m. one company of the 5th/6th Royal Scots (14th Brigade) crossed the canal and river at the site of the Brie bridge. This it did in spite of machine-gun fire and having to wade for a short distance through water three feet deep. The company then cleared the Germans out of Brie, bombing the dug-outs and capturing 7 prisoners and 8 machine guns. Meanwhile a second company had crossed by a temporary

---

[1] In these operations the brigades were really brigade groups with mounted troops, artillery and engineers attached.

footbridge north of Brie, and the two companies established a line on the high ground about two thousand yards east of the village, north of the Brie–Mons en Chaussée road. After hearing about 9.30 a.m. of the successful crossing of the 15/Highland L.I., Major-General Lambert issued orders for the 14th Brigade to occupy some German trenches which ran past the western end of Athies Woods northward along the spur north-east of Brie, in order to assist the passage over the Somme of the 97th Brigade, which was to come up on its right. This involved only a short advance by the companies of the Highland L.I. and Royal Scots, the extension to the south, not quite so far as Athies Woods, being provided by the two remaining companies of the latter battalion. The 97th Brigade sent two companies of the 1/5th Border Regiment over the Somme by the passage at Brie in the 14th Brigade area, and at 12.45 p.m. they began working southwards, capturing Remé Wood, in order to clear the way for the 2/K.O.Y.L.I. It was not, however, owing to opposition, until 3 p.m. that the latter battalion managed to cross at Cizancourt and St. Christ ; it then pushed on, and the enemy gave way, running hard to escape. By nightfall the 2/K.O.Y.L.I. had established a line fifteen hundred yards east of Ennemain, two and a half miles from the river, with the French on its right and the whole of the 1/5th Border Regiment on its left ; it had captured 105 prisoners.

At 6 p.m. the 32nd Division issued orders for an advance to a line 3 miles onward through Devise–eastern end of Mons en Chaussée–Cartigny ; but they reached the troops too late for compliance. The 1/Dorsetshire, however, the reserve battalion of the 14th Brigade, sent to fill the gap between this brigade and the 97th, on reaching the front about 3.45 p.m., ascertained by patrols that Mons was unoccupied ; so Br.-General Evans, who had just come to the battalion headquarters, ordered the Dorsetshire to go forward, take possession and occupy the divisional objective east of the village. This they did by 9.15 p.m. against very little opposition, the Germans fleeing when machine-gun and rifle fire was opened. It was then discovered that the troops on either flank had not come up ; but the 1/Dorsetshire, throwing back defensive flanks, remained where it was.

Meantime the engineers and pioneers of the 32nd Division had reconstructed the bridges at St. Christ and Brie, so that the whole division and a considerable number of French troops had been able to cross at these places.

The 5th Australian Division, in the Péronne sector, sent fighting patrols forward at 5 a.m. under cover of a smoke screen, and they captured Doingt and Bussu after slight resistance. Further advance was opposed in the usual way by machine guns and isolated field guns, but the division came up abreast of the 32nd.

In the III. Corps, according to orders, the 47th Division moved first, sending its 141st Brigade as advanced guard at 5.30 a.m. through the 142nd to reach the highest ground east of the Canal du Nord marked by the Aizecourt le Haut–Nurlu road. Its progress was expected to assist the 74th Division, on its right, to make a good advance. Considerable resistance was experienced from the factory and the well-organized quarries north-west of Cat Copse and on the right flank ; but a line from Cat Copse past the west of the quarries and thence northwards through Ville Wood was reached about 8.30 a.m. On the left, the 12th Division was on the move and so secured that flank, but as the 74th Division had not yet started, a defensive right flank was formed. A message giving the situation was sent to the 74th Division, but at 10.15 a.m., as its troops had not appeared, the 140th Brigade was ordered up to take over protection of the right flank.

The 230th Brigade (Br.-General A. A. Kennedy) had been detailed by the 74th Division for the advanced guard, and on receipt at 9.45 a.m. of the message of the 47th Division it at once moved forward through the 231st (Br.-General C. E. Heathcote), which also proceeded to advance, but was recalled to the duty of right flank guard by a divisional message. A trench system east of Aizecourt le Haut had been given as the first objective ; but it was 1 p.m. before this village was captured and 4 p.m. before the 230th Brigade was on its first objective. Proceeding on across a valley at 6 p.m. to reach the second objective, a trench system east of Driencourt, it encountered field-gun fire (both H.E. and gas) and machine-gun fire, and came to a stop roughly a quarter of a mile short of the objective, only the extreme left near Save Wood reaching it.

Meantime the 47th Division had been making arrangements for a further advance by both the 140th and 141st Brigades, in conjunction with the 12th Division on the left. The heavy artillery was turned on to the quarries and northern part of Ville Wood and then on to the high ground beyond, between l'Epinette Wood and Nurlu ; during the afternoon, too, the CXII. Brigade R.F.A. (25th Division[1]) succeeded in crossing the Canal du Nord, to give the two brigades effective short-range support. Thus when, at 7 p.m., the brigades advanced in a violent thunderstorm, they reached their objective everywhere, the high ground along the Aizecourt le Haut–Nurlu road. So eager for water were the men in this and other divisions that they caught the rain of the storm in their ground sheets to drink.

The relief of the 18th Division by the 36th and 35th Brigades (Br.-Generals C. S. Owen and A. T. Beckwith) of the 12th (Major-General H. W. Higginson) during the night of the 4th/5th September was carried out ; but their assembly was with difficulty completed to time owing to great darkness and the gas shelling of the woods in the Tortille valley. After a 20-minute bombardment, the 35th Brigade (7/Norfolk and 9/Essex leading), advanced up the slopes at 6.45 a.m. under a barrage, the heavy artillery and field howitzers shelling Nurlu and the trench system west of it. On reaching the flat ground in front of Nurlu strong opposition was encountered, and the attack was finally brought to a standstill by violent fire and thick belts of wire. A similar fate befell the 7/R. Sussex, the leading battalion of the 36th Brigade, which went forward about 8 a.m. ; but by 5 p.m. it had filled the gap between the 47th Division and the 35th Brigade. The 7/R. Sussex and the 1/1st Cambridgeshire, now up, and the right of the 35th Brigade, were warned to attack Nurlu at 7 p.m. in co-operation with the 47th Division ; but the attempt to do so was unsuccessful.

The divisions of the Fourth Army had therefore made an advance varying from fifteen hundred to three thousand yards; after the first moves they had found little opposition on the right, where the Somme line had been weakly held, whilst on the left resistance was still obstinate.

---

[1] This division, less its R.A. and R.E., was being re-formed in England.

THIRD ARMY[1]

In the Third Army on the 5th September, though a great deal of patrol work took place, there were only two small operations. In the 17th Division sector, the 7/Lincolnshire (51st Brigade, Br.-General R. M. Dudgeon), attacked south-eastwards under a barrage at 9.30 a.m. from the extreme left of the divisional front to complete the capture of the enemy's trenches, near the canal tunnel, between Equancourt and Ytres. The operations came to a standstill after an advance of about a thousand yards ; but when continued at 8.30 p.m. by the 7/Border Regiment, the enemy was taken by surprise and the whole position captured.

In the IV. Corps sector a convergent attack by one company of the 1/7th Lancashire Fusiliers (125th Brigade) and three companies of the 1/Otago (2nd New Zealand Brigade) at 5.30 p.m. succeeded in completing the capture of Neuville Bourjonval and in advancing the line to a depth of five hundred yards on a 3,000-yard frontage. At night the corps front was reorganized so that it was held by two divisions, the 37th and New Zealand ; the 42nd Division was then withdrawn to join the 5th in reserve.

The VI. Corps found that the Spoil Heap on the west bank of the canal on the front of the 2nd Division had been evacuated ; but attempts to establish posts along the western bank met with no permanent success.

FOURTH ARMY

General Rawlinson had made representations to G.H.Q. that in view of the strenuous fighting of the past month by the Australian and III. Corps, and the extensive frontage now held by the former, it would be difficult, without reinforcements, to maintain an active pursuit affording no respite to the enemy's rear guards and preventing the destruction of roads and railways. He was at once informed that the 6th Division (Major-General T. O. Marden), which had just arrived in the III. Corps area from the Second Army, although earmarked as G.H.Q. reserve, together with the 5th Cavalry Brigade,[2] was placed at his disposal, and that

---

[1] See Sketch 24.

[2] The 5th Cavalry Brigade (Br.-General N. W. Haig), which was in the Third Army area, arrived south of Albert on the 6th ; on the 8th it moved to Querrieu (7 miles north-east of Amiens), where it remained until the 26th.

the IX. Corps (Lieut.-General Sir W. Braithwaite, in succession to Lieut.-General Sir Alexander Gordon, who had fallen ill),[1] would be reconstituted and inserted between the French First Army and the Australian Corps, whilst the 5th and 3rd Australian Divisions would be relieved by the 4th and 1st from rest areas.[2]

In the late afternoon of the 5th therefore the Fourth Army issued orders for the Australian and III. Corps to " press the pursuit as rapidly and vigorously as possible and " give the enemy's rear guards no respite ".

The great question was, on which of the available lines of the old British front and of the Hindenburg Position opposite it, the enemy would make a stand. His retirement, pivoting now on Havrincourt, being well under way,[3] the whole of the Fourth Army and the V. Corps of the Third Army made fair progress on the 6th and 7th September, the IV. Corps on the 6th only ; on the 8th the enemy's resistance stiffened again.

A series of lines was defined by the Fourth Army[4] as the successive objectives to be reached daily, but they were to be regarded as a general guide only and not to be rigidly adhered to by divisions if greater progress could be achieved. Actually they nearly marked the daily progress, and on the evening of the 7th the corps were exactly on the line for that day except the extreme right, which was a little beyond it, and the extreme left which was partly in front and partly behind it, the total distance covered since the morning of the 5th having been nine to ten miles.

---

[1] Br.-General G.S., Br.-General W. J. Maxwell-Scott till 23rd September, then Br.-General A. R. Cameron ; D.A. and Q.M.G., Br.-General J. C. Harding-Newman ; C.R.A., Br.-General G. Humphreys ; C.H.A., Br.-General G. B. Mackenzie ; C.E., Br.-General G. S. Cartwright.
The IX. Corps heavy artillery, under Br.-General G. B. Mackenzie, was in action with the French XXXVI. Corps, on the British right, from 23rd August until 5th September. It then concentrated near Amiens, moving to the front on the 11th.

[2] After the Battle of the Chemin des Dames in May–June, the IX. Corps headquarters had returned to the British zone, but by the end of July was without troops.

[3] During the night of the 5th–6th the German *Second Army*, retiring east-northeastward slightly obliquely to the front of the Fourth Army, reached the line Pontru (12 miles from the Somme and just in front of the Hindenburg Position)–Trescault (2 miles south of Havrincourt), leaving only small rear guards, amounting to no more than five battalions and one field artillery brigade (B.O.A., p. 542.) The *Seventeenth Army*, north of the *Second*, had reached its new line on the night of the 3rd/4th.

[4] See Sketch 23. From this point Sketches 23 and 24 should be used alternatively.

On the 6th, the three divisions of the Australian Corps, the 32nd (unrelieved and occupying all its original front), the 5th Australian and 3rd Australian, moved off early about 6 a.m. with the 97th, 14th and 11th Australian Brigades as advanced guards[1]; but there was some little hesitation about starting in the III. Corps, and it was not until after a bombardment of the Templeux la Fosse–Nurlu position that the 74th, 47th and 12th Divisions went forward at 8 a.m., at first in attack formation. Although occasionally enemy machine guns and snipers fired, no real opposition was offered to either corps, and the later advance was covered in the Australian Corps by the 13th Light Horse and the Corps Cyclist Battalion, and in the III. Corps by the Northumberland Hussars and XXII. Corps Cyclist Battalion. The only capture of note was four guns and one officer and forty men by the 12th Division.[2] The V. Brigade R.A.F. again did good service driving off the enemy planes, destroying at least eight, and shooting or forcing down all the enemy's observation balloons, besides ·bombing and machine-gunning his retreating troops. A more serious danger than the enemy's fire arose from the filthy state of the huts and shelters abandoned by the Germans; they were fouled and fly-infested beyond description, so that until they could be cleaned and disinfected there was fear of an epidemic of dysentery and enteric, if not of cholera. At night, as another exhibition of German culture, the horizon ahead was red with the flames of burning villages.

In the Third Army on the 6th,[3] it was found that the enemy had withdrawn on the whole front of the V. Corps, and the 21st (vice the 38th, relieved) and 17th Divisions advanced up the Fins gap, and over the high ground on either side, including the Equancourt trenches, almost without opposition. The New Zealand Division of the IV. Corps went considerably farther, passing through Metz en

---

[1] The 8th Australian Brigade was detailed in the 5th Australian Division and should have passed through the 14th, but arrived so tired that the latter offered to take its place.

[2] They belonged to the *6th (dismounted) Cavalry Division*, which had arrived by rail from the Ypres sector on the previous evening.

[3] See Sketch 24.

Couture and most of the southern part of Havrincourt Wood ; the 37th Division (Major-General H. Bruce Williams) also pushed, but not so far, into the northern part of the wood. In the VI. Corps on this and the three following days there was patrol action, but no change in the situation.[1]

On the 7th the divisions of the Fourth Army started between 7 and 8 a.m., and the Australian Corps, with no more opposition than on the previous day, reached the objective line near an old British reserve line which seemed lightly held ; the 97th Brigade (32nd Division) on the right went a thousand yards beyond the objective, and, the enemy being on the run, in conjunction with the French on the right, captured Villeveque at the elbow of the valley of the Omignon. At night the 14th Brigade was relieved, the right of the 5th Australian Division taking over its frontage.

The 5th Australian Division captured the large village of Bernes. The 3rd Australian Division, now on the left of the Australian Corps, secured Montigny Farm and Hervilly. On the extreme left of the Army, however, where the Hindenburg Position was nearest, the 12th Division was checked about 1.30 p.m., when past Saulcourt, by heavy fire from the double village of Epéhy–Peizière, now an outlyer of the Hindenburg Position. At 2.45 p.m. Major-General Higginson gave Br.-General Incledon-Webber (37th Brigade, which was making the attack) verbal orders not to press it to the final objective, Epéhy itself, if strong opposition continued, but to consolidate. Towards evening a little more ground was gained by infiltration, but as the 21st Division (Third Army), on the left, was still somewhat behind, further effort then ceased.

In the Third Army the 21st and 17th Divisions (Major-Generals D. G. M. Campbell and P. R. Robertson) of the V. Corps advanced about three thousand yards, took Heudicourt and Dessart Wood with some opposition from German rear guards, and came up abreast of the New Zealand Division (IV. Corps), which, being ahead of its neighbours, did not move. The 37th Division made a further advance through Havrincourt Wood and also came up level with the New Zealanders.

---

[1] On the 6th Br.-General W. E. Ironside left the 99th Brigade on orders to proceed home for employment in N. Russia.

On the 8th September the enemy's artillery became active again and the progress made was small, falling much short of the objective for the day.   It became of importance to ascertain whether this check was due to the obstinacy of the rear guards or to the enemy having decided to make another stand, either on or in front of the Hindenburg Position from which he had made the March offensive. Active patrolling was carried out, but observation, both ground and air, was hampered by the weather, which broke and continued unfavourable until the 15th.   The 32nd Division, on its reduced front between the French and the Amiens–Vermand high road, gained a little ground by establishing posts in Jean Devaux Woods, a thousand yards ahead, and northwards.   Patrols of the Australian Corps cyclists entered Vermand during the morning without opposition, and found the enemy holding the villages on the left bank of the Omignon and on the high ground to the north. In the III. Corps the 74th Division reached the outskirts of Templeux le Guerard and Ronssoy Wood, but were driven back again by a counter-attack.   The 58th Division (Major-General F. W. Ramsay), whose left, the 174th Brigade (Br.-General A. Maxwell), passed through the 12th Division and took over its front, advancing under an artillery barrage,. in conjunction with the 21st Division (Third Army) on its left, could not get within a thousand yards of Epéhy.   In spite of machine-gun fire, parties of the 7th and 8/London took prisoners of two battalions of the *Alpine Corps*, which had evacuated the latter village, but being unsupported, they could not remain there.   On this day the 47th Division (III. Corps) began to entrain for transfer to the Fifth Army.

In the Third Army the 21st Division and the right of the 17th managed to swing forward about a thousand yards on the right, but then met strong opposition ; the V. Corps drew the conclusion that the enemy was making a stand on the line Peizière–Vaucelette Farm–Chapel Hill–Gouzeaucourt,. and could not be moved except by an attack in force, which was arranged for next day.   Northward, in the IV. Corps, New Zealand patrols pushed through to the edge of Havrincourt Wood, but were withdrawn at night so as to be out of the way of the next day's barrage.   The 63rd Brigade (Br.-General E. L. Challenor) of the 37th Division made a short advance in Havrincourt Wood and occupied the whole of the western bank of the canal in the divisional sector.

In the Fourth Army the 9th September passed uneventfully. The 32nd Division, on the right, pushed some posts forward to connect with the French at Étreillers ; the 5th and 3rd Australian Divisions limited their operations to active reconnaissance ; as also did the III. Corps.

The right wing of the Third Army, the 21st and 17th Divisions of the V. Corps and the New Zealand Division of the IV. Corps, made a considerable advance, pivoted on Havrincourt Wood, by an organized attack made in the dark at 4 a.m. Each division was supported by four brigades of field artillery, whilst four brigades of heavy artillery shelled selected points, and those of the III. Corps (Fourth Army) kept Peizière under bombardment. The attack was carried out by the 64th, 52nd, and 3rd New Zealand (Rifle) Brigades. Some gas shelling, which affected the eyes, made it difficult to keep direction in the darkness ; but in the early stages this darkness prevented the enemy's machine-gun fire from being very effective, and good progress was achieved. Then opposition made itself felt and counter-attacks began ; all the gains therefore could not be held and the objective, which included Chapel Hill and a line of trenches running N.N.W. from it, was not quite reached. The New Zealanders captured Gouzeaucourt Wood and again advanced to the eastern edge of Havrincourt Wood ; but they could not secure the sunken cross roads at Dead Man's Corner whence devastating enfilade fire was proceeding.

For the next day, the 10th, only a few local enterprises were planned. The night of the 9th/10th September was very dark and rain fell in torrents ; mud hampered movement, and, as the roads were scarcely recognizable owing to war and weather, and few landmarks were visible, some units, detailed to attack, lost their way in moving to their jumping-off places. In the end, only a little ground was gained on the extreme flanks of the Fourth Army.

In the 32nd Division, the 97th Brigade was to clear the enemy out of the valley of the Omignon in the divisional sector and from the western edge of Holnon Wood and the woods between Attilly and Marteville, establishing machine guns in these so as to deny them to his use. The 10/Argyll & Sutherland Highlanders and the 2/K.O.Y.L.I. were

entrusted with the task. Starting at 5.30 a.m., the trees of
Holnon Wood being just visible, they had complete initial
success on the right and nearly so on the left, the Argyll
suffering only two casualties. Attilly was mopped up, the
Germans being seen retiring in large numbers from it towards
the northern part of Holnon Wood, and part of Dead Wood
was taken. Machine-gun fire from the intervening copses
prevented junction between the two battalions, and into the
gap the enemy, until 5 p.m., made persistent attempts to
penetrate, supported by artillery fire, which fortunately fell
either behind or in front of the 97th Brigade. Not only
were all his counter-attacks repulsed, but the remainder of
Dead Wood was also captured.

The 5th and 3rd Australian Divisions, being about to be
relieved by the 4th and 1st, did not attempt any serious
operation. The change of brigades in front line was carried
out on the night of the 10th/11th September.

The III. Corps had given verbal orders early on the 9th
for the renewal on the 10th at 5.15 a.m. of the attempt to
capture Epéhy and Peizière and the railway embankment
east of them by the advanced guard of the 58th ; the
advanced guard of the 74th Division, on its right, was to
co-operate by seizing during the previous night the two long
spurs which jut out south-westwards from the Ronssoy–
Epéhy ridge towards Templeux Wood and Ste. Emilie ; and
it was hoped that the 21st Division (right of the Third Army)
would take part by attacking the trench system north of
Peizière—which it did not do. The 16/Devonshire and
14/Black Watch of the 229th Brigade (74th Division) during
the night duly captured the greater part of the spurs above
mentioned ; but the later attack of the 175th Brigade, under
a field-gun barrage, ended in failure. Men of the 2/2nd and
2/4th London managed to enter both Epéhy and Peizière,
but the battalions were eventually forced to fall back almost
to their starting line, mainly owing to the fierce resistance
offered by the *Alpine Corps* with machine guns and snipers
in the ruins of the houses. At 1.30 p.m. Major-General
Ramsay ordered the attack to be renewed and furnished
two battalions to the 229th Brigade as reinforcements ; but
the casualties incurred had been so heavy that an organized
attack was considered by Br.-General Corkran (173rd) to be
out of the question, and he instructed his battalions to gain
ground by infiltration with the help of Stokes mortars. On

the right the 3/London (173rd Brigade) captured the German trenches south-east of Epéhy, but no other success was obtained. It was evident that the enemy meant to stand on the old British Main Line.

In the Third Army the bad weather and other troubles already mentioned caused the renewed attack on the Chapel Hill position to be postponed from 4 a.m. to 5.15 a.m. ; but even at the latter hour, although the artillery fired the barrage, the infantry of the 17th Division was not ready to advance, and the 21st Division, which did start, lost the barrage owing to darkness, missed its direction, and failed in its attack.

Between the 11th and 17th September the activities of the Fourth Army were limited to minor operations in preparation for an attack which was to take place on the 18th ; the IX. Corps (with the 32nd and 6th Divisions, the latter from G.H.Q. reserve) came into official existence on the 11th, and took over from the Australian Corps the sector south of the Brie–Vermand road.

The Third Army during the 11th made some small advances to improve the line and in preparation for further attack. The right of the 21st Division (V. Corps) at 3 a.m. pushed forward under a barrage to get touch with the left of the Fourth Army ; it drew level, but a pocket of the enemy held out obstinately between the two Armies until the night of the 12th/13th. The 2nd Division of the VI. Corps (whose southern boundary had been shifted fifteen hundred yards farther south with a view to an attack on Havrincourt) carried out a preliminary operation under a barrage in order to draw nearer to that village, gaining ground to the south-west of it and capturing the eastern bank of the canal, there dry, near the Spoil Heap. The 57th Division (Major-General R. W. R. Barnes) of the XVII. Corps, using the 170th and 171st Brigades (Br.-Generals A. L. Ransome[1] and F. C. Longbourne), under a barrage, secured Moeuvres ; but the attempt to cross the canal and establish a line beyond it failed ; although the canal was reached, the troops were compelled to fall back.

---

[1] Assumed command, *vice* Br.-General G. F. Boyd, on 5th September.

It was now a week since the G.H.Q. order of the 3rd September had been issued directing that the enemy's outposts and rear guards should be driven in and his dispositions ascertained, but forbidding deliberate operations on a large scale pending the resumption of the Allied offensive.[1] The fighting which had ensued had shown that the enemy had by the 10th retired as far as he intended to go, and was back in a position, much of it the Hindenburg Position, which he had held before the offensive of the 21st March 1918, and could only be forced from it by a deliberate assault backed by all available artillery and tanks.

This had been expected by Maréchal Foch, who on the 8th September had sent to Sir Douglas Haig an addendum to his Directive of the 3rd September[2] which ran :

" In carrying out their operations south of the Scarpe " the British Armies will first take as objective the line " Valenciennes, Solesmes, le Cateau–Wassigny [that is " the line of the German Hermann Position].[3]

" The German retirement having been accentuated " in the last few days, it is to be expected that the " Allied troops will be in contact with the enemy's " principal line of resistance all along the front, in a day " or two.

" The preparation of an offensive aiming at the " seizure of this line and pushing beyond it to the " objectives indicated should therefore be undertaken " at once. It is of importance to launch this offensive " without delay, in order to catch the enemy before he " has had time to re-organize to any great extent.

" The Field-Marshal Commanding-in-Chief of the " British Armies is requested kindly to report the date " selected for these operations, also the general dis- " positions he proposes to adopt, so that the Marshal " Commander-in-Chief of the Allied Armies may be " able, if desirable, to organize corresponding action of " the French forces immediately on the right of the " British Armies ".[4]

---

[1] See p. 421.

[2] See p. 443.

[3] See Sketch 11.

[4] The combined operations on the Western Front were not the only operations in hand : the final Macedonian offensive began on 15th September, and the final Palestine offensive on the 19th. The Italians, in spite of Maréchal Foch's urging, did not begin their offensive until 24th October.

On receipt of this communication G.H.Q., on the same day, requested the five Army commanders to

" forward a short report based on the information
" obtained in the recent advanced-guard actions, on :

" (a) the enemy's dispositions and probable in-
" tentions, particularly in regard to the position on
" which he is likely to stand and give battle ;

"·(b) the general state of the hostile troops.

" Army commanders will further submit their pro-
" posals and recommendations for deliberate offensive
" operations as may be considered advisable by them
" on the fronts of their respective Armies ".

The replies of the Army commanders who had been principally engaged furnish a good appreciation of the situation.

To begin on the right, General Rawlinson for the Fourth Army pointed out : that the Germans had six lines of defence[1] which they could hold if they had sufficient men available and if the morale of the troops was good enough to warrant their being placed out in front of the elaborately prepared defences of the Hindenburg Position. These six lines were, from west to east :

(a) *The old British Reserve Line*, which had already been pierced in the centre near Hesbecourt, where it was only held by machine guns. The whole line could probably be gained without serious difficulty. The wire lay east of it.

(b) *The old British Main Line*. This the enemy had held with great determination in the spring of 1917. It would probably be difficult to capture unless his morale was very low. Most of the wire was east of the trenches, but some, the German wire of 1917, was west. In this line were the strong localities of le Verguier, Basse Boulogne and Epéhy.

(c) *The old British Outpost Line*, which would not present much difficulty and would probably fall at the same time as the British main line, if that was strongly attacked with adequate forces well supported by artillery.

(d) *The Advanced Hindenburg System*. Originally an outpost line to the main Hindenburg Line and when first constructed not intended to be held against a

---

[1] See Sketch 26.

determined attack.[1] In 1917 the outposts were given
orders to withdraw to the main line if attacked in force,
and higher commanders were definitely instructed not
to bring on a battle in front of the main Hindenburg
Line. The importance of the advanced Hindenburg
System to the British for the purposes of observation,
and the great advantages accruing to them from its
capture, were now fully realized by the enemy. Since
the spring of 1917 the advanced system had been very
materially strengthened, so that the policy had probably
been changed. Moreover, the enemy now placed more
reliance on defence in depth than he had in the previous
year. If troops were available and morale was sufficiently good, it was possible that this advanced system, now
well provided with wire and dug-outs, and no longer an
outpost line, would be held with determination.

(*e*) *The Main Hindenburg System*, of which the canal
and its tunnels[2] formed the basis of the defence. Its
strength precluded its capture except by a carefully
prepared attack on a wide front with strong forces with
tanks and plenty of artillery. It could not be rushed ;
on the other hand, the possession of every detail of the
scheme of defence between St. Quentin and Bellicourt
would render the task much less difficult.

(*f*) *The Reserve Hindenburg System*. Probably not
completed ; consequently it might be possible, if the
main system was captured and the attack pressed, to
gain possession of, or break into, the reserve system on
the same day.

The report went on to draw attention to the fall in the
German morale as a result of the attack on the 8th August
and subsequent operations which had necessitated a prolonged retirement, and to the severe losses, in most cases not
replaced, which had been inflicted.[3] Nevertheless, experiences in March and April had shown that on every day on

---

[1] This information came from the copy of the defence scheme of the
Hindenburg system drawn up early in 1917 and captured by the Fourth
Army on 8th August 1918.

[2] The St. Quentin canal and the tunnels at le Tronquoy and Bellicourt.

[3] The Fourth Army was opposed by about seven divisions between
Beauvois and Heudicourt. Of these seven divisions, six were in the line
for the second time since 8th August and one division, mainly engaged on
the Third Army front, was fresh. The number of rifles opposing the Fourth
Army was estimated to be 11,610. Since 8th August twenty-one
Continued at foot of next page.

which no attack took place improvement and recuperation became possible, and that good troops, although temporarily their morale might be shaken, would not withdraw from a position without being pressed. Taking all these factors into account, General Rawlinson considered that if the Advanced and Main Hindenburg Systems were to be attacked, it was essential to " hustle " the Germans out of the positions west of these two lines—especially out of the old British main and outposts lines—as quickly as possible. Such action would deprive them of time in which to organize and to make preparations for holding the Advanced and Main Hindenburg Systems, for which purpose some of the divisions that had been badly defeated might be employed. It would also enable the positions to be captured without undue loss ; whereas if time was given the defenders might hold on with determination and cause serious casualties. An interval must elapse on getting close to the Advanced and Main Hindenburg Systems to give time for reconnaissance, organization, rest and improvement of communications, before they could be attacked. In General Rawlinson's view it was most important that this pause should occur when the British were close to the real Hindenburg system and not when still some distance from it. He therefore urged, most strongly, that he should be allowed to undertake operations with the IX., Australian and III. Corps at the earliest possible moment in order to secure the old British outpost line, and especially Holnon Wood, le Verguier and the high ground north of it, the high ground east of Hargicourt and the commanding villages of Ronssoy and Epéhy. Until this line had been won it would be difficult to estimate the possibilities of attacking the Advanced and Main Hindenburg Systems, and probably the deciding factor would be the morale of the enemy holding them and the advanced lines west of them. In General Rawlinson's opinion, the advanced positions could be won at no great cost if attacked with determination on a wide front and with

Continued from previous page.
divisions had been withdrawn to reserve, of which four had been resting for over three weeks, six between two and three weeks, five between one and two weeks, and six under one week. Seven of the twenty-one divisions had been engaged twice and one division three times since 8th August. Owing to casualties, battalions had been reduced to three companies in eight divisions. It was considered that only five of these twenty-one divisions were fit at the moment for operations, their rifle strength amounting to 10,440.

adequate artillery support. Until they had been captured and the cost of success was known, and until the Fourth Army was in possession of ground from which the Advanced and Main Hindenburg Systems could be observed, it was not possible to say whether they could be attacked with any reasonable prospect of success.

General Byng replied for the Third Army on the 9th. He considered that the enemy was fighting to gain time to resuscitate his demoralized divisions, to recuperate and to make preparations either for an offensive or a better thought out retirement than the one imposed on him : his divisions therefore had been told to hold on as long as possible and to counter-strike, a policy which gained time but was wasteful in men : his main stand opposite the Third Army would no doubt be on the Hindenburg Position :[1] his next solid defence line would be the Schelde canal : beyond this there was no strong defence line ready : he would therefore endeavour to hold a position west of St. Quentin–Cambrai–Douai as long as possible.

The general state of the enemy's troops General Byng considered poor : many would surrender if they dared and many fought extremely badly : every division as it arrived fought well for a couple of days and then became demoralized by the never ceasing action forced upon it : this demoralization of the enemy would not last unless he was constantly attacked and harassed, and therefore continuous offensive action must be our rôle.

General Byng's proposals were for offensive operations to get astride of the Hindenburg Front System by an attack east of the Canal du Nord as soon as possible. If this succeeded in gaining part of the Hindenburg Front System, he hoped that it might be exploited by an advance of the First Army. When the line of the Schelde Canal was reached, it would depend to a very great extent on the condition of the enemy's troops whether this line should be attacked frontally or should be turned.

In the case of the Second Army, plans had been under consideration for some days. On the 26th August, after the German retirement in the Lys salient had got well under way,[2] Sir Douglas Haig had been in conference with Belgian G.H.Q., and found H.M. King Albert anxious to take

---

[1] See End-paper B.
[2] See Sketch 21.

offensive action. A week later, on the 2nd September, Maréchal Foch sent a letter by hand to the British Commander-in-Chief and to Lieut.-General Gillain (Chief of the General Staff, Belgian Army), pointing out that the enemy's withdrawal, combined with the paucity of the German troops in Flanders, their exhaustion and their lack of reserves, might very shortly bring about a situation favourable for exploitation. In view of the evident speeding up of the German retirement, it seemed to him probable that the Second Army and the Belgian Army could at small cost occupy the high ground east of Ypres : besides the advantages which would accrue by the unexpected extension of the Allied offensive to the north of the Lys, the line thus captured would afford an excellent jumping-off position for later operations. He therefore asked that a plan of such an attack should be studied, so that it could be launched at the earliest possible moment, and by surprise.

G.H.Q. passed on these instructions to General Plumer early on the 5th September, giving as objective " the " Passchendaele–Clercken Ridge and, if possible, the high " ground about Gheluvelt ". The force available was put at eight Belgian divisions and not more than two British divisions, and he was informed that the whole operation would be under his control.

The receipt of these instructions brought General Plumer to G.H.Q. by 11 a.m. He had his own plans, and wished to continue his efforts to press the enemy back between Armentières and the Yser—his front extended from opposite Armentières to beyond Ypres—and to recapture Messines. But Sir Douglas Haig, being anxious that the Belgian Army should co-operate, supported Maréchal Foch's views as to the objective, and directed General Plumer to keep two good divisions on his left to co-operate with the Belgian right, and told him that he should be prepared to move a division later by sea to Ostend and then occupy Bruges, pushing its left to the Dutch frontier, but keeping connection with the British–Belgian Armies.

On the 6th and 7th September, fires in Douai and the burning of Wervicq and villages east of it seemed to point to a German withdrawal to the Haute Deule Canal Line or beyond it.[1] On the 8th more fires were seen north-east of

---

[1] The portion of the canal south of Lille is called the Haute Deule ; it runs first south-west and then south-east to Douai (20 miles south of Lille).

Lille ; prisoners stated that preparations were being made to fall back to Passchendaele ridge and to evacuate Douai. General Plumer's plan for the immediate continuance of the advance of the Second Army seemed therefore entirely to meet the case. But on the 9th Maréchal Foch came for a conference to Second Army headquarters at Cassel.[1] Before the meeting he had a private talk with Sir Douglas Haig in which he said—as the British Commander-in-Chief already knew—that King Albert, with whom he had had an audience that morning, was anxious to advance. He proposed, therefore, to offer the King the command of the Allied forces engaged in the Flanders operations, " with the collaboration " of General Degoutte and the staff of the Sixth Army ". General Degoutte's duties were subsequently defined as " Chief of the Staff to the King of the Belgians ".[2] Sir Douglas Haig agreed that General Plumer should take orders as regards operations from King Albert ; he declined, however, to provide three cavalry divisions for Flanders, as he wished his mounted troops to act with his main forces ; but he promised to provide some motor machine-gun batteries.

At the conference Maréchal Foch explained his plan, handing in a short Note of its features to Sir Douglas Haig, to General Plumer and to General Gillain.[3] To clear the country between the Lys and the coast, and the coast itself, it said : first a base must be secured from which exploitation could be carried out : this would be a line running from the Ypres–Comines canal to Clercken, passing over the high ground at Zandvoorde and Gheluvelt, Passchendaele ridge, Houthulst Forest, and it would be attacked by nine Belgian and two British divisions. Exploitation would then be carried out rapidly by a column of Belgian troops and three French cavalry divisions moving through Thourout on Bruges to cut the German communication with the coast,

---

[1] Besides Maréchal Foch and Sir Douglas Haig, there were present : Generals Gillain and Maglinse (Belgian C.G.S. and D.C.G.S.), General Weygand, Lieut.-General Sir H. Lawrence (C.G.S.) and Major-General J. H. Davidson (General Staff Operations).

[2] F.O.A. vii (i), p. 307. The King's command was given as " Belgian Army, British Second Army, three French divisions, and a French cavalry " corps (3 divisions) ". F.O.A. vii. (i), Annexes 1074 and 1043. " Degoutte failed to exercise much influence over the King and General " Sir H. Plumer, who required no mentor ". (*Army Quarterly*, Vol. XXXVII., p 204.)

[3] See Sketch 27.

and by the mass of the reserves (probably three French divisions) making for Thielt via Roulers, whilst the British Second Army formed a protective flank along the Lys from Menin to Courtrai. Thus the successive stages would be the lines Menin–Roulers–Thourout, Courtrai–Thielt–Bruges, and then the area round Ghent to the Dutch frontier. " This offensive ", continued the Note, " which fits into its " place in the general battle of the Allied Armies actually " in progress and in process of development, must, on account " of the operations already arranged for these Armies, be " launched between the 20th and 25th September ", and secrecy and rapidity in its execution were enjoined.

General Plumer, who knew the ground intimately, objected to Zandvoorde–Gheluvelt being included in the initial line, saying that Hill 60–Polygon Wood and thence along the ridge to Broodseinde was the longest advance (two miles shorter than that proposed) which could be undertaken in the first instance with the divisions at his disposal. Maréchal Foch concurred with him, but the wording of the Note was not formally amended and he was finally told that a direct attack on the Messines–Wytschaete Ridge should not be made, although pressure must be maintained on the enemy holding it.

General Plumer, having received orders from Sir Douglas Haig for offensive action, in his report submitted on the 11th September in compliance with the G.H.Q. memorandum of the 8th, made no recommendations, but exhaustively enumerated the enemy defence lines, giving their nature and condition. The present front line, he said, might be regarded as an outpost line only, on no part of it was there an organized trench system : he had no definite evidence pointing to a withdrawal from it, but a stand on it seemed unlikely to be of long duration : it was probable that if the retirement were resumed the enemy would give battle on the line Lille defences–Bondues–Wervicq–Gheluvelt–Zonnebeke–Staden. As regards the German morale, he discriminated between the divisions, but said that the withdrawal from the Lys salient had lowered it throughout, and that discipline was now on a lower level than in the early summer : no satisfactory explanation had been given to the German troops for the retirement, which must be ascribed to the continuous pressure of the Second Army towards the line La Bassée–Armentières–

Kemmel during August and to the decrease in German man-power which necessitated the shortening of the front.

On the 13th the Intelligence Branch reported that the enemy opposite Lens was disposed in depth, and seemed to be expecting attack ; that in front of La Bassée he was gradually falling back, but was holding on to his positions about Messines and Wytschaete. During the afternoon Lieut.-General Lawrence (C.G.S.) visited General Plumer at Cassel, and handed him formal written instructions that, for the forthcoming operations, the Second Army would be included in the command of King Albert : in all other respects his responsibilities towards Sir Douglas Haig would remain unaltered.

General Plumer mentioned that he had discussed with Vice-Admiral Sir Roger Keyes (commanding the Dover Patrol) the possibility of an Allied landing on the Belgian coast. Both of them, he said, considered such an operation impossible on an open beach ; but they agreed that it might be feasible to rush four monitors carrying two infantry battalions and machine guns into Ostend harbour, although not until the Belgians were within striking distance on the land side.

NOTE I

THE FRENCH, 4TH–11TH SEPTEMBER

(End–paper B and Sketch 20)

" During the night of the 3rd/4th September the enemy began
" the retirement which, from information received, G.Q.G. had
" been expecting for several days. . . . On the 4th the enemy
" gave up ground in front of the First and Third Armies, in front
" of the right of the Tenth, on the whole front of the Sixth [Vesle
" front] and before the extreme left of the Fifth [west of Fismes
" on the Vesle]. On the other hand, he continued resistance in
" front of the left and centre of the Tenth Army [which was
" ahead of the First and Third Armies, which had hung back, so
" that their front formed a great re-entrant 12 miles in depth].
" In the face of this event, General Fayolle ordered that the
" pursuit should be begun and carried out with the greatest
" possible energy."

He gave the First, Third and Tenth Armies an eastward direction, but the Sixth was to push northwards.

Q* 2

During the following days the Sixth Army made slight progress, as far as the Aisne, and its front then became stabilized ; but the Tenth, Third and First swung forward towards the Hindenburg Position, the Third and First coming up into the general line of the French Tenth and British Fourth Armies, the left of the First then more or less keeping pace with the right of the British Fourth Army.

On the 7th September, General Pétain informed General Fayolle that the G.A.R. would soon suffer reduction : " the retirement " made by the enemy towards the Hindenburg Position entails " the entry of the G.A.R. into a new phase. Henceforward the " First and Third Armies will be operating in the devastated area, " where the maintenance of a large force is temporarily impractic- " able. On the right bank of the Oise our front will be consider- " ably shortened, the re-entrant of the First and Third Armies " obliterated, and part of it will encounter the obstacle formed " by that river above La Fère. From the offensive point of view " the situation of the Tenth Army alone is interesting ; for its " right wing can manoeuvre to outflank the defences of the " Chemin des Dames [Aisne Position] and of the Ailette river " behind it ". He gave warning that the Third Army would be brought out of the line and placed in G.Q.G. reserve " as soon as " contact has been taken with the Hindenburg Position north of " the Oise."

Late on the 7th General Fayolle issued instructions, in his turn, that " there is no necessity to halt in front of the Hindenburg " Position until it is known whether or not the enemy means to " defend it ; nevertheless, as it is likely that he has developed " the position into a formidable refuge for his defeated troops, " it should not be approached without precaution nor before all " the artillery is up."

The First Army, next the British, was instructed not to employ in the front line more than two divisions each of the XXXVI. and XXXI. Corps, and only one of the X. Corps ; the main bodies of these divisions were to halt in a position of resistance selected by the Army, " in front of which each division should push only " an advanced guard (divisional cavalry, a regiment of infantry, " and a brigade of artillery) ".

F.O.A. then says :

" The information collected by G.Q.G. between the 8th and " 11th gave the definite impression that the German retirement " would stop at the Hindenburg Position : a great quantity of " artillery was already placed in that position, and the trenches " and wire had been reconditioned ".

The 11th September, therefore, found the Tenth Army and the right wing of the Third close up to the Hindenburg Position, and the left wing of the Third and right of the First, both of which had been delayed for two days on the Crozat canal, with the left of the First, approaching the position.

NOTE II

THE GERMANS, 4TH–11TH SEPTEMBER

(End–paper B and Sketch 11)

The German troops " began to occupy the new position on the " 4th September, but completion of the occupation dragged on for " many days ". The main bodies of the *Second Army* reached the line Pontru (5 miles north-west of St. Quentin)–Trescault (4½ miles north of Villers Guislain) on the night of the 5th/6th, and the *Eighteenth Army* arrived on the night of the 6th/7th in the Hindenburg Position between La Fère and Pontru. South of the Oise, the *Ninth Army* retired during the 4th/5th, and the right of the *Seventh* on the night of the 3rd/4th, so as to blunt the salient near Vailly on the Aisne. To give the necessary time to reach the new position considerable resistance was offered by the rear guards. Near Epéhy–Peizière (see Sketch 23) and southwards the *6th (Dismounted) Cavalry Division* and the *Alpine Corps* held on to the high ground and checked the III. Corps. On the other flank of the Fourth Army, the *79th Reserve Division* had to give ground before the 32nd Division.

Crown Prince Rupprecht (ii., p. 441), relates on the 5th September that that morning a battalion of the reliable *44th Reserve Division*, near Havrincourt, had bolted, shouting " the English are coming ", and that the examination of the letters of the *183rd, 3rd Naval, 26th Reserve* and *83rd Divisions* showed that their morale was bad, and that little reliance could be placed on them.

On the 6th September, a conference took place at O.H.L. at Avesnes, at which the Chiefs of the General Staffs of the three Groups of Armies were present   General von Lossberg (p 357), gives the following account :

" General Field-Marshal von Hindenburg first spoke " shortly and stressed the great seriousness of the situation. " He then left the further conduct of the conference to " General Ludendorff. The latter impressed me as being in " a very nervous state, completely different from his former " determined manner [Kuhl also reported to Crown Prince " Rupprecht (ii., p. 442) that Ludendorff ' looked very bad " ' and overtired ']. The troops came in for a good deal of " condemnation from his mouth. He made the troops and

" their leaders responsible for the events of the past days,
" without recognizing that his own faulty leading bore the
" main blame for what had happened. He gave notice that
" an O.H.L. order would be issued reducing infantry batta-
" lions from 4 to 3 companies, as reinforcements, both of
" officers and men, were lacking. The baggage also would
" be cut down. Ludendorff demanded sharp measures
" against shirkers.

" He then sketched the plans of O.H.L. for the Hermann
" and Hunding–Brunhild Position, also the Antwerp–Meuse
" Position, and requested the views of the three Chiefs of the
" Staff on the matter. In my statement I reported that
" General von Boehn on his daily visits to the front with me
" had assured himself that the Hindenburg Position was
" much dilapidated, had very little wire, and that on account
" of the condition of the troops a lengthy resistance in it
" could no longer be expected. The construction of the
" Hermann Position had not yet been begun. A long
" resistance there could not be hoped for when further retire-
" ment became necessary. On these grounds Boehn's Group
" of Armies suggested that, after the loss of the Hindenburg
" Position, the whole German front from Verdun to the
" sea should be brought back to the Antwerp–Meuse Position,
" about 45 miles shorter, in one bound, and that this position
" should be constructed without delay.

" Before the retirement as much material as possible
" should be sent back, and during it all railways, bridges
" and other communications destroyed. I based this
" proposal mainly on the assumption that the German Army
" could only gain sufficient time to carry out the re-organiza-
" tion and resting of its units by putting a long distance
" between itself and the enemy. General Ludendorff,
" however, turned the proposal down and stuck to his plan
" to construct the Hermann and Hunding–Brunhild Posi-
" tion, and to go back to it after the loss of the Hindenburg
" Position. This was a grave mistake ; for the Hinden-
" burg Position was overrun on the 8th October, and then
" the northern wing of the German Army collapsed
" (*brachzusammen*) during the retirement to the Meuse
" through the continuous pursuit of the enemy ".

On the 9th September, Lieut-Colonel Wetzell, Chief of the
Operations Section O.H.L. and Ludendorff's strategic adviser,
requested to be relieved of his duties, on the grounds of Ludendorff's constant use of the telephone to interfere with operations
without hearing what he had to say. Wetzell's successor was
Major von Bronsart (Rupprecht ii., p. 443).

CHAPTER XXIII

The Approach to the Hindenburg Position

The Battles of Havrincourt and Epéhy

12th–18th September 1918

(Map 4 ; Sketches 24, 26, 28)

Officially " The Battles of the Hindenburg Line " commence on the 12th September ; but the fighting in which the Fourth and Third Armies took part between that date and the 26th was preliminary in its nature, for the purpose of gaining possession of the outlying defences of the Hindenburg Position and obtaining observation over it before the general attack of the Allied Armies was launched. The action of the Third Army on the 12th is honoured with the name of the " Battle of Havrincourt ", and that of the Fourth Army on the 18th with that of the " Battle of Epéhy".

After the small preliminary move of the 2nd Division, already mentioned, on the evening of the 11th to secure the line of the canal near the Spoil Heap,[1] an attack was made by the extreme left of the V Corps, the IV Corps and the VI Corps of the Third Army at 5.25 a.m. on the 12th to capture the Trescault and Havrincourt spurs, which ran parallel to the front. The former spur, the highest ground in the neighbourhood, extended from Gouzeaucourt Wood to about eight hundred yards east of Trescault ; then came the widish valley of the stream called Grand Ravin, a feature in the Battle of Cambrai in 1917, with Havrincourt on its northern slope, and beyond it the Havrincourt spur, trending west of north towards No. 7 Lock on the canal.

The attack, which, after hard fighting, was highly successful, started from the fronts of the New Zealand, 37th and 62nd Divisions, and was carried out by the 3rd New Zealand (Rifle) Brigade (Br.-General H. Hart), the 111th (Br.-General S. G. Francis), the 186th (Br.-General J. L. G. Burnett) and the 187th (Br.-General A. J. Reddie). It was well covered by artillery, the three divisions being supported by six, four and eight brigades of field artillery, respectively, and by

---

[1] See Sketch 24.

one, four and four brigades of heavy artillery, after concentrations of fire had been put down during the night on Havrincourt, Trescault and other villages and on the enemy's communications.[1]

The first objective of the 3rd N.Z. Brigade, a line of trenches about six hundred yards away, was taken fairly easily ; but beyond this, progress over the further half mile was very difficult owing to intense fire and because the detachment of the 38th Division, which should have covered the right, was driven back by counter-attack. Fighting went on, with many more enemy counter-attacks, until 7 p.m. when, with artillery assistance, the left reached the final objective, and the right and centre were not far from it. Heavy casualties had been inflicted on the enemy and 490 prisoners captured. A further enemy counter-attack at 10.30 p m. entailed the loss of a little ground in the centre.

The 111th Brigade had managed to establish outposts on the eastern edge of the north-east horn of Havrincourt Wood during the night of the 11th/12th, and the advance at 5.25 a.m. was made from this line. At first there was little opposition ; but Trescault, which lies below the Trescault spur on its western side, and a strongpoint east of it offered an obstinate defence. On the right and in the centre the objective was reached about 8 a.m., the left being bent back to get touch with the 62nd Division. All gains were held, although at 6.30 p.m. fifty of the enemy, in a counter-attack, also made on the 62nd Division, actually entered the British trenches.

The brigades of the 62nd Division (Major-General Sir R. D. Whigham), brought in on the right of the 2nd Division (Major-General C. E. Pereira), had taken Havrincourt on the 20th November 1917 in the Battle of Cambrai. Major-General Whigham's operation orders recalled this by saying " the 62nd Division will recapture Havrincourt village ". The brigades had a somewhat complicated task, having in

---

[1] New Zealand Division : 1, II (Army) and III Brigades N.Z. F.A. ; 210th and 211th (42nd Division) and 223rd (63rd Division) Brigades R.F.A. and LVI Brigade R.G.A., under Br.-General G. N. Johnston.

37th Division : 123rd and 124th Brigades R.F.A. (37th Division), XV (5th Division), 317th (63rd Division), and XXXIV, LVII, XC and XCII Brigades R.G.A., under Br.-General F. Potts.

62nd Division : XL and XLII (3rd Division), 210th and 212th (62nd Division) Brigades R.F.A., V, LXXVI, XCIII and 232nd (Army) Brigades R.F.A., and XXXIX, LX, LXX and LXXXIV Brigades R.G.A., under Br.-General A. T. Anderson.

front of them the Hindenburg Position, which ran for fourteen hundred yards across the Grand Ravin, then passed in front of Havrincourt, and along Havrincourt spur to the canal, which beyond this point was inside the enemy's lines. It was decided to make the attack from the south-west, because from Havrincourt Wood (inclusive) southwards the IV. Corps was already across the canal, and the wood itself provided good cover for assembly. Sufficient time for reconnaissance and to lay tapes through the wood was available on the 11th. Major-General Whigham's plan was to advance from the position gained on the 11th north-eastwards on both flanks of Havrincourt—the moat of the chateau formed a serious obstacle on the southern side—then change direction eastwards to the final objective beyond the front system of the Hindenburg Position, and mop up the village from the west.

In the 186th Brigade, the 5/Duke of Wellington's (less 2 companies in brigade reserve) and the 2/4th battalion of the same regiment led. Advancing at first northwards, they turned eastwards with the left near the southern edge of Havrincourt and by 7.30 a.m., against considerable opposition, had captured the Hindenburg front system.

The 2/4th Hampshire, detailed to capture Havrincourt, followed behind the left, and at 7.15 a.m., when the heavy artillery lifted off the village, began operations. It had no difficulty in taking the chateau, but had stiff fighting in other parts, and was not established on the eastern edge until 11.30 a.m. An attempt made by the 9/Durham L.I. (Pioneers) to carry the brigade line forward about half a mile beyond the Hindenburg front system was only partly successful, and in the end, owing to casualties, any gains were abandoned. The 187th Brigade, on the left, sent forward the 5/K.O.Y.L.I. (plus a company of 2/4th K.O.Y.L.I.), and the 2/4th York & Lancaster. Some casualties were suffered in the assembly positions from the enemy counter-preparation, and the later advance eastward was checked for a time by enfilade fire from a strongpoint a quarter of a mile south of Havrincourt, which had to be taken.[1] After this the attack went well, and here also the objective was reached by 7.30 a.m., and the 2/4th K.O.Y.L.I. extended the line

---

[1] Sergeant L. Calvert, M.M., 5/K.O.Y.L.I., was awarded the V.C. for rushing forward alone, capturing two machine guns and killing the detachments.

to the right, but could not make connection with the 186th Brigade over the open ground intervening until nightfall.

At 6.30 p.m. the enemy made a determined effort to recapture Havrincourt, part of a fresh division, the *20th*, attacking, accompanied by low-flying aeroplanes, after a violent bombardment.[1] The onslaught struck mainly the 2/4th Hampshire (186th Brigade) and the 5/K.O.Y.L.I. (187th) ; it was repulsed by rifle and machine-gun fire, and finally broken by artillery fire. The 62nd Division, therefore, held Havrincourt and the Hindenburg front system north and south of it. The general advance of the Third Army had averaged nearly a mile on its five-mile front, but had not quite reached the final objective everywhere.

On the 13th September, the day after the American First Army had launched its successful attack against the St. Mihiel Salient, Sir Douglas Haig sanctioned the strongly urged proposal in General Rawlinson's report that the Fourth Army[2] should be allowed to attack the enemy's outpost positions on the ridges between le Verguier (in the centre of the Australian Corps front) and Epéhy (on the left of the III Corps front) as soon as possible—the 18th was settled on—and that he would arrange for the co-operation of the French First Army.

On the same day, the Commander-in-Chief replied to Maréchal Foch's communication of the 8th.[3] He stated that he was taking steps to engage the enemy at the earliest possible date : the Third Army had attacked on the 12th and had captured Trescault and Havrincourt, but the opposition had been serious : resistance on the whole battle front of the Third and Fourth Armies was stubborn, and it was evident that to dislodge the enemy a carefully prepared attack was necessary : he was making arrangements to deliver such an attack on a front extending from the right of the Fourth Army to Gouzeaucourt in the sector of the right corps of the Third Army, with eight or nine divisions in the front line : the object of this attack would be to capture

---

[1] The *20th Division*, after 10 days' rest, was brought up as *Eingreif* division to Ribecourt and then to support the *52nd Reserve*, which was relieved on the night of the 17th/18th by the *6th Division*.

[2] See Sketch 26. Sketch 24 should now be used alternately.

[3] See p. 457.

the high ground as well as the fortified positions and defences west of the Schelde (St. Quentin) canal, that is the front of the main Hindenburg Position : he was arranging for the French First Army to extend the attack to the south : north of Havrincourt, the Third Army was endeavouring by means of minor operations to gain a footing on the eastern bank of the Canal du Nord : he intended to continue operations with the main weight against the defences between St. Quentin and le Catelet, the sector of the main Hindenburg Position opposite the Fourth Army, and directed on the railway centre of Busigny (10 miles east of le Catelet) : to obtain effective results, the French First Army must attack strongly up the Oise valley towards la Fère (12 miles south of St. Quentin), and he hoped that Maréchal Foch would reinforce it sufficiently for this purpose.

At a conference at 11 a.m. on the 15th, at General Byng's headquarters at Villers l'Hopital (7 miles north-west of Doullens), with the commanders of the First, Third and Fourth Armies, Sir Douglas Haig further explained what he had in mind, subject to modification when more had been learnt about the enemy's dispositions after the attack of the Fourth Army on the 18th. The Third Army, he said, would support the later attack of the Fourth Army against St. Quentin–le Catelet by advancing eastwards towards Solesmes (20 miles east of Inchy), and the First Army would take Bourlon Wood (4 miles E.S.E. of Inchy) and cover the left of the Third Army, by holding a line on the Scarpe and Schelde as far as Valenciennes (25 miles north-east of Inchy). General Rawlinson now informed him that General Debeney (French First Army) had stated he would be unable to support the attack on the 18th owing to the weakness of his Army.[1] As the French Third Army had, owing to the shortening of the French front, been brought out of the line on the 14th, and its XV and XVIII Corps absorbed into the First Army,[2] the reason for the First Army being too weak to attack is not apparent. This information the Commander-in-Chief telegraphed to Maréchal Foch, drawing

[1] At 7 p.m. on the 15th General Fayolle issued an instruction (F.O.A. vii (i), Appendix 1150), in which he said " The resources of the First Army, " very reduced both in artillery and infantry, do not permit of any general " action ; only local operations are possible ".   Only the left wing would be " active ", and its mission was (1) to drive the enemy back to the Hindenburg Position ; (2) to support the attacks of the Army Rawlinson and advance in union with it.

[2] F.O.A. vii. (i), p. 315.

attention to the last portion of his letter of the 13th. At a meeting with the Generalissimo on the following day he repeated his request for the assistance of the French First Army, when Maréchal Foch confirmed that it was very weak, as its Army artillery had been transferred to other Armies— if there was to be any success, General Pétain was determined that it should be French and not British—but he would see that General Debeney was sufficiently strengthened to enable him to cover the Fourth Army's right, and he slightly altered the Allied boundary so that the whole of the important high ground, Fayet–Gricourt (both N.N.W. of St. Quentin), required as a gun position for the later attack on the main Hindenburg Position should be in the area of the Fourth Army.[1]

The formal order for the attack on the 18th was then issued by G.H.Q. It contained only four paragraphs :

" (1) The First, Third and Fourth Armies will " co-operate so as to establish themselves within striking " distance of the enemy's main defences on the general " line St. Quentin–Cambrai.

" The Third Army commander will be responsible for " co-ordinating his operations with those of the First " and Fourth Armies.

" (2) In order that the task of capturing the heights " of Bourlon Wood may fall to one Army, the First " Army will extend its front southwards to a point " which will be arranged in consultation direct between " the First and Third Army commanders. First Army " will report the arrangements made.

" Separate instructions will be issued regarding the " artillery to be transferred from Third to First Army.

" (3) Special instructions regarding the co-operation " between the French First Army and British Fourth " Army have been issued separately.

" (4) The lines of demarcation between Armies will " be as shown on the attached map ".[2]

---

[1] On the 16th Maréchal Foch addressed a letter (F.O.A. vii. (i), Appendix 1151) direct to the First Army, over the heads of Generals Pétain and Fayolle, informing it of the new boundary, and adding : " General " Debeney will have as first preoccupation to support constantly with " his left the attack of the right of General Rawlinson, with whom he " should remain in closest touch ". Nothing was said about increasing the strength of the First Army.

[2] Not reproduced.

The operation orders of the Fourth Army had been issued on the 13th, with a continuation on the 14th.

General Rawlinson, who had discussed the attack with his corps commanders at an informal conference on the 12th, gave two objectives,[1] which corresponded roughly to the old British main line and the old British outpost line, with the Advanced Hindenburg System as the Line of Exploitation.

Between the 12th and 17th a fair amount of ground was gained in small preliminary affairs, particularly on the right where the newly formed IX. Corps (Lieut.-General Sir W. P. Braithwaite) advanced over four thousand yards, in order to secure a good jumping-off line. On the 13th September, the 3rd Brigade (Br.-General Sir W. A. I. Kay) of the 1st Division (Major-General E. P. Strickland), on the left, established a line of posts from the northern part of Holnon Wood to the Omignon, and pushed the line forward slightly on the 14th. On the 15th, the 6th Division, on the right, captured trenches on the western edge of Holnon and the 1st Division secured Maissemy and trenches east of it. At 5.30 a.m. on the 17th an attempt was made by the 6th Division, then occupying the eastern edge of Holnon Wood, in co-operation with the French 34th Division, to establish a line east of Savy Wood–east of Holnon–Badger Copse, and thence north-westwards to the boundary with the 1st Division, as this would be a favourable jumping-off line for the 18th. In spite of a violent thunderstorm, which began at 12.30 a.m., accompanied by a gale and torrential rain, the troops were in position in time. The advance of the 18th Brigade (Br.-General G. S. G. Craufurd), representing the 6th Division, was made under a creeping barrage without any preliminary bombardment, and fighting continued until after 10 p.m. The 1/West Yorkshire and 11/Essex reached their objectives ; but, owing to the failure of the infantry of the French 34th Division to make any attempt to advance on this day[2] when it should have captured Round Hill,

---

[1] See Sketch 28.

[2] The affair is not mentioned in F.O.A., which says (vii (i), p. 316), " no action on the 17th north of the Oise deserves mention ". Its Map 27 shows no advance between the 12th and 18th. But the British " preparatory move to seize Holnon " is duly recorded. When Br.-General Craufurd sent a copy of his orders to the French infantry commander on his right, a staff officer, then with the regiment, stated positively that the weather was too bad and the French were not going to attack. In this decision they persisted and made no movement of any sort, although the general commanding the 34th Division assured the 6th Division that his men would attack and his artillery did co-operate.

which commanded the hollow in which Holnon lies, the West Yorkshire, in spite of very heavy losses, were unable to retain the village, which changed hands several time, but a line west of it was held.

On the Australian Corps front, on the 12th September, the 1st Australian Division (Major-General T. W. Glasgow) had occupied Jeancourt without encountering much opposition, and on the 13th the 4th Australian Division (Major-General E. G. Sinclair-Maclagan) pushed forward the line several hundred yards east of Bihucourt and up to Jeancourt, securing the ridge between these two villages.

There was artillery activity in this period on the III Corps front, and on the 17th September the 74th and 58th Divisions suffered many casualties from mustard gas ; but little else happened. On the 12th Lieut.-General Butler had resumed command of the corps on return from sick leave, Lieut.-General Godley returning to the XXII Corps.

Until the 15th September the weather had been too unfavourable for aerial photography ; but on that day it had cleared so that by the evening of the 17th photographs of the German defences along the whole Fourth Army front to a depth of four thousand yards on a front of approximately thirteen miles had been distributed to the eight divisions which were to take part in the offensive on the 18th.

Roughly the German position, held by fourteen divisions,[1] lay on a long ridge extending from St. Quentin via Villeret, Ronssoy to Epéhy, with the St. Quentin canal behind it. The ridge had many long sinuous spurs projecting to the front and to the rear, the Villeret spur, after running west, turning south to le Verguier parallel to the front, and the valleys marked by Gricourt, Pontru, Pontruet, Hargicourt, Templeux le Guerard and Ste. Emilie–Malassise Farm run into the ridge, so that the various lines of the enemy position ran over a series of spurs and valleys, but was on reverse slopes where possible.

The two objectives bristled with fortified localities ; in or near the first, roughly the old British main line, stood Selency, Fresnoy le Petit, le Verguier, Villeret Woods, Hargicourt, Ronssoy, Basse Boulogne and Epéhy–Peizière ;

---

[1] Twelve in the line and two in reserve.

in or near the second, the old British outpost line, were Gricourt, Berthaucourt, Pontru, Ascension Farm, Villeret, Cologne Farm, Malakoff Farm, le Sart Farm, le Tombois Farm, and Little Priel Farm. In the line of exploitation, that is the Advanced Hindenburg System, were also numerous localities ; but it was not considered likely that this line would be reached on the first day unless the enemy's defence collapsed, and, in fact, only the 4th Australian Division did advance so far. In general, the trenches and wire were so overgrown with grass and weeds as to make it difficult to locate them from the ground.

A creeping barrage, with 10 per cent. smoke shell, was arranged to the first objective, where a long pause of over an hour would be made ; but no preliminary bombardment was to be fired, reliance being placed, as on the 8th August, on surprise, on powerful artillery concentration, including intense counter-battery work, and on the use of tanks at places where resistance was expected to be greatest. A total of 1,488 guns and howitzers was available,[1] but no more than 20 tanks of the 2nd Battalion, as it was desired to reserve the bulk of the machines for a later attack on the Main Hindenburg System ; but a number of dummy tanks made of canvas on wooden frames were placed near the starting line and dragged forward a short distance before dawn. Four tanks were allotted to the IX Corps and eight each to the Australian and III Corps, but they were not to go beyond the first objective, except in the case of the left division of the Australian Corps. For machine-gun barrages divisions made their own arrangements.

The first part of the night of the 17th/18th was fine, and the R.A.F. squadrons made many bombing attacks on the villages opposite the Fourth and Third Armies ; but about

---

[1] Field Artillery :

				18-pdrs.	4·5-inch howitzers.
IX Corps	..	..	..	210	48
Australian Corps		..	..	270	90
III Corps	..	..	..	270	90

Heavy Artillery :

			Guns		Howitzers			
			60-pdrs.	6″	6″	8″	9·2″	12″
IX Corps	..	..	36	4	50	18	12	—
Australian Corps	..	..	48	12	96	24	18	2
III Corps	..	..	36	12	94	30	16	2

1 a.m., when the assembly of the infantry was nearly completed, the weather changed and rain began to fall heavily. At 5.20 a.m., zero hour, the rain still continuing, a thick mist hung in the valleys. When, about 9.30 a.m., the weather cleared, a grey cloudy day followed ; visibility remained poor, so that the only flying which could be done was ranging and indicating targets to the artillery. The ground was soft and slippery, so that the tanks, in particular, were severely handicapped. The enemy's fire was always heavy and at more or less close range. It was particularly difficult to obtain information, runners and returning wounded proving the best source ; thus it was hours after events had happened at the front that they became known to divisional headquarters, and the direction of the battle lagged even more than ordinarily.

On the right, the 6th Division of the IX Corps was specially at a disadvantage : first because, owing to the lack of the promised French assistance, the division had failed on the 17th to make good the starting line selected ; secondly, because the two attacking brigades, the 71st and 16th (Br.-Generals P. W. Brown and H. A. Walker), had had no opportunity to reconnoitre or even see the ground beforehand ; and thirdly, because Holnon Wood, lying just behind the front line and extending practically the whole three thousand yards of the divisional frontage, was so drenched with gas as in the dark to force the brigades to pass north and south of it in order to reach their assembly positions. The ground in front, stretching away for three thousand yards to the ridge overlooking St. Quentin, the final objective was devoid of cover except for a few copses, which provided shell-traps rather than protection, and the Germans had well-concealed trenches, and behind them a number of quarries, off which they had mined safe quarters for their reserves. Dominating the line of advance on the right flank stood Manchester Hill and Round Hill in the French sector, whilst to the right front lay a strong combination of trenches, known as " The Quadrilateral ",[1] at the end of a spur overlooking Selency. This village and Francilly Selency were on comparatively low ground, and Fayet nestled in a hollow of the Quadrilateral spur.

---

[1] The Quadrilateral was a system of trenches enclosing a group of cottages which had themselves been turned into a keep. The eastern face was a high bank tunnelled for the passage of troops and guns.

In view of the difficulties on the right of the 71st Brigade, the 2/Durham L.I. and two companies of the 1/West Yorkshire of the 18th Brigade were attached to it.   The 2/Durham L.I., which with the 2/Sherwood Foresters led the attack, succeeded in forcing its way through Holnon village ; but the French 34th Division, on its right, made only a very half-hearted attempt and got no farther than the jumping-off line for the previous day ; it did not therefore capture either Manchester Hill or Round Hill, and the enfilade fire from these coigns of vantage compelled the Durham, after very heavy casualties and in spite of reserves being employed, to fall back almost to their starting line.   The arrival at night of a large draft of reinforcements from home enabled a position east of Holnon to be secured ; but the total losses of the battalion for the day amounted to more than the number of the original attackers.   The 2/Sherwood Foresters soon reached the western face of the Quadrilateral, but during the rest of the day could make no further progress. The 9/Norfolk, which was to take the second objective, was caught by the German barrage and only part of it came up on the left of the Sherwood Foresters, the rest forming a reserve in a sunken road.   The 1/Leicestershire (the reserve battalion) was used at 12.30 p.m. to dig a trench from Badger Copse southward, in order to protect the right of the 16th Brigade, and lost many men by shelling during its advance from the western side of Holnon.

The front to be attacked by the 16th Brigade was high ground in the form of a horseshoe, flanked by the Quadrilateral and Fresnoy le Petit, and two of the four tanks were sent against each of these strongholds.   The 2/York & Lancaster was to capture the first objective by a direct advance, and the 1/Buffs and 1/Shropshire L.I. passing through it were then to establish themselves on the second.   At 6.30 a.m., due praise being given to the " splendid barrage ", the occupation of the first objective was reported ; actually the line reached in the mist was nearly four hundred yards short of it except on the left.   There the York & Lancaster penetrated into the eastern outskirts of Fresnoy ; but this advantage was lost by a counter-attack about 10 a.m.   The tanks were unable to give any help ; the two sent against Fresnoy were ditched and broke down ; one of the others suffered the same fate, and the fourth was shot into flames. The two battalions in second line came forward soon after

7 a.m. in thick mist, suffering severely from fire on both flanks, and during the morning five German planes flew along the line near Fresnoy and bombed and then machine-gunned the line. Thus, in spite of efforts continued until 5 p.m., the Buffs and the Shropshire were unable to advance much beyond the line reached by the York & Lancaster, and eventually they were ordered to consolidate it.

The 1st Division, with the 1st and 2nd Brigades (Br.-Generals W. B. Thornton and G. C. Kelly) in the front line, each employing two battalions, experienced an initial difficulty. Its advanced troops had before Zero made progress some six hundred yards beyond the line laid down by the Fourth Army; so as to ensure that the barrages of the neighbouring divisions did not fall on the flank battalions, they were ordered to drop back, and the 1st Division barrage, after falling, had to wait until that on the flanks drew level. Misunderstanding, however, occurred and some barrage fire fell on the centre battalions. The failure of the 6th Division to hold Fresnoy affected the right of the 1st Brigade; but, except on that flank, in spite of much machine-gun fire, the four leading battalions, the 1/L. North Lancashire, 1/Cameron Highlanders, 2/K.R.R.C. and 2/R. Sussex, reached the first objective between 7.30 a.m. and 8 a.m. Lateral communication over the Omignon and its marshes between the brigades was cared for by the 409th Field Company R.E. At 8.30 a.m., the time fixed for the move from the first objective, the advance was resumed; but Fresnoy continued to hold up the right, and on this flank the L. North Lancashire remained on the watch to defeat counter-attacks for the rest of the day. The right of the Camerons was also pinned down, but the left reached a sunken lane leading into Berthaucourt, and, reinforced by two companies of the 2/Black Watch, formed a defensive flank in the gap between the first and second objectives. This flank was completed by throwing back the right of the K.R.R.C., which, with the Sussex, had reached the second objective.

Resistance on the right seemed to increase, but on the left to be diminishing; about midday, therefore, the 2/R. Sussex sent forward patrols, followed by two platoons, for exploitation. Moving into the valley east of the second objective and up the opposite slope, they found trenches strongly held, and just as a patrol entered them, the Germans, after building up a firing line in front of Pontruet by dribbling men forward a few at a time, essayed to launch a counter-attack against the K.R.R.C., which struck also the right of the Sussex. Their purpose was detected and defeated by the covering artillery, whose forward observing officer was with 2nd Brigade headquarters, and the infantry completed their discomfiture.

An outpost line was formed by the Sussex to connect the right of their new line with the second objective ; and at midnight two companies of the battalion attacked once more in order to establish touch with the right of the Australian Corps, which had made splendid progress, and had reached the line of exploitation.

The brigades of the 4th and 1st Divisions of the Australian Corps were disposed differently in order to deal with special features of their front.[1] The 12th Australian Brigade (Br.-General R. L. Leane), on the right, made the attack on a one-battalion front, the 48th Battalion carrying it to the first objective, the 45th to the second, and the 46th to the line of exploitation. The 4th Australian Brigade (Br.-General C. H. Brand) advanced on a three-battalion front, the 13th and 15th Battalions passing round le Verguier to the first and second objectives, whilst the 16th mopped up the village, and the 14th then moved through the leaders for exploitation. The 3rd and 1st Brigades (Br.-Generals H. G. Bennett and I. G. Mackay), of the 1st Australian Division, were each disposed on a front of two battalions, the other battalions leap-frogging the leaders at the first objective.

The barrage was excellent, and such resistance as there was came as usual from a few machine-gun posts ; but with the assistance of the eight tanks, the whole of the first objective, though defended by more troops than the Australians deployed, was secured by 7.35 a.m., and 450

---

[1] The strength of all Australian units was low, as reinforcements were not coming along. The Australian Government, on the advice of Generals Birdwood and Monash, had rejected the proposal to reduce brigades to three battalions, using the fourth to bring them up to establishment, as such a change would complicate tactics and destroy *esprit de corps*.

The battalions of the 1st Division averaged 18 officers and 339 men ; of the 4th, 19 officers and 405 men.

Just before the battle, a ship being available, each of these divisions had entrained about two hundred married men for home leave.

prisoners of the *1st Reserve* and *119th Divisions*, 60 machine-guns and several field guns were taken in the elaborately fortified le Verguier alone.[1]

At 8.30 a.m. the four brigades again advanced under a barrage. Considerable resistance was offered in the ruins of Villeret, which was overcome with the help of a tank; and a maze of trenches round Cologne Farm, where another tank was very useful, took some time to clear ; but before 10 a.m., when the protective barrage ceased, the whole of the second objective had been secured and a further large number of prisoners taken.

Lieut.-General Monash hardly expected that " exploitation " could effect much against the many-lined German defences, but each of the divisions then pushed forward two battalions, in order to reach a position looking down on the St. Quentin Canal. The 46th and 14th Battalions of the 12th and 4th Brigades (4th Australian Division) made good progress at first, and the left of the 14th got into the Advanced Hindenburg System and started bombing down the trenches ; but resistance then began to stiffen, and Major-General Sinclair-Maclagan wisely postponed further operations until 11 p.m., when the same two battalions captured the whole of the third objective with over three hundred prisoners. The 10th and 9th Battalions of the 3rd Brigade (1st Australian Division) advancing with the 4th Australian Division obtained a footing in the Hindenburg trenches and by 10 a.m., the 1st Brigade being held up by machine-gun fire, had captured nearly the whole of the Cologne Farm ridge, but elsewhere did not quite gain the third objective, although they went far enough to obtain the desired observation over the canal and the southern tunnel entrance. They established connection with the III Corps, whose right had reached only the second objective, at Malakoff Farm.

The Australian Corps, besides obtaining a very commanding position which the enemy meant to hold, had captured

---

[1] Sergeant M. V. Buckley, 13th Battalion, was awarded the V.C. for most conspicuous bravery : with a Lewis gun he dealt with seven enemy posts on the southern side of le Verguier, and was " in a measure " responsible for his battalion's success ".

Private J. P. Woods, 48th Battalion, also received the V.C. for capturing and holding an enemy strongpoint in a vital tactical position, garrisoned by 25 men and six machine guns, and thus contributing to his battalion's success.

during this day 4,243 prisoners, 76 guns, over 300 machine guns and 30 trench mortars, its own casualties being only 1,260.

In the III Corps (Lieut.-General Sir R. H. K. Butler) the deduction had been drawn from prisoners' statements that the enemy on its front expected attack on the 18th and had no intention of making any further voluntary retirement. For this decision there were, no doubt, at least two reasons. In the first place, Ronssoy, Lempire, Epehy and Peizière were very strong, having been thoroughly prepared for all-round defence and provided with good wire and dug-outs by the British in the winter of 1917–18 ; and the area around them, which had formed part of the Battle Zone of March 1918, was a maze of trenches. Secondly, it was of vital importance to retain this front, as it covered the tunnelled portion of the St. Quentin canal, over which a tank attack could therefore be made without meeting the then insuperable obstacle which the canal presented elsewhere.

Lieut.-General Butler at first intended to attack with three divisions ; but, owing to the strength of the enemy's defences and the large size of the villages which must be mopped up, he finally decided to employ all four, trusting to receiving the 46th Division, in G.H.Q. reserve in the III Corps area, in case of emergency.

Enemy gas added to the difficulties of assembly on a wet and dark night. The dispositions of the divisions varied, the 74th Division allotted two brigades to the front line ; the 18th, one ; the 12th, two ; and the 58th, one. The 74th strengthened its two brigades by attaching to each of them a battalion from the third brigade. Only eight tanks were available and, none being allotted to the 74th Division, it improvised some dummies of wood and painted canvas, which were thought to have a useful effect on the enemy.

The feature of the attack of the 230th and 231st Brigades of the 74th Division was that the 15/Suffolk of the 230th Brigade side-slipped southwards into the Australian area during the night of the 16th/17th (the 18th Division putting a battalion into the line to fill the gap thus left), so that it could advance east-north-eastwards. At zero hour (5.20 a.m.) this battalion in a very short time swept through Templeux le Guerard and the Quarries, taking the Germans completely by surprise and capturing a number of prisoners. The other battalions of the brigade, the 10/Buffs and 16/R. Sussex, left their trenches and closed up to the barrage line half an hour before Zero. The Sussex went on to the first objective, capturing between four and five hundred unwounded prisoners. The Buffs then leap-frogged the 15/Suffolk, now in front of it, and the 12/Somerset L.I. (229th Brigade), the Sussex, and without much difficulty, reached the second objective ; two companies of the Buffs even went beyond it, but had to be withdrawn in the evening owing to British artillery fire falling on them.

The 16/Devonshire (229th Brigade) and 25/R. Welch Fusiliers, on the 231st Brigade front, were on the first objective by 7.35 a.m., taking many prisoners without much resistance, the 24/Welch following to mop up Ronssoy. The 10/Shropshire L.I. and the 25/R. Welch Fusiliers, at 8.30 a.m., made for the second objective ; but resistance stiffened, the barrage was lost, and under the fire of many machine guns the advance of the 231st Brigade came to a standstill. A bombardment of the second objective was then arranged, and the Shropshire, towards 4 p.m., gained ground first on the extreme right and later the rest of its assigned frontage, and, as the 18th Division on the left had not come up, the Welch Fusiliers formed a defensive flank to connect it with the Shropshire.[1]

On the left wing, as on the right, of the Fourth Army, the advance made was not so good as in the centre.

The 18th and 12th Divisions had the formidable task of capturing the Ronssoy–Epéhy position.[2] These localities are on a well-marked ridge. Ronssoy is the southern of a group of four long villages, the others being Basse Boulogne, Lempire and la Pauerelle, which form four arms around a central cross-roads. Epéhy, with Peizière adjoining on the north-west, is a large oblong of houses. From Ronssoy a spur projects westwards (with Ronssoy Wood on its north slope), and from Epéhy another, south-westwards, the two enclosing a triangular valley or, rather, "basin". This basin it was intended to avoid in the initial attack.

---

[1] For most conspicuous gallantry in attacking machine-guns, Lce.-Sergeant W. Waring, M.M., 25/R. Welch Fusiliers, was awarded the V.C. posthumously. The battalion suffered serious casualties in officers and n.c.o.s. Reduced to 120 men, it was reorganized in two companies under second-lieutenants.

[2] Held by the *2nd Guard Division* and *Alpine Corps*, the former had reached Ronssoy on the night of 11th/12th September, after ten days' rest.

The attack of the 18th Division (Major-General R. P. Lee) was led by the 54th Brigade (Br.-General A. J. Tyler), which sent forward only the 7/R. West Kent (of the 53rd Brigade attached), under a barrage fired by four brigades of field artillery, along the south side of the Ronssoy spur.[1] On reaching the eastern edge of the village, whose capture was to be aided by four tanks, it was to halt, covered on the north by an enfilade barrage, when the 2/Bedfordshire was to pass through it and two other battalions form on the left. The whole line, under a renewed barrage, would then proceed to the first objective, which ran north and south through the centre of Lempire, the 55th Brigade (Br.-General E. A. Wood) later passing through to secure the second.

The enemy's barrage was very thin and few casualties occurred during the advance, although, owing to the mist, the West Kent lost their own barrage. Resistance encountered in a spinney west of Ronssoy Wood led to the 2/Bedfordshire, following in rear, becoming involved in the fighting, which was now continuous; but the battalions, in spite of losses, went on to the first objective, three tanks (the fourth had mechanical trouble) giving great assistance in the capture of Ronssoy, where, however, mopping up, in which the 24/Welch (231st Brigade) assisted, took a long time, as many Germans were hiding in the cellars. The 11/Royal Fusiliers and 6/Northamptonshire, which were to extend the line to the left, after moving first northwards, reached their forming-up line in time to benefit by the barrage, which crept forward at 7.16 a.m. They at once came under lively shelling at short range and galling machine-gun fire, but after they had driven the enemy out of Ronssoy Wood and, with the help of two of the tanks, had cleared Basse Boulogne, the right reached the refused left flank of the 74th Division. From this point, after la Pauerelle had been captured by the help of a tank which was returning from the front, the 54th Brigade line ran north-westwards to Quid Copse, on the top of the ridge. Patrols then worked northwards and established touch with the 12th Division.[2]

---

[1] 110th, LXXXII, 290th and 291st.

[2] For great gallantry in attacking machine-gun posts single-handed on this day, and for initiative and leadership on 21st September, when he was killed, Lce.-Corporal A. L. Lewis, 6/Northamptonshire, was awarded the V.C. posthumously.

It had been laid down in corps orders, following Fourth Army instructions, that the 55th Brigade should leap-frog the 54th on the first objective at 8.30 a.m., the general hour of advance to the second objective. Major-General Lee had represented that this programme did not allow sufficient time for the completion of the attack on Ronssoy and adjoining villages, nor sufficient space for the forward flow of the troops, in view of the limited width of ground available in the early stages ; but his protest was overruled. The 8/East Surrey of the 55th Brigade, therefore, went forward, soon reached the outskirts of Ronssoy and assisted to clear it of Germans, but could push only a short distance beyond. By 11 a.m. Br.-General Wood had concentrated his three battalions in sunken roads and trenches east of the village, and reported the situation. After various times of attack had been proposed, divisional headquarters, about 3 p.m., decided that an attempt to advance to the second objective should be made by the 55th Brigade, under a barrage, at 5 p.m. Unfortunately, by this hour a fresh German division[1] had arrived on the scene, and, although the right of the attack went well, the left made little progress, largely owing to enfilade fire. The result was that the parties in advance of the first objective were in danger of being cut off. At 7 p.m., therefore, orders were given by the 55th Brigade that all troops east of the first objective should be withdrawn to it by 9 p.m., and this was successfully carried out. An attempt was made during the night by the 6/Northampton-shire to seize a copse, in advance of the left of the divisional front, but it failed.

The orders to the 12th Division were simple : it was to take Epéhy—whilst the 58th Division took Peizière—and, if possible, push on to the line of exploitation. The 36th and 35th Brigades (Br.-Generals C. S. Owen and A. T. Beckwith) were to advance as far as the first objective, when the 37th (Br.-General A. B. Incledon-Webber) would pass through them. The method to be employed for the execution of these orders was, however, complicated. The first move-ments of the two brigades were to be divergent. The starting line for the 36th Brigade was to be the embankment of the western of the two railways which run into Epéhy from the

---

[1] The *121st*, which had been resting since 2nd September, was put in to counter-attack.

south, through the " basin ", previously mentioned, out of
sight of the village—that is, it was to move south-eastwards.
At zero hour (5.20 a.m.) the brigade was to send forward two
companies on its left to clear the area on the northern slope
of the basin between the front line and the railway, and the
advance of the brigade from the railway was to commence
at 6.50 a.m. The 35th Brigade was to attack Epéhy from the
south-west—that is, to move north-eastward—and it was
expected that it would be able to advance from the village
to the first objective also at 6.50 a.m., the dividing point
between it and the 36th being the junction of the two
railways. The barrage of the 36th Brigade was to open on
the top of the ridge (marked by Malassise Farm) at zero
hour, but at 6.50 a.m. would be adjusted to creep in front
of the attackers, in conjunction with the barrages on either
side.[1]

In spite of the rain and darkness, the preliminary moves
were successful, and, in the 36th Brigade, posts of the 9/Royal
Fusiliers and 7/R. Sussex were, between 10 and 11 a.m.,
established on the ridge on either side of Malassise Farm,
which, however, remained in the enemy's hands.

The 35th Brigade (7/Norfolk and 9/Essex, with the 1/1st
Cambridgeshire in reserve to mop up Epéhy), soon lost the
two tanks allotted to it, one developing mechanical trouble
and the other receiving a direct hit soon after it started.
One of the tanks working with the 58th Division, about
7 a.m., caused confusion and delay as, after entering Epéhy
from the north, it lost its bearings, and began firing on the
troops of the 35th Brigade, with the result that a gap arose
between the 12th and 58th Divisions. The Germans were,
however, cleared out of the southern part of Epéhy, though
some clung to a line of posts on the northern edge and others
hid in cellars until opportunity should occur to resume action.
Heavy casualties were suffered by both sides, and the
5/R. Berkshire (36th Brigade) and two companies of the
divisional pioneers (5/Northamptonshire) were sent up to
reinforce. About 5.30 p.m. a party of the enemy, about a
hundred and fifty strong, was seen to be making off north-
eastwards, and shortly before 8 p.m. the village, or rather

---

[1] The 36th Brigade was supported by the LXXXIII Brigade R.F.A.
of the 18th Division ;   the 35th, by the LXII. (18th Division), 112th
(25th Division) and 231st (46th Division), and the 139th Heavy Battery
R.G.A. (60-pdrs.), under the C.R.A. of the 12th Division (Br.-General
H. M. Thomas).

the ruins of it, was reported clear. The railway east of it was then occupied by the 5/R. Berkshire and 5/Northamptonshire. The *Alpine Corps*, containing twelve *Jäger* battalions, had been turned out of a stronghold which it had been ordered to hold to the last, by five British battalions.

The 37th Brigade, which was to have passed through the line at the first objective, began to advance for that purpose at 5.30 a.m., sending the 6/Queen's south of Epéhy and the 6/R. West Kent north of Peizière. These battalions did not, however, attempt to become involved in the fighting, which was still taking place west of the first objective. At 12.30 p.m. brigade orders were issued for the 6/Queen's, with the 6/Buffs, to attack south of Epéhy at 3.30 p.m. ; but these battalions were brought to a stop by fire from Quid Copse and Malassise Farm ; so at 6 p.m. it was decided to withdraw them behind the railway embankment from which the 36th Brigade had started.

The 58th Division detailed the 173rd Brigade to make the attack on Peizière and gave it the support of two brigades, R.F.A. and one R.G.A., with two tanks.[1] The 2/2nd London led the attack, with two companies of the 3/London on its right, covering in all three hundred yards, the 2/24th London providing the moppers-up.[2]

Good progress was made at first, the two tanks giving valuable assistance, one eventually turning south and occasioning confusion in the 12th Division, as we have seen. It was only gradually established at brigade quarters from conflicting statements that by 7.30 a.m. the 2/2nd London had pushed through Peizière, and that the 3/London and 2/24th London were engaged in clearing the ruins and occupying the strongpoints in the village ; as sign that it had been captured the Germans were shelling it. The enemy still clung to the first objective, and, although formal attacks were made by the 173rd Brigade at 9 p.m. and at 2 a.m. (on the 19th) in order to reach it and get abreast of the Third Army, it was not wrested from him.

---

[1] The LXIII (12th Division) and 108th (Army) Brigade R.F.A. and the LXXXV R.G.A. (12 60-pdrs. and 12 6-inch howitzers) under the C.R.A. of the 58th Division (Br.-General J. McC. Maxwell).

[2] On 12th September the 2/4th London, hitherto one of the units of the 173rd Brigade, had been absorbed by the 2/2nd London, and replaced by the 2/24th London from the 66th Division.

The attacks of the outer wings of the Fourth Army, although they had gained ground, had therefore failed to reach the second objective; on the extreme flanks they had not even reached the first. No attempt had been made to utilize the complete success in the centre of the Army, where the Australians had broken into the enemy's well-organized defensive belt, to help the wings which were hanging back.

The total number of prisoners taken by the Fourth Army on the 18th September was over seven thousand : IX Corps, 559 ; Australian Corps, 4,243 ; III Corps, 2,300.

The right only of the Third Army[1] (General Hon. Sir J. Byng) co-operated with the Fourth Army on this day, as the centre was already up to the advanced works of the Hindenburg Position and the left had actually bitten into it. Considerable success was attained.

The attack was made by the V Corps (Lieut.-General C. D. Shute), protected on the left flank by two companies of the IV Corps, and as soon as its date was fixed the enemy was softened for it by the gas shelling of as many of his batteries as possible on the nights of the 15th/16th, 16th/17th, and 17th/18th. Three objectives were given : two bounds being thus made to reach the continuation of the first objective of the Fourth Army, and the third to the top of the ridge overlooking the valley of the upper Schelde in which runs the St. Quentin canal, would bring the Third Army in line with the second objective of the Fourth Army. The first objective, where a pause of 18 minutes was to be made, included Chapel Hill and was about five hundred yards only from the front line ; the second, where a pause of 15 minutes was allowed, included Vaucelette Farm and Chapel Hill Crossing on the railway, and ran past the western outskirts of Gouzeaucourt, that is another six hundred yards ahead in the south and double that distance in the north ; the third objective, a mile farther on, for the right and centre only of the V Corps, started at Limerick Post on the Army boundary, ran past the western outskirts of Villers Guislain to Gauche Wood, and then turned westwards along the northern edge of the wood back to the

---

[1] See Sketch 24.

second objective. Gouzeaucourt was not to be attacked ; for if the second objective and Gauche Wood were taken, the village would be encircled on three sides and would probably be evacuated. Exploitation was to be limited to rounding up prisoners and capturing material.

The orders for the attack of the V. Corps were issued on the 15th September. It was to be made by the 21st, 17th and 38th Divisions (Major-Generals D. Campbell, P. R. Robertson and T. A. Cubitt), the last being brought back into the line for the purpose. The 33rd Division (Major-General R. J. Pinney) from the Second Army and one brigade of the 38th Division were kept in reserve. The artillery available was fifteen brigades of field artillery and six of heavy.[1]

The artillery programme comprised a hurricane bombardment of trench mortars, a creeping barrage of 18-pdrs., with a searching barrage of 18-pdrs. and 4·5-inch howitzers, and another of 6-inch howitzers and 60-pdrs., respectively two to five hundred yards and four to eight hundred yards beyond the creeping barrage. From zero hour (5.20 a.m.) to Zero + 30 minutes, 4·5-inch howitzers were to place a smoke screen on the whole corps front, and from the latter hour onward the right division was responsible for a smoke screen to cover the ridge on the southern boundary, the centre division for one to cover Villers Guislain and Villers Hill south of the village, and the left division for another to cover Gonnelieu.

To strengthen the machine-gun barrage, two companies each of the 33rd Machine Gun Battalion were allotted to the 17th and 21st Divisions.

The III. Brigade R.A.F. (Br.-General C. A. H. Longcroft), besides its usual duties, provided one squadron of low-flying aeroplanes to co-operate in the infantry attack beyond the second objective. No tanks were available, but their absence did not militate against the success of the Third Army.

---

[1] 21st Division (C.R.A. Br.-General H. W. Newcome) : field brigades, XCIV. and XCV. (its own), LXXII., 315 and II. New Zealand (Army), with the XXXV. Brigade R.G.A.

17th Division (C.R.A. Br.-General P. Wheatley) : field brigades, 156th and 162nd (33rd Division), 122nd (38th Division) and XVIII. and XXXIV. (Army), with the XXII. Brigade R.G.A.

38th Division (C.R.A. Br.-General T. E. Topping) : field brigades, 121st (38th Division), LXXVIII. and LXXIX. (17th Division), and XCIII. and 155th (Army), with the XVII. Brigade R.G.A.

The remainder of the heavy artillery carried out counter-battery work.

In the 21st Division sector, the 62nd Brigade (Br.-General G. H. Gater), with all three battalions in line (2/Lincolnshire, 12th/13th Northumberland Fusiliers and 1/Lincolnshire), in spite of machine-gun fire, was completely successful in capturing the first and second objectives, retaking Vaucelette Farm, which it had held in the German offensive of the 21st March, with many prisoners, without suffering heavy casualties.[1]

Beyond the second objective the frontage of the division widened out from 1,500 to 3,000 yards, and at 7.31 a.m. the 110th and 64th Brigades· (Br.-General H. R. Cumming and C. V. Edwards) passed through the 62nd to continue the advance. The 58th Division (Fourth Army), on the right, although it had taken Peizière, had failed, as already mentioned, to reach its first objective, the southern continuation of the second objective of the 21st Division. In consequence, the 6/Leicestershire, on the right, was held up by enfilade fire and could get no farther than the road about a thousand yards short of the third objective. The 1/Wiltshire, next on the left, reached the third objective, but was counter-attacked and fell back far enough to join on to the Leicestershire. The attack of the 1/East Yorkshire and 9/K.O.Y.L.I., of the 64th Brigade, went well and they gained the third objective except on its extreme right, which was drawn back to connect with the 110th Brigade. In addition to its gain of ground, the 21st Division had taken 694 prisoners and 15 guns ; but a pocket of Germans remained in a trench between its two brigades. As the attempts to push on during the night made by the 58th Division were unsuccessful, the 110th Brigade cancelled the orders which had been issued for an advance in the early morning of the 19th.

The plan of the 17th Division was for the 52nd Brigade (Br.-General W. Allason) to take the first objective, the 50th Brigade (Br.-General A.R.C. Sanders) to pass through it and capture the second, and, similarly, the 51st Brigade

---

[1] The formation of the 2/Lincolnshire is recorded in its diary : it attacked on a frontage of 300 yards with three companies in front line and one in support in rear of the right company (the right company of the division). The front companies moved in two lines, with two platoons in each line ; platoons had two sections in the front wave and the Lewis gun section in the second wave.

(Br.-General R. M. Dudgeon), to secure the third. Each brigade put all its three battalions in line on the one-mile frontage.

The 9/Duke of Wellington's, 12/Manchester and 10/Lancashire Fusiliers in the initial attack of the 52nd Brigade met with considerable opposition from machine guns, especially from Chapel Hill; but by 5.50 a.m. they had taken the first objective with over six hundred prisoners. At 6.10 a.m. the 50th Brigade passed through and the 6/Dorsetshire and 10/West Yorkshire reached the second objective somewhat easily; but the 7/East Yorkshire, on the left, suffered a good deal from artillery fire and met with stiff opposition from the enemy on the Peizière–Gouzeaucourt road, and the battalion was still fighting there when the 51st Brigade advanced, passing through the second objective at 7.47 a.m. The 10/Sherwood Foresters, on the right, took its objective easily with many prisoners at a cost of only thirty casualties. The 7/Border Regiment, in the centre, was strongly opposed in Gauche Wood, which lies across the long spur between the valleys in which Villers Guislain and Gouzeaucourt are situated, with good observation from its northern edge. Eventually 6-inch trench mortars had to be brought up to knock out a machine-gun nest formed of four derelict British tanks. The wood was then cleared by bombing and the final objective gained. The 7/Lincolnshire, on the left, finding the 7/East Yorkshire (50th Brigade) still held up short of the second objective, sent one company to outflank the resistance from the north, and the East Yorkshire were then, about 9 a.m., able to advance again and two hundred prisoners were taken. The Lincolnshire, though they had lost the barrage, duly occupied their objective, the northern edge of Gauche Wood, about 10 a.m. They were left in peace; but the centre of the brigade (the left of the Sherwood Foresters and the Border Regiment) was counter-attacked about 2 p.m. and lost the front trenches, which were, however, all regained, and further counter-attacks in the evening were repulsed. The 17th Division had thus captured all its objectives, with 1,069 prisoners and 3 guns.

The 38th Division had only the first and second objectives to take, without any pause, and it sent in the 114th Brigade (Br.-General T. R. C. Price) and the 113th (Br.-General H. E. ap Rhys-Pryce), the former on a three-battalion and the latter on a two-battalion frontage.

The 15th, 14th and 13/Welch took the first objective easily, and, although resistance then stiffened, it was overcome and all three battalions reached their final objective. The 13/Welch suffered considerably from machine-gun fire on its left flank throughout, as the 113th Brigade (14th and 16/R. Welch Fusiliers) had not kept touch, and a gap had arisen between the brigades. Only the right and centre companies of the 14/R. Welch Fusiliers gained the first objective, the left company and those of the 16th entered it in places, but were unable to hold on and fell back to their starting line. At 3.20 p.m. after half an hour's renewed bombardment, part of the first objective was regained by bombing, and after dark the 13/R. Welch Fusiliers relieved the 16th and formed a flank between the 14th in the first objective and the original front line.

On the left of the 38th Division, the 5th Division (recently transferred from the XI to the IV Corps) sent forward two companies of the 2/K.O.S.B. (13th Brigade), under a barrage, to make a protective flank as arranged. They both reached their objective, but, as the 38th Division had failed to come up, after suffering heavy casualties they had to fall back.

After the V. Corps had received reports of the capture of their objectives by the 17th Division and the right of the 38th Division, it issued orders at 12.55 p.m. for these formations to push forward northwards along the ridge on the eastern side of Gouzeaucourt so as to continue the encirclement of the village, and 9 p.m., when there would be moonlight, was agreed on as zero hour. Orders could not, however, be forwarded to the front line troops of the 114th Brigade in time ; so that the attack was made by the 17th Division alone and carried out by the 6/Dorsetshire and 10/West Yorkshire of the 50th Brigade under a barrage. Quentin Redoubt, more than half a mile ahead, was taken and held by the former ; and the West Yorkshire, which were delayed by machine-gun fire and lost the barrage, captured the southern end of a trench, which led past the redoubt ; but these were the only results of the night attack.

The enemy on the rest of the Third Army front had not been quiescent during the V. Corps' attack, and had attempted diversions against the left of the IV. Corps and right of the VI. in the hope, perhaps, of recovering Havrincourt,[1] and against Moeuvres in the 52nd Division sector. At 3.30 p.m. he opened a heavy bombardment, using gas freely and battering positions and communication trenches in the Havrincourt sector. At 4.30 p.m. he shortened range on to the front and support trenches of the 112th Brigade (Br.-General A. E. Irvine) of the 37th Division (Major-General H. Bruce Williams), and the whole front of the 9th and 8th Brigades (Br.-Generals H. C. Potter and B. D. Fisher) of the 3rd Division (Major-General C. J. Deverell). Fifteen minutes later a large number of aircraft flew over the British trenches dropping bombs and firing machine guns, and at 5 p.m., that is at the same time as the counter-attack of the *121st Division* against the 55th Brigade near Ronssoy, German infantry made a determined advance ;[2] some of the front line posts were overwhelmed and small penetrations made. Only north of Havrincourt did the enemy succeed in reaching the support trench of the front Hindenburg System, and he then tried to bomb along it. Everywhere the Germans were thrown back and cleared out, and by 11 p.m. the whole line was re-established.[3]

The counter-attack against Moeuvres was made at 5.30 p.m., and at first penetrated into the position ; but the enemy was driven out during the night by bombing.

The V. Corps alone had captured 1,848 prisoners, besides twenty-four guns, so that the total for the day on the Fourth and Third Army fronts was over nine thousand, and very substantial progress had been made towards securing a jumping-off line for the attack on the main Hindenburg Position.

NOTE I

THE FRENCH ON THE 18TH SEPTEMBER

(Sketch 28)

The French did very little on the 18th. The Official History devotes only 12 lines to the day, and of these four refer to the

---

[1] " Regt. No. 92 ", p. 533, says that the *20th Division* was brought up to retake Havrincourt, " the possession of which was of special importance " for the holding of the Hindenburg Position ".

[2] Prisoners were taken of the *6th* and *20th Divisions.* The former was quite fresh, having been resting since 4th August, whilst the latter had been out of the front line since the 1st/2nd September, although one regiment had been engaged on the 12th.

[3] See Note II at end of Chapter.

British success. The extreme left of the French First Army made an advance of about twelve hundred yards over a 3-mile frontage but failed to take, indeed did not try to take, either Manchester Hill or Round Hill. A similar advance was made by the extreme right of the Tenth Army north of the Aisne near Vailly.

NOTE II

THE GERMANS ON THE 18TH SEPTEMBER

(Sketches 24 and 28)

German accounts make much of the determined defence of Holnon on the south and of Epéhy on the north ; except in regimental histories, no mention is made of four divisions (at least), three fresh, the *6th, 20th* and *121st*, and one tired, the *185th*, being thrown into the fight, nor of the failure of the counter-attack at 5 p.m. of the three fresh divisions. The expulsion of the *Alpine Corps* from Epéhy is accounted for by asserting that it was attacked " by at least three British divisions " accompanied by tanks and low-flying aeroplanes ". (B.O.A., p. 546), and admitting that the divisions on either side of the *Alpine Corps* gave way. Actually, the attackers were the 35th Brigade with two battalions attached and two tanks for mopping up. The *Leib Infantry Regiment* of the *Alpine Corps* states that the bombardment was singularly effective ; " sections " of trench were flattened out in a minute, exits of dug-outs " blown in, remnants of walls collapsed, machine guns and trench " mortars were covered up by earth and rubbish, and ammunition " dumps exploded "

The *1st Guard Grenadier Regiment* of the *2nd Guard Division* on the left of the *Alpine Corps*, defending Ronssoy, Basse Boulogne, Lempire, and la Pauerelle, attributed the British success to the fog which " prevented early knowledge of the " advance and neutralized our weapons and defence," a commentary to be remembered in considering the German success on the 21st March.

As regards the counter-attack against the 3rd Division and a brigade of the 37th, " Regt. No. 92 " (p. 533) of the *20th Division* states, " in spite of the elaborate preparations, the counter-attack " did not get farther than the first deployment, and directly after " leaving the jumping-off line received heavy machine-gun and " rifle fire. Simultaneously came enfilade fire from the right " and left. The supporting artillery fire was wholly ineffective. " So the attackers advanced little more than a hundred yards."

According to " Regt. No. 60 " (p. 265), the *121st Division* was brought up in lorries to relieve the *38th Division*, which had been driven back in the early morning. The counter-attack was made

R*

at 5.15 p.m. with Malakoff Farm as the objective ; it was brought to a standstill by artillery fire in front and machine-gun and rifle fire against the right flank. A second attempt which had been ordered was abandoned.

General von der Marwitz was removed from command of the *Seventeenth Army* on the 22nd September. " His supersession " was due to the failure of his left wing, three rotten[1] divisions on the 18th September." (Gallwitz, p. 382.) This seems to refer to the abortive counter-attack of three divisions (nearly fresh) near Havrincourt at 5 p.m. on the 18th.

---

[1] " *Angekränkelte* "—an unusual word, used in translating Shakespeare's " *Sicklied* o'er with the pale cast of thought ".

CHAPTER XXIV

The effect on the Germans of the success achieved on the 18th September became evident during the following days. The wings of the Fourth Army, which had for various reasons, notably the inaction of the French First Army on the right and the strength of the Epéhy position on the left, had not reached the final objective, as the Australian Corps in the centre had done. Between the 19th and 26th, however, they were able to push forward in spite of the strength of the enemy defences on ground which he had selected and fortified at leisure.[1]

It was essential, in order to attain a good line for operations against the main Hindenburg System, that the wings should gain possession of its outlying works ; so at 9.30 p.m. and 8.50 p.m. respectively, on the 18th the commanders of the IX. and III. Corps issued orders for the continuation of the attack. The Australian Corps, not being required to go farther, was able to proceed with consolidation and with minor adjustments of its line for the purpose of improving observation, whilst crushing the feeble German attempts made against its outposts.

---

[1] The German divisions opposing the Fourth Army are shown on Sketch 28. The numbers have been taken from the Intelligence maps and verified by German regimental histories. It was not found feasible to show those opposite the Third Army in the same way, as the data are incomplete ; the partial list from south to north is as under :

201st Division	Relieved *6th Cavalry Division* 6th/7th September.
87th Division	Put in on 18th September near Villers Guislain after six days' rest.
6th Cavalry Division	Put in on 25th September after rest since 4th September.
Jäger Division	Put in on 12th September after two weeks' rest.
113th Division	Put in on 10th September after six weeks' rest.
6th Division	Put in on 16th–18th September after rest since 4th August on relief of *52nd Division*.
20th Division	Re-entered line on 12th September after two days' rest.
49th Reserve Division	Put in on 1st September after a short rest.
1st Guard Reserve Division	Relieved by the *7th Cavalry Division* on 22nd/23rd September.

497

On the 19th,[1] the weather being dull and overcast, the IX. Corps and the French XXXVI. Corps, on its right, were unable to make any progress, except that the latter captured the villages of Essigny le Grand, Contescourt and Castres, three miles south of the international boundary. Round Hill and Manchester Hill therefore remained untaken, and the flank of the 6th Division still open and exposed. Lieut.-General Braithwaite came to the conclusion, in view of the strength of the outer defences of the Hindenburg Position, that a trench warfare attack in conjunction with the French, after a methodical bombardment, was the least costly solution. In agreement, General Fayolle (G.A.R.), on the 20th, ordered General Debeney " to unite the major part of " the heavy artillery at his disposal in the area between the " Somme and Holnon so as to assist and follow the British " advance. At the same time the field artillery on the flanks " will be reinforced by the artillery of the divisions in second " line. . . . Efforts should first be concentrated on Croupe " 138 [Manchester Hill] ".[2] Arrangements were thus made for a combined attack on the 24th.

In the IX. Corps, the 46th Division, in reserve, was brought up on the left, taking over the front of the 4th Australian Division on the night of the 21st/22nd, and the 32nd Division (lately with the Australian Corps) was allotted to it as reserve. A reorganization of the artillery was also carried out, four Army field artillery brigades, the field artillery brigades of the 5th Australian Division, two R.G.A. brigades and two siege batteries being transferred from the Australian to the IX. Corps,[3] and during the 21st, 22nd and 23rd a deliberate observed bombardment was fired.

The 20th and 21st passed quietly. On the 22nd the Germans, at 7 p.m. under a heavy barrage, gained a footing

---

[1] See Sketch 28.

[2] F.O.A. vii. (i), p. 318.

[3] This gave a total of :

6th Division front	..	5 field and horse artilllery and one R.G.A. brigades.		
1st	,,	,,	..	6 field and horse artillery and one R.G.A. brigades.
46th	,,	,,	..	6 field and horse artillery and one R.G.A. brigades.

Corps heavy artillery : 5 R.G.A. brigades and one R.M.A. battery, and four siege batteries (one 15-inch howitzer, two 12-inch howitzers and eight 6 inch guns).

in the outpost line east of Berthaucourt in the 1st Division's area, but were at once thrown out ; on the 23rd, although there was some bickering and much machine-gun fire, no alteration in the line took place.

The objectives of the IX. Corps on the 24th included Selency (previously in the French sector), the Quadrilateral, Dee Copse, Gricourt (exclusive, but it was nevertheless captured), Pontruet (the long spur, with a knoll at its extremity, stretching westwards between it and Gricourt gave observation over much of the ground behind the British front line) and Ste. Hélène ; and for the French, Dallon, Manchester Hill and Francilly Selency.   Zero hour was 5 a.m.

The French XXXVI. Corps took Round Hill, but failed to capture Manchester Hill, and secured Dallon and Epine de Dallon, but only part of Francilly Selency.   The task set to it and, to the 18th and 16th Brigades of the 6th Division[1] proved more difficult than foreseen, as many belts of wire were found to be uncut, having been cunningly concealed in hollows and at the bottom of trenches, and the enemy was expecting attack.   Of the four tanks of the 13th Battalion allotted to the 18th Brigade, one was knocked out at once; the other three entered the Quadrilateral and were put out of action there.   The 2/Durham L.I. and 1/West Yorkshire, of the 18th Brigade, were after a time driven back to their starting line ; but a company of the 11/Essex put in on the left cut its way through the wire and, bombing down a trench which formed a prolongation of the western face of the Quadrilateral, eased the situation.   A bombing contest ensued and continued all day and into the night.   At 11 p.m., however, in moonlight, the 1/Leicestershire (71st Brigade but attached to the 18th) attacked under a barrage, in the sector of the 2/Durham L.I., the West Yorkshire going forward again with it, and they captured the trench west of Selency and the western face of the Quadrilateral, which had held up the advance so long and caused so many casualties.   The 1/Shropshire L.I. and 2/York & Lancaster of the 16th Brigade were more easily successful in their attack in spite of enfilade fire from the Quadrilateral, and they reached their objective, the prolongation northward of the eastern face of

---

[1] Against the German *25th Reserve Division* and another, unidentified on its right.

that work.[1] Bombing attacks were then made by the Shropshire and 1/Buffs against the northern face of the Quadrilateral in order to help the 18th Brigade ; but it was not until evening that this face was captured. At 5.30 p.m. the 2/York & Lancaster co-operated in the attack of the 1st Division which resulted in the capture of Gricourt. Of the four tanks with the 16th Brigade, one was hit, ditched and set on fire after going only six hundred yards ; two, after liquidating a few machine-gun posts, were put out of action. The fourth later attacked a gun in Dum Copse which was enfilading the line, but was hit and its petrol ignited ; the crew then engaged the gun with Hotchkiss fire and killed the detachment, the gun itself being captured later.

The 1st Division, whose objective extended from a trench on the western side of Dee Copse to Pontruet (exclusive), had no easy task.[2] Of the twelve tanks allotted to it seven only went into action, the crews of three being completely prostrated by fumes on their way to the starting-point, one having mechanical trouble and one being hit. Three helped in the capture of Fresnoy le Petit, one being set on fire there ; later two went into Cornouillers Wood and four gave useful assistance in Pontruet and in the section south of that village. Of the total of twenty with the IX. Corps, nine tanks came or were towed out of action to the rallying point.

The 3rd and 2nd Brigades, after being shelled during assembly in the dark, had heavy fighting ; but in the end they secured the line assigned to them. Their troubles on the right came mainly from a strongpoint in Fresnoy and a large nest of machine guns in Cornouillers Wood, which held out until 10.30 p.m. and 5.30 p.m. respectively, in spite of tank attacks ; on the left flank Pontruet, which was not captured by the 46th Division, for a time belched enfilade fire into the flank of the 2nd Brigade.

By about 10.30 a.m. the 2/Welch of the 3rd Brigade was at Dee Copse and the 1/Gloucestershire around Fresnoy and in Marronier Wood ; the 2/R. Sussex and 1/Northamptonshire of the 2nd Brigade held the Gricourt–Pontruet road, with defensive flanks thrown back, and the 2/K.R.R.C. had

---

[1] The formation was two waves, each of two companies and in two lines, with a hundred yards between waves and fifty yards between lines.

[2] Against the German *11th* and *197th Divisions* and the left of the *79th Reserve Division*.

mopped up Arbousiers Wood as far as the western end of Cornouillers Wood, which was separated from Marronier Wood by a 200-yard clearing. The 2/K.R.R.C. was then relieved by the 1/Cameron Highlanders (1st Brigade), that it might be available as brigade reserve. But before this battalion could rejoin the Sussex and Northamptonshire, who by now were very weak, an enemy force about four hundred strong made a determined counter-attack on the right of the brigade. It was splendidly met by the men of the right of the Sussex, who, when their ammunition began to run short, though one to five, charged with the bayonet, and drove the Germans into flight leaving fifty prisoners behind. After this success, the situation of the 2nd Brigade began to improve ; machine guns and trench mortars were brought into action against Pontruet, and effectively served to reduce the hostile enfilade fire ; later the occupation of Gricourt and trenches east of it by the 3rd Brigade eased matters on the right flank.

Pontruet is a rambling village covering an area about five hundred yards long and nearly as much wide ; it lies at the bottom of the shallow valley of the upper Omignon, with Berthaucourt and Pontru west of it, overlooked on the south by the long spur between it and Gricourt, on the north by the Ste. Helène spur and commanded on the east from the spur above Bellenglise. The attack of the 46th Division (Major-General G. F. Boyd) against it was made by the 5/Leicestershire (138th Brigade), moving south-eastwards so as to take the German trenches in flank, with the 6/Sherwood Foresters on its right and on the left the 5/Lincolnshire (138th Brigade), which had occupied the houses of Ste. Helène on the evening of the 23rd and was to clear the trenches north-east of these houses, whilst the 5/Sherwood Foresters (139th Brigade), starting seventeen minutes after Zero, was to mop up the trenches west of Pontruet as far as the barrage (which included smoke) put down on the western half of the village would permit. The Leicestershire were baffled in the darkness and smoke by a new German trench, known as Forgans Trench, bristling with machine guns, which had been dug during the night. Some of the Leicestershire penetráted into this trench and began to bomb their way along it ; others forced their way into Pontruet, where, after about seventy minutes' fighting they worked their way into the northern portion, taking a hundred prisoners and four machine guns. When, towards 9 a.m., the smoke cleared and the light improved, the position of the Leicestershire became critical. They were sniped and machine-gunned from the south, with the result that those in Pontruet fell back to a position along the northern portion of the western edge, where they established touch on the right with the 5/Sherwood Foresters, which, with the 6th, was held up by fire of all kinds. The men in Forgans Trench, after building a block in it, rallied between the northernmost point of the village and Ste. Hélène, where the 5/Lincolnshire was established.[1]

For the remainder of the day the position of the 46th Division remained almost unchanged. The enemy re-occupied Forgans Trench in strength and also dribbled small parties round the south side of Pontruet into trenches in its western half. To check any attack from Forgans Trench, it was heavily shelled for an hour, with the desired effect. An attempt was made at 7.30 p.m. by a company of the 6/Sherwood Foresters and some of the 5/Leicestershire to enter the village from the Ste. Hélène side, but it resulted in failure, and at 2.30 a.m. (25th) the village was evacuated, although posts north and west of it were still held.

During the night of the 24th/25th and early morning of the 25th, the 6th Division resumed the attack, and about 8 a.m., without firing a shot, captured 3 officers and 104 other ranks, who had lost their way, bringing the total of prisoners taken by the IX. Corps on the 24th and 25th up to 33 officers and 1,400 other ranks. By 10.30 a.m. patrols were pushing forward into Selency and the copse surrounding the chateau, and later these two localities were occupied. Bomb fighting continued all day in the Quadrilateral, but by midnight the

---

[1] For most conspicuous gallantry in the fighting around Forgans Trench, Lieut. J. C. Barrett, 5/Leicestershire, was awarded the V.C.

Pontruet was defended by 6 companies and 1½ machine-gun companies of the *262nd Reserve Regiment* of the *79th Reserve Division*, which held the Gricourt (exclusive)–Pontruet sector. The boundary of the *Eighteenth* and *Second Armies* ran on its northern side, and the *79th Reserve Division* had been ordered to give special attention to holding the village (" Res. " Regt. No. 262 ", p. 280). Sketch 22 in the history of the regiment shows two trenches, one running in rear of Gricourt and in front of Pontruet, with another, about 250 yards farther forward, with a flank (probably Forgans Trench), turned back facing north-west to join on to the first. The village was thought to have been lost, but a few parties still clung to it until the general retirement in the night of the 25th/26th.

whole area had been cleared.   Two counter-attacks made in
the morning against the 2/K.R.R.C. (1st Division on the
spur south of Pontruet), and another in the afternoon, were
repulsed with heavy loss.

On the 26th the French XXXVI. Corps made a short
advance north of the St. Quentin canal, and took Manchester
Hill; during the evening the 6th Division pushed forward
patrols north and south of Fayet without any opposition;
and the 1st Division occupied the eastern edge of Pontruet
without much resistance.   A general retirement of the enemy
to the true Hindenburg Position had taken place.   The IX.
Corps of the Fourth Army was now overlooking St. Quentin
and the main German defences beyond the St. Quentin canal.

In addition to some minor improvements of its positions,
important changes were meantime taking place on the
Australian Corps front.   On the 22nd and 23rd the American
27th and 30th Divisions (Major-Generals J. F. O'Ryan and
E. M. Lewis) of the American II. Corps (Major-General
G. W. Read) arrived in the Fourth Army area from the
Second Army, and on the night of the 23rd/24th the 30th
relieved the 1st Australian Division in the line; on the night
of the 24th/25th the American 27th Division took over the
front of the 74th and 18th Divisions of the III. Corps, the
command of the composite American and Australian Corps
passing to Lieut.-General Sir John Monash at 10 a.m. on
the 25th.

The III. Corps had had fighting at least as fierce as that
of the IX. Corps and similar success in swinging forward.
At 8.50 p.m. on the 18th Lieut.-General Butler issued orders
for the continuation of the attack in order to reach the
second objective of the 18th, and then the line of exploitation,
and thus get a footing in the outer defences of the Hindenburg
Position.   Shortly after the despatch of these orders, it was
learned that the first objective though captured had not been
retained; so at 11.55 p.m. fresh instructions, reducing the
scope of the operation, were sent out.   The 74th Division
was now to consolidate the position which it had secured,
but with a view to further advance; the 18th and 12th were

to attack under a barrage, at an hour later fixed at 11 a.m. (19th), with the object of clearing Lempire and securing a line running north by Yak and Zebra posts to No. 12 Copse, and so joining on to the 58th Division, which was to occupy the first objective during the night. This last task the 173rd Brigade was unable to effect ; but attacking again at 11.20 a.m. (19th), it succeeded, after a prolonged bombing contest, in accomplishing it by 7 p.m. The 53rd Brigade (18th Division), which had gained a little ground on either side of Malassise Farm during the night, and the 37th and 35th Brigades (12th Division), on its left, starting at 11 a.m., after very stiff fighting, managed to occupy the line assigned to them except that No. 12 Copse remained in the enemy's possession.

On the 20th a number of more or less isolated trench struggles took place, and X, Y and Z Copses, fire from which had galled the right of the 18th Division, were evacuated by the enemy and occupied ; but otherwise little ground was gained, as the enemy was too strongly dug-in on the second objective (the old British advanced line) to be stirred without another organized attack. At 1.45 p.m., therefore, Lieut.-General Butler issued orders for a combined attack on the 21st : at 5.40 a.m. by the 74th and 18th Divisions, the 1st Australian Division on the right, then in the midst of a relief, agreeing to conform by a slight advance by two battalions. The aim of these divisions was to reach a line just short of the line of exploitation, marked by Quennemont Farm, Guillemont Farm and the Knoll, whilst the 12th and 58th formed a left flank back to Kildare Post on the boundary line with the Third Army. Most of the advance would be down slopes exposed to fire from the German main position and cross-fire from defended localities. Four tanks of the 5th Brigade were made available for the attack on Gillemont Farm and seven for the Knoll, a smoke barrage being put down to screen their action.

The barrage of field guns and a few medium howitzers was not effective against the German wire and trenches. After a long struggle, the 230th Brigade of the 74th Division was by 2 p.m. back on its starting line, many Lewis-gun teams sacrificing themselves to cover the retirement of their comrades. The 231st by evening had got no farther than the second objective ; and not until 12.15 a.m. (22nd) did it finally take the work east of Basse Boulogne, also called the Quadrilateral, which had changed hands several times, and with it over two hundred prisoners and thirty machine guns. The tanks had not been able to help ; for two broke down before going into action and the other two struck mines before they were half-way to the objective.

The 54th and 53rd Brigades of the 18th Division had much the same experience : they got within a hundred and twenty yards of the second objective, took and lost le Sart Farm, but failed to take le Tombois Farm, although operations were carried on into the night and until nearly 4 p.m. next day (22nd), when a party of the 2/Bedfordshire attacked a pocket of Germans left between the battalion and the 6/Northamptonshire, killed about two hundred and captured nearly as many. The brigade then repulsed two counter-attacks. Of the five Mark V. tanks, only one, with two Mark V* reached Guillemont Farm,[1] when as no infantry had come up they returned, the Mark V. machine being put out of action whilst doing so.

The 37th and 36th Brigades of the 12th Division also had a desperate struggle. The former did not quite reach the second objective on the 21st ; but, after bombing attacks during the night and several attempts on the 22nd, it secured the line desired about 3 p.m., large numbers of Germans running away. The 36th Brigade, after a day's fighting, gained the second objective, including No. 12 Copse, by an attack at midnight, which lasted until 2 a.m. (22nd).

The fight of the 175th Brigade (with the 1/4th Suffolk, the divisional pioneer battalion, attached) of the 58th Division was even more prolonged. It was aided on the right by the progress of the 12th Division, but hampered at first on the left as part of the 19th Brigade (33rd Division) of the Third Army drifted into its sector. The 2/10th and 12/London nevertheless kept straight on and dug in about four hundred yards short of the objective. Fire was so intense that nothing further could be done until 9.30 p.m. on the 22nd, when, in rain and darkness, the 9/London (175th Brigade) attacked through the 2/10th and 12th. Although the battalion of the 33rd Division which should have co-operated on the left did not appear, the 175th Brigade by 2.30 a.m. (23rd), had taken all its objectives between Catelet Copse and Limerick Post.

---

[1] One broke down during the approach march, two were hit soon after starting, and the fourth struck a land-mine.

During the 19th and 20th only desultory encounters took place on the front of the Third Army : in the V. Corps, the 33rd Division relieved the 21st Division and right of the 17th on the night of the 19th/20th, and the next night the 38th Division was withdrawn, the 17th Division extending to the left to take over the one-brigade frontage which it had occupied. The front of the V. Corps was now held by the 33rd and 17th Divisions.[1]

On the 21st the 19th and 98th Brigades (Br.-Generals C. R. G. Mayne and J. D. Heriot-Maitland) of the 33rd Division co-operated in the attack of the 58th Division (Fourth Army) under the same trench warfare conditions. After an advance of about a quarter of a mile the 1/Queen's (whose right company drifted into the 58th Division area) and 1/Cameronians (19th Brigade) were stopped by uncut wire and heavy fire, and could make no further progress ; the 2/Argyll & Sutherland Highlanders (98th Brigade) gained a little ground by bombing down trenches from the north, but, seeing no signs of the 19th Brigade, withdrew again. After dark, at 7.45 p.m., two companies of the 5/Scottish Rifles (19th Brigade), under a barrage, successfully took Meath Post, still short of the objective, with 42 prisoners, established some posts farther east, cleared the trenches on either side, and built defensive blocks in them. The same two companies of Scottish Rifles entered and occupied the trenches farther north evacuated by the Argyll. An attack of the 19th Brigade was arranged in conjunction with the 58th Division for 9.30 p.m. on the 22nd ; but, as already mentioned, the 2/Worcestershire, the battalion selected (attached to the 19th from the 100th Brigade) was unable to reach the forming-up position in time, and its advance was postponed until 5 a.m. on the 23rd, when it found Limerick Post evacuated. The 2/Argyll duly advanced at 9.30 p.m. ; but, counter-attacked in force at 9 a.m. on the 23rd and running short of bombs and ammunition, had eventually to fall back ; it was, however, 4 p.m. before the struggle came to an end. To fill the gap between the two brigades the 16/K.R.R.C. (100th Brigade, Br.-General A. W. F. Baird, which had relieved the 19th during the night1 of the 22nd/23rd) and the 1/Middlesex attacked at 3 a.m.

---

[1] In the early morning of the 20th, Br.-General A. R. C. Sanders, commanding the 50th Brigade, was killed whilst returning from a visit to Quentin Redoubt.

on the 24th, but failed to retain the trenches which they won. No change in the situation occurred during the 25th and 26th September. The end of the fighting was therefore that the front line of the 33rd Division ran along the trench which had been the third objective on the 18th, but it was broken by a large enemy pocket on both sides of the inter-brigade boundary, the Heudicourt–Honnecourt road.

During the period 19th–26th September comparative quiet reigned farther north on the front of the IV. and VI. Corps of the Third Army ; but gas drums were discharged into the enemy lines, and shelling and patrol encounters took place. In the XVII. Corps, the 52nd Division (Major-General J. Hill) re-took Mœuvres on the evening of the 19th, finding a post of the 5/Highland L.I., isolated on the 17th, still holding out.[1]   At 3.30 p.m. on the 21st, after a heavy bombardment, the enemy[2] attempted to recover Moeuvres, but could do no more than drive in some posts. The situation was restored by counter-attack and further enemy attempts on the 23rd, 25th and 26th were unsuccessful.

To sum up, in the fighting for the outer defences of the Hindenburg Position, the resistance of the Germans in prepared positions had proved by no means comparable with that at the Somme in 1916 or at Passchendaele in 1917, so that by or before the evening of the 26th September the Fourth and Third Armies had reached a good jumping-off line in front of the main German position from Selency and Pontruet to Trescault, Havrincourt and Moeuvres, and at 10.30 p.m. on the 26th the preliminary bombardment was begun on the fronts of the Fourth, Third and First Armies.

On the 22nd Sir Douglas Haig, after the success gained by the American First Army at St. Mihiel on the 12th–15th and by the Fourth Army on the 18th, had informed Maréchal Foch that he was prepared to carry out the operation assigned to him on the 4th September in the general scheme of operations : that is the attack of the principal enemy

---

[1] The commander of the post, Corporal D. F. Hunter, was awarded the V.C., and his six men the D.C.M.

[2] *1st Guard Reserve Division.*

defences on the front St. Quentin–Cambrai[1] : the First
Army[2] would, at a date to be fixed later (27th September
was selected), in the first instance capture the heights of
Bourlon Wood and then operate so as to protect the left of
the Third Army ; the Third Army[3] on the same day would
advance in the direction of the general line Le Cateau–
Solesmes, that is eastwards ; the Fourth Army, protected on
the right flank by the French First Army, would deliver the
main attack two days later against the enemy defences on
its whole front. The British Commander-in-Chief was well
aware of the serious nature of the task and had on the 21st
been warned by Lord Milner, the Secretary of State for War,
during a visit to G.H.Q. that the recruiting situation was
bad and that if the British Army was used up there would be
no men for the following year ; but he had carefully weighed
the favourable and unfavourable factors. His views are
recorded in his despatch of the 21st December 1918 :

" The results to be obtained from these different
" attacks [by the Americans west of the Meuse, in the
" Argonne, by the French west of the Argonne, by the
" British and by the Allied forces in Flanders] depended
" in a peculiarly large degree upon the British attack in
" the centre. It was here that the enemy defences were
" most highly organized. If these were broken, the
" threat directed at his vital systems of lateral com-
" munication would of necessity react upon his defence
" elsewhere.

" On the other hand, the long period of sustained
" action through which the British Armies had already
" passed had made large demands both upon the troops
" themselves and upon my available reserves. Through-
" out our attacks from the 8th August onwards, our
" losses in proportion to the results achieved and the
" numbers of prisoners taken had been consistently and
" remarkably small. In the aggregate, however, they
" were considerable, and in the face of them an attack
" upon so formidably organized a position as that which
" now confronted us could not be lightly undertaken.
" Moreover, the political effects of an unsuccessful

---

[1] See p. 443.
[2] See Sketch 24.
[3] See Frontispiece.

" attack upon a position so well known as the Hinden-
" burg Line would be large, and would go far to revive
" the declining morale not only of the German Army
" but of the German people.

" These different considerations were present to my
" mind. The probable results of a costly failure, or,
" indeed, of anything short of a decided success, in any
" attempt upon the main defences of the Hindenburg
" Line were obvious ; but I was convinced that the
" British attack was the essential part of the general
" scheme, and that the moment was favourable.

" Accordingly I decided to proceed with the attack."

REFLECTIONS

The progress made by the British Armies, an average of
25 miles on a front of 40 miles, between the 8th August and
the 26th September, fifty days, but mostly in the period
21st August to 18th September, twenty-nine days, had
exceeded the expectation and hopes of the troops concerned,
accustomed as the older hands were to small gains of ground
at great cost. At the Somme the average advance had been
only 8 miles on a 12-mile front in $4\frac{1}{2}$ months. The British
casualties in the 1916 battle had been roughly 420,000 ; in
the fighting of 8th August–26th September 1918, about
180,000. The advance had been frontal over country which
had been the scene of the Battles of the Somme in 1916, of
the German retreat to the Hindenburg Position in 1917, and
of the great German offensive of March 1918. The ground,
besides being traversed by the south-north course of the
Somme and the Canal du Nord, and affording a multitude of
small features and localities suitable for concealment of men
and guns, was seamed with the trenches and wire of former
positions, which furnished a succession of lines admirably
suited to an enemy carrying out a series of delaying actions.

Very heavy casualties had been inflicted on the enemy ;
unlike in all previous offensives, a very large number of
prisoners taken, and the enemy had not at his disposal
sufficient reinforcements to make the depleted units up to
establishment again, nor sufficient reserves to give the tired
and fought-out divisions rest, or even sufficient sleep. But,
attrition apart, the success gained was only what the

Germans would call an "ordinary victory"; nothing decisive had been accomplished, except that the Germans from O.H.L. to the soldier in the ranks had lost faith in final victory.

Strategically the main offensive was made at the wrong place, because the Army that was most fighting-fit happened to be holding that front.[1] It was not necessary to push forward directly in front of Amiens in order to relieve the railway situation there. In view of the facts that the only completed German second position, the Hindenburg (Siegfried) Position started near Soissons and faced west, that the direction of the German communications was from west to east, and that the main part of the German forces were west of Reims (149 divisions out of 201 on the 1st August),[2] an offensive east of Reims offered the best results. Such an offensive (Meuse–Argonne) was carried out by the American First Army and French Fourth Army, but not until the 26th September; and another, even farther east, in Lorraine, north-eastward past the eastern side of Metz, by the French Eighth Army, supported by the Tenth Army, was not ordered by Maréchal Foch until the 29th October, and was never launched at all.[3]

Maréchal Foch, on several occasions, pointed out the good results to be expected from the extension of the front of a successful battle. An offensive immediately east of Reims, where General Mangin with the French Fourth Army had just completely defeated a German attack, would have extended the success of the French in their operation for the obliteration of the Soissons salient of the 18th July–7th August; but it does not appear to have been considered. The Generalissimo, gravely hampered by having under his command Armies which were not homogeneous as his opponent's were, allotted the August offensive to the British; for the Americans were not ready and the French had been engaged in costly fighting since the 27th May, and in General Pétain had a commander who would not urge them on. No thought seems to have been given to obtaining enveloping effect by, say, an attack of the French Third Army northward and the British Fourth Army eastward, whilst the French First Army, between them, held back;

[1] See Sketch 1.
[2] See Map 2.
[3] F.O.A. vii. (ii), pp. 328 *et seq.*

or, better still, a wider pincer attack by the French Tenth and British Third Army. Nor was working the two wings alternately considered.

Instead of the French–American Armies attacking the flank of the German Western Front and the British profiting by their action, the British Armies had therefore to make a frontal attack on a position which had behind it as a retrenchment the Hindenburg Position. The plan had the one great advantage that the German strategists did not expect such a movement, and the preparations for it having been made with appropriate secrecy, they were completely surprised. Even more might have been effected had General Debeney, on the British right, employed more than one corps, and that belatedly, on the 8th August. Subsequently, too, he hung back and gave scant assistance, and the other French Armies which were engaged, the Third and the Tenth, entered the battle in succession, only on the 10th and 18th respectively, as the British advanced. The general result[1] was that as the British advanced, with Debeney's Army lagging behind, the French Third and Tenth Armies merely wheeled to the right, and contributed no flanking effect. This may have been the extension of the battle that Maréchal Foch contemplated. The true extension—to the left by the British Third and First Armies—was proposed and carried out by Sir Douglas Haig and in the circumstances was the proper strategy. The operation, however, was at first opposed by Maréchal Foch, who wished the British Fourth Army to continue to press forward eastwards in spite of strong opposition, which seems evidence that he conceived the rôle of General Rawlinson to be to sweep the Germans away from the front of the French First, Third and Tenth Armies. In fact he exhibited his high displeasure that the Fourth Army was perforce halted by withdrawing the French First Army from the command of Sir Douglas Haig, under whom it had been placed for the 8th August operations. On Sir Douglas Haig's appeal he did, however, impress on General Pétain, and, over his head, on General Debeney direct, that the French First Army should give more assistance to the British ; he did not, however, ensure that General Pétain did not weaken instead of strengthening that Army, and his mere words had no effect. General Debeney certainly issued orders for attack, but took no measures to see that they were executed, and on

[1] See Sketches 12 and 19.

the 15th and 16th September, at least, the troops themselves of the division next to the British refused to go forward.[1] Proper co-ordination by the Generalissimo of the efforts of the British and French Armies was lacking both strategically and tactically ; he had undoubtedly serious difficulty in obtaining willing compliance with his orders from General Pétain ; yet on the 26th June to obviate that very difficulty the Commander-in-Chief of the French Armies had been placed by M. Clemenceau " purely and simply under the " direct orders of General Foch ".[2]

Although Sir Douglas Haig's orders did not achieve a spectacular envelopment, they aimed at one. The Third Army was to break through and then, if possible, push southwards in order to outflank the enemy forces opposing the Fourth Army, whilst the First Army protected its outer flank and the Cavalry Corps accentuated the enveloping movement. The threat to the enemy flank led, however, to the retirement on the night of the 26th/27th August of the two German Armies opposite the British attack, and further retirements to the Hindenburg Position, although General Ludendorff had intended to hold the Somme–Canal du Nord line for the winter.

More, it seems now, might have been made of the great initial success of the Canadian and Australian Corps on the 8th August, either to help forward the III. Corps or to achieve a genuine break-through—just as more might have been made of the success of the XIII. Corps, on the right of the Fourth Army, on the 1st July 1916 at the Somme. Of the disorder into which the Germans had fallen there was ample evidence. General Rawlinson, perhaps awed by his remembrance of the stout defence of the Germans in the battles on the same ground in 1916, at first treated the enemy with too much respect. His object was to gain certain defence lines and consolidate and hold them against counter-attack, although Sir Douglas Haig urged him to do more. He certainly had to bear in mind that on the right General Debeney was going to make the French zero hour later than his, and then engage only part of his Army, and was unlikely to give much assistance ; whilst on the left the plans of the III. Corps had been upset by a serious attack made on it two days before the battle, and this corps was still in contact

---

[1] See p. 475 footnote.
[2] See " 1918 " Vol. III, p. 187, footnote 3.

with the enemy, with no chance of effecting a surprise, and therefore might not be able to advance as far as the others. Remembering the later stages of the Somme and what he had heard of the experiences of Passchendaele, General Rawlinson was no doubt confirmed in his views that short advances well covered by artillery were more likely to succeed than the launching of divisions into the blue with unlimited objectives.

Throughout the early part of the battle the commander of the Fourth Army did not by any means see eye to eye with the Commander-in-Chief, who desired that the Fourth Army should take risks and push on. On the 19th August, before the offensive of the Third Army, Sir Douglas Haig paid a visit to General Byng to warn him against " a repeti-" tion of the loss of opportunity which had occurred in the " Fourth Army ", and on the 22nd he issued definite instructions to all Armies that " each division should press " on even if its flanks were temporarily exposed " and " risks " which a month before would have been criminal to incur " ought now to be taken as a duty ".

The British Army has invariably been asked to undertake great enterprises—in the Peninsula, in the Crimea, and in S. Africa—with insufficient means. It must not be over-looked that, unlike the Germans in March 1918, Sir Douglas Haig and, on a smaller scale, General Rawlinson had not rows of divisions in second and third line ready to pass through and exploit the successes of the first line, and that the Germans after the 8th August, owing to the reserves at their disposal and by thinning unattacked fronts, were able to attain actual numerical superiority in divisions to oppose the Fourth and Third Armies.[1] This disadvantage could only have been balanced by bringing French divisions to the direct help of the British, which was not, judging by the events of March 1918, a very efficacious remedy. The nine divisions of the Fourth Army in the front line had behind them five divisions (including one American) in the corps reserves, but only one, the 32nd, in Army reserve ;[2] and the commander of the Canadian Corps urgently begged for this one on the evening of the first day of battle to exploit his

[1] The German divisions were weaker in men than the British, but owing to the number of machine guns, stronger in fire power.

[2] The 17th and 63rd, also originally available, were sent to the Third Army.

success. Although at first released, it was in a few hours withdrawn from him by the General Staff of the Fourth Army. Thus a great opportunity, as far as can be judged, was missed and the whole subsequent course of the battle affected. When the Germans were on the run on the 8th they were not kept on it ; they recovered themselves, so that when the 32nd Division was put in on the 11th, in changed circumstances, it merely suffered heavy losses without compensating return. The cavalry, too, was handled on the 8th August with excessive caution, and not required to do much more than ride ahead after the first phase and make good the infantry's final objective. The distribution of the tanks into small packets certainly gave some assistance to the infantry—the German infantry did just as well on the 21st March without tanks—but brought no decisive results. What might have been is indicated by the successful raid of the 17th Armoured Car Company, which caused great confusion behind the German lines. Sir Douglas Haig did issue orders that the cavalry should be kept together in large bodies ; but no such orders were given as regards tanks, although their massed employment was earnestly advocated by the senior officers of the Tank Corps. The tanks, however, were a new weapon, mechanically still imperfect and slow, and tactically still an uncertain instrument ; a very large number were soon knocked out. Materially they achieved little ; their moral effect, however, was tremendous, so that the German infantry saw and heard them when they were not present, and always exaggerated their numbers.

The failure on the whole to exploit successes and make use of penetration at one spot to assist neighbouring fronts still struggling with the enemy, and generally to try to make flanking rather than frontal attacks, is less a matter of controversy. As a whole, the operations were a gigantic drive in line, or line of advanced guards, which went on until the enemy resistance stiffened ; so, on the 3rd September, the Commander-in-Chief ordered that " no deliberate " operations will be undertaken for the present ", and the troops were to be rested in view of a first-class offensive in the near future.

The leaders of the fighting troops were well aware of the value of envelopment and of flank attacks, and made use of them, as the narrative shows : for instance, Lieut.-General Sir J. Monash's (Australian Corps) plan for turning the

Somme Line from the north via Péronne ; Major-General Lipsett's (3rd Canadian Division) avoidance of frontal attack in the opening phase of the 8th August ; and Br.-General A. A. Kennedy's (230th Brigade) flank attack on the 18th September which swept through Templeux le Guerard and the Quarries. Villages and defended localities were " pinched out " and then " mopped up " by troops in second line, and strongpoints and machine-gun nests approached from the flanks or rear whenever it was feasible. The German regimental histories time after time attribute the collapse of the battalion fronts to attack from the flank. The capture of Rifle and Hamon Woods by the 9th Canadian Brigade on the 8th August ; the capture of Morlancourt by the 1/1st Cambridgeshire on the 9th August ; the capture of Chuignolles and Chuignes by the 1st and 3rd Australian Battalions on the 22nd August and of Mont St. Quentin by the 5th Australian Brigade (in strength only a battalion) on the 31st August ; the seizure of the high ground above Miraumont on the night of the 23rd/24th August by the 64th Brigade ; and the forcing of the passage of the Somme by the 14th and 97th Brigades of the 32nd Division on the 5th September are excellent examples of the enterprise of the divisional leaders.

On the whole the leading of the Canadian and Australian officers and n.c.os. was superior to that of the British regimental cadres, and no doubt for the reason that they had been selected for their practical experience and power over men and not for theoretical proficiency and general education.

The early morning was the favoured time for attack, because the German machine guns, in particular, would be blanketed ; and the young soldiers who formed the majority of the troops do not seem to have suffered harm from continuous loss of sleep at night which assembly for dawn attack entailed. It is worthy of record that the German regimental histories one and all complain that the frequent early morning fog handicapped the defence ; their earlier plea that it adversely affected the attack on the 21st March 1918 seems therefore to fall to the ground.

The enemy system of defence was to hold ground by fire in depth, artillery and machine guns furnishing not only the framework but also the main resistance. Few attacks were therefore made, fog or no fog, without a creeping barrage. Its range often formed the limit of the infantry advance ;

for the actual position of the German defences not being accurately known, and it being difficult in the semi-open warfare to pass back information quickly, the artillery, although the guns were pushed well up for the purpose, could not, as already pointed out, support the infantry as closely or as speedily as in trench warfare. But whenever the enemy attempted to hold a marked line, like the Drocourt–Quéant Position, for instance, the British artillery immediately obtained, and retained, the upper hand.

For the first time both sides used low-flying aeroplanes to assist infantry attacks by machine-gun fire and the throwing of small bombs.

The daily advances being small the rearward services had no great difficulty in supplying the troops and evacuating casualties; but the engineers were fully employed in removing delay-action mines, in repairing roads, building bridges and providing water-supply. This last, indeed, proved a most important duty, for on the Santerre uplands water was scarce and the few wells very deep, and the enemy did not hesitate to defile the sources of supply. The future depended on whether the supply of the Allied Armies with food and ammunition could be maintained; no doubt existed that they could overcome the already half-beaten enemy.

CASUALTIES AND PRISONERS

It has not been found possible to compile a complete table of casualties by divisions. The following summaries are available:

CASUALTIES

FIRST ARMY, 8TH AUGUST–26TH SEPTEMBER

Period	Killed		Wounded		Missing		Died of Injuries		Injured	
	Officers	O.Rs.	Officers	O.Rs.	Officers	O.Rs.	Officers	O.Rs.	Officers	O.Rs.
8th to 31st August ..	59	624	294	6,885	11	169	1	23	8	261
1st to 26th September	166	2,918	793	15,845	14	1,520	2	27	17	408
Total ..	225	3,542	1,087	22,730	25	1,689	3	50	25	669

THIRD ARMY, 8TH AUGUST–30TH SEPTEMBER

Period	Killed		Wounded		Missing		Died of Injuries		Injured	
	Officers	O.Rs.	Officers	O.Rs.	Officers	O.Rs.	Officers	O.Rs.	Officers	O.Rs.
8th to 20th August ..	2	78	28	573	1	7	–	–	-	–
21st August to 30th September	782	9,438	2,536	56,148	87	7,385	3	29	33	737
Total ..	784	9,516	2,564	56,721	88	7,392	3	29	33	737

FOURTH ARMY, AUGUST AND SEPTEMBER

Period	Killed		Wounded (evacuated)		Missing	
	Officers	O.Rs.	Officers	O.Rs.	Officers	O.Rs.
August ..	415	5,263	1,936	40,782	84	2,516
September ..	313	4,262	1,010	22,313	47	3,123
Total ..	728	9,525	2,946	63,095	131	5,639

	Officers	Other Ranks
First Army	1,365	28,680
Third Army ..	3,472	74,395
Fourth Army ..	3,805	78,259
Total	8,642	181,334

TANK CORPS CASUALTIES

Between 8th August and 27th September, the casualties of the Tank Corps were 408 officers and 1,759 other ranks. In this period 582 tanks were handed over to salvage, of which only 14 were struck off the strength as irreparable.

WESTERN FRONT CASUALTIES

Between 21st March and 20th September, 1918, the number of battle casualties on the Western Front for the British and Overseas forces amounted to 27,470 officers and 584,216 other ranks, and the total number of prisoners taken up to 23rd September had been 5,300 officers and 223,222 other ranks.

PRISONERS TAKEN IN AUGUST AND SEPTEMBER

BY FIRST ARMY

	Officers	Other Ranks
August	90	4,012
September	299	12,805
Total	389	16,817

BY THIRD ARMY

	Officers	Other Ranks
8th–20th August ..	—	80
21st–30th September	1,110	41,246
Total	1,110	41,326

BY FOURTH ARMY

	Officers	Other Ranks
August	684	29,752
September	547	20,981
Total	1,231	50,733
GRAND TOTAL ..	2,730	108,876

NOTE I

THE FRENCH, 19TH–26TH SEPTEMBER

(Sketches 20, 28)

" On the 19th September the First Army resumed the attack " on its whole front. North of the Somme in the Dallon area the " enemy offered stout resistance and his artillery barrages pre- " vented any progress ; but a little to the south Coutescourt,

" Castres and Essigny le Grand were captured. In front of the
" Tenth Army [the Third Army had been withdrawn] the
" enemy stood fast on the plateaux north of the Aisne."

At 7.50 p.m. on the 19th, General Pétain telegraphed to
General Fayolle (G.A.R.[1]) : " the requirements of the operations
" as a whole have led me to withdraw the greater part of its
" resources (moyens) from the G.A.R., and for the moment on
" its part of the front the situation demands that the troops
" should be rested and the strictest economy of men and muni-
" tions observed, in view of future efforts. In consequence, the
" resources left with the G.A.R. should be utilized solely on the
" left of the First Army, whose mission is to support the British
" Fourth Army, and on the front of the Tenth Army, in order
" that it may retain its gains in the Allemant area at Vailly [on
" the Aisne, 10 miles east of Soissons]. On the rest of the front
" the troops will organize the ground captured." (F.O.A. vii. (i.),
" Annexe 1210.)

In accordance with these instructions, as stated in the text,
General Fayolle ordered General Debeney (First Army) to mass
the major part of his artillery (field and heavy) on his left. " From
" this moment the left of the First Army hurried on its prepara-
" tions for the offensive to be carried out in combination with
" the British, and a calm followed in the Dallon area." Thirty-
five heavy groups and the artillery of eight divisions were arrayed
between the Somme and the British right.

On the 24th, " the XXXVI. Corps, in liaison with the British
" Fourth Army, in spite of obstinate resistance of the enemy,
" seized Francilly Selency, Epine de Dallon and entered Dallon.
" On the 25th the enemy launched violent counter-attacks to the
" east of Savy Wood, which were repulsed ; at 3 p.m. the attack
" was resumed on the whole front, which completely cleared up
" Dallon."

NOTE II

THE GERMANS, 19TH–26TH SEPTEMBER

In German accounts these days are represented as marked by
successful defence. Various regimental accounts state, however,
that the divisions were withdrawn into the main Hindenburg
Position in a general retirement on the night of the 25th/26th.
The *Alpine Corps*, after a " complete defence victory " at Epéhy
against three British divisions (actually the attack was made by

---

[1] Originally containing the First, Third, Sixth and Tenth Armies ; on
19th September it had only the First and Tenth.

two weak British brigades—by German nomenclature, regiments) ; it was, however, withdrawn on the night of the 22nd–23rd and relieved by the *8th Division*, brought down from the Ypres sector, and sent to rest at Le Cateau. " There it found the " *5th Bavarian Division*, which had also been pulled out. The " troops were again terribly used up. Casualties and sickness, " caused by exhaustion, dirt and poor food, had thinned their " ranks." (B.O.A., pp. 546–7.)

On the 20th, during a visit, General Field-Marshal von Hindenburg told Crown Prince Rupprecht that " the reinforcement " situation filled him with anxiety ; but the French as well as the " British were at the end of their man-power." The Prince adds in his diary, " I think he is wrong on the latter point and under- " estimates the military capacity of the Americans." (Rupprecht ii., p. 448.)

ORDER OF BATTLE

8th August, 1918

FIRST ARMY

(GENERAL SIR HENRY HORNE)

I. CORPS (Lieut.-General Sir A. HOLLAND) :
1st Division (1, 2, 3)[1] to IX. Corps, 4th September.
11th Division (32, 33, 34) to XXII. Corps, 29th August.
55th Division (164, 165, 166).

VIII. CORPS (Lieut.-General Sir AYLMER HUNTER WESTON) :
8th Division (23, 24, 25).
20th Division (59, 60, 61).
24th Division (17, 72, 73).

XVII. CORPS (Lieut.-General Sir CHARLES FERGUSSON, Bt.) (to Third Army 23rd August) :
15th Division (44, 45, 46).
51st Division (152, 153, 154) to XXII. Corps 29th August.
52nd Division (155, 156, 157).
57th Division (170, 171, 172).

XXII. CORPS (Lieut.-General Sir A. GODLEY) (re-formed 29th August) :
11th Division (32, 33, 34) from I. Corps.
51st Division (152, 153, 154) from XVII. Corps.

SECOND ARMY

(GENERAL SIR HERBERT PLUMER)

II. CORPS (Lieut.-General Sir C. JACOB) :
33rd Division (19, 98, 100) to V. Corps 18th August.
34th Division (101, 102, 103) to XIX. Corps 30th August.
49th Division (146, 147, 148) to reserve 27th August.
American 30th Division to Australian Corps 1st September.
14th Division (41, 42, 43) from 17th August.
35th Division (104, 105, 106) from X. Corps 1st September.

X. CORPS (Lieut.-General R. B. STEPHENS) :
30th Division (21, 89, 90).
35th Division (104, 105, 106) to II. Corps 1st September.
36th Division (107, 108, 109).

---

[1] These numbers give the brigades.

XV. CORPS (Lieut.-General Sir B. de LISLE) :
 9th Division (26, 27, S. African).
 29th Division (86, 87, 88).
 31st Division (92, 93, 94).
 40th Division (119, 120, 121).

XIX. CORPS (Lieut.-General Sir H. E. WATTS) :
 6th Division (16, 18, 71) to IX. Corps 1st September.
 41st Division (122, 123, 124).
 American 27th Division to Australian Corps 4th September.
 34th Division (101, 102, 103) from II. Corps 30th August.

THIRD ARMY

(GENERAL THE HON. SIR JULIAN BYNG)

IV. CORPS (Lieut.-General Sir G. M. HARPER) :
 37th Division (63, 111, 112).
 42nd Division (125, 126, 127).
 62nd Division (185, 186, 187).
 63rd Division (188, 189, 190) to XVII. Corps 31st August.
 New Zealand Division (1, 2, 3rd (Rifle) N.Z.).
 5th Division (13, 15, 95) from XI. Corps 13th August.

V. CORPS (Lieut.-General C. D. SHUTE) :
 21st Division (62, 64, 110).
 38th Division (113, 114, 115).
 17th Division (50, 51, 52) from Australian Corps 20th August.
 33rd Division (19, 98, 100) from II. Corps 18th August.

VI. CORPS (Lieut.-General Sir A. L. HALDANE) :
 Guards Division (1 Gds., 2 Gds., 3 Gds.).
 2nd Division (5, 6, 99).
 3rd Division (8, 9, 76) from XIII. Corps 13th August.
 59th Division (176, 177, 178) to XI. Corps 26th–28th August.
 52nd Division (155, 156, 157) from XVII. Corps on 22nd, back to XVII. Corps 25th August.
 56th Division (167, 168, 169) from old XXII Corps.
 57th Division (170, 171, 172) from XVII. Corps on 22nd, back to XVII. Corps on 25th August.

XVII. CORPS (Lieut.-General Sir CHARLES FERGUSSON Bt.) (from First Army 23rd August) :
 51st Division (152, 153, 154) from old XXII. Corps.
 52nd Division (155, 156, 157) from VI. Corps.
 56th Division (167, 168, 169) from old XXII. Corps.
 57th Division (170, 171, 172) from VI. Corps.
 63rd Division (188, 189, 190) from IV. Corps 31st August.

FOURTH ARMY

(GENERAL SIR HENRY RAWLINSON, BT.)

III. CORPS (Lieut.-General Sir R. H. K. BUTLER) :
  12th Division (35, 36, 37).
  18th Division (53, 54, 55).
  47th Division (140, 141, 142).
  58th Division (173, 174, 175).
  74th Division from XI. Corps 1st–2nd September.

CANADIAN CORPS (Lieut.-General Sir. A. CURRIE) (to First
    Army at end of August) :
  1st Canadian Division (1, 2, 3 Cdn.).
  2nd Canadian Division (4, 5, 6 Cdn.).
  3rd Canadian Division (7, 8, 9 Cdn.).
  4th Canadian Division (10, 11, 12 Cdn.).
  32nd Division (14, 96, 97) to Australian Corps 20th August.
  4th Division (10, 11, 12) from XIII. Corps 26th/27th
    August.
  15th Division (44, 45, 46).
  51st Division (152, 153, 154).

AUSTRALIAN CORPS (Lieut.-General Sir J. MONASH) :
  1st Australian Division (1, 2, 3 Aust.).
  2nd Australian Division (5, 6, 7 Aust.).
  3rd Australian Division (9, 10, 11 Aust.).
  4th Australian Division (4, 12, 13 Aust.).
  5th Australian Division (8, 14, 15 Aust.).
  17th Division (50, 51, 52) to V. Corps 20th August.
  32nd Division (14, 96, 97) from Canadian Corps 20th
    August.

IX. CORPS (Lieut.-General Sir A. GORDON, succeeded on
    13th September by Lieut.-General Sir W. P. BRAITH-
    WAITE) (re-formed 4th September, 1918) :
  1st Division (1, 2, 3) from I. Corps.
  6th Division (16, 18, 71) from XIX. Corps.
  32nd Division (14, 96, 97) from Australian Corps 11th
    September.

FIFTH ARMY

(GENERAL SIR W. R. BIRDWOOD)

XIII. CORPS (Lieut.-General Sir T. L. N. MORLAND) :
  3rd Division (8, 9, 76) to VI. Corps 13th August.
  4th Division (10, 11, 12) to Canadian Corps 25th August.
  19th Division (56, 57, 58).
  46th Division (137, 138, 139).

XI. CORPS (Lieut.-General Sir R. HAKING) :
 5th Division (13, 15, 95) to IV. Corps 13th August.
 61st Division (182, 183, 184).
 74th Division (229, 230, 231) to III. Corps 1st/2nd
  September.
 59th Division (176, 177, 178) from VI. Corps 26th–28th
  August.

CAVALRY CORPS
(Lieut.-General Sir CHARLES KAVANAGH) :
 1st Cavalry Division (1, 2, 9).
 2nd Cavalry Division (3, 4, 5).
 3rd Cavalry Division (6, 7, Cdn.).

APPENDIX II

G.H.Q. OPERATION ORDER OF THE 29th JULY, 1918

O.A.D. 900/3

General Sir H. S. RAWLINSON, Bt.,
Commanding British Fourth Army
General DEBENEY,
Commanding French First Army

1. An operation will be carried out by the British Fourth and French First Armies with the object of disengaging Amiens and the railway Paris–Amiens.

The enemy between the rivers Somme and Avre will be attacked with the utmost vigour and driven back in the direction of Ham.

The line Méricourt–Harbonnierès–Caix–Quesnel–Hangest will be seized as quickly as possible and organized for defence.

2. When the line Méricourt–Hangest is secured, the British Fourth Army, keeping their left flank on the Somme, will press the enemy in the direction of Chaulnes.

The French First Army, with its right on the Avre will, in the same manner, press the enemy in the direction of Roye. Special attention is to be paid to the maintenance of connection between the French and the British Armies.

3. The dividing line between the two Armies will be as shown on the attached map.[1]

4. All details as regards objectives and the execution of the attack will be arranged between the General Officers Commanding British Fourth and French First Armies, who will submit their plans to British G.H.Q. without delay.

---

[1] Not reproduced. See Map 1 and Sketch 2.

5. In order to enable this operation to be carried out the British Fourth Army is being reinforced by the Canadian Corps (4 divisions), 1st Australian Division, and the Cavalry Corps (3 divisions).

The French·First Army is being reinforced by four French divisions.

6. The date on which the operation will be carried out will be notified shortly.

7. It is of the first importance that secrecy should be observed and the operation carried out as a surprise.

8. Please acknowledge receipt.

H. A. LAWRENCE,
Lieut.-General,
Chief of the General Staff.

APPENDIX III

FOURTH ARMY OPERATION ORDER OF 31st JULY, 1918

1. The Fourth Army will attack the enemy's position between Morlancourt and the Amiens–Roye Road (inclusive) on a date to be notified later.

Objectives and boundaries between corps, and between the Fourth Army and First French Army, are shown on attached map.[1]

2. The III, Canadian, Australian, and Cavalry Corps will carry out this attack.

3. The following tank units are allotted to corps for this operation :—

10th Tank Bn.	.. ..	III. Corps.
5th Tank Bde.	.. ..	Australian Corps.
4th Tank Bde.	.. ..	Canadian Corps.
3rd Tank Bde.	.. ..	Cavalry Corps.
9th Tank Bn.	.. ..	In Army reserve.

and will receive their orders direct from the formation to which they are allotted.

4. In conjunction with the attack by the Fourth Army, the First French Army will attack the enemy's position between the Amiens–Roye Road (exclusive) and the Avre Valley.

5. All further orders as regards carrying out this operation will be issued in the form of instructions.

6. Acknowledge by wire.

A. A. MONTGOMERY,
Major-General,
General Staff, Fourth Army.

---

[1] Not reproduced. See Map 1 and Sketch 2.

APPENDIX IV

FRENCH FIRST ARMY INSTRUCTION OF
31st JULY, 1918[1]

(TRANSLATION)

1st Army Staff	Army Hqrs.,
3rd Section	31st July, 1918.
No. 2859/3	
SECRET.	

Personal and Secret Instruction No. 520 for the
Commanders of the XXXI., IX. and X. Corps

1. The XXXI. Corps is about to execute an operation against
the high ground near Moreuil. This operation will be exploited
by the capture of the debouches on the right bank of the Avre
on the whole front of the Army.

2. The XXXI. Corps, starting from the junction of the Luce
with the Avre,[2] will carry the high ground around Point 110[3],
and will pursue its attack on Mezières and the Bois de Genon-
ville.[4] It will continue its offensive in the direction of Hangest.

Moreuil will be captured by encirclement.

The IX. Corps will clear the St. Ribert spur[5]; it will carry
Fillescamps Farm[5] and Braches. Its mission is to secure the
passages of the Avre at Braches and above, and to push on to the
right bank in order to join on to the XXXI. Corps and prepare
the entry of the X. Corps.

These operations will take place on zero day.

3. On zero day+1 the XXXI. Corps will continue its advance
in the direction of Hangest and Arvillers.

The X. Corps, taking advantage of the advance of the IX. Corps,
will send the 152nd Division to attack Hargicourt and the Bois de
Bouillancourt,[6] with the mission to capture the passages at
Pierrepont and to establish itself as far forward as possible on the
plateau between the Avre and the R. des Doms.[7]

The 152nd Division will connect north of the Avre with the
right of the XXXI. Corps by extending across the front of the
troops of the IX. Corps. As the XXXI. Corps gradually advances,
it will remain the mission of the X. Corps to cover its right by

---

[1] See Sketch 4.
[2] The Avre is just off the northern edge of Sketch 4.
[3] Two miles north of Moreuil.
[4] South-east of Moreuil.
[5] These places are midway between la Neuville and Moreuil.
[6] Just to the south of Hargicourt.
[7] This stream enters the Avre at Pierrepont. It is shown, but not
named, on Sketch 4.

holding the valley of the Avre and the plateau between the Avre and the des Doms. The 152nd Division, and the 166th if necessary, will be employed on this mission.

4. As soon as the junction between the X. and XXXI. Corps is assured, the IX. Corps will be withdrawn from the front, but its artillery will remain provisionally in Army reserve.

5. The corps commanders will have all preparations made with the greatest secrecy in order to obtain the effect of surprise.

Each corps commander will receive a separate order fixing the resources placed at his disposal and giving information as to the special nature of the operation.

The officers detailed to work on the preparations will be nominated by the corps by name, the orders will be written or typed by the officers concerned, the use of the telephone is forbidden. Any indiscretion will be very severely punished.

DEBENEY.

APPENDIX V

MEMORANDUM BY THE CHIEF OF THE GENERAL STAFF, 25TH JULY, 1918

BRITISH MILITARY POLICY

1918–1919

General Staff,
    War Office,
        25th July, 1918.

BRITISH MILITARY POLICY
1918–1919

Introductory

1. The object of this Paper is to examine the situation of the
Military Forces of the British Empire in relation to the future
course of the war and to determine the principles which should
govern its organisation, distribution and strategical employment.

2. In the absence of a " directive " from the point of view of the Allies as a whole, such as can appropriately be issued only by the Supreme War Council, the problem must be treated principally from the purely British standpoint and its solution must to that extent be incomplete. But, the nearer we get to the end of the war, the more necessary is it to keep in mind the ultimate aspects of the situation from the British side, so that the policy of our war aims and the strategy of our war effort may harmonise in securing for the British Empire the best possible position at the dawn of peace.

3. It is proposed to deal with the subject under four headings, corresponding to four well-defined phases of action :

(a) The present phase, i.e. the immediate necessities of the situation now confronting us.

(b) The period of preparation, which must intervene between the present period of crisis and the culminating phase of decisive effort.

(c) The decisive phase, for the culminating moment of which the entire Allied effort should be concentrated.

(d) The situation of the British Empire after the war.

Section A. The Present Phase

4. The Crown Prince's attack which began on the 15th July, constituted the fifth of the great assaults which have marked the enemy's offensive on the Western Front this year. After a week's hard fighting this attempt may be said to have been definitely neutralised, thanks to the high qualities of leadership of the General Commanding-in-Chief and the fine fighting spirit of the Allied troops.

5. As the result of these operations the Germans may be said to have lost the initiative in that particular part of the field, and the threat to Paris has been greatly lessened. The enemy's reserves are, however, still formidable, and Prince Rupprecht who, out of a total of 79 divisions under his command, has 26 divisions in reserve fresh and fit for fight (24th July, 1918) has still to be reckoned with.

It is known that preparations have been in hand for some time for an attack on the British Front in Flanders, as well as between Montdidier and Noyon, and these signs continue to develop. It remains to be seen whether, in view of the serious reverse sustained by the Crown Prince, this attack will materialise in the immediate future as an isolated operation, or whether the German High Command will call a halt and wait to reconstitute the greatest possible number of divisions for a combined effort.

Indications obtained in the fighting of the last two or three weeks tend to show that the German companies are in many cases under strength. It is unlikely that their 1920 class can be available in large numbers until about the middle of October unless they take the very undesirable course of putting in boys averaging even less than $18\frac{1}{2}$ years of age and with less than the minimum of four months' training.

On the whole it appears doubtful whether the Germans can do more than make one further attack on the grand scale this year.

6. The possibilities that may arise as the result of these operations are as follows :

(i) The German offensive may be fought to a standstill before any strategical decision has been obtained, leaving the Allied Armies in effective touch with each other, holding a line from the North Sea to Switzerland, covering the Channel Ports and Paris.

(ii) The British Army may be forced to abandon the Channel Ports, either—

(a) As the result of a successful attack on the British front, or

(b) In order to keep touch with the French and Americans South of the Somme.

This could hardly be achieved without great loss to our arms both in men, material and moral, but a considerable portion of our forces could probably be reckoned on for further operations as the facilities for embarking personnel at the Ports in case of emergency are surprisingly great. Thus, a large proportion of the troops that could not be moved by land to south of the Somme could be transported by sea to Havre or to Ports still further west in order to re-establish connection with the main Allied Forces.

(iii) The enemy may capture Paris, or bring it under such effective fire as will deny the use of the railway communications through it and stop the working of the extensive munition works which are concentrated in its vicinity.

(iv) The enemy may effect the complete separation of the British and French Armies, the former being driven back to positions covering the Channel Ports, the latter falling back to the south.

(v) The enemy may effect a breach in the line on some part of the Front, east of Paris, cutting the French army in two and entailing a return to the conditions of open warfare.

7. Alternatives (iv) and (v) would probably result in the decisive defeat of the French and might involve the loss of a considerable portion of the British and American Armies. Alternative (iii) would probably have such serious political and

industrial results as to cripple the French powers of resistance. But, even should the French be compelled to make peace, the British Empire and America could still carry on effective maritime and economic war, though the withdrawal of their troops from France would be a delicate matter and might entail considerable sacrifices. Our military effort would then have to be exerted on the Eastern Front as well as in Mesopotamia and Palestine. The results to be obtained by this would almost entirely depend on the extent to which Allied intervention through Siberia had previously materialised.

8. In the case of alternative (ii), i.e. the loss of the Channel Ports, the Allies could still continue operations in France though at a great disadvantage owing to the unfavourable naval situation thereby created. Our position would be prejudiced not only by the insecurity of our cross-channel communications and the practical cessation of traffic to the Port of London, but by the adverse effect on the submarine situation in the Atlantic, which would probably reduce to a considerable extent the forces that America could maintain in France. So much so that there would probably be a substantial surplus of American troops over and above what could be transported to or maintained in France which could then be profitably employed on the Far Eastern Front, provided the latter had been reconstituted.

9. It is evident therefore, that from both these points of view the Far Eastern Front acquires serious importance.

10. Assuming, as we reasonably may, that the first possibility becomes an accomplished fact and that the German advance is stayed without achieving any far-reaching strategical results, the immediate pre-occupation of the Allies must be to secure such a margin of safety for our line in France as will remove all anxiety as to our position. This will enable us to devote our efforts uninterruptedly during the ensuing period to preparation for the decisive phase and if necessary to detach troops to other theatres without misgiving.

11. This will involve a series of operations with limited objectives designed to push the Germans back from in front of the vital strategical objectives, such as the Channel Ports, the Bruay coal mines, the Amiens centre of communication and Paris. The plans for these operations as well as the moment of their execution must be defined by the Allied Commander-in-Chief, but it is obvious that they should take place before the end of this campaigning season. It is also certain that they will require the active co-operation of every man and gun that we can keep in the field until late in the Autumn. There is, therefore, no possibility of sending any divisions to operate in other theatres until this aim is accomplished.

Section B. The Period of Preparation

12. Having removed all immediate anxiety as to the situation in France and obtained a sufficient margin of safety for our strategical position on the Western Front, a period of preparation should ensue during which all the Allied resources should be husbanded, organised and trained for the culminating military effort at the decisive moment. This will not be a period of passive defence, far from it, but it will be a period during which no final decision is attempted.

13. The first question that arises is—when is this decisive effort to be made. That is to say, will it be possible to accomplish it in 1919 or must we wait until 1920.

14. The principal factor in the problem is of course the development of the military power of America expressed in terms of the number of divisions that she can raise, train, equip, transport to France, command and maintain in the field. The progressive increase in this factor has to be balanced against the progressive decrease which from now onwards must be anticipated in the man-power of France and England.

15. All calculations as to these numbers must of necessity be unsatisfactory as there are so many uncertain factors dependent on problems of shipping, manufacturing resources, wastage of our own and the enemy's forces in the interim and so forth, but as far as it is possible to judge we are justified in assuming that by June, 1919, America may have 15 replacement divisions and 65 fighting divisions fit for the line (vide, App. 1). The limiting factors appear likely to be the equipment and supply of the force rather than the provision of the actual number of men, while the creation of the necessary commanders and staffs must be a matter of the greatest difficulty. According to a recent calculation by the British Section at Versailles, the Allied situation by the 1st July, 1919, may be as follows :

				Divisions	Rifles
British	..	..	..	44	400,000
French	..	..	..	65	461,000
Belgian	..	..	..	5	42,000
Portuguese	..	..	..	2	20,000
American	..	..	..	65	780,000
Total Allies		..	..	181	1,703,000
German	..	..	..	170	1,230,000

This estimate is based on the assumption that the Germans are some 200,000 under strength at the present moment, that they cannot enrol Russian troops in any considerable numbers, nor induce their Allies to fight for them in the West, but that they may bring over 10 or 12 divisions from the East, and reincorporate large numbers of released prisoners.

16. According to this reckoning, even allowing nothing for Belgians or Portuguese, the Allied Forces on the Western Front should have a superiority of about 400,000 rifles by the 1st July, 1919, and should be able to maintain at least that superiority during the remainder of the year.

17. If the whole of the 100 divisions which President Wilson has undertaken to provide can be placed in the field during the summer of 1919, this will add another 15 fighting divisions to our total, and increase the Allied superiority to 580,000 rifles.

18. If Allied intervention in Siberia has materialised sufficiently to reconstitute an effective Eastern Front in Russia—even partially—our superiority in the West may well amount to 650,000 rifles.

19. Taking the most conservative of these estimates, a superiority of 400,000 rifles, or the equivalent of some 50 German divisions may not of itself be considered overwhelming. It may be argued that in view of the enemy's far more favourable strategical position and ample room for manoeuvre before any vital strategical objectives are reached, we could not, with only that relative preponderance, hope to reach a decision. At the same time that superiority, if properly supported by the fullest equipment of every mechanical auxiliary, and efficiently directed under one supreme command, will give us a fair chance of achieving substantial military success, while if the more favourable contingencies should arise our success should be decisive.

More important even than the actual numerical superiority will be the ascendancy in *moral* which cannot fail to be acquired by the Allied armies as they realise the great numbers of young, vigorous and enthusiastic men that come steadily pouring in across the Atlantic week by week and month by month. The enemy's discouragement at seeing the balance turn against him at this late period of the war, after all the sacrifices he has made, will be proportionately great.

20. In any case the arguments against deferring the crisis to 1920 are so strong as to be irresistible. The war weariness in Great Britain, the exhaustion of France and Italy, and the impatience of America, who will by that time have been at war for over two years, will oblige us to strike in 1919 or to stop the war.

21. On the other hand if the Germans are allowed another year to consolidate their position in Russia and Asia, they will have time so to exploit that vast reservoir of raw material and

man-power as will enable them, to a great extent, to counter the relative increase in Allied strength in the west, while their prospects after the war will be immeasurably brighter.

I have no hesitation in saying therefore, that as basis of calculation, we should fix the culminating period for our supreme military effort on the Western Front not later than 1st July, 1919.

22. Having decided this question the next problems that arise are :—

(i) What are the Central Powers likely to do in the meantime while we are preparing for our decisive blow ?

(ii) What must the Allies do to frustrate such action ? and

(iii) Is there any action that we can profitably take during the preparatory phase in any of the subsidiary theatres without prejudice to the concentration and development of our maximum forces for the main effort ?

From the moment when the German offensive is definitely arrested a period of equilibrium will gradually supervene which will last through the winter. During this period the Germans need have no immediate anxiety as to their military position in France, although they will have lost their numerical superiority and they can if they so desire detach considerable forces for operations in other theatres. But by March, 1919, the balance will begin to swing heavily against them. (Vide, App. II.)

23. If once the conviction begins to dawn on the German mind that a decision in their favour is not to be obtained this year on the Western Front they cannot fail to realise that their chances of ever obtaining one are relatively slight. But the General Staff will not lightly abandon their ideal and, although they are no gamblers, they may risk a sudden stroke in the hopes of bringing about such a complete change in the political situation as will enable them to win a German peace. The opportunity for such a stroke is afforded in the Italian theatre.

Recent calculations show that 14 German divisions can be concentrated per month on the Italian front, and that a maximum of 93 divisions can be supplied on that front.

With such a force, German Divisions being sent either in addition to, or partly in substitution of, the Austrian divisions at present there, the Germans might hope to inflict such a decisive defeat on the Italians as would force them to relinquish the struggle. Having eliminated Italy, the Austrian army would be released either to reinforce the Germans in the west or to take part in a campaign for the capture of Salonica, though this is not considered probable.

24. A sudden attack on Italy towards the close of this year is, therefore, a possibility to be seriously reckoned with. It is conceivable even that it might be made as an alternative to the sixth and final effort in France, if things go badly with the Germans

and the chances of success in the West do not appear to them commensurate with the sacrifices entailed.

25. It is less probable that a hostile offensive will be undertaken in the Balkans, except as a sequel to the elimination of Italy. The enemy would have little difficulty in maintaining a larger force there, say another 12 divisions, but neither the Austrians nor the Bulgarians are considered able or willing to undertake an offensive in Macedonia without strong compulsion and a very substantial backing from German troops. Such a dispersal of force would hardly be undertaken unless the political situation in Bulgaria should become so menacing as to necessitate German intervention. On the other hand the strategical situation of the Allies in this theatre is unsatisfactory. They are occupying a long line with insufficient depth behind it and for the most part forming front to a flank, since they are based on Salonica. A comparatively short advance by the enemy down the Vardar valley would sever the communications of the larger part of the force with their base, and cut the Allied army in two.

26. Turning to Palestine and the Middle East, it is scarcely probable that any large number of German troops will be sent to reinforce the Turks in those theatres, owing to the delay entailed in their passage to and from the west and to the comparatively small results which could be accomplished in a limited time. It is more likely that the Germans will adhere to their policy of employing the minimum German forces in the East, using whatever troops they do send there to stiffen Turkish units and stimulate their offensive activities. There were signs recently of a conflict of interests between the Germans and the Turks in the Caucasus ; Baku being the bone of contention. The Germans being nervous as to the effect of a Turkish occupation, which might have led the Armenian population to destroy the oil wells, were exerting pressure to prevent the Turkish advance on the town and endeavouring to induce them to send troops to Palestine. The latest information is, however, to the effect that these differences have been composed. Now that Germany has established herself firmly in Southern Russia and controls the Black Sea, her route to the East no longer runs through Egypt or even Syria, and it is more important for German interests to advance in Mesopotamia, Persia and Trans-Caspia than in Palestine. Her immediate interests centre in gaining control of Baku and the Caspian navigation, which gives access to the Volga waterway as well as to Trans-Caspia and the Ferghana cotton.

The only part of the Mesopotamian theatre which is closed in winter is the mountain range on the Persian frontier. The occupation of Baku turns the passes of these mountains and if the enemy gains control of the Caspian his communications in Northern Persia will be superior to ours.

On the whole, it is probable that whatever offensive efforts the Germans can induce the Turks to undertake are more likely to be diverted towards Mesopotamia and Persia than to Palestine.

27. It is apparent from the above considerations that apart from the enemy's gradual assimilation and exploitation of the resources of the East, the principal danger to the Allies, during this Autumn and Winter, lies in Italy. To meet this two measures are recommended. In the first place, the communications by road and rail between France and Italy should be improved to facilitate the rapid transfer of troops from one theatre to another and all staff arrangements worked out in full detail, including the accumulation of the reserves of supplies and material necessary to free the railways for the transport of troops in the emergency. Action has already been taken by the Military Representatives at Versailles to get these measures put on a proper footing (*Vide*, Joint Note 22) and the matter has recently been brought to General Foch's personal notice.

Secondly, a group of three or four British Divisions in addition to the three already there should be sent to Italy the moment that they can be spared from France, that is as soon as we have secured the necessary margin of strategical safety already referred to. These divisions should be stationed in Italy during the whole of the preparatory phase and will form a British Reserve. They will then be immediately available to meet a German offensive in Italy and well placed to reinforce the Macedonian front or even Palestine in case of necessity, while the change of scene and climate, added to the unrivalled facilities for training, will be of immense benefit to the troops.

28. In Macedonia, the main precautions to be taken are to carry out the instructions already given by the Supreme War Council as to the organisation of defensive works covering Old Greece, and the establishment of the bases and Lines of Communication necessary to maintain the Allied armies in the event of Salonica being lost. So far in spite of being urged to do so by the British Government, the Allied Commander-in-Chief in that theatre has refused to tackle the question. The problem is admittedly difficult, because it would take many months to evacuate the vast accumulation of stores, supplies, hospital establishment, etc., from Salonica and, while this base will never be voluntarily abandoned before an attack develops, if the latter is successful it will be practically impossible to do so afterwards.

29. In Palestine and Mesopotamia we are well situated for defence and the situation need cause us no immediate anxiety, but our line of communications with North-west Persia is so bad that our troops there will always be liable to defeat, until a railway has been made by which reinforcements can be brought up.

30. We now come to the question of how we can best employ the means at our disposal during the period of comparative stagnation on the Western Front that must occur while we are gathering our forces for the final round. Can we take a leaf out of the German book and concentrate successfully against one or other of her Allies in the hope of knocking them out altogether and forcing them to conclude a separate peace ? Can we not do to Austria, Bulgaria or Turkey what Germany did to Servia, Russia, Roumania and almost to Italy ? The suggestion is an attractive one, but we are faced at the outset with the inconvenient fact that the cases are in no way comparable. For, while the Allies of the Entente were isolated by their geographical positions from all hope of assistance in their time of need, the interior lines of the Central Powers enable either of them to be reinforced by Germany with certainty and speed. Germany, indeed, can move troops to any of the other theatres far more quickly and surely than we can send them from the Western front.

31. In Italy, as in France, our activities during the preparatory phase should be confined to such limited operations of local importance as may be necessary for the tactical improvement of our line and in order to keep ourselves informed of the enemy's dispositions and intentions. In France, in particular, these will want careful watching for, once the balance has definitely begun to turn in our favour it is highly probable that the Germans will seek to readjust their line by a systematic withdrawal, such as they executed in the winter of 1916–17, in order to avoid the risk to which they would be exposed if extended along their present salient front in face of superior numbers. Our answer to this manœuvre should be to follow up vigorously with the aid of tanks in large numbers, which can break through the enemy's rearguards and dislocate his plans. With the greatly increased equipment of these weapons that the Allies ought to have next year, added to what may well be overwhelming superiority in the air, the Germans should find it no easy matter to effect such withdrawals successfully.

32. The question as to whether it would be expedient to undertake offensive operations in the Balkans turns largely on the political aspects of the case. The situation there appears to be that the moral of the Bulgarian troops is far from high and they have no desire whatever to take the offensive themselves, nor could they be persuaded to do so without a very strong backing of German troops. Yet they would fight stoutly in defence if we attacked. An Allied offensive might also have the effect of causing Bulgaria and Turkey, between whom there is considerable friction at present, to settle their differences. Bulgarian national feeling would also be roused if the Greeks and Serbs took a prominent part against them.

33. Our operations would further be handicapped by the interminable political jealousies between Italian, French, Greek, and Serbian interests in this theatre.

34. It is fairly clear that unless our offensive produced far-reaching military results it could not achieve any useful political consequences. To produce these results it is essential that it should take place at a time when Germany could not with safety detach many troops from the Western front, otherwise even if we reinforced our armies for the operations (and the Allies are at present inferior in numbers by some 30,000 rifles) the enemy's interior lines would enable him to reinforce more rapidly and to neutralise our efforts. Thus it will not be until the spring of 1919 that conditions will be favourable for an offensive in the Balkans. It is in the spring too that our troops are at their fittest and have recovered from the effects of the malaria, which incapacitates so large a proportion during the summer and autumn.

The most promising venture in this theatre would appear to be an advance in Albania, first to Durazzo, then Scutari, finally Lovchen, where the main Austrian destroyer and submarine stations at Cattaro could be destroyed by shell fire. The feature of this theatre is that it is the one spot where our communications would be superior to the enemy's.

35. On the whole, I am averse to undertaking an offensive at present in the Balkans, and recommend that we economise British troops to the utmost in this theatre by the gradual substitution of Indian units as fast as they can be made available. The troops thus released will want a considerable period in which to recuperate and recover from the effects of their long sojourn in that fever-stricken district before they are fit for the arduous demands of the coming campaign in France.

36. Turning to the possibilities in the East, the question of whether it would be possible temporarily to reinforce General Allenby this Autumn by three or four divisions, with a view to assisting him in operations against the Turks has already been studied, and I have reluctantly come to the conclusion that no useful purpose can be served by doing so before the end of this year. General Allenby was asked to state his proposals in such an eventuality, on the understanding that the reinforcing divisions would have to be withdrawn in the spring. In reply he suggested a series of operations with the following objectives :—

(i) The line Jisr ed Damieh–Nablus–Tul   Keram–Nahr Iskanderuneh. This he hoped to reach with his present force of seven divisions and four cavalry divisions, commencing operations about the middle of September, but he hoped that the artillery of the three or four reinforcing divisions could reach him before that date in order to enhance his chances of success.

(ii) On the arrival of the three or four reinforcing divisions the advance would be continued first to the line Beisan–Haifa, and afterwards to

(iii) the line Tiberias–Acre. This was the furthest line that General Allenby considered he could reach with the forces at his disposal and hold after the reinforcing divisions had been withdrawn. He also considered that this line should be reached by the end of November as after that date the rains would make operations very difficult. Therefore the first move must be made not later than the middle of September.

37. The urgency of rectifying our precarious situation in France, which will require the active employment of all our forces there until late in the Autumn, added to the necessity of providing a reserve in Italy as soon as the former exigencies have been met, renders it impossible for any reinforcing divisions to reach Egypt until the end of November at the earliest.

38. A further consideration is that sufficient railway material, locomotives and rolling stock cannot be made available to maintain General Allenby's force on the Tiberias–Acre line, in view of the more urgent demands of other theatres.

39. Moreover the final advance proposed by General Allenby, i.e. to the line Tiberias–Acre, does not appear to promise any great results. It gives us no important strategical objectives, while it lengthens our lines of communication by a vulnerable 60 miles. In addition to this it would bring our front by so much nearer to the enemy's broad gauge railhead at Rayak, while it fails to give us control of the Hedjar line to Deraa, for General Allenby does not include Deraa in his objective no doubt because he does not consider the force at his disposal would be sufficient to hold it.

40. Should the Germans elect to reinforce the Turks during the Spring of 1919, and attack us on this line, we should be considerably embarrassed and might be forced to keep several divisions in Palestine at a time when they were wanted for the decisive battle in the West.

In any case the suggested operations would produce nothing more than a series of tactical successes, the political results of which would be insignificant. I therefore consider that our policy in Palestine should for the present continue to be one of active defence. Looking to the future, the importance of Aleppo as a strategical objective has greatly diminished since the Central Powers have obtained possession of the Caucasus and the railway to Tabriz, which provides them with an alternative and in some respects a better line of operations against Persia and India than by the Euphrates or the Tigris routes from Aleppo and Nisibin.

Should they also succeed in making good Baku and the command of the Caspian they will be in a position to control the Trans-Caspian railway up to the very borders of Afghanistan.

On the other hand, the importance to us of consolidating our position in Mesopotamia and Persia, establishing secure communications with the Caspian, and gaining control of the Caspian itself, has acquired ever increasing importance from this very fact. Indeed it is not too much to say that both with a view to winning this war and to securing the safety of India for the next generation we should devote our efforts to this theatre rather than to Palestine.

41. Our position in Palestine derives its chief importance in relation to the security of Egypt. We are well situated for defence as we now stand, holding the shortest line between the Mediterranean and the Dead Sea, the latter forming a secure defence for 60 miles on our right flank. In a few weeks' time our front will be served by a double line of standard-gauge railway, giving us a great advantage in this respect over the Turks.

42. In one respect only could our position be improved, namely, by extending our right so as to secure the Hedjaz railway in the neighbourhood of Amman, in order to establish permanent connection with the Arabs and consolidate our influence and political relations with them.

The advance to the line Jisr ed Damieh–Tul Keram, proposed by General Allenby, is probably a necessary preliminary to operations for the occupation of Amman.

43. With the exception of these two operations I am forced to recommend that our policy in Palestine should for the present be confined to one of active defence.

44. I can, however, conceive that in the event of a serious hostile advance being made against us in Persia or Mesopotamia we might with advantage undertake a counter-offensive in Palestine in order to regain the initiative and to compel the enemy to detach troops from his own line of operations. As long as no large force of German troops were so employed we might thus hope to bring the enemy's offensive to a standstill, in view of the dwindling numbers that the Turks can maintain in the field. Preparations should therefore continue to meet this eventuality.

45. I have already alluded to the grave menace to the British Empire created by the collapse of Russia in the Middle East. Our military situation in Mesopotamia gives no grounds for anxiety

as regards direct attack in the immediate future, for we have a large superiority in strength over the Turkish forces in that theatre, in fact too large to be strategically sound, viz., 73,000 rifles or 115,000 combatants.

We have also ample room to manœuvre in front of Baghdad, and very fair communications behind us. On the other hand, if the Germans succeed in occupying Baku and in obtaining control of the Caspian and the Trans-Caspian railway, they have an effective line of operations which turns the whole of our position in Persia and Mesopotamia and gives them direct access to the Afghan border.

Apart from the immense economic advantages they would thus secure, particularly in regard to the Ferghana cotton, of which at least a year's supply is lying ready to their hand, the ultimate military threat to India would in that case be formidable.

46. We, on our part, are making strenuous efforts to establish a line of communication from Baghdad to the Caspian, via Hamadan and Kasvin, with a view to gaining control of the Caspian ourselves. As the War Cabinet are aware, the most urgent instructions have been issued to General Marshall to consider this his main objective and to concentrate the maximum force possible in Northern Persia. The problem is mainly one of transport and supply, as the Turks, although in occupation of Azerbaijan and the railway to Tabriz, are showing no great activity at present south of this. There is evidence, however, to show that the Germans are urging them to occupy Enzeli, and it is not impossible that they may attempt to do so.

47. The despatch of a small force to Baku has been sanctioned, admittedly as a gamble, but the stakes involved are so valuable as to make the hazard justifiable. For the present the greatest force that General Marshall can maintain in Northern Persia will be about a brigade of infantry, a regiment of cavalry, and a few batteries of artillery, with some armoured cars and aeroplanes. We must spare no effort to improve our communications and increase our equipment in motor transport with a view to maintaining there ultimately a force of one or two divisions.

48. It is only right to consider whether by undertaking an offensive up the Euphrates or the Tigris we could facilitate the operations towards the Caspian. I am afraid that an advance either towards Aleppo or Mosul would not materially influence the situation. All our recent experience goes to prove that attacking the Turks in this theatre is like striking a jelly-fish, which stings and floats away, only to drift back when the pressure is removed. The enemy now has a secure line of communication via the Black Sea to the Caucasus and Tabriz. Even if we occupied Mosul we could not threaten the Turks in Azerbaijan during the winter, as

the passes would be closed. Again, we could make no appreciable advance on either line without pushing forward the railway concurrently and this we cannot do without diverting railway material that is urgently required elsewhere. But much more serious than this is the question of advancing our railways any nearer to the enemy's railheads and being forced to give battle to the Central Powers with every advantage in the way of reinforcement and supply on their side. This consideration applies not only to the present campaign, but has a most important bearing on the future.

49. If at the end of the present war we have pushed our railways round the mountains of Afghanistan, or across the deserts of Mesopotamia, to link up, or nearly so, with the enemy lines from Europe, we shall have broken down the physical barriers which nature has provided for the defence of India. By making it easy for a hostile army to deploy at will on our very threshold we shall have for ever committed the British Empire to an unlimited liability for defence. It will be necessary to keep ready on our frontiers a great army in a state of constant readiness for there will be no time to reinforce our outposts before the weight of invasion bursts upon them.

My view, therefore, is that we should not operate further up the Euphrates or the Tigris; that our programme of railway construction should be devoted in the first place to pushing the line from Khanikin to Hamadan and the Caspian; secondly, to completing the Basra–Baghdad line by the Euphrates route, so as to release transport now largely employed in collecting the Hillah harvest for use towards the Caspian and to build up a complete and secure line of communication for the defence of Baghdad and our operations in Northern Persia; thirdly, in order of importance is the completion of the line to Tekrit and possibly to the Jebel Hamrin at Shoreimieh in order to provide an alternative line of supply for any operations it may be necessary to undertake towards Kirkuk. The construction of this line may have some further advantage as a threat against Mosul and mislead the enemy as to our intentions in that direction.

50. In Northern Russia we cannot do more than prosecute the adventure upon which we have embarked with the handful of troops which is all that we can spare. The fruits of this enterprise can only be reaped if Allied intervention in the Far East becomes a reality.

For Siberia we are already providing a brigade of all arms, mostly through the prompt and generous response of Canada. The only possible reinforcement for this force would be a division from Mesopotamia, which could at present be spared, but would eventually have to be replaced, possibly from Palestine. If the despatch of this division would induce the United States and Japan to make a really determined effort to reconstitute the Eastern front in European Russia, the risk would be worth taking, but not otherwise, for once committed to the Far East these troops could scarcely be brought back before the end of the war.

Section C.   The Decisive Phase on the Western Front

51. I have already given my reasons for taking July 1st, 1919, as the date by which we should complete our preparations for the decisive struggle. This date is a basis of calculation only, for the exact time, as well as the plans and scope of the operations, must be laid down by the General Commanding-in-Chief the Allied Armies in France. ˙ To discuss these plans is beyond the scope of this Paper, but we may appropriately consider the principles on which the organisation of the British Forces should be based, in order to ensure that in the coming campaign our diminishing reserves of man-power are employed to the best advantage.

52. We are at the present moment pledged to General Foch to keep the maximum number of divisions in the field in order to assist in tiding over the existing crisis and to enable him to keep the battle machinery running by the process of " roulement." To carry out this pledge and maintain 59 divisions in being in addition to two cadre divisions training Americans, we are keeping some divisions below strength, and filling up others with second-rate material. Such a system is as pernicious and wasteful as running a motor car on a flat tyre, and I recommend that the moment the crisis is over we should make drastic reductions in the number of our formations, and maintain only that number of divisions in the field which we can with certainty keep up to strength and fully effective.

53. As our resources in man-power diminish it is surely prudent to economise what remains by endowing them to the fullest extent with the most effective man-killing equipment—such as machine guns, tanks and aeroplanes. In this connection we must look to the Royal Air Force to take an ever increasing part in co-operating with our infantry in ground fighting.

54. We must also compensate for smaller numbers by better training. Too much stress cannot be laid on the latter point, for no perfection of equipment can make up for inadequate training, as the Germans have proved to our cost in this year's campaign and as every war, in every age, in every theatre, has proved over and over again.

55. To ensure the necessary degree of training we must have a large proportion of our units out of the line. To be able to do this we must economise our commitments in the out-theatres and use the preparatory period to bring back as many British troops as possible to Europe. The principal source of such reinforcements is to be found in Salonica. Our four British divisions there should be completely replaced by Indian formations before next June. The 54th Division in Palestine should either be brought bodily to Europe or converted to an Indian division by the same date, and the British battalions thus released sent to France or Italy as may be thought desirable.

56. In accordance with the above principles the following concrete proposals are put forward and have been submitted for the consideration of Field-Marshal Sir Douglas Haig.

(a) *Infantry*

Infantry battalions to be maintained at a minimum establishment of 900 other ranks. This will be the ruling factor in deciding the number of divisions that can be kept in the field. While it is not possible at the moment to say definitely what this number will be, it may be assumed to be about 43, including 10 Dominion divisions and those in Italy. In any case I prefer to take a conservative figure, and if our wastage proves to be less or the supply of recruits greater than what we have allowed for, the surplus should go to increasing our establishment of machine guns and tanks.

(b) *Machine Guns*

Our army has been allowed to fall far behind the French, Americans and Germans, in the proportion of heavy machine guns to rifles, the figures being as follows :—

	M.G.	Rifles
British (as proposed by Sir Douglas Haig for the reduced number of divisions)	1	to 90
French ..	1	to 52
American	1	to 71
German	1	to 70

I consider that to rectify the disparity in a vital weapon an increase of machine-gun personnel should be made even at the expense of infantry—certainly in place of cavalry.

(c) *Artillery*

Field artillery to be provided on the basis of four brigades per division instead of two, and a proportion of army brigades.

Heavy artillery will not exceed the number of guns now in France.

(d) *Cavalry*

The following re-organisation of the existing cavalry corps of three cavalry divisions is proposed :—

(i) The reduction of one cavalry division, the regiments so released to be utilised as machine gun or tank units so as to retain their identity.

(ii) One cavalry division to be broken up and its nine regiments allotted as corps cavalry, the need for which has been greatly felt during this year's campaign. This leaves one cavalry division intact, and the cavalry regiments of a second division in existence but distributed among the army corps and divisions.

(iii) The cavalry corps headquarters to be abolished and an Inspector with a small staff to supervise training provided.

(e) *Tanks*

The scheme put forward for General Foch's approval involves an Allied tank attack on a 50-mile front by a force of 70 divisions and 8 cavalry divisions supported by some 10,500 tanks. Of this striking force it is proposed that the British contingent should be 20 divisions and one cavalry division, with about 3,000 tanks, in addition to about 7,300 mechanical tractors for the cross-country transport of ammunition and rations. The organisation, equipment and training of these 20 divisions which amounts to about half of the total British force in France should have priority over all other requirements. The total British tank personnel required will be 35,000. In deciding between the various conflicting demands for man-power the principle should be adopted of ensuring the complete realisation of the above programme both in trained personnel and material at the expense, if needs be, of the other half of the British Army not earmarked for the striking force.

Section D. The Situation of the British Empire after the War

57. An essential part of every plan of operations is the scheme for the consolidation of the objective after it has been reached. The British Empire in Egypt and India reached its objectives long before this war, which it has waged in self-defence. But this defence has of necessity been an active one and has advanced our strategical frontiers far beyond their original limits. The end of the war will leave us with a much more formidable enemy on our distant marches than we had to encounter before and it will tax our resources to the utmost to preserve our frontiers inviolate.

58. One thing is certain. Whatever concessions it may be contemplated to make to Germany as to the return of any of her colonies, a matter in which the Navy and the Dominions are chiefly concerned, under no circumstances can we afford to withdraw beyond our present railheads in Palestine or

Mesopotamia. We have to remember that in the next war we may be fighting Germany alone and unaided, while she will have Turkey and perhaps part of Russia, if not on her side, at least under her thumb. In such circumstances Germany, with no preoccupation in Europe, could concentrate great armies against Egypt or India by her overland routes, which are beyond the reach of our sea power. Our only chance will then consist in possessing such room for manœuvre beyond the confines of our dependencies as will give us time to assemble sufficient forces for their defence. In the same order of ideas is the warning already sounded against allowing our own railways to be pushed forward to within touch of the enemy railheads at Rayak, Nisibin, or Tabriz (*vide* Section B, para. 48) and in the terms of peace we should define the limits of the enemy's railway activities for the future.

59. Equally vital is it for our future security that the end of the war should find us with a line of railway in existence from Baghdad to the Caspian, or within reasonable distance of completion. With this in our hands, or at least under our political control, we shall be able not only to interdict the German advance through Trans-Caspia, but to keep touch with and lend active support to those elements in Russia which have still spirit enough to call themselves a nation and maintain their independence against the German Empire.

60. This brings us finally to the factor which will decide the future. Even when the German armies are soundly beaten in the West and driven out of France and Belgium, it is difficult to see how we could force such terms on the Central Powers as would loosen their hold in the East or close the road to Egypt and India. Unless by the end of the war democratic Russia can be reconstituted as an independent military power it is only a question of time before most of Asia becomes a German colony, and nothing can impede the enemy's progress towards India, in defence of which the British Empire will have to fight at every disadvantage. The resurrection of Russia can only be brought about by Allied intervention in Siberia and the re-creation of an Eastern Front. Failing such intervention and the re-birth of a Slavonic State, the Germans will be free to exploit both the material resources and the man-power of what was once Russia, not only for economic purposes but to swell the ranks of their armies. With this double increment of recuperative power Germany will be practically independent of maritime blockade and will be able completely to outstrip the rest of Europe in the reconstruction of their economic and military resources. Thus at no distant date Germany will be in a position again to threaten the peace of civilisation and consummate the domination of half the world.

Conclusions

61. The conclusions arrived at in this Paper may be summarised as follows :—

(i) At the earliest possible moment we must regain sufficient ground in front of the vital points in France to free us from anxiety, and enable us to make satisfactory preparations for our own offensive.

(ii) Having done this we should husband our resources during the preparatory period, making arrangements so that by the end of this period we can concentrate the maximum forces in the West, equip them to the fullest extent with every mechanical auxiliary, and ensure them the most thorough training before making our supreme effort. During this period a British reserve of three or four divisions should be stationed in Italy.

(iii) Although our calculations must necessarily be based on many uncertain factors, we may reckon on a numerical superiority of 400,000 rifles by next July if things go reasonably well. In view of this and other considerations, it would be unwise to defer the attempt to gain a decisive victory until 1920. For purposes of calculation the 1st July, 1919, should, therefore, be taken as the date by which all preparations are to be completed for the opening of the main offensive campaign.

(iv) Beyond improving our position in Palestine by gaining possession of the Hejaz railway about Amman and consolidating our connection with the Arabs no extensive operations in the subsidiary theatres should be undertaken during the preparatory period. British formations in Macedonia should be replaced by Indians as fast as the latter can be provided and the troops thus liberated employed as seems best to further the main object in view.

(v) The most urgent task in the meantime is the establishment of British control of the Caspian and of a secure line of communication to it from Baghdad.

(vi) Looking to the period after the war it is imperative for the future security of Egypt and India that a wide no-man's-land should be maintained between our present railheads in those theatres and those of the enemy, while no effort should be spared to build up behind our present front as complete and secure communications as the means at our disposal will allow. For it is ultimately on the physical obstacle presented by that no-man's-land and the relative superiority of our communications behind our existing front that the defence of our Empire will largely depend.

(vii) The reconstitution of Russia in some form as an armed and independent State, strong enough to withstand

German infiltration and aggression is a vital British interest. If the war closes without this being accomplished the future of the British Empire will be seriously menaced, and we shall ultimately have to fight at the gravest disadvantage.

(viii) Lastly, I am aware that in many of the matters I have touched on I have been trenching on the domain of policy, which is beyond the bounds of my responsibility. My excuse for so doing is that the ultimate security of the British Empire depends on the extent to which British policy and British strategy are made to harmonize in defence of British interests. Unless our strategy is based on a sound, sane and clearly-defined foreign policy the sacrifices we have made in this war and the efforts we may put forth in the future will avail us little. It is to policy that we must look to deny the vital lines of advance to potential enemies, to create the neutral zones and call into being the Buffer States that will provide that no-man's-land before our outposts and render abortive all hostile intentions and activities for years to come.

HENRY WILSON,
C.I.G.S.

General Staff,
War Office, S.W.1.
25th July, 1918.

ANNEXURE

AMERICAN ARMY

1. *Situation, 1st August :* 5 Corps (30 Divisions)+2 Divisions (56,000) less 147,000 ancillary services.

Situation, 1st September : 6 Corps (36 Divisions) (i.e., 1st Army complete+1 Corps).

Situation, 1st October : 7 Corps (42 Divisions).

2. After September, no programme has been laid down, but the possibility of having 100 divisions in France by 1st July, 1919, is being studied in America. It is assumed that no division which arrives after 1st April will be fit for the line by 1st July and, therefore, the question resolves itself into transport during the six months, October–March.

To bring one corps of six divisions a month (183,000)+10 per cent. initial reinforcements means approximately transporting 200,000 men per month. To this must be added Army troops and a continually increasing number of reinforcements, so that even assuming shipping for 300,000 to be available, a rate of one corps per mensem appears the limit.

This would give a total of 42+36 divisions landed by 1st April fit for action on 1st July, i.e. 78 divisions.

3. The limiting factor is not, however, personnel but the transport of horses, equipment and ammunition and above all the maintenance of over three million Americans in France. The supply of the one million already in the country is causing some anxiety, and though up to one million may be offset against a corresponding reduction in the strength of the other allies, there still remains a balance of at least one million extra to be maintained.

For this reason it is considered that 78 should be regarded as the maximum number of American divisions which can be relied upon for action on 1st July, 1919, of which 65 would be combat divisions and 13 depot divisions. This would mean 2 Armies, each of 30 divisions (strength 1¼ millions each) plus 15 combat and 3 depot divisions, giving a total of over 3,175,000 rations. the figure on which it is understood that General Pershing is at present basing his calculations for 1st August, 1919. In the graph attached (Appendix II)[1], which is otherwise based on figures supplied by Versailles, 65 combat divisions are taken.

4. It is important that the Americans should work to a figure of 100 divisions in France. It does not, of course, follow that this number will actually ever be constituted on the Western Front.

The number will depend on the severity of the fighting, and it is immaterial to the *comparative* strengths whether the Americans increase from 78 to 100 whilst the Germans decrease slowly or whether the Americans remain stationary whilst the Germans drop by an extra 20–30 divisions. The essential fact is that, however heavy the fighting, we shall be able to maintain our formations up to strength, whilst the Germans will presumably not. The figures on which the graph is based allow for heavy fighting as from March, 1919, onwards because, although it is not our intention to begin operations on a great scale until July, it is quite possible that the Germans may attempt to hamper our preparations by forestalling us with an offensive of their own.

This will be a reversal of the conditions which obtained in 1917 and went far towards crippling our offensive.

General Staff,
    War Office, S.W.1.
       25th July, 1918.

---

[1] Not reproduced.

APPENDIX VI

FOURTH ARMY GENERAL STAFF INSTRUCTIONS, 31ST JULY, 1ST AUGUST AND 4TH AUGUST, 1918

GENERAL INSTRUCTIONS[1]

[FIRST PART]

1. *Secrecy*

(*a*) It is of first importance that secrecy should be observed and the operation carried out as a surprise.

Commanders will take all possible steps to prevent the scope or date of the operation becoming known except to those taking part. Any officer, N.C.O., or man discussing the operation in public, or communicating details regarding it to any person, either soldier or civilian, not immediately concerned, will be severely dealt with.

(*b*) All movement of troops and transport in an easterly direction will take place by night, whether in the forward or back areas of the Fourth Army, on and after 1st August, except where absolutely necessary to move by day.

(*c*) G.O.C., 5th Brigade, R.A.F., will arrange with corps for aeroplanes to fly over Fourth Army area during days when flying is possible, and to report to Corps H.Q. any abnormal movement of troops or transport within our lines.

(*d*) Work on back lines will be continued as at present, so that there may be no apparent change in our attitude.

(*e*) The Canadian Corps and divisions in reserve to III. Corps will not open any wireless stations till after Zero.

(*f*) Commanders will ensure that the number of officers reconnoitring the enemy's positions is limited to those for whom such reconnaissance is essential.

Nothing attracts attention to an offensive more than a large number of officers with maps looking over the parapet and visiting O.Ps.

Commanding officers of units holding the front line should report at once to higher authority any disregard of these orders.

2. *Reserves.*

(*a*) In drawing up plans, arrangements must be made on the fronts of the Canadian and Australian Corps for all troops taking part in the attack, whether in support or reserve, to be prepared to move forward at Zero so as to avoid any delay in the forward movement.

---

[1] See Map 1 and Sketch 2.

3. *Artillery*

(*a*) Instructions which deal with technical Artillery details will be issued by G.O.C., R.A., Fourth Army, to G.Os. C.R.A., of corps.

(*b*) The following will be the strength of the Artillery placed at the disposal of corps :—

| | *Field Artillery* | *Heavy Artillery Brigades.* | | | | | *6-in. Gun Btys.* | *12-in. How. Btys. Mk. IV on road mountings* |
		Mobile	*Mixed*	*8-in.*	*9.2-in.*	*Total*		
Canadian Corps	17 Bdes.	3	2	3	1	9	3	1
Australian Corps	18 Bdes.†	2	2	3	2	9	4	1
III. Corps	17 Bdes.	1	3*	3	1	8	3	1

* Less 1 section 6-in. How. at Artillery School.

† Less 1 battery at Artillery School.

(*c*) Ammunition will be dumped at or near gun positions as follows :—

	Rounds
18-pdr.	600
4.5-in. How.	500
60-pdr.	400
6-in. Guns	400
6-in. Hows.	400
8-in. Hows.	400
9.2-in. Hows.	400
12-in. Hows.	200

Arrangements should be made to commence dumping this ammunition as soon as feasible. Echelons will be kept full.

(*d*) Attention is called to the importance of all artillery instructions being issued in sufficient time to permit of subordinate formations being afforded ample time to study them and to work them out in detail. No changes in the artillery programme at a late hour should be permitted without very urgent reason.

(*e*) Boundaries between corps as regards bombardment and counter-battery work coincide with the boundaries between corps shown on map issued with Fourth Army No. 20 (G), dated 31/7/18.[1]

(*f*) *Barrages* (*Field Artillery*).—The timing of Field Artillery barrages will be regulated as follows :—

> (i) North of the Somme by III. Corps.
> (ii) Between the Somme and the Luce by the Army.
> (iii) South of the Luce by the Canadian Corps.

---

[1] Not reproduced.

As regards (ii), all Field Artillery lifts will be 100 yards.

The Field Artillery barrage will come down at zero, 200 yards beyond the infantry tape line.

The first two lifts will be at zero+3 and zero+5.

The next eight lifts will be at 3-minute intervals.

From the eleventh lift, inclusive, until the green line[1] is reached, lifts will be at 4-minute intervals.

Corps will arrange the 4.5-in. howitzer barrage to fit in with the above.

A protective barrage will be maintained in front of the green line until zero+4 hours, after which all barrages will cease.

(g) *Barrages* (*Heavy Artillery*).—In view of the nature of the enemy's defences on this front, the fire of the majority of the heavy howitzers employed for purposes other than counter-battery work should be used during the barrage to engage special strongpoints or localities rather than to form a creeping barrage. At the same time, some 60-pounder guns and howitzers should be employed to deal with fugitives from the creeping barrage.

(h) *Normal activity*.—Active counter-battery work and harassing fire will be maintained.

Such registration as is necessary should be carried out under cover of this fire.

The necessity for concealing the increase in the number of guns on the Army front must be borne in mind, and on no account should a large number of guns be employed at any one time. This must be remembered in connection with counter-preparation and S.O.S. plans.

Normal fire should, so far as possible, be carried out from positions other than the permanent positions of batteries.

(j) *Counter-Battery Action*.—At least two-thirds of the available heavy artillery should be employed for counter-battery purposes.

Heavy concentrations of fire will be directed on the different groups of enemy artillery.

The importance of strong counter-battery work on the flanks must be borne in mind. On the southern flank this will be carried out in co-operation with the French.

All corps will devote special attention to the problem of dealing with the hostile artillery after the objectives have been gained. This involves close co-operation with the R.A.F. The conditions prevailing on the fronts of the Canadian and Australian Corps are likely to be those of open warfare.

(k) *Close Support of the Infantry*.—It will be necessary to move forward guns in close support of the infantry.

The general principle to be followed will be that some 18-pounders and 4.5-in. howitzers should be advanced as soon as possible under orders of the infantry brigadiers ; Divisional

---

[1] The first objective.

Artillery under the orders of the C.R.A. of the division, with one or more 60-pounder batteries to follow. These should be strengthened in due course by the advance of more Field Artillery, 60-pounders, and 6-in. howitzer batteries.

(*l*) *Action in case of Bombardment by Hostile Artillery previous to Zero.*—Each corps will prepare a plan for dealing with the hostile artillery should a heavy development of hostile fire take place on zero night.

The decision to put the plan into execution rests with corps.

If the hostile batteries responsible are located in the counter-battery area of another corps, arrangements for counter action will be made direct between corps concerned.

(*m*) In the event of wet weather, corps will arrange for a proportion of smoke to be used in their barrage in order to cover the advance of the tanks.

(*n*) Heavy artillery fire on all villages east of the red line and south of the railway, except Le Quesnel, will cease at $0+6\frac{1}{2}$ hours.

Heavy artillery fire on Le Quesnel will cease at $0+7\frac{1}{2}$ hours.

4. *Tanks*

(*a*) The allotment of supply tanks for infantry has been made and communicated to G.Os.C. 4th and 5th Tank Brigades and 10th Tank Battalion.

(*b*) The advance of the tanks up to the infantry tape line must be covered by the action of the R.A.F., so as to avoid the noise of the tank engines being heard by the enemy.

Detailed programmes as regards this will be arranged between the G O.C. 5th Brigade R.A.F. and Corps.

(*c*) The 17th Armoured Car Battalion is placed at the disposal of the Australian Corps, and will join 5th Tank Brigade shortly.

5. *Communications*

(*a*) All possible arrangements will be made so that once the advance has begun, communication may be maintained by visual signalling, mounted messengers, etc.

Mounted messengers have been found the most reliable, and corps will arrange for the distribution of these from their own resources.

(*b*) When divisional and brigade H.Q. advance, their position must be clearly marked by distinguishing flags.

(*c*) Red flares will be used by all corps for communication with aircraft.

(d) The following light signals will be employed by corps as stated :—

Signal	Meaning
(i) *Cavalry Corps*	
White star turning to red on a parachute fired from 1½-in. Very pistol.	" Advanced troops of cavalry are here."
(ii) *III. Corps*	
(a) No. 32 grenade, green over green over green.	S.O.S.
(b) No. 32 grenade, white over white over white.	Success signal, i.e., " We have reached objective."
(c) One white Very light.	" Barrage is about to lift."
(iii) *Canadian Corps*	
(1) No. 32 grenade, red over red over red.	In addition to being employed for S.O.S., this signal will also mean—
	(a) " We are held up and cannot advance without help."
	(b) "Enemy is counter-attacking."
	Remark : In the case of (a) a smoke rocket (No. 27 grenade) will also be fired in the direction of the obstruction to indicate its position.
(2) No. 32 grenade, green over green over green.	(a) " Lift your fire, we are going to advance."
	(b) " Stop firing."
(3) Three white Very lights in quick succession.	" We have reached this point."
(iv) *Australian Corps*	
(1) No. 32 grenade, green over green over green.	S.O.S.
(2) No. 32 grenade, white over white over white.	Success signal, i.e., " We have reached objective."

(e) Special care must be taken by the artillery on the left and right flanks of the Canadian and Australian Corps respectively, that all officers and N.C.Os. are acquainted with these signals so that no mistake may arise as regards the difference in the S.O.S. signals of the two corps.

(f) Pigeons are allotted as follows :—

Cavalry Corps ..	2 lofts at Vignacourt[1]	..	140 birds.
III. Corps ..	2 lofts near Holliens-au-Bois		128 birds.
Canadian Corps	1 loft at Pont de Metz .. ⎫ 1 loft at Flixecourt (M.88).. ⎬		236 birds.
	1 loft at Villers Bocage .. ⎭		
Australian Corps	2 lofts at Allonville Wood .. ⎫ 1 loft at Bertangles.. .. ⎬		228 birds.
3rd Tank Brigade	1 loft at Flixecourt (M.24)..		70 birds.
4th Tank Brigade	1 loft at Vaux .. .. ⎫		140 birds.
5th Tank Brigade	1 loft at Vaux .. .. ⎭		

Should more birds be required for the use of tanks than allotted above, they will be provided by corps out of their own resources

(g) The Army will be responsible for cable communication between A.H.G. and Cavalry Corps H.Q. (N.29, d.0.7, S.E. of Longueau). Cavalry Corps will be responsible for laying and maintaining cable communication, thence to 3rd Cavalry Division H.Q. (near Cachy). At least two lines will be laid. When Cavalry Corps H.Q. move forward, the responsibility for this communication will be taken over by the Army.

6. Maps

(a) The following special maps are being prepared and will be issued to all concerned on 4th or 5th August in sufficient numbers to meet all requirements :—

(i) 1/40,000—covering the area approximately La Houssoye–Peronne–Mesle–Mailly Raineval.

These maps will show the following information regarding hostile dispositions so far as they are known :—

Corps, divisional, brigade, and battalion H.Q.
Battalions and companies.
Rest billets.
Battery positions.
Detraining stations.
Railheads.
Dumps.
Aerodromes.
Hospitals.

(ii) 1/20,000—(for use of Canadian Corps)—Blangy Wood–Framerville–Warvillers–Moreuil.

---

[1] See Map 3.

7. *Roads*

(*a*) Special parties will be told off by Canadian and Australian Corps to repair the Amiens–Roye and the Amiens–Villers Carbonnel roads, respectively, so that they may be ready for use at the earliest possible moment.

(*b*) The Amiens–Longueau–Villers Bretonneux road, as far east as cross roads in N.26.C [south-east of Longueau] will be reserved for the exclusive use of the Cavalry Corps from 9.30 p.m. " Y " day to 8 a.m. " Z " day.

After 8 a.m. " Z " day it will be at the disposal of the Australian and Cavalry Corps. The Australian Corps will control the traffic on it.

H.Q., Fourth Army,
 31st July, 1918.

[SECOND PART]

8. *Date and Hour of Attack*

(*a*) Zero hour will be communicated to corps in writing at 12 noon on " Y " day.

(*b*) Watches will be synchronised by the General Staff, A.H.Q., with Corps H.Q., 5th Brigade R.A.F. H.Q., and First French Army H.Q. on the telephone at 12 noon and 6 p.m. on " Y " Day.

9. *Reliefs*

(*a*) The relief of the 4th Australian Division by the Canadian Corps will be carried out as follows :—
 Two brigades in support on night 4th/5th.
 Transfer of command at 10 a.m. on the 5th.
The brigade in line will be withdrawn on Y/Z night under arrangements to be made between Canadian and Australian Corps.

(*b*) The 65th Brigade, American 33rd Division, will be transferred to the III. Corps and be concentrated in the III. Corps area on the 6th August.

The 33rd American Division will not be employed in the attack.

10. *Army Policy after Reaching Objectives*

(*a*) After reaching the furthest objectives[1] shown on the map issued with Fourth Army, No. 20(G), dated 31/7/18, preparations to meet any possible counter-attack will immediately be taken in hand and the line gained consolidated.

A regular system consisting of front, support and reserve lines will be constructed.

---

[1] The Amiens Outer Defences. See Map 1 and Sketch 2.

This system will become the Main Battle Position of the Fourth Army until further orders, and will be prepared for defence as such.

11. *Special Companies, R.E.*

(*a*) Special Companies, R.E., are allotted to corps as follows :—

Canadian Corps	No. 2 Special Company.
Australian Corps ..	Nil.
III. Corps..	" D," " H," " Z " and No. 1 Special Companies.

(*b*) O.C. Special Companies, R.E., Fourth Army, is placed at the disposal of III. Corps, and has been ordered to report to III. Corps H.Q. at once.

H.Q., Fourth Army,
　1st August, 1918.

[THIRD PART]

12. *R.A.F.*

(*a*) The action of the R.A.F. during forthcoming operations will be as follows :—

The 5th Brigade R.A.F. will have at its disposal :—

(i) Six Corps Squadrons distributed :—

1 per corps—III.Corps ..	..	35th Squadron.
Canadian Corps	..	5th Squadron.
Australian Corps	..	3rd Australian Squadron.
1 to work with tanks ..	..	8th Squadron.
1 to work with cavalry ..	..	6th Squadron.
1 to feed machine guns with S.A.A. on the red and blue lines of the III. and Australian Corps ..		9th Squadron.

(ii) 22nd Wing (8 Scout Squadrons) will be exclusively employed in engaging ground targets by bombing and machine-gunning on the whole Army front.

(iii) 1 day bombing squadron ..	..	205th Squadron.
1 night bombing squadron ..	..	101st Squadron.
(iv) 1 Reconnaissance squadron..	..	48th Squadron.

In addition, the scouts of the 9th Brigade will maintain constant patrols at height over the front of attack, reinforced, if need be, by machines of the 3rd Brigade.

Finally, four day-bombing squadrons and three night-bombing squadrons will be loaned from other wings for co-operation purposes.

The low-flying scouts of 22nd Wing will be detailed at first in even distribution on each corps front of attack, this disposition being changed later, if necessary, to meet special circumstances which may arise. They will operate in two phases, i.e. from Z to Z+4 eastwards from the green line, and from Z+4 eastwards from the red line.

In each phase very favourable targets will be engaged irrespective of the boundaries demarcated by the green and red lines.

(b) The following will be the special markings of machines on special duty :—

(i) Machine working with tanks—black band on middle of right side of tail.

(ii) Machine working with cavalry—2 streamers on both inside struts.

(iii) All contact patrol machines—rectangular panels 2 feet by 1 foot on both lower planes about 3 feet from the fuselage.

(iv) Machines carrying S.A.A. for machine guns of Australian Corps will have the underside of both lower planes painted black for a distance of $2\frac{1}{2}$ feet from the tips.

13. *Cavalry*

(a) The first mission of the Cavalry Corps on " Z " day will be to secure the line of the outer Amiens defences, and hold it until relieved by the infantry of the Canadian Corps.

The general line of advance of the cavalry, and objective are shown on the map issued with Fourth Army, No. 20 (G) of 31st July.[1]

(b) Cavalry Corps H.Q. will be established as follows :—

At 8 p.m. " X " day—Yzeux.

At 9 p.m. " Y " day—N.29.d.0.7 (500 yards S.E. of Longueau).

(c) 3rd Cavalry Division, with one battalion "whippet" tanks, is forthwith placed under the orders of Canadian Corps.

(d) Bivouac areas for Cavalry Corps on " X "/" Y " night are shown on attached map marked " A."[1]

(e) Concentration areas for the 1st and 3rd Cavalry Divisions on " Y "/" Z " night, together with track reserved for the cavalry advance from the concentration area, are shown on attached map marked " B."[1]

Canadian Corps will arrange for this track to be kept clear for the use of the cavalry.

The 3rd Cavalry Division will be responsible for the preparation of this track. Work on it must not be begun until " Y "/" Z " night.

---

[1] Not reproduced.

(*f*) The 3rd Cavalry Division, with battalion of " whippets " attached, will revert under command of the Cavalry Corps as soon as the whole of the red line on the Canadian Corps front has been reached by the infantry.

(*g*) The closest touch must be kept by the Cavalry Corps with the right Australian Division (5th).

(*h*) All the villages in the area south of the Amiens–Roye Road will be under heavy French artillery fire on " Z " day. Cavalry will, therefore, not go south of this road.

(*j*) The Cavalry Corps will arrange for one cavalry brigade of 1st Cavalry Division, with one company " whippets," to be placed under the command of the Australian Corps from 9 p.m. " Y "/" Z " night.

This brigade will revert under command of the Cavalry Corps when the infantry of the Australian Corps have reached the Red line.[1] If the whole of the 1st Cavalry Division is required south of Amiens–Chaulnes railway to exploit success gained before that time, it will rejoin its division without waiting for the infantry of the Australian Corps to reach the Red line.

A. A. MONTGOMERY,
Major-General,
General Staff, Fourth Army.

H.Q., Fourth Army,
4th August, 1918.

APPENDIX VII

FOURTH ARMY ADMINISTRATIVE ARRANGEMENTS OF 6TH AUGUST, 1918

Details of administrative arrangements will be issued under the following headings :—

Section	*Section*	*Section*
A. Railways.	G. Water.	L. Veterinary.
B. Railheads.	H. Ordnance.	M. Traffic Control.
C. Roads.	I. Labour.	N. Prisoners of War.
D. Canals.	J. Medical.	O. Accommodation.
E. Ammunition.	K. Remounts.	P. Civilian Inhabitants.
F. Supplies.		

H. C. HOLMAN.
Major-General,
D.A. & Q.M.G., Fourth Army.

6th August, 1918.

---

[1] The second objective.

A.—RAILWAYS

1. *Amiens-Albert line.*

    (*a*) Is repaired to Bonnay.

    (*b*) Will be repaired to Heilly about 8th August.

    (*c*) Corbie and Heilly stations are repairable.

    (*d*) Most forward railhead at present is Lamotte Brebiere.

2. *Amiens-Chaulnes line.*

    (*a*) Is repaired to Petit Blangy.

    (*b*) Old Blangy siding is being restored.

    (*c*) Most forward railhead at present is Longueau.

3. *Amiens-Clermont line.*

    (*a*) Is in running order throughout, but is not used owing to proximity of enemy.

    (*b*) Boves station can be taken into use if required.

    (*c*) Most forward railhead at present is Longueau.

4. Further·repairs to these lines will be undertaken by Army.

B.—RAILHEADS

1. The following advance railheads will be opened when the situation admits :—

Lines			Railheads
Amiens–Albert..	..	..	Corbie.
Amiens–Chaulnes	..	..	Longueau.
			Blangy.
			Villers Bretonneux.
Amiens–Clermont	..	..	Boves.

2. The attached (Table I) shows the railheads on zero day.

C.—ROADS

1. Roads will be repaired by Corps as follows, immediately the tactical situation admits :—

    (*a*) III. Corps ..   .. Corbie–Sailly Laurette.

    (*b*) Australian Corps   .. Amiens–Villers Carbonnel.

    (*c*) Canadian Corps   .. Amiens—Roye.

2. Corps will reconnoitre lateral communications as soon as possible, repair temporarily those required for immediate use, and report to A.H.Q. those which they propose to put under permanent repair.

3. Companies now working on defences under corps will not be sent to work on zero day, but will be held in readiness for work · on forward roads as soon as the situation admits.

TABLE I.—RAILHEADS ON ZERO DAY

Formation	Ammunition	Supplies	R.E. Stores	Ambulance Trains	Stone
Tank Corps.				Wounded will be evacuated in trains nearest to C.C.S. to which they are taken.	
3rd Brigade	} Flesselles	Third Army Prouzel Poulainville	Third Army Prouzel Poulainville		—
4th Brigade					
5th Brigade					
Cavalry Corps.				Saleux, or Longueau, or Amiens, or St. Roch, or Crouy.	
1st Cavalry Div. ..	} Saleux	} St. Leger-les-Domart Saleux St. Leger-les-Domart	} Prouzel or Vecquemont		—
2nd Cavalry Div. ..					
3rd Cavalry Div. ..					
Corps Troops ..					
III Corps.					Poulainville Vignacourt and Ville le Marclet }
12th Div.	} Flesselles and Poulainville	} Poulainville	} Poulainville	} Vignacourt and Pernois	
18th Div.					
47th Div.					
58th Div.	} Vignacourt	} Vignacourt			
Corps Troops ..					

TABLE I—RAILHEADS ON ZERO DAY (continued)

Formation	Ammunition	Supplies	R.E. Stores	Ambulance Trains	Stone
Australian Corps. 1st Australian Div. 2nd Australian Div. 3rd Australian Div. 4th Australian Div. 5th Australian Div. Corps Troops ..	Saleux and Flesselles	Ailly-sur-Somme Lamotte Brebiere Poulainville Ailly sur Somme Lamotte Brebiere Ailly-sur-Somme	Poulainville, Vecquemont and Montieres	Vignacourt or Saleux or Longueau, or Amiens, or St. Roch or Crouy or Longpre les Corps Saints.	Hangest, Montieres, Longueau and Petit Blangy, if ready.
32nd Div... ..	Flesselles	Hangest	Poulainville	Vignacourt and Pernois	—
Canadian Corps. 1st Canadian Div. 2nd Canadian Div. 3rd Canadian Div. 4th Canadian Div. Corps Troops ..	Bacouel	Prouzel Saleux Prouzel	Prouzel	Saleux or Longueau or Amiens or St. Roch or Crouy	Longueau and Boves, when open

D.—CANALS

1. The Somme canal is now open for barges to the steel tank bridge at Lamotte Brebiere, but the quay at this place cannot be used until this bridge is removed.

2. The canal will be utilised under Army arrangements and corps concerned will be informed.

E.—AMMUNITION

1. The numbers and natures of guns to be supplied with ammunition are given in Fourth Army Secret No. 32 (G), dated 31st July, 1918.

2. The numbers of rounds per gun to be dumped at or near the guns are :—

18-pdr. ..	.. 600	6-inch How.	..	400
4.5.-in. How.	.. 500	8-inch How.	..	400
60-pdr. ..	.. 400	9.2-in. How.	..	400
6-in. Gun	.. 400	12-inch How.	..	200

When these amounts have been drawn and echelons are complete, further drawings are to be confined strictly to the amounts required to replace actual, NOT estimated, expenditure.

3. The following amount of ammunition will be held in reserve for the Cavalry Corps at Saleux :—

					Rounds
13-pdr. H.E.	..	..	..	..	10,000
13-pdr. Shrapnel	..	..	..	..	20,000
Total		..	..	..	30,000

4. Ammunition railheads, dumps and refilling points are given in Table II attached.

5. Attention is drawn to Fourth Army Standing Orders (A. and Q. Branch), Part I, paras. 613, *et seq.* [Not available].

Ammunition for Tank Corps

6. The following total amounts of ammunition will be maintained for Tank Corps at Flesselles :—

					Rounds
6-pdr. H.E.	..	..	..	..	50,000
6-pdr. Case	..	..	..	..	10,000
S.A.A. ..	..	..	..	..	5,000,000
Pistol, Webley	..	..	..	..	100,000

F.—SUPPLIES

Cavalry Corps

1. All Cavalry Divisions will work on the double echelon system.

2. All units will carry three days' Iron Rations, and 20 lb. oats per horse, on man, horse, and A2 Echelon.

3. Issues to complete to above scale have been authorised as follows :—

Item	Quantity	From
Oats ..	480,000 lb.	G.H.Q. Reserve, St. Riquier
Iron rations	48,000 rations	Army Reserve, La Folie

4. Proportion of fresh to preserved rations on pack train, will be as 35 per cent. is to 65 per cent.

All Corps

5. The following extra supplies have been issued to Corps through D.D.S. & T., Fourth Army :—

Item	Cavalry Corps	III. Corps	Canadian Corps	Australian Corps
Chloride of Line ..	—	—	—	5 tons
Solidified alcohol ..	12,000	62,000	36,000	60,000
P. of W. rations ..	—	—	—	3,000
Pea Soup and Oxo	—	—	—	50,000
Rum, gallons ..	—	—	900	1,500
Iron rations .'.	42,000	12,000	38,000	19,000
Petrol tins for water	1,300	6,000	8,000	7,900

Supplies for Tank Corps

6. The following quantities of petrol, oil and grease have been issued :—

(a) *To 4th Brigade at Saleux—*

Petrol A.	80,000 gallons
Price's Engine Oil ..	4,000 gallons
Steam Cylinder, Thick ..	10,000 gallons
Vacuum A.	8,000 gallons
Grease	20,000 lbs.

(b) *To 5th Brigade at Poulainville—*

Petrol A.	80,000 gallons
Price's Engine Oil	4,000 gallons
Vacuum A.	8,000 gallons
Steam Cylinder, Thick ..	10,000 gallons
Grease	20,000 lbs.

7. The following reserve of petrol, etc., has been ordered up from Rouen, and will commence to arrive on 8th August, 1918. Twelve truck-loads will be put into Longueau, for 4th Brigade, the remainder into Prouzel, for whole of tanks :—

Petrol A.	40,000 gallons
Price's Engine Oil	2,000 gallons
Vacuum A.	4,000 gallons
Steam Cylinder, Thick ...	5,000 gallons
Grease	10,000 lbs.

G.—Water

1. A map showing initial and forward water facilities has been issued to those concerned.

2. Sterilisers and 30-cwt. Garford lorries have been allotted as follows :—

	Sterilisers	Garford Lorries
Cav. Corps	–	20
III. Corps	2	20
Canadian Corps	3	20
Australian Corps	4	1

3. The following locations are suggested for the sterilisers in the forward area :—

Corps	River	No.	Location	Map reference
III. Corps	Ancre	1	Mericourt l'Abbe	
	Ancre	1	Treux	
Australian	Somme	2	Sailly Laurette..	
Corps	Somme	1	Cerisy	
	Somme	1	Varie-sous-Corbie	
			or	[By
			Bouzencourt ..	Coordinates.
Canadian	Luce	1	Domart.. ..	Omitted].
Corps		1	Hangard ..	
		1	Demuin ..	
			or	
			Aubercourt ..	

4. Sites for these locations will be reconnoitred as soon as circumstances permit.

5. It should be remembered that :—

   (a) Suction lift for pumps should not exceed 6 feet below ground level.

   (b) A hard standing is required, if possible off the road, for the lorry, which weighs 5 tons when full.

   (c) Suitable traffic routes must be provided for water carts, without interfering with main traffic.

   (d) Horse water points must not be in the immediate neighbourhood of the source of supply.

H.—Ordnance

Gun Park

1. An Advanced Gun Park will be formed at Longueau.

2. The following stores, to be sent up as soon as circumstances admit, are packed ready at Calais. They fill a special train, which can be dispatched six hours after receipt of order.

Store	*No.*
60-pdr. equipments, complete with all essential stores	2
6-inch. How. equipments, complete with all essential stores	2
18-pdr. equipments, complete with all essential stores	12
4.5-inch How. equipments, complete with all essential stores	6
13-pdr. R.H.A. equipments, complete with all essential stores	4
60-pdr. Ammunition wagon and limber	1
18-pdr. Ammunition wagons and limbers	4
4.5-inch How. Ammunition wagons and limbers ..	2
13-pdr. R.H.A. Ammunition wagons and limbers ..	2
Vickers guns, complete	50
Lewis guns, complete	200
Hotchkiss guns, complete	30
3-inch Stokes motars, complete	6
Hotchkiss gun strips (30-round)	5,000
Vickers gun barrels	100
Vickers gun belts..	400
Vickers gun belt boxes	200

3. The personnel required to receive these stores at Longueau will be provided by the D.D.O.S., Fourth Army.

4. The main gun park at Pont Remy will be moved forward to Longueau as soon as the situation makes the measure desirable.

Extra Stores

5. Table III attached, shows the Ordnance stores and tentage demanded by, and issued to, corps, etc., in addition to establishments or stocks held by them.

6. Workshops are allotted as follows :—

Formation	*Description of shop*	*Shop Nos.*	*Location*
III. Corps.. ..	Light.	20, 29,	Pierregot.
	Light.	23, 47,	Cardonnette.
	Medium.	10, 17.	Vaux–Amienois.
Australian Corps ..	Light.	18, 53,	Amiens.
	Light.	17, 22,	Boutillerie.
	Medium.	2, 25.	Montieres.
Canadian Corps ..	Light.	8, 26,	St. Fuscien.
	Light.	2, 24,	Sains.
	Medium.	1, 7.	Saleux.
Cavalry Corps ..	Light.	15	Picquigny.

TABLE II.—AMMUNITION RAILHEADS, DUMPS AND REFILLING
POINTS

| Formation | Railheads | Dumps | Refilling Points | |
			Heavy and Siege	Field
Fourth Army	Flesselles. Hangest. Vignacourt.	Bois du Gard. Soues–Picquigny road. Flesselles.	— — —	— — —
III. Corps	Flesselles. Poulainville	*Field Artillery—* A.17.b.9.9. B.20.d.6.2. *Heavy and Siege Artillery—* B.8.b.8.6. A.6.d. H.11.d.1.1. H.12.a.7.9.	Battery positions	I.35.b.7.6. C.19.a.4.4. J.7.d.4.5. I.18.d.4.2. B.30.b.6.7. C.11.a.5.5. U.21.c.8.3.
Australian Corps	Saleux and Flesselles.	*Field Artillery—* G.24.b. G.36.c. R.26.d. *Heavy Artillery—* G.6.c. R.21.c.	Battery positions	H.16.d. N.19.d. N.6.c.
Canadian Corps	Bacouel.	—	Battery positions	M.36.a.15.3. M.36.d.4.6. T.1.d.4.3.
Cavalry Corps	Saleux.	Saleux.	—	—

TABLE III.—ORDNANCE STORES AND TENTAGE DEMANDED BY, AND ISSUED, TO CORPS, ETC., IN ADDITION TO ESTABLISHMENTS OR STOCKS HELD BY THEM

Item	III. Corps	Canadian Corps	Australian Corps	A.C.A.A.	Area Comdt. Cavillon	Area Comdt. Saleux
Harness, lead, sets	54	—	—	—	—	—
Lewis guns, S.A.	—	100	100	—	—	—
Wire cutters, S.A.	—	3,600	—	—	—	—
Wire cutters, L.H.	—	500	—	—	—	—
Wire cutters, Mark V	70	150	300	—	—	—
Yukon packs	—	—	60	—	—	—
Racks for carrying water tins	328	500	230	—	—	—
Hot food containers	60	—	400	—	—	—
Waterbottles with carriers and slings	5,000	40,000	20,600	—	—	—
Packsaddles	280	150	230	—	—	—
Ration bags	12,000	—	—	—	—	—
Water carts and harness	—	—	20	—	—	—
Gloves, barbed wire	80	2,400	—	—	—	—
Tarpaulins	—	150	—	—	—	—
Carriers, ammunition, emergency, 18-pdr.	300	—	—	—	—	—
Carriers, ammunition, emergency, 4.5-inch	450	—	—	—	—	—
Tents	450	400	450	107	12	12
Trench shelters	300	600	2,100	—	500	500

I.—LABOUR

British labour companies, now employed on defences under corps, will not proceed to work on zero day, but will be held in readiness for work on forward roads directly the situation admits.

J.—MEDICAL ARRANGEMENTS

The following is the allotment of C.C.Ss., etc., to corps.

	Casualty Clearing Stations (for sick and wounded)	Ambulance Convoys	Advanced Depot of Medical Stores	Laboratories
III. Corps	Nos. 4 and 41 (Pernois)	No. 10 and 20 cars from No. 1 M.A.C.*	No. 13 (Vignacourt)	No. 19 Mob. Lab. (Vignacourt)
Canadian Corps	Nos. 4 and 47 (Crouy)	No. 42* and 20 cars from No. 1 M.A.C.*	No. 14 (Crouy)	No. 5 (Can.) Mob. Lab. (Crouy)
Australian Corps	Nos. 20 and 61 (Vignacourt)	No. 3 and 20 cars from No. 1 M.A.C.*	No. 13	No. 5 (Can.) Mob. Lab.
Cavalry Corps	Nos. 4 and 47 (Crouy)	No. 42	No. 14	No. 5 (Can.) Mob. Lab.

* Arrives 7th August 1918.

No. 12 Casualty Clearing Station will receive all N.Y.D.N., N.Y.D., Gas, S.I.W., Ophthalmic, Dental, Nose, Ear and Throat, Venereal and Dysentry cases.

Nos. 53 and 55 Casualty Clearing Stations and No. 41 Stationary Hospital will receive cases of sick from units in the back areas.

Each Casualty Clearing Station receiving sick and wounded from Corps has been reinforced by three surgical teams and eight nursing sisters.

Application for additional ambulance cars, medical equipment, etc., should be made to D.M.S., Fourth Army.

Two ambulance trains will be garaged at each of the following sidings : Crouy, Vignacourt, Pernois. Four more trains will be available if required.

K.—REMOUNTS

1. Urgent demands for remounts will be wired direct to D.D.R., Fourth Army.

2. Complete train loads of remounts will be despatched from the Base to :—

    (a) Vignacourt.

    (b) Aily-sur-Somme.

3. Horses in numbers less than a train load will be drawn from Remount Depot, Abbeville. Conducting parties must be provided by the formations drawing the remounts. They will stage the night at Picquigny.

L.—Veterinary

1. Veterinary Collecting Posts will be arranged by corps according to requirements.

2. Veterinary Evacuation Stations will be located as follows :—

Formation	Place	Method of Evacuation
Fourth Army V.E.S.	Picquigny ..	By road to Abbeville.
III Corps .. ⎱ Australian Corps ⎰	Olincourt Chateau	By rail from Vignacourt.
Canadian Corps ..	Saleux	By rail from Saleux.

M.—Traffic Control

1. The following traffic control units are at present attached to the Fourth Army.

Half No. 2 Traffic Control Squadron.
One troop attached III Corps.
Half troop in Army Reserve.
No. 2 Traffic Control Company.
Half company attached Australian Corps.
Half company attached Canadian Corps, and in Amiens district.

2. Another Traffic Control Company has been applied for and will be used for traffic work at railheads in case of an advance.

3. Attention is drawn to A.R.O. 2039 [traffic control], which will be rigidly enforced.

N.—Prisoners of War

Cages

1. Army and Corps prisoner of war cages are located as follows :—

Formation	Main Cage	Advanced Cage
Fourth Army ..	Poulainville. Flesselles. Flixecourt.	— — —
III Corps ..	Molliens.	Behencourt.
Canadian Corps ..	Boves.	Boves–Gentelles road.
Australian Corps ..	Vecquemont.	Aubigny.

Evacuation

2. Prisoners of war will be evacuated under divisional arrangements to Corps Headquarters and thence to the Army cage at Poulainville, under corps arrangements.

3. Only those required for further interrogation will be sent to Flixecourt. The remainder will be despatched by rail from Poulainville.

4. Flesselles is mainly an overflow cage. If it is necessary to use it, the prisoners not wanted will be railed away from Flesselles.

5. Infantry Divisions will take over prisoners of war captured by the Cavalry, and give a receipt for the numbers.

O.—ACCOMMODATION

1. Corps will be responsible that all tents and trench shelters in their areas are collected and safeguarded directly they are vacated, and taken forward if and when required.

2. Tents and trench shelters which are not taken forward will be collected at a suitable place to be selected by corps, placed under guard, and held in reserve. A.H.Q. will be notified of the numbers of tents and trench shelters in these reserves.

3. No tents or trench shelters are to be removed from the areas administered directly by the Army. Commanding Officers will be held responsible that this order is obeyed.

P.—CIVILIAN INHABITANTS

Examination, Evacuation, and Feeding of Civilians in captured Territory

1. Attention is drawn to Fourth Army Standing Orders (A. & Q.), 502–535, which must be observed.

2. The following points must receive special attention (G.H.Q., M.3663, 25.3.17) :—

   (*a*) A.P.M.s of Divisions will report at once by despatch rider, to P.M., Fourth Army, the presence of civilians in captured territory.

   (*b*) A.P.M.s must be on the spot at least as soon as the Intelligence.

   (*c*) Use of Gendarmerie in guarding civilians.

   (*d*) Posting of " Orders".

   (*e*) Use of learners in Provost duties as Town Majors in forward localities. Their main duties will be :—

   (i) To ascertain the number of inhabitants under their control.

(ii) To ensure that no civilian gets away.

(iii) To arrange for daily check roll.

(iv) To send daily reports to A.P.M. Corps, repeated to P.M., Army.

(v) To arrange for distribution of rations and to obtain receipts for same.

(f) Civilians found in a town which has been utterly destroyed will be evacuated as soon as possible.

(g) In towns left with sufficient houses to accommodate the civilians, it may be necessary only to evacuate those who were non-residents of the place; but, if the place is under shellfire, the whole population will be evacuated.

(h) Civilians found in open country without shelter will be evacuated at once.

(i) Civilians will be evacuated as follows :—

First stage.—From the captured towns or villages to some place where transport can be got up.

Second stage.—To railhead, by transport, arranged by the corps concerned.

Third stage.—From railhead, in empty trucks, to the Examination Centre, where they will be met by an officer specially detailed to look after them.

An A.P.M. " Learner," with Gendarmes and an Interpreter, will accompany each party from the captured territory to the Examination Centre, where they will hand them over to the French Authorities. They will then return under orders issued by the A.P.M. Corps concerned. Corps A.P.M.s will arrange to send information regarding the evacuation and the expected times of arrivals at railheads and Examining Centre to P.M., Fourth Army, and R.T.O. concerned.

Examination

3. Civilians allowed to remain in recaptured villages or towns will be examined by I (b) Army or corps ; those evacuated will be examined by I (b) Army, and none will be allowed their liberty until the Intelligence Officers are satisfied as to their being above suspicion.

Examination may take place at all or any of the following places :—

(a) The captured town.

(b) Collecting points along the road to railhead.

(c) Examination centre.

4. It must be impressed on all M.P.s that they must work in the closest touch with, and do everything possible to meet the wishes of, the Intelligence.

Circulation of Civilians during an Advance

Barrier line

5. A barrier line, consisting of a chain of posts manned by the French Provost, has been established, to prevent the civilian population now in the " Forbidden Zone " moving forward with the troops. No civilians will be allowed EAST of this line until further orders.

Intelligence Police and Provost Agents will patrol the line.

Examining Posts

6. Only in exceptional cases will civilians be allowed to cross the line of Examining Posts from East to West or West to East.

7. Passes will not be accepted unless they bear the British Square stamp.

8. The exceptional cases would include :—

    (*a*) Persons who are absolutely necessary for revictualling the Communes.

    (*b*) Doctors.

    (*c*) Midwives.

    (*d*) Government employees on duty.

Movement within the " Forbidden Zone "

9. Civilian circulation will be reduced to a minimum within the " Forbidden Zone", in order to facilitate the movements of troops.

10. Only such carts as are necessary for revictualling will be allowed on traffic circuits and they must travel at stated hours.

APPENDIX VIII

G.H.Q. OPERATION ORDER OF 5TH AUGUST, 1918

O.A.D. 900/14

General Sir H. S. Rawlinson, Bt.,
    Commanding British Fourth Army.

General Debeney,
    Commanding French First Army.

1. In continuation of Operation Order No. O.A.D. 900/3, dated 29th July ; in view of the more extensive nature of the operations which are being undertaken by the French as described verbally to Army Commanders today, it is probable that in the event of an initial success the battle will develop into one of considerable magnitude.

In order to maintain the fight and to take full advantage of any success gained, three British divisions are being assembled in general reserve close behind the battle front. Further divisions are being held in readiness behind the rest of the British front to move south as circumstances may require.

2. The first object of the operation is to disengage Amiens and the Paris–Amiens railway line by pushing forward and seizing the old defensive line Hangest–Harbonnieres (*vide* O.A.D. 900/3, dated 29th July).

The next object is to push forward in the general direction.of the line Roye–Chaulnes *with the least possible delay*, thrusting the enemy back with determination in the general direction of Ham, and so facilitating the operations of the French from the front Noyon–Montdidier.

3. Please acknowledge receipt.

H. A. LAWRENCE,
Lieut.-General,
Chief of the General Staff.

FOURTH ARMY OPERATION ORDERS OF 6TH AUGUST, 1918

1. The continuation of Fourth Army Order No. 20 (G), dated 31/7/18.

2. In view of the more extensive nature of the operations which are being undertaken by the French, as described verbally to Corps Commanders today, it is probable that, in the event of initial success, the battle will develop into one of considerable magnitude.

3. In order to maintain the fight, and to take full advantage of any success gained, three British Divisions are being assembled by G.H.Q. in General Reserve close behind the battle front (32nd, 17th, 63rd). Further divisions are being held in readiness behind the rest of the British Front to move south as circumstances may require.

4. The first object of the operation is to disengage Amiens and the Paris–Amiens railway line by pushing forward and seizing the old Amiens defence line Hangest–Harbonnieres–Méricourt (*vide*, Fourth Army No. 20 (G), dated 31/7/18, para. 1 and map).

5. The next object is to push forward in the general direction of the line Roye–Chaulnes with the least possible delay, thrusting

the enemy back with determination in the general direction of Ham, and so facilitating the operations of the French from the front Noyon–Montdidier.

6. With the above object in view, the Cavalry Corps, as soon as they have accomplished their first mission (*vide* Fourth Army No. 32 (G), para. 13 (*a*)), will push forward in the direction of the line Roye–Chaulnes with the least possible delay.

7. The Canadian Corps, which will be reinforced if necessary by further divisions, will press on in support of the cavalry, keeping close touch with the French on their right.

8. The Australian Corps, pivoting on the Somme between Méricourt and Etinehem, will swing forward their right so as to keep touch with the advance of the Canadian Corps.

9. The III Corps will push forward, as early as possible, and gain the old Amiens defence line between Etinehem and Dernancourt. This position will be consolidated and form a defensive flank to the forward movement of the Fourth Army South of the Somme.

10. Acknowledge by wire.

A. A. MONTGOMERY,
Major-General,
General Staff, Fourth Army.

APPENDIX X

G.H.Q. OPERATION ORDER OF 8TH AUGUST, 1918

General Sir H. S. Rawlinson, Bt., G.C.V.O., K.C.B., K.C.M.G., Commanding Fourth Army.

O.A.D. 900/20

1. Having secured the old Amiens defence line,[1] Quesnel–Caix–Harbonnieres–Morcourt, the Fourth Army will push forward to-morrow and establish itself on the general line Roye–Chaulnes–Bray-sur-Somme–Fernancourt.

Outposts will be thrown forward well to the east of this latter line and touch maintained with the enemy.

Particular attention should be paid to the left flank and a strong position established north of the river Somme.

2. The French First Army on your right is continuing its attack to-morrow with its left in the direction of Roye. French forces will also operate on the front Montdidier–Autheuil.

---

[1] See Map 1 and Sketch 2.

3. The cavalry will continue to operate under your orders and will act on your right flank in such a manner as to facilitate the advance of the French First Army.

J. H. DAVIDSON,
Major-General for Lieut.-General,
Chief of the General Staff.

APPENDIX XI

FOURTH ARMY OPERATIONS ORDERS OF 8TH AUGUST, 1918[1]

1. The Fourth Army will push forward to-morrow and establish itself on the general line Roye–Chaulnes–Bray-sur-Somme–Dernancourt. Particular attention should be paid to the left flank, and a strong position established north of the river Somme. South of the Somme, outposts will be thrown forward well to the east of the above line and touch maintained with the enemy.

2. The First French Army on the right is continuing its attack to-morrow with its left in the direction of Roye.

French forces will also operate on the front Montdidier [three miles south of Gratebus] – Autheuil [16 miles south-east of Montidier].

3. The boundary between the Fourth Army and the First French Army will be the Amiens–Roye road (inclusive to Fourth Army).

4. The cavalry will operate on the right of the Fourth Army in such a manner as to gain the objectives allotted to the Canadian Corps and to facilitate the advance of the French First Army.

5. The Canadian Corps will advance to-morrow with their right on the Amiens–Roye road (inclusive) and their left on the Amiens–Nesle railway (inclusive), view a view to establishing themselves on the general line Roye–Hattencourt–Hallu.

6. (a) The Australian Corps, conforming in the first instance to the advance of the Canadian Corps, will advance to-morrow with a view to establishing themselves on the general line Lihons–Framerville–Méricourt.

---

[1] See Map 1 and Sketch 2.

(*b*) When the III Corps have reached the general line L.26–L.7–E.29–Dernancourt,[1] the Australian Corps will advance their left flank and occupy the general line Lihons–Chuignolles.

7. The III Corps will advance to-morrow to the general line L.26–L.7–E.29–Dernancourt[1] and consolidate a strong position as a defensive flank to the Fourth Army, which will be held at all costs.

8. The G.O.C. Canadian Corps will decide the hour at which the advance of his Corps will commence, informing the Cavalry Corps and Australian Corps as early as possible.

The G.O.C. III Corps will decide the hour at which the advance of his Corps will commence, informing the Australian Corps as early as possible.

9. Acknowledge by wire.

A. A. Montgomery,

Major-General,

General Staff, Fourth Army.

Appendix XII

FOURTH ARMY OPERATION ORDERS OF
9th AUGUST, 1918, No. 1[2]

1. Our troops, according to latest reports, have reached the approximate line Bouchoir – Warvillers – Rosières – Framerville–Méricourt (exclusive).

The French First Army, according to latest reports, have reached the general line Pierrepont–Arvillers and will continue their advance to.morrow. French forces will also be attacking to-morrow on the front south of Montdidier.

2. The Fourth Army will continue its advance with the object of establishing itself on the general line Roye–Chaulnes–Bray–Dernancourt.

3. The dividing line between the First French Army and the Fourth Army will be the Amiens–Roye road as far east as la Cambuse cross roads, thence north of Goyencourt and south of Gruny (see also attached map).[3]

---

[1] The line L.26–L.7–E.29 runs roughly from the eastern side of Etinehem Spur to a point a mile and a half north-west of Bray and Somme, and thence to one two thousand yards south of Meaulte.

[2] See Sketches 7 and 4.

[3] Not reproduced.

4. The cavalry will operate on the right of the Fourth Army in such a manner as to gain the objectives allotted to the Canadian Corps and to facilitate the advance of the First French Army.

5. (a) The Canadian Corps will advance to-morrow with their right on the Amiens–Roye road (inclusive) as far as the La Cambuse cross roads, thence north of Goyencourt and south of Gruny, and their left on the Amiens–Nesle railway (inclusive).

(b) The 32nd Division is released from G.H.Q. reserve and placed at the disposal of the Canadian Corps.[1]

(c) The 13th Tank Battalion is transferred to the Canadian Corps from Army reserve forthwith.

6. (a) The Australian Corps, conforming in the first instance to the advance of the Canadian Corps, will advance to-morrow with a view to establishing itself on the general line Lihons–Framerville–Méricourt.

(b) Orders regarding the further action of the Australian Corps' left will be issued later.

7. Orders as regards the action of the III Corps will be issued alter, when the result of the attack this afternoon is known.

8. The Canadian Corps will fix the time for the advance to commence, and inform the Australian Corps, Cavalry Corps, and French First Army as early as possible.

9. Acknowledge by wire.

A. A. MONTGOMERY,

Major-General,

General Staff, Fourth Army.

APPENDIX XIII

FOURTH ARMY OPERATION ORDERS OF
9TH AUGUST, 1918, No. 2[2]

1. In continuation of Fourth Army, No. 20 (G), dated 9th August.[3]

2. The Australian Corps will take over from the III Corps as far north as the Corbie-Bray road (exclusive), as far east as K.17 central, thence the boundary will run to L.8 central (*see* attached map).[4]

---

[1] This was subsequently cancelled.
[2] See Sketch 7.
[3] Appendix XII.
[4] Map not reproduced. K 17 is the road junction half a mile east of the Brickyard on the Corbie–Bray-sur-Somme road. From this point the boundary was to run north-east.

3. The transfer will take place and command pass at 8 a.m., 10th August.

4. (a) On the transfer taking place the following troops will forthwith be transferred from the III Corps to the Australian Corps :—

131st Regiment, 33rd American Division.
58th Divisional Artillery.
5th A.F.A. Brigade.
51st Brigade R.G.A.

(b) As soon as possible after the transfer of front has taken place the III Corps will transfer to the Australian Corps the 66th Brigade H.Q., 132nd Regiment, and 124th M.G. Battalion of the 33rd American Division.

5. The Australian Corps will advance their left flank to-morrow and occupy the general line Lihons–Chuignolles.

6. The III Corps, if not already in possession of it, will advance to the general line L.7–E.29–Dernancourt.[1] This advance will conform with the advance of the Australian Corps.

7. G.O.C. Australian Corps will decide the time when this advance will commence, and will inform the III Corps as early as possible.

8. The dividing line between counter-battery zones will be the E. and W. grid line through L.7.c.0.0.

9. Acknowledge by wire.

A. A. Montgomery,
Major-General,
General Staff, Fourth Army.

Appendix XIV

G.H.Q. OPERATION ORDER OF 10th AUGUST, 1918[2]

O.A.D. 900/22

General Sir H. S. Rawlinson, Bt.,
Commanding British Fourth Army.
General Debeney,
Commanding French First Army.
General The Hon. Sir J. H. G. Byng,
Commanding British Third Army.

---

[1] The line L7 – E29 runs from a point a mile and a half north-west of Bray-sur-Somme to one two thousand yards south of Meaulte.

[2] See Sketches 12 and 15.

1. The offensive operations of the French First Army and the British Fourth Army will be continued with a view to securing the general line Guiscard–Ham–Peronne and gaining the crossings of the river Somme.

The French Third Army will be co-operating on the right of the French First Army with a view to exploiting the success of that Army and·clearing the neighbourhood of Noyon of the enemy.

2. The dividing line between the French First Army and British Fourth Army will be as laid down in O.A.D. 900/21, dated 9th August, 1918,[1] extended due eastwards to Ham (inclusive to French).

That portion of the British Fourth Army north of the Somme will conform to the general movement.

3. The British Third Army will carry out raids and minor operations in order to ascertain the enemy's intention on the Albert–Arras front, and will take immediate advantage of any favourable situation which the main operations may create and push advanced guards in the general direction of Bapaume.

J. H. DAVIDSON,

Major-General for Lieut.-General,

Chief of the General Staff.

APPENDIX XV

FOURTH ARMY OPERATION ORDERS OF 10TH AUGUST, 1918[2]

1. Our line has been advanced to-day, according to the latest reports received, to La Cambuse cross roads–centre of Parvillers–Fouquescourt (exclusive)–Chilly–Lihons (inclusive)–Framerville–(inclusive)–Méricourt (inclusive)–Bois des Tailles (inclusive)–Dernancourt.

2. The French, according to the latest reports received, have reached the line Conchy les Pots–Bus–Marquivillers–Andechy.

3. The Fourth Army has been ordered to press on to the Somme between Ham (exclusive) and Peronne and establish bridgeheads on the right bank of the river.

---

[1] Not printed here.

[2] See Sketch 8 ; and for the French Sketch 4.

4. The First French Army is advancing on our right with its left directed on Ham (inclusive).

The boundary between the First French Army and the Canadian Corps will be Gruny–Marche Allouarde–Billancourt–Languevoisin–Offoy, all inclusive to Canadian Corps.

5. The Cavalry Corps (less one Brigade) will advance to-morrow with a view to assisting the Canadian Corps to secure the line of the Somme from Offoy (inclusive) to St. Christ (exclusive).[1]

6. The Canadian Corps will continue its advance with a view to securing the line of the Somme and establishing bridgeheads on the right bank between Offoy (inclusive) and St. Christ (exclusive).[1]

7. (a) The Australian Corps will continue its advance with a view to securing the line of the Somme between St. Christ (inclusive) and Bray and establishing bridgeheads on the right bank of the river.

(b) The Cavalry Corps will place one Brigade of Cavalry at the disposal óf the Australian Corps forthwith to assist in the above operations.

8. The boundary between the Canadian Corps and Australian Corps will be Chaulnes–Marchelepot–Cizancourt (all inclusive to the Canadian Corps).

9. (a) The III. Corps will establish a strong position on the general line L.26–L.7–E.29–Dernancourt,[2] which will be held at all costs as a defensive flank to the Fourth Army.

(b) In the event of the left flank of the Australian Corps north of the Somme being advanced, the III. Corps will conform.

10. The G.O.C. Canadian Corps will decide on the hour at which the advance tomorrow will commence, which should be as early as possible.

11. Acknowledge by wire.

A. A. MONTGOMERY,

Major-General,

General Staff, Fourth Army.

---

[1] For these places see End–paper A. Offoy is eight miles S.S.E. of St. Christ.

[2] The line L26 – L7 – E29 runs roughly from the eastern side of the Etinhem spur to a point a mile and a half north-west of Bray-sur-Somme, and thence to one 3 miles south of Albert.

APPENDIX XVI

FOURTH ARMY OPERATION ORDERS OF 11TH AUGUST, 1918[1]

1. According to latest reports received the Fourth Army has reached the following line :—

La Cambuse–western outskirts of Damery–Parvillers (exclusive) – Fouquescourt (inclusive) – Chilly (inclusive) – Lihons (inclusive) – Rainecourt (inclusive) – Mericourt (inclusive)–ridge west of Bray–Amiens Outer Defences at Dernancourt.

2. The First French Army, according to the latest reports received, has reached the following line :—

West of Tilloloy [4 miles S.S.W. of Roye] (exclusive)– Dancourt (exclusive) – Armancourt (exclusive) – Andechy (inclusive)–La Cambuse [1½ miles north of Andechy].

3. The enemy's opposition is stiffening all along the Fourth Army front, and two more fresh divisions have been identified today.

4. The advance of the Fourth Army to the Somme will not be continued until all available artillery can be brought up in support and the number of tanks now with Corps increased.

Further orders as regards the future advance will be issued later.

Any minor improvements to the line now held will be made at the discretion of Corps Commanders.

5. The 13th Tank Battalion will rejoin the 5th Brigade Tank Corps under arrangements to be made between the Canadian and Australian Corps.

6. The whole of the Cavalry Corps is being withdrawn into reserve and will be situated as follows (vide Fourth Army Telegram, No. G.862 of 11th August) :—

Cavalry Corps H.Q., St. Fuscien [4 miles south of Amiens].

One division in the Somme Valley between Rivery and Vecquemont [east of Amiens, north of the Ancre].

One division about Ignaucourt and Cayeux.

One division in the Noye Valley between Ailly [10 miles south of Amiens] and Boves [8 miles south-east of Amiens].

7. The 3rd Brigade Tank Corps will come into Army Reserve and be located at E.20.a.2.8 north of le Quesnel.

8. Acknowledge by wire.

A. A. MONTGOMERY,
Major-General.
General Staff, Fourth Army.

---

[1] See Sketch 8 ; and for the French, Sketch 4.

APPENDIX XVII

MARÉCHAL FOCH'S INSTRUCTION OF 12TH AUGUST, 1918[1]

(Translation)

G.Q.G., A., 12th August, 1918.

Maréchal Foch, Commander-in-Chief of the Allied Armies to Field-Marshal Haig, Commander-in-Chief of the British Armies in France, and to General Pétain, Commander-in-Chief of the Armies of the North and North-East.

The maximum results possible must be obtained from the battle now in progress, and the deep penetration obtained on the 8th, 9th and 10th August by the British Fourth Army and the French First Army must be exploited for all it is worth.

1. The results required have already been laid down as regards the area between the Somme and the Oise by General Directive No. 2.[2] They are to throw the enemy back on the Somme and seize the passages of the river at Ham and below it.

In view of the resistance offered by the enemy, there is no question of obtaining these results by pressing uniformly all along the front ; this would only lead to being weak everywhere.

On the contrary, it is a matter of using concentrated and powerful action at the most important points of the area, that is to say those whose possession would increase the enemy's disorganization, in particular would disturb his communications. These operations should be rapidly and strongly mounted by the rapid assembly and employment of the means available and appropriate to the nature of the resistance encountered (tanks, artillery, infantry in good condition . . .).

The operations of this nature to be undertaken are :—

(a) *As soon as possible*, an attack to gain possession of the road junction of Roye (that is to say, the Champien plateau to the east of that town) ; this attack will be executed by the French First Army and the right of the British Fourth Army, and be supported and exploited on the south by the French Third Army with a view to clearing the Noyon area.

(b) *Without delay*, an attack by the centre of the British Fourth Army from the area Lihons–Herleville, in a north-easterly direction for the purpose of capturing the Amiens–Brie main road, or at least keeping it under the fire of field guns. This action is to be combined with a thrust of the left of the British Fourth Army, eastward, in order to clear the enemy out of the loop of the Somme.

[1] See End–paper A.
[2] See " 1918 " Vol. II, p. 116.

2. These results may be increased to vast proportions by an extension of the attacks to the two flanks of the battle now in progress, on the one hand to the north of the Somme, on the other hand to the east of the Oise :

(*a*) To the north of the Somme, the attack of the British Third Army in the general direction of Bapaume–Péronne may have as consequence the outflanking of the defence which the enemy will no doubt put up on the Somme, and force him to make an even more definite retirement.

(*b*) To the east of the Oise the attack of the French Tenth Army in the direction of Chauny and the Chauny–Soissons road, in order to force the enemy to abandon the whole of the hilly and wooded massif extending between Noyon, Guiscard and Tergnier. These two attacks should be prepared with the greatest energy and without delay ; they will be launched as soon as the preparations permit.

The results obtained by the French Third Army with only its own resources show what can be attained by the extension of the offensive on the flank of a successful attack.

Since the 15th July, the enemy has engaged 120 divisions in the battle. There is an opportunity to-day which may not recur for a long time, and which demands from all an effort that the expected results fully justify.

The Commanders-in-Chief of the British and French Armies are requested to inform the Maréchal Commander-in-Chief of the Allied Armies on what dates and in what strength the attacks indicated above can be carried out. Our interests demand that they should take place as soon as possible and with the least interval of time possible between them.

Foch.

Appendix XVIII

G.H.Q. OPERATION ORDER OF 13th AUGUST, 1918[1]

O.A.D. 907

General The Hon. Sir J. H. G. Byng, K.C.B., K.C.M.G., M.V.O., Commanding Third Army.

The Field-Marshal Commanding-in-Chief directs that you should prepare an attack on the Moyenneville–Ablainzevelle front to be delivered at the earliest possible date.

---

[1] See Sketch 10 ; and for the French, Sketch 12.

The object of this attack is to break the enemy's defences on the front mentioned, and, if circumstances permit, to exploit the success gained in the direction of Bapaume.

These operations would be carried out subsequent to a successful attack by the French First Army and the British Fourth Army on the front Roye–Chaulnes as described in Operation Order, No. 900/23, dated 12th August (a copy of which has been sent to you)[1] and, in conjunction with those operations, aim at throwing the enemy back to and beyond the line Bapaume–Péronne.

In order to enable you to exploit a success gained and carry out the mission entrusted to you, the 3rd, 5th and 63rd, and later the 17th Divisions will be placed at your disposal, together with the Cavalry Corps (comprising 1st and 3rd Cavalry Divisions).

You will be informed without delay regarding the number of tanks and the amount of artillery which can be made available.

The outline of your plan of operations should be submitted as early as possible.

H. A. LAWRENCE,
Lieut.-General,
Chief of the General Staff.

APPENDIX XIX

G.H.Q. OPERATION ORDER OF 15TH AUGUST, 1918[2]

O.A.D. 907/2

General Sir H. S. Horne, K.C.B., K.C.M.G., Commanding First Army.

General The Hon. Sir J. H. G. Byng, K.C.B., K.C.M.G., M.V.O., Commanding Third Army.

General Sir H. S. Rawlinson, Bt., G.C.V.O., K.C.B., K.C.M.G., Commanding Fourth Army.

Lieut.-General Sir C. T. M. Kavanagh, K.C.B., C.V.O., D.S.O., Commanding Cavalry Corps.

Major-General H. J. Elles, C.B., D.S.O., Commanding Tank Corps.

---

[1] This gave the gist of Maréchal Foch's Instruction given in Appendix XVII.
[2] See Sketch 10.

1. In view of the enemy's withdrawal on the Third Army front, and the consequent change in conditions on the front of that Army, O.A.D. 907, dated 13th August, 1918, addressed to Third Army,[1] is modified as stated below.

2. The Third Army will press the enemy back energetically in the direction of Bapaume. This operation will be carried out without delay and every effort made to prevent the enemy from destroying road and rail communications.

The following additional troops are being placed at the disposal of the Third Army for the above purpose :—

> Cavalry Corps (less 1 division).
> Five battalions of tanks (156 tanks).
> 63rd Division.
> 17th Division, on relief in Fourth Army.
> 3rd Division ⎱ held temporarily in G.H.Q. reserve.
> 5th Division ⎰

3. The First Army[2] will be prepared to take advantage of any withdrawal, either in front of that Army or in front of the Third Army, by following up and pressing the enemy in the direction of Monchy-le-Preux, or, if conditions are favourable, delivering an attack on Orange Hill and Monchy-le-Preux. Preparations for this latter attack should be commenced at once.

For this purpose three battalions of tanks (105 tanks) are being placed at the disposal of First Army.

4. The Fourth Army will continue its preparations for attack south of the River Somme in accordance with O.A.D. 900/26, dated 14th August, 1918,[3] and will take advantage of any opportunities which may arise for gaining ground and driving the enemy back towards the River Somme.

North of the River Somme the Fourth Army will take advantage of a further hostile retirement on the front of the Third Army and, in co-operation with that Army, take steps to press the enemy and follow him up closely.

5. The Cavalry Corps, less 3rd Cavalry Division, will be placed at the disposal of the Third Army and be disposed in the first instance as follows :—

Corps H.Q.	Auxi-le-Chateau [30 miles west by south of Arras].
2nd Cavalry Division	To Auxi-le-Chateau area.
1st Cavalry Division	One brigade tonight, 15th/16th, and the remainder tomorrow night, 16th/17th, to the Third Army.

---

[1] Appendix XVIII.
[2] See Sketch 14.
[3] Not printed here.

Arrangements for the above moves will be made by Cavalry Corps direct with Armies concerned.

The 3rd Cavalry Division will remain for the present in the Somme Valley under the orders of the Fourth Army.

H. A. LAWRENCE,

Lieut.-General,

Chief of the General Staff.

APPENDIX XX

COMMANDER-IN-CHIEF'S TELEGRAM OF
22ND AUGUST, 1918

O.A.D. 911

General Sir H. Horne,
      First Army.
General Sir H. Plumer,
      Second Army.
General The Hon. Sir J. Byng,
      Third Army.
General Sir H. Rawlinson,
      Fourth Army.
General Sir W. R. Birdwood,
      Fifth Army
Lieut.-General Sir C. T. McM. Kavanagh,
      Cavalry Corps.

I request that Army Commanders will, without delay, bring to the notice of all subordinate leaders the changed conditions under which operations are now being carried on, and the consequent necessity for all ranks to act with the utmost boldness and resolution in order to get full advantage from the present favourable situation.

The effect of the two very severe defeats, and the continuous attacks to which the enemy has been subjected during the past month, has been to wear out his troops and disorganise his plans.

Our Second and Fifth Armies have taken their share in this effort to destroy the enemy, and already have gained considerable ground from him in the Lys sector of our front.

Today the French Tenth Army crossed the Ailette and reports that a Bavarian division fled in panic, carrying back with it another division which was advancing to its support.

Tomorrow, the attack of the Allied Armies on the whole front from Soissons to Neuville–Vitasse (near Arras) is to be continued.

The methods which we have followed, hitherto, in our battles with limited objectives when the enemy was strong, are no longer suited to his present condition.

The enemy has not the means to deliver counter-attacks on an extended scale, nor has he the numbers to hold a continuous position against the very extended advance which is now being directed upon him.

To turn the present situation to account, the most resolute offensive is everywhere desirable. Risks which a month ago would have been criminal to incur, ought now to be incurred as a duty.

It is no longer necessary to advance in regular lines and step by step. On the contrary, each division should be given a distant objective which must be reached independently of its neighbour, and even if one's flank is thereby exposed for the time being.

Reinforcements must be directed on the points where our troops are gaining ground, not where they are checked.

A vigorous offensive against the sectors where the enemy is weak will cause hostile strongpoints to fall, and in due course our whole army will be able to continue its advance. This procedure will result in speedily breaking up the hostile forces and will cost us much less than if we attempted to deal with the present situation in a half-hearted manner.

The situation is most favourable ; let each one of us act energetically, and without hesitation push forward to our objective.

Addressed to all Army commanders.

D. H.

11.30 p.m.

APPENDIX XXI

MARÉCHAL FOCH'S NOTE OF 30TH AUGUST, 1918[1]
(Translation)

G.Q.G.A.,

30th August, 1918.

Commanders-in-Chief of the Allied Armies.

NOTE[2]

I.

The operations which, on the 24th July, it was decided to undertake in the course of the summer and autumn of 1918 were suitable to the situation at that time.

---

[1] See Sketch 1.

[2] F.O.A. VII (1), Annex 896. It bears the remarks :—" Left with " General Pershing on the 30th Oct." " Copy taken to G.Q.G. by Colonel " Desticker at 9 a.m. on the 31st."

To-day, the favourable development of the two first of these operations has thrown the enemy well beyond the first objectives which were selected ; the battle extends from Reims to the Scarpe on a front of 120 miles, and the enemy is retiring, giving manifest proofs of his disorganization.

It is of the greatest importance to exploit this favourable situation to the utmost, continuing and extending the battle to the Meuse and bringing into it all the Allied forces in one great convergent attack.

For this purpose :—

(1) The British Armies, supported by the left of the French Armies, will continue to attack in the general direction St. Quentin–Cambrai.

(2) The centre of the French Armies will continue vigorous action to throw the enemy beyond the Aisne.

(3) The American Army and the right of the French Armies, operating on the Meuse and westward, will attack in the general direction of Mezières.

II.

The operations mentioned in paragraphs (1) and (2) above are in the course of execution. Those mentioned in paragraph (3) should include :—

(i) The attack of the American Army on the right bank of the Meuse. This holds good and should be launched as soon as possible, making use of all the preparations already made, so as to give no respite to the enemy.

But this attack will be reduced in scope so that it will go no further than the line Vigneulles–Thiaucourt–Régniéville,[1] which will give the desired results : these are the freeing of the Paris-Avricourt railway and a sufficiently good base for future operations.

Thus, considerable Allied forces will be left available for the principal operations in the direction of Mezières.

(ii) An offensive covered on the east by the Meuse in the general direction of Mezières, on both banks of the Aisne, including :—

(a) An attack between the Meuse and the Argonne carried out by the French Second Army reinforced by

---

[1] This line was the base of the St. Mihiel Salient. The original objective line was nine miles farther north and more than double the length.

American troops (4 to 6 divisions), to be prepared at once and launched as soon as possible after that of Mezières.

(*b*) A French-American attack to be made from the Argonne to the Souain road [15 miles west of the Argonne], to be similarly prepared without any delay so that it can be launched a few days after the preceding one.

This attack will be carried out :—

On the right by an American Army operating astride the Aisne ;

on the left by the French Fourth Army operating as far as west of Souain road.

III.

These operations, in order to have their full success, should follow one another quickly without leaving the enemy time to recover himself. They should be prepared with the greatest energy. To carry them out it is necessary first of all to make the necessary reduction in the original plan for the St. Mihiel operation, to settle on the new plan and to carry it out, also to work out the resources which will be left available for other operations.

The General Commanding the American Expeditionary Force is, therefore requested, without delay, to decide on this new plan and to inform the Maréchal Commanding-in-Chief the Allied Forces what American troops will be employed at St. Mihiel.

It would seem, as far as can be foreseen, that there will be required :—

(i) Eight or nine divisions for the reduced St. Mihiel operation ;

(ii) four to six divisions to support the French Second Army at Verdun ;

(iii) eight to ten divisions for the American Aisne Army.

The St. Mihiel attack should be ready to begin on the 10th September ; the two others from the 15th to the 20th September.

In order to simplify and speed up communication between the High Commands, General Degoutte and General Malcor, of the artillery, are placed at the disposal of General Pershing. These officers, who are fully acquainted with the situation of the French Armies and their resources, and also with the zones of action in question, are furnished with sufficient powers to ensure the rapid solution of all questions.

FOCH.

APPENDIX XXII

FOURTH ARMY OPERATION ORDERS OF
30TH AUGUST, 1918[1]

III. Corps.
Australian Corps.
5th Brigade, R.A.F.

1. The Fourth Army will continue to press back the enemy's rear guards, maintaining the principal pressure on the north towards the high ground between Nurlu and the Bois de Buire. The V. Corps have been directed on Honnecourt.

2. The high ground between Nurlu and Templeux La Fosse will be attacked from the west by III. Corps and from the south-west by the Australian Corps, these Corps mutually assisting each other by encircling movement when strong opposition is met with.

3. South of the railway bridge at Peronne the Australian Corps, while seizing any opportunity for extending its footing on the right bank of the Somme, will not commit itself for the present to a general advance.

If an advance is made north of Peronne, the Australian Corps will pivot on that place and form a flank on the high ground north of the Cologne Valley, thus, protecting the advance on Templeux La Fosse and Nurlu.

4. North of the railway bridge at Peronne the Australian Corps will effect a crossing of the river at as many places as possible, and work north-east up the spurs between the Bois de Buire, Nurlu and Epine de Malassise (west of Moislain).

5. The left of the Australian Corps, which is now advancing up the spur from Clery towards Epine de Malassise, will not advance beyond the Moislains–Bouchavesnes road, and will be relieved as early as possible on the high ground in C.21 and C.16[2] by the III. Corps.

6. The III. Corps will press forward eastwards towards Nurlu and Bois de Nurlu as rapidly as possible.

7. The attached map[3] shows the boundaries between corps and between Fourth Army and neighbouring Armies. They are not meant to be rigidly adhered to whenever the tactical situation demands that either corps can gain ground by crossing beyond its boundary.

---

[1] See Sketch 17.
[2] South-west of Epine de Malassise.
[3] Not reproduced.

8. The boundary of counter-battery zones will be the same as the corps and inter-Army boundaries.

9. Acknowledge by wire.

A. A. Montgomery,
Major-General,
General Staff, Fourth Army.

Appendix XXIII

9th DIVISION OPERATION ORDERS OF 15th AUGUST, 1918[1]

1. On F day, an operation will be undertaken to improve our position by making a further advance southwards along the Hoegenacker Ridge.

The 29th Division is co-operating on our right.

2. The first objective is shown by a Red Line on Map. R. issued herewith. When this has been secured a further advance will be made on the right to the line shown in Blue on Map R.[2]

3. *Artillery.*—(a) The field artillery engaged in the frontal barrage will consist of 9th Divisional Artillery, 113th A.F.A. Brigade, 119th A.F.A. Brigade and one brigade 39th Divisional artillery.

(b) Co-operation of 29th Division, 1 Brigade, R.F.A., puts down an enfilade barrage which will move forward in conformity with the advance of our frontal barrage ; 2 Brigades R.F.A. sweep eastwards across the ground to be attacked and ultimately form a protective barrage on the northern portion of the continuous Black Line on Map. R[2].

(c) Under detailed instructions to be issued by C.R.A., 9th Division Field Artillery mentioned in paragraph (a) above will put down a barrage of H.E. and smoke at Z minus 1 minute on the line shown thus –o–o–o–o–o–o–o on Map R[2].

(d) At Z plus 3 minutes the barrage will lift 50 yards and continue to advance at the rate of 50 yards per minute until it reaches the line shown thus on Map R[2]—where the barrage will pause from Z plus 12 to Z plus 15 minutes.

---

[1] These Orders are reproduced as typical of the period. It has not been thought necessary to indicate the position of the trenches, or of the areas defined by co-ordinates which are mentioned.

[2] Not reproduced. The objectives are shown on Sketch 22, but not the artillery lines or the trenches mentioned.

(c) At Z plus 15 minutes the barrage will continue its advance at the same rate as before until it reaches the protective barrage line shown by a continuous Black line on Map R². The protective barrage will continue on this line until Z plus 35 to cover consolidation and re-organisation. Each battery will change to shrapnel on reaching the protective barrage line.

(f) At Z plus 45 all artillery brigades (less 50th Brigade and one gun of each 18-pdr. battery of brigades forming the protective barrage north of point Y) will put down a barrage of H.E. and smoke on the protective barrage line west of point Y. At Z plus 46 this barrage will advance by lifts of 50 yards and continue to advance at the rate of 50 yards a minute till it reaches the line shown thus –o–x–o–x–o–x on Map R². Each battery as it reaches this line will change to shrapnel. The protective barrage on this line will continue until Z plus 70, after which hour F.A. brigades under the orders of 9th and 29th Divisions will take over the protection of the fronts held by their respective Divisions.

(g) Under orders of the G.O.C. 29th Division, the artillery covering the advance of that division, west of the Meteren Becque, will conform with the movement of artillery covering the advance of the 9th Division.

(h) At Z plus 70 all firing will cease, unless asked for. After this, areas to a depth of 600 yards will be swept out every half hour for 1½ hours at the rate of 100 yards a minute.

(i) The S.O.S. line will be the final protective barrage line, that is, –o–x–o–x–o–x line south and west of point Y and the continuous Black Line north of it.

(j) C.R.A., 9th Division, acting in conjunction with C.R.A., 29th Division, will arrange to smoke Outtersteene, Terrapin House and other enemy O.Ps.

(k) *Co-operation by XV. Corps Heavy Artillery.*—One (6-gun) 60-pdr. battery firing shrapnel in enfilade will barrage the front of our advance, keeping 300 yards ahead of the Field Artillery barrage.

One 6-inch How. battery will fire on the area about x.28.b.5.8. from Z to Z plus 12. Other batteries of heavy hows. will assist in the moving barrage during the advance and will bombard selected points.

4. *Infantry.*—(a) *Preparatory Movements.*—(i) On the night 14th/15th, S.A. Brigade will withdraw two companies from the Roukloshille Switch to Thieushouk.

(ii) On the night 15th/16th, 29th Division will take over the front west of the Meteren Becque. The divisional boundary on completion of the relief will be—Meteren Becque—inclusive to

9th Division from the present front posts to Brahmin Bridge and thence the Brahmin Bridge–Moolenacker road inclusive to 9th Division to the present divisional boundary about X.19 central, thence as at present.

(iii) Two battalions (less two companies) 26th Brigade will move up to the right Brigade Sector on the night E/F and will come under the orders of G.O.C., 27th Brigade.

" A " Battalion will be accommodated in and in front of the " Z " line and will act as reserve to 27th Brigade.

" B " Battalion (less two companies) will be accommodated in the Courte Croix–Union–Cholic Trench and will not be employed in front of the " Z " line without previous reference to Divisional Headquarters.

" A " Battalion Headquarters will be at X.7.a.3.1.

" B " Battalion Headquarters will be at Fletre.

(v) On the night of E/F, one battalion S.A. Brigade will move to assembly position to be selected by G.O.C. 27th Brigade and will come under his orders on arrival at the assembly position. This battalion will take part in the attack.

(vi) All infantry posts south of Scots Trench will be withdrawn by 5 a.m. on " F " day.

(b) The attack will be carried out by two battalions 27th (Lowland) Brigade on the right and one battalion S.A. Brigade (attached to 27th Brigade) on the left.

(c) The infantry will leave assembly positions in Scots Trench at Zero.

(d) A simultaneous advance will be made by troops of the 29th Division west of the Meteren Becque, which will form the boundary between the divisions. In order to ensure connection between the two divisions at least one section of 27th Brigade will advance with the 29th Division on the right of the Becque ; a similar party of 29th Division will advance with 27th Brigade on the left of the Becque.

(e) Troops of the 29th Division will take over from 27th Brigade the front from the Becque to F.3.b.2.1, as soon after it has been captured as possible. The boundary between divisions will then run as follows : F.3.b.2.1., F.3.b.2.6., X.26.central, then as at present.

5. *Machine Guns.*—Under instructions to be issued by O.C., 9th Battalion M.G.C., one machine gun company in positions about Axemill will put down a frontal barrage covering the infantry advance on the left and conforming with the artillery barrage.

After the objective has been reached this company will be given an S.O.S. line covering the front of the left assaulting battalion.

One company, 9th Battalion M.G.C. will put down an enfilade barrage on the front of the right and centre assaulting battalions, which will advance in conformity with the field artillery barrage. The 29th Division is arranging for at least one other machine gun company to take part in this enfilade barrage.

O.C., 9th Battalion M.G.C. will detail eight guns to act under orders of G.O.C., 27th Brigade as forward guns.

Machine gun barrages will open at Zero.

6. *Light Trench Mortars.*—(a) L.T.M. batteries of 26th and S.A.Brigades will come under orders of G.O.C. 27th Brigade at 9 p.m. on E/F night.

(b) L.T.M. batteries of 26th, 27th and S.A. Brigades will be formed into a group under the orders of O.C., 27th L.T.M. Battery.

(c) The 29th Division have agreed to allot sufficient space for one L.T.M. battery in the trench running from X.26.b.5.8. to X.26.b.8.9.

7. *R.A.F.*—(a) A contact patrol will go over at Z plus 30 minutes and at Z plus 70 minutes.

(b) It will be marked as follows :—Black flap on trailing edge of under plane and coloured streamer on tail.

(c) All troops detailed to go through to the Red Line and also those detailed to go to the Blue Line will be provided with Red Flares and pieces of tin about 8 inches square.

(d) When the contact plane goes over it will call for signals by sounding a kláxon horn or firing a white Very light. The infantry in the front line then light flares in groups of three or more and will shine their pieces of tin, or Vigilant periscopes if the sun is shining. This signal is more clearly visible than flares.

(e) A counter-attack patrol will watch the front from zero hour onward until dusk. A Red Very light dropped from the plane means that the hostile infantry is about to attack.

(f) (T) Popham signalling panels will be put out by 27th Brigade H.Q. and by H.Q.s of all battalions under orders of G.O.C. 27th Brigade.

8. *Defence of the Line.*—From the time when the battalion of S.A. Brigade attached to 27th Brigade is in assembly positions on the night E/F, the boundary between the Right and Left Brigade Sectors will run as follows :—X.22.a.6.3.—X.16.c.0.1—X.15.d.7.4. and thence as at present.

9. Prisoners and captured documents will be sent under brigade escort to Q.33.d.6.3 where they will be taken over by a divisional escort and examined by the Divisional Intelligence Officer.

10. Watches will be synchronised at X.7.a.3.1 at 10 p.m. on the night E/F and again at Z minus 4 hours. Representative officers from 29th Division, 9th Division Artillery, 27th and S.A. Infantry Brigades and 9th Battalion M.G.C. will attend. Representative officer from R.A.F. will attend at Z minus 4 hours.

11. The following signals will be used :—

Objective gained	Blue· smoke, rifle grenade.
Lengthen range 100 yards	White to Green, rifle grenade.
S.O.S. by day	Red smoke, rifle grenade.
S.O.S. by night	Ordinary S.O.S. signal.
S.O.S. if in mist	Short blasts on strombos horn in addition to light signals.

12. *Reports.*—27th Brigade will report departure of infantry from assembly positions and will report progress of operations frequently.

13. Headquarters will be established as follows :—

Adv. Div. H.Q. .. .. Cholic Cottage, X.7.d.3.7. from Zero minus 1 hour until further notification.

27th Inf. Bde. Adv.

H.Q. .. .. .. Kelso Cottages, X.14.b.85.45.

G.O.C., 27th Brigade will report as soon as possible the location of H.Qrs. of the Brigade Reserve Battalion, Right Assaulting Battalion and Right Assaulting Company.

14. F Day and Zero hour will be notified later.

15. Acknowledge.

T. C. MUDIE,

Lt.-Colonel,

General Staff, 9th (Scottish) Division.

Issued through Signals at 8 a.m.

GENERAL INDEX

A

Administrative arrangements, 17
Air, 8, 20, 40, 451 ; units, 25 ; command of, 26 ; instructions for 8th Aug., 34 ; in Battle of Amiens, 47, 51, 52, 83–4 (bombing of Somme bridges), 87, (casualties), 95 ; 9th Aug., 95 ; bombing, 119 ; numbers, 121 ; comments, 157 ; Battle of Albert, 181, 183, 198, 212, 213, 220, 237, 265 ; Battle of the Scarpe, 298, 306, 327, 336, 356, 364 ; at Drocourt-Quéant, 397, 398, 404, 410, 416 ; Hindenburg Position, 476, 477, 490
Albert, Battle of, 179 ; 2nd day, 196 ; 3rd day, 211
Albert, H.M., King of the Belgians, 174, 461, 463, 465
Albert, town, 196, 197, 201
Albrecht of Württemberg, Duke, 176
Alexander, Major-Gen., E. W., V.C. (M.G.R.A., First Army), 297
Allason, Br.-Gen. W. (52nd Bde.), 247, 300, 491
American Army, shifts towards St. Milhiel, 2 ; divisions with French, 4 ; First Army formed, 5 ; divisions with British, 5 ; employment, 29, 107, 108, 111, 112, 130 ; liaison force, 165 ; 3 divisions leave British, 166, 171 ; policy as regards employment of, 316 ; Army to be formed, 354 ; divisions with Second Army, 428 ; with Fourth Army, 503. *See also* Arms & Formations index
Amiens, Battle of, 1st day, 40 ; use of reserves, 86 ; 2nd day, 93 ; 3rd day, 119 ; 4th day, 142 ; end, 152 ; comments, 154
Amiens, defence lines, 12 ; control of city, 17. *See also* Amiens, Battle of
Ammunition, artillery, available, 23 ; expenditure during Aug., 424
Ancre, river, 192–3, 196, 201, 202, 233, 243, 249
Anderson, Br.-Gen. A. T. (C.R.A., 62nd Div.), 470
Anderson, Major-Gen. W. Hastings (M.G.G.S., First Army), 297

Armoured cars, 53, 61, 64, 66, 68 (description), 94, 183, 190, 514
Army Service Corps, units, 24
Artillery, strength, 22 ; ammunition, 23 ; in support, 34, 36, 62, 77, 184–6, 188, 192, 197, 200, 213, 220–24, 243, 244, 249, 265, 272, 277, 305, 306, 325–6, 365, 380–1, 392, 398, 401–2, 404, 407, 423–4, 431, 470, 477 (Fourth Army 18th Sept.) ; transfer, 143 ; strength 20th Aug., 180 ; minor reorganization, 490, 498
Arz v. Straussenberg, Gen. (Austrian Chief of General Staff), 178
Atkinson, Major-Gen. E. H. de V. (C.E., First Army), 297.

B

Baird, Br.-Gen. A. W. F. (100th Bde.), 506
Baker-Carr, Br.-Gen. C. D'A. B. S. (I Tank Bde.), 188
Banks, Lieut.-Col. T. M. (10/Essex), 322
Bapaume, 301, 334, 338 ; battle dates, 355 (f.n.)
Barker, Br.-Gen. M. G. H. (53rd Bde), 80, 208, 321, 438
Barnes, Major-Gen. R. W. R. (57th Div.), 336, 406, 456
Barrett, Lieut. J. C., V.C., 502
Barron, Br.-Gen. N. G. (C.H.A., XVII Corps), 304
Bases, 35
Beak, Comdr. D. M. W., V.C. (Drake Battn.), 406
Beckwith, Br.-Gen. A. T. (35th Bde.), 200, 320, 448, 486
Beecham, Capt., M.C. (13/Welch), 439
Belgrave, Lieut.-Col. J. D. (G.S.O.1, 12th Div.), 130
Bell, Br.-Gen. A. H. (6th Cdn. Bde.), 49, 307, 308
Bell, Major-Gen. G. (American 33rd Div.), 74
Below, Gen. v. (*Seventeenth Army*), 181, 204

612 INDEX TO ARMS, FORMATIONS, AND UNITS

Sketch 1

GENERAL FOCH'S PLANS
24th July 1918

SCALE OF MILES

PRINCE RUPPRECHT

CROWN PRINCE

v. GALLWITZ

DUKE OF WÜRTTEMBURG

Belgian
Dunkirk
Calais
Boulogne
Abbeville
Wiry
Flixecourt
AMIENS
Beauvais
Ypres
Kemmel
Hazebrouck
Robecq
Festubert
la Bassée
Aubers
Lille
Arras
Monchy
Preux
Albert
Bapaume
Cambral
Péronne
Grancourt
Bray
Chaulnes
Ham
Royes
Montdidier
Noyon
Lassigny
Guiscard
Valenciennes
HERMANN
HUNDING
Oise
SIEGFRIED
S.Quentin
WOTAN
CANAL
Mezières
Rethel
Laon
Soissons
Aisne
POSITION
BRUNHILD
REIMS
Château Thierry
Marne
Châlons
Verdun
St.Mihiel
Avricourt
PARIS
Seine

G. A. C.
R.
A.
A. E.
E.
F.
G.

① ② ③ ④

Ordnance Survey 1939.

Compiled in the Historical Section (Military Branch)

Sketch 2.

AMIENS 1918: 8th August

REFERENCE

Line on 8th August British French German
At Zero
At 9 p.m.

Scale of Miles
½ 0   1   2   3   4   5   6

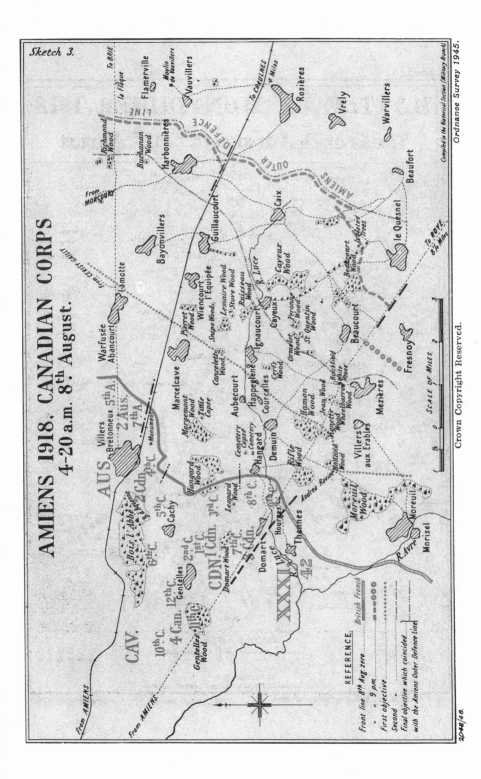

Sketch 3.

AMIENS 1918. CANADIAN CORPS
4-20 a.m. 8th August.

Ordnance Survey 1945.

Compiled in the Historical Section (Military Branch)

Crown Copyright Reserved.

REFERENCE.

British   French
Front line 8th Aug zero ——— ———
   "   9 p.m. ▬▬●●●●
First objective ••••••••
Second
Final objective which coincided
with the Amiens Outer Defence line ———

SCALE OF MILES.

2048/46.

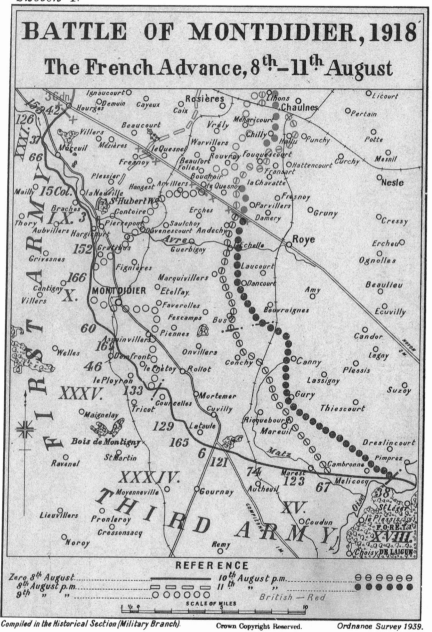

Sketch 4.

BATTLE OF MONTDIDIER, 1918
The French Advance, 8th–11th August

REFERENCE

Zero 8th August .... 10th August p.m. ....
8th August p.m. " .... 11th " " ....
9th " " .... British — Red

SCALE OF MILES

Compiled in the Historical Section (Military Branch).   Crown Copyright Reserved.   Ordnance Survey 1939.

Sketch 5.

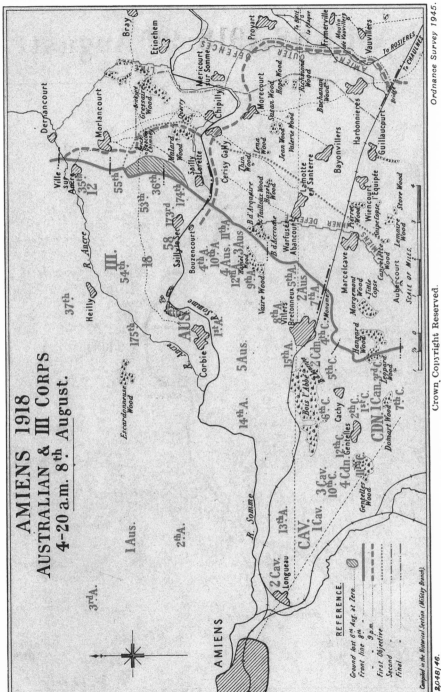

AMIENS 1918
AUSTRALIAN & III CORPS
4–20 a.m. 8th. August.

REFERENCE.

Ground lost 6th Aug. at Zero.
Front line 8th ....
        ,,   9 p.m. ....
First Objective ....
Second ....
Final ....

SCALE OF MILES.

Compiled in the Historical Section (Military Branch).

Ordnance Survey 1945.

Crown. Copyright Reserved.

2,048/46.

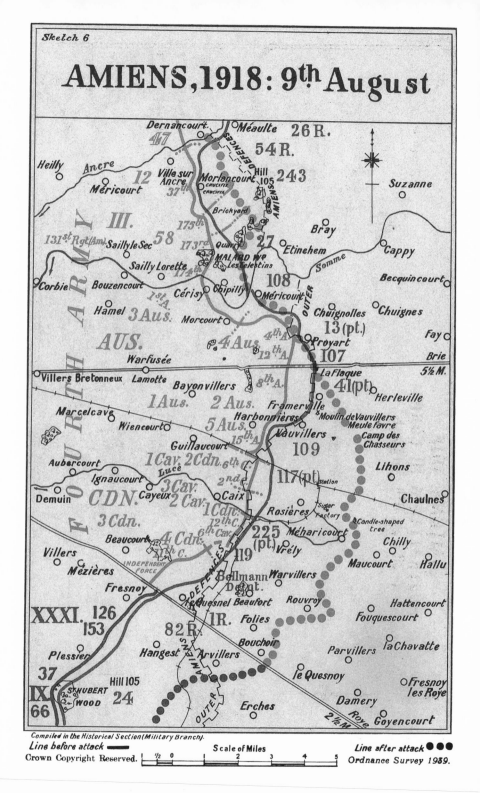

Sketch 6

AMIENS, 1918: 9th August

Line before attack ▬▬▬

Scale of Miles

Line after attack ●●●
Ordnance Survey 1939.

Sketch 7.

AMIENS 1918: 10th August

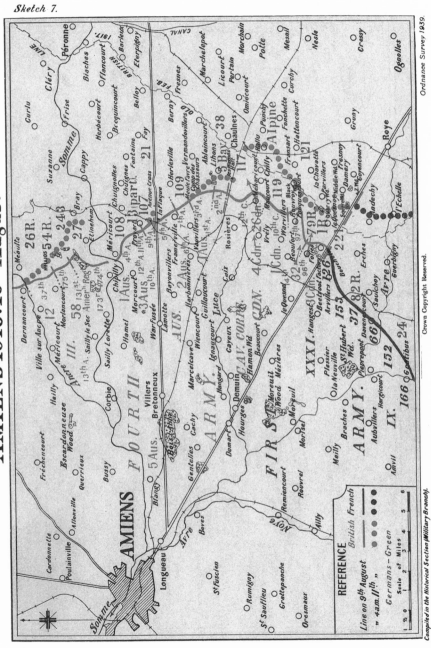

Ordnance Survey 1939.

Crown Copyright Reserved.

Compiled in the Historical Section (Military Branch).

REFERENCE

Line on 9th August
" 4am.11th "

British French

Germans — Green

Scale of Miles
0   1   2   3   4   5   6

Sketch 8.

AMIENS 1918: 11th August

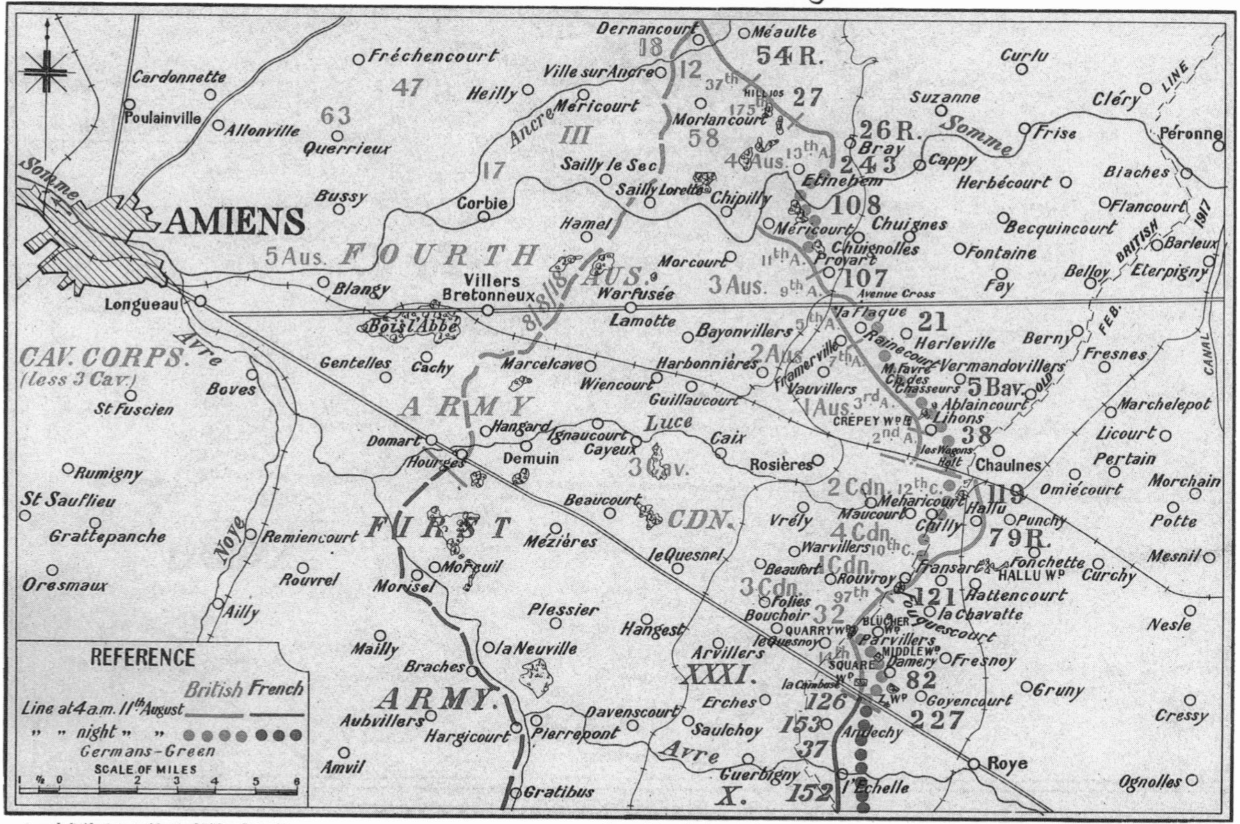

Ordnance Survey 1939.

Crown Copyright Reserved.

Compiled in the Historical Section (Military Branch)

REFERENCE

Line at 4 a.m. 11th August
" " night " " "
Germans—Green

British   French

SCALE OF MILES

The Advance: 8th–20th August, 1918.

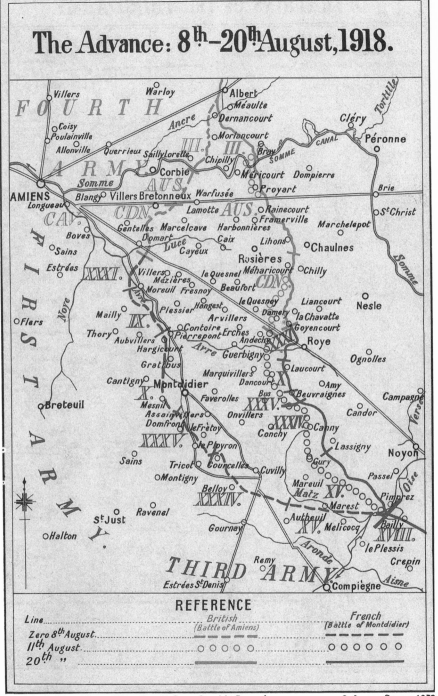

REFERENCE

Line	British (Battle of Amiens)	French (Battle of Montdidier)
Zero 8th August		
11th August	o o o o o	o o o o o o
20th "		

Scale of Miles

10 — 5 — 0 — 5 — 10

OPERATIONS OF THE THIRD ARMY.

Sketch 10.

REFERENCE.

British Line morning 21st August	————
First Objective of Third Army 21st August	+++++++
British Line morning 22nd August	2
„ „ evening 23rd „	3

To ARRAS

Minorca Trench

Neuville Vitasse

Mercatel

Super Factory

St. Martin

59

39

Boisleux St. Marc

Henin

Boiry Bacquerelle

Boisleux au Mont

52

Bareilles

XVII.

21 R.

3

Berles au Bois

62

Gds.

Blaireville

Adinfer Wood

R. Cojeul

Hamelincourt

234

St. Leger

Bienvillers au Bois

VI. **2**

Ayette

Moyenneville

Hamel Work

R. Sensée

Holly Copse

Monchy au Bois

Mory Copse

Hannescamps

2 Gd. Res.

Courcelles

Ervillers

Mory

5

Essart

3

2

Béhagnies

Fonquevillers

Ablainzevill

Logeast Wood

Gomiecourt

Sapignies

37

63

Cemetery

Achiet le Grand

Sapignies Switch

Bucquoy

54 Bav.

37

Bihucourt

Favreuil

Monument

IV. Salient

Achiet le Petit

Biefvillers

Monument Wood

NZ

Puisieux

NZ

Avesnes les Bapaume

63

Serre

German

42

HILL 140

Beauregard Dovecote

Irles

Grevillers

BAPAUME

Beaumont Hamel

183

Miraumont

Loupart Wood

Thilloy

Ligny Thilloy

Former

Beaucourt

Bois d'Hollande

Baillescourt Fm.

Pys

Warlencourt

Butte de Warlencourt

le Barque

21

Grandcourt

le Sars

Luizenhof Fm.

V. Hamel

St. Pierre Division

17 **16 R.**

Courcelles

Destremont Fm.

Eaucourt l'Abbaye

Factory Corner

17

Mesnil

Thiepval

Pozières

Windmill

Martinpuich

Flers

Gueudecourt

38

Authuille

3 Nav.

High Wood

Lesbœufs

Ovillers

Bazentin le Petit

Avuluy

Crucifix Corner

Contalmaison

Bazentin le Grand

Delville Wood

Morval

la Boisselle

Longueval

Ginchy

ALBERT

Mametz Wood

Guillemont

Bouleaux Wood

Combles

FOURTH ARMY

Compiled in the Historical Section (Military Branch).

SCALE OF MILES.

Ordnance Survey 1945.

Crown Copyright Reserved.

Sketch II.

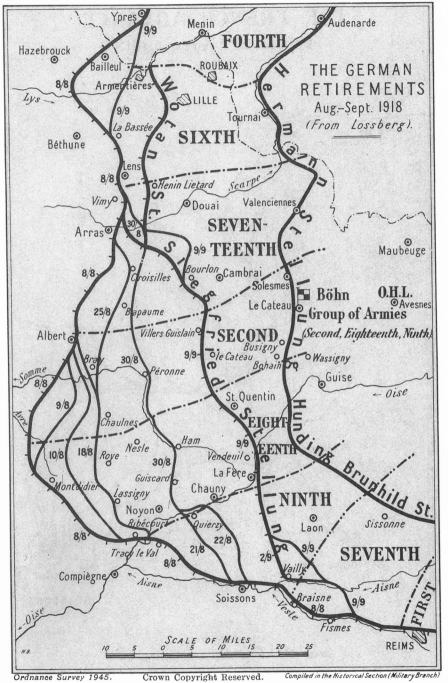

SCALE OF MILES

Ordnance Survey 1945.   Crown Copyright Reserved.   Compiled in the Historical Section (Military Branch)

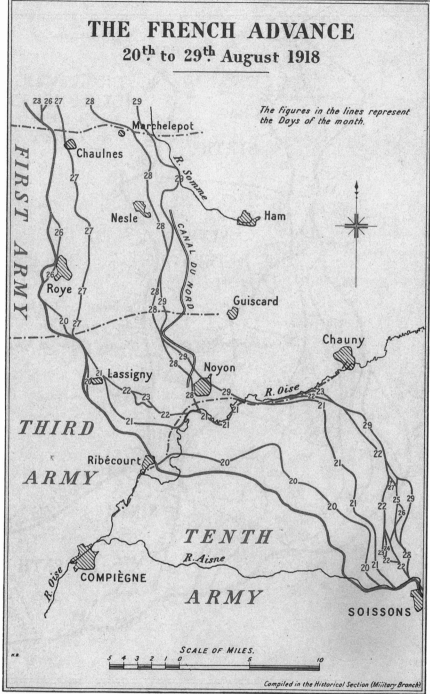

THE FRENCH ADVANCE
20th to 29th August 1918

The figures in the lines represent the Days of the month.

FIRST ARMY

Marchelepot

Chaulnes

R. Somme

Nesle

Ham

CANAL DU NORD

Roye

Guiscard

Chauny

THIRD

Lassigny

Noyon

R. Oise

ARMY

Ribécourt

TENTH

R. Aisne

COMPIÈGNE

R. Oise

ARMY

SOISSONS

SCALE OF MILES.
5 4 3 2 1 0   5   10

Compiled in the Historical Section (Military Branch)

OPERATIONS
OF THE
THIRD AND FIRST ARMIES

SCALE OF MILES.

REFERENCE.
British line evening 23rd Aug. 1918
   "   "   morning 24th   "   " ———4———
   "   "   25th   "   " ———5———
   "   "   26th   "   " ———6———
   "   "   27th   "   " ———7———

Compiled in the Historical Section (Military Branch).

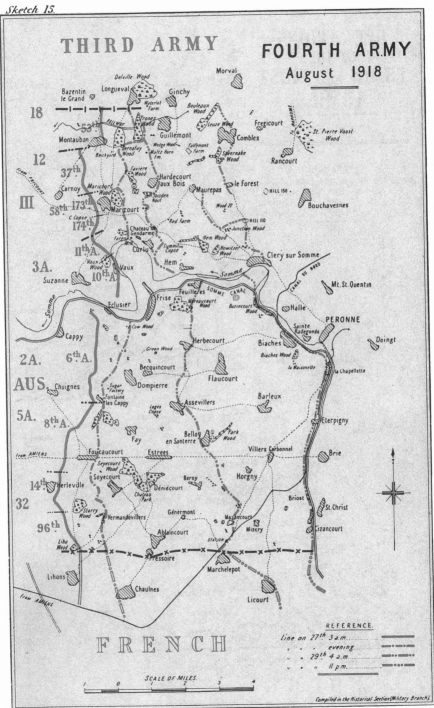

THIRD ARMY

FOURTH ARMY
August 1918

THIRD ARMY ·— Delville Wood · Morval · Bazentin le Grand · Longueval · Ginchy · Waterlot Farm · Bouleaux Wood · 18 · 53rd · RAILWAY · Trones Wood · Leuze Wood · Fregicourt · St. Pierre Vaast Wood · Montauban · Guillemont · Combles · Wedge Wood · Falfemont Farm · Maltz Horn Fm. · 12 · Brickyard · Bernafay Wood · 37th · Faviere Wood · Trones Wood · Hardecourt aux Bois · Maurepas · le Forest · HILL 150 · Carnoy · Maricourt Wood · Boisden haut · Red Farm · Wood 77 · Bouchavesnes · III · 58th · 173rd · Maricourt · C Copse · HILL 110 · 174th · Chateau de Gendarme · Junction Wood · Ferrons Park · Hem Wood · Howitzer Wood · 11th A. · Summit Copse · Curlu · Clery sur Somme · 3A. · Vaux Wood · Hem · Somme · Mt. St. Quentin · 10th A. · Suzanne · Vaux · Somme · Eclusier · Frise · Feuilleres · SOMME CANAL · Halle · CANAL DU NORD · Mereaucourt Wood · Bazincourt Wood · PERONNE · Cappy · Cow Wood · Herbecourt · Sainte Radegonde · Doingt · Green Wood · Biaches · 2A. · 6th A. · Becquincourt · Biaches Wood · la Maisonette · AUS · Chuignes · Sugar Factory · Dompierre · Flaucourt · la Chapellette · Fontaine les Cappy · Barleux · 5A. · 8th A. · Loges Copse · Assevillers · Eterpigny · Fay · Belloy en Santerre · Park Wood · Foucaucourt · Estrees · Villers Carbonnel · Brie · from AMIENS · Seyecourt Wood · Soyecourt · Berny · Horgny · 14th · Herleville · Deniecourt · Briost · 32 · Chateau Park · Genermont · Mazancourt · St. Christ · Starry Wood · Vermandovillers · Misery · Cizancourt · 96th · Ablaincourt · STATION · Lihu Wood · Pressoire · Marchelepot · Lihons · from AMIENS · Chaulnes · Licourt

FRENCH

REFERENCE.
Line on 27th 3 a.m.
" " evening
" 29th 4 a.m.
" " 11 p.m.

SCALE OF MILES
1 0 1 2 3 4

Compiled in the Historical Section (Military Branch).

Crown Copyright Reserved.

Ordnance Survey 1945.

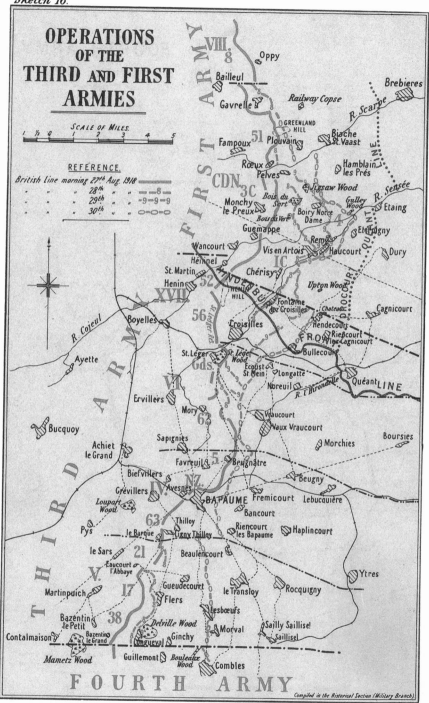

Sketch 16.

OPERATIONS
OF THE
THIRD AND FIRST
ARMIES

SCALE OF MILES.

REFERENCE.
British Line morning 27th Aug. 1918 ———
  "   "   "   28th   "   —8—
  "   "   "   29th   "   —9—9—9
  "   "   "   30th   "   ⊙⊙⊙

FOURTH ARMY

Crown Copyright Reserved.

Compiled in the Historical Section (Military Branch)

Ordnance Survey 1945.

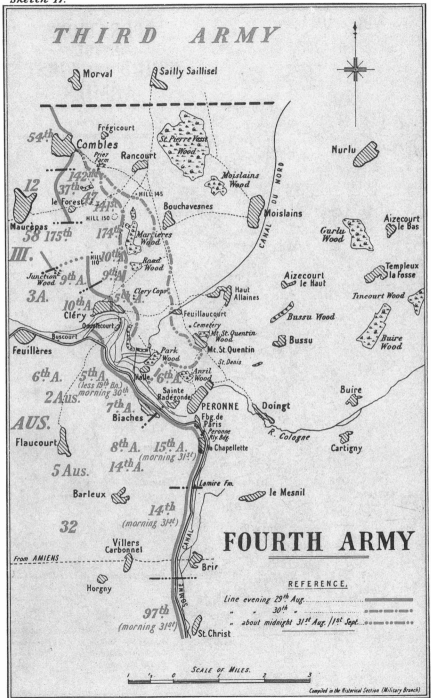

THIRD ARMY

Morval

Sailly Saillisel

Frégicourt

54th

Combles

Rancourt

Prier Farm

St. Pierre Vaast Wood

Nurlu

12

142nd

37th

le Forest

47th

141st

HILL 145

Bouchavesnes

Moislains Wood

Moislains

Gurlu Wood

Aizecourt le Bas

Maurepas

58 175th

HILL 150

174th

Marrières Wood

Road Wood

Aizecourt le Haut

Templeux la fosse

III.

HILL 110

10th A.

9th A.

9th A.

Haut Allaines

Bussu Wood

Tincourt Wood

Junction Wood

3A.

10th A.

5th A.

Cléry Cops.

Feuillaucourt

Bussu

Buire Wood

Cléry

Omiécourt

Cemetery

Mt. St. Quentin Wood

Buscourt

Feuillères

Park Wood

Mt. St. Quentin

St. Denis

6th A.

5th A. (less 19th Bn.) morning 30th

Halle

6th A.

Anvil Wood

Buire

2 Aus.

7th A.

Biaches

Sainte Radegonde

PERONNE

Doingt

Cartigny

AUS.

Fbg. de Paris

Flaucourt

Peronne Rly. Bdg.

5 Aus.

8th A.

15th A. (morning 31st)

la Chapellette

R. Cologne

14th A.

32

14th (morning 31st)

Lamire Fm.

le Mesnil

From AMIENS

Villers Carbonnel

CANAL

Brie

Horgny

97th (morning 31st)

SOMME

St. Christ

FOURTH ARMY

REFERENCE.

Line evening 29th Aug. ....

" " 30th ....

" about midnight 31st Aug./1st Sept. ....

SCALE OF MILES.

Compiled in the Historical Section (Military Branch).

Ordnance Survey 1945.

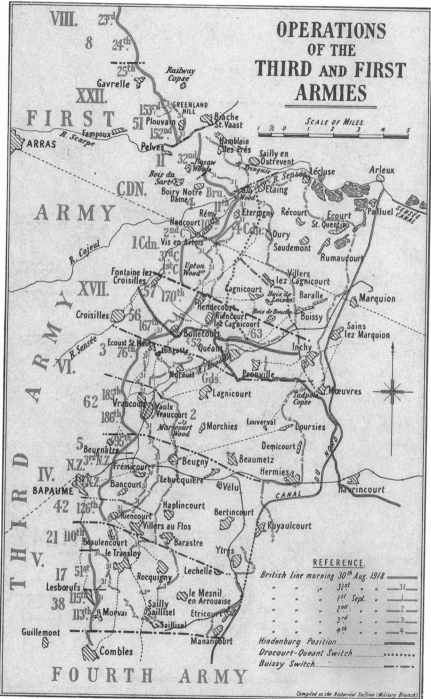

Sketch 18.

OPERATIONS
OF THE
THIRD AND FIRST
ARMIES

SCALE OF MILES.

REFERENCE.

British line morning 30th Aug. 1918	
" " " 31st	31
" " " 1st Sept.	1
" " " 2nd	2
" " " 3rd	3
" " " 4th	4

Hindenburg Position
Drocourt-Quéant Switch
Buissy Switch

Compiled in the Historical Section (Military Branch).

Ordnance Survey 1945.

Sketch 19.

Crown Copyright Reserved.

Ordnance Survey 1945.

THE FRENCH ADVANCE
30th Aug.–26th Sept.
1918

The figures in the lines represent
the days of the month.

Hindenburg line ∿∿∿∿

SCALE OF MILES.
0 1 2 3 4 5 ____ 10 ____ 15

Compiled in the Historical Section (Military Branch).

    Ordnance Survey 1945.

Sketch 21.

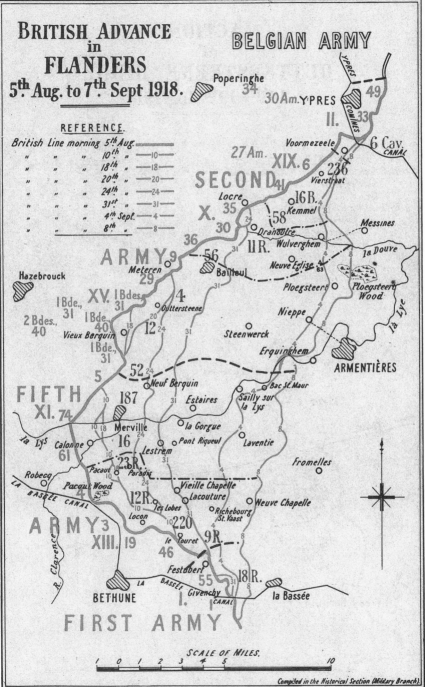

BRITISH ADVANCE
in
FLANDERS
5th Aug. to 7th Sept 1918.

BELGIAN ARMY

Poperinghe 34

30 Am. YPRES
II. 49
33

REFERENCE.

British Line morning 5th Aug. ——————
  "   "   "   10th "   —— 10
  "   "   "   18th "   ———— 18
  "   "   "   20th "   —— 20
  "   "   "   24th "   —— 24
  "   "   "   31st "   —— 31
  "   "   "   4th Sept. —— 4
  "   "   "   8th   "   —— 8

27 Am. XIX. 6
Voormezeele 6 Cav.
CANAL

SECOND 41
236
Vierstraat

X. 35
Locre
16 B.
Kemmel
58
Messines

30
24
Dranoutre
la Douve

36
II R.
Wulverghem
Neuve Eglise 63
Ploegsteert
Wood

ARMY 9
56
Meteren 29
Bailleul
Ploegsteert

Hazebrouck
XV. 1 Bdes.
1 Bde., 31 31 4
31   Outtersteene
Nieppe
la Lye

2 Bdes., 1 Bde.
40   40
Vieux Berquin 18 12 24 31
1 Bde.,
31
Steenwerck
Erquinghem
ARMIÈRES

5 52 24
Neuf Berquin Bac St. Maur

FIFTH
XI. 74 187
10
Estaires
Sailly sur
la Lys

10 18
Merville 24
la Gorgue
Laventie

Calonne
61 16
Pont Riqueul
Fromelles

Robecq
Pacaut
Paradis 23 R
10
Vieille Chapelle
Lacouture
Neuve Chapelle

Pacaut Wood
4 12 R
10
les Lobes
Richebourg
St. Vaast

ARMY 3
Locon
10 220
XIII. 19
le Touret 9 R
46
Festubert

BETHUNE
LA BASSÉE CANAL
55 18 R
Givenchy
I. CANAL
la Bassée

FIRST ARMY

SCALE OF MILES.
1 0 1 2 3 4 5   10

Compiled in the Historical Section (Military Branch).

Ordnance Survey 1945.

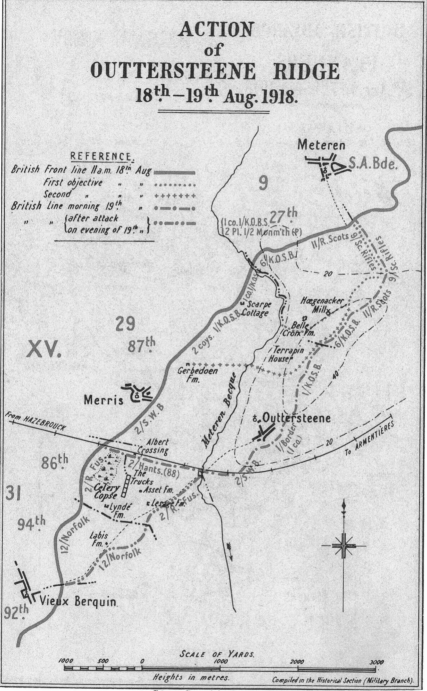

ACTION
of
OUTTERSTEENE RIDGE
18th – 19th Aug. 1918.

REFERENCE.
British Front line 11a.m. 18th Aug
First objective " "
Second " "
British line morning 19th
" " { after attack
on evening of 19th " }

Meteren
S.A.Bde.

9

27th
(1 co. 1/K.O.B.S.
12 Pl. 1/2 M.onm'th (?)

11/R.Scots
9/Sc.Rifles
9/Sc.Rifles

6/K.O.S.B.

20

Scarpe Cottage
2 coys. 1/K.O.S.B.

Hœgenacker Mill

6/K.O.S.B. 11/R.Shots

Belle Croix Fm.

Terrapin House

40

29
87th

Gerbedoen Fm.

1/K.O.S.B.

XV.

Merris

2/S.W.B

Outtersteene

1/Border (1 co.)

20

To ARMENTIÈRES

From HAZEBROUCK

Albert Crossing

2/Hants. (88)

2/S.W.B

86th

2/R.Fus.

The Trucks

Asset Fm.

Celery Copse

31

Lynde Fm.

Leose Fm. 2/R.Fus.

94th

Labis Fm.

12/Norfolk

12/Norfolk

92th   Vieux Berquin.

SCALE OF YARDS.
1000 500 0   1000   2000   3000

Heights in metres.   Compiled in the Historical Section (Military Branch).

FOURTH ARMY
September 1918.

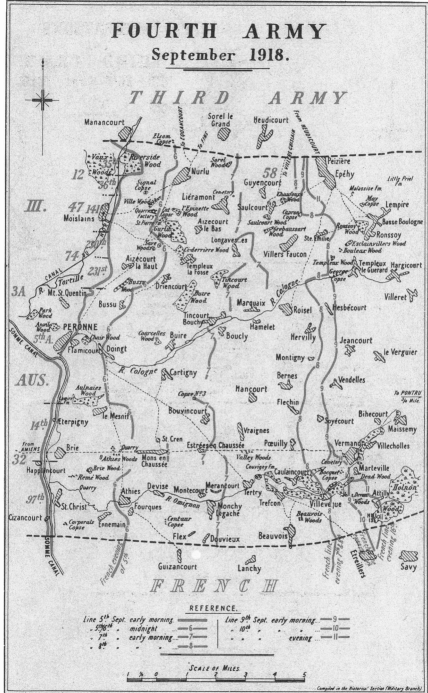

THIRD ARMY

FRENCH

REFERENCE.

Line 5th Sept. early morning	Line 9th Sept. early morning — 9
" 5th/6th midnight — 6	" 10th evening — 10
" 7th early morning — 7	" evening — 11
" 8th — 8	

SCALE OF MILES.

1/2 0 1 2 3 4 5

Compiled in the Historical Section (Military Branch)

Ordnance Survey 1945.

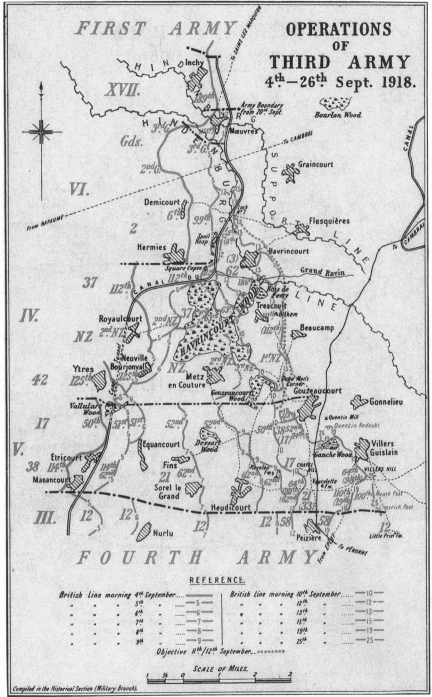

OPERATIONS
OF
THIRD ARMY
4th — 26th Sept. 1918.

FIRST ARMY

FOURTH ARMY

REFERENCE.

British Line morning 4th September		British line morning 10th September	
" " " 5th "		" " " 12th "	
" " " 6th "		" " " 13th "	
" " " 7th "		" " " 15th "	
" " " 8th "		" " " 19th "	
" " " 9th "		" " " 25th "	

Objective 11th/12th September

SCALE OF MILES.

Compiled in the Historical Section (Military Branch).

Ordnance Survey 1945.

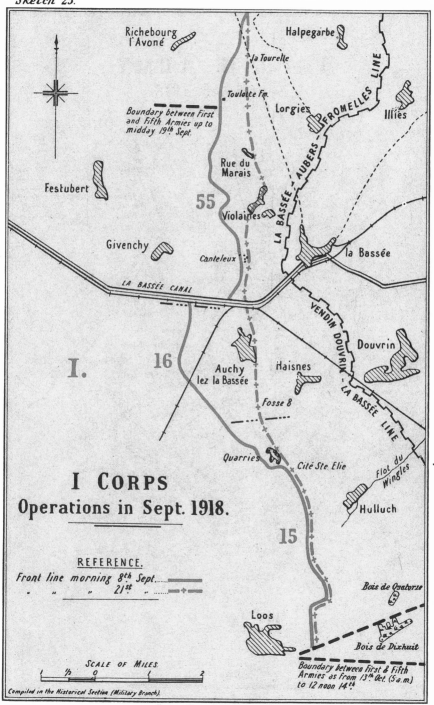

Sketch 25.

Richebourg l'Avoné

Halpegarbe

la Tourelle

Toulette Fm.

Boundary between First and Fifth Armies up to midday 19th Sept.

Lorgies

FROMELLES LINE

Illies

Rue du Marais

55

Violaines

Festubert

LA BASSÉE AUBERS

Givenchy

Canteleux

la Bassée

LA BASSÉE CANAL

VENDIN DOUVRIN

Douvrin

I.

16

Auchy lez la Bassée

Haisnes

LA BASSÉE LINE

Fosse 8

Quarries

Cité Ste. Elie

Flot du Wingles

Hulluch

I CORPS

Operations in Sept. 1918.

15

REFERENCE.

Front line morning 8th Sept.

" " " 21st "

Bois de Quatorze

Loos

Bois de Dixhuit

SCALE OF MILES.

Boundary between First & Fifth Armies as from 13th Oct. (5 a.m.) to 12 noon 14th

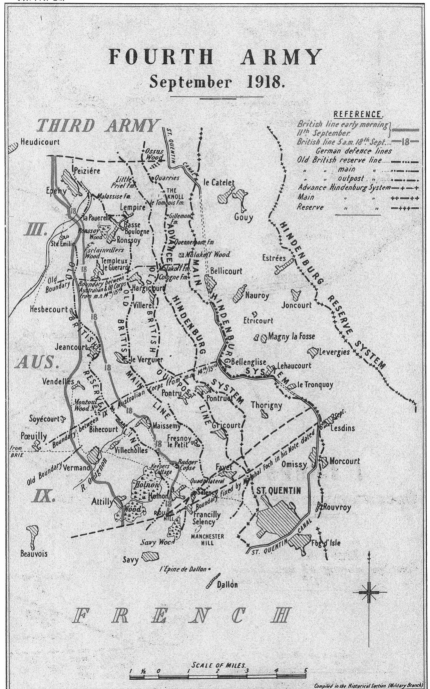

FOURTH ARMY
September 1918.

THIRD ARMY

REFERENCE.
British line early morning } 11th September
British line 5 a.m. 18th Sept. ___18
German defence lines
Old British reserve line
  "   "   main   "
  "   "   outpost   "
Advance Hindenburg System
Main   "   "   "
Reserve   "   "   "

Heudicourt
Peiziére
Epehy
Little Priel Fm.
Malassise Fm.
Lempire
la Pauerelle
Basse Boulogne
Ronssoy Wood
Ronssoy
Ste. Emilie
Esclainvillers Wood
Templeux le Guerard
Old Boundary
Boundary between Australian & III Corps from m.n.H 15th
Hargicourt
Villeret
Hesbecourt
Jeancourt
le Verguier
Vendelles
Montouit Wood No.1
Soyécourt
Bihecourt
Pœuilly
from BRIE
Villecholles
Vermand
Old Boundary
Attilly
Holnon
Hétnon
Holnon Wood
Rouen
Ossus Wood
Quarries
THE KNOLL
le Tombois Fm.
Gillemont Fm.
Quennemont Fm.
Malakoff Wood
Malakoff Fm.
Cologne Fm.
le Catelet
Gouy
Estrées
Bellicourt
Nauroy
Etricourt
Magny la Fosse
Bellenglise
Lehaucourt
le Tronquoy
Pontru
Pontruet
Thorigny
Maissemy
Gricourt
Fresnoy le Petit
Fayet
Keepers Cottage
Badger Copse
Quadrilateral
Selency
Boundary fixed by Marshal Foch in his Note dated 6th Sept.
Francilly Selency
Rouy le HILL
Savy Wood
MANCHESTER HILL
Savy
l'Epine de Dallon
Dallon
Joncourt
Levergies
Lesdins
Morcourt
Omissy
ST. QUENTIN
Rouvroy
Fbg d'Isle
Beauvois
Boundary between
Australian Corps from m.n 14th/15th

HINDENBURG RESERVE SYSTEM
HINDENBURG MAIN SYSTEM
HINDENBURG OUTPOST SYSTEM
BRITISH RESERVE LINE
OLD BRITISH MAIN LINE
OLD BRITISH OUTPOST LINE
ST. QUENTIN CANAL

III.
AUS.
IX.

FRENCH

SCALE OF MILES.
1 ½ 0 1 2 3 4 5

Compiled in the Historical Section (Military Branch)

Ordnance Survey 1945.

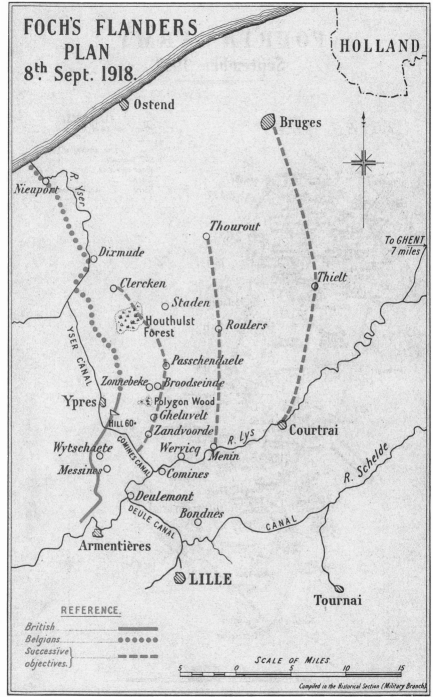

Sketch 27.

FOCH'S FLANDERS
PLAN
8th Sept. 1918.

HOLLAND

Ostend

Bruges

Nieuport

R. Yser

To GHENT
7 miles

Dixmude

Thourout

Thielt

Clercken

Staden

Houthulst
Forest

Roulers

Passchendaele

Zonnebeke

Broodseinde

Ypres

Polygon Wood

Gheluvelt

Zandvoorde

HILL 60·

YSER CANAL

Wytschaete

Wervicq

R. Lys

Courtrai

Messines

Menin

R. Schelde

COMINES CANAL

Comines

Deulemont

Bondues

CANAL

DEULE CANAL

Armentières

LILLE

Tournai

REFERENCE.

British
Belgians
Successive
objectives.

SCALE OF MILES.

5   0   5   10   15

Compiled in the Historical Section (Military Branch).

Crown Copyright Reserved.   Ordnance Survey 1945.

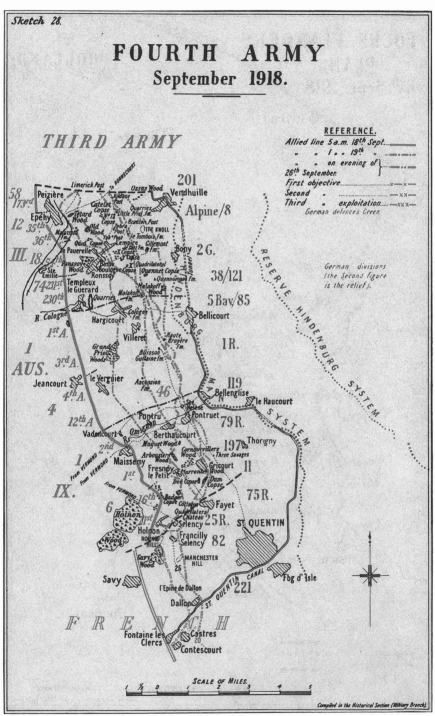

Sketch 28.

FOURTH ARMY
September 1918.

THIRD ARMY

REFERENCE.

Allied line 5 a.m. 18th Sept.	
„ „ 1 „ 19th	
„ „ on evening of 26th September.	
First objective	x x
Second „	xx
Third „ exploitation	xxx
German defences Green.	

German divisions
(the Second figure
is the relief).

RESERVE HINDENBURG SYSTEM

201
Vendhuille
Alpine/8
Bony 2 G.
38/121
5 Bav/85
Bellicourt
1 R.
119
Bellenglise   le Haucourt
79 R.
197
Thorigny
II
75 R.
St. Quentin
25 R.
82
221

Limerick Post
Peizière
58
173rd
12 35th
Epéhy
36th
III. 18
74 21st
230th
1st A.
1
AUS. 3rd A.
4   4th A.
12th A.
Jeancourt
2nd
IX.   1st
6   16th
Holnon
Holnon
Wood
Savy
Ronssoy
Templeux
le Guerard
Hargicourt
Villeret
le Verguier
Ascension Fm.
46
Pontru
Vadancourt
Berthaucourt
Maissemy
Fresnoy
le Petit
Fayet
Selency
Francilly
Selency
Savy Wood
Manchester Hill
l'Epine de Dallon
Dallon
Fontaine les Clercs
Castres
Contescourt

FRENCH

SCALE OF MILES.

Compiled in the Historical Section (Military Branch).

Crown Copyright Reserved.

Ordnance Survey 1945.

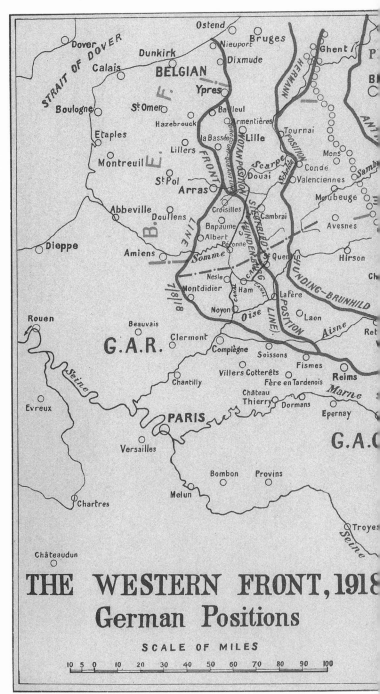

THE WESTERN FRONT, 1918

German Positions

SCALE OF MILES

10 5 0   10   20   30   40   50   60   70   80   90   100

Compiled in the Historical Section (Military Branch).
2048/46.

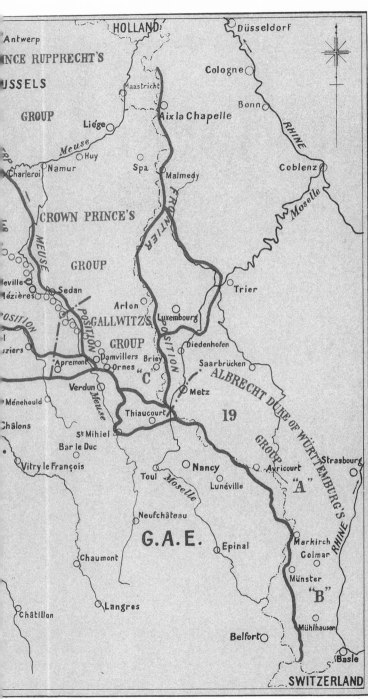

Ordnance Survey 1939.